KILL NOW, TALK FOREVER:

DEBATING SACCO AND VANZETTI

BY

Richard Newby

KILL NOW, TALK FOREVER

Frankfur**Ter`**
Lippm**A**nn
H. **L**. Mencken
Las**K**i

Fraenkel
D **O**s Passos
B. **R**ussell
Einstein
Lo **V**ett
A. M. Schl**E**singer, Jr.
Kaise**R**

DEBATING SACCO AND VANZETTI

Anna N. Davis Aldino Felicani Carlo Tresca John N. Beffel Eugene Lyons Heywood Broun Morris L. Ernst Isaac Don Levine A. Lawrence Lowell Alvan T. Fuller Upton B. Sinclair James Rorty Samuel E. Morison Gardner Jackson William G. Thompson Ben Shahn Herbert B. Ehrmann Tom O'Connor Michael A. Musmanno Robert M. Hutchins Edward H. James Alexander Meiklejohn Zona Gale Mme. Curie Max Lerner David Starr Jordan Roger Baldwin Herbert G. Wells Anatole France John Galsworthy John Dewey Edmund Wilson Bernard DeVoto Bennett Cerf Malcolm Cowley William A. White Jane Addams George Seldes James T. Farrell John Dever Robert P. Weeks Katherine A. Porter Edna St. Vincent Millay Maxwell Anderson Louis Joughin Edmund M. Morgan Bruce Bliven Sylvester Gates Horace M. Kallen Max Eastman William F. Buckley Robert H. Montgomery James Grossman Francis Russell David Felix Roberta Strauss Feuerlicht Ronald Steel Kenneth S. Lynn William O. Douglas Nunzio Pernicone Robert D'Attilio Eric Foner John P. Roche Daniel Aaron James E. Starrs Dorothy Gallagher Oliver W. Holmes Charles E. Wyzanski, Jr. Michael S. Dukakis James D. Forman Robert M. La Follette Paul Avrich

Edited by Richard Newby

First published by AuthorHouse 03/30/07

ISBN: 0-7596-0791-5 (e-book)
ISBN: 0-7596-0792-3 (Paperback)
ISBN: 1-4208-4393-1 (Dust Jacket)

Library of Congress Control Number: 2003094255

This book is printed on acid free paper.

Printed in the United States of America
Bloomington, IN

Edited by
Richard Lee Newby
Associate Professor of English Emeritus
Illinois State University

This book is for
Marilyn Provart Newby, professor/wife
Our children: John, David, Kent, Jane
Their spouses: Pam, Gail, Kelly, Tim
Our granddaughters: Sarah, Diana, Helen, Katherine,
Kendall, Kelsey
Our grandson: Kolin Backues Newby
And their contemporaries
All 21st-century jurors

In memory of Gail South Newby

Reports on Scholarship of Richard Newby

"Richard Newby is a first-rate scholar. He gets to the center of subjects. His book excerpts important documents on Sacco and Vanzetti and highlights new evidence he discovered in 2005." Robert H. Ferrell, Distinguished Professor Emeritus of History, Indiana University, Bloomington

"Kill Now, Talk Forever seems to have some of the aspects of a case book, with its excellent research/study/writing topics and its very useful transcripts. I could see it being adopted by school libraries as a reference text." Anthony Arthur, Professor of English Emeritus, California State University at Northridge. Arthur is the author of *Radical Innocent : Upton Sinclair* (2006) and five other books.

"Author Richard Newby does not directly analyze the Sacco and Vanzetti trial. The unique structure of the book leaves it to the reader to determine whether Sacco and Vanzetti were guilty and whether they received a fair trial." Review in *Wisconsin Lawyer*, Vol. 77, No. 9 (September 2004) by Major Joshua E. Kastenberg, USAF JAG Corps.

An appointed referee judges "Sleuthing Sacco-Vanzetti: Sidelong History and Judge Wyzanski's Opinion," an article Newby submitted to Linda Cooke Johnson, editor of *The Historian* (Michigan State University) on 20 October 1997: "The article reveals deep research in the relevant records and a masterful command of the details of the case. This piece is obviously the product of a long, intense engagement with this subject. Moreover, it is an article obviously motivated by a desire to get to the facts at issue, stripping away the detritus of decades of myth-making."

"The controversial Sacco and Vanzetti case is thoroughly explored in *Kill Now, Talk Forever: Debating Sacco and Vanzetti*, edited by Richard Newby (2002)." George Brown Tindall and David Emory Shi, authors of *America: A Narrative History*, 7th edition, W. W. Norton & Company, 2007.

PERSPECTIVES

Tell your friends, write to your congressman, to the political bosses of your district, to the newspapers. Demand the truth about Sacco and Vanzetti. John Dos Passos, <u>Facing the Chair</u>.

The execution of Sacco and Vanzetti would cry out against us for centuries to come just as the witchcraft executions have. Samuel Eliot Morison, Harvard historian. Letter to William G. Thompson. The Thompson Papers, Harvard Law School Library.

I know of no canon of legal etiquette or of common sense that counsels against a disinterested and scientific discussion of a case. Felix Frankfurter, Professor of Law, Harvard Law School. <u>Illinois Law Review</u>, December 1927.

I have no doubt in my own mind that they were wholly innocent. I am forced to conclude that they were condemned on account of their political opinions and that men who ought to have known better allowed themselves to express misleading views as to the evidence because they held that men with such opinions have no right to live. Letter to Gardner Jackson. 28th May 1929. <u>The Autobiography of Bertrand Russell 1914-1944.</u> Vol. 2. Bertrand Russell. British pacifist, mathematician, philosopher.

I did the Preface [to Appel's first volume of the transcript] with the hope that students of political science and law would be encouraged to mine the record so as better to understand what went on at that trial. William O. Douglas, Associate Justice of the United States Supreme Court. Letter to Ramsey Clark. June 25, 1970. <u>The Douglas Letters</u>.

The question of their guilt or innocence is still being debated, but that they were tried in an atmosphere of hysteria before a biased court is indisputable. Daniel Aaron, Professor of English, Harvard University. <u>American Heritage</u>, July/August 1996.

[E]ven a genius will, on occasion, be wrong.... . Keep in mind that whenever someone presents an opinion about the truth of an issue or the wisdom of an action—that is, whenever someone presents a judgment—you not only have a right to judge his [her] view by the evidence. You have an <u>obligation</u> to do so. Vincent Ryan Ruggiero, <u>The Art of Thinking</u> (1984), p. 64.

CONTENTS

PART I
EVIDENCE BY THE COMMONWEALTH

PART II
EVIDENCE BY THE DEFENSE

PART III
DOCUMENTS IN THE SACCO-VANZETTI CASE

YALE UNIVERSITY
SCHOOL OF LAW
NEW HAVEN CONNECTICUT

December 26, 1930

Professor Felix Frankfurter
Harvard Law School
Cambridge, Mass.

Dear Felix:

Many thanks for your note of the 22d. . . . As you know, I have for the past year and a half been more actively pursuing my long conceived plan of getting the records and facts in cases in which innocent persons have been convicted of crime. I have now, . . . complete facts in some thirty-five such cases. Fifteen or more are now in process of completion, and I am hoping to have them all ready, . . . within a few months.

The name Sacco-Vanzetti will not appear in the book, but this is my humble contribution to preventing another such case.

. . . I want to dedicate this book to John H. Wigmore and yourself. You have both had a part in it. . . . You gave me the final impetus to start actually after the cases and get the work done. I do not know the exact ethics of dedication, but I would not so dedicate a book without asking your consent. It is my present feeling that I shall not ask Mr. Wigmore. I do not know whether you have any compunction about appearing on the same page with Wigmore and in a joint relation, but personally I shall get some kick out of the dedication, . . . I think it will give some people a certain amount of amusement, which will temper the somewhat tragic stories that the book will tell. It will also remind those who know something about the subject that it has to some extent to do with the Sacco-Vanzetti case; and yet, by leaving that case entirely unmentioned, it will, I think, drive the lesson more vividly home. . . Very sincerely yours, (Signed: Edwin Borchard)
[Source: Edwin Montefiore Borchard Papers, Manuscripts and Archives, Yale University Library. See pp. xxxviii, 68, 224, 617]

ACKNOWLEDGMENTS

Addison Wesley Longman. Selections from The Art of Thinking: A Guide to Critical and Creative Thought by Vincent Ryan Ruggiero. Copyright © 1984 by Harper & Row, Publishers, Inc. Reprinted by permission of Addison Wesley Educational Publishers, Inc.

Adler & Adler. Letter to Ramsey Clark, June 25, 1970. The Douglas Letters Copyright © 1987 by Melvin I. Urofsky. Reprinted by permission of Melvin I. Urofsky.

American Civil Liberties Union. "To American Friends of Justice." 2/19/1921. Excerpts of this letter reprinted by permission of John W. Roberts, Executive Director, American Civil Liberties Union of Massachusetts.

American Legion Magazine. "Sacco-Vanzetti Again" by William F. Buckley. Selections reprinted by permission of William F. Buckley and The American Legion Magazine, © October 1960.

Antioch Review. "The Tragedy in Dedham: a retrospect of the Sacco-Vanzetti trial." Antioch Review, © Vol. 15, (Winter 1955). Reprinted with permission of the publisher.

Paul P. Appel, Publisher. THE SACCO-VANZETTI CASE: Transcript of the Record of the Trial of Nicola Sacco and Bartolomeo Vanzetti in the Courts of Massachusetts and Subsequent Proceedings 1920-7. Mamaroneck, N. Y., 1969. Selections reprinted by courtesy of Paul P. Appel, whose six volumes have made a significant contribution to Sacco-Vanzetti scholarship.

Robert Bentley, Inc. Boston: A Documentary Novel of the Sacco-Vanzetti Case by Upton Sinclair. Copyright © 1928 by Upton Sinclair. Reprinted by permission of McIntosh and Otis, Inc.

Boston Herald. "Suicide Bares Bomb Arrests," (5/3/20) and "Contradicts Story Clearing Vanzetti in Bridgewater Crime" (1/13/29). Reprinted with permission of the Boston Herald.

Boston Public Library. Robert D'Attilio. "La Salute e in Voi: the Anarchist Dimension"; Nunzio Pernicone. "Introductory Remarks"— both passages from KF 224.S2S24, "Sacco-Vanzetti: Developments and Reconsiderations—1979"; John Dos Passos, Facing the Chair, p. 110 X.Fel 35; Bartolomeo Vanzetti—HV6533.M4A6 1921X. Reprinted by courtesy of the Trustees of the Boston Public Library.

Boston University Law Review. Common Sources of Error in the Examination and Interpretation of Ballistics Evidence, Volume 26:2 (1946) 207-48, by Charles J. Van Amburgh. Selections reprinted with permission. ©1946 Trustees of Boston University. Forum of original publication.

Bridgeport Post. "Bridgeport Man Thinks Shell Photos Beat Sacco-Vanzetti." Selections from news item of August 4, 1927. Reprinted by permission of Rick Sayers.

Marshall Cavendish Corporation, 1995. America in the 20th Century: 1920-1929 by Janet McDonnell. Reprinted with permission of the publisher.

The Christian Century. "STILL NO PROOF" by Alfred P. Klausler. Copyright © 1962 Christian Century Foundation. Selections from the September 26, 1962, issue of The Christian Century reprinted by permission of the publisher.

The Christian Science Monitor. "'Innocence and Betrayal'—was it a myth" by Francis Russell. March 10, 1966. Selections reprinted with permission of the publisher

Commonweal. "The intellectual mob for the defense" by David Cort. March 18, 1966. Selections reprinted by permission of Gregory Wilpert, Business Manager, Commonweal Foundation.

Massachusetts Archives
Summary of Sacco-Vanzetti Collections

PS11/Series 2084X Division of State Police. Sacco and Vanzetti case file, 1920-1977.
Materials include reports and interviews conducted by police before the trial, partial trial transcript, photographs, materals related to the bombing of Judge Webster Thayer's home in 1932, witretaps of Felix Frankfurter's phone, publicatons from and surveillance of the Sacco-Vanzetti Defense Committee, reports on the funeral of Sacco and Vanzetti, and requests for use of the Sacco-Vanzetti papers and exhibits. Photocopies of the collection are in box 4 - use of originals in boxes 1 & 2 is restricted. A finding aid is attached to the RLIN record in PS11 binder.

AG1/Series 2062X Attorney General's Office. Sacco and Vanzetti case file, 1919-1976.
This series includes legal records, reference materials and correspondence related to the case. A finding aid is attached to the RLIN record in AG1 binder.

GO7/Series 938X Governor's Legal Office. Subject files of the legal counsel, 1963-1978.
Gov. Dukakis files (1975-1979: MSD 2-253) include working papers, correspondence, and clippings relating to a review of the case on the fiftieth anniversary of the execution of Sacco and Vanzetti, leading to issuance of a gubernatorial proclamation on July 19, 1977.

GO22/Series 315X Governor's Advisory Committee on the Sacco-Vanzetti Case.

HS9.01/Series 289X Massachusetts State Prison. Commitment registers: v. 16, 1918-1927.

HS9.01/Series 305 Massachusetts State Prison. Inmate case files, 1910-1941.

PR27/PO28X Thayer family files, 1927-1938.

Massachusetts Suprene Judicial Court Archives. Commonwealth v. Sacco and Vanzetti: Records, 1919-1928. [See p. xliv in this handbook.]

FOREWORD

This book begins with the primary source—The Sacco-Vanzetti Case: Transcript of the Record of the Trial of Nicola Sacco and Bartolomeo Vanzetti in the Courts of Massachusetts and Subsequent Proceedings, 1920-7, Paul P. Appel, Publisher, Mamaroneck, N. Y., 1969. [See Holt's 6 vols., 1928-1929.] Volume I has pages 1-1092. (Justice Douglas's prefatory essay, "The Sacco-Vanzetti Case: Some Forty Years Later," runs from p. xv to p. l.) Vol. I contains the jury selection and evidence by the prosecution, The Commonwealth of Massachusetts, in the Dedham trial. The Commonwealth rests its case, concludes its presentation of evidence, on page 941; and counsel William Callahan begins his opening statement for the defense on the same page. Pages 947-1092 contain evidence by the defense.

Volume II has pages 1093 to 2266v. Pages 1093-2077 contain further evidence by the defense. The rest of volume II contains the Commonwealth rebuttal and reply (2078-2121), closing arguments by the defense and the Commonwealth (2122-2238), defense motions (2238), Judge Thayer's charge to the jury (2239-2265), the jury's verdict (2265-2266), and appendix (2266a-2266f). The index in volume II is keyed to both volumes I and II.

Volume III has pages 2267 to 3478. The defendants' Exceptions from Volume I are in pages 2269 to 2876. Exceptions from volume II are in pages 2877 to 3476. Demurrer is on pp. 3434-3436. Motion for Severance and Separate Trial of the defendants Sacco and Vanzetti is on pp. 3437-3443. Demand for Bill of Particulars is on pp. 3470-3471. Volume III is indexed in volume IV.

Volume IV has pages 3479 to 4359s. Defendants' Exceptions (continued from vol. III) are on pp. 3479-3495. Between p. 3482 and p. 3483 are two fold-out maps. The larger and more detailed map is a drawing of the crime scene—"Plan of Pearl Street South Braintree May 21, 1921 C. B. Breed Civil Engineer." Preceding this drawing is the "Plan of Johnson House West Bridgewater, Mass," the Johnson house being the scene of a major episode which prompted much post-trial debate.

Crammed with legal disputes, volume IV has the first five supplementary motions for a new trial: the Ripley motion (3536,3548-3593) and decision (3594-3604); the Gould motion (3496-3512) and decision (3513-3527); the Goodridge motion (3733-3887) and decision (3887-3891); the Andrews motion (3892-3949) and decision (3950-3960); the Proctor-Hamilton motion (3539, 3604-3732z) and decision (3704-3724). All five motions were heard by trial judge Webster Thayer, then a Massachusetts practice, and denied. Judge Thayer's ruling on the Switch of Gun Barrels, an episode not in the Holt volumes, is on pp. 3732bb-3732tt. Photos of shells, Vanzetti's gun, and bullets appear on pp. 3732b-3732z.

The appeal on the conviction of Sacco and Vanzetti was made in January 1926 before the Supreme Judicial Court for the Commonwealth. The Brief for the Defendants was argued by William G. Thompson (3961-4151). The Brief for the Commonwealth was argued by Assistant District Attorney Dudley P. Ranney (4153-4267).

On May 12, 1926, the Supreme Judicial Court for the Commonwealth upheld the Dedham verdict of July 14, 1921 (4269-4359). On May 13 Thompson appealed the Supreme Court's May 12 decision (4359a-4359c), requesting a re-hearing. The Supreme Judicial Court denied Thompson's request for a re-hearing on May 27,1926 (4359d). Index for volume IV is on pp. 4359f-4359s.

Volume V has pages 4360 to 5621. The volume has these documents: Madeiros' motion for a new trial (4361-4721) and Thayer's decision (4722-4777); Thompson and Ehrmann's appeal of Thayer's denial of the Madeiros motion for a new trial (4782-4861); Ranney's Brief for the Commonwealth (4863-4877); Decision on this appeal by the Supreme Judicial Court of the Commonwealth (4880-4894); Proceedings Upon Motion for Imposition of Sentences, which includes pre-sentencing statements by Sacco and Vanzetti (4895-4905); Petition for Exercise of Governor's Executive Power (4906-4947); Proceedings Before the Governor's Advisory Committee [stenographic minutes are not complete] (4948-5348); Hearing Before Governor's Advisory Committee (5349-5378); **Decision** of Gov. Alvan T. Fuller (5378c-5378h); **Report** by Fuller's Advisory Committee (5378i-5378z); Proceedings in State Courts after Governor's Decision (5379-5503); On Petitions for Certiorari (5505-5525); Petitions for Habeas Corpus (5527-5538); Copy of Docket Entries (5539-5545); General Appendices (5547-5597). Trial exhibits are on p. 5606. Cumulative index is on pp. 5599-5621.

Volume VI, the supplemental volume, has stenographic minutes of Vanzetti's preliminary hearings on the Bridgewater crime, May 18, 1920 (1-35), and an incomplete transcript of his trial at Plymouth for this crime (37-336). It has two letters to Governor Fuller from defense attorneys Thompson and Ehrmann (339-361), the Pinkerton reports (363-394), a transcript of the minutes from the inquest at Quincy on April 17, 1920 (395-467), an Index (469-473), and a Chronology (475-482). Its bibliography on the Sacco-Vanzetti case from1920 to1967 is on pp. 487-524.

Now to my purpose. This 2007 handbook will make you better informed about the joint trial of Sacco and Vanzetti than the Dedham jurors. Since July 14, 1921, champions of Sacco and Vanzetti have challenged the jury's verdict on Sacco's .32 Colt pistol, Vanzetti's .38 H. & R. revolver, the six murder bullets, and selected witnesses. All Sacco-Vanzetti champions genuflect before Felix Frankfurter, who in 1927 pronounced magisterially on the 1921 verdict without knowledge of accessible primary sources, new evidence. (Frankfurter never told his 1925 pupil, Sylvester Gates, to research in Dexter, Maine.) Against the partisans' 85-five-year record of complaint, readers will find here several pieces of new evidence mingling with well-known documented artifacts of Sacco and Vanzetti history. Both are represented in my 52 research topics, addenda, and other critical items.

This handbook shows my faith in your skill and industry to find the historical truth of the Sacco-Vanzetti case in the primary source, the transcript of the Dedham trial, a document read by comparatively few in the twentieth century. Here is your chance to study the testimony in the transcript—all the critical evidence presented at the trial. Having this bedrock evidence at hand, you meet the first rule of research: begin at the beginning. So this book, initially, bypasses summaries of the case in history books and reference works, all secondary sources, each one of which you will be able to test for accuracy and fairness once you have mastered the Dedham transcript. Armed with this handbook, you may become the final historians of this disputed case.

To honor Mr. Appel, I sometimes cite **Appel** to stand for **Transcript of the Record**. (So: Appel, VI: 1 means volume 6 of the transcript, page 1.) Editorial comments are in brackets. Boldface means my emphasis of a textual item. Bracketed items within the testimony are added for clarity. Example: Q. Where did you see it [the bandit car]? The number within brackets tells the page of an **Appel** volume or of another source. Q = Question. A = Answer. Court = Thayer.

I am grateful to specialists in the Interlibrary Loan Department at Milner Library, Illinois State University: Carol Hartzell, Carol Ruyle, and Pat Lee. I appreciate the assistance given me by other specialists at Milner Library: Vanette Schwartz, Katherine Weir, James Huff, Jean Macdonald, Joan Winters, and Stanley Gutzman.

I thank Stephen Z. Nonack, Head of Reference, Library of the Boston Athenaeum.

I thank librarians at the Boston Public Library: Andy Schmidt, Reference Librarian, Social Sciences Department; Giuseppe Bisaccia, Curator of Manuscripts; Roberta Zonghi, Keeper of Rare Books and Manuscripts; Henry F. Scannell, Reference Librarian, Microtext Department. I thank M. Leanne Alexander, Reference, Iowa State University; Bill Boles, The Boston Globe; Dennis Lien, University of Minnesota Libraries; Shyamala Balgopal, Reference, University of Illinois; David A. Ferris, Curator of Rare Books, Harvard Law School Library.

I thank Elizabeth Van Tuyl, Historical Collections, and Betty D. Goldman, Bridgeport Public Library, Bridgeport, Connecticut; and I thank reference librarians, Bloomington Public Library, Bloomington, Illinois.

I thank J. Michael Comeau, Massachusetts Archives, Boston, Massachusetts. I thank Bill Talentino, Goodnow Public Library, Sudbury, for putting me in touch with Lt. Edward Montague, Massachusetts State Police, the Department's representative to the future Massachusetts State Police Museum at New Braintree, Massachusetts.

I extend my thanks to YIVO INSTITUTE FOR JEWISH RESEARCH for their documentation of Dr. Kallen's publications with The World Book Encyclopedia.

For her three maps, three processed photos, and four sections of Breed's Plan I give special thanks to cartographer Jill Freund Thomas, Department of Geography-Geology, Illinois State University.

For offering his judicial expertise, I thank Ronald C. Dozier, Circuit Judge, Circuit Court of Illinois, Eleventh Judicial Circuit, McLean County.

I am indebted to Professor James E. Starrs for a copy of EXAMINATION OF FIREARM RELATED EVIDENCE: THE

NICOLA SACCO AND BARTOLOMEO VANZETTI CASE—1983 Report of Firearm Examination Panel, AFTE Journal (Volume 17, Number 3) July 1985.

I am grateful for insights given me in letters by David E. Kaiser, in letters by David Felix, in brief notes by Paul Avrich, in three letters by the late Francis Russell.

I thank Carol Feurtado, Outreach Committee of the Dexter Historical Society, for sending me on 13 May 2003 a photocopy of the news item from the 5 February 1914 issue of The Eastern Gazette, a Dexter weekly reporting the 3:00 A.M. fire that gutted the grocery store of Frank N. Morgridge in Dexter, Maine, on 1 February 1914. I also thank Carol for sending me the "Ninety-Eighth Annual Report of the Municipal Officers of the Town of Dexter For the Year Ending March 1, 1914." Within this 98th annual report, pp. 54-55, is the "Report of the Engineers of Fire Department," an excerpt of which is this statement on p. 55: "February 1, 3:00 A.M.,—This alarm was for a bad fire in the store of F.N. Morgridge, near the old depot, and the department was given a long, hard run. The store was in flames when the alarm was rung in,... The building was badly burned on the first and second floors...." I thank Maggie Frazier, Reference Department, Bangor Public Library, for sending me a photocopy of the news item on the Morgridge fire from the 2 February 1914 issue of the Bangor Daily News. I thank the Town of Dexter for preserving two primary sources, discovery of which came from a curiosity piqued by pp. 1556-1568 in the Transcript of the Record, grocer "Morgridge" having been ignored by authors of U.S. history textbooks for 75 years. I thank Phil Getchell, Bangor Public Library, for a photocopy of p. 6 from the Bangor Daily Commercial (02/02/1914) with the headline: CAT SAVES LIFE IN DEXTER FIRE. The News item states: "Amos Morgridge...with difficulty...aroused his brother-in-law, Elbridge Atwater and his wife who resided with him." It adds: "Mr. and Mrs. Morgridge were in Parkman [birthplace of Frank Morgridge] at the time of the fire." Lastly, I thank Sally Vermaaten, Harvard Law School Library.

I owe a great debt to my wife, Marilyn Provart Newby, Professor Emerita of Art, Illinois State University, who gave expert assistance, designed the cover of the handbook, typed much of it, and titled it.

A NOTE TO THE READER IN 2007

New evidence in this book includes three unpublished letters from Edwin M. Borchard to Felix Frankfurter, 1927-31, Frankfurter's Oxford letter to Borchard, November 9, 1933, and a letter dated June 17, 1921, from Charles C. Palmer of Dexter, Maine, to the District Attorney at Dedham, Massachusetts. I bring these letters to the center stage of Sacco and Vanzetti history alongside evidence of the fire that gutted the grocery store of Frank N. Morgridge of Dexter, Maine, on February 1, 1914. (The "triangular" stage which Harvard historian Arthur M. Schlesinger draws on page xi in *The Legacy of Sacco and Vanzetti* ignores Dexter, hometown of Elbridge Atwater and Rexford Slater, defense witnesses on Vanzetti's revolver.) I add to the testimony of nine witnesses: Elbridge Atwater, John Faulkner, Austin Cole, Albert Frantello, William Heron, Peter McCullum, Joseph Rosen, Joseph Scavitto, and Charles Van Amburgh. I update the book further with assessments of Sacco and Vanzetti by Paul Avrich, John F. Neville, and Michael Miller Topp.

I add letters by Upton Sinclair to Robert Minor (1928) and to John Beardsley (1929). I also add bricolage.

The Sacco and Vanzetti case is poorly understood by most Americans. To correct this national scandal, *Kill Now, Talk Forever* excerpts key testimony from the stenographic minutes of the 1921 Dedham trial. It presents a wide range of opinion in the exhaustive post-trial debate, tapping into scholarly journals, history books, book reviews, reference works, encyclopedias, newspapers, magazine articles, essays, editorials, letters, historical fiction, a 1959 legislative hearing, a 1979 Boston conference, a 2005 book in the Bedford Series in History and Culture, and primary sources from the Dexter Historical Society. New evidence I discovered in three places (Dexter, Harvard, and Yale) sheds new light on the Plymouth and Dedham trials. Now you can tell if U.S. history textbooks and encyclopedias get it right on Sacco and Vanzetti.

Richard Newby
Normal, Illinois
January 20, 2007

INTRODUCTION

Nicola Sacco and Bartolomeo Vanzetti were arrested on a streetcar in Brockton, Massachusetts, on May 5, 1920. Both were Italian immigrants who became ultramilitant anarchists. Sacco carried a loaded .32 calibre Colt automatic pistol in the waistband of his trousers when he was arrested. Vanzetti carried a loaded .38 calibre Harrington & Richardson revolver in his back pocket. Sacco had in his pocket twenty-three live rounds that fit his Colt; Vanzetti had four shotgun shells on him. This arrest at 10:05 P. M. marked the beginning of the Sacco-Vanzetti case, America's long debate over two criminal trials.

At the first trial—held in Plymouth, Massachusetts, from June 22 to July 1, 1920—Bartolomeo Vanzetti of North Plymouth was found guilty of assault with intent to rob and murder at Bridgewater on December 24, 1919. Vanzetti did not testify. For firing a shotgun at a payroll truck, Vanzetti was sentenced on August 16, 1920, to serve 12 to15 years in the Charlestown State Prison.

At the second trial—a joint trial held in Dedham, Massachusetts, from May 31 to July 14, 1921—Nicola Sacco of South Stoughton and Vanzetti (now a convicted felon) were found guilty of murdering paymaster Frederick A. Parmenter and his guard Alessandro Berardelli on April 15, 1920, in South Braintree. The prosecution contended Sacco and Vanzetti and three other bandits escaped in a stolen 7-passenger Buick with the Slater & Morrill payroll of $15,776.51. After eight motions for a new trial were denied, Sacco and Vanzetti and a third convicted murderer were electrocuted in the first twenty-seven minutes of August 23, 1927.

On April 9, 1927, Judge Thayer sentenced Sacco and Vanzetti to die on July 10, a sentence which set the stage for the last feverish summer of appeals. Disturbed by the long legal battle and the issue of doubt, some of Massachusetts' most respected citizens urged Governor Alvan T. Fuller to appoint an advisory committee on the case. On June 1 he appointed three men: Robert Grant, retired probate court judge; Abbott Lawrence Lowell, President of Harvard University; and Samuel W. Stratton, President of the Massachusetts Institute of Technololgy. Fuller directed his advisory committee to review both the transcript of the trial and the eight appeals of the verdict, then give him a report of their judgment on the two questions at issue: the fairness of the trial and the justness of the verdict. Fuller would grant executive clemency (commute the death sentences) or deny clemency (carry out the death sentences) based upon the report of his advisory committee. Fuller also had authority to pardon Sacco and Vanzetti.

On June 3, 1927, the ballistics expert, Major Calvin Goddard, brought his newly developed comparison microscope to Dedham and compared Bullet 3 and Shell W of the Dedham trial with bullets and shells test fired through Sacco's gun at Lowell on June 18, 1921. Goddard said Bullet 3 and Shell W were fired from Sacco's Colt.

Independently, Fuller began his own review on April 23, 1927, and was kept tied to the case until the last hour before execution. With help from his attorney and his secretary, he interviewed eleven jurors, the trial judge, and some 100 witnesses of the South Baintree crime. He also interviewed Plymouth trial witnesses and Plymouth jurors. After he talked with John Vahey and James M. Graham——defense attorneys at Vanzetti's Plymouth trial——he concluded that Vanzetti himself had made the decision not to take the witness stand at Plymouth. This conclusion Vanzetti disputed.

If Fuller did not conduct an exhaustive review, he did interview many concerned about the fairness and justness of both the Plymouth and Dedham trials. Among these was Roy E. Gould, who, though a putative eyewitness of the South Braintree crime, had not been called to testify at Dedham. Upon request, Fuller agreed to a joint interview with Gardner Jackson and Aldino Felicani. (Jackson and Marion Denman Frankfurter published The Letters of Sacco and Vanzetti in 1928. Felicani, on May 6, 1920, founded the Sacco-Vanzetti Defense Committee.) Jackson, who left a reporter's job at the Boston Globe in 1926 to direct public relations for the Sacco-Vanzetti Defense Committee, was one of many persistent visitors to Fuller's office. The pugnacious Jackson also confronted Fuller's Advisory Committee.

In July, Fuller conducted interviews both in his office and on the road. He questioned ballistics experts who had testified at Dedham, and he read legal documents submitted by William G. Thompson and Herbert B. Ehrmann——attorneys who represented Sacco and Vanzetti before Fuller's Advisory Committee. (Thompson, who had lectured at the Harvard Law School, became chief attorney for the defense on November 25, 1924, when the radical lawyer Fred H. Moore lost favor with the Saccos.) In his surprise visit to the Charlestown prison on July 22, Fuller talked with Sacco, Vanzetti, and Celestino F. Madeiros in the warden's office.

Enter Celestino Madeiros. Madeiros, a convicted murderer like Sacco and Vanzetti, while waiting to be retried for his crime of November 1, 1924, in Wrentham, Massachusetts, confessed in a prison note of November 18, 1925, that he and a gang from Providence, Rhode Island, committed the South Braintree crime, not Sacco and Vanzetti. This confession generated eighty-eight affidavits; and a motion for a new trial for Sacco and Vanzetti was argued before Judge Thayer from September 13 to 17, 1926. Thompson and Assistant District Attorney, Dudley P. Ranney, debated the thesis that the South Braintree crime had been committed by Madeiros and the Joe Morelli gang of Providence. Thayer denied this motion on October 22, 1926. Thompson and Ehrmann lost the appeal on denial of this sixth motion on April 5, 1927. On April 9, Sacco and Vanzetti were permitted to speak before Thayer pronounced their death sentences.

Fuller heard varied pleas in his Executive Chamber, the first pleaders being Rosa Sacco and Elias Field. In one meeting he heard angry words from Tom O'Connor (to which Fuller replied in kind), forensic reporter who would trumpet the innocence of Sacco and Vanzetti for the rest of his life. In another, he heard Joseph Rosen, Dorchester cloth peddler and Vanzetti's first alibi witness at the Dedham trial. He heard Louis and Tony Fortini of Plymouth, men not found in the transcript of the Plymouth trial. (The transcript of the Plymouth trial is incomplete. Vanzetti boarded his first four years in Plymouth with the Brini family. In 1918-1920 he boarded with Frank and Mary Fortini. Mary, an alibi witness for Vanzetti at his Plymouth trial, came to plead with Fuller.) He heard Beltrando Brini, Vanzetti's 13-year-old alibi witness at the Plymouth trial; and he heard Beltrando's anarchist father, Vincenzo Brini (under threat of deportation in 1918), who had welcomed anarchists Galleani, Tresca, and Giovannitti to his North Plymouth home. He heard Agostino Ferrante, Italian consul; James Mede, ex-convict; Robert Reid, Thomas Doyle, George Woodbury, and Harry M. Schaub—investigators for the defense; Atwater and Slater, witnesses on Vanzetti's H. & R. revolver; Mrs. Rantoul, who would submit an affidavit on the prejudice of Thayer. He heard "mystery witnesses" alluded to darkly in the Boston Herald and in Upton Sinclair's Boston; and he heard John F. Moors,

Boston banker and member of the Harvard Corporation. On July 29, he heard William G. Thompson and Herbert B. Ehrmann plead eight hours for the convicted Sacco and Vanzetti. He last heard Thompson and Ehrmann plead on August 22, the day he heard Congressman Fiorello H. La Guardia.

On July 26, Fuller walked the crime scene at South Braintree, taking measurements to check against testimony in the transcript, after which he paid a second visit to Vanzetti at the Charlestown prison. Sacco refused to discuss the case with him. Elsewhere, not averse to speaking out, was poet Edna St. Vincent Millay—duly arrested for picketing, a fate she shared with authors John Dos Passos, Dorothy Parker and Katherine Anne Porter. Millay told Fuller in an afternoon interview on August 22 how the Governor of Maine had made a tragic mistake by failing to commute a condemned man's death sentence. That evening she sent Fuller a letter with a refrain in hexameter: "Which way would He have turned, this Jesus of your faith?"

Working apart from the Governor, Fuller's advisory committee read trial papers to prepare for the private hearings they would hold in the Council Chamber of the State House in Boston. The hearings began on July 11, 1927, three days after the committee visited the crime scene and interviewed Sacco, Vanzetti, and Madeiros in the Charlestown prison. Counsel for the Commonwealth of Massachusetts—Ranney—and counsel for Sacco and Vanzetti—Thompson and Ehrmann—debated various points of the two trials. Each side questioned Dedham trial witnesses. Thompson and Ehrmann questioned Frederick G. Katzmann, formerly District Attorney for the Southeastern District of Massachusetts and prosecuting attorney at both the Plymouth and Dedham trials. But Thompson and Ehrmann were absent when the advisory committee questioned Judge Thayer (July 12) and ten Dedham jurors, a condition set by the advisory committee. (One juror was dead, one was out of state. The committee lacked subpoena power.) On July 13—the same day they pleaded with Fuller—Minnie Kennedy and Louise Kelley, not called as trial witnesses, told the advisory committee the man they saw by the bandit car below their first-floor factory window on April 15, 1920, was neither Sacco nor Vanzetti.

Lowell, the dominant member of Fuller's committee, on July 14 challenged the banquet testimony by two of Sacco's alibi witnesses—Bosco and Guadagni. Bosco answered this challenge by producing a newspaper item which verified the banquet date in his Dedham testimony. Bosco's answer, critics say, exposed Lowell's bias. In 1948, Louis Joughin would fault a Lowell biographer for deleting this episode.

Jeremiah J. McAnarney, Vanzetti's attorney at the Dedham trial, did not meet the advisory committee. Nor did Fred H. Moore, Sacco's attorney. But Jeremiah's brother, Thomas F. McAnarney, Vanzetti's co-counsel at Dedham, met the advisory committee and answered questions by Thompson, Ehrmann, Grant, Lowell, and Ranney. So did a second brother, Judge John W. McAnarney. Albert H. Hamilton, engaged to do ballistics studies for the defense in 1923, told the advisory committee his test results exonerated Sacco, the thesis of the Proctor-Hamilton motion.

Hamilton was challenged by James E. Burns, defense ballistics expert at Dedham, who, after reviewing new studies of the bullets and shells, amended his trial testimony, telling Fuller's committee that one murder-scene shell—Fraher Shell W—had been fired from Sacco's gun. Burns is not in the truncated committee minutes, but according to reporter Wendell D. Howie, Boston Evening Transcript (August 10), Burns "tacitly admitted [to Fuller] that the fatal shell and the test shells fired in the Sacco gun had identical markings." Burns had given a similar statement to the Bridgeport Post on August 4.

Joseph Rosen, the major alibi witness for Vanzetti, came before the advisory committee on July 21 and testified he stayed in a rooming house at Whitman on the night of April 15, 1920, after his midday sale of cloth to Vanzetti in North Plymouth. Assistant District Attorney Ranney did not cross-examine him.

Several witnesses at the hearings of the advisory committee called Webster Thayer a prejudiced judge. His accusers included Brahmin lawyer Arthur D. Hill; Lois B. Rantoul, who spoke for the Greater Boston Federation of Churches; Frank Sibley and Elizabeth Bernkopf, reporters for the Boston Globe and the International News Service, respectively; Robert Benchley, drama critic and humorist; James Richardson, professor of law at Dartmouth College; George U. Crocker, prominent Boston attorney. All but Hill and Richardson signed affidavits as to Thayer's prejudice. A final affidavit was signed by John Nicholas Beffel, radical journalist. Motion 8, built from these affidavits, Hill argued on August 8 and Thayer denied on August 9. (Motion 7, which alleged collusion between the U.S. Department of

Justice and the Commonwealth of Massachusetts to conceal evidence, was denied jointly with Motion 6.)

The motion on Thayer's prejudice came after Thompson and Ehrmann's June/July allegation to both Fuller and Fuller's committee: that someone in the prosecution—before the trial—had secretly removed both the bullet that killed Berardelli and a spent crime-scene shell and substituted another bullet and shell. This allegation in 1927— that the Commonwealth used false trial exhibits, Bullet 3 and Shell W—some Sacco-Vanzetti scholars take seriously.

On July 27, Fuller received three brown envelopes from his advisory committee, their report upholding the guilty verdict at Dedham. That same day, Alfred Dreyfus, himself a victim of gross injustice, signed a French communique which said the United States "must take into account the world's opinion" (NY Times, 7/28/27: 8). To some, Sacco and Vanzetti had become international heroes.

The committee's report signalled defeat, and defense effort redoubled with execution imminent. (Thayer had moved the execution date from July 10 to August 10.) Hill, who assisted Thompson in 1923, became chief defense counsel on August 4, teaming with Felix Frankfurter, who worked behind the scenes. (Frankfurter's involvement in the appeal process is documented by transcripts of wiretaps made on his telephone by Massachusetts state police.) Seeking a ruling from the United States Supreme Court—all appeals of the verdict having failed in Massachusetts—Hill, Thompson, and Michael Musmanno visited the vacationing U. S. Supreme Court Justice Oliver Wendell Holmes, who refused to grant a writ of habeas corpus, a writ which would have stayed execution. That was August 10, when execution was reset for midnight August 22. On the same day, the Sacco-Vanzetti Liberation Committee appealed to the Pope in a cablegram which read: "Sacco and Vanzetti are as innocent as Jesus Christ" (NY Times, 8/11/27: 2).

The six years between conviction and execution brought protests from such intellectuals as Marie Curie, Albert Einstein, John Dewey, Anatole France, and H. G. Wells. Fuller stood unmoved by well-organized protests from abroad, by public demonstrations in the U. S., by thousands of letters—many begging for clemency—and by pleas of Rosina Sacco. Bombings and death threats did not deter him.

Petitions grew. On August 21 Hill drove to Maine and was denied a petition for a writ of habeas corpus by Holmes' colleague on the Supreme Court, Justice Harlan Fiske Stone. The same day, Hill and

Richard C. Evarts were denied a stay of execution by a third member of the U. S. Supreme Court, Justice Louis D. Brandeis, a friend of Felix Frankfurter, Harvard Law School professor. The next day, defense counsel Elias Field and Musmanno were denied a stay of execution by Superior Court Judge James H. Sisk. Justice Holmes denied two more petitions for stay of execution on August 20 (by Hill and Evarts) and August 22 (by John Finerty).

"There were no constitutional grounds for federal intervention and whatever his personal feelings he [Holmes] did not have a judicial reason to postpone the execution." Joseph P. Lash, <u>Dealers and Dreamers: A New Look at the New Deal</u> (New York: Doubleday, 1988): 62. See Holmes's notes, transcript: pp. 5516, 5532.

In April, Michael A. Musmanno, a Pittsburgh lawyer, joined the fight to save Sacco and Vanzetti. Through Thompson he soon met Fuller, debated the case with him, and left the Governor's office depressed. Still, he worked intensely in the last hours of appeal. On August 21 he pleaded for a stay of execution in a personal telephone call to Chief Justice William Howard Taft in Quebec. Taft told him to put his specific request in a telegram. This he did at 9:30 P.M. The same day, he sent three telegrams to President Coolidge at his summer White House in Rapid City. Getting no reply, he tried to talk with Coolidge by telephone and was told by a presidential secretary that the Sacco-Vanzetti case was not a federal matter. When he offered to fly to South Dakota, he was told the President would not see him. (The Sacco-Vanzetti Defense Committee had appealed to Coolidge by telegram on August 9, and had asked Col. Charles A. Lindbergh—see the subhead in the <u>Boston Herald</u>, August 9—"to appeal to President in behalf of Sacco and Vanzetti.") On the morning of August 22, Musmanno received Taft's long telegram of denial. It came just two days after he tried to file a writ of certiorari with the United States Supreme Court, in recess until October. Acting in haste, Musmanno had failed to bring Commonwealth court records with him to Washington (NY Times, 08/21/1927: 17).

Failing to persuade earthly powers, Musmanno, one hour before the not-to-be-stopped execution, confronted Fuller on his decision to electrocute: "And on that decision will you stand for all time?" "For all time," replied Fuller. Facing that finality, Musmanno left the State House at 11:03 P.M. on August 22. When he recalled the pre-execution hour in his aggrieved epilogue, After Twelve Years, he wrote: "The tramp of the centurions could be heard on the hill of Golgotha." This claim of martyrdom, which atheists Sacco and Vanzetti had asserted through Christian allusions in their letters from prison, was boosted at their funeral by mourners wearing red arm bands with the black letters:

REMEMBER
JUSTICE
CRUCIFIED
AUGUST 22, 1927

Frankfurter gave the Sacco-Vanzetti case respectability and intellectual force. A man of keen judicial insight and impeccable academic credentials, he was appointed to the United States Supreme Court by President Franklin D. Roosevelt in 1939, where he served until August 28, 1962. His brilliance was first officially recognized when he was chosen to join the staff of the Harvard Law Review as a second-year student at the Harvard Law School, a high honor. In 1914 at the age of thirty-one he was appointed to the faculty of the Harvard Law School. He was much esteemed by the judicially astute Justice Louis D. Brandeis, who, because of a conflict of interest, could not help Sacco and Vanzetti—a dual conflict, say historians who have read the Brandeis-Frankfurter correspondence. To the end of their lives, both Justices kept their belief in the innocence of Sacco and Vanzetti. (A similar dogmatic faith—the men were "probably innocent"—was to be expressed in 1969 by Associate Justice William O. Douglas in his prefatory essay to Appel's first volume of the Dedham trial transcript.)

Loyal to principle, Frankfurter placed his name on the February 19, 1921, statement by the New England Civil Liberties Committee, whose parent is the American Civil Liberties Union. This pre-trial statement argued: 1. There is no substantial evidence against Sacco and Vanzetti, 2. The Commonwealth of Massachusetts is putting these men on trial because they are Italian immigrants who belong to a radical group. In his capacity as Harvard Law School professor, Frankfurter validated the 1921 ACLU opinion on the Sacco-Vanzetti case by writing a scathing criticism of Thayer and Katzmann in the March 1927 issue of the Atlantic Monthly, calling the Dedham trial a mockery of justice. Convinced by Frankfurter's analysis, H. G. Wells wrote in the London Sunday Express on June 5, 1927: "Sacco and Vanzetti are as innocent of the Braintree murder ... as Julius Caesar."

Frankfurter's 24-page article, fast expanded to a book of 118 pages, argued the need for a new trial to avert a miscarriage of justice. (Brandeis got his copy of Frankfurter's book—The Case of Sacco and Vanzetti—on March 7, 1927, the book intellectuals called their "bible.") In both article and book, Frankfurter endorsed Thompson and Ehrmann's thesis that the South Braintree murders had been committed by Madeiros and the Morelli gang.

When Frankfurter was challenged in 1960, he resumed his fight to exculpate Sacco and Vanzetti. In his "Note on Republication," June 5, 1961—Universal Library Edition, Grosset and Dunlap, January 1962—Justice Frankfurter observed: "And Sacco-Vanzetti have probably the unique distinction for men convicted for robbery-murder of having a favoring account of themselves in the Dictionary of American Biography." He called his book a "document in the history of the case," considered its republication reasonable, adding that he could not "disown" what he wrote in 1927. This 1962 reprint would be his final appeal to history.

Neither daunted nor impressed by Frankfurter's book, Boston attorney Robert H. Montgomery, after his epistolary dispute with Justice Frankfurter in 1958, set out to inculpate Sacco and Vanzetti in his 1960 book—Sacco-Vanzetti: The Murder and the Myth. This massive challenge to Frankfurter, the first of four challenges in the 1960s, came after a 33-year silence by apologists for the Commonwealth of Massachusetts, excepting Ethelbert Grabill's booklet. Recognition of Montgomery as a worthy challenger to Frankfurter would come tardily from editors of reference books. Some editors of encyclopedias have yet to recognize him. On the trial verdicts, one of these authorities is right, and the other authority is wrong. With the help of this handbook, you can tell the world which one is right.

NOW TO THE COURTROOM

Members of a jury must listen intently at a murder trial in order to find out who is telling the truth. As a 21st-century juror, you must read these selections from Appel's published trial record carefully. Remember! The transcript of Sacco and Vanzetti's trial is the authority to which Frankfurter appealed—he called it "the incontrovertible official record"—when he lectured John H. Wigmore, dean of Northwestern University Law School, in the <u>Boston Herald</u>, April 26,1927. In defending his article in the <u>Atlantic Monthly</u> against Wigmore's attack (Wigmore called Frankfurter "the plausible pundit of the leading law school"), Frankfurter advised Wigmore that whenever a human opinion (that is, Thayer's) is in conflict with "the stenographic record of the trial, the official record of the trial must prevail." After you have read the record of the Dedham trial and studied the Plymouth transcript, you will be qualified to judge between these 1927 disputants in the case: Frankfurter and Wigmore.

Borchard Joins Sacco-Vanzetti Debate

On May 2, 1927, Edwin M. Borchard, Yale Law School professor, wrote to Frankfurter: Thank you for your note of the 27th enclosing your exchanges with Wigmore. Wigmore, unhappily, is a casualty of the war. It seems a great pity that so useful a man should have permitted himself to be paralyzed by the late catastrophe. . . . Indeed, his emotions have led him into a careless contempt of fact. . . . He so grossly misrepresents the laws of certain foreign countries in a matter in which there is now complete information available that I regard it as almost inexcusable. The misrepresentation is due to the fact that he desires to make a case, and is, therefore, careless of facts. I regard Wigmore as a tragic pity. The same attitude of mind is reflected in his articles on the Sacco-Vanzetti case. [Source: Edwin Montefiore Borchard Papers, Manuscripts and Archives, Yale University Library.]

CHRONOLOGY

1919

June 2	Attorney General Palmer's house in Washington, D. C. is bombed. Bombing across U.S.
June 24	Luigi Galleani, anarchist leader, and eight of his disciples are deported to Italy.
November 7	First of the Palmer Red raids.
November 23	Buick belonging to Francis J. Murphy is stolen in Needham.
December 22	License plates (used at Bridgewater) stolen from Hassam's garage, Needham.
December 24	Attempted holdup in Bridgewater.

1920

January 2	Red raids in 33 cities.
January 6-7	License plates belonging to Warren H. Ellis (used at South Braintree) stolen from car, Needham.
Jan. or Feb.	Sacco is told by his employer, George Kelley, that he is being investigated by Federal agents.
February 25	Friends of Sacco and Vanzetti, Elia and Salsedo, anarchist printers, are detained in New York by Department of Justice for questioning about pink circulars found at bomb sites.
April 15	Holdup and murders of Parmenter and Berardelli in South Braintree.
April 16	Coacci, an anarchist arrested by Stewart in 1918, is taken from the Coacci house by Inspector Root of the Immigration Service. He is deported from New York City on April 18.
April 17	Discovery of abandoned Murphy Buick in Manley Woods, West Bridgewater.
April 19	Boda's Overland is towed from Coacci house to be repaired at the Johnson garage in Elm Square, West Bridgewater.

April 20	Stewart interviews Boda at Coacci house, suspects him of South Braintree crime, and decides to set a trap for him at Johnson garage.
April 25	Vanzetti is sent by a committee to New York City to learn about Salsedo and Elia. He returns on April 29.
May 2	Meeting in East Boston of Sacco, Vanzetti, Orciani, Felicani, and others to discuss Vanzetti's report of his New York trip.
May 3	Salsedo jumps 14 floors to his death in New York City after giving Dept. of Justice names of anarchist bombers and admitting he printed pink circular "Plain Words."
May 4	Sacco gets oneway passport (foglio di via) for himself, wife, and son at Italian Consulate in Boston.
May 5	Sacco and Vanzetti are arrested on a streetcar in Campello, a part of Brockton.
May 6	Orciani arrested.
May 7	John P. Vahey of Plymouth is hired as Vanzetti's counsel. James M. Graham is hired as Sacco's counsel.
May 11	Orciani, having a work alibi, is released.
May 18	Preliminary hearing of Vanzetti for Bridgewater holdup held at Brockton. Vanzetti is held for the grand jury.
May 26	Sacco's preliminary hearing for South Braintree murder held at Quincy. Sacco is held for the grand jury.
June 11	Vanzetti indicted by Plymouth County grand jury for assault with intent to rob and for assault with intent to murder at Bridgewater.
June 22-July 1	Vanzetti is tried in Superior Court at Plymouth for attempted holdup at Bridgewater. Vanzetti pleads not guilty but does not testify. Jury returns verdict of guilty on both counts.
August 16	Vanzetti is sentenced 12 to 15 years in Charlestown prison for Bridgewater crime.
August 19	Fred H. Moore, upon recommendation of Carlo Tresca, is named chief defense counsel for Sacco and Vanzetti.
September 11	Sacco and Vanzetti indicted by Norfolk County grand jury for the South Braintree murders.
September 16	Wall Street bomb explosion.

November 22   American Civil Liberties Union supports defense after hearing report by Mary Heaton Vorse.

1921

February 19   New England Civil Liberties Committee, whose parent is the American Civil Liberties Union, sends out an appeal for money to aid defense, calling projected trial political.

May 31-July 14   Trial of Sacco and Vanzetti.

October   Mass demonstrations in Europe against verdict.

1927

April 26   Edwin M. Borchard of the Yale Law Faculty publishes his April 21st letter to Governor Fuller in the <u>Yale Daily News</u>. He urges Fuller to appoint an advisory commission on the Sacco and Vanzetti case. In his April 26 letter to Felix Frankfurter, Borchard says he is astonished that theYale campus conveys the general impression "that the men were really guilty." Borchard says Yale's "Liberal Club is taking an active part in setting campus opinion straight" by publishing his letter to Fuller in the college campus paper.

2003

March 9   Newby finds new evidence in Maine.

2005

July 19   Newby finds Frankfurter's 1933 Oxford letter to Borchard and Palmer's letter relating what Rexford Slater told him on June 17, 1921.

THE SACCO-VANZETTI CASE

TRANSCRIPT OF THE RECORD
OF THE TRIAL OF
NICOLA SACCO AND BARTOLOMEO VANZETTI
IN THE COURTS OF MASSACHUSETTS
AND SUBSEQUENT PROCEEDINGS
1920-7

Prefatory Essay by William O. Douglas
Associate Supreme Court Justice

VOLUME I
Pages 1 to 1092

Second Edition

BIBLIOGRAPHY
1920-1967

PAUL P. APPEL, PUBLISHER
Mamaroneck, N. Y.

1969

COMMONWEALTH OF MASSACHUSETTS

Superior Court, Criminal Session,

Norfolk, ss.   Thayer,

J., and a Jury.

Docket Nos. 5545 and 5546.

COMMONWEALTH vs. SACCO
COMMONWEALTH vs. VANZETTI

STENOGRAPHIC MINUTES OF TRIAL

Indictments charging the defendants with murder were returned September 11, 1920.

The trial, held at Dedham, began May 31, 1921, and was concluded July 13, 1921, each of the defendants being found guilty.

Records relating to the Sacco-Vanzetti case in other repositories:

Boston Athenaeum, 10 1/2 Beacon Street., Boston, MA 02108. Finding aid in Supreme Judicial Court reference files - see Libby Bouvier.

Aldine Felicani collection (Sacco-Vanzetti Defense Committee records, 1920-1929), Boston Public Library, 666 Boylston St., Boston, MA 02117

Sacco-Vanzetti case records, Harvard Law School Library, Langdell Hall, Cambridge, MA 02138. Finding aid in Archives series control file for PS11/Series 2084X; also included as part of AG1/Series, 2062X. RLIN record in PS11 binder.

A.L. Lowell papers, Harvard University Archives, Pusey Library, Harvard University, Cambridge, MA 02138. (see GO22/Series 315X above)

Ballistics materials are at State Police Headquarters.

Federal Bureau of Investigation, Washington, DC.

[Source: Jennifer Fauxsmith, Reference Archivist, The Commonwealth of Massachusetts, Archives Division, 220 Morrissey Boulevard, Boston, Massachusetts 02125. (617) 727-2816. See p. xxii in this handbook.]

Records at Harvard University

Sacco-Vanzetti Case Records,1920-1928, Finding Aid. Harvard Law School Library, Cambridge, MA 02138. See Box 23-2
Correspondence, 1921-1923: C. C. Palmer to Ranney June 17, 1921.
See also Box 23-23 Correspondence, July, 1927: Ranney to Frank N. Nay July 14, 1927 [Ed. See p. 413 in this book.]

FIRST DAY

COMMONWEALTH OF MASSACHUSETTS

NORFOLK, SS.

SUPERIOR COURT

CRIMINAL SESSION
Thayer, J. and a Jury.

COMMONWEALTH

V.

SACCO

COMMONWEALTH

V.

VANZETTI

APPEARANCES:

Frederick G. Katzmann, Esq., District Attorney; Harold P. Williams, Esq., Assistant District Attorney; Wm. F. Kane, Esq., Assistant District Attorney; George E. Adams, Esq., Assistant District Attorney, for the Commonwealth.

Fred H. Moore, Esq., and Wm. J. Callahan, Esq., for the defendant Sacco.

Jeremiah J. McAnarney, Esq., and Thomas F. McAnarney, Esq., for the defendant Vanzetti.

Dedham, Mass., May 31, 1921.

[Editor: The sitting opens. Preliminaries of the trial begin.]

THE CLERK. Mr. Crier, you will make the opening proclamation.

(The Crier makes opening proclamation.)

THE CLERK. Mr. Crier, make proclamation to all persons summonsed as jurors to answer to their names.

(The crier makes proclamation to persons summonsed as jurors.)

THE COURT. Gentlemen, you have been summonsed as jurors. You will kindly give me your attention while I address you concerning **the qualification of jurors**. [1]

[T]he cases to be tried are indictments between the Commonwealth of Massachusetts and Nicholas Sacco of Stoughton and Bartolomeo Vanzetti of Plymouth. The charges in the indictment allege the killing by them of one Frederick A. Parmenter and Alessandro Berardelli at Braintree sometime in April, 1920, by the use of a revolver. The penalty upon conviction of this alleged crime is death.

I now beseech you, gentlemen, to follow me with the greatest possible attention in order that each of you may answer certain questions that will be put to you by the Court not only intelligently, but also truthfully and conscientiously. There are five of these questions. . They are as follows:——

1. Are you related to either party? That is, to either of the defendants, Nicola Sacco or Bartolomeo Vanzetti, or to either of the deceased, Frederick A. Parmenter or Alessandro Berardelli?

2. Have you any interest in the trial or result of these indictments?

3. Have you expressed or formed any opinion upon the subject matter alleged in either or both of these indictments?

4. Are you sensible of any bias or prejudice therein?

5. Are your opinions of such a character as to preclude you from finding a defendant guilty of a crime punishable by death? [2]

Capital punishment upon conviction of murder has been **the law** of Massachusetts for generations past. The law demands this penalty not in a spirit of vengeance or revenge, but rather as a punishment that is consistent with the character and the gravity of the crime committed... [4]

It [the law] seeks to select 12 jurors who will stand between these parties, the Commonwealth on the one hand and these defendants on the other, with an unyielding impartiality, with absolute fairness and unflinching courage in order that truth and justice shall prevail, ... [6]

MR. KATZMANN. May I have the indictments, Mr. Clerk?

(The clerk hands indictments to Mr. Katzmann.)

If your honor please, the Commonwealth presents for trial **two indictments**, respectively number 5545 and 5546, charging these two defendants, Nicholas Sacco and Bartolomeo Vanzetti with the murder, on the 15th of April, 1920, at Braintree, of Alessandro Berardelli and an indictment, 5546, the same two defendants, with the murder of Frederick A. Parmenter, at the same place. [6]

[Ed. Court advised defense that the indictments "follow the statutory form for murder" {7}. McAnarney first filed a demurrer and then two additional motions. {8} Judge Braley of Massachusetts Supreme Judicial Court clarified (May 12, 1926) in Appel, IV: 4311: "[E]ach defendant also moved for a bill of particulars and demurred to the indictment."]

(Noon recess.)

AFTERNOON SESSION

[Ed. Jury selection begins.]

THE CLERK. Nicola Sacco and Bartolomeo Vanzetti, you are now set to the bar to be tried. These good men whom I shall call are to pass between the Commonwealth and you upon your trial. If you object to any of them you must do it as they are called and before they are sworn.

You each have the right to challenge 44 of the jurors peremptorily and so many of the others as you have good cause to challenge.

MR. KATZMANN. If your Honor please, I offer Mr. Joseph Ross, interpreter, to act as interpreter when required, and ask that he be sworn.

THE COURT. ... Mr. Ross is appointed... .

(The clerk administers oath to the Interpreter.) [9]

(Examination is then made by the Court of the first 500 persons summonsed as jurors.)

THE CLERK. That is the last man. [10]

[Ed. Seven jurors are selected from these 500. The remaining five jurors are selected from 200 male citizens of Norfolk County summoned by court order. See pp.10-45. Jury members: Alfred Atwood, real estate dealer; John Dever, salesman; John Ganley, grocer; George Gerard, photographer; Wallace Hersey, real estate dealer; Harry King, shoe worker; Frank Marden, mason; Lewis McHardy, mill worker; Frank McNamara, farmer; Seward Parker, machinist; Walter Ripley, stockbroker; Frank Waugh, machinist.]

THE COURT. Mr. Sheriff, I have given you instructions to allow the jurors selected to read no account in any paper whatsoever of this trial. [24]

[Ed. Moore's motion that the Commonwealth used a method "not in compliance with the statute" in summoning the Dedham jurors is denied. {45} Jury is brought to Court to hear Thayer's instructions.]

(The 12 jurors come in at 1:35 a.m.) [46]

THE COURT. . . .[A]fter we begin the evidence I do not want you then to discuss at all any part of the evidence.... [Y]ou must remember that while the evidence of the Commonwealth is being introduced, you are only hearing one side, that is all. You have not heard any of the testimony relating to the defence, ... You should wait before you discuss the evidence in these cases until you have heard all the evidence, ... so that when you cross the threshold into your jury room your minds are in a state of absolute impartiality... [46] [Y]ou must all keep together and you should never separate.... You must converse with nobody.

We are now in a Massachusetts court. These men are going to be tried in the court room.

Massachusetts guarantees protection to all citizens.... It is one of the boasts of the American law that the rich, the poor, the high, the low, the learned, the ignorant, all shall receive the same rights, the same privileges, and we must see to it that a trial of that kind is held according to American law and according to American justice and nothing must be done by anybody in any way whatsoever to mar or impair a fair, honest trial. The defendants are entitled to it.... You may swear the jurors. [47]

THE CLERK. (To the Jurors.) You each of you solemnly swear that you shall well and truly try and true deliverance make between the Commonwealth and the prisoners at the bar whom you shall have in charge according to your evidence. So help you God....

THE COURT. ... You just notice, gentlemen, the oath given to the officers.

THE CLERK. (To the officers.) You each of you solemnly swear that you will keep this jury together in some convenient place until they shall return into Court; that you will not suffer any person to speak to them nor speak to them yourselves, that you will not furnish them with any refreshments or suffer any to be furnished to them except by order of the Court. So help you God! [48]

FIFTH DAY. June 6, 1921.

[Ed. Katzmann's motion that jury, officers, and counsel view the crime scene is accepted. Court appoints Ripley jury foreman. Indictments are read before the June 6 trip.] [49]

THE CLERK. Gentlemen of the jury, harken to the indictment found against the prisoners at the bar by the grand inquest for the body of this county: [49] NORFOLK, SS."——

THE COURT. Wait just a minute.
[Conference at Bench between Court and Counsel.]

THE COURT. Sheriff Capen, I have made an order here, and I wish you would come around, because **you are going to be custodian of the weapons and also the bullets**, and they are to be kept in your possession and not to be taken from your possession by anybody. Counsel for the defendants have made a motion to that effect, that they be given an opportunity to have the bullets and weapons examined by their expert. I have granted that motion.... [50]

[Sheriff Capen joins Court and Counsel at Bench.]

And therefore, **you will not allow them to go out of your custody**. They can, in your immediate presence, have them for examination, and after their experts have examined them sufficiently, then you will return them to Captain Proctor. That is the order of the Court.

...

They will be put in your possession, ... I cannot conceive of anybody thinking of changing the condition of either of the weapons or the bullets. That goes with the orders, Sheriff, so bear that in mind.

The motion for separate trials is overruled, ... [50]
[Ed. Motion for separate trials of defendants made by Callahan and Moore on behalf of Sacco.]

THE CLERK. [Reading indictment.] [52]

"COMMONWEALTH OF MASSACHUSETTS.

NORFOLK, SS.

At the Superior Court begun and holden at Dedham within and for the County of Norfolk, on the first Monday of September, in the year of our Lord one thousand, nine hundred and twenty, the jurors for the Commonwealth of Massachusetts on their oath present that Nicola Sacco of Stoughton, in the County of Norfolk, and Bartolomeo Vanzetti, of Plymouth, in the County of Plymouth, on the 15th day of April, in the year of our Lord one thousand, nine hundred and twenty, at Braintree, in the County of Norfolk, did assault and beat Frederick A. Parmenter, with intent to murder him by shooting him in the body with a loaded pistol and by such assault, beating and shooting, did murder Frederick A. Parmenter, against the peace of said Common-[52] wealth and contrary to the form of the Statute in such case made and provided.
A true bill,

John B. Whalen
Foreman of the Grand Jury.

[Ed. The indictment for the murder of Parmenter is concluded on p. li.]

1

FREDERICK G. KATZMANN,
District Attorney.

September 11, 1920.

Returned into said Superior Court by the Grand Jurors and ordered to be filed.

Attest, R. B. Worthington, Clerk." [53]

[Ed. Indictment for the murder of Berardelli is on page 53 of volume I.]

To these indictments, the prisoners at the bar have pleaded not guilty, and for trial put themselves upon the country, which country you are. You are sworn to try the issue. If the defendants are guilty, you will say so; and if they are not guilty, you will say so and no more. Good men and true, stand together and hearken to your evidence.

THE COURT. Let the officers be sworn. [53]

[Ed. To prepare the jury for the trip to view the crime scene and "other places and vicinities" deemed "material" (p. 49), assistant district attorney Harold Williams identifies landmarks on a map.]

MR. WILLIAMS. So this morning we are going to take you down to the scene of this alleged crime... [54]

[T]he crime or crimes, which we are about to try, involve the ... alleged shooting of two men. That shooting took place at South Braintree on the 15th day of April, 1920, ... [54]

Now, South Braintree is on the Plymouth Division of the New York, New Haven & Hartford Railroad.... [I]t is the next station south of Braintree.... East Braintree is some mile or two down here, to the east... [55]

As you cross the tracks [in S. Braintree], you will note ... a water tank.... As you go down further, you will notice Rice & Hutchins factory on the right, a cement and brick structure; and as you go further down the hill and by these cross-streets, you will notice Slater & Morrill factory No. 2, ... [55]

You will have pointed out to you when you go down these tracks, the water tank, this space here [excavation site in 1920], which is now, ... occupied by a building, a fence which runs along the southerly side of Pearl Street here [indicating], these poles which are shown in the map, the Slater & Morrill factory with a little **cement gasoline house** in front of it, ... [and] the flagman's shanty which you will note here on the westerly side of the track, the gates,—that is, the railroad gates,—at the track, the various buildings up Pearl Street... [56]

[Ed. Williams traces for the jury the presumed escape route of the bandit car—a route the jury will travel on June 6—naming streets on the route: Pearl, Washington, Hancock, Pond, Granite, Randolph Avenue, Oak, Chestnut. He mentions the Tower Hill district, North Stoughton, Brockton Heights (part of Brockton), Pearl Street in Brockton Heights, Marshall Corner in southwest Brockton. From here the jury will travel to West Bridgewater, turn onto Manley Street and cross a railroad track, beyond which stands Manley Woods, where the Commonwealth said the bandit car was found—about 14 miles from South Braintree.]

[W]e will then proceed ... to a house further down in West Bridgewater on the corner of Lincoln and South Elm Streets. It will be referred to ... as the Coacci house. You will look at the house and the shed, ... or barn ... [and] size up the ... measurements of that shed or barn. [57]

[B]etween the place in the woods where we will stop and this house you will go through a little village, ... called Cochesett. [58]

Then leaving the Coacci house we will go east a short distance, less than a mile, to a square called Elm Square. You will be asked to look at ... a garage which is situated in the Square. [58]

Then from Elm Square we will go a very short distance north again toward Brockton, crossing the railroad tracks and show you two houses, one called the Johnson house, ... which is over the railroad tracks, and ... a neighboring house called the Bartlett house...

[W]e will go to another railroad crossing in West Bridgewater, which is over in the northeasterly side of West Bridgewater, called the Matfield railroad crossing, ... [58]

[Ed. Judge Thayer {58} invites counsel for the defendants "to make a brief opening…" Jeremiah McAnarney declining, Thayer instructs the jury before June 6 trip.]

THE COURT. An opening statement is merely a statement made with a view to explaining to a jury the issues involved, . . An opening statement is never evidence, …

You must judge these cases according to the evidence which comes from the lips of witnesses who take the witness stand and who testify under oath.... [59]

We are in a court here of law and of justice, where we must follow certain rules. Counsel have a right to object. The law gives them that right to object. It is the duty of counsel to keep out incompetent testimony. It is their duty to see to it that only legal testimony is admitted for the consideration of the jury, and whether the Court sustains the objection or overrules the objection, you will allow no inference whatsoever to be drawn on that account. [59]

Calendar of Events

May 1921

Su	Mo	Tu	We	Th	Fr	Sa
1	2	3	4	5	6	7
8	9	10	11	12	13	14
15	16	17	18	19	20	21
22	23	24	25	26	27	28
29	30	31				

June 1921

Su	Mo	Tu	We	Th	Fr	Sa
			1	2	3	4
5	6	7	8	9	10	11
12	13	14	15	16	17	18
19	20	21	22	23	24	25
26	27	28	29	30		

July 1921

Su	Mo	Tu	We	Th	Fr	Sa
					1	2
3	4	5	6	7	8	9
10	11	12	13	14	15	16
17	18	19	20	21	22	23
24	25	26	27	28	29	30
31						

Two dates are conjectural--noted by (?)

May 2 Maine State Police employ C. C. Palmer of Dexter.

May 27 Orciani talks to Atwater & Slater in Dexter, Maine. **(?)**

May 31 Sacco & Vanzetti trial opens at Dedham, Mass.

June 13 Mrs. Fred Moore talks to Atwater & Slater in Dexter. **(?)**

June 17 Palmer reports Atwater & Slater left Dexter for Boston.

June 18 Atwater & Slater view Vanzetti's revolver in Dedham court.

June 21 Palmer reports Atwater & Slater are back in Dexter.

June 22 Callahan gives his opening statement; he omits Dexter.

June 30 Atwater testifies on Vanzetti's H. & R. revolver & a holster.

July 1 Slater testifies on Vanzetti's H. & R. revolver & a holster.

[See pp. 249, 409, 412-413.]

Opening Statement by Harold P. Williams. Tuesday, June 7, 1921.

We have now cleared away the preliminaries of this case and are prepared to introduce real evidence upon which you will base your verdict. [62]

We now come down to the evidence which is to be presented in court and is to be presented by word of mouth... . The difference between so-called direct and circumstantial evidence is that in direct evidence the witness testifies directly to what he has seen, the real point at issue. If it is by stabbing he says "I saw that man stab." The witness to the circumstantial evidence simply testifies to the circumstances, from which circumstances you, as the judges and jurors, draw the inferences which you would naturally draw from those circumstances. [62]

... We are starting in on the trial of a case where the lives of two men who are now in the court room may be involved. Nothing could more impress us with the seriousness of what we are about to do. And the attorneys for the Government are as acutely conscious of the seriousness of this as you can possibly be. It is their duty to present evidence to you, but no pride of profession, gentlemen, no desire to win a case, I assure you, will influence them in presenting the evidence... . [63]

And gentlemen, this crime, this alleged crime——because until it is proved it is only alleged——took place, ... on the 15th day of April, 1920, at about three o'clock in the afternoon. The place was South Braintree, the southerly part of the town of Braintree in Norfolk County. On that day money had been received by Slater & Morrill, shoe manufacturers, occupying that upper factory near the South Braintree Station, for the purpose of making out their pay roll, and paying their employees. [63]

The money came out by express ... early in the morning, and was received by the local agent of the American Express at the Station shortly after nine o'clock in the morning... . The amount involved was some $15,776 and odd cents. The local express agent, a Mr. Neal, with his driver, received it at the station and took it across to his office, which is in the part of the Slater and Morrill building which is nearer the cobbler [63] shop.

[O]n that morning as he went into his office he noticed standing in front of the building, ... a large, black automobile, apparently a seven-seater, standing ... between his door and the Slater & Morrill door, with its engine running, and he observed a man standing ... near the car, a rather slight man with ... [an] emaciated, yellowish face, ... [64]

Neal went into his office and changed the money and ... came out again, with the money for Slater & Morrill. At that time the man was still standing there by the car. Neal came out of his door and walked northerly to the middle entrance of the ... building and went into the Slater & Morrill offices. The man watched him, and as Neal ... went into the middle entrance, the man got into the machine. The engine, if you recall, was still running, and drove in a northerly direction... . up toward Holbrook Avenue... . And that was about 9:30. [64]

The money was taken into the Slater & Morrill Company. The pay envelopes were made up by the pay mistress... . The exact amount was put into the envelopes, and ... the moneys so allotted were put into two boxes, perhaps two and one-half feet long, a foot and a half deep, a foot wide, ... [64]

The acting paymaster at that time ... was Frederick A Parmenter. The man employed to accompany him, ... from factory No. 1 up there by the station down the hill to factory No. 2... . was Alessandro Berardelli, a man of Italian descent, and at three o'clock, ... Mr. Parmenter and Mr. Berardelli left the Slater & Morrill factory with these boxes to make the payments in the lower factory... . [64] each with a box filled with the money and the pay envelopes... . [65]

The scene shifts ... down the hill... . [I]n front of Rice & Hutchins factory were two men leaning against the fence ... . They were two short men, perhaps five feet, six or seven, rather stocky, described as ... being 140 and 160, ... [wearing] caps, dark clothes, caps somewhat lighter than their clothes, of apparent Italian lineage. [65]

Parmenter and Berardelli stopped and talked with a friend of theirs just after leaving the railroad crossing... . They came down to where the two men were, ... and these two men on the [pipe] fence stepped out and approached them... . [O]ne of the men seized hold of Berardelli, shots were fired by these two men, Berardelli fell wounded, Parmenter ran across the street and fell wounded on the other side of the street. [65]

[Ed. Williams mentions Mrs. Nichols, Colbert house, Colbert Avenue, and Italian laborers "excavating for the cellar" of the restaurant.] [66]

Berardelli had four bullets in him at the autopsy. Parmenter had two. [66]

As Parmenter was shot, he dropped his box and ... ran towards the excavation... . One of the bandits followed him across the street and ... shot him in the back. [67] ... [O]ne of the bandits, a fellow who had lost his cap, a short, swarthy man, ... was standing in front of Berardelli with a pistol, and fired two shots at the prostrate man. That man, gentlemen, who shot Berardelli ... is described and identified as Nicola Sacco, the defendant on the left. [68]

... While that was going on, this big, black car which Neal alleged he saw early in the morning, was down below the Slater & Morrill factory... . As Berardelli fell dead—... *that car approached driven by this light-haired man with an emaciated face.* It was a seven-passenger 1920 Buick with a top, that is, the canvass [sic] top up, with the back up and with the curtains up on both sides, ... [68]

There were two men in the car, the driver and a man we cannot describe, in the back seat. The car crawled up to the scene of the shooting. The two bandits, the man who had shot Berardelli when he was on the ground and the fellow who chased Parmenter ... came back, took up the two boxes, and piled them into the car. [68]

There is some evidence that there was another bandit on the other side of the street over behind the brick pile... . [T]here then being five men in the car, it proceeded up the street to the crossing. [68]

As it went up the street a man in the Rice & Hutchins factory, ... got the number 49,783 on back... . [T]hey noticed that the rear window ... that isinglass window, ... was out, and a gun or the barrel of a rifle or shotgun protruded from the window in back... . [69]

[T]he gate-tender was at his post in the little shanty on the other side of that track. The gates were up. He had heard the shooting and at the same time he heard an approaching train... . [H]e started to wind his crank to lower that gate. At that time the car was just entering upon the other side of the crossing, and the men in the car hollered at him and intimidated him so that he did not close the gates, and they proceeded up across the crossing. As they came across he noticed on the front seat an Italian with a moustache, ... with a slouch hat on, whom he identified as the other defendant, Bartolomeo Vanzetti.... [69]

People up in the corner window of Slater & Morrill's factory where you went yesterday—Miss Devlin and Miss Splain—looked out of the window right down on that car as it went past them and will tell you that that man ... leaning out under the curtain with his revolver raised, with his cap off, and shooting at the crowd ... was the defendant Nicola Sacco.... [69]

The car, gathering headway, ... reached the corner of Hancock Street by the drug store, turned down Hancock Street to the left. [69]

[Ed. Williams traces (p. 70) the route of the bandit car: Hancock Street, hair pin turn, Pearl Street, Pond Street, Granite, Oak, North Main Street toward Randolph, "crossing down Chestnut Street," Tower Hill district, the turnpike, North Stoughton "towards the Bridgewaters," Brockton Heights.]

We next find them at Matfield Crossing where we went yesterday. The crossing-tender [Reed], ... noticed them coming down the grade there towards the crossing at the same time that a train was approaching, and ran across the crossing with his stop signal, that big signal with the "Stop" on it, [and] this big car ... stopped. He held them there until the train got by. And then the man who was on the front seat and whom he describes as Bartolomeo Van- [70] zetti, said: "What to hell are you holding us up for?" [71]

They were gone about three minutes, ... and came back and over the same crossing, ... and the crossing-tender observed them again coming back with Vanzetti in the front seat, ...

They are checked up on North Pearl Street [below Brockton Heights] around quarter of four. The Matfield Crossing incident took place around 4:10, ... [71]

After the bodies had been removed, ... a cap was found on the road beside the body of Berardelli. Some empty shells were found on the road [Pearl Street]. [71]

Shelley Neal had seen this car in the early morning, ... Sometime after ten o'clock, ... it was seen coming up Holbrook Avenue and turn into Hancock Street... And the gentleman who was on the front seat of the car at that time or was in [71] the car and was noted to be in the car by an intelligent and reliable witness [Dolbeare] was the defendant Vanzetti.... [72]

Now, where had the car been from the time that Neal saw it roll away from in front of his office ... at 9:30, to where this witness saw it coming up Holbrook Avenue between 10 and 11? Here is where East Braintree comes into this story ... There was a gentleman who took the train at Cohasset on that morning at 9:20, who got into the smoker, ... [of] the South Shore train that came up from Plymouth, ... the place where the defendant Vanzetti lives, ... [72]

[T]he gentleman from Cohasset [Faulkner] was attracted by the man across the way leaning forward and touching the man in front of him and saying, "Is this East Braintree?" ... [T]he gentleman from Cohasset told the man who had made the inquiry that the East Braintree station was one or two or three stations ahead. [72]

[H]e was an Italian, he had an Italian look, and he had a moustache... . And he got off the train at East Braintree... . And the gentleman from Cohasset will ... tell you that that man who got off at East Braintree station ... about 9:50 was the defendant Bartolomeo Vanetti... . [72]

[Ed. Williams says Vanzetti exited train at East Braintree station "with his grips" on April 15, that Dolbeare saw him in the Buick on Holbrook Avenue "sometime after ten o'clock."] [72]

There were two strangers, ... in around South Braintree that morning ... seen up there leaning against the ... drug store, ... [72] [T]he owner of the building [Tracy], ... will tell you that one of those men is the counterpart of the defendant Nicola Sacco. [73]

Further down the street ... [t]he car was seen ... about 11:30 ... between the Slater & Morrill factory No. 2 and between Rice & Hutchins' factory, headed up the hill, and there were two men at that time working around the car, the ... emaciated faced driver, and another man, who was fooling around the car, and you will be told by a witness [Lola Andrews] that that second man who was fooling around the engine is the defendant Nicola Sacco or his double. Sacco was seen in the railroad station that morning at sometime. [73]

Where was Sacco supposed to be this day? ... Vanzetti was a fisherman and peddled fish at times in Plymouth. Sacco ... comes from South Stoughton, and he is a shoe worker... . in what is called the "3 K" factory... . in South Stoughton. [73]

Early in the week of April 15th—the 15th was Thursday ... Sacco ... asked to get off on Thursday. He was allowed to get off on

Thursday, and Sacco was away from his job in the 3-K factory all day Thursday. [73]

April the 17th came on Saturday... [T]hat day two men...on horseback ... went up that little wood road that we traversed yesterday, and there they found ... a 1920, seven-passenger, black Buick car with the top up, with no number plates on it, with the rear window, that long window of isinglass in back, out of it, and with a bullet hole in the right-hand side in back, shot from the inside to the outside, and that car there found is identified by the witnesses of the shooting as the car involved in the shooting.... [73]

[I]t was owned by ... Murphy in Natick. It was stolen from Murphy on November 23, 1919, and was never traced until the time it was discovered in the woods. The numbers 49,783 which were on the car at the time of the shooting, but ... not on the car at the time it was found, were stolen from a man in Needham named Ellis ... in the early part of 1920. [73]

We next hear of Sacco on the evening of May 5th.... [J]ump for a moment to the Coacci house which you viewed yesterday.... [I]n the early part of 1920 it was inhabited by a family by the name of Coacci, and there lived at that house with the Coaccis a man by the name of Mike Boda. [73]

Mike Boda had ... an Overland car, but sometime in the early part of April ... 1920, he was observed driving a larger car, ... of the description of this 1920 Buick. He was seen at one time driving it early in the morning. A large car with four dark complexioned men in it was observed several times driving up to the Coacci house on Sunday evenings and the men getting out there. [74]

After the South Braintree shooting police officers visited the Coacci house and the shed [April 20] and...discovered the remains of curtains which had been nailed over the four windows of the shed... [T]hey found inside evidence ... of the dirt floor having recently been raked over, ... [74]

There was some talk with Boda [by Stewart and Brouillard], and then Boda for a time disappeared. But on May 5th Mrs. Simon Johnson ... was awakened by a knock on her door, ... in that little house beside the railroad crossing on North Elm Street near Elm Square.... Boda, when he left the scene within a day or two after the shooting, left his Overland car at Mrs. Johnson's Garage [April 19].

lx

She came out of the door of her house, ... and there was Mike Boda standing beside the telegraph pole, and down here on the Brockton side was a motor-cycle with a side car ... with the light streaming on Mike Boda, and beside that motor-cycle and the side car was ... Orcciani, ... from Hyde Park; and as she saw Boda ... and ... Orcciani standing there, she saw two men come over that bridge by Boda on the other side of the road from her, and one of those men was Nicola Sacco, and he had with him his co-defendant, Bartolomeo Vanzetti. [74]

By reason of some pre-arranged plan, ... [74] she went over to the Bartlett house—the next house up towards Brockton, ... and as she went Sacco and Vanzetti followed alongside of her on the other side of the street where the railroad track is. She turned into the Bartlett house and was there for ten minutes, ... When she came out Sacco and Vanzetti were watching opposite the Bartlett house. [75]

She came out...and there was something said in a foreign language, ... and they followed back with her on the other side of the street.... [75]

[Ed. She sees Boda and Orcciani get on motorcycle and ride north.]

Later that evening a street car was proceeding up North Elm Street towards Brockton under the direction of ... Cole, a conductor, ... Sacco and Vanzetti got aboard the car.... [Cole] recognized them as two men who had boarded the car at the same place ... on ... April 14 or ... April 15 previously. [75]

They rode in the car that night of May 5th to Brockton and were ... arrested when they reached Campello, by Brockton police officers. They were searched, and on Sacco was found a Colt automatic pistol, ... tucked down, ... inside his trousers. It was fully loaded ... [I]t was a 10-shot pistol, 32 calibre. There were 22 loaded cartridges in his hip or pants' pocket. Vanzetti had on him a loaded 38 Harrington & Richardson revolver. There were no extra cartridges for the revolver found on Vanzetti. They were taken to the Brockton Police Station and booked. [75]

On the next day, which is May 6, ... witnesses from South Braintree were brought to the Brockton Police Station, and several identified Sacco as the man who had participated in the shooting and was in the abandoned car after the shooting. Vanzetti was also identified at that time. Vanzetti and Sacco had known each other for some period before this. During the few days immediately preceding the joint arrest, Vanzetti had been at Sacco's house in West Stoughton, and their stated reasons, ... for going to West Bridgewater that night, was to go down and see a man named Peppy or Poppy whom Vanzetti thought lived in West Bridgewater, ... Orcciani was seen with his motor-cycle and side car—the number, ... was 861— at Sacco's house [75] ... on ... the day of the arrest ... or on the previous day. [76]

The contention of the Government ... is that this crime was committed by five men; that use was made of this stolen Buick ... which ... had been kept in the curtained shed at the Coacci house in West Bridgewater; that on the morning of the murder ... it was taken from the Coacci house and was driven to South Braintree; that they picked up Vanzetti at the East Braintree station; that the men who guided and drove that car were very familiar with the localities of West Bridgewater and the roads leading to and from that section; ... [T]hey proceeded by those back roads, Oak Street and Chestnut Street, until they got to the old turnpike, ... a direct means of access to the West Bridgewater locality ... and then either started to take Vanzetti over to Plymouth and for that reason went over the Matfield crossing or went over there with the idea of ... disposing of something in the Matfield River—[They] went over there and found it was inadvisable ... came back over the Matfield crossing and subsequently abandoned their car in the region adjacent to the Coacci house. [76]

I have mentioned ... a cap ... found at the scene of the shooting near the body of Berardelli ... [W]itnesses who know ... the cap that Sacco was in the habit of wearing will tell you that the cap found at the scene of the shooting is similar to the cap that Sacco wore. [76]

There were six bullets found in these two men... . The two in Parmenter were fired from a Savage automatic pistol. It is perfectly easy to tell from what type of gun a cartridge is fired by reason of the marks left on the bullet by the rifling of the gun or pistol. They have certain ridges in the pistol which makes depressions in the bullet, and the distances between those depressions or ridges give you a clue as to the kind of gun ... from which the bullets came. And the bullets in Parmenter's body [were] ... of 32-calibre. [76]

Three of the bullets in Berardelli's body came from a Savage automatic of 32-calibre, but the bullet ... that caused Berardelli's [76] death, the bullet that was fired as he was crouched on the ground ...

that entered in behind his shoulder and went down through his body and lodged in his intestines, ... was fired from a 32-Colt automatic pistol. And when Sacco was arrested ... he had on his person, tucked down inside his trousers, a fully-loaded Colt automatic pistol of 32-calibre, and he had twenty-two additional bullets for that pistol in his pants' pocket. [77]

[G]entlemen, when you listen to the witnesses on both sides, ... you will size up their opportunities of observation and what they apparently have remembered, how they tell it, and from that and from your own instinct you will say whether or not they are telling, or attempting to tell, the truth. [77]

... First-degree murder is a killing perpetrated with deliberately premeditated malice aforethought, that is, with an unlawful motive or purpose which has been premeditated, which has been thought out beforehand, deliberately thought out.... . [77]

The Commonwealth has **no evidence** of any eye witness that saw Vanzetti fire any gun. They have direct evidence of Sacco shooting at Berardelli, but their evidence connecting Vanzetti with this murder connects him with the gang that perpetrated the murder and puts him in the car, puts him there, and you may fairly ask me if he did not shoot anybody, is he guilty of murder? [78]

The law is this, gentlemen. If two or more conspire to kill and do any joint act looking towards the killing and do kill, one is as guilty as the other... . The man who drove the car up to assist them ... is just as guilty as the man who fired the shot. Every one of this group who participated in this hold-up, in this shooting, if they knew that shooting was intended, if there was resistance to the robbery, or if there was not resistance, are guilty of murder as much as if they had actually held the gun. [78]

Watch the witnesses carefully and ... try to forget as far as you can when you are listening to the evidence that this is anything more than any other case because you have got to size up evidence in the same way in a murder case as you have in a case of petty larceny. The same principles are involved in listening to your witnesses and in gauging your evidence, ... [G]et out of each witness what you can and find out from each witness what the real truth is, ...

[Mr. Williams is called to the bench by the Court.]

THE COURT. Also the degreee of proof required, and also that the defendants are entitled, as a matter of law, to the presumption of innocence [78] until the Commonwealth has established beyond reasonable doubt that the defendants are guilty.

MR. WILLIAMS. His honor ... reminds me that I have failed to state to you the position of the defendants at the bar.... . The fact that they have been indicted by a Grand Jury, that has nothing to do with the case... [79]

The defendants are presumed to be innocent... . They do not become guilty until evidence is offered before you gentlemen to overcome that presumption of innocence, ... The evidence must be so strong as to maintain that burden of proof which is upon the Government in a case of this kind. It is not mere preponderance of the evidence in a criminal case. It is what we call proof beyond reasonable doubt, ... [79]

[I]f you find after evidence, sufficient evidence has been submitted to overcome the presumption of innocence which now rests upon them that they have been proved guilty beyond a reasonable doubt, it is your duty, of course, to so declare. [79]

[Ed. Exhibits 1-9, photographs of crime scene, admitted in evidence, pp. 81-84. Exhibits 10-16, photographs of Buick discovered in Manley Woods, admitted in evidence, p. 89.]

[Ed. Court denies McAnarney's motion that Vanzetti be tried separately from Sacco.] [93].

PART I

EVIDENCE BY THE COMMONWEALTH

1. SURVEYOR, PATHOLOGIST, AGENT, PAY-MISTRESS

Edward B. Hayward, Sworn. June 7, 1921.

Q. (By Mr. Williams) What is your name? A. Edward B. Hayward.
Q. What is your profession or business?   A.   Surveyor and civil engineer... .
Q. At my request, some day in the late winter or early spring, did you make a plan of the vicinity of the crossing at South Braintree on Pearl Street? A. Yes.
Q. And is that plan ... tacked there on the board the plan which you then made? A. Yes, sir.
Q. Did you make the measurements for that plan? A. Yes, sir. [96]
Q. Have you in connection with this case made plans for the defendants' attorneys? A. Yes, sir.
Q. Let me ask you again, that scale is what? A. One inch equals 20 feet.
MR. WILLIAMS. I offer that plan, if your honor please.
MR. JEREMIAH McANARNEY. No objection.
[Admitted.]
[The map is admitted in evidence and marked "Exhibit 17."]
Q. Will you step over here? [Witness leaves witness stand and goes to map on wall.]
Q. Give me the distance from the middle of Pearl Street across the tracks?
A. Just the tracks across the street?
Q. Yes, just the tracks from the outer rail on one side to the outer rail on the other side?
A. Sixty-seven feet.
Q. Now, will you give me the distance from the nearest rail of those tracks down to the first pole shown in the plan going east from the tracks? A. 14 feet.
Q. The distance from that pole to the next pole, going east? A. 107 1/2 feet.
Q. And from that pole to the next pole? A. 123.
Q. And from that pole to the pole down by the Slater & Morrill factory? A. 125.

3

Q. Have you marked on there where the end of the iron fence [pipe fence] in front of the Rice & Hutchins factory is? A. The east end?

Q. Are you sure that is the east end? If you don't know, just say so, . . A. I am not certain about it. That is the fence to that point there. Whether it is an iron fence, … I could not say. [97]

Dr. George Burgess Magrath, Sworn. June 7, 1921.

Q. (By Mr. Williams) What is your full name? A. George Burgess Magrath.

Q. Where do you live? A. In Boston, 274 Boylston Street. [108]

Q. What is your profession? A. I am a graduate of the Harvard Medical School, holding a degree of Doctor of Medicine. The branch of medicine in which I am engaged is known as pathology.

Q. Do you hold any official position at the present time? A… . I am Medical Examiner for Suffolk County, and instructor in legal medicine in Harvard University… .

Q. At the request of Mr. Katzmann did you participate in the autopsy on the body of Frederick A. Parmenter? A. Yes, sir.

Q. And did you also at his request at some time participate in the autopsy on the body of Alessandro Berardelli. A. Yes.

Q. Now, take the autopsy on Parmenter first, and I will ask you when that took place?

A. On April 16, 1920, beginning at 7:00 p.m., in Quincy, … [109]

[Ed. Dr. Magrath testified he found two wounds on Parmenter's body—one "on the left-hand side of the chest in front," the other on "the right and back part of the body."] [110]

Q. What, in your opinion, caused these wounds? A. They were both wounds, in my opinion, made by a bullet, each by a bullet… .

Q. Which wound was that [which one was fatal]? A. That of the right-hand side of the back. [111]

Q. When was it [autopsy on Berardelli], Doctor, and where was it?

A. On April 16, 1920, beginning at 11:00 a.m., in Randolph, …

Q. Who was present at that autopsy, Doctor? A. Doctor John C. Frazer of Weymouth, medical examiner for the Fourth Norfolk District; Dr. Frederick E. Jones of Quincy, Medical Examiner for the Third Norfolk District; Dr. George V. Higgins, of Randolph, associate Medical Examiner for the Third Norfolk District; …

Q. Will you tell the jury, Doctor, what was done at that autopsy, what your observations were?

Dr. Magrath tells how he marked the four Berardelli bullets.

A. ... As my operating proceeded and I came upon a bullet, the location of this bullet ... and character were noted and described and the bullet marked on its base with the point of a needle, a numeral, a Roman [112] numeral, in the order in which it was taken out. Thus, the first bullet recovered was marked "I", a small scratch on the base. Succeeding bullets so taken out as they were come upon were similarly and appropriately marked. Two was marked—the second was marked with a Roman "II" and three with a Roman "III" and the fourth with the Roman "IIII", or four vertical lines. [113]

Dr. George Burgess Magrath, Direct Examination, Continued.
June 8, 1921.

Q. (By Mr. Williams) And because one bullet is numbered "II" and you number a wound "II", that does not mean that that bullet was the one that caused that wound? A. No. I can explain. The wounds on the outside of the body—they were all wounds of entrance made by bullets going in—were given a number ... before the inside of the body was looked at. Thus, the wound of the back left upper arm was numbered "I". The wound of the left shoulder, behind, was numbered "II". The wound on the left side lower down behind was numbered "III". The wound of the right side of the back or right shoulder was numbered "IV".... . [115]
Q. Let me show you these bullets, Doctor, and see if you can identify them as the bullets removed from the body of Berardelli (handing bullets to the witness).
MR. WILLIAMS. May we have a little light, Sheriff?
(The sheriff turns on the lights.)
THE WITNESS. I identify that (indicating) as the bullet which I numbered "III" by placing three vertical marks upon it, on the left base. [118]
Q. Is there any objection to me showing this bullet to the jury? A. None whatever. I am not sure that light in the jury box will show the light marks. If it doesn't, use the lens.

5

MR. WILLIAMS. I offer this bullet, which we will call No. III.

THE WITNESS. Yes.

THE COURT. You may show it to counsel first, please.

(Mr. Williams shows bullet No. III to counsel for defense.)

(Bullet No. III is admitted in evidence and envelope containing the bullet is marked "Exhibit 18.")

Q. What kind of a bullet is that? A. It is a jacketed bullet, ... consistent with ... 32 calibre.

MR. WILLIAMS. (To the jury.) Mr. Foreman, just look at that bullet and see if it is flattened in any way and look at the mark on the base...

Q. I will ask you, Doctor, to save possibly a longer examination of other bullets, if the other marks on the other bullets which you are about to examine are Roman numerals similar in character to that No. III on the bottom of that bullet? A. They are; the number 4 being represented by four vertical lines ...

Q. And that bullet No. III, Doctor, which I have just offered in evidence, is the bullet from which wound? A. From the wound on the back of the right shoulder, the wound numbered 4, ...

Q. Doctor, if you will replace that in the envelope marked "Bullet No. III." Now, if you will examine envelope marked "Bullet No. II" and tell us what you find there. A. This envelope contains a jacketed bullet bearing two marks which I placed upon its base, known as No. "II" of my record.

Q. What calibre bullet? A. Consistent with 32.

Q. And from what wound was that [bullet 2] taken?

A. From the wound of the back of the left upper arm.

Q. That is wound No. 1? A. That is wound No. 1.

MR. WILLIAMS. I offer this bullet, if your Honor please.

[Mr. Williams shows bullet to counsel for the defense.]

[Bullet marked "II" is admitted in evidence and envelope containing same is marked Exhibit 19.]

MR. WILLIAMS. [Showing Exhibit 19 to the jury.] Just pass it around to show its general appearance, gentlemen. That is all you need to do, ... unless you care to do otherwise. [119]

Q.... . Will you now look at [the] envelope which is marked "I" and tell us what you find there? A. A jacketed bullet of a size consistent with 32 calibre, which on its base bears number "I" placed there by myself, and is the bullet which I took out from the muscles of the chest, ...

6

[bullet having] entered the body through wound of the left side of the back ... described as wound number "II".

MR. WILLIAMS. I offer this bullet, if your Honor please.

[Mr. Williams shows bullet to counsel for defense.]

[Bullet numbered "I" admitted in evidence and envelope containing same is marked Exhibit 20.]

MR. WILLIAMS. ... I will start this around, gentlemen [showing bullet, Exhibit 20, to the jury].

Q.... . Open the envelope marked "Bullet No. IIII" and tell us what you find there. A. This is a jacketed bullet of a size consistent with 32 calibre, marked with four vertical lines, placed

there by myself. This was the fourth bullet recovered from the body of Alessandro Berardelli. I found it in the belly wall ... and traced it to the wound of the left side of the back numbered and described as "III."

MR. WILLIAMS. [To the jury.] Can you gentlemen see with that little glass there or would you rather have the big one? I offer this bullet, if your Honor please.

[Bullet numbered "IIII" admitted in evidence and envelope containing same marked Exhibit 21.]

MR. WILLIAMS. Bullet marked No. "IIII" becomes Exhibit 21. [Showing Exhibit 21 to the jury.]

Q. Now, Doctor, you will note I have returned each bullet to its proper envelope? A. Yes, sir.

Q. And returned them into the custody of the sheriff [handing to the sheriff]. Doctor, what, in your opinion, caused these four wounds ... in the body of Alessandro Berardelli?

A. The entrance of four separate bullets.

Q. What, in your opinion, was the cause of Berardelli's death? A. The effect of a wound on the right side of the back or shoulder penetrating along the aorta, causing hemorrhage and shock.... .

THE COURT. Which wound would you say that was, according to your number, Doctor?

THE WITNESS. Number four [caused by Bullet 3].... . [120]

Q. Doctor, a question was put to you by one of the counsel for the defendants in the ante-chamber, which leads me to to ask you this: How do you account for the apparent lop-sidedness or flattening on one side of one or more of the bullets which were exhibited to the jury and which were found by you in the body of Berardelli? A. The flattening to which you refer is exhibited by Bullet No. III, which entered the

7

body through wound No.IIII of the back of the right shoulder and took the course diagonally downward to the left and slightly forward lodging in the region of the left hip inside. As I found it, it lay sidewise against the flat surface of the hip bone, and in my opinion the flattening of the bullet was due to its striking that bone side on.... [126]

[Ed. McAnarney cross-examined Magrath about powder marks, not bullets. {132} Dr. Nathaniel S. Hunting testified that he removed a 32 calibre bullet from the abdomen of Parmenter, marked it with a "cross on the base," and gave it to Scott of the State Police. {133} This became Bullet 6 (Exhibit 24), kept in envelope marked "Bullet X." {134} Dr. Frederick Ellis Jones testified that a nurse, never identified, found a bullet on the floor of the Quincy City hospital operating room. Jones said that on June 7, 1921, he scripted "the figure 5 on the base of the bullet." {134} Bullet 5 was admitted and marked Exhibit 25. Williams gave envelope marked "Bullet X" to Sheriff Capen. Jones testified he gave bullet 5, 32 calibre, to Officer Scott of the State Police. The Court said these bullets must stay in the custody of the Sheriff so that defense experts might examine them. {135} Williams put bullet 5 into envelope marked "No 5" and returned it to Sheriff Capen.] [136]

Mr. Shelley A. Neal, Sworn. June 8, 1921.

Q. (By Mr. Williams) Were you agent for the American Railway Express Company on April 15th of last year? A. Yes....

Q. And that morning, as local agent for the American Express, did you receive any package or parcel or bundle or safe with money from Boston? A. Yes, sir.

Q. In what sort of a receptacle did the money which you received from Boston that day arrive?

A. In an iron box about 12 inches high, 18 inches wide and 2 feet long.

Q. What time did it arrive in Braintree?

A. The train is due I believe at 9:18, but that was usually late. I should say about 9:25.

Q. Where did you receive the safe that morning, or the box?

A. Out of the baggage car door of the train.

Q. Did you receive it over at the South Braintree station? A. Yes.

Q. When you received it, where did you go with it, if anywhere? A. The driver that is with me took one end of the box, I took the other.

We put it in our express wagon, … . After pushing it in near our front seat, we both got on the seat of the wagon and started for the office. [137]

Q. Where was your office at that time? A. Well, diagonally across from the station, the lower story of the building occupied by Slater & Morrill nearest the Pearl Street side… .

[The Hampton House [is] north of Pearl Street and to the west of the New York, New Haven & Hartford right of way. This is a four-story frame building. The ground floor, southeast corner, is occupied by the American Express Company. The second floor by the Slater & Morrill, Inc. offices. The third and fourth floors by the cutting rooms of Slater & Morrill, Inc. The entrance to the office of the American Express Company is through the doorway on Railroad Avenue nearest the southerly end of the building. The doorway nearest to the north is the entrance to the offices and factory of Slater & Morrill, Inc. Appel, III: 2270.]

Q. When you got over by your office, what did you do? A. Backed the team up in front of the door, took out the safe, took it into my office, broke the seal on it, took the key that we have that comes in a sealed package, opened the safe and took Slater & Morrill's payroll out.

Q. What did you do then? A. I locked the safe up, leaving the **other payroll** in there, then came out the door. Do you want the story just as it is?

Q. I am just asking you what you did, …

A. I took the money under my arm then and started to make the delivery.

Q. The Slater & Morrill door was the next door north from your entrance, … the middle entrance of the building? A. The middle entrance, yes.

Q. Now, Mr. Neal, as you came across from the station to your office, did you notice anybody or anything in front of your building?…

A. … I noticed a large number of automobiles.

Q. Yes. A. More than generally appeared there that time in the morning… .

Q… . Now, what else did you see? A. Standing directly in front of Slater & Morill's door was this newly varnished car, **Buick car**. [138]

Q. What type of car was it? A. It was a Buick, about 7-passenger car.

Q. See anybody there around the car? A. There was one man sitting in the car.

9

Q. Now, when you got to your office, did you see anybody?

A. Saw another man standing in Slater & Morrill's doorway.

Q. Will you describe that man? A. He stood here, a man possibly an inch or two taller than I am, slight in frame, very slight, slim, light hair, hair that,——well, extremely light, blue eyes, very downcast expression like. That is, he did not look at me up straight... He had a soft hat, ...a black overcoat... . The coat was buttoned up tight, both hands in his overcoat pockets down so I could not even see the wrists, right close down. He stood there when I was passing the cars, and also stood there when I made delivery of the money.

Q. What was his complexion, did you notice? A. Of a very sallow complexion, ... My first impression was that he was a tubercular patient. [139]

AFTERNOON SESSION

Mr. Shelley A. Neal, Direct Examination Resumed.

THE COURT. Immediately upon the adjournment of the court this noon, information came to the Court that people were told they could not take notes at this trial. Whoever gave any such orders did so absolutely without authority. These trials are public, the courts belong to the people, they have a right to know what is going on in their courts. If anybody wants to take notes during this trial they are at perfect liberty to do so, and so far as the Court is concerned, as long as people conduct themselves with proper decorum, they are welcome in this court to hear and to know what is going on. You may proceed with the witness.

Q. As you proceeded with your box or bag from your entrance to the Slater & Morrill entrance of the building, will you tell the jury what you noticed regarding that car which you have told us was a large Buick car, and any men in or around that car? [140]

[Ed. The witness digressed about his buttoned coat and 38 revolver and was told by the Court: "Pay attention to the question kindly and answer nothing else."]

THE WITNESS. The car was standing there close up against the sidewalk, the walk in front of the building, right directly in front of the door.

Q. Of which door? A. Facing north.

Q. Of which door? A. The main door to Slater & Morrill's factory, going upstairs. It occurred to me—

Q. ... You can't say what occurred to you. What you saw is what we want to know. A. That car was there and with the back,—I looked at the car very particular as I wanted to see, make sure whether there was another man in the car or [140] not. I could see one man sitting at the wheel and this other man standing in the doorway. I had to walk opposite the door going into the car before I could gain my point, to make sure that there was not a man in the back seat.

Q. Was there a man in the back seat? A. There was not... .

THE COURT. What the witness said "before I gained my point" may be stricken from the record, on the ground that it is not responsive.

Q. Now, what did you observe as to the man in the front seat, ...?

A. He was sitting with his one hand on the driving wheel, the engine of the car running. He did not turn in any way, did not seem to look at me... . I could see nothing only the back of his head... .

Q. You went up and I assume delivered your bag or box? A. Yes, sir.

Q. To Slater & Morrill's. To whom did you give it, ...? A. To Margaret Mahoney... .

Q. What did you see in reference to this car and these two men as you came out of the building?

A. As I got half way down the stairs a man that was standing still in the position that he had been from the time [141] I came from the depot stepped off of the step, opened the rear door of the car and got in and sat down and closed the doors. Immediately the car started.

Q. And in which way did it go? A. North... .

Q. I say, again that is toward Holbrook Ave.? A. Yes.

Q. Was there any rear window in the car at that time? A. Yes, sir. [142]

Q. What time was it when this car with these men in it, as you have described, drove off north?

A. About 9:33.

Q. Did you later on that day see that same car? A. In my judgment, I did ... [while] sitting in my office ... at the ... window.

Q. At what time of day did you see that same car?

A. About 3:05. [From inside of Hampton House.]

Q. Where was the car at that time and what ... were its movements?

A. Coming across the railroad track on Pearl Street, going [west] up Pearl Street. [143]

Q. Will you describe the car as it looked at that time [3:05]? A. At that time it was considerably more dust on it, the car, than what was in the morning, but ... it [was] the same car. [144]

Miss Margaret Mahoney, Sworn, June 8, 1921.

Q. (By Mr. Williams) What is your name? A. Margaret Mahoney [of North Easton].

Q. You are employed by Slater & Morrill? A. Yes.

Q. Are you the pay-mistress ... or paymaster for that concern?
A. Yes.

Q. And were you occupying that position on April 15th of last year?
A. Yes... .

Q. On April 15, 1920, what position did Mr. Parmenter occupy with Slater & Morrill?
A. Assistant paymaster.

Q. What position did Alessandro Parmenter [Berardelli] occupy with that firm on that date?
A. Special officer... .

Q. On April 15 did you make up the payroll? A. Yes.

Q. Did you make it up from money brought in by Mr. Neal from the American Express Company? A. Yes.

Q. How much of a payroll did you make up and send down to the lower factory on that day?
A. $15,776.51.

Q. In what shape did you put it up? A. It was in two steel cases. I placed it in two steel cases.

Q. In what shape was it inside the cases? A. In two wooden boxes.

Q. What was it inside the boxes? A. In pay envelopes.

Q. That is, there was a pay envelope for each employee? A. Yes.
[168]

Q. And was the exact amount due the employee at that time in cash?
A. Yes.

Q. That would be in bills? A. Yes, sir.

Q. And in change, I take it? A. Yes.

Q. How large were those tin boxes in which the wooden boxes were placed in which the money was placed? A. About 2 feet long, about 1 ft. high, and about 8 inches wide.

Q. Have you any idea how heavy those boxes were that day ...?

12

A. Well, no, I could not say exactly how heavy, but they are quite heavy... .

Q. Did Berardelli and Parmenter come to your department, to your office, and get those boxes that day? A. Yes, they did.

Q. What time did they get there? A. At 5 minutes of 3 they left my desk.

Q. Do you remember how those gentlemen were dressed when they left your desk at 5 minutes of 3? A. Parmenter wore a sort of mixed overcoat, mixed brown, and a soft hat, and Mr. Berardelli wore a black overcoat and a soft hat.

Q. Who took the boxes of those two men? A. Parmenter took the two boxes on leaving me... .

Q. Did Berardelli come into your office at that time? A. He did, yes...
.

Q. Do you know if Berardelli owned any shooting weapon? A. Yes.

Q. And what did he own, to your knowledge. A. A revolver. [169]

Q. At what times do you recall having seen it on Berardelli? A. Why, at one time when we were riding down in the car [to the lower factory] I asked him if he had his——

Q. What you said to him I presume is not competent, but what you saw is.

A. I saw him take it out of his trousers pocket.

Q. What did he do with it, do you remember? A. Put it back in again.

Q. When was that, do you remember? A. That was--

MR. JEREMIAH McANARNEY. How is that significant in this case?

THE COURT. I do not see what significance it has in this case. If you can explain, I should be glad.

MR. WILLIAMS. We offer to show Berardelli had a revolver, that he customarily carried it.

THE COURT. Is there any claim of self-defense or anything of that kind here?

MR. JEREMIAH McANARNEY. Never have heard it suggested.

THE COURT. (Continued.) That required Berardelli to use a revolver?

MR. JEREMIAH McANARNEY. Nothing of the kind.

MR. WILLIAMS. There is some testimony, if your Honor please, to be introduced later regarding a revolver which makes this material.

THE COURT. If you say it is, I will hear it. It may be later. I can't see now.

[Ed. See Thayer's ruling, p. 42, that the revolver may be material evidence.]

Q. At what other time or times did you see a revolver on Berardelli? A. Well, at another time when we went from the main factory, went from factory No. 1 to factory No. 2, in which he removed it from his overcoat into his trousers pocket on arriving at the main factory.
Q. How long before he was killed was that? A. Within two months or more before it happened. [170]

Cross-Examination.

Q. (By Mr. Jeremiah McAnarney) Usually you went down with the payroll, didn't you? A. Yes.
Q. You did not this day? A. No, I didn't.
Q. Had that happened before, within say a month of this occurrence?
A. Yes, I had not gone down for at least two or maybe three weeks before that.

Redirect Examination.

Q. (By Mr. Williams) Was it approximately the same amount of money in each box?
A. I should say so, yes.... [Ed. The payroll was never recovered.]
THE COURT. Any questions?
MR. JEREMIAH McANARNEY. No. [171]

2. THE PLYMOUTH TRAIN

John W. Faulkner, Sworn. June 13, 1921

Q. (By Mr. Williams) Where do you live, sir? A. Cohasset.

Q. What is your business or occupation? A. Pattern maker... .

Q. Do you recall the date of the so-called South Braintree shooting? A. Yes, sir.

Q. Where were you on that day? A. I was going from Cohasset to the Watertown Arsenal.

Q. What time did you leave your home in the morning? A. Why, I got the 9:23 train, ...

Q. From what station? A. Cohasset.

Q. A train going in what direction? A. To Boston... .

Q. Do you remember what car of that train you got into? A. I always ride in the smoking car.

Q. And where in the smoker did you sit [on April 15]? A. Second seat on the left hand side.

Q. From which end? A. At the baggage end. [425]

Q. Was that one of those half-and-half smokers, with part for a baggage car in that end?

A. Baggage, with a toilet on the right hand side... .

[Ed. See letter from N.Y. N.H. & Hartford R.R. to McAnarney on p. 220.]

Q. Now, ... as you were traveling ... towards Boston from Cohasset, was your attention directed to any conversation across the way? A. Why, yes. As we come in East Weymouth, the fellow on my right asked me if this was East Braintree. I said no. He said, "The man behind me wants to know if it is East Braintree."

Q. Did you look at the man behind? A. Yes, I took a look at the man behind.

Q. Where was he sitting? A. In the single seat next to the toilet... .

Q. What kind of a looking man was that? A. Why, he looked like a foreigner, with a black mustache, and cheek bones. [426]

Q. Where did you see that man that was sitting in the single seat in front of the toilet after that day? A. In the Plymouth jail.

Q. When did you see him? A. Why, I looked it up, and it was July 20th [1920].

Q. Do you see that man that you saw in the train that day, and which you subsequently saw in the Plymouth jail, in the court house here?
A. Yes, sir.
Q. Where do you see him? A. Sitting right over there.
Q. Where? A. With the black mustache.
Q. Sitting where? A. In the cage.... . To the left of me.
Q. The man known as Vanzetti? A. Yes, sir.
Q. Are you sure that is the man you saw in the train that day? A. That is the man.
Q. Now, will you tell the jury what talk you had at that time with the man on the train?
A. The only conversation we had was when we come to each station he wanted to know if—
Q. What did he say, and what did you say? A. He wanted to know if it was East Braintree when we come to East Weymouth and Weymouth Heights. I told him at the start, at Weymouth, when we came to it I would let him know. When we come to it, I did tell him, "This is East Braintree."
Q. What did he do? A. He got up and got out.... .
Q. What did he do when he got off, if you know?
A. He got off the train, went on the station platform, and dropped his bag.
Q. What kind of a bag? A. An old bag, 16 or 18 inches long.... . An old leather bag. [427]

Cross Examination.

Q. (By Mr. McAnarney) You were doing what? A. I had an accident [while working on a submarine] at the Watertown Arsenal, and I was having my hand fixed, going to the post hospital at Watertown.
Q. There are a lot of Italians live in Cohasset? A. There are very few Italians. [428]
Q. Only two Italians in "H" department [where you worked on a submarine in Fore River]?
A. That is all where I worked. [432]

Cross Examination.

Q. (By Mr. Moore) Now, this thing attracted your attention, did it?
A. When he asked the question, and got so servous [sic] after we left the different stations. I told him it [East Braintree] would be in three or four stops.
Q. When this rather peculiar thing happened, did you note anybody that was on the train other than this man? A. Nobody that I knew.
Q. How about the man ... opposite you, who was that man?
A. ... He said he ... didn't know the stations around there. [433]

Redirect Examination.

Q. (By Mr. Williams) Did the South Braintree shooting have any connection in your mind with what had occurred at the East Braintree station that next day? [Objections overruled.]
THE WITNESS. Well, it had that much on my mind that I thought that was one of the crowd that came up in the train with me. [443]
Q. When did you have that thought? A. Why, as soon as I read the paper. [444]

Cross Examination

Q. (By Mr. McAnarney) ... I wanted to ask him if he had ever seen anyone that looked like that photograph [of Joseph Scavitto] before?
A. I suppose I have seen somebody looks like it, yes...
Q. He looks to a foreigner to you, don't he? A. Why, yes.
Q. Looks a little like the man you saw get off the train at East Braintree? A. Similar.
Q. Quite a lot like him, don't he? A. Looks quite a lot like him. [444]
Q. He looks so much like the man you can't say whether he is or not?
A. I wouldn't say.
MR. JEREMIAH McANARNEY....I show the photograph—may I introduce it as a chalk to the jury?
THE COURT. You may. [445] [Ed. See reference to Scavitto, p. 97.]

17

Daniel F. Ahern, Sworn. June 15, 1921.

Q. (By Mr. Williams) What is your occupation?
A. Chief train dispatcher for the Boston Division, New York, New Haven & Hartford Railroad.
Q. At the request of my office, have you brought here the train schedules of the so-called South Shore trains for April 15th, 1920?
A. I have the train sheets. [540]
Q. Give us the names of the stations, and ... the different times at the ... "reporting points," Mr. Ahern, ... Go right through from Plymouth to Braintree. A. Starting at Plymouth, the train stops at Seaside, Kingston, Highland Creek, South Duxbury, Duxbury, Green Harbor, Marshfield, Marshfield Centre, Sea View, Marshfield Hills, Greenbush, Scituate, Egypt, North Scituate, Beechwood, Cohasset, a flag stop at Black Rock, North Cohasset, Nantasket Junction, Hingham, West Hingham, East Weymouth, Weymouth Heights, Weymouth, East Braintree, and Braintree.
Q. Now, at what stations are there reporting points, and what time did it reach those reporting points? A. It left Plymouth at 8:14, Kingston at 8:24, South Duxbury at 8:32, Duxbury 8:36, ... Scituate 9.05, ... Cohasset 9:22, ... East Weymouth 9:43, and arrived at Braintree at 9:55. [541]
Q. Where is the Braintree station with reference to the South Braintree station?
A. It is a little over a mile north of South Braintree.... [542]
Q. And what was the number of that train? A. 5108.
Q. Just one other question. Do you know where Matfield station is?
A. Yes, sir.
Q. Where is that? A. That is on the main line between Boston and Provincetown, approximately two and one-half miles south of Campello.
Q. Between what stations does that station lie? A. Between Campello and Westdale.
Q. Is it, speaking more generally, between Brockton and Bridgewater?
A. Yes, it is.... [542]

3. PRE-CRIME WITNESSES

Harry E. Dolbeare, Sworn. June 14, 1921.

Q. (By Mr. Williams) What is your occupation or business?
A. Piano and musical instruments repairing.
Q. How long have you lived in South Braintree, Mr. Dolbeare?
A. About twenty-five years,—since '96.
Q. Were you living there on the 15th day of April, 1920? A. I was.
Q. At any time in the morning on April 15th—and that you remember is the day of the shooting? A. Yes, sir.
Q. Did you see a car with a number of men in it? A. I did. [488]
Q. Have you any idea when? A. Well, it was between ten and twelve.... I don't say to a minute.
Q. And where was the automobile, ... when you first saw it? A. I saw it make the turn from Holbrook Avenue into Washington Street. [Ed. Toward South Braintree Square.]
Q. How many did you see in it? A. Five.
Q. Can you tell where they were located in the car?
A. Two were on the front seat and three in the back part of the car. [489]
Q. Did you see anybody ... that you could describe ... to the jury, in the car? A. I did.
Q. And where did you see anybody that you now refer to? A. In the back part of the car.
Q. Will you describe him to the jury? ... A. He looked like a foreigner, and he had a very heavy mustache, quite dark.... .
Q. You, as I understand, were summoned as one of the veniremen in this case? A. I was.
Q. What day was that? A. Thursday, June 2.... .
Q. Did you at that time see the man that you saw in South Braintree that day? A. I did.
Q. Where did you see that man [on June 2]? A. In the dock.
Q. Do you see him now? A. I do.
Q. Will you tell the jury where you see him? A. It is the farther one of the two.
Q.... . [W]hich one do you mean? A. The one on my left, the one with the mustache.

19

Q. The one known as Bartolomeo Vanzetti? A. Yes, sir... .

Q. Is there any doubt in your mind he is the man you saw that day in South Braintree?

A. Not a particle... . [490]

Mrs. Lola R. Andrews, Sworn. Saturday. June 11, 1921.

Q. (By Mr. Williams) Where do you live? A. Quincy... . in the Alhambra building. [332]

Q. What is your occupation at the present time? A. At present, attendant for an invalid.

Q. And what did you do before then [October 1920]? A... . [W]orked in a shoe factory. [332]

Q. Did you ever work for Slater & Morrill or Rice & Hutchins?

A. ... [F]or Rice & Hutchins.

Q. Did you work for them after that [April 15] or before?

A. ... [A]fter the 15th of April.

Q. Now, for any reason were you in South Braintree on the 15th day of April?

A. Yes, sir, I was... .

Q. What time of day did you go to South Braintree? A. It would be between half past 11 and somewheres around quarter of 12 that I was there... .

Q. From the South Braintree station [after arrival], where did you go?

A. From the South Braintree station, I went to the Slater factory.

Q. Which one? ... A. This factory I went into was below the Rice & Hutchins factory... .

[The Slater & Morrill, Inc. main factory...faces Pearl Street on the south side. This is a four-story frame building, ... The distance from ... the one-story **concrete building** ... in front of Slater & Morrill's to the east side of track No. 6 ... is 385 feet. Appel, III: 2271.]

Q. Who was with you? A. A lady by the name of Campbell.

Q. Mrs. Julia Campbell? A. Yes, sir. [333]

Q. How long did you stay in the Slater factory?

A. I would say I wasn't in there more than, in my judgment, 15 minutes, possibly not that.

Q. What were you doing in there? A. Inquiring for work... .

Q. Where did you go after you came out of the Slater factory?

A. To the Rice & Hutchins factory... .

Q. How long were you in there? A. I was in there about the same time, … 15 minutes.

Q. Now, Mrs. Andrews, … tell the jury if you saw or talked with anybody either before you went into the Slater & Morrill factory, or afterward? A. If I saw or talked with anybody? …

Q. Now, did you see anybody before you went into the factory?
A. Yes, sir.

Q. And will you tell the jury whom you saw and where you saw them? Under what circumstances?

A. As I went into the Slater & Morrill factory I saw a car standing by the roadside of the Slater factory, … and there was a man working on the car, at the front part of it, and there was another man there with him. I passed by them and went into the factory, and as I came back from the factory the same man was standing there at the same place where I first went in. [334]

Q. Which way was the automobile headed? A. Headed [west] towards the track.

Q. … I want you to place the men when you went into the factory.

A. As I saw them when I went into the factory? [335]

Q. Yes. A. As I went into the factory, the first man was bending over the front part of the car, which I would call the hood, and the other man was sitting in the back of the car.

Q. Can you describe the appearance of either of those men? A. The man that was bending over the hood was a dark complexioned man, and I would say medium height, smooth face.

Q. Can you tell how he was dressed? A. In dark clothing.

Q. Could you tell about the man whom you say was inside the car…?
A. He was … very light.

Q. Could you say anything more about him? A. He was thin, … emaciated like he was sick, …

Q. Where was the car when you came out? A. At the same point as it was when I went in.

Q. Where were the men at that time? A. The light man was behind the auto as I came out, standing behind, and the other man was down under the car, like he was fixing something… .

Q. Did you have any talk with either of those men at that time?
A. Yes, sir.

Q. Which man? A. With the man who was fixing the car.

21

Q. Was he the light man or the dark man? A. No, sir, he was the dark man.

Q. Where was he when you had the talk with him?

A. When I had the talk with him, he was under the car.

Q. Did he get up at any time? A. Yes, sir.

Q. I mean, when you had your talk with him, did he get up?

A. I spoke to him and he got up, as I spoke to him.

Q. Will you tell the jury what talk you had with him? A. I asked him if he would please show me how to get into the factory office, that I did not know how to go.

Q. What did he say? A. He told me,——he asked me which factory I wanted, the Slater? I said "No, sir, the Rice & Hutchins." [336]

Q. Anything more? A. That is all the conversation.... .

Q. Have you seen the man you talked with that morning since? I am referring to the dark man with whom you talked? A. I think I have, yes, sir.

Q. Where did you see him? A. I saw him at the Dedham jail, first.

Q. Have you seen him since then? A. Yes, sir, I have.... .

Q. Do you see him in the court room now? A. I think I do, yes, sir.... .

Q. Just point to the man you mean? A. That man there (indicating).

Q. Do you mean—

[The defendant Sacco stands up in the cage and says: "Take a good look. I am myself."] (He actually said: "I am the man? Do you mean me? Take a good look.")

Q. Then you mean the man who just stood up and made the remark. A. Yes, sir.

Q. The man they call Sacco? A. Yes, sir. [337]

Q. Tell the jury what, if anything, he said? A. He said to go in the driveway and told me which door to go in, it would lead me to the factory office.

Q. Where did you go then? A. After I talked with him?

Q. Yes. A. I went into the Rice & Hutchins factory.

Q. Now, this Mrs. Campbell who was with you is a lady of what age, roughly?

A. I would say she would be 69.

Q. And where is she now, do you know? A. At Stockton Springs, Maine. [338]

Q. At what time did you have this talk with the defendant ...?

A. ... about quarter of 12.

22

THE COURT. [To the jury.] It should be my duty, I think, to caution you, gentlemen, that the testimony of the witness should have no effect whatever so far as the defendant Vanzetti is concerned. It appears from no evidence at present that he was there, and therefore it is evidence against Sacco only.... [340]

Cross-Examination.

Q. (By Mr. Moore) Mrs. Andrews, I talked with you at your home on the 14th day of January [1921] in Quincy, did I not? A. Yes, sir.

Q. And at that time you told me freely and frankly and fully everything that you knew about this matter. Is that correct? A. Why, I don't just remember what I told you. [340]

Q. Let me get this. Calling attention to this plan, do you recognize these locations? This [indicating] is the railroad track up here, Rice & Hutchins factory here [indicating]. You walked on down past Rice & Hutchins, on down Pearl Street to the Slater & Morrill factory?
A. Yes, sir... .

Q. Now, as you passed the front of the car, you did not see any particular man there, you did not see a man at the time that you passed, except, as I understand you to say, he was underneath the car? A. Yes, sir.

Q. So that at the time you went down you saw no man there?
A. At the time I went down, I did see a man there. [342]

Q. Didn't you just tell me the man that was underneath the car?
A. Not going down.

Q. When was he underneath the car? A. He was underneath the car, as I was coming out of the factory, not as I was going down.

Q. I see. You want to withdraw that statement that he was under as you went down?

MR. KATZMANN. One moment.

A. No, sir.

MR. KATZMANN. One moment, Mrs. Andrews, please.

MR. MOORE. I just wanted, reading back a trifle, she might not have intended to say that.

MR. KATZMANN. She did not say it.

MR. MOORE. Previously here she did say so.

MR. KATZMANN. Not as of the time she went in.

[The question is read.]

THE COURT. That is not a proper question. You may ask her if she wants to. You assume she wants to withdraw. Just ask her that question.

MR. KATZMANN. There is a further objection. It assumes she had said something the Commonwealth respectfully submits the witness did not say.

MR. MOORE. I will re-frame that question.

THE COURT. I guess you better.

Q. If you have stated in any previous answer to any previous question of mine, Mrs. Andrews, that the man was under the car when you went down, you did not intend to so state?

A. But I never stated that, Mr. Moore. [343]

Q. Now, the car at that time was in what condition with reference to being closed or open?

A. The side curtains were down on it.

Q. ... [T]he side curtains were on the car? A. They were down, they were not rolled up... .

Q. How far forward did the curtains go? A. Almost, . . to the front of the seat... .

Q. Up to the back of the front seat? A. Yes, sir. [344]

Q. Did I show you on the date I talked with you [Jan. 14] a photograph that you would now ... say was the photograph of the defendant?

A. Why, I don't understamd that, Mr. Moore... .

Q. I say, did I show you a photograph on the date that I talked with you that you are now prepared to tell the jury was the photograph of the man you saw on April 15th? A. Yes.

Q. And did you tell me on that date that any photograph that I showed to you was the photograph of the man that you saw on April 15th?

A. I did not, no, sir.

Q. What? A. I did not tell you.

Q. You didn't tell me? A. No, sir.

Q. On the contrary, you did say that it was not the photograph, did you not? A. I did not. [357]

Lola R. Andrews, Continued. June 13, 1921.

[Ed. Next, Moore questioned Andrews about her visit to the Brockton jail, about what she saw and did at the South Braintree depot, the location of the bandit car, and the men by that car.]

Q. (By Mr. Moore) Yet you couldn't see even the face of the man you were directing your question to [about Rice & Hutchins]? A. Why, sir, I saw his face when he got up.

Q. You had to call him up before you were able to see his face at all, weren't you?

A. He was getting up when I spoke, getting up from under the auto.... . [375]

Q. ... Mrs. Andrews, you don't claim that there was any intimidation, or threats, or coercion, or inducements, or anything of that kind ... offered to you ... at the time you and I talked?

MR. KATZMANN. To that I object, if your Honor please.

THE COURT. Hasn't she answered that repeatedly? [378]

Q. Did I offer you anything of any kind or character, whether it would have been a hairpin or the world? A. You mean, did you offer me anything at all, is that what you mean?

Q. Yes, anything, anything?

A. The only thing you offered me was to go down and see Mrs. Campbell for my vacation.... .

Q. Do you mean to state that I ... attempted to ask you to go down there to Maine, ...?

A. ... You asked me for Mrs. Campbell's address, which I gave you. You then asked if I knew where Stockton Springs was...You asked me how I would like to go down there. I told you I couldn't go at that time. You said, "How would you like a little vacation?"

Q. Now, have you said it all?

A. I have only answered what you asked me. You asked me if there was any inducements. [379]

Q. Go ahead, and tell the jury [the statement you allege I made to you]. This is not a question of integrity between you and I; this is a question for the jury. A. You asked me why I was afraid I would lose my work if I took the vacation to Maine, ... You said if I lost my work, you would see I got a position as good as I had now, or better. That is what you said to me. [380]

Q. [D]id I show you a large group of photographs among which were three separate and distinct photographs of the defendant Sacco, at the time I talked with you [Jan. 14]?

A. I don't remember.... .

Q. [D]id you see any photograph, ... which you even suggested ... to me in any way was the photograph of the man you saw on April 15th,

1920? A. The only way that I can answer you is, that I did show you one that I said resembled the man that I saw.

Q. And, as to that one, you said that, while he resembled, he was not the man?

A. No, sir, I didn't make that statement to you.

Q. Do you remember that there was two people with me ...? [382]

A. There was two men, ...

Q. And a young lady who ... took her notes by stenotype machine, ...?

A. Yes, sir. [383]

[Ed. Next, Moore asked about Andrews' work experience. Jeremiah McAnarney (see pp. 387-412 in the transcript) tried to get Andrews to admit she told Stewart—after she had seen Sacco at the Brockton police station—that Sacco was not the man she saw at South Braintree. {406} She denied this. {406} And she denied McAnarney's suggestion that Brockton jail employees had led her to Sacco, assistance which tainted her identification. {405} McAnarney asked Andrews to give the exact position of the bandit car by the Slater factory. {390-398} Then this.]

THE WITNESS. I feel faint.

MR. KATZMANN. She feels faint.

THE COURT. I think she should have a rest... .

(The witness collapses, and is removed from the court room.) [412]

[Ed. Recalled on June 14, Andrews was cross-examined further by McAnarney. {446-452} On redirect examination, Andrews said she gave her "time book" (Rice & Hutchins' work record) {457} to Moore when he visited her in Quincy. Moore denied this. {458} Williams argued that Andrews was frightened by an Italian visitor to her lodging late at night "two or three days" before Moore interviewed her. Williams said this experience affected Andrews' ability "to ... recall testimony given" {456} to Moore at her Quincy lodging. Subject to recall, Andrews exited trial on p. 460.]

William S. Tracy, Sworn. June 14, 1921.

Q. (By Mr. Williams) Where do you live? A. South Braintree, 158 Tremont Street.

Q. What is your occupation? A. Real Estate.

Q. Were you pursuing that occupation on the 15th of April of last year? A. I was... .

Q. Will you tell the jury what you did that morning? A. [V]ery soon after half past eleven I had occasion to go to the store, to Dyer & Sullivan's store. [Opposite corner to Torrey's drug store.]

Q. Where is that store? A. That store is on the corner of ... Hancock and Pearl Street... . [W]hen I returned home I found it was necessary for me to come back again and go to another store ... and I did so, and then returned home.

Q. What time did you get ... to the corner of Hancock and Pearl Street, the first time?

A... . [A]bout twenty minutes of twelve.

Q. How long were you there at that time? A. Well, I might say three minutes. [498]

Q. What time did you come back to about the same place after your trip home?

A... . [I]n about two minutes after.

Q. Do you know if there is a drug store at the corner of Pearl and Hancock? A. I do.

Q. On which corner is that? A. It is on the northeast corner of Washington and Pearl... .

Q. Who owns the building? A. I do. [Drug store is in building owned by Tracy.]

Q. Did you notice anybody in that vicinity on either of your trips? A. I did, sir.

Q. And on which, the first or the second? A. The first and second and third.

Q. ... Describe them and what you noticed them doing, if anything?

A. Well, on the first trip down there I noticed two men with their back to the store window.

Q. You refer to what store? A. The Torrey Store. [W. A. Torrey & Company.]

Q. That is the drug store? A. The drug store nearest the northeast corner. There is another window on the other side of the store, and, as a rule, men don't stand with their backs to those windows. [Ed. The Court ordered the last remark stricken from the record.]

Q. ... I just want you to tell us what you saw that morning. A. What I saw? [499]

27

Q. Yes. A. I saw two men standing with their back to the window of that store, …and I went into the store and did my errand in there and came back, and I went in a driveway back of the drug store and backed out and came around as near the corner as I could, so I observed those people within 20 feet, and I then went home and … came back again and drove right by that corner and went to the bakeshop on Pearl Street.

Q. Did you see the two men when you came back? A. They were both standing there, …

Q. Mr. Tracy, will you tell this jury what the personal appearance of these two men that you saw in front of the drug store was? A. Well, the two men were dressed respectably, … The man nearest the drug store was the shorter of the two, …

Q. What can you say as to their faces?

A. Well, they were,—one was a little darker than the other. [500]

Q. Have you ever seen either one of those men since? A. I have.

Q. Where? A. I saw one in the,—in the county house [jail] over here.

Q. When did you see him in the jail? A. On the 15th day of February.

Q. Of this year, of course? A. Yes, sir. [Ed. Tracy accompanied to jail by Officer John Scott.]

Q. Now, do you see in court today the man you saw in the jail at the time? A. I do.

Q. And what do you say as to his identity with the man you saw that day at South Braintree?

A. While I wouldn't be positive, I would say to the best of my recollection that was the man.

Q. Which man do you refer to? A. The man at this side.

Q. Where? A. In the cage.

Q. You mean the man described as Nicola Sacco? A. Yes. [501]

William J. Heron, Sworn. June 14, 1921.

Q. (By Mr. Williams) What is your business or occupation?

A. Railroad police officer.

Q. And by what company are you employed? A. New York, New Haven & Hartford.

Q. Were you in South Braintree on the day of the shooting, April 15th of last year? A. Yes, sir.

Q. What time did you arrive in South Braintree on that day? A. About 12:27… .

28

Q. What did you do when you got off the train? A. I went inside and walked around, hung around there for a few minutes. I got hold of [518] a young fellow that was sitting up on the Union News box, and took him inside of the office. I asked him his name... .

Q. Did you see anybody ... while you were there in the South Braintree station? A. Yes, sir.

Q. And who did you see there, other than the fellow you apprehended? A. Two men sitting there beside the gent's toilet.

Q. Will you describe the men you saw sitting there, and tell the jury what they were doing?

A. One of them was about 5 feet 6 inches, weighed about 145 pounds, Italian. The other fellow was about 5 feet 11; ... weighed about 160. They were smoking cigarettes, one of them.

Q. Do you know which one was smoking? A. The tallest one.

Q. Did you notice anything else they were doing?

A. Well, they acted kind of funny to me, nervous... .

Q. Have you seen either one of those men that you saw in the station that day since? A. One.

Q. Which one of those that you saw there in the station? A. The smallest one.

Q. And where did you next see that man?

A. In the Quincy court, coming in shackled to State Officer Scott.

Q. When was that, . .? A. Oh, probably five weeks or six weeks afterwards [after April 15].

Q. Do you see that man that you saw there in the station that day, and later saw in the Quincy court, here in court today? A. Yes, sir.

Q. Where? A. In the cage. [519]

Q. Do you know his name? A. Sacco.

Q. Which one is he? A. The smallest one, without the mustache.

Q. Are you sure he is the man you saw in the station that day?

A. Pretty sure.

Q. ... Have you any question in your mind that he is the man?

A. No. [520]

Cross-Examination.

Q. (By Mr. Moore) You didn't see, ... any of these men [defendants] for a lapse of six weeks after that date [04/15/1920]? A. No, The day they were brought into Quincy was the day I saw them, ...

Q. Who directed your attention to them at Quincy? A. I made a remark when he [Sacco] came out of the car, and somebody heard it, I guess.

Q. Who did you make the remark to? A. Well, there was about a dozen of us standing on the steps.

Q. Well, who did you make the remark to? A. I don't know... [523]
[Ed. Sacco's preliminary hearing of the South Braintree charge held in Quincy, 05/26.1920.]

Cross-Examination.

Q. (By Mr. McAnarney) Why did you not tell Mr. Reid what you knew about this case?

A. Why, I didn't have to. [Ed. Reid: investigator for Moore.] [535]

Re-Direct Examination.

Q. (By Mr. Williams) ... Where were you with reference to the Quincy court house at [537] the time of that hearing? A. ... I was inside. When the automobile drove up to the door, I went out on the front steps.

Q. Did you see Sacco come in that day [05/26/20]? A. Yes, sir.

Q. [W]hat was this remark ... you made to a number of people thereabouts?

MR. McANARNEY: Does your Honor think that competent?

THE COURT: You drew it out. I won't say you, but one counsel drew it out in cross-examination, the fact that he made some remark to several people who where there, and it was followed up further by questions as to the names of those people, if the witness could give them....

(The question is read.)

A. When he [Sacco] got out of the car, I said, "Gee, that is the fellow I saw down at South Braintree the day of the shooting." [538]

4. WITNESSES AT GROUND LEVEL

Annie Nichols, Sworn. June 10, 1921.

Q. (By Mr. Williams) What is your full name? A. Annie Nichols.

Q. And where do you live? A. South Braintree.

Q. Whereabouts in South Braintree? A. I live at 4 Colbert Avenue now, South Braintree.

Q. Did you live in South Braintree on April 15th of 1920? A. Yes, sir. [At 13 Curtis Place.]

Q. Do you know how far from Pearl Street your house was? A. ... It may be 150 feet, ... [256]

Q. Is the house you were living in on April 15th last the house which is now in back of the restaurant? A. Yes, sir.

Q. Where were you about three o'clock on the afternoon of April 15th, ...? A. I was at home.

Q. In what part of the house? A. In the kitchen.

Q. Which side of the house was the kitchen on? A. Facing the street [Pearl Street].

Q. Now, will you tell the jury, Mrs. Nichols, what you saw and heard relating to the shooting that afternoon ...? A. As I was in the kitchen, I just happened to look out of the window, and I saw Mr. Berardelli and Parmenter coming along, and as they come down the street this man that was standing against the [pipe] fence stepped up to Mr. Berardelli, and he spoke to him.

Q. Spoke to whom? A. Berardelli. He came along first, and then I didn't see any more. I sat down, and as I sat down I heard these shots. I rushed out on to the piazza, and when I got there Mr. Parmenter had his hands up. He ran across the street—

Q. When you say "he"— A. Mr. Parmenter ran across the street, and this man chased him and put two shots into him. As he ran across the street—

Q. When you say "he'— A. Mr. Parmenter ran across the street. The laborers ... were working right in front of the cellar. As he ran, there was a shot came from the pile of bricks there.

Q. Where was the pile of bricks? A. Right at the corner, right at this side of the water tower.

Q. I will show you Exhibit 8, and ask you if that picture shows where the pile of bricks was?

A. Right there [indicating picture].... .

Q. You are pointing to the corner of the fence right by the water tower?

A. **The bricks were piled up there**.

Q. You heard a shot from there? A. Yes. I heard the shot, and then the laborers all rushed back towards my house, and then the auto-[257] mobile, it seemed as though it came right along.

It came right up the hill. They threw the boxes in.

Q. When you say "they", who do you mean? A. These two men I saw standing there threw the boxes into the automobile, and were gone. That is all I know.... .

Q. Now, as the first man, as the first bandit chased Parmenter across the street, where was Berardelli? A. Lying on the ground. [258]

Q. Did you see anybody get into the automobile?

A. I think I saw the third man get in from the brick pile, get down and get in. [259]

Cross-Examination.

Q. (By Mr. McAnarney) You say the Italians didn't move, the laborers didn't move, until after a shot was fired from the brick pile? A. That is when they rushed back to my house.

Q. Your house is about 150 feet from the street? A. About that.

Q. The **brick pile** was about [the] edge of the street? A. Yes.

Q. Please tell us how you were able to tell at a distance of 150 feet where a shot came from?

A. Well, by the sound.

Q. You could tell by the sound of a shot that it came from a pile of brick that was right beside the street rather than from a person standing in the street,—you could tell that the shot came from the pile of brick, do you mean that? A. Well, I heard three shots.

Q. True, you heard a shot, but you had no way of knowing that shot came from that pile of brick or from either side of the road, Madam, had you? A. No, only just as they fired, that the laborers were there, and it scared them back.... .

Q. You really don't know where it [that shot] was fired from, do you? A. That is where the sound came from. The men rushed back. [261]

Redirect Examination.

Q. (By Mr. Williams) I forgot to ask you, Mrs. Nichols, if you noticed how these bandits were dressed. I am referring to the two you saw across the street there. A. I think they had dark suits, and a cap, light cap.

Q. ... Are you referring to both? A. Those two men I saw standing at the fence had dark suits and wore a cap.

Q. ... Did one have a cap, or both have caps? A. No, they both had caps. [263]

Recross Examination.

Q. (By Mr. Moore) Now, both of these men had their coats on, overcoats? A. No, sir, they didn't have no overcoat on.... [264]

Q. But you have seen the photographs— A. I have never seen the photographs.

Q. You have seen the defendants?

A. Yes, in the papers, but nobody ever showed me any photographs... .

Q. And on the view from the point on your porch, you can make no effort or attempt to say these are the men that you saw? A. No, sir.

Q. [By Mr. Williams] Mrs. Nichols, when was it you observed the caps on these men?

A. Why, as I saw them standing against the fence there. I saw them standing there.

MR. WILLIAMS. That is all. Thank you. [265]

Mr. Hans Behrsin, Sworn. Saturday, June 11, 1921.

Q. (By Mr. Williams) At the present time you are chauffeur for Mr. Slater of Slater & Morrill? A. Yes, sir.

Q. Were you chauffeur for that gentleman on the day of the shooting last year? A. Yes, sir.

Q. Were you with that car [Slater's Marmon Car] on Pearl Street shortly before that shooting? A. Yes, I was down below, by the factory, filling in gasoline.

Q. Whereabouts were you filling in gasoline?

A. That is right by the factory, right below the end of the shoe factory. [324]

Q. Do you mean by that, that little **cement house**? A. Yes, sir, exactly.

Q. At what time were you down by the cement house with this car of Mr. Slater's?

A. I should say about, it was about three o'clock [when he filled the Marmon's gas tank].

[The distance from ... the one-story concrete building ... in front of Slater & Morrill's to the east side of track No. 6 ... is 385 feet. The distance from the same point ... to the extreme east corner of the Rice & Hutchins 5-story brick factory ... is about 182 feet. Appel, III: 2271.]

Q. Who helped you to put in the gas? A. Louis Wade.

Q. After you got through filling up your car with gasoline, where did you go?

A. I started the car and go up across the track, over to the garage.

Q. Did you see anybody as you went up Pearl Street toward the railroad tracks? A. Yes.

Q. Whom did you see? A. I seen two fellows sitting on the fence... . on the left-hand side.

Q. Whereabouts did you see them sitting on the fence? A. It was on the,—almost on the end of Rice's factory. [325]

[The Rice & Hutchins factory ... building is square with the points of the compass, while Pearl Street at this point runs slightly to the north of east... . To the north of the Rice & Hutchins 5-story brick building on the south side of Pearl Street there is an iron **pipe fence**, then a gravel sidewalk, then a gravel gutter and roadway with a macadamized surface in the center of Pearl Street. Appel, III: 2271]

Q. Can you tell us how they were dressed or how they looked? A. The one was dressed with an army shirt on ... the color of an army shirt ... and I did not notice ... what the other was.

Q. Did you notice what they had on their heads? A. They had—... they had something on their heads, ... I think it was caps, but wouldn't say for sure. [326]

Q. Where did you stop your car? A. Right as I passed by the grass, by the garage where the cobbler shop is on the corner. [327]

Q. Will you say to the jury what you saw of the other car which then came up Pearl Street?

A. ... I should say it was a Buick car, ... It wasn't going very fast. I do not think the car was in good order, ... [T]he back curtains were down and flopping around ... [T]here were about five ... in there ... [T]here was some one in the back there beckoning with a gun or shotgun ... through the back light where you got the celluloid glass, ... That was broken out. [328]

Lewis L. Wade, Sworn. June 9, 1921.

Q. (By Mr. Williams) What is your full name? A. Lewis L. Wade.
Q. What is your occupation? A. Shoemaker.
Q. Employed by whom? A. Slater & Morrill.... about 15 years,—16.
Q. You then were employed by them April 15th of last year? A. Yes, sir
Q. And in what factory? A. Slater & Morrill's, Number 1.
Q. When you say "Number 1," you mean the one down the hill?
A. Yes, sir. [201]
Q. And where were you immediately before the shooting? A. ... I was in the **cement house**.
Q.... . Can you point out on that picture where the cement house is ...?
A. Right there (indicating).
MR. WILLIAMS. The witness points out the cement house right there **in front of** Slater & Morrill's factory.
Q. What were you doing there?
A. Well, at that time I was filling up Mr. Slater's car with gasoline.
Q. What time of the day was it? A. Well, about seven minutes of three.
Q. Anybody there with you? A.... . His chauffeur [Behrsin].
Q. Where did the car go then [after you put in 8 gallons of gas]?
A. It went down the hill, then up the road, and up Pearl Street.... .
Q. ... [W]hat did you next see or hear? A. Well, ... I hung the hose up, ... and came out of the cement house. I was just snapping the lock on it.
Q. On the door of the house? A. Yes, sir... I heard a shot—it sounded like a shot.
Q. What did you do then? A. Then I turned, and I saw—I heard [202] a lot of noise up there first.... . [S]ome Italians working across the road ... made a lot of noise, and I thought they were fighting first, but as I looked I could see Berardelli on the sidewalk.
Q. Tell us ... what you saw, ... A. As I turned there and looked up the road, I saw Parmenter run, and as he ran across the road he ran like

that (illustrating), ... The horses were out over the gutter and the truck was on the sidewalk—and as he ran by it, I couldn't see him no more. I looked at Berardelli, and he was in a crouching position. That means his left arm was up here, and he was down like that. And this man was standing, ... not at the most over five feet, anyway, from him, and he was in a crouching position. He was ... jumping back and forth, and I saw him shoot. Then I saw him shoot again.

Q. In what direction? A. Towards the man on the sidewalk, Berardelli... Berardelli stood in an angle of north-east, and the man that was shooting him was facing south. And the next thing that I saw was a car came up Pearl Street, and stop—Well, it didn't exactly stop... . And there was a man at the wheel... . he was a pale-faced man, ... He looked to me like a man that had sickness ... and this man that was shooting Berardelli went out on the side of the road and picked up the money box, I call it, and lifted it up with two hands and put it into the car, and he got into the car, ... I would not say for sure whether he shot again or not, but I think so, and I should take it that he shot at the man on the road. Then I turned into the office to call emergency, and after I called them I ran out. I went to where Berardelli lay, ...

Q. Where was he lying at that time? A. He was lying on the sidewalk in the middle of Rice & Hutchins, on the north side... . [H]e was exactly between that stump and the telegraph pole with the fire alarm box on it, only he was on the sidewalk. [203]

Q. Will you describe that man you saw shooting at Berardelli?

A. Why, he was kind of a short man, had black hair, he was bareheaded, ... and I would say that he weighed probably 140 pounds ... . The man ... was probably 26 or 27 ... . He had a gray shirt on... . And he needed a shave, ...

Q. Have you seen that man you saw shooting at Berardelli that day since then?

A. ... I thought I saw him... . [a]t the Brockton police station.

Q. How long after the shooting? A. Well, I think it must have been a month. [204]

Q. And will you tell the jury if the man you saw in the Brockton police station, which you say in your judgment was the man who did the shooting that day, is in the court room?

A. I would not say for sure.

Q. What is your best judgment? A. Well, he resembles,—looks somewhat... .

Q. Which man [looks like the South Braintree shooter]? A. The man on my left in that cage... .

Q. What is his last name? A. Sacco... .

Q. Is he, in your best judgment, the man you saw shooting at Berardelli that day?

MR. McANARNEY: I object. [205] [Ed. Debate follows.]

(The question suggested by the Court is read.) ... (The question is again read.)

A. Well, I ain't sure now. I have a little doubt... . [206]

[Ed. Wade said his doubt began 3 or 4 weeks ago after he saw a man who "resembled" Sacco.

After more debate appears this statement.]

THE COURT: (To the Jury.) Gentlemen, I should explain to you the purpose of this inquiry. This is not in any way evidence of the fact. Under the statute, although the prosecution calls a witness, if a witness has made contradictory statements outside, inquiries may be made with reference to those statements, solely with one view, and that is, to attack the credibility of the witness. It is not affirmative evidence of anything; ... [207]

Cross-examination.

Q. (By Mr. Jeremiah McAnarney) ... You were some 70 paces, I believe you testified in the preliminary examination, away from where the shooting took place, weren't you? A. Yes. [213]

Q. Had the man who was in front of Berardelli changed his position from the time you saw him standing, as you testified about 5 feet or something from Berardelli, . .?

A. He was changing it all the time there as I was looking at him.

Q. In what way, please? A. He was jumping back and forth, ... in a space probably 4 feet; ...

Q. Now, what did he finally do; ...? A. He was stooping over, like that (indicating).

Q. After he got through with that motion ... what did he do next?

A. He took about two or three steps and picked up a box and put it in the automobile. [214]

Q. You testified in the Quincy District Court on the 26th of May, 1920, didn't you? A. Yes, sir.

[Ed. McAnarney directs Katzmann to a page in the transcript of Sacco's preliminary hearing on May 26.]

MR. JEREMIAH McANARNEY Take page 31, Mr. Katzmann, the fourth question from the top.

"Q. Do you say this is the man or can you say positively whether he is or not?

A. I do not want to make a mistake. This is too damn serious, but he looks like the man."

Does that call your attention to the question and your answer? A. Yes, I remember that.

Q. Now, did you later down have this question put to you:

"Q. Will you say he is the man?"

and you answered,

"No, I will not say so"?

You so answered at Quincy last May, a year ago, didn't you? A. I do not know, it is so long ago. [216]

Redirect Examination.

Q. (By Mr. Williams) I am now showing you, Mr. Wade, what purports to be the official transcript of the record in the Quincy Court. [Ed. After 3 questions, this follows.]

Q. Now wait. I wish to call your attention to the question and answers in between the two that Mr. McAnarney put to you. Were you asked in the lower court,

"Q. You will not say positively he is the man, will you?"

and you answered,

"A. I do not want to answer that. Must I answer that question?"

Was that asked and did you so answer? A. It must have been asked or it would not have been there. Of course, it is so long ago. [217]

....

. . .

Q. Did you then answer,

"A. I may be mistaken but still I don't think so. He looks like the man in every description."

A. I must have said that.

Q. Have you any doubt you said it? A. No.

Q. Mr. Wade, was that answer that you then gave true? A. At that time. [218]

[Ed. See Wade's testimony at Inquest held at Quincy District Court on April 17, 1920, Appel, VI: 440-444. Wade said (p. 442) "That's the man" when shown photo 2 by state police.]

Mr. James F. Bostock, Sworn. June 9, 1921.

Q. (By Mr. Williams.) What is your name? A. James F. Bostock.

Q. Is your work connected with machinery in shoe factories? A. I am a mill-wright.

Q. Were you in South Braintree on that day [April 15, 1920]? A. Yes.

Q. Did you do any work there that day? A. Yes, sir. [185]

Q. And in which factory or factories? A. Slater & Morrill's.

Q. Which factory? A. Both factories.

Q. That is, the one at the railroad station and the one down the hill?
A. Yes, sir.

Q. And where did you see them [Berardelli and Parmenter] in the afternoon?

A. Why, I met them in the afternoon. I left the factory at three o'clock or thereabouts.

Q. Now, will you tell the jury ... what you saw in connection with this shooting?

A. ... [A]s I came from the [lower] factory there was a man filling Mr. Slater's car with gasoline and they flowed it over the car, ...

Q. Whereabouts were they doing that? A. Right at the end of the factory where there is a cement house, ... [186]

Q. Go ahead, if you will. A. I ... watched him fill that car. Then I crossed the street, and as I came up the street there was a pair of horses with one of these scoops. A man was hollering at the horses, ...

Q. Where were those horses, ?

A. Those horses stood where they were digging out a restaurant... .

Q. Go on from that point. A. I walked up the street, and there is a fence on my right-hand side where there is a tank that the railroad use ... and I was on just **this side of the tank.**

[The view from the Hampton House east down Pearl Street is in part obstructed by a high board fence extending along the **north side** of Pearl Street, from a point immediately east of the railroad gate, and extending east to a point east and north of the water tank. Appel, III: 2271.]

Q. When you say "this side", what do you mean by "this"? A. I mean to the **east** of the tank. I saw Parmenter and Berardelli coming down the street and as I walked towards them Parmenter says to me, "Bostock, when you go up by, you go into the other factory and fix the pulley on the motor," and I says to him, "I am going to get this quarter past three car to Brockton to do a repair job," and as I started to turn around to leave, I heard two or three shots fired, and as I swung around there were two men shooting at him. [187]

Q. ... [T]ell us what happened. A. As I looked down there, this Berardelli was on his knees in a crouched position as though he was guarding with his hand over his head, ... and this man stood off... . and fired at him almost as if the man was touching him when he fired at him. [188]

Q. What did you see this man you saw standing over Berardelli did [sic] after that? A. Why, he stood there over him. He shot, ... at Berardelli probably four or five times. He stood guard over him.

Q. And then what happened? A. I started to walk in the direction towards him. Probably I was away from him 50 or 60 feet, ... and ... they swung around and shot at me twice... .

Q. Where was the second [bandit]? A. [H]e probably stood away from him [Berardelli] five or 10 feet. He stood looking down the road and ... made a beckon in that direction. [189]

Q. How many bandits—using that term again—did you see on the road at any time? A. Four.

Q. During the shooting? A. Three on the road. I saw the two that done the shooting and one other got off the running-board or got out of the auto, ... but he got out and helped throw the two cans, or boxes, ... that had the pay roll, in... .

Q. You meant the **third man** you saw? A. The third man, yes. He got up, and when he got to within about probably 10 or 15 feet he came out of that automobile and run to where the other two stood, and he picked up one can and one of the bandits who stood took the other, and the man who was with them got into the back seat of the car, and as I say, as he came towards the railroad crossing he crawled from the back seat to the front seat... . [190]

Q. Where were you at that time as it reached the crossing? A. I was at the end of this fence... .

Q. You say "the fence." You are now pointing to the **wooden fence** by the water tank? A. Yes, sir, ... If I laid out at arm's length I could have touched the spokes of the car as it passed me.

Q. What did you observe as to the car or the inmates of the car, ...? A. ... I went back to where Berardelli was laying, but as it passed me I noticed it, the back end glass was broken out and the covering on one side was flying out and then one of the bandits laid over on the outside of the car, out in about that direction [indicating], firing ... all the way up the street.

Q. What part of the car was he firing from? ... [191] A. ... [F]rom the front end. [192]

[Short recess.]

James F. Bostock, Continued

Q. (By Mr. Williams) Did you see any of these bandits ... as you came up the street from Slater & Morrill's? A. Why, yes. [193]

Q. Where were they at that time? A. Leaning on the [iron pipe] fence. [See photo, p. 163.]

Q. Step right down in front of the jury, and point out where you saw them leaning on the fence at that time.

(The witness stands in front of the jury, and indicates a picture.)

A. I should say they stood about there, right about opposite that telegraph pole.... One stood leaning on the fence in that position, and the other stood leaning towards him....

Q. Did you see any of the men who were doing the shooting do anything with their gun either during the shooting or after, except shoot? A. Why, I should say one of them filled his gun.

Q. Do you know which one that was? A. I should say it was the one that shot at Berardelli... .[194]

Q. Were you taken to the Brockton police station at any time? A. Yes, sir.

Q. Did you look at the defendants at that time? A. Yes, sir.

Q. Could you tell whether or not they were any of the men? A. No, sir, I could not tell ...

Q. Did you pick up any shells there? A. Yes, I picked up some shells.

Q. Where abouts did you pick them up? A. I picked them up just close to where the shooting was, about two or three feet from the shooting.

Q. What did you do with them? A. I think Mr. Fraher had them.

Q. Mr. Fraher? A. I left them in Slater & Morrill's office.

Q. How many did you pick up? A. Three or four.

Q. You turned them over to Mr. Fraher?

A. No. I left them in the office of Slater & Morrill, in one of the desks.

Q. Is that all you found there? A.... . I saw some others picked up. I saw some others had some others, but that is all I picked up. [195]

Q. Did you see Berardelli do anything during the shooting, . .?

A. No, I did not. I thought he spoke to them. He acted to them as though he knew the men and spoke to them... .

Q. You say you have known Berardelli for some time? A. Yes, sir.

Q. Do you know whether or not he had a revolver?

A. I have seen him with a revolver in the shop, yes.

Q. How many times have you seen him with a revolver? A. I have seen him a number of times. I have joshed him with the revolver,—— asked him if he carried it to shoot rats.

Q. Where was it his custom to carry the revolver, if you know?

MR. McANARNEY. How is that important?

THE COURT. I don't see [its materiality].

MR. WILLIAMS. [I]t will be material as the trial progresses.

THE COURT. Step to the desk and inform me wherein its materiality may appear later.

(Conference at the bench.)

THE COURT. You may inquire.

MR. WILLIAMS. What was the question?

(The question is read.)

A. In his hip pocket.

Q. How long before the shooting had you last seen the revolver in Berardelli's possession?

A. I think the Saturday night [April 10] before the shooting. [196]

Q. What kind of a revolver was it, do you know?

A. ... It was a 38 calibre revolver, that is all I can tell you. I don't know. I never owned one.

Q. What did it look like? A. It was a nickel-plated revolver.... .

(Mr. Williams shows a revolver to the witness.) ...

Q. Can you say whether or not the revolver that you saw in Berardelli's possession was similar in appearance to the revolver I now show you?

[Ed. After Moore's objection was overruled, Bostock answered.]

A. Well, I should say it is a revolver similar to that, yes; that kind of a revolver. [197] [Ed. Revolver is Exhibit 27, p. 102.]

Cross-Examination.

Q. (By Mr. McAnarney) You had known Berardelli how long? A. . . .
I should think five or six months.

Q. When did you first know that he carried a revolver? A. Why, I have seen
him with a revolver a good many mornings when I went there. I knew he
was an officer, and I have seen him with a revolver. I joshed him about it, ...

Q. Then you got used to seeing him carry a revolver? A. Yes... .

Q. You knew he always carried a gun? A. Yes, I knew... [198]

Q. Well, I now ask you did he any of these times take the revolver out?
A. One time he took the revolver out.

Q. Which time? A. The first time I asked him [if he carried a gun]... .

Q. Did he hold it in his hand, or lay it on a desk or any place? A. I
had it in my hand.

Q. You took the gun out of his hand? A. No, I did not take the gun
out of his hand. He showed it to me. He handed it to me. I had the
gun Berardelli carried in my hand... .

Q. Have you a distinct recollection of anything on that revolver? A.
No, sir, not one particularly. I couldn't tell it if I saw it again.

Q. And that is the only time you saw it? A. Yes, sir. I have seen it a
number of times in his possession.

Q. But you couldn't tell it again? A. No, sir.

Q. And you don't know whether this is the revolver? A. No, sir. [200]

James E. McGlone, Sworn. June 10, 1921.

Q. (By Mr. Williams) What is your business? A. Teamster.

Q. Do you recall the day of the South Braintree shooting last year?
A. Yes, sir. [265]

Q. Where were you on that afternoon? A. I was taking stone from
where the restaurant is now.

Q. How far from the edge of Pearl Street, ... was this excavation being
made? A. About thirty feet.

Q. How large an excavation was it? A. A hundred feet square.

Q. Now, ... assuming you were standing in the excavation ... [w]hat
would be the first thing to your right? A. There was a little **water
tower** there.

Q. Anything around the water tower? A. Chimney brick they were
carting for the restaurant.

43

Q. How big a [**brick**] **pile** was it, do you remember?

A. Well, I guess it must have been ten or twelve 5-ton truckloads... .

Q. Did you have a 2-horse drag? A. I had a 1-horse drag. [266]

Q. Now, what was the first you heard or saw of this shooting? A. I was kneeling down putting the stone on the drag, and I heard one or two shots fired. I turned and looked across the street, and I saw two or three up against the fence towards the Rice & Hutchins shoe shop. I heard a couple more shots fired, and there was a fellow had hold of this guard by the shoulder.

Q. A fellow what? A. One of these fellows had hold of the guard by the shoulder, and there was a couple of shots fired.

Q. At that time, do you mean? A. Yes, sir. The next thing I saw, two fellows running with a black bag, ... and there was a machine coming up over the hill slowly, and when the machine got up by this telegraph pole they jumped in with the bag.

Q. Which telegraph pole is that?

A. The telegraph pole right at the corner of Rice & Hutchins shoe shop.

Q. Now, what else did you see? A. Parmenter started across the street, and he started to holler. He came over where I was and he started to go down, and I put my arm around his shoulders and put him down on the ground, and I got a double blanket off one of Loud's teams and put underneath his head ... Then we took and spread the blanket out after some more fellows came, and we carted him over across the street into Colbert's house. [267]

Q. Can you give us any idea about the machine? A. What I saw ... was about a 7-passenger and the isinglass in back was out, and I think it was **a rifle** sticking out of the back end of it... .

Q. Did you see more than two bandits that day?

A. Well, I think I made a mistake on that [He said two bandits on p. 268]. There was **three**.

Q. And where did you see the third? A. The third was the one that had hold of this guard, and then there was two, I meant to say, that ran with the boxes. [269]

Cross-Examination.

Q. (By Mr. Moore) Mr. McGlone, do you see in this court room any of the men that you saw April 15? A. No, sir, I do not. [274]

3rd Redirect Examination.

Q. (By Mr. Williams) Any other reason [you are unable to identify these men]? A. Well, I can't say that they are the men or they are not the men, because I ain't sure. [276]

3rd Recross Examination.

Q. (By Mr. McAnarney) You were close enough so you saw the side, and you noticed the side of the revolver was flat, didn't you? A. That was facing right straight towards me. [277]

Q. You were looking right attentively at those men, weren't you?

A. Yes, but I did not get a good look at them to identify them. I can't say those are the men. I can't say they ain't the men.

4th Redirect Examination.

Q. (By Mr. Williams) What did the Italian laborers do after the shooting commenced?

A. After the shooting commenced?

Q. Well, when the shooting commenced? A. They all started to jump behind those double carts.

They had double carts there. They all left their work and started to beat it back farther. [278]

Mr. Horace A. Colbert, Sworn. June 10, 1921.

Q. (By Mr. Williams) Where do you live? A. At present, 23 Summer Street, South Braintree.

Q. Where were you living on the 15th day of April, 1920? A. No. 4 Colbert Avenue. [288]

Q. Can you point out on this plan where your house was on that day? That is the house here, the first house around the curve on Colbert Avenue? A. Yes, sir... .

Q. Where were you at the time the shooting began, if you know?
A. I was standing in the doorway between my kitchen and dining room.

Q. What did you hear? A. I heard some shots, and I turned around and came back, and I saw some men running out of the cellar.

Q. What did you do? A. I went to the door to look out, and I thought the shooting was in the cellar, and I watched them running behind the house.

Q. Who were the men who were running? A. The men that were digging the cellar.

Q. Which way were they running? A. Towards the house. The houses where Mrs. Nichols lived and Frank Graves, in the other house.

Q. What did you then do? A. I looked around to see what was making them run. I saw two men out in the street going from the gutter up onto the sidewalk. Each one had a money box. They walked up the street this way. [Indicating]. The car came up by them... .

Q. Did you get a look at their faces? A. No, sir, I did not. I saw them back to. [289]

Q. ... Did you see either of the victims of the shooting afterwards?
A.... I saw Parmenter.

Q. Where did you see him? A. Lying side of a tip cart belonging to McGlone.

Q. What did you do with him? A. When I got out there the two McGlone boys were there. They had a horse blanket and they were putting it under his head, and I told them to lay the blanket out and they put Parmenter on and to take him into my house. They did that, ...

Q. Did you see Berardelli's body? A. They brought it into the house some time after they brought Parmenter in. [290]

Cross-Examination.

Q. (By Mr. Jeremiah McAnarney) After the shooting, did quite a number of people come out of both factories? A. Yes... .

Q. The street was practically packed, wasn't it?
A. Fairly well, around the front of my house and in front of the cellar. [291]

5. WITNESSES AT FACTORY WINDOWS

Edgar C. Langlois, Sworn. June 10, 1921.

Q. (By Mr. Williams.) What is your occupation or profession?

A. Foreman of a shoe factory.

Q. Slater & Morrill's? A. Rice & Hutchins.

Q. Rice & Hutchins. What was your position or occupation on April 15th, the day of the South Braintree shooting? A. Foreman. [278]

Q. ... If you did hear it [the shooting], where were you in the factory?

A. Within two or three feet of the window.

Q. What floor, I meant?

A. Second floor from the street level. The third floor rising from the cellar.

Q. Does that picture you have got in front of you show Rice & Hutchins factory? A. Yes.

Q. Perhaps you can show the jury.

THE COURT. Where were you?

THE WITNESS. The second floor from the street level or third floor from the cellar... .

Q. Near which window? A. The second window, ... That middle window, it seems to me... .

Q. Now, will you tell the jury in your own way what you heard, what you did and what you saw?

A. Well, I heard some noise and thinking it was blasting out there, a kind of queer report, too quick for blasting, and I opened the window; calling my attention I looked. There I seen two men shooting. I ran to the telephone that is 75 feet away, probably, and got the operator and told them to call the police, and came back. Then I seen some more shooting there, but I kept looking in and out all the time, pushing my help away. That is about all. I seen the auto coming up a little farther down.

Q. ... As you opened that window, what picture did you get as you looked down on the street?

A. Well. I seen this man Berardelli and the two men firing at him, one in back, one in front.

Q. Where was Berardelli? Suppose you are now looking down from that window you then opened out... . A. Directly underneath me. [279]

47

Q. Where was Berardelli standing in relation to that **iron fence**? A. In the middle of the sidewalk, I should say... .

Q. Where were the men that were shooting at him? A. One was, one in front, one in the back. [280]

Q. There were two, as I understand it? A. Two men, both were firing rapidly... .

Q. Where was Berardelli when you got back [from telephoning]? A. The same place.

Q. Standing up? A. Yes, well, just creeping down... .

Q. Sagging, you mean? A. Sagging down. [281]

Q. Did you see anything distinguished about the back of that automobile as you saw it going up the street? A. The **window** was pulled out.

Q. Yes. Anything else? A. There was **a gun** in there.

Q. ... Where did you see the gun? [283] A. It was a long-barreled gun probably a couple of feet long, coming in the center of the window.

Q. Will you describe ... the appearance of either or both of these men with guns that were down below your window? A. Short and dark complexioned, curly or wavy hair, about five feet, eight or nine inches, about 140 or 145 pounds... .

Q. Could you identify either or both of those men if you saw them again? A. No, sir. [284]

Lewis Pelser, Sworn. Afternoon Session. June 10, 1921.

Q. (By Mr. Williams) What is your full name? A. Lewis Pelser. [Town: Jamaica Plain.]

Q. Where do you work? A. Rice & Hutchins shoe factory. [Employed about two years.]

Q. Were you working there on April 15th of last year, the day of the shooting? A. Yes, sir.

Q. What floor were you working on? A. I would call it the **first floor**. There is a basement underneath it.

Q. And what did you first know that day with reference to the shooting, either by hearing something or seeing something?
A. Well, I heard something first, and then I opened the window afterwards.

Q. Which window did you open? A. I opened the middle window, this middle window right here.

Q. That is the middle window in the end of Rice & Hutchins' factory?
A. Yes, sir.
Q. What had you heard before you opened that window?
A. I heard about three shots before I opened the window... .
Q. And what did you see when you looked out? A. I seen this fellow shoot this fellow. It was the last shot. He put four bullets into him. [292]
Q. You saw this fellow shoot this fellow. Who was the man that was shot? A. Berardelli... .
Q. What did you see there ["looking down towards Pearl Street"]?
A. I saw him lying down.
Q. Who? A. Berardelli, after the shooting. [Ed. Pelser had learned his name was Berardelli.]
Q. How was he lying, do you remember?
A. He was lying on his left side, and then he rolled over on his back. [293]
Q. Could you describe what it [bandit's gun] looked like? A. It was a bright gun, a brand new gun it looked like.
Q. What color? A. Whitish color... .
Q. Will you describe that man that you saw there who was doing the shooting? A. Well, he was about two or three feet away, and he stood like that, and put the last bullet in him... .
Q. Yes, describe his appearance. A. He was kind of crouched down.
Q. I don't mean the way he was standing, but the way he looked?
A. You mean his description?
Q. Yes, that is just what I do mean. A. He had a dark green pair of pants and an army shirt tucked up. He had wavy—hair pushed back, very strong hair, wiry hair, very dark.
Q. What complexion? A. Dark complexion.
Q. How far were you from him at that time? A. Oh, about seven feet away....
Q. You say an army shirt tucked in? A. Tucked around the neck.
Q. What do you mean by an army shirt?
A. One of those brown army shirts they have in the army.
Q. You say, tucked in around the neck?
A. He had the collar pushed up, and I think he had a pin in it... .
Q. Do you see in the courtroom the man you saw shooting Berardelli that day? A. Well, I wouldn't say it was him but he is a dead image of him. [Pelser points to Sacco in the cage.] [294]
Q. Do you know what his name is? A. Well, I have heard it was Sacco... .

49

Q. Now, what did you see that man on the street do after he shot, as you say, the fourth shot ...?

A. He ran towards the automobile. The automobile was coming up slowly.

Q. What did you see happen when the automobile came?

A. He started to fire. He put a bullet over towards where Parmenter fell.

Q. Who did? A. The fellow that was doing the shooting.

Q. That same fellow? A. Yes.

Q. What did Parmenter do? A. He fell there in the lot where the restaurant is now.

Q. Did you see him fall? A. Yes, sir. [295]

Q. After he put a bullet over there, what did you see him do?

A. Then he flashed a gun over towards the factory.

Q. What factory? A. Rice & Hutchins. Then he jumped into the automobile, and put two bullets right over the window where I was standing... .

Q. What did you see it [bandit car] do, I mean? A. I took the number of the car.

Q. Where was the car when you took the number? A. It was no more than about five or six feet.

Q. What was the number on the car? A. 49783. [Pelser said he saw the front license plate.]

Q. Did you make a note of it at the time? A. Yes, sir. [296]

Q. Did you see anybody in the car? A. No, I didn't see anybody. I was too anxious to get away. I was kind of scared myself... .

Q. Did you make a memorandum yourself of the number, or did you call it out to some one?

A. Well, I put it on a cutting board. [297]

Cross-Examination.

Q. (By Mr. Moore) Mr. Pelser, on March 26 of this year did a gentleman call on you, Mr. Reid, and talk with you with reference to the facts of this case? A. To my house?

Q. Yes. A. Yes, sir. [Ed. Reid: investigator for chief defense counsel Fred Moore.] [299]

Q. Why was it that you didn't tell Mr. Reid the facts? A. Because I didn't want to tell my story.

Q. Why? A. Because I didn't like to go to court... .

Q. Did you tell Mr.Reid a falsehood ... to avoid being called as a witness ...? A. Yes, sir. [300]

[Ed. Moore quotes from Reid's notes of his interview of Pelser on March 26, 1921.]

Q. [Reading.] Question: "The shooting was all over by the time you opened the window?" Answer: "Yes." Did you so state to Mr. Reid? A. Yes, sir.

Q. Was that the truth? A. No, it was not... .

Q. [Reading.] Question: "Did you see the man who did the shooting? Answer: "No; they were just gone." Did you so state to Mr. Reid? A. Yes, sir.

Q. Why did you tell Mr. Reid that, Mr. Pelser? A. Because I didn't know him well enough... .

Q. He told you that he represented the defendant? A. Yes... .

Q. Why did you tell Mr. Reid that you ducked under the bench? Now, Pelser, isn't it the truth that you did duck under the bench? A. No, sir.

Q. Didn't you tell counsel for the Commonwealth in direct examination that you got scared?
A. Yes, sir.

Q. Then you ducked under the bench, didn't you, sir? A. Yes, sir.

Q. Why didn't you tell the jury half a second ago that you did duck under the bench?
A. Well, I didn't.

Q. Didn't you just now tell me that you did? A. No, sir. That is what I told Mr. Reid. [301]

Q... . [W]hy did you tell the story that you told this jury today after March 26th, the date of this statement? A. Because I knew if I come up here I would have to tell the truth.

Q. Didn't you feel there was any obligation upon you ... to tell Mr. Reid the truth? A. No, sir. [302]

Q... . [Y]ou were willing to tell a deliberate untruth to a man representing the defendants?
A. I didn't know him well enough to talk to,—to know who he was until he told me. [304]

Q. [After citing Reid again.] Then you did get down underneath the bench?
A. At the last part of it [the shooting]. [305]

Cross-Examination.

Q. (By Mr. McAnarney) So far as you know, you were the only man that got the number of that automobile, weren't you? A. Yes, sir.
Q. And still you were hiding along the 26th of May last so that you would not be called, and you didn't want to tell the truth to Mr. Reid? A. Yes, sir. [315] [Ed. See debate, pp. 316-323.]

Mary E. Splaine, Sworn. June 9, 1921.

Q. (By Mr. Williams) Were you employed as bookkeeper by Slater & Morrill on April 15th of last year? A. Yes sir.
Q. At that time where was the bookkeeper's office or room where you worked? A. It is in the southeast corner of the building, on Railroad Street. [Upper factory, Hampton House.]
Q. On which floor? A. The second floor. [220]
Q. After you saw them [Parmenter and Berardelli] go down the street there, what did you next see or hear ...? A. I heard some shots, which sounded like back firing from an auto.
Q. After you heard them, what did you do? A. I stood up in the middle of the office, and then I walked to the window on the south side. [221]
Q. What can you say as to the [bandit] car at that time, . .? A. I took it to be a touring car.
Q. What do you say about the tops or curtains? A. The top and the curtain, the top was up. The back curtains were up but the curtain between the back seat and the middle seat was not buttoned down. That was where the man appeared, between those two places. [222]
Q. ... Can you tell better ... what you mean by that picture [which shows the side of the auto]?
A. ... It was in this space here where the man's body appeared, right where this curtain is.
Q. Where the first curtain is? A. Yes, sir, the first curtain right there (indicating). That curtain was not buttoned down. In this place was where the man's form appeared.
MR. MOORE. Refer to the Exhibit number.
MR. WILLIAMS. Referring to Exhibit 10.
THE COURT. May I see that, please?
(Mr. Williams hands Exhibit 10 to the Court.)
THE COURT. Mr. Williams, I understand that this is the—

MR. WILLIAMS. She says that where that first curtain was the man,—that was not buttoned down, the man's body appeared here, as I understood you?

THE WITNESS. Yes.

THE COURT. Thank you.

Q. Did you see that man that appeared at that place? A. Yes, sir.

Q. Can you describe him to these gentlemen here? A. Yes, sir. He was a man that I should say was slightly taller than I am. He weighed possibly from 140 to 145 pounds. He was a muscular,—he was an active looking man. I noticed particularly the left hand was a good sized hand, a hand that denoted strength or a shoulder that—

Q. So that the hand you said you saw where? A. The left hand, that was placed on the back of the front seat, ... He had a gray, what I thought was a shirt,—had a grayish, like navy color, and the face was what we would call clear-cut, clean-cut face. Through here [indicating] was a little narrow, just a little narrow. The forehead was high. The hair was brushed back and it was between, I should think, two inches and two and one-half inches in length and had dark eyebrows, but the complexion was a white, peculiar white that looked greenish... .

Q. Did you ever see that man after that? A. Yes. [223]

Q. Where did you see him? A. I saw him in the police station in Brockton... .

Q. I want you to look around the court room and see if you see in the court room the man that you saw that day in the automobile?

A. Yes, sir, the man sitting nearest to me on this side of over there... .

Q. The man with the mustache, or the man without the mustache?

A. No, sir, the man without the mustache... .

Q. Are you sure? A. Positive... .

Q. What is the name [of the man] you learned? A. Nicola Sacco. [224]

Cross-Examination.

Q. (By Mr. Moore) Well, now, this man leaning against the forward seat of the car, back of the forward seat of the car, I understand you to say he was not firing anything? A. I did not see him fire. He was not leaning against the front seat of the car. He was leaning out of the car. He was steadying himself against the front seat. [230]

Q. Then his both hands were inside of the body of that car, were they?
A. I saw his right hand,—I mean his left hand, inside the car, I do not know anything about his right hand.

Q. Do you remember testifying on the preliminary examination in this case as follows, in response to questions asked, I believe, by counsel, by Mr. Adams?

[Ed. Moore is about to cite the transcript of the preliminary hearing for Sacco held at the Quincy court on May 26, 1920]

MR. KATZMANN. The page?

MR. MOORE. Page 50. At the bottom of page 50.

"A. He stood there with one hand resting on the front seat and the other hand discharging."

A. No, sir, I never said that in Quincy.... [231]

Q. At any rate, these matters that I have directed your attention to in your testimony [at the hearing in Quincy court] are all matters of error in the record? A. Those things to which I have taken exception are errors.

Q. Including this statement:

"Q. Do you say this is the man? A. I will not swear positively he is the man.

Q. You did not get a sufficient look to say positively this is the man?

A. I would not swear positively he is the man."

A. I did not answer that question that way [at Quincy].

Q. Do you want to say that this is not a correct transcript of your testimony?

A. I should say that was an incorrect transcript of that answer. [233]

[Short recess.]

Mary E. Splaine, Continued.

Q. (By Mr. McAnarney) While you were there [at Captain Proctor's office in Boston] you were shown some photographs? A. Yes, sir, pictures. [243]

Q. You identified that photograph as the photograph of the man you saw leaning out of the car? A. No, sir, not in detail....

Q. Later you learned that man was in Sing Sing at the time of this—I don't know the word he used, but you learned it was not Sacco? A. I learned the man was not at large. [244]

Q. So, in describing this man whose picture you saw in the Rogue's Gallery, and whom you learned was in jail for some other offence, you said then to … Captain Proctor and others, he bore a striking resemblance to the man you saw leaning out of the car? A. In some features…. [245]

Mary E. Splaine, Continued. June 10, 1921.

Q. (By Mr. McAnarney) [Citing the Quincy court transcript] And when you used those words,
"I don't think my opportunity afforded me the right to say he is the man," you meant it?
A. Yes, sir, I did. [249]

Redirect Examination.

Q. (By Mr. Williams) Now, will you tell these gentlemen how you reconcile in your own mind the answers which you made in the Quincy Court and the answer which you made to me in this court? A. Well, from the opportunity—[251] [McAnarney's objection prompted rephrasing.]
Q. … [W]hat did you mean here yesterday when you said that you did positively identify the defendant as the man whom you saw at South Braintree? A. From the observation I had of him in the Quincy Court and the comparison of the man I saw in the machine, on reflection I was sure he was the same man. [252]

Recross Examination.

Q. (By Mr. McAnarney) … You are most certain now, aren't you?
A. I am positive he is the man, certain he is the man. I admit the possibility of an error, but I am certain I am not making a mistake. [253]

Miss Frances J. Devlin, Sworn. June 14, 1921.

Q. (By Mr. Williams) Were you employed on April 15th, last year, the day of the shooting?
A. Yes, sir.
Q. And by whom were you employed and in what capacity on that date? A. By the Slater & Morrill factory, as bookkeeper.
Q. Were you in the same room Miss Splaine worked in? A. Yes, sir. [460]

Q. Where were you when you heard the shots? A. Right at the window... .

Q. Will you point out on either picture No. 4 or picture No. 1 ... at what window you were?

A. This window here. [Indicating.] ... .

MR. WILLIAMS. [Showing to the jury.] ... The witness points to the window nearest the corner on the railroad side of the Slater & Morrill factory of the Hampton House. [461]

Q. Now, ... tell the jury in your own way what you saw in reference to that automobile ...

THE WITNESS. I saw the man in the back seat get up and lean toward the gate-tender, and then ... he came on the nearer side of the automobile, and he was stretched out, with a gun in his hand, shooting into the crowd. Then the automobile passed from my sight. [462]

Q. Will you describe to the jury the ... appearance of that man that you saw leaning out?

A. He was a dark man, and his forehead, the hair seemed to be grown away from the temples, and it was blown back ... he had a white complexion and [was] a fairly thick-set man, ...

Q. Have you seen that man since that time? A. Yes, sir.

Q. Where did you see him? A. At the Brockton police station... .

Q. Will you look around the court room and see if you see that man in the court room?

A. Yes, sir.

Q. Will you point out to the jury where you see that man to-day?

A. The man on this side of the cage [Indicating], on the inner side as you go out.

Q. The man who is smiling? A. Yes, sir.

Q. That man you know is Sacco? A. Yes, sir.

Q. And are you sure that is the man? A. Yes, sir. [464]

Cross-examination.

Q. (By Mr. Jeremiah McAnarney.) After you had been examined in the Quincy court, do you recall the last question that was asked of you, and I now give it, page 49.

"Q. Do you say positively that he is the man?"

And your answer:

"A. I don't say positively."

Did you so state at Quincy? A. Yes, sir. [466]

Redirect Examination.

Q. (By Mr. Williams) Miss Devlin, . . Have you at any time had any doubt of your identification of this man?
MR. JEREMIAH McANARNEY. That I object to, if your Honor please.
THE COURT. You may answer.
MR. JEREMIAH McANARNEY. Your honor will save my **exception**?
THE COURT. Certainly. [477]
THE WITNESS. No. [478]
[Ed. McAnarney objected {477} and was overruled. Then he asked the Court for an **exception**.]
[A bill of exceptions is a written statement, certified by the judge to be correct, of all the evidence and occurrences at the trial necessary and appropriate to give to the appellate court sufficient information to enable that court to determine whether the several acts of the trial judge complained of {as in McAnarney's complaint here} were erroneous in point of law and prejudicial to the complaining party. In Massachusetts a bill of exceptions is first prepared by the complaining party and filed in court within the time specified by law... . Appel, III: 2265]
THE COURT. [To the jury.] I again caution you, gentlemen, that the testimony of the last witness at the present time has no effect against the defendant Vanzetti... and the evidence which has been offered heretofore in regard to Vanzetti, you will give that no consideration so far as the other defendant is concerned, Sacco. [480]
[Ed. Earlier, the Court denied motion by defense for separate trials.]

Mark Edward Carrigon, Sworn. June 9, 1921.

Q. (By Mr. Williams) What is your name? A. Mark Edward Carrigan.
[Ed. Index shows Carrington.]
Q. Were you employed by Slater & Morrill the date of the shooting, last year? A. Yes, sir.
Q. April 15? A. Yes.
Q. What position did you then occupy with that company? A. Shoe cutter.
Q. Where was your place of work?
A. In the centre of the room, directly over the main entrance to the office, on the third floor.

Q. That is the building up by the station [Hampton House]? A. Yes, sir.

Q. Did you know Frederick A. Parmenter and Alessandro Berardelli?

A. I knew Mr. Parmenter, but I did not know Berardelli.... .

Q. What time did you see Parmenter on that afternoon?

A. I should say around three o'clock. [172]

Q. Will you tell these gentlemen what you saw Parmenter and the man with him do at that time?

A. I saw Berardelli and Parmenter leaving the office with two tin boxes, going from where we were working, the cutting department in the office building, down to the factory.... .

Q. As they went across the yard and approached the crossing, what did you see them do?

A. I saw Parmenter start to talk to a man for just a short time, possibly two or three seconds.

Q. Whereabouts did he stop? A. Right on the middle of the railroad crossing.

Q. Where was the last that you saw them? A. About at the entrance of the driveway to the Rice & Hutchins shoe factory. [173]

Q. Now, what did you next see or hear in connection with the occurrences of that afternoon?

A. ... I heard the report of, you might say, a backfiring of a motorcycle, or something like that. [174]

Q. Did you go to any window there? A. ... I went to the last window [corner window ... "towards Pearl Street"].

Q. Now, what did you see when you got to that window?

A. I saw the automobile coming up the street. [175]

Q. Can you describe the car to the jury ...? A. The car I seen was ... a seven passenger car. It was an extra big car, ... kind of dusty, although there was some shine to it, ...

Q. How many men did you see in the car? A. All I seen was one man.

Q. And can you tell us a little more definitely where that man was placed and what part of him you saw? A. Well, he was in the front seat with the driver, and he was kind of in a crouched position, ... He had hold of either the windshield or might have had hold of the top, pointing out like that [indicating].

Q. What did he have in his hand, if anything? A. He had some kind of a gun.

Q. ... Describe him to us as best you can. A. I thought ... he looked like a farmer—I mean, a foreigner, and he had black hair. It was kind of long. It looked as though it was combed back, but the wind had blown it. [176]

Q. Have any hat or cap on? A. He had no hat on. [177]

6. THE ESCAPING BANDIT CAR

Michael Levangie, Sworn. June 13, 1921.

Q. (By Mr. Williams) You work in South Braintree also? A. Yes, sir.

Q. What is your employment? A. Gate tender.

Q. New York, New Haven & Hartford? A. New York, New Haven & Hartford Railroad Company.

Q. Were you gate tender for the New Haven on April 15th of last year? A. Yes, sir.

Q. Were you on duty at the crossing in the afternoon of that day? A. Yes, sir, three o'clock.

Q. At any time did you hear anything connected with the shooting? A. I was busy then, and I heard some shots, and I didn't know … whether it was an automobile backfiring or a motorcycle.

Q. Where were you when you heard these noises? A. Cleaning my window.

Q. Windows of what? A. Of the shanty where I work. [413]

Q. Can you give us any idea how many of those sounds you heard? A. 12 or 15 shots.… .

Q. At any time, did you look down the road? A. It stopped for a second, and then it begun again, so I turned around and looked that way ["where the noise was"].

Q. And which way was that from you? A. East.

Q. Now what did you see as you looked east? A. I saw one man coming behind **a pile of bricks,** walking quite fast, and shooting as he went across the road. [414]

Q. … Then did you see anything else? A. I heard a bell of a train then.

Q. What do you mean by that? A. A bell on my shanty for a train approaching.

Q. Some signal? A. Yes.

Q. Then what did you do? A. Put down my gates.

Q. What did you do to put down your gates? A. Turned the crank.

Q. Where did you go turn the crank? A. Right on the post where the gate was.

Q. That is, you stepped over to the nearest gate——… to the shanty? A. Yes.

59

Q. Now, when you got to the gate, what did you start to do? A. To turn it down,—turn the crank so the gate would go down. [Ed. Crank lowered the gates on both sides of the track.]

Q. Which direction was the train coming? A. From Brockton.

Q. Then what happened next? A. I looked around, ... and ... I saw an automobile coming up.

Q. Where did you see the automobile coming? A. Right up the hill.

Q. Now, go ahead and tell us everything that happened ... A. It came right up the hill as far as the gate. Of course, I had my gates down, and the first thing I knew, there was a revolver pointed like that at my head. I looked back at the train to see if I had a chance enough to let them go. I saw there was [a] chance to let them go, and I let them, and I put my gates back again where they belonged. [That is, "away down."] [415]

Q. Did you see anybody in that machine? A. I saw one man.

Q. Where abouts did you see him? A. Driving the machine.

Q. Will you describe the man that you saw as it came across the crossing? A. Dark complected man, with cheek bones sticking out, black hair, heavy brown mustache, slouch hat, and army coat... .

Q. How near were you to that man at any time,—what was the closest? A. I didn't measure it, but I should say it was about 10 or 12 feet.

Q. Have you ever seen that man since? A. Yes, sir.

Q. Where have you seen him since that time? A. Brockton police station.

Q. Where have you seen him since then? A. Right there... .

Q. Which one [which defendant do you mean]? A. The one on the left.

Q. With the mustache? A. Yes, sir. [417]

Q. The one that is known as Vanzetti? A. That is the fellow. I didn't know his name, but that is the fellow. [418]

Cross-Examination.

Q. (By Mr. McAnarney) ... Now, what happened in this automobile? A. I was going to stop them from coming across. I wasn't going to put up the gates, and I saw this revolver, and I put them up... .

Q. You think this thing was pointed from somewhere back of the front seat?

A. Behind the driver... .

Q. You saw his arm? A. I saw his hand as far as that (indicating) with the revolver in it.

Q. Pointed straight at you? A. Pointed at me, yes.

Q. ... Are you sure that it wasn't pointing at something above your head, calling your attention to a bird up there? A. No, sir. [420]

Q. Are you quite sure he was not pointing to an airplane going up back of you? A. No, sir... .

Q. How did you know but he was beckoning to you to come over to him?

A. I knew better than that.

Q. You knew that meant to put up the gates? A. Yes, sir. [421]

Louis DeBeradinis, Sworn. June 14, 1921.

Q. (By Mr. Williams) What is your occupation? A. Shoemaker.

Q. Where did you carry on your business on April 15th of last year.

A. 88 Pearl Street.

Q. Did you hear the shooting? A. Yes, sir... .

Q. Then what did you do [after the shots]? [480] A. ... I went around to the door outside, ...

Q. When you went outside, where did that bring you, . .? A. On to Pearl Street. I went to the center door, and looked to the railroad track... .

Q. ... [T]ell what you saw ... A. When I saw the machine coming ahead, . . [t]he man was outside of the car, and when they come over this side of the railroad track the body was outside of the car, but the feet, down to the feet, was inside of the car, and the one hand holds on himself by the window shade of the car, and the other hand had the revolver. When they came by in front of my store, this man pointed a revolver at my face, and he pulled the trigger, but the revolver did not fire. He didn't have any more bullets. [481]

Q. Do you wish to say what ... language you used [at Brockton police station]? A... . I said, "No, I can't say sure I saw Sacco. The one I saw was light, and Sacco was dark... ." [485]

Q. Well, do you now say that the man you saw on Pearl Street that day, who shot at you, looked like the defendant Sacco? A. Yes, sir, as I say. [487]

Cross-Examination.

Q. (By Mr. McAnarney) You are sure that it was a light-haired, thin man who pointed the revolver at you? A. Yes, sir, sure. [487]

Carlos E. Goodridge, Sworn. June 15, 1921.

[Ed. C. E. Goodridge is an alias for Erastus Corning Whitney. See Appel, IV: 3733-3891.]

Q. (By Mr. Willliams) What is your full name, please? A. Carlos Edward Goodridge.

Q. What is your occupation? A. Salesman.

Q. Did you at any time live in South Braintree or Braintree? A. Yes, sir.

Q. And did you live there on April 15th, 1920, the day of the shooting? A. Yes, sir...

Q. Where was [sic] you at that time? A. At that time I was in Mr. Magazu's pool-room.

Q. And where was that pool-room? A. On Pearl Street. [542]

Q. ... Now, what was the first thing you heard of the occurrences of that afternoon?

A. I heard the report of something similar to a gun. In fact, I heard several of them.

Q. What did you do? A. Well, I left the pool table and went to the window looking out towards the railroad station, in the direction the sound came from.

Q. Did you see anything? A. No, sir.

Q. What did you do then? A. I went back to the table, picked up the cue again and took two or three shots, and then I heard another report.

Q. Now, tell what you did and what you saw. A. I went to the door and stepped out, and ... there was an automobile just this side of the railroad crossing coming towards me.

Q. ... [T]ell the jury what you saw ... A. ... Just as I stepped out half way on the sidewalk, ... a fellow poked a gun over towards me, and I was probably within twenty feet of it, or twenty-five. I went back into the pool-room... .

Q. Now, where was the man that poked the gun at you? A. Well, I couldn't say exactly whether he was directly in the front seat, or in the front seat leaning over—the back of the seat leaning over. [543]

Q. Will you describe the appearance of that man...? A. Well, as I got him on a side view, he was a dark complexioned fellow, with dark hair, and he had his face—kind of a peculiar face, that came down pointed. [544]

Q. Did he have any hat on? A. He had no hat on... .

Q. Have you seen that man since then? A. Yes, sir.

Q. Where did you see him since? A. In this court room.

Q. And when was that? A. Last September or October... .

Q. Where in the court room did you see him?

A. I saw him when he was brought in here to be arraigned... .

Q. Will you look around the court room and see if you see that man in court today?

A. The gentleman on the right, in the cage... .

Q. Do you mean the man with the mustache or the man without the mustache?

A. Without the mustache. [545]

Cross-Examination.

Q. (By Mr. McAnarney) What business were you in in Braintree at that time? A. Selling Victrolas... .

Q. Are you not a defendant in a criminal case in this court? A. No, sir.

MR. KATZMANN. One moment...

THE COURT. That is not a competent question.

MR McANARNEY. I think it would be if he was.

THE COURT. Oh, no. A man that has been convicted, then you can use that record—

MR. McANARNEY. If your Honor please—...[Ed. McAnarney and Moore got exceptions.]

THE COURT. ... The law is the same for all witnesses, and you can't attack any witness's credibility except by showing a record of conviction, and the record of conviction means a sentence, a judgment pronounced by the court, and until there has been [546] a judgment pronounced by the court, the evidence is not competent. Therefore, I exclude it. [547]

Mr. Francis Charles Clark, Sworn. June 15, 1921.

Q. (By Mr. Williams) Do you remember the day of the South Braintree shooting? A. I do.

Q. And where were you on the afternoon of that day? A. At Tucker Hill.

Q. At what? A. At North Stoughton, on Tucker Hill. [Ed. North of North Stoughton.]

Q. What were you doing that day, what occupation were you following?

A. I was driving a baker wagon... .

Q. In which direction were you then going? A. I was going south [towards Stoughton]... .

Q. Will you tell the jury what you saw in reference to any car, ...?

A. When we were driving on the right-hand side of the road there, this auto did not blow his horn ... and passed us on our left, took the wrong side of the road, .. going at a pretty good rate of speed, ... [573]

Q... . Just what you saw. A. [W]e noticed that the **rear window** was out of the auto, ... the curtains were down on the right-hand side, ... flapping.

Q. Did you take the number [on license plate]? A. I did not take it, but the man that was with me took it, and I read it off to him. [Ed. Elmer Pool rode on a horse-drawn wagon with Clark.]

Q. What did you do with that number when it was taken?

A. Wrote it down on the side of the wagon.

Q. Do you remember that number today? A. I remember a 49 in it. I could not say whether that was the first number or not. [575]

Julia Kelliher, Sworn. June 15, 1921.

Q. (By Mr. Williams) How old, are you, Miss Kelliher? A. Sixteen... .

Q. And where were you on that afternoon [April 15, 1920]?

A. Coming home from school.

Q. You said you live in Brockton, didn't you? A. Yes, sir.

Q. On Pearl Street? A. Yes, sir. [590]

Q. Will you tell the jury what you saw of that automobile [when it passed you about 3:45 at the corner of West Elm and Pearl]? A. Well, it was before four in the afternoon, and as we were coming home ... an automobile ... was coming at a high rate of speed, and we turned around, and ... saw it coming ... over the hill, and there was a lot of dust raised, ... and as it went past us I took the number... . [T]he number plate was all mud spattered. We took the number.

Q. What number plate did you take the number from? A. We got some from the front and some from the back. We got most of it from the back.

Q. What did you do with that number when you got it? A.... . [W]e wrote it in the sand, and I guess I wrote it down when I got home.

Q. Did you communicate that number to anybody? A. To my father.

Q. Did you see Lieutenant Carey ... of the Brockton police? A. Yes.... the following Sunday.

Q. Did you tell him the number? A. Yes, I did.

Q. ... [D]o you remember ... what the number was? A. I know it was 83 on the end, and I knew there was a 9 and 7. I don't know which order they came in. [591]

Austin T. Reed, Sworn. June 15, 1921.

Q. (By Mr. Williams) Where do you live? A. East Bridgewater... . 113 Belmont Street... .

Q. Do you know what you were doing on that day [April 15, 1920]?

A. Crossing tender.

Q. Where abouts? A. At Matfield... .

Q. ... [E]mployed by the New York, New Haven & Hartford Railroad, I presume? A. Yes, sir.

Q. What stations lie on either side of the Matfield station?

A. Campello and Westdale.

Q. Campello on the north, I take it, and Westdale on the south?

A. Yes. [594]

Q. Now, that afternoon,—I am speaking of the afternoon of the shooting, was your attention directed to any automobile that approached that crossing? A. Yes, sir.

Q. What time of day did that occur? A. 4:15.

Q. From which direction was the train coming? A. From Westdale, from the south... .

Q. And where were you when you saw that train approaching?

A. ... by a window in the shanty.

Q. What did you do then?

A. I got up to see if there was any automobiles coming, and I saw an automobile up the street.

Q. What did you do then? A. I went out to stop it. [Reed carried a "Stop" sign with a handle.]

Q. What happened as you stood there with your sign at the side of the track? A. Why, I had to walk across the track onto the west side and as I saw this automobile wasn't going to stop, it didn't have time enough to get by ahead of the train. I had my sign in my hand, and as they approached they did not seem to want to stop then.

Q. Yes. A. And one of them in the automobile asked me, "What to hell I was holding him up for?" He pointed his finger at me, and they ... seemed quite anxious to get by.

Q. Where were you when that man spoke to you?

A. I was on the west side of the track, in the middle of the road.

Q. Where was the automobile then? A. Up the street about 40 feet away from there.

Q. Was the automobile stopped, ...?

A. It was,—the engine was running, but it had come to a stop. [595]

Q. Where was this man that spoke to you? A. He was on the seat, aside of the driver.

Q. ... [A]t what point ... did the train go by? A. The train went by between the automobile and myself, because I stepped ... back to the side where the shanty is.

Q. Then what did you see [after the train went by]? A. This automobile came by, and they swung up aside of the shanty, and he pointed his finger at me again.

Q. Who? A. And he says, "What to hell did you hold us up for?" And they beat it down the street and went down Matfield Street.

Q. Was it the same man who had spoken to you before, ...? A. This is the same man.

Q. How near was he to you when he made that second remark to you by your shanty?

A. Within about four feet of the doorway... .

Q. ... [W]hich fork of the road was Matfield Street? A. That right-hand side.

Q. And did you see the machine again? A. Yes, sir. It came back on the left-hand side. [596]

Q. How long after you noticed it going down the right fork down Matfield Street did you see it coming down the left fork, Belmont Street [a triangular route]? A. About three minutes.

Q. What did it do? A. It went over the crossing, up towards [West] Bridgewater again.

Q. Where did you last see it? A. It got out of sight [in about 220 yards] up over Matfield.

Q. How many men, do you know, were in the machine? A. Five.

Q. Will you describe the appearance, ... of that man who spoke to you those two times?

A. He was a dark complected man, kind of hollow cheeks, with high cheek bones, had a stubbed mustache. And kind of a stubbed mustache, bushy. His hair was black... .

Q. Have you ever seen that man since that day? A. Yes, sir.

Q. Where did you see him after that time? A. Brockton police station.

Q. Do you see that man in the court room now? A. Yes, sir.

Q. Where is he sitting? A. The man with the first arm off the side of the cage.

Q. You refer to Vanzetti? A. Yes.

Q. Are you sure he is the man you saw that day at Matfield? A. Yes.

Q. Any doubt in your mind? A. No, sir... .

Q. Do you know what make of car it was? A. It was what I call a Buick.

Q. Have you ever seen that car since, as far as you know? A. Yes, sir.

Q. Where did you see it? A. Down to Plymouth.

Q. When did you see it down there? A. At the trial. [597]

Cross-examination.

Q. (By Mr. Jeremiah McAnarney) This was the 4:10 train to Boston, due 4:10 at Matfield?

A. Yes. [605]

Richard Newby

The Borchard-Frankfurter Connection

YALE UNIVERSITY
SCHOOL OF LAW
NEW HAVEN, CONNECTICUT

Edwin M. Borchard
Professor of Law   April 26, 1927.

Professor Felix Frankfurter,
    Harvard Law School,
      Cambridge, Mass.

Dear Frankfurter:

    I wonder whether you could not get for our library, a copy of the records in the two Sacco Vanzetti appeals which went up to the Supreme Judicial Court. If you could help us out in this respect, you would add to our library resources and, I think, aid the cause of justice. We are getting many inquiries for the records here and cannot satisfy the requests. Your courtesy would be deeply appreciated.

    I enclose to you herewith, a copy of my letter to the Governor, which was sent off Friday. Campus opinion here at Yale was much confused; indeed to my astonishment, there seems to be a general impression that the outcry against the verdict was merely that of dissatisfied radicals, and that the men were really guilty. The Liberal Club is taking an active part in setting campus opinion straight, and has brought about the publication of the enclosed letter in the Yale Daily News, a college campus paper.

Very sincerely yours,   Edwin M. Borchard

[Source: Edwin Montefiore Borchard Papers, Manuscripts and Archives, Yale University Library. Borchard's letter to Governor Fuller, April 21, 1927, appeared in *The Yale Daily News* on April 26, 1927 (Vol. L, No. 155). See pp. xii, xxxviii, 506.]

7. THE ABANDONED BUICK AND STOLEN PLATES

Mr. Charles L. Fuller, Sworn. June 16, 1921.

Q. (By Mr. Williams) What is your occupation? A. Brockton Enterprise. [Newspaper]

Q. Do you recall the time or the date of the South Braintree shooting, …?

A. I think it was the15th. I won't be certain as to that.

Q. Do you recall any horseback trip or ride which you took shortly after that time? A. Yes, sir.

Q. And what day or date did you take such a ride? A. Saturday, on the 17th of April.

Q. And who was with you, if anybody?

A. Mr. Wind. [617] [Ed. Testimony of Max E. Wind is omitted.]

Q. And whereabouts was that [your ride]? A. Just over the railroad track on Manley Street... . We took the by-path that leads off Manley Street to the right, going towards West Bridgwater.

THE COURT. What street did he say?

MR. WILLIAMS. Manley Street. M-a-n-l-e-y.

THE WITNESS. We turned to our right into this path … [W]e came … across the automobile headed toward us. The path was so **narrow** that we had to get off our horses. [618]

Q. Now, will you describe the automobile which you found?

A. It was a Buick.

Q. Yes. A. Seven passenger, …

Q. Will you tell the jury what you noticed in regard to that car, …?

A. … [T]he car had the appearance of having been out over night... . [A] little dampness around the radiator top. There was some dust on the car. There were no number plates. The rear window was out. The right-hand curtain was loose. [619]

Q. … [D]id you see any tracks in the path, any tire tracks?

A. You mean at the entrance or inside the—…

Q. Of which entrance?

A. Of the south, with smaller tires,—tracks to the south of that south entrance.

Q. What do you mean by "smaller tired tracks"?

A. Well, they would not be called a Buick track, ...

Q. Well, tracks of a smaller tire? A. Yes sir, tracks of a smaller car, smaller tire... .

Q. And from which side did the smaller tracks come in?

A. From the southern side of that south entrance.

Q. Which side were the larger tracks?

A. They appeared to be the other side, the north side of the south entrance. [621]

Q. Any glass? A. Yes, the glass was at the bottom on the floor.

Q. Please tell us about that. A. The glass was at the bottom of the car, when I saw it.

Q. What glass? A. From the rear, from the rear curtain, the back, the top at the back.

Q. And where did you see that? A. That was on the floor of the car, when I saw it. [622]

Mr. William S. Hill, Sworn. June 16, 1921.

Q. (By Mr. Williams) What is your occupation? A. Police officer.

Q. In the city of Brockton? A. Brockton, yes, sir.

Q. Were you on the police force of the city of Brockton April 17th of last year? A. Yes, sir.

Q. Did you go to West Bridgewater on that day? A. I did... .

Q. Who went with you? A. City Marshal Ryan.

Q. Whereabouts in West Bridgewater did you go? A. On Manley Street.

Q. Whereabouts on Manley Street? A. Why, down near the Poor Farm there, in Cochesett [village belonging to West Bridgewater], I believe toward West Bridgewater.

Q. When you got down there on Manley Street, where did you go?

A. We left the car at the side of the road, and went up a cart path about six hundred feet, I should say, and found a Buick car.

Q. Now, will you describe the car you found there in the woods? A. It was a seven passenger Buick; I should say a 1920 model, black; ... [635]

Q. Did you take the number of the car at that time?

A. When we got to the station after I had driven it back.

Q. What did you do with the car? A. Mr. Fuller … got in and backed it out of this woods road, and … I got in and drove it to the station, and the City Marshall followed in his car.

Q. Did you find anything else about the car? A. No, sir,—yes, I found down there in the garage, I found a bullet hole in the right rear door. [636]

[Ed. The Court ruled, 640-643, on the competency of the Buick found in Manley Woods, stating that the probative value of the Buick, as evidence, rested with the jury. After the Court granted "exceptions for each defendant" {643}, Court, jury, counsel, and stenographer went outside to the rear of the court house, where Williams spoke to the jury about features of the Buick.]

MR. WILLIAMS. [To the Jury.] … Notice which way the back door opens; notice … this hole in the right rear door, … [645] Please notice these extra seats here, … [647]

[The jury returns to the court room.] [647]

[Ed. Defense elected, p. 645, to have Sacco and Vanzetti remain in the court room.]

Mr. Francis J. Murphy, Sworn. June 16, 1921.

Q. (By Mr. Williams) In 1919, did you own a Buick car? A. I did.

Q. … What was the Massachusetts registration number? A. 123,000.

Q. What became of that car, as far as you know? A. I lost it at Needham, visiting in Needham. The 23rd of November, 1919, the car was taken… .

[Ed. The jury retire. In their absence, Moore argued that the theft of Murphy's car was an "independent crime" and that "the Government will not attempt to prove that theft {at Needham} in and of itself was in any wise traceable to … either of these defendants." {662} He argued there was no evidence that put either defendant in Needham, where Murphy's Buick was stolen. {663} Thayer then made this ruling:]

THE COURT. … I will admit the evidence for the purpose of proving ownership. Of course, the fact it was stolen is not competent or as having any bearing against these defendants.

MR. MOORE. Reserve an exception, please?

MR. JEREMIAH McANARNEY. For both defendants?

THE COURT. For both defendants.

[The jury returns to the court room.] [664]

Q. Was there any engine number on the car? A. There was.

Q. What was the engine number? If you have any memorandum, you may refer to it.

A. 560,490.

Q. Do you know whether that number is on now? A. It is.

Q. It is on there now? When did you look? A. This morning.

Q. Was there any chassis or factory number on there?

A. There was a number on the rear of the frame, 513,915.

Q. Is that number on there now? A. It is not. [665]

Mr. Warren H. Ellis, Sworn. June 16, 1921.

Q. (By Mr. Williams) Where do you live? A. 602 Webster Street, Needham, Mass.

Q. What is your occupation? A. A clerk.

Q. Did you live in Needham in 1920? A. Yes, sir.

Q. Did you own any ... number plates of Massachusetts registration for a motor car?

A. Yes, sir.

Q. On what date did you possess such plates? A. From January 1st until January 6th.

Q. How many plates did you have? A. Two plates.

Q. What was the registration number on those plates? A. 49783.

Q. For what year was the registration? A. 1920.

Q. When did you last see your number plates? A. Wednesday evening, January 6th, 1920.

Q. Where? A. In my own garage, back of the house.

Q. Have you any knowledge of what became of them after January 6th? A. They were——...

THE WITNESS. I have not. They disappeared in January after that. [667]

8. THE JOHNSON HOUSE AND MIKE BODA

Ruth C. Johnson, Sworn. June 16, 1921.

Q. (By Mr. Williams) Where do you live? A. West Bridgewater.

Q. Whereabouts in West Bridgewater? A. Elm Square, North Elm Street. [A tar road.]

Q. Are you married? A. Yes.

Q. Your married name is Mrs. Simon Johnson? A. Yes, sir.

Q. In what direction from Elm Square is your residence? A. Towards Brockton. [673]

Q. What was your husband's business on ... May 5 of last year?

A. He was working in the garage at Elm Square [with his brother Samuel].

Q. Is there any railroad track near your house? A. Yes, on the [right-hand] side of the house, it runs along the side [as Ruth faces North Elm Street].

Q. Well, suppose this is the street going to Brockton: your house is on the left-hand side going [north] to Brockton? A. Yes, sir.

Q. Is there any street railway track there? A. Yes. [Interurban.]

Q. Where is that? A. It faces the front. [Ed. Tracks run east of, and parallel to, tar road.]

Q. Where does that street railway track run? A. To Bridgewater and Brockton.

Q. Does that track go through Elm Square? A. Yes, [south] right through to Elm Square.

Q. Where were you on the night of May 5? A. I was home.

Q. Do you remember what time your husband went to bed that night? A. Around nine o'clock.

Q. Did anything happen that night? A. Well, somebody knocked at the door.

Q. What time did somebody knock at the door? A. It was about twenty minutes past. [674]

Q. What? A. Nine.

Q. Then what happened? Tell us, please.

MR. MOORE. I object.

THE COURT. You may go ahead, I will save your rights.

MR. MOORE. You will save us an exception, your Honor?

MR. McANARNEY. An exception for both.

A. I went to the door after I heard a knock, and asked who it was.

Q. Did you see someone there? A. Do you mean after I opened the door?

Q. Yes. A. No, not when I first opened it.

Q. Did you at any time after you opened the door see somebody? A. Yes.

Q. Where did you see someone? A. Standing up by the bridge [spanning the railroad track].

Q. Tell us ... more as to the location of the front of your house and the objects around it, ...

A. The bridge is just before you get to my house. [Ed. Bridge is south of Johnson house.]

Q. Coming from which way? A. From Elm Square. [675]

Q. I will ask you first, how far is your front door to the nearest side of North Elm Street?

A. About three yards and a half, about.

Q. Is there any pole anywhere around there? A. Yes.

Q. Where is the pole?

A. There is one right at the corner of the bridge, on the same side as my house.

Q. Now, tell us what you did see, and what you did ... . A. I saw a man standing by the pole, and he walked towards me ... I looked and saw two more coming over the bridge on the car track. So, as the man by the pole came up to me, I didn't say anything at first and he didn't. When he got right up to me, I said my husband would be right out. [676]

Q. What did he say? A. He didn't say anything to me, but he kind of called out "His wife."

Q. Called out his what? A. Called out "His wife." The man ... called out "His wife."

Q. And where were those other two men you saw coming from the bridge at that time?

A. Walking on the car track... . Towards Brockton.

Q. In front of your house? A. Yes.

Q. Now, will you tell us what happened from that time on? A. Well, I stepped out of the door, and I started towards Brockton. These two men seemed to come right along with me, only on the other side of the street. I was on the left-hand side, and they were on the right-hand side. Then I went over to the next house.

Q. Well, did you see anything before you got over to the next house?
A. Yes

Q. Just tell us what you saw? A. There was [a] bright light shining on to the bridge.

Q. Just tell us about that, where it came from and what it was?
A. I saw a light shining, and there isn't any light near my house at all.

Q. No street light? A. No street light ... I glanced towards Brockton and I saw a large light shining towards me, and I couldn't see what was behind it. [677]

Q. What did it shine on, or what did it light up, as it shone there?
A. Well, it lighted up the whole street and kind of the side of my house.

Q. Light up this pole you spoke of? A. Yes, that was right on the corner of the bridge, the pole.

Q. You say you walked towards Brockton. Go ahead.
A. As I went by the motorcycle, I glanced up.

Q. Now, wait a minute. You say "the motorcycle". You haven't said anything about a motorcycle yet. A. Well, the light was on [shone from] a motorcycle.

Q. What kind of a motorcycle was it?
A. I don't know what kind it was, but it had a side car. [678]

Q. Now, ... tell the jury what you did? A. I passed the motorcycle and kept walking until I got to the next house. There is a big driveway there.

Q. Where were those other men that you spoke of? A. They walked right along with me.

Q. How far away from you were they, Mrs. Johnson? A. About three yards and a half.

Q. You were walking along the road? A. Yes.

Q. On what part of the road? A. On the left-hand side going towards Brockton.

Q. On which side of you were these men walking? A. On the right.

Q. What did you do when you got to the Bartlett house [next house north]?
A. I knocked at the door. [Ed. Distance from Johnson door to Bartlett door about 200 feet.]

Q. What did you do then?

MR. MOORE. I object, your Honor.

THE COURT. You may proceed.

A. I knocked at the door.

MR. MOORE. You will save us an exception?

THE COURT. Certainly.

MR. McANARNEY. An exception.

A. I knocked at the door, and somebody opened the door.

Q.... . Where were these two men when you went into the Bartlett house?

A. They were right opposite me on the car [streetcar] track.... .

Q. You did go into the Bartlett house? A. I did.

Q. When you went into the Bartlett house, did you do anything in reference to the Bridgewater police?

MR. MOORE. I object.

MR. WILLIAMS. I will put it in this form.

Q. What did you do after you went into the Bartlett house?

A. I telephoned.

MR. MOORE. I object.

THE COURT. You may inquire, "What did you do?"

A. I telephoned.

MR. MOORE. I will reserve an exception. [679]

MR. McANARNEY. Exception.

Q. To whom? A. West Bridgewater police.

MR. McANARNEY. Your Honor will note an exception?

THE COURT. Certainly.

Q. Did you later come out of the Bartlett house? A. Yes.

Q. How long were you in the Bartlett house before you came out?

A. [A]bout ten minutes.... .

Q. Now, after you came out, Mrs. Johnson, what did you do? A. I walked down the [50-foot] driveway, and as I got to the end of the driveway two men walked alongside of me.

Q. What two men? A. The same that followed me up.

Q. ... [I]s the Bartlett house on the same side of the street as your house? A. The same side.

Q. And as you walked along on the same side going back, what did you notice about the two men?

A. I could see them plain. They were on the car track.

Q. What were they doing? A. Just walking along as I did.

76

Q. Did you notice anything about the motorcycle as you went back towards your house? A. Yes.

Q. Tell us what you did notice about that? A. It had turned towards Brockton on the car track side, and the light was shining right in my face, and the two men that were walking with me.

Q. Which side had it been on, ... when you went up to the Bartlett house?

A. On the right, going towards Elm Square.

Q. Now, which side was it on when you went back [south] towards your house?

A. On the right going towards Brockton. [680]

Q. Now, what happened as you went along there going back to the house?

A. As I got up to the motorcycle I heard it was running. Then I saw the two men stop.

Q. Stop where? A. At the motorcycle.

Q. Could you see them at that time?

MR. MOORE. I object. There is no designation of persons here. When she says "two men",—

THE COURT. I understood that the evidence—that there is to be evidence offered tending to prove that these two defendants were there. Am I right, Mr. Williams?

MR. WILLIAMS. Yes.

MR. MOORE. But, there is no testimony here. The relationship after the—It is very ambiguous—this method of designation.

THE COURT. That may be a fair suggestion. Do I understand these two men about whom you are testifying, or about whom the witness is testifying, in going up to the Bartlett place and returning, are the two defendants?

MR. WILLIAMS. I had to get them back into the motorcycle light before I could identify them, if your Honor please. That is why I went along this way.

THE COURT. I didn't ask you what you had to do; I asked you if you had evidence—

MR. MOORE. I object to these statements of evidence, your Honor, the statement that counsel just made that he had to get back to the light of the motorcycle before he could identify them is a unique way of presenting evidence.

77

THE COURT. Counsel vary, I notice, as to their method of putting in evidence. You may proceed.

Q. Could you see them at that time? A. Yes

Q. Now, where were they then? A. Side of the motorcycle.

Q. Was there a man with them by the motorcycle? A. Yes.

Q. How many men there? A. There were three all together.

Q. By the motorcycle? A. By the motorcycle.

Q. Now could you see the faces ... of any of those men there by the motorcycle there at that time? A. Yes.

Q. Now, will you describe to the jury the appearance of any of the men there at the motorcycle that you then saw? Take them one by one, ... A. Well, he was short——

Q. Which one? A. The one that I saw most of all.

Q. Yes. A. He was short, and his face was kind of blue, as though he had just shaved. He had an overcoat and a derby. That is all I can say. [681]

Q. Did you ever see that man you have described after that? A. Yes.

Q. Where did you see him after that? A. At the Brockton police station.

Q. When? A. The next night [May 6, 1920].

Q. What time the next night, do you remember?

A. I think I got up to the police station about half past seven.

Q. Anybody with you. A. My husband... .

Q. Now, do you see that man you saw on North Elm Street with the motorcycle, and you later saw in the Brockton police station, here in court today? A. Yes.

Q. And where do you see him? A. Right there.

Q. Just point, please. A. Right there, on this side.

Q. The man with the moustache, or the man without a moustache? A. Without.

Q. Do you know what his name is now? A. Sacco.

Q. Are you sure he is the man you saw that night? A. Positive.

Q. You have described Sacco. Now, describe the other one, if you can.

A. I didn't see him. He was on the other side.

Q. Tell us anything you did see about him.

A. He had a long overcoat and soft hat, that is all I could see.

Q. Now, could you see the man with the motorcycle? A. No.

Q. Did you see him at any time that night, the man on the motorcycle?

A. Well, just his coat and hat, that is all.

Q. Tell us what kind of a coat and hat he had on... .

A. He had a mackinaw coat, and soft hat pulled down over his face.

Q. Now, did you see that man afterwards? A. Yes, sir.

Q. Where did you see him? A. At the Brockton police—

MR. MOORE. I assume now you are referring to persons other than the defendants. [682]

THE COURT. I don't know. What is the fact?

MR. WILLIAMS. This is a man who is not one of the defendants, if your Honor please.

THE COURT. Well, wherein is that competent?

MR. WILLIAMS. I wish to show at the present time who was in the company of the defendants at that time, if your Honor please.

MR. MOORE. I object.

THE COURT. The four men who were there?

MR. WILLIAMS. The four men.

MR. MOORE. I object, your Honor.

THE COURT. I will allow you to show that, if it is simply to show all the men in that party, that is, the four men.

MR. WILLIAMS. Yes.

THE COURT. I will allow that.

MR. MOORE. Reserve an exception.

THE COURT. Certainly.

MR. McANARNEY. An exception... .

Q. What was his name? A. Sino or Scino.

Q. Did you ever see it spelled? A. Yes, in the paper... .

Q. See if this sounds familiar, A-r-c-i-a-n-i, or am I wrong? A. I think that was the way it was spelled in the paper. [Ed. Transcript shows both Orcciani and Orciani.]

Q. You saw him at the Brockton police station that night? A. Yes. [Ed. Arrested on May 6.]

Q. What did he have on at that time? A. Mackinaw coat and a soft hat.

Q. Now, ... what else did you see happen? A. Well, I walked right along up to my front door, and my husband was talking to a man ["The man that was standing by the pole"].

Q. Do you know who he was? A. Yes.

Q. Who? A. Boda. [Ed. Mike Boda is a pseudonym for Mario Buda. See Avrich, <u>Sacco and Vanzetti: The Anarchist Background</u>, p. 207.]

MR. MOORE. I object, your Honor.

THE COURT. Simply for the purpose of showing the names of the four people who were there, you may inquire. [683]

MR. MOORE. Exception.

MR. McANARNEY. Exception.

Q. Boda? A. Boda.

Q. Do you know his first name? I think they call him Mike, I am not positive. [684]

Simon E. Johnson, Sworn. June 17, 1921.

Q. (By Mr. Williams) You are the husband of the last witness?

A. I am.

Q. How far from Elm Square do you live? A. Why, it is less than a quarter of a mile... .

Q. Which side of the street is the street-car track? A. On the opposite side from the house.

Q. That street-car track runs between Bridgewater and Brockton?

A. Between Elm Square and Brockton line. [702]

Q. Is there a bridge near your house over the [N.Y. N.H. & Hartford] railroad track? A. Yes.

Q. Will you describe that bridge ... A. It is an iron girder with wooden flooring, and ... the corner of the bridge is about fifteen feet [south and east] from the door of my house... .

Q. Are there any street lights there? A. No.

Q. Do you remember the night of May 5 of last year? A. I do.

Q. Where were you that night? A. In bed.

Q. Your wife has said something about a knock on the door. Do you recall that occurrence?

A. Yes.

Q. About what time did that happen? A. Why, I should say about 9:20 or 25.

Q. Did you and your wife have any talk in regard to that knock? Just answer Yes or No, please. A. Yes.

Q. And after such talk as you may have had, what did she do, . .? A. She went to the door.

Q. What did she do then, do you know ...? A. Asked who it was.

Q. Did she come back and speak to you? A. Yes.

Q. Did you later get up? A. Yes.

Q. Did you dress? A. Yes.

Q. Did you go outdoors? A. Yes, sir.

Q. Now, will you tell the jury what you saw when you went outdoors?
A. Why, I met a man coming towards the door.

Q. From what direction? A. From the direction of the bridge [to Johnson's right]. [703]

Q. Who was he? A. Mike Boda.

Q. Now, who is Mike Boda?

MR. MOORE. I object.

Q. Well, where does Mike Boda live?

MR. MOORE. I object to that, your Honor.

THE COURT. That may be answered.

MR. MOORE. Your Honor will save an exception.

MR. McANARNEY. Any conversation with Boda, so far as the defendant Vanzetti—

THE COURT. This is not a conversation with Boda.

MR. McANARNEY. He is coming to it. Your Honor suggested last night we could expedite matters.

THE COURT. I will adopt that suggestion in this way: Without your repeatedly objecting to this particular line of inquiry, I will save your rights.

MR. McANARNEY. To any inquiry from this witness as to conversation with Boda.

THE COURT. That is right,—if I admit any. I have not admitted any yet.

MR. McANARNEY. I know, but I think I know what my brother is coming to.

Q. Where did Mike Boda live? A. At that time?

Q. Yes. Do you know where he was living at that time?

A. At that time he said he lived in South Boston.

Q. Where did he live before that?

MR. McANARNEY. That I object to. This is all subject to the same objection.

THE COURT. Sure, but on account of your objection to what has been said, you may strike from the record that conversation that he lived at South Boston.

Q. Where did he live previous to that?

MR. MOORE. I object to that, your Honor. That is directly contrary to the rule your Honor just announced because it could be no information other than described by conversation.

THE COURT. I don't know about that.... . He might have seen the man in the house.

MR. MOORE. We have no way of controverting it.

THE COURT. He may be speaking of his own knowledge.

Q. I am asking you of facts within your own knowledge, Mr. Johnson, now.

THE COURT. If you know, you may answer.... . [704]

A. Corner of South Elm and Lincoln.... .

Q. Where is Lincoln Street? A. In West Bridgewater.... .

THE COURT. South Elm and what?

A. Lincoln. Why, about a mile from Elm Square.

Q. In which direction? A. I should say about southwest.

Q. How long had you known Mike Boda? A. Why, since the December, 1919, wouldn't it be?

Q. What business were you then in? A. Garage business.

Q. Now, can you describe...the place at the corner of South Elm and Lincoln Street where Boda lived? A. Why, it is an almost square house, and sets right on the corner.... .

Q. Anything there but a house? A. Why, kind of a shed or barn-like.... .

Q. How many times did you talk with him [Boda]? A. Twice, I believe.

Q. Can you describe his physical appearance to the jury? A. I think so.... .

Q. What? A. He was a slight built man, five or five feet and an inch or two inches tall, weighting about 125.

Q. Can you describe the way he was customarily dressed? A. He was generally well dressed.... .

Q. How was he dressed that night? A. In a shabby dress. [705]

Q. What kind of clothes? A. Why, old clothes, dark clothes, khaki shirt, and an old slouch hat.

Q. Did you ever go to the place where Boda lived on the corner of South Elm and Lincoln Streets? A. Yes.

Q. When was that? A. April 19th.... .

Q. Now, what did you do there?

MR. MOORE. I object, your Honor. The difficulty is, I don't want to keep objecting, but April 19th this date is, your Honor.

THE COURT. I know, but going there that is of no particular consequence. I suppose it is leading up to something.

MR. MOORE. Yes, your Honor.

THE COURT. Then, of course, if it leads up to nothing that is connected with this case, I will exclude it and have it stricken from the record, but I assume that eventually it is going to have some relationship to this case... . with that assurance, you may proceed.

MR. MOORE. An exception, plesae [sic].

MR. McANARNEY. In order that it may be clear, of course, we don't know what is going to follow, and at present, I take it, this will go in under the rule that all evidence by this witness of anything between he and Boda is excepted to.

THE COURT. I will let it go under this rule, ... that if the Commonwealth introduces no evidence tending to prove that this evidence has any relationship to any issue in the indictments on trial, upon your motion I will order it stricken from the record. I think that is the customary and usual method in matters of this kind.

MR. MOORE. May I suggest, your Honor, that this is a little bit more than the usual situation where evidence is going to be connected. I direct your Honor's attention specifically to the date, April 19th, four days after April 15th, and I think your Honor will recognize the significance of that.

THE COURT. Oh, yes, but that is of no consequence. I have said that. It is the evidence that comes later. I suppose there is some, but so far as going there in 1919 or 1918, that in and of itself is of no conse- [706] quence. There must be some connection here between the evidence offered and the issues involved in these indictments. In other words, this evidence must be connected with some other evidence which comes pertinent to the issues on trial, and, as I understand Mr. Williams, he has that evidence. Is that right?

MR. WILLIAMS. It is so, if your Honor please.

THE COURT. With that assurance, you may go ahead, with the understanding if the connection is not made, upon your request I will strike it from the record... .

[Ed. Moore and McAnarney are given exceptions by the Court.]

Q. Now, what did you do there? A. I went to get his car.

Q. Whose car? A. Boda's car... .

Q. Now, did you get his car that day? A. I did.

Q. What kind of a car was it? A. Overland... . [1914 model]

Q. Where did you find the car when you went there?

A. In a shed-like back of the [Coacci] house, aside of the house.

Q. Are you familiar with the premises ... where you say Boda lived?
A. Why, yes, somewhat.

Q. [Showing witness photographs] Let me show you these pictures, and ask you if they represent those premises? A. These two do... .

Q. These two pictures I now show you represent the premises where Boda lived at that time?
A. Yes.

[The pictures are marked Exhibits 5 and 6 for identification.]

Q. Will you describe to the jury the size and the interior of that shed from where you took the car? A. Why, that part of the shed was large enough for about two cars, and where the Overland was I think there was boards under the wheels... . [707]

Q. Now, what was the condition of the earth in the floor, except where the Overland was actually standing? A. Why, I should judge it had been raked up. It was quite soft... .

Q. Where did you take that Overland car? A. To the Elm Square garage.

Q. And how long did you keep it there? A. It is still there... .

Q. And how far was that garage from your house? A. Why, less than a quarter of a mile.

Q. Right in Elm Square? A. Right in Elm Square.

Q. Did Boda know you had taken that car? A. He was there when I took it... .

Q. Now, my question is, did Boda ever come for the car?
A. Well, he came to get it May 5th. [708]

Q. Did you see Boda that night [May 5]? A. Yes... .

Q. Did you see anything or anybody else on ... North Elm Street, at that time and place? A. Yes.

Q. Now, tell us what you saw? A. I saw a motorcycle, and three men near it.

Q. And where was that? A. North of the house.

Q. Well, whereabouts with reference to the street, how far from the house? A. Why, it was near the street car track, I should judge around thirty feet from the house... .

Q. Can you describe the motorcycle any more in detail? A. Just a motorcycle and sidecar.

Q. Where with reference to the motorcycle were the three men?
A. Why, one was on the motorcycle and two were in the sidecar.

Q. Now, did you have some talk with Boda at that time? A. Yes.

Q. Now, you need not answer this until my friends have a chance to object. Was that talk in reference to his automobile? A. Yes.

Q. Well, I wanted to give them a chance to object.

MR. McANARNEY. This is all subject to the exception, I understand?

THE COURT. That you ask as a fact? You are not asking for the conversation?

MR. WILLIAMS. No, if your Honor please.

MR. McANARNEY. The whole interrogation of this witness is under the general exception?

THE COURT. Oh, yes.

Q. Now, after you had that talk with Boda, what did you see happen …? A. Why, Boda left me … went to the motorcycle and got in the sidecar, and they [Orciani and Boda] drove off.

Q. Now, what happened to the other two men you say were standing by the motorcycle?

A. They started towards the bridge.

Q. That is, going— A. Going south.

Q. That is, the Elm Square direction? A. Yes…. [709]

Q. Did Boda get his car that night? A. No.

Q. Had it been repaired? A. Yes, sir.

Q. Where did you go later that night? A. I went down to the garage.

Q. Where did you go after that? A. Brockton police court—police station.

Q. Did you see anybody there? A. Yes.

Q. Who did you see there? A. The two in the cage….

Q. Where were they at that time? A. In a room in the police station.

Q. What time of night was that?

A. Why, it must have been between ten and eleven; I don't know just what time it was.

Q. Did you see Boda again that night? A. No, sir.

Q. Have you ever seen Boda since? A. No….

Q. Did you see your wife on North Elm Street that time? A. That night?

Q. Yes. A. Yes.

Q. What did you see her doing? A. Walking towards the house.

Q. Towards your house? A. Yes….

Q. … Where was she with reference to the Bartlett house?

A. Why, … a little more than halfways between.

Q. Which way was the motorcycle headed at that time? A. North. [Towards Brockton.]
Q. Was there any searchlight at that time? A. Headed north, yes. [711]

Cross-Examination.

Q. (By Mr. Jeremiah McAnarney) You said to us that the ground in that place where the car was kept at the Coacci house had seemed to have been raked over,—the earth? A. Yes.... [714]
Q. Now, Boda came there to get his car, didn't he? A. Yes.
Q. There were no 1920 number plates on it? A. No.
Q. You advised him not to take the car and run it without the 1920 plates, didn't you? A. Yes.
Q. Now, your wife, while you were talking with Boda, your wife had been up to the Bartlett's house and eventually came back? A. Yes. [715]

Redirect Examination.

Q. (By Mr. Williams) Now, Mr. Johnson, you need not answer this question until the Court has passed upon it. What talk did you have with Boda in front of your house that night?
MR. MOORE. Objected to, if your Honor please.
THE COURT. Is there any claim that that was within hearing distance of either or both of the defendants?
MR. WILLIAMS. Well, I am asking the question, if your Honor please, in view of Mr. McAnarney's——
THE COURT. He has only asked, as I recall,——he has only referred to the fact that there was a conversation.
MR. WILLIAMS. Then a little further than that, he asked this witness if he did not advise Boda.
THE COURT. Oh, I remember, about the number plates. [718]
MR. JEREMIAH McANARNEY. Yes.
MR. WILLIAMS. Now, I want the whole conversation.
THE COURT. Why are they not entitled to it, Mr. McAnarney?
MR. McANARNEY. All this conversation, I understand, if your Honor please, with reference to Boda goes in subject to our exception?

THE COURT. Not with reference to this particular part, because you opened that up. [719]

[Ed. This debate takes up an additional 3.5 pages. Examination of Simon Johnson is suspended in favor of Napoleon Ensher. Johnson's recall is put next for continuity.]

Mr. Simon E. Johnson, Recalled. June 21, 1921.

Q. (By Mr. Williams) I recall you, Mr. Johnson, to ask you what conversation you had with Boda regarding the taking of this car—

MR. MOORE. Objected to.

Q. —at the time you talked with him in front of your house on the evening of May 5, 1920?

MR. MOORE. I object.

THE COURT. I will hear you.

[Ed. After an exchange between McAnarney and the Court, the Court ruled:]

THE COURT... I should not allow it if it had not been for that cross-examination.... [874]

MR. JEREMIAH McANARNEY. This is cross-examination. Clearly I have a right to summarize on that.

THE COURT. Oh, there isn't any question about that. The cross-examination was perfectly proper, and according to my view the argument is perfectly proper that you intend to make or which is open to you to make. Now, that being true, you having opened that up, hasn't the Commonwealth the right now in reply to it to show the entire conversation that has reference to the nondelivery or the delivery of the car that night?

MR. JEREMIAH McANARNEY. Without taking more time, I think my position is clear to your Honor.

THE COURT. Oh, yes, I think so.

MR. JEREMIAH McANARNEY. And my rights on that you will reserve.

THE COURT. All right. But I am going to give you the right,—I do not know what this evidence may disclose. It may not have any bearing. It might have a bearing, because your inquiry related to the fact of the failure to take away that car that night because of the want of number plates. Now, this conversation must have some reference to that thing, namely, the failure to take away the car on that night.

MR. JEREMIAH McANARNEY. I assume Mr. Williams knows what his witness will testify to.

THE COURT. I suppose so, and if the evidence does not disclose that, then you may have the right to have the evidence stricken from the record.

MR. JEREMIAH McANARNEY. If your honor please, I don't know but what I would be with propriety making this request, that if Mr. Williams' knowledge is such that that is not what the witness will testify to, that the question should not be put.

THE COURT. ... I am going to assume, as I have assumed for both sides, that counsel in good faith tell the Court what their evidence will tend to prove.

MR. JEREMIAH McANARNEY. I did not mean he would not put that in good faith, but I meant if he has knowledge that that answer is going [875] to incorporate things that were not inquired about by me, then that he should tell us, or at least so swing his question to avoid something that does not belong in the record.

THE COURT. Well, I will watch it very carefully and see. If there is, I will, upon motion, have it stricken from the record.

MR. JEREMIAH McANARNEY. There was an objection and exception, I understand.

THE COURT. Oh, yes.

[The question is read as follows:

"Q. I recall you, Mr. Johnson, to ask you what conversation you had with Boda regarding the taking of his car at the time you talked with him in front of your house on the evening of May 5th, 1920?"]

Q. Will you state that conversation?

THE COURT. Now, limit this conversation as much as you can to the question about, and the question refers to the taking of that car on that night. You may proceed, please.

A. When he came, he said he came for his car.

Q. Just speak up.... A. He said he came for his car, and I asked him if he had any number plates. He said "No." "Why," I said, "You can't take it without number plates." "Well," he said, "I will take the chance." And I said, "All right. As soon as my wife gets back I will go down [to the garage] with you," and then when my wife came back from the Bartlett house, he said, "Never mind, it is too late. I will send somebody for it tomorrow." That was practically all of it. [876]

Mr. Napoleon Joseph Ensher, Sworn. June 17, 1921.

Q. (By Mr. Williams) What is your name? A. Napoleon Joseph Ensher.

Q. Where do you live? A. West Bridgewater.

Q. Whereabouts in West Bridgewater?

A. I am on the corner of—on Lincoln Street, West Bridgewater.

Q. Are you acquainted with the corner of Lincoln Street and South Elm?

A. I am not very far from there.

Q. How far do you live from there? A. I should judge 700 feet.... Possibly a thousand.

Q. Do you know ... Mike Boda? A. Why, what do you mean, "know him"?

Q. Do you know what he looks like? A. Seen him once or twice. [722]

Q. How many times have you seen him? A. Two or three times.

Q. Do you know where he lived in 1920?

MR. MOORE. I object, your Honor.

THE COURT. You may answer.

MR. MOORE. Reserve an exception.

A. Why, yes, I think he lived down at the corner.

Q. Whereabouts at the corner? A. Well, I should call it Mr. Puffer's house, a building owned by Mr. Puffer, corner of South Elm and Lincoln Street.... [Ed. This is the Coacci house.]

Q. Do you know when Boda first came to West Bridgewater?

MR. MOORE. That I object to.

THE COURT. You may answer.

MR. JEREMIAH McANARNEY. Save an exception.

MR. MOORE. Save an exception.

THE COURT. Certainly.

A. Why, some time during the fall.

Q. The fall of what year? A. I do not know. I think it must have been 1919. [723]

Q. Do you know whether any other people lived in the same house with Boda? A. Yes, another young man.

MR. MOORE. I object, if your Honor please.

THE COURT. You may answer. Of course, if there is no connection with this later, this alleged crime of course it is incompetent. I suppose there is going to be some connection. This is only something leading up to something... .

Q. What is the name of the other man who lived there? A. I don't know, sir.

Q. Was there any other family that lived in that house? A. Well, as far as I know there was another lady and child that was supposed to be this other man's wife; his name I don't know.

Q. Let me show you two pictures and ask you if you know what those pictures represent (showing pictures to the witness)? A. (Witness examines pictures.) Why, this one here (indicating) is the house, and this (indicating) was the barn and shed, and this (indicating) was the same building.

Q. The house and barn of what place? A. Of the Puffer place in which these people lived.

MR. WILLIAMS. I am referring to, for the purposes of the record, the pictures I had marked for identification Nos. 5 and 6.

Q. Do you know whether or not Boda had an automobile while he was there? A. Yes, sir.

MR. JEREMIAH McANARNEY. Objected to, if your Honor please.

THE COURT. The evidence is already in, isn't it, that he had,— what?

MR. WILLIAMS. An Overland.

MR. JEREMIAH McANARNEY. "While there."

MR. WILLIAMS. While he lived there. [724]

THE COURT. Didn't the last witness [Simon Johnson] say he went down there to this same place and got this Overland?

MR. MOORE. We objected at that time. We are simply making the same objection to the same line of testimony.

THE COURT. You may answer.

MR. MOORE. Save an exception.

Q. What kind of machine was it? A. He told me an Overland.

THE COURT. Well, that may be stricken out... .

Q. Have you ever seen that machine? A. Yes.

Q. How many times?

THE COURT. I will excuse the jury and I will hear counsel on the evidence to be offered later.

[The jury retire from the court room and the following argument takes place in their absence.]

THE COURT. ... I will hear you now, Mr. Williams, as to what this evidence is leading up to.

MR. WILLIAMS. If your Honor please, it is leading up to a situation which possibly you do not recall, but which I set forth in my opening remarks to the jury.

THE COURT. I had some doubt when I heard it, as to its competency.

MR. WILLIAMS. We shall offer to show that this man Boda lived at the corner house there which your Honor recalls we took the jury to see, the so-called Coacci house; that he came there in the early part of December, 1919, and stayed there until about April 20, 1920; that while there he was seen driving a large Buick car of the type which is of interest to us in this case; that he was associated with one Orciani, that he was associated with Sacco, and we shall ask the jury from the evidence which we present to draw the inference that the car which Boda was then driving was the car concerned in this murder, and we shall tie up the car and Boda, by evidence of other association between these four men, Sacco, Vanzetti, Orciani, and Boda.

THE COURT. Have you any evidence to show that the car Boda was driving was the same car or evidence tending to prove it was the same car, same Buick car to which evidence has been given by the prosecution?

MR. WILLIAMS. We can show it was the same kind of car. We cannot show any closer than that. I mean, by any distinctive features of the car, other than it was a large, dark Buick car.

THE COURT. Anything about the window in the rear? [725]

MR. WILLIAMS. No, we cannot show that, so far as I know.

THE COURT. What evidence have you to show, in any way, to connect either Orciani or——what is the other man's name?

MR. WILLIAMS. Mr. Boda.

THE COURT. ——Boda, with either of the defendants?

MR. WILLIAMS. We have other evidence regarding that, which will be introduced later.

THE COURT. Well, what is it?

MR. WILLIAMS. We shall show them together at Stoughton.

THE COURT. Now, who were together?

MR. WILLIAMS. Orciani, Boda——let me say we shall show Orciani, Sacco and Vanzetti together at Stoughton on May 4, I think the date it [sic].

91

THE COURT. With what car? .... .

MR. WILLIAMS. With a motorcycle at that time. We cannot place the four men together at any time in this particular Buick car.

THE COURT. Or one of this type?

MR. WILLIAMS. Or one of this type. We can show Boda had a car of that type, was seen driving it; can show the association between the men I have indicated. We will further show that this car was stolen on November 23, 1919, was seen driving through Dedham in the direction which has been indicated in court to your Honor; that Orciani was then living in Hyde Park, that Boda was then, if I am correct, living with Orciani, that he subsequently moved to the Coacci house about the first of December; that thereafter——

THE COURT. Are you going to show that the number to which the Dedham policeman testified was the number on any car that Orciani had?

MR. WILLIAMS. No, we cannot show that. We will further show that after Boda moved to the Coacci house, curtains were on the windows of this shed. That is, the windows were curtained off, and that there were marks of another car kept in the shed.

THE COURT. Have you any evidence tending to prove that either Boda or Orciani or Coacci had any relationship as to any issue involved in these indictments?

MR. WILLIAMS. We cannot place them in South Braintree, if that is what your Honor means.

THE COURT. I am very much in doubt.

MR. WILLIAMS. I also call to your Honor's attention the place where the car was found in the woods, and the Coacci house where Boda lived, the relation between that place and Elm Square and the Johnson house.

THE COURT. How far was it?

MR. WILLIAMS. About three-quarters of a mile from the Coacci house to Elm Square. The Johnson house, if you remember, a few hundreds yards beyond there. It was a little over a mile and a half from the [726] Coacci house to the place in the woods off Manley Street, where the car was found.

THE COURT. The difficulty with me is to find some relationshp between this car Boda had and the car used at the day or time of the alleged shooting. There is the great difficulty, Mr. Williams. I am very

92

much in doubt about its competency. Beyond the fact that it was a touring car of a Buick model, is there—

MR. WILLIAMS. No, not as to the car Boda was seen driving.

THE COURT. What is there that you claim shows any logical connection between the car Boda was driving and the alleged shooting, anything more than Boda was driving a Buick car?

MR. WILLIAMS. We show this: let me start with the car. Supposing there is nothing about the South Braintree murder in evidence at the present time. We start with a man named Boda driving a large car in that general direction and keeping it, as we will offer evidence which we say tends to show, in a shed under conditions which show that he was intending to conceal the keeping of it. We show that Boda was associating with a man named Orciani and a man named Sacco. We show that Vanzetti was associating with Sacco and with Orciani. We show that those men were associating together under certain circumstances in that general vicinity on May 5, three weeks after the shooting. We show that Sacco and Vanzetti—we will show that Sacco and Vanzetti were down in that vicinity on the night of April 14, the night before the shooting, or the night of April 15, the night of the shooting; and we will ask the inference that it was that car used by those associated gentlemen which was concerned in the murder and we shall endeavor to show that Sacco and Vanzetti—

THE COURT. Is there any claim that there was any concert of action between Orciani and Boda and the defendant?

MR. WILLIAMS. Only that by reason of the association of Sacco and Vanzetti with these men, particularly Boda, who had such a car, we shall ask the jury to draw the inference that that was the car which was concerned in the South Braintree shooting.

THE COURT. Inference based on what?

MR. WILLIAMS. On the association of the men and linking up those men with this car which Boda was driving.

THE COURT. How much evidence have you as to the association?

MR. WILLIAMS. We have two or three instances of their being seen together at Stoughton.

THE COURT. Have they ever been at his house—have you any evidence that they have ever been at his house or barn where this automobile was kept?

MR. WILLIAMS. We have evidence of one or more occasions where on a Sunday night or Sunday nights where a car with four dark men

93

was [727] seen to drive up to that Coacci house. We cannot show they were the particular men you have spoken of.

THE COURT. That is not enough to identify either of these defendants. There are a good many Italians who are dark men.

MR. WILLIAMS. Mr. Katzmann suggests I have not indicated the nature of the testimony as to when Boda was seen driving this Buick car, which was shortly before the South Braintree shooting.

THE COURT. But he [Boda] is not connected in any way with the murder. Anybody else driving a Buick car, if it was a 7-passenger car, would stand almost in the same relationship.

MR. WILLIAMS. He would, if it were not for the geographical significance of the locality.

THE COURT. But there is not one identifying feature. For instance, a window out in the rear, or any other thing.

MR. WILLIAMS. That was taken out. Our evidence shows that was taken out the day of the shooting. It may be remote, if your Honor please, but it has seemed to us——

THE COURT. I am afraid of it. The only question that disturbed me at all. I am not going to admit that at the present time. I want to consider it. That is a very disturbing question. Nothing hitherto has been troublesome at all, not in the least.

MR. WILLIAMS. Then, if your Honor please, I will suspend with this witness and put on another witness.

THE COURT. I wish you would.

MR. WILLIAMS. Which will take up a different phase of the case. Mr. Ensher, I will suspend with you temporarily, if you will step from the courtroom. Hold yourself in readiness to be recalled to the stand.

(Mr. Ensher leaves the stand and examination is suspended.)

THE COURT. The jurors may return, please.

(The jurors return to the court room.) [728]

9. ARREST ON THE STREETCAR

Mr. Austin C. Cole, Sworn. June 17, 1921.

Q. (By Mr. Williams) What is your full name? A. Austin Cole....

Q. Where do you live? A. My home is in South Easton. [728]

Q. What was your occupation in ... April and May, 1920? A. Conductor.

Q. Employed by what company? A. The Eastern Massachusetts Street Railway.

Q. What division of that railway did you work on during those months? A. Brockton.

Q. Were you a regular conductor? I mean, have a regular route or not? A. No, a spare.

Q. ... What ... are the duties of a spare conductor?

A. Well, run on any line out of the Campello barn... .

Q. Do you recall the night of May 5, 1920? A. Yes, sir.

Q. Were you running as a conductor on some route that night?

A. Yes.

Q. What route? A. Bridgewater.

Q. ... What points did you run between? A. School Street, Brockton and Bridgewater Center.

Q. What was the route you took between those points? A. Campello, Main Street to Campello, and from Campello, Copeland Street, through to the West Bridge Water line.

Q. What street did you go through after leaving Copeland Street?

A. North Elm Street.

Q. That is a continuation of Copeland Street? A. Yes, sir.

Q. Did you go through Elm Square? A. Yes, sir... .

Q. How far is Bridgewater from Elm Square? A. Well, it is a 15 minute run on the car... .

Q. How far is it from Elm Square to School Street, Brockton?

A. I should say between four and five miles. [729]

Q. What was your running time from Elm Square to School Street?

A. Half an hour... .

Q. The whole trip from Bridgewater to Brockton ... would be three-quarters of an hour?

A. Yes, sir... .

Q. ... Do you know the defendants Sacco and Vanzetti?

A. Well, I do not know their—

Q. I do not mean to speak to, but do you know who they are?

A. I know who they are. [730]

Q.... Did you see Sacco that night [May 5, 1920]? A. Yes.

Q. Where did you see him for the first time? A. Sunset Avenue, West Bridgewater.

Q. Did you see Vanzetti there that night? A. Yes.

Q. Where did you see him? A. Sunset Avenue, West Bridgewater.

Q. On which trip and which way was your car going?

A. It was the 9:30 out of Bridgewater, for Brockton.

Q. Due at Brockton what time? A. 10:15.

Q. Now, will you tell the jury what you saw of the defendants that night, what you saw them do, anything you observed regarding them?

A. They got on the car at Sunset Avenue.

Q. I am going to stop you right at the start and ask you where Sunset Avenue is?

A. Well, it is about half way between Elm Square and the Brockton and West Bridgewater line.

Q. Can you tell us how far it is in miles from Elm Square to Sunset Avenue?

A. I should say around, not quite a mile and a half.

Q. Is there a regular stopping place there at Sunset Avenue?

A. There is a white pole, yes.

Q. Now, ... will you answer my previous question? A. They boarded the car at Sunset Avenue and Sacco offered me a quarter. I changed it for him. I said, "To Brockton?" He said, "Yes." I said it would be thirty cents. He said, "I know it." He has a nickel in his other hand. He throws the thirty cents into the cash box and asks for two transfers. I give him the two transfers. They went in and sat down. Next time I noticed them was at the Campello police station when Officers Connolly and Vaughn came in and took them off to—[731]

Q. Had you ever seen Sacco before that night of May 5? A. Yes, sir.

Q. Had you ever seen Vanzetti before that night? A. Yes, sir.

Q. Do you know what day or night it was that that you saw him [Sacco] before?

A. ... [I]t was Wednesday or Thursday before April 19.

Q. Do you know what dates those would be, Wednesday or Thursday?

A. The 14th or 15th, I think. [732]

Q. How can you say it was one of those two nights?

A. Because I was running down on the Bridgewater line those two nights, I know.

Q. Any other nights along there? A. No, sir. [733]

AFTERNOON SESSION.
Austin C. Cole [continued]
[Direct Examination Resumed.]

Q. (By Mr. Williams) You say they were taken off the car the subsequent night, which was May 5, at Campello? A. Yes, sir.

Q. You were in the car when they were arrested? A. Yes, sir.

Q. Can you tell the jury about that arrest, ...? A. Officer Vaughn got on at Tremont Street through the rear door, and Connolly got on at Calmer Street, one street above. [734]

Cross-Examination.

Q. (By Mr. McAnarney) ... Now, you thought the man with Sacco was somebody that you knew, didn't you? A. Yes, sir.

Q. You thought he was who? A. I thought he was a Portugee [sic] fellow that I knew.

Q. Name what? A. Tony.

Q. Tony what? A. I couldn't tell you.

Q. How long had you known Tony? A. Oh, off and on I should think for a dozen years or so.

Q. You thought Vanzetti was some one you had known for a dozen years? A. At the first glance...

Q. Where does Tony live? A. In West Bridgewater, so far as I know.

Q. Where did you live at that time? A. When?

Q. At that time? A. What time do you refer to?

Q. April? A. I lived at Campello.

Q. Did you ever live in West Bridgewater? A. Yes, sir.

Q. How long did you live in West Bridgewater? A. For about fourteen years, or so. [737]

Q. The second glance [at Vanzetti] proved to you it was not [Tony]? A. Yes, sir....

[Mr. McAnarney shows a photograph (of Joseph Scavitto) to the witness.]

Q. Have you ever seen anyone that looked like that photograph?
A. Yes, sir.

Q. Who? A. Vanzetti.

Q. To your best judgment, that is a picture of the man you saw get aboard that car, isn't it? A. I can't say positive, because I didn't get a side view of him.

Q. Then, you didn't get a side view of the man that got on your car? A. No sir....

MR. McANARNEY. I would like to have that marked for identification. [738]

[The picture is shown to the jury.] [739]

Earl J. Vaughn, Sworn. June 17, 1921.

Q. (By Mr. Williams) You are a member of the Brockton police force? A. Yes, sir.

Q. Do you remember the night of May 5, 1920? A. Yes, sir.

Q. Were you in Campello, that part of Brockton that is called Campello, that night? A. I was.

Q. Will you tell the jury anything you did or observed in connection with the defendants that night? A. Well, I can tell about the arrest, that is all.

Q. That is what I am asking you? A. Well, the telephone——

THE COURT. Speak up.

Q. [Continued] We got a telephone call that the two men we wanted were on the Bridgewater car.

So Officer Connolly and myself boarded the car, and took these two men off.... and placed them under arrest, and we took a gun out of Vanzetti's pocket. That is about all.

Q. Who boarded the car [streetcar] first? A. Officer Connolly.

Q. Where did you get on the car? A. I got on at Calmer Street and he got on at Peckham.

Q. How far down from Calmer is Peckham? A. About one car stop. [749]

Q. Did you personally search either one of them? A. Yes, sir.

Q. Which one did you search? A. I searched Vanzetti.

Q. Did you find anything on him at that time? A. I found the gun.

Q. Where did you find it? A. In his [right] hip pocket.

Q. What did you do with that gun afterwards? A. Turned it in to the station.

Q. Whom did you turn it in to?

A. I turned it in to Officer Connolly, and he turned it in to the station. [750]

Michael J. Connolly, Sworn. June 17, 1921.

Q. (By Mr. Williams) Are you a member of the Brockton police force? A. I am... .

Q. Do you remember the night of May 5th of last year? A. I do.

Q. Where were you stationed that night? A. Campello.

Q. Did you receive any telephone call that evening? A. I did.

Q. About what time? A. Three minutes of ten.

Q. Do you know where the call came from? A. The central station.

Q. After receiving that call, what did you do?

A. Put on my hat and coat and went out to meet the Bridgewater car.

Q. What time was that Bridgewater car due, do you know? A. It was due out of the avenue at 10:04. That brings her on to Main Street, Campello, at 10:04.

Q. 10:04. Did you, as a matter fact, get aboard that Bridgewater car? A. I did.

Q. Whereabouts? A. At Keith's Theatre in Campello.

Q. Do you know the defendants Sacco and Vanzetti? A. I do.

Q. ... [D]o you recognize them [Sacco and Vanzetti] here in the court room? A. I do.

Q. Will you tell the jury what you did after boarding the car, . .? A. I boarded the car at Keith's theatre. I got on the front end... . I looked the length of the car to see if I could see two foreigners, which the telephone had said had tried to steal or take an automobile in Bridgewater. [Ed. This was stricken out.]

Q. Well, you looked down the car, and what did you see and do?

A. I seen Sacco and Vanzetti sitting on the end seat, the left-hand end seat... .

Q. It was on the left-hand going from the back to the front? A. By looking from the front to the back. I came in that way, and they were sitting on the end seat. I went down through the car and when I got opposite to the seat I stopped and I asked them where they came from. [751] They said "Bridgewater." I said, "What was you doing in Bridgewater?" They said, "We went down to see a friend of mine." I said, "Who is your friend?" He said, "A man by the—they call him 'Poppy'." "Well," I said, "I want you, you are under arrest." Vanzetti was sitting on the inside of the seat.

Q. ... [Y]ou mean toward the aisle or toward the window?

A. Toward the window.... and he went, put his hand in his hip pocket and I says, "Keep your hands out on your lap, or you will be sorry."

THE DEFENDANT VANZETTI. You are a liar!

THE WITNESS. They wanted to know what they were arrested for. I says, "Suspicious characters." We went,—oh, it was maybe about three minutes' ride where the automobile met the car coming from the central station. Officer Vaughn got on just before, and when he got on I told him to stand up, and I told Officer Vaughn to fish Vanzetti; and I just gave Sacco a slight going over, just felt him over, did not go into his pockets, and we led them out the front way of the car.

Q.... Was anything found on either man at that time?

A. There was a revolver found on Vanzetti.

Q. What was done with that revolver?

A. It was handed over to me and I handed it over to the police.

Q. ... Who handed it over to you at that time? A. Officer Vaughn.

Q. From whom did Officer Vaughn take that revolver? A. From Vanzetti.

Q. And from what part of Vanzetti, if you saw? A. From the left hip pocket, back pocket.

Q. Was that gun handed to you at that time? A. Handed to me when he got outside the car.

Q. Did you examine it then or not? A. I kept it in my hand and used it on the men to the station.

Q. Did you note at that time whether or not it was loaded? A. I did.

Q. And was it or was it not? A. It was....

Q. Go ahead, then. A. I put Sacco and Vanzetti in the back seat of our light machine, and Officer Snow got in the back seat with them. I took the front seat with the driver, facing Sacco and Vanzetti.

Q. What do you mean? You say you were in the front seat with the driver?

A. Yes. I turned around and faced Sacco and Vanzetti.

Q. All right. A. I told them when we started that the first false move I would put a bullet in them. On the way up to the station Sacco reached his hand to put under his overcoat, and I told him to keep his hands outside of his clothes and on his lap. [752]

100

Q. Will you illustrate to the jury how he placed his hand? A. He was sitting down with his hands that way [indicating], and he moved his hand up to put it in under his overcoat.

Q. At what point? A. Just about the stomach there, across his waistband, and I says to him,

"Have you got a gun there?" He says, "No." He says, "I ain't got no gun." "Well," I says, "keep your hands outside of your clothes." We went along a little further and he done the same thing. I gets up on my knees on the front seat and I reaches over and I puts my hand under his coat but I did not see any gun. "Now," I says, "Mister, if you put your hand in there again you are going to get into trouble," He says, "I don't want no trouble." We reached the station, brought them up to the office, searched them... .

Q. Did anybody search Sacco in your presence? A. They did.

Q. Who? A. Officer Spear. I searched Vanzetti. In his right-hand coat pocket—[753]

Q. ... [D]escribe to the jury what was done regarding the searching of them in the office... .

A. I searched Vanzetti. In his right-hand pocket I found four shells. Three Peters.

THE COURT. What is that?

THE WITNESS. Three Peters and one Winchester.

Q. What kind of shells? A. Shotgun shells.

Q. Do you know the gauge? A. 12 gauge... .

Q. I show you that revolver [found on Vanzetti] and ask you if you—

THE COURT. There are no cartridges in it?

MR. MOORE. I object... .

Q. Showing you that revolver, I ask you if you know what revolver that is?

MR. MOORE. I object, your Honor.

THE COURT. You may answer.

A. Yes.

MR. MOORE. Reserve an exception, please... .

MR. JEREMIAH McANARNEY. Your Honor will save an exception to both.

THE COURT. You both except. I have not ruled on it yet.

MR. JEREMIAH McANARNEY. All right, we will await your ruling.

THE COURT. Will the answer to the question be to the effect that the revolver was found on one of the defendants?

MR. WILLIAMS. I expect the witness will answer that is the revolver that was found on Vanzetti.

THE COURT. Then he may answer.

MR. MOORE. Reserve an exception. [756]

THE COURT. I will save your exception.

THE WITNESS. That is the revolver that was found on Vanzetti.

Q. How do you know that is the revolver? A. I marked it

Q. How did you mark it? A. With a knife cut in the handle.

Q. Do you see that knife cut there? A. I do.

Q. Will you point it out?

MR. JEREMIAH McANARNEY. In order that there be no time taken, I would like to reserve an exception to any description or evidence in regard to that revolver.

THE COURT. All right. You object to its competency on any ground, I take it?

MR. JEREMIAH McANARNEY. I do, yes.

THE COURT. You object also on the ground it is incompetent for any purpose, both of you?

MR. JEREMIAH McANARNEY. Yes, sir.

THE COURT. All right.

MR. WILLIAMS. I offer it in evidence.

MR. JEREMIAH McANARNEY. Well, the objection goes to the offering in evidence, also, of course.

THE COURT. Oh, sure.

MR. WILLIAMS. I offer this in evidence and ask it be marked.

[The revolver is admitted in evidence and marked "Exhibit 27."] ... .

Q. Now, will you point out to the jury the mark you put on it? A. It is a knife cut right in the round part of it.

[Mr. Williams shows revolver to the jury.]

Q. Was it loaded at that time? A. It was.

Q. How many bullets were in it? A. Five.

Q. What did you do with the bullets?

A. I took them out and kept them until I handed them over to the state police.

Q. Do you remember to whom you handed them? A. Yes.

Q. To whom? A. Mr. Scott. [Ed. References to envelope holding these bullets on pp. 774, 778 of transcript.]

Q. What calibre revolver is that? A. .38

Q. Do you remember what kind of bullets were in that?

MR. MOORE. I object.

THE COURT. Well, do you know?

THE WITNESS. I have it in notes.

THE COURT. Well,—

Q. If you have any memorandum, you can refer to it.

THE COURT. You may use it to refresh your recollection.

MR. MOORE. Reserve an exception, if your Honor please.

THE WITNESS. There is two Remingtons and three U. S. [Ed. Bullets in Vanzetti's gun.]

Q. Do you know what "U. S." stands for? A. United States, I think. [757]

MR. WILLIAMS. I am just asking now about the cartridges. We have spoken about four 12-gauge shotgun shells.

THE COURT. There was no objection to the admission of those. Did you intend to object?

MR. MOORE. I intended to have this objection run to all revolvers and cartridges.

THE COURT. I don't know. You kept objecting right along, but did not object to that, so I did not know whether you intended your objection to run to that or not.

MR. MOORE. We were objecting, your Honor,—I think there was an objection to the four shotgun shells.

THE COURT. I have not heard one. You see if there is anything on the record.

MR. MOORE. If not, let it be understood that there is an objection to any testimony—

THE COURT. That is why I wanted it called to your attention. I will hear you now, Mr. Williams, why the four shells should stay in.

MR. WILLIAMS. I have not offered them as yet, but I will take it up. He simply described what he found in his pockets.

MR. MOORE. Let me suggest, if I may be permitted, your Honor, that the objection to this revolver and to the shells in connection with this revolver, in part, at least, the same character of objection runs to the revolver and those shells as runs to the other four shells that your Honor has in mind, not in its entirety. There is a further objection to the four 12-gauge shells that does not apply to these, but there is a very

103

valid objection, I feel, to the introduction of this revolver and the .38 calibre shells.

THE COURT. So far as the four shells are concerned, the shells used in an ordinary shotgun, I take it.

MR. WILLIAMS. As I understand from his testimony.

THE COURT. Is that what you meant?

THE WITNESS. The first shells, these shells I described now—

THE COURT. No, the four shells you talked about.

THE WITNESS. Yes, those were ordinary shotgun.

THE COURT. A shotgun. I will exclude that. You will give it no consideration whatsoever, with reference to the four shotgun shells.

MR. WILLIAMS. If your Honor please, you bear in mind that the testimony shows that there was protruding from the rear window of this car a barrel there of a shotgun or rifle. [758]

THE COURT. Do you find any evidence of a shotgun? As I get it, it was a rifle… .

[Ed. After exchange between Moore and the Court, Mr. Williams spoke.]

MR. WILLIAMS. If your Honor please, Mr. Katzmann directs my attention specifically to the testimony of Hans Behrsin, the chauffeur, who testified. [759]

THE COURT. Let the stenographer, … look it over during sometime and call it to my attention.

MR. WILLIAMS. In the meantime, do I understand the testimony which he gave about finding those [four shotgun] shells is in or stricken out?

THE COURT. It is out. [760] [Ed. Two shotgun shells admitted on p. 939 of transcript.]

Merle A. Spear, Sworn. June 18, 1921.

Q. (By Mr. Williams) You are a police officer? A. I am.

Q. Of the city of Brockton? A. The city of Brockton.

Q. … Do you remember the evening of May 5, 1920? A. I do.

Q. Were you on duty that night? A. I was.

Q. And where were you on duty? A. In the police station.

Q. That is the central station or the Campello? A. The central station.

Q. In response to some telephone call did you go to some place from that station? A. I did.

Q. Where did you go?
A. To meet the car coming out of Keith Avenue from Bridgewater at ten o'clock.
Q. Did you yourself board the car? A. I did not.
Q. Did you see the defendants that night? A. I did.
Q. Now, will you tell the jury when you saw the defendants, where, what you did in respect to them, and what you observed regarding them? A. I saw the defendants in the cross seat on the right-hand side of an electric car, just as they got up to come forward, coming out of the car.
Q. What police offcers, if any, were with them at that time?
A. Officers Connolly and Vaughn. And they got into the auto that I had stopped across the front end of the [electric] car.
Q. What kind of an auto was it [you traveled in]? A. A Dodge touring car. [779]
Q. The top up? A. The top up, yes, sir. And I drove them to the police station from there.
Q. Now, what was done with them on the drive to the police station or what did you hear any of them say, if anything? A. Why, on the way up, probably half way up, through some talk of one of the police officers about keeping their—... .
MR. MOORE. I object to what the police officer said... .
THE COURT. Of course, what the police officer says you may say is of no consequence. It is what a defendant says or does that has its competency... .
MR. WILLIAMS. I understand this is by reason of what some police officer said... .
THE COURT. You may state what the police officer stated... .
A. I think that Officer Snow told Sacco on the way up— [Ed. Snow is not a witness.]
MR. MOORE. I object.
THE COURT. Go ahead.
A. —to keep hands where he could see them.
MR. JEREMIAH McANARNEY. Your Honor will save my rights on that.
THE COURT. Certainly.
MR. MOORE. An exception.
Q. He said what? A. To keep his hands where he could see them.

Q. Yes. A. Officer Connolly got up. He was sitting on the front seat with me, and got up and reached in back....

Q. Did you observe the defendants? That is, were the defendants in your view at any time during the ride from the car to the police station? A. They were not.

Q. Did you hear them say anything?

A. I heard Sacco say to Officer Snow, "You need not be afraid of me." [780]

Q. Now, what was done [at the police station] in respect to searching the defendant...?

A. I helped to search Sacco.

Q. Will you describe ... what you did ... to Sacco, where you did it and what you found, ...?

A. At the desk in the central police station they were brought and searched, and I first,—we took a number of automatic cartridges from his right hip pocket. I took an automatic revolver.

THE COURT. How many, did you say?

THE WITNESS. Later counted twenty-three. From in his waist I took an automatic .32 Colt revolver.

Q. What? A. A Colt revolver, automatic revolver....

Q. Where did you take it from? A. From inside his waist, in here, to this side [indicating].

Q. Now, just where was it? I want to be sure of this.

A. Inside of his waist, to the button, to the right....

Q. In what condition was the gun which you took from him?

A. Fully loaded....

Q. How many shots were in it? A. There was eight in the clip, and one in the barrel.

Q. You now say it was a revolver? A. A Colt automatic revolver.

Q. Did you make any mark on that gun when you took it? A. Not when I took it.

Q. Did you while it was in your possession? A. I did.

Q. Whereabouts? A. On the stock I put the initials "M.S.", I think.

Q. Now, will you look at the gun I show you and see if you find any mark on there by which you can identify it? A. [Witness examines gun.] I do.

Q. Will you tell the jury what gun that he is? [sic] A. The gun I took from Sacco. [781]

Q. How many bullets does that hold, do you know?

A. I took eight from the clip and one from the barrel.

Q. What did you do with them, Mr. Spear?

A. I turned them over to the state police, the next evening, the evening of May 6th.

Q. Do you know which member of the state police you turned it over to? A. Scott, I think.

Q. Was anybody present when you turned it over to Scott? A. Proctor was there.

Q. Captain Proctor? A. Yes.

MR. WILLIAMS. I offer this gun, if you please. I will put a tag on it after I show it to the jury.

THE COURT. I understand you object to the competency?

MR. MOORE. To the same.

THE COURT. On any ground, on every ground?

MR. MOORE. Yes, if your Honor please, we make an objection.

THE COURT. You object.

MR. MOORE. Yes.

THE COURT. And on the ground it is not competent for any purpose whatever?

MR. MOORE. Yes, your Honor.

THE COURT. All right. Your objection is overruled and exception noted.

MR. JEREMIAH McANARNEY. To both.

THE COURT. Certainly.

[The pistol found on Defendant Sacco is admitted in evidence and marked "Exhibit 28."]

[Mr. Williams shows Exhibit 28 to the jury.]

MR. WILLIAMS. [To the jury.] You can see the mark which the witness says he put on the stock. You see, by holding it with the barrel to the left of each one of you, there are scratches that show,—if you want a glass, here it is [handing glass to the jurors.] There is no other light we can have over in this corner. [782]

Q. I don't want any misunderstanding about it, that is why I am pressing it. Do you know what make those bullets were you found in the hip pockets? A. Four different makes.

Q. Do you have in mind what they were? A. There were **sixteen of Peters** make.

Q. Sixteen of Peters? A. Yes.

107

Q. Yes. A. **Seven of U. S.,**—United States make.

Q. Sixteen Peters and seven U. S. A. There were **six of Winchester,** and there were **three of the Remington.**

Q. Three Remington,—Peters, U. S., and Winchester? A. Yes.

THE COURT. Three of what?

THE WITNESS. Remington,—"U.M.C.", I think, is a further mark on them... .

Q. Well, will you just examine these cartridges ... and tell the jury what ... the calibre is, ... [handing bullets to the witness]? A. [Witness examines bullets.] .32 calibre... .

Q. Are those bullets of the same type of bullet you took from that gun? A. Yes.

Q. From his pocket and pistol? A. Pocket and gun.

Q. No identifying marks on them, as I understand? A. No.

[Mr. Williams shows bullets to defendant's counsel.]

MR. WILLIAMS. [To the jury.] I am just going to show you, gentlemen, the four types of bullets which the witness says he described. The pistol becomes Exhibit 28.

Q. Mr. Katzmann suggests I have not asked you the calibre of this. Will you please tell us what the calibre of this gun is? A. .32 calibre.

Q. .32 calibre, Colt automatic? A. Yes. [783]

Q. You simply grouped all together those that were in the [Sacco] pistol and those that were loose in the pocket? A. I did.

Q. Were the bullets loose in the pocket or were they in some receptacle?

A. They were loose in the pocket.

[Mr. Williams returns bullets to sheriff.] [784]

10. THE LORING CAP AND BERARDELLI'S GUN

Fred L. Loring, Sworn. June 18, 1921.

Q. (By Mr. Williams) What is your business or profession? A. Shoe worker.

Q. Where do you work? A. Slater & Morrill's.

Q. Were you working there on the day of the so-called South Braintree shooting?

A. Yes, sir. [796]

Q. Was your attention called to the shooting that afternoon?

A. I heard them speaking about it, and looking out of the window, so I went up there… .

Q. Did you know Alexander [sic] Berardelli? A. I did… .

Q. Did you see the body of Berardelli there? A. Yes, sir.

Q. Where was it? A. Right near the telephone post there, right—well—… .

Q. Now, you are referring to a pole east of Rice & Hutchins' factory, or west?

A. It is east here—[797]

Q. And which direction from the pole was it? A. Towards the railroad track.

Q. That is what we call west? A. West… .

Q. How far is that pole you refer to from the nearest corner of Rice & Hutchins factory?

A. I should think it was about 20 feet.

Q. Where was the body of Berardelli lying …? A. Right in the gutter, but on the sidewalk.

Q. Now, when you arrived at the scene, was there anything which you noticed on the street near the body of Berardelli? A. A cap.

Q. Where was the cap? A. It was about 18 inches from Berardelli's body, towards the street.

Q. Did you do anything in regard to that cap? A. Yes. I picked it up.

Q. What did you do with it? A. Carried it down to the shop, kept it about an hour, looked it over, and finally … gave it to Mr. Fraher… .

(Mr. Williams hands a bundle to the witness.)

Q. Will you open that bundle, and see if you can tell the jury what it is? A. That is the cap… . Found beside the body… .

MR. WILLIAMS. I offer this, if your Honor please.

(Mr. Williams submits the cap to counsel for the defendants.)

MR. McANARNEY. Well, we object to its introduction, if your Honor please. [798]

THE COURT. On what ground?

MR. McANARNEY. A general objection

THE COURT. Anything else? Any specific objection to which you desire to call my attention wherein it is incompetent?

MR. McANARNEY. It is generally incompetent,—identification, who it belonged to, who it did not belong to, and so forth.

THE COURT. Are you going to offer evidence tending to prove that cap belonged to either of the defendants?

MR. WILLIAMS. I am, if your Honor please.

THE COURT. Then I will admit it, reserving, of course, the right, if the connection is not made, to have all the evidence in regard to the cap stricken from the record. That is the policy we have adopted up to the present time, and I see no reason I should not follow it for both sides. [799] [Ed. Debate over the cap is resolved in this way.]

THE COURT. ... Supposing you mark it for identification, with the understanding that if evidence is offered tending to prove that this cap belonged to one of the defendants that it may be admitted in evidence?

MR. WILLIAMS. I am perfectly content.

THE COURT. Would you agree to that?

MR. McANARNEY. No objections to its being marked for identification whatever. [800]

Mrs. Sarah Berardelli, Sworn. June 20, 1921.

Q. (By Mr. Williams) You were the wife of Alexander Berardelli? A. Yes, sir.... [806]

Q. At some time before the shooting, do you know whether or not your husband had done something with the gun which he carried? A. Why, yes, three weeks before he got shot, why, he brought it in the place to have it repaired....

Q. Where was it taken? A. I forget the name of the place....

Q. Can you describe to the jury where the place was? A. I think it is on the corner of Washington Street and I don't know what the other street is....

Q. Was the name Iver Johnson Company? A. Yes, sir.

Q. Now, did anyone go with your husband when he took the gun there? A. Myself....

Q. Well, do you know what the matter with the gun was? A. Yes.

Q. What was it? A. It was a spring broke... . [807]

Q. Now, at some time after that did he do anything about getting the gun back?

A. No. He returned the check to Mr. Parmenter.

Q. And when you say the "check", what do you mean? A. The check for the gun he was supposed to take it out. He gave it to Mr. Parmenter to take it out... .

Q. He gave the receipt check to Mr. Parmenter? A. Yes, sir... .

[Mr. Williams shows a cap to the witness.]

Q. Did you ever see that cap before? A. No.

Q. Is that your husband's cap? A. No.

[Ed. Williams shows Mrs. Berardelli the cap Loring testified he found.]

MR. McANARNEY. What number is that you are referring to?

MR. WILLIAMS. I am referring to cap marked for identification No. 11. You may inquire. [808]

Cross-Examination.

Q. (By Mr. McAnarney) ... Now, when was it that you and your husband were in Boston and your husband left the revolver to be repaired, what month...? A. It was in January, I think.

Q. Well, what [gun] did he have in February or January after he took this revolver in?

A. Mr. Parmenter let him take another one... .

Q. You don't know whether he got that revolver back, or not? A. No. He returned the ticket to Mr. Parmenter, and I don't know if Mr. Parmenter got it for him, but I know Mr. Parmenter let him take another one [gun]. [809]

Lincoln Wadsworth, Sworn. June 20, 1921.

Q. (By Mr. Williams) Were you employed in Boston in March or April of last year? A. I was.

Q. And by whom were you employed? A. Iver Johnson Sporting Goods Company.

Q. Where is their store located ...? A. 155 and 157 Washington Street, Boston.

Q. In what capacity were you employed at that time?

A. At that time I had charge of the pistols and repairs to firearms.

Q. At some time a few weeks before April 15th of last year, was a gun brought in by one Alexander [sic] Berardelli? A. Yes.

Q. And on what date was such gun brought in? A. 20th day of March... .

Q. Did you receive that gun? A. I can't say.

Q. Did you make a record of the gun when it was brought in? A. I did.

Q. Have you that record before you? A. Yes.

Q. Was that record correct when it was made? A. So far as I know, it was correct... .

Q. Will you read that record to the jury?

MR. McANARNEY. I object.

THE COURT. How is that competent?

MR. WILLIAMS. Why, as showing the type of gun received, and the details regarding the receipt.

THE COURT. He can use it to refresh his recollection, but how is it evidence? [813]

Q. Well, using that record, Mr. Wadsworth, to refresh your recollection, will you tell the jury as to the facts as to that revolver being brought in?

MR. McANARNEY. To that I object, your Honor, and ask your Honor to save us an exception.

THE COURT. On what grounds, if you please ...?

MR. McANARNEY. If your Honor please, in view of the nature of this evidence and the relation of the defendant or defendants to the control or whatever they had to do with the matter now to be introduced, we object to it.

THE COURT. It is not introduced at all as evidence that the defendants had anything to do with.

I may be in error, but I suppose the purpose is to show that a certain revolver was taken there, and something may have been done to that revolver, and it may be that one thing that was done on that revolver may be a method of identifying this particular gun.

MR. WILLIAMS. That is the purpose of it, if your Honor please.

THE COURT. In other words to show that the particular gun left there was Berardelli's gun and is the gun that has been introduced here in evidence. Is that your purpose?

MR. WILLIAMS. Yes, your Honor, absolutely.

THE COURT. I will hear it.

MR. McANARNEY. Save an exception

MR. MOORE. Exception.

A. 38 Harrington & Richardson revolver, property of—

MR. WILLIAMS. Please keep your head up, or speak a little louder,—... .

A. [Continued] The record shows that a 38 Harrington——

THE COURT. I said the record could not be introduced.

Q. You are using the record to refresh your recollection, and then testify.

A. 38 Harrington & Richardson revolver, property of Alex Berardelli, was brought in for repairs, and sent up to the shop on March 20, 1920.

Q. You made the record yourself, as I understand it? A. Yes. [814]

Q. Will you tell the jury what type and calibre that revolver is. I now show you and I am referring to Exhibit 27.

[Mr. Williams hands a revolver to the witness.]

A. That is a 38 Harrington & Richardson auto. "Auto" refers to automatic extractors. That is the particular name of that revolver.... .

Q. Can you tell the jury whether or not the revolver which was brought in on that date is of the same type and calibre of revolver as the one I have now shown you?

MR. McANARNEY. To that I object... .

THE COURT. I suppose you are going to show, are you not, later by evidence tending to prove that the revolver in front of the witness was the same revolver that Berardelli had at the time of the alleged shooting?

MR. WILLIAMS. I am, if your Honor please.

THE COURT. With that assurance, the witness may answer... . [Ed. Exceptions are saved.]

MR. McANARNEY. I want to say now, if your Honor please, if it is in within [sic] our right to ask to have that stricken from the record if the connection is not made, while I realize it must be in some instances, it seems on grave and important matters that the connection should be made before the evidence is offered, and then we won't be in that uncertain frame of mind to have the jury asked to disregard that which they have heard.

THE COURT. Well, in all these kind of cases it has been the established rule to admit evidence, not only upon the assurance of the district attorney, but upon the assurance of counsel for the defendant. That is done because every witness ought not to be recalled. The Court has a right to rely upon an assurance made, that it is made in good faith, and that when an attorney says he has that evidence he honestly believes that he has, and that is the reason why the courts have acted upon that assumption for much longer than I have been a member of the Bar. You may proceed.

113

MR. McANARNEY. Your Honor will save me an exception.

MR. MOORE. And me an exception. [815]

Q. ... Will you tell us whether or not that revolver [Exhibit 27] which I have shown to you answers the description of the revolver brought in that day? A. It does... .

Q. Now will you tell us [after question is reworded]? A. It is the same calibre and make... .

MR. McANARNEY. [Ed. After exceptions assured.] No questions, if your honor please. [816]

[Ed. No cross-examination of witness.]

George F. Fitzemeyer (Fitzmeyer), Sworn. June 20, 1921.

Q. (By Mr. Williams) What is your occupation or business?

A. Gunsmith.

Q. For whom do you work? A. Iver Johnson Sporting Goods.

Q. How long have you been with them? A. Thirty years or more... .

Q. Now, in what capacity are you employed by them? A. Foreman of the gun shop... .

Q. Whereabouts is that gun shop located?

A. The fifth floor, corner of Cornhill and Washington Street.

Q. What duties do you have to perform with regard to guns brought in for repairs? A. Give them out to my different men to repair. I repair most all the revolvers myself. [816]

Q. Do you make any record when you repair revolvers? A. Yes, sir.

Q. Have you your records with you? A. Yes, sir... .

[The witness produces a record book.]

Q. If a gun was left say at three o'clock in the afternoon or thereabouts, when would you receive it? A. I would receive it next morning about quarter to nine, ... or, perhaps, a little earlier.

Q. Now, referring to any records you may have of March 21, 1920, will you tell us whether or not you received any Harrington & Richardson revolver on that date for repairs?

A. March 19 I received——

Q. Not the 19th. The 21st, I think. A. Do you want the number of the repair job, the ticket?

Q. No. I am referring to the 21st of March. A. My record is the 19th.

Q. No; I am referring to the 21st. A. 21st? Anything on the 20th?

Q. Anything on the 20th? A. It may be I entered this on the 20th. I may have repaired this next morning, for all I know. I have it marked in with the 19th. Yes, I guess it is the 20th,—between the 22nd and the 19th.

Q. You received a Harrington & Richardson revolver? A. Yes, sir. "H. & R," I call it... .

Q. ... Did you receive more than one Harrington & Richardson revolver during that time for repairs? A. Two. [817]

Q. Well, hasn't your attention been called, Mr. Fitzemeyer, before going on the stand, to repairs made on a certain Harrington & Richardson revolver? A. Yes, sir.

Q. And haven't you found a record of that particular revolver? A. Yes, sir.

Q. Have you the record before you? A. Yes, sir.

Q. Now, will you tell the jury, referring to your record to refresh your recollection, when that revolver was received, what was done upon it, and what was done with it?

MR. McANARNEY. To that I object.

A. My book shows the 19th—

THE COURT. Just a minute. I suppose you claim that this was the Berardelli revolver?

MR. WILLIAMS. Yes, if your Honor please. I am trying to trace it from this record to the record of the witness.

THE COURT. Of course, it isn't competent unless that fact is established.

MR. WILLIAMS. I appreciate that.

THE COURT. With that assurance, you may proceed.

MR. McANARNEY. Your Honor will save an exception.

MR. MOORE. Exception.

THE COURT. Certainly.

Q. All right, Mr. Fitzemeyer, will you go ahead? A. H. & R. revolver 32, new hammer, half an hour... .

Q. On what date? A. Mine is marked the 19th.

THE COURT. What is that about a hammer?

A. New hammer.

Q. 19th? A. It may be the 19th. It is between the 22nd and the 19th... .

Q. What do you mean to say,—that it was between the 19th and the 22nd? A. That job was done—I have "19th" and then marked "22nd", starting over marking the record again. I don't put down every morning when I start in.

Q. You mean your 19th record covers the days up to the 22nd, is that what you mean?

A. Yes, sir, that is what I mean.

Q. What have you to connect that job with the Harrington & Richardson which came in downstairs on the 20th? [818]

MR. McANARNEY. I object.

THE COURT. You must ask him if he can, and then he can refresh his recollection... .

Q. Can you identify that particular revolver which you are now testifying about, and that job upon it, with the Harrington & Richardson revolver received downstairs on the 20th?

A. No, sir, I cannot.

Q. Well, now, you say there were two Harrington & Richardson jobs done or received by you or received by you during that interval between the 19th and the 22nd? A. Yes, sir.

Q. What was the other one? A. There was two of them marked together, two H. & R. revolvers tied together, that is, two in one repair job. "New main spring, new friction spring, repairs, an hour and a half on two."

Q. What calibre guns are those? A. I didn't make a record.

Q. Well, can you tell us—Is there any number on either which will help us to check up with any record they may have downstairs?

A. Yes, sir, my repair number.

Q. Would that repair number be on the books downstairs? A. Yes, sir.

Q. What is your number of your 32 Harrison [sic] & Richardson job? A. 94765.

[Mr. Williams shows a book to the witness.]

Q. Now, I wish you would look at the record downstairs, and see if you can identify the job with that? A. 94765.

MR. WILLIAMS. Do you want me, Mr. McAnarney, to recall the previous witness to simply identify that number?

[Mr. Williams shows book to Mr. McAnarney.]

MR. McANARNEY. I will agree that if he was here he would say the number is 94765... .

MR. WILLIAMS. It is agreed that if the previous witness, Mr. Wadsworth, were here on the stand, he would testify that the number attached to the revolver purporting to have been received from one Alex Berardelli was No. 94765,—repair number. [819]

Q. Now, have you repair job number 94765? A. Yes, sir... .

Q. Will you tell the jury what was done to that revolver in the way of repairs?

A. It is just marked on my book as "New hammer and repairs." ... .

Q. Do you know ... why you should have made a record "32-calibre" [and not 38-calibre]?

MR. McANARNEY. I object.

THE COURT. Excluded.... [820] [Ed. Exchange between Court and Williams.]

Q. What, if any, distinctions are there between a 32 & 38 Harrington & Richardson revolvers?

MR. McANARNEY. I object, if your Honor please.

THE COURT. You may answer.

MR. McANARNEY. Your Honor will save an exception, please.

MR. MOORE. Exception.

THE COURT. Certainly.

THE WITNESS. Shall I answer?

MR. WILLIAMS. Yes.

A. No difference. It is a larger frame.

Q. What is a larger frame? A. Larger frame, one shot more and one calibre.

Q. Which is the one shot more? A. One shot less in the 38.

Q. The 38 has how many shots? A. Five.

Q. And the 32? A. Six. [821]

[Mr. Williams hands a revolver to the witness.]

Q. Let me show you revolver No. 27, Exhibit No. 27, and ask you to inspect that gun. Now, will you tell us if, in your opinion, any repairs have been made to that revolver recently?

A. Well, a new hammer, I should call it, a new hammer.

Q. And how can you tell a new hammer has been put in there?

A. Well, the firing pin does not show of ever being struck... .

Q. How much larger is the frame of the 38? A. Well, there isn't much difference.

Q. Can you tell us in some unit of measurement how much difference there is in the size of the frame? A. It isn't more than a quarter of an inch all through the frame, barrel and all.

Q. In what way, do you mean? A. I mean in the width of it.

Q. Do you know whether you repaired the revolver received under that repair number yourself? A. Do I know if I repaired it?

Q. Yes. A. Yes, sir.

Q. You were repairing the revolvers ... at that time? A. Yes, sir, I do all of the revolver work.

Cross-Examination.

Q. (By Mr. McAnarney) You said something about the number of guns or revolvers that you repair in the course of a day. About how many? A. Oh, twenty-five or thirty, or more.... [822]
[Short recess.]

George F. Fitzemeyer, Recalled.

Q. (By Mr. Williams) Mr. Fitzemeyer, is there any part of your testimony ... which you desire to correct? A. Yes, there is.
Q. What is it? A. On the size of the frames. 38 and 32 are the same size frame in an ejector,—hand ejector. The other model is a Premier and it is a smaller frame.

Recross Examination.

Q. (By Mr. Jeremiah McAnarney) How many different styles, length of barrel and so forth, do they make of those guns,—any idea?
A. ... There is over a half dozen, length of barrel and length of cylinder, 32 long and 32 short and 22, from 22 up.
Q. Then, ... there are at least half a dozen different models, makes and sizes? A. Yes, sir.

Redirect Examination.

Q. (By Mr. Williams) What is that particular model [Exhibit 27], so that we may have that in the record? A. That is what we call a police model, 38 police model.
Q. 38 Police model. A. A break-open hand ejector. Break-open ejector; break-open,—there (indicating) is your ejector. [823]

Mr. James H. Jones, Sworn. June 20, 1921.

Q. (By Mr. Williams) What is your business? A. Firearms salesman and manager of the department for Iver-Johnson Sporting Goods Company, Boston. [823]
Q. Were you the manager last—were you in April and March? A. I was.
Q. How long have you been the manager of that department?

118

A. [A]bout four years, now.

Q. At the request of our office, have you looked up the gun which was concerned in the repair job in your store No. 94,765? A. I have... .

Q. Can you tell the jury whether or not that gun was re-delivered?

A. To the best of my knowledge it was delivered.

Q. And how can you tell the jury then that, to the best of your knowledge, it was delivered?

A. Because the gun is not in our place of business now.

MR. JEREMIAH McANARNEY. I ask that be stricken out. I object to the question and answer.

THE COURT. I will hear all this evidence in the absence of the jury. (The jury retire.) [824] ... .

THE COURT. Of course, these questions are not evidence in the case at all. Go ahead, Mr. Williams.

Q. Now, if that gun had not been delivered, what would you have done with it? A. It would have been left in our draw until the first of the year, after stock-taking time. At that time the repair jobs would be taken out and put into a draw in the office and held there for a while, and then sold.

Q. Do you keep a record of sales that are made?

A. We keep a record of every sale of revolvers that is made, an absolute record.

Q. Is there any record of the sale of this revolver?

A. There is no record of any sale of that revolver.

THE COURT. Have you looked personally, yourself, to see whether that revolver is at your place of business?

THE WITNESS. I did.

THE COURT. So you can say that at the time you searched it was no where on the premises?

THE WITNESS. It was nowhere on the premises.

THE COURT. And you have got no record it was ever delivered?

THE WITNESS. I haven't any record in the book here of its being delivered, no sir. [825]

THE COURT. All right. Let the jury return. [833]

(The jury returned to the court room.) [Ed. After McAnarney read from Bostock's testimony.]

THE COURT. You may read, Mr. Stenographer, the last question.

(The question is read as follows: "Q. And how can you tell, then, that, to the best of your knowledge it was delivered?")

THE COURT. That question and the answer have been stricken from the record. Mr. Williams will put some new questions.

Q. Have you personally made a search of the store to see whether or not that revolver is now in the possession of Iver-Johnson? A. I have.

Q. And what has your search disclosed? A. I cannot find the revolver in the store, in any part.

Q. When did you make such search? A. At the time the officers came to make the investigation.

Q. Has your concern any established custom regarding the disposition of revolvers or guns which are not delivered or called for after repairs are made upon them? Yes or no.

MR. JEREMIAH McANARNEY. That I object to.

THE COURT. Answer yes or no.

MR. JEREMIAH McANARNEY. Save an exception.

Q. Just yes or no. A. Yes. [833]

Q. What is that custom? A. To sell them after——

MR. JEREMIAH McANARNEY. That is subject to the exception——

THE WITNESS. To sell revolvers——

THE COURT. Wait one minute. If guns are not delivered within a certain time, what do you do with them? You may ask that question.

Q. If guns are not delivered within a certain time, what do you do with them?

THE COURT. I will save your rights.

MR. JEREMIAH McANARNEY. Save my rights.

Q. What do you do with them? A. At stocktaking time, the first of the year, we take the revolvers from the repair draw and put them in a desk in the office on the third floor, and they are held there for awhile and then sold.

Q. Do you keep records of guns which are sold?

A. We keep records of all guns sold, whether they are second-hand or new.

Q. Have you any record of this gun being so sold? A. We have not.... . [Ed. Exception saved.]

Q. Was this gun ever sold? A. That gun was not sold from our store.

Q. Well, what do you mean by that? A. As a second-hand gun. As a new gun it might have been sold from any store.... .

Q. That is what I mean, your store. A. The gun was not sold in our store.

Q. You say it is not in your possession now? A. It is not in our possession now.... [834]

MR. JEREMIAH McANARNEY. No questions by the defense, sir.

THE COURT. That is all, sir. [835]

11. POLICE CHIEF MICHAEL STEWART

Michael E. Stewart, Sworn. June 20, 1921.

Q. (By Mr. Williams) You are chief of police of the Town of Bridgewater? A. I am.

Q. Do you recall the date of the arrest of these defendants? A. I do.

Q. And that date was what? A. May the 5th, 1920.

Q. They were arrested some time in the evening? A. Yes, sir.

Q. And on that same evening, did you see either one of the defendants? A. I seen both of them.

Q. What time did you see them? A... .—it was very close to eleven o'clock... .

Q. Where were they at that time?

A. When I see them they were in the emergency room at the Brockton police station... .

Q. With whom did you talk first? A. The defendant Vanzetti.

Q. Was anybody present when you had a talk with him? A. Yes, sir.

Q. Who was present ...? A. There was Officer LeBaron of Bridgewater, Officer Spear and Connolly of Brockton, Officer Lawton and Davenport of West Bridgewater, ... and Simon Johnson of West Bridgewater. [840]

AFTERNOON SESSION.

Michael E. Stewart (Continued.)

THE COURT. You may state your agreement, if you please, Mr. Katzmann, so that it may be a part of the record.

MR KATZMANN. It is agreed between the Commonwealth and both of the defendants that in response to the question put to the witness now upon the witness stand, Michael E. Stewart, to repeat the conversation at the Brockton police station between himself and the defendant Vanzetti on May 5, 1920, he would give the following questions that he put to the defendant Vanzetti and the following answers which the defendant Vanzetti, as the witness Stewart would testify, made to those questions

THE COURT. I suppose it is also agreed that the testimony should have exactly the same effect as evidence as though the witness himself [Stewart] testified to it on the witness stand?

121

MR. McANARNEY. That is correct.

MR. KATZMANN. Mr. Stewart, you may sit down, if you want to. (The witness leaves the stand.) [842]

[Ed. Here are selected questions Stewart asked Vanzetti on the night of May 5 at the Brockton police station.]

MR. KATZMANN. (Reading)

"I am going to ask you some questions. You are under arrest for crime. You are not obliged to answer them unless you see fit, and if you do, what you say may be later used against you.

"Q. What is your nationality? A. Italian.

"Q. What is your name? A. Bartolomeo Vanzetti... .

"Q. Where do you live? A. 35 Cherry Street, Plymouth.

The witness Stewart would testify that he then said:

"It was at that point I warned the defendant. I had asked him some questions previous to the warning." ...

"Q. "What is your business? A. Am fish peddler. [842]

"Q. Were you in West Bridgewater tonight. A. I think so. I am not sure. I am not acquainted.

"Q. Who was with you? A. My friend.

"Q. Who is he? A. Aco Sacco.

"Q. What were you doing in West Bridgewater? A. I went to Bridgewater to see my good friend.

"Q. Who is your friend in Bridgewater? A. Poppy.

"Q. What is his first name? A. ... I don't know his name. They call him just 'Poppy', what you call a nickname.

"Q. Where does he live in Bridgewater? A. I don't know.

"Q. How long have you known him? A. A long time. I worked with him in the cordage company in Plymouth... [Ed. From spring 1914 to January 1915.]

"Q. And you don't know his name? A. They call him 'Poppy'. He is a strong, big man; . .

"Q. When did you leave Plymouth? A. Sunday morning... .

"Q. Where did you go? A. Boston... .

"Q. Who did you go to see in Boston? A. Nobody. I go to see my friend in South Stoughton.

"Q. Do you mean Sacco? A. Yes. He is going to Italy. I get a letter from him, and he asked me to come as he is going to Italy soon. I did go to his house I think Monday, I am not sure."

122

MR. MOORE. Pardon me... . [Ed. Moore's copy differs.] It is in substance the same.

THE COURT. As I have already told you several times, Gentlemen, this has no relevancy whatsoever against Sacco. This can only be considered at the present time against ... the defendant Vanzetti. [843]

"Q. What time did you leave Stoughton to go and see 'Poppy'?
"A. Maybe half past three.

"Q. How did you go? A. Electric car... ."

"Q. What did you do then [after arrival in West Bridgewater]?
"A. Well, we come to a square, and it was lights. I say, 'Maybe my friend is sleeping,' so we went back... . [844]

"Q. Did you see a motorcycle that night in West Bridgewater"—

MR. MOORE. I object, your Honor to that question.

THE COURT. Admitted. Do you want an exception to that?

MR. MOORE. Yes, sir.

THE COURT. You may have it.

MR. KATZMANN. I will read the question: (Reads.)

"Q. Did you see a motorcycle that night in West Bridgewater?
"A. No... .

"Q. Do you know Mike Boda?

MR. MOORE. The same exception?

THE COURT. Exception noted.

MR. KATZMANN. (Reading.)

"A. No.

"Q. Do you know Raphael Coacci?" [Ferruccio Coacci.]

MR. MOORE. I object to that, your Honor, for the same reason.

THE COURT. Unless there is some connection here shown with Coacci, it is of no consequence, Gentlemen, whether he knew him or not.

MR. KATZMANN. (Reading.)

"A. No.

"Q. Have you been to the Coacci house in West Bridgewater?
A. No." ... [845]

"Q. Were you ever in Hyde Park? A. No.

"Q. Were you ever in Needham? A. No."

If the witness Stewart were on the stand he would now testify that the defendant Vanzetti was at this point taken back to his cell, and another man was brought in, and that after Chief Stewart had a talk with this other man, the defendant Vanzetti was again brought back to him, and he asked him the following questions,—questions of the defendant Vanzetti:

(Mr. Katzmann continues reading.)

"Q. Do you remember that when you left the car in West Bridgewater, Sacco said you were in Elm Square? A. No.

"Q. Did you see Sacco go to a sign board, and when he came back he said he was in Elm Square? A. No. We didn't look at the sign. I saw no sign.... [846]

MR. KATZMANN. It is agreed, if your Honor please, that Chief Stewart, the same night at the Brockton police station, asked the following questions and received the following answers from the defendant Sacco, and that my reading of them is to have the same force and effect as if Mr. Stewart on the stand testified that he asked these questions and received these answers. It has the same force and effect as evidence.

(Mr. Katzmann reads as follows:)

"My name is Stewart. I am a police officer. I am going to ask you some questions, which you are not obliged to answer, and if you do answer, what you say may be used against you in court.

"Q. What is your name. A. Nicola Sacco....

"Q. Where do you live? A. South Stoughton.

"Q. Where do you work? A. 3-K....

"Q. Do you know Bartolomeo Vanzetti? A. Yes. He is my friend.

"Q. Was he visiting at your home today? A. Yes. He came to my house Tuesday.

"Q. Were you in West Bridgewater tonight? A. I think so. I am not sure. I don't know the place....

"Q. What time did you leave your house? A. After supper.... Maybe half past six.

"Q. What did you go to West Bridgewater for? A. My friend, Mr. Vanzetti, go to see his friend, and he asked me to come.

"Q. Who is his friend? A. I don't know. I never see him.

"Q. Did you see him [Poppy] tonight? A. No. We ride a long ways, and get off the car at Elm Square.

"Q. How did you know it was Elm Square? A. I read the sign.

"Q. What did you [do] then? A. We walked a long ways. We go to the square. My friend says we is too late, maybe his friend sleeping. So we walked back....

"Q. Who were the men on the motorcycle tonight in West Bridgewater?"

MR. MOORE. I object, your Honor. I reserve an exception.

THE COURT. What was the question? [847]

MR. KATZMANN. "Who were the men on the motorcycle tonight in West Bridgewater?"

THE COURT. What is the answer?

MR. KATZMANN. "A. I no see any motorcycle."

THE COURT. That may stand.

MR. MOORE. Reserve an exception.

MR. KATZMANN. (Reading resumed.)

"Q. Weren't you with some men on a motorcycle tonight?"

MR. MOORE. Objection.

MR. KATZMANN. (Reading.)

"A. No, I no see."

THE COURT. Exception noted.

MR. KATZMANN. (Reading.)

"Q. Do you know Mike Boda?"

MR. MOORE. The same objection, your Honor.

THE COURT. Exception noted.

MR. KATZMANN. (Reading.)

"A. No.

"Q. Ferruccio Coacci?"

MR. MOORE. The same objection, and exception.

THE COURT. Yes.

MR. KATZMANN. (Reading.)

"A. No."

THE COURT. ... At the present time Coacci has absolutely nothing to do with this case... .

[T]his evidence can be considered at the present time only against the defendant Sacco. It has no relevancy whatsoever against the defendant Vanzetti... .

MR. KATZMANN. (Reading.)

"Q. You had a revolver in your pocket when arrested?

MR. MOORE. Objection. [Moore was overruled and his exception was noted.] [848]

MR. KATZMANN. (Reading.)

"A. Yes... .

(Mr. Katzmann shows book from which he is reading to counsel for the defendants, and then continues reading as follows:) ... .

"Q. Where did you get the revolver you had?"

MR. MOORE. Same objection.

THE COURT. Admitted. Exception noted.

MR. KATZMANN. (Reading.)

"A. I buy a long time ago.

"Q. "Where?"

MR. MOORE. Objection.

THE COURT. Admitted, and exception noted.

MR. KATZMANN. (Reading.)

"A. Near Hanover Street in Boston. I don't know the name." ... .

(Michael E. Stewart again takes the witness stand, and his examination is resumed as follows:) [849]

Q. (By Mr. Williams) Mr. Stewart, how did you take the notes from which you have testified? A. The most of the Vanzetti conversation I wrote out as he talked; the conversation with the defendant Sacco I wrote either that night or the next morning. It is not clear to me which.... .

Cross-Examination.

Q. (By Mr. Jeremiah McAnarney) You have stated that in one instance here you wrote some out at night and that was about one o'clock, wasn't it? A. Sometime after midnight, I should judge.

Q. Sometime in the next day you wrote,—your memory jumps from what took place at midnight and put it into that book? A. I wrote the greater part of the Vanzetti——

Q. Pardon me. You did not write it all. One of them, you did not write all, I understand you.

A. Yes, I finished—

Q. Part of it you wrote the next day? A. Yes... . around nine o'clock in the morning.

Q. Substantially writing from recollection what was said the night before? A. Yes... .

Q. Well, you later rewrote it, did you not? A. I did, yes. [850]

Q. Where are the original notes you made that night about one o'clock? A. Destroyed.

Q. What? A. I destroyed them when I copied them... .

Q. Now, who do you say was there when you were going through this writing first?

A. Chief Davenport, of West Bridgewater. [851]

12. SUPERINTENDENTS KELLEY AND FRAHER

Mr. George T. Kelley, Sworn. June 20, 1921.

Q. (By Mr. Williams) Where do you live? A. Stoughton, Massachusetts.

Q. What is your business? A. Superindendent of a shoe factory.

Q. Known as what? A. 3-K Shoe Company.

[Ed. George Kelley is son of Michael Kelley. See Chapter 27.]

Q. Do you know the defendant Nicola Sacco? A. Yes, sir. [851]

Q. How long have you known him? A. I have known him for ten or twelve years.

Q. Was he employed at the 3-K in Stoughton, in the early spring and summer of 1920?

A. Yes, sir... .

Q. In what capacity was he employed? A. When he first went to work for us he was employed as an edge trimmer... Then he has worked taking care of the boiler nights, part time, not staying all night, but part time... .

Q. How near did you live to Sacco? A. Oh, probably one hundred feet, a little more... .

Q. Did Sacco work on Thursday, April 15th? A. No, sir.

Q. Had you had some talk prior to that day [April 15] about his being absent some day during the week? A. Yes, sir.

Q. Do you remember what day? A. ... Monday or Tuesday... . [N]ot any later than Tuesday.

Q. What was said by him and ... by you, Mr. Kelley? [Ed. Williams rejects Kelley's answer.] [852]

Q. Just say "He said" ... That is the proper way to testify to a conversation. A. Thank you. He said he would like to have one day off that week to go in to see the consul in regard to passports. I told him at that time that if he was caught up he may have the day off... . It went along about Wednesday, and he came to me and said he was going in to-morrow. That would be Thursday, and if possible, would be back again to his work Thursday, to which I said, "Very well... ."

Q. You say he did not work Thursday? A. He did not work Thursday, no, sir.

Q. Did he come back any time during the day? A. No, sir, not at the factory.

Q. That is what I mean. A. Yes. Do you want me to go about Friday?

Q. Yes. A. Then Friday morning I went to him early and asked him how he got along and he told me that he was trying to get back Thursday but on account of the crowd that was there waiting for passports, it was impossible for him to come out so he could get up to work Thursday afternoon... . I took the excuse as being all right... . [Ed. Kelley repeats this statement in Recall, p. 1684.]

Q. What kind of a cap have you seen him wearing? A. I have seen him wear a dark cap... .

Q. Well, have you in talking it over with anybody, described it in any different terms or more in detail than that? A. I have said of a salt and pepper design... .

Q. What have you seen in regard to this cap, if anything?

A. Nothing more than coming in to work and hanging it up on a nail. [853] [Ed. This is the Loring cap. See pp. 112, 136 in this handbook.]

Q. What can you tell us in regard to its condition? As to whether it was old or new clean or dirty? A. Why, I should say it was naturally dirty... .

Q. Do you know if anything had occurred to his cap by reason of being hung on a nail?

A. No, sir.

Q. Have you examined the lining of this cap? A. I did.

Q. What do you notice to be the condition of the lining? A. Torn.

Q. Do you know a man named Orciani? A. Yes, sir.

Q. When did you first see him to know him?

MR. MOORE. I object, your Honor.

A. I was introduced to him one night.

MR. KATZMANN. Wait, there is an objection.

MR. WILLIAMS. I beg your pardon.

THE COURT. You may answer.

MR. MOORE. Save an exception.

THE WITNESS. I was introduced to him one night, by Mr. Sacco.

Q. Where? A. In the back of my,——or in his yard.

Q. Whose yard? A. Mr. Sacco's.

Q. Do you know what night it was?

A. Well, it was a Monday or a Tuesday night, previous to the arrest, I think... .

Q. Did you see anything of a motorcycle that night? A. Yes, sir.

MR. MOORE. I object, your Honor.

Q. Did Sacco say anything about it?

MR. MOORE. Save an exception. [854]

THE COURT. Is this the statement of the defendant in regard to a motorcycle?

MR. WILLIAMS. Yes.

THE COURT. You may,—when was it?

MR. WILLIAMS. Two days or so before the arrest. There was an objection, I understand, to my previous question. I did not hear it clearly. The witness has answered. Perhaps we better go back, if your Honor please... .

[The question was read as follows:

"Q. Did you see anything of a motorcycle that night? A. Yes."]

THE COURT. The answer may stand.

MR. MOORE. Save an exception.

THE COURT. That is, "Yes, sir," he saw a motorcycle. That may stand.

MR. WILLIAMS. What was the next question?

[The question is read as follows:

"Q. Did Sacco say anything about it?"]

THE COURT. You may answer.

THE WITNESS. He made no comment on the motorcycle until I asked him.

THE COURT. What did he say? What did you say; what did he say? He is entitled to have just what the conversation was.

THE WITNESS. Yes, sir. I asked him why he didn't wear an overcoat.

Q. Asked who? A. Sacco. On account of its being a cool night, on account of riding in a motorcycle I asked him why he didn't have an overcoat. He said he did not intend to ride home with it, but he went to see his friend, who brought him home in the motorcycle.

Q. Do you know to whom he was referring when he said "his friend"? A. Orciani.

Q. Was Orciani there at the time? A. Yes, sir, he was there. He introduced me to him.

Q. Did you see that motorcycle at or around the factory or at or around Sacco's house before Sacco's arrest? ...first, ... that particular motorcycle, did it have any attachments to it by which you can describe it? A. Only a side car.

MR. MOORE. I object... .

THE COURT. You may answer.

MR. MOORE. Reserve an exception... .

Q. It had a side car. Do you know what color the motorcycle was?
A. Red. [855]

Q. Did you see a red motorcycle with a side car at Sacco's house again before Sacco's arrest?

A. Yes, sir.

Q. When? A. The day previous, I would say.

Q. The day previous to what? A. Of his arrest... .

Q. It is agreed here he [Sacco] was arrested on Wednesday, the 5th of May, late in the evening. A. Yes.

Q. Now, does that help you to recall the time you saw that motorcycle standing there?

A. I should say that motorcycle, to the best of my recollection, was there Wednesday afternoon.

Q. Do you know how long it was there that afternoon?

A. The greater part of the afternoon. I did not see it leaving the yard... .

Q. Any other time you seen the motorcycle there? A. I have seen it several times, but I couldn't say what dates they were. [856]

MR. WILLIAMS. If your Honor please, I offer this cap in evidence. It has been marked for identification, and I now offer it as an exhibit.

MR. JEREMIAH McANARNEY. I object... . [Ed. Court asked for rephrasing.]

Q. Mr. Kelley, ... is the cap I show you alike in appearance to the cap worn by Sacco?

A. In color only... . [Ed. Court said this answer was not responsive to the question.]

Q. In its general appearance, is it the same? A. Yes.

MR. WILLIAMS. I now offer the cap, if your Honor please.

THE COURT. Admitted.

MR. MOORE. Save an exception.

MR. JEREMIAH McANARNEY. Save an exception.

[The cap is admitted in evidence and marked "Exhibit 29."] [Ed. This is the Loring cap.]

MR. WILLIAMS. [Passing Exhibit 29 to the jury.] Notice the outside and inside. You may inquire. [857]

Cross-Examination.

Q. (By Mr. Jeremiah McAnarney) Well, you said you never saw this cap before?

A. I did not say any such thing. [857]

Q. Now, at one time, Sacco worked there, as you said, something as a watchman, or something?

A. Yes, sir. Nightwatchman. [858]

Q. Did you have any conversation with Sacco in reference to his procuring and having a gun with him while he was acting as watchman?

MR. KATZMANN. That may be answered yes or no.

Q. Whether you did yourself? A. No. [864]

Q. Specifically in regard to Sacco, what did you know about him [on gun ownership]?

A. I never knew he had a gun for the use of protecting the factory.

Q. I believe you said something about you knew he had a revolver or a gun?

A. But I did not know he was using it doing his duty. That is what I'm getting at... .

Q. I call your attention to this sheet of paper [showing to the witness] and ask you to recognize the handwriting. A. Yes, sir.

Q. That is whose handwriting? A. My sister's,—Margaret's.

Q. Your sister. And what does she do at the factory? A. She has charge of the payroll... .

Q. Now, would you glance through that and tell us how steady he worked, or, ... what time was he away from work, if you can get it easier that way, ...?

A. Well, ... the only time that he was out was the week of Christmas of 1920.

Q. You do not mean 1920, do you? A. Wait a minute... . [Witness examines record.] ... I think it was probably 1919, the Christmas of 1919. [866]

Redirect Examination.

Q. (By Mr. Williams) Do you recall any other day of his being out before this time during the year 1920? A. What do you mean, previous to Christmas or——

Q. No, no. I am referring to the year 1920. A. Yes.

Q. The next day he was out was the 15th day of April? A. Yes.

Q. Was there any other day that year, Mr. Kelley, before that time?

A. Yes. I think he was out one day previous to that.

Q. And when? A. It wasn't very,——probably a week.

Q. About the week before? A. I think so... .

Q. What makes you recall he was out about a week before?

A. Simply because there was some conversation about leaving one day a week or half a day... . He and I had an agreement he should take and get out as long as the work was kept up, and if my memory serves me right, after that conversation took place, why, I think he was out a day previous to that Thursday [April 15].

Q. And the last time he was before that, he was out was during the Christmas week of 1919?

A. Yes. [871] [Ed. This topic reappears in trial.]

[Ed. See the scholarly work by Paul Avrich, <u>Sacco and Vanzetti: The Anarchist Background</u> (Princeton, N.J., 1991), especially pp. 67-68. Note Avrich's references to George Kelley and the "elder Kelley" on p. 68. Later references to this book will be cited as Avrich.]

Tuesday, June 21, 1921.

THE COURT. It is agreed all the experts on guns may be present in court while the testimony is being offered. [873]

Mr. Thomas F. Fraher, Sworn. June 21, 1921.

Q. (By Mr. Williams) What is your business or occupation?

A. Superintendent, Slater & Morrill.

Q. Where were you at the time [of the shooting]?

A. On the upper,——in the upper factory, the same side as the railroad track... .

Q. Do you know a man named Bostock? A. James Bostock, yes.

Q. Shortly after the shooting, did Bostock deliver anything to you? A. Four empty shells.

Q. Shells of what general character?

A. Well, **four brass shells**; I should say they were .32 calibre.

Q. You took those shells? A. I took those shells.

Q. What did you do with them? A. I kept them until Captain Proctor of the state police arrived, and turned them over to him. [882]

Q. Were they delivered the same day to him?

A. The same day, about an hour and a half afterwards.

Q. Do you know what kind of head gear Berardelli and Parmenter had on the day of the shooting?

A. Soft felt hat.

Q. How long before the shooting did you see them?...

A... . Well, I had seen them more or less all that morning and at about noontime. [883]

Francis Russell's Letter, August 1, 1988
(Handwritten on Harvard Club of Boston stationery)

Sandwich, 1: VIII 88

Dear Mr. Newby--

Thank you for your letters & enclosures. Long ago I wrote to the Enc. Americana editor, suggested an update on the S-V case (I did the Hardy update for them). Instead they got a senile old partisan (himself a decent enough man--alas, his name for the moment escapes me) to write the piece.

I think the best approach to those reference areas is to state the cold facts without comment--the ballistics tests, Tresca's admission, Gambera's confession, etc. Eventually the truth will have to out. You may be interested to know that shortlly before his death Judge Wyzanski wrote me a long letter saying I had convinced him of Sacco's guilt. He did add, though, that because of Proctor's testimony he still considered the trial unfair.

An English priest sent me the TLS. Just the old pre-conceived notions, held with such emotional intensity. I also saw Avrich's review, again from one emotionally impervious to facts.

You ask about D'Attilio. He is an amiable nobody who lives obscurely & fiddles round with the "great book." He does know a lot about Italian anarchists but will not accept the factuality of the FBI files and maintains that deep in the archives are hidden proofs of innocence. (Signed. Sincerely, Francis Russell)
[Ed. The "senile old partisan" is Fraenkel. Reference to the TLS is Brogan's review, p. 571. See Avrich's review, p. 577. See Wyzanski, p. 630. See p. 560.]

134

13. THE COMMONWEALTH'S BALLISTICS EXPERTS

Mr. William H. Proctor, Sworn. June 21, 1921.

Q. (By Mr. Williams) Are you connected in some way with the state police? A. I am.

Q. And in what capacity? A. I am Captain in the Department of Public Safety, in charge of the Division of State Police. [884]

Q. At some time, Captain, after the South Braintree shooting, did you go to South Braintree and to Brockton? A. I did.

Q. And did you receive at South Braintree and at Brockton certain articles? A. I did.

Q. Do you know Mr. Fraher of the Slater & Morrill Company? A. I do.

Q. Did you receive anything from Mr. Fraher? A. I did.

Q. What did you receive from him?

MR. JEREMIAH McANARNEY. That I object to, if your Honor please, for the sake of the record.

Q. You may answer, Captain. A. I received four empty shells.

THE COURT. That may be stricken out. I sustain that objection.

MR. WILLIAMS. The question, if your Honor please—

THE COURT. I will see counsel at the desk.

MR. WILLIAMS. These are cartridges, four cartridges were found at the scene of the shooting.

THE COURT. Shells,—he means cartridge shells? All right. That may stand.

Q. Will you look at the envelope which I am now showing you and ask you if you can identify what is found inside (handing envelope to the witness)? A. I can.

Q. And what are they ...? A. They were given me by Thomas Fraher at the Slater & Morrill factory at East Braintree,—South Braintree, on April 15, 1920.

Q. And have they been in your possession since that time?

A. Until I turned them over to the sheriff in this court.

THE COURT. The witness has testified, as I recall it, of picking up some shells.

135

MR. WILLIAMS. Mr. Bostock testified to picking them up and he turned them over to Mr. Fraher and Mr. Fraher to Mr. Proctor.

THE COURT. All right.

(Mr. Williams shows the shells to counsel for the defense.)

MR. WILLIAMS. I offer these, if your Honor please.

MR. JEREMIAH McANARNEY. They are excepted to, if your Honor please.

THE COURT. Admitted.

(Four empty shells are admitted in evidence and marked "**Exhibit 30**.") [885]

Q. Now, Captain, will you look at those **four** empty shells ... and tell the jury what they are? A. (Witness examines shells.) ... These are shells ... ammunition adapted to automatic pistols, 32 calibre. There are **two Peters** and **one U. M. C.**, and **one W. R. A.**, **Winchester**... .

[Ed. The Winchester shell is called **Shell W**, the W.R.A. Fraher spent cartridge of Bullet 3.]

Q. ... What is "U. M. C."? A. That is the Remington, Union Metallic Cartridge Company... .

Q. ... Are they [the four empty shells] all 32 calibre? A. They are. [886]

Q. Now, Captain, did you receive any articles purporting to have been connected with this shooting at the Brockton police station? A. I did.

Q. And where and in what manner did you receive them? A. I received them upstairs in the Brockton police station. John Scott,—— State Officer Scott was present, and some Boston,——Brockton police officer handed them to him and he to me.

Q. And what were they?

A. The automatic pistol in question, and some cartridges, automatic cartridges, 32-calibre.

Q. Do you remember how many of the automatic cartridges there were? A. 32.

Q. What kind of automatic pistol was it? A. It was this pistol (indicating).

Q. A Colt automatic? A. A Colt automatic.

Q. Has that been in your possession since then? A. Until I turned it over to the sheriff here.

Q. Will you look at this envelope of cartridges and see if you can identify those (handing envelope to the witness)? A. (Witness examines envelope.) That is the same envelope and it looks like the same amount of cartridges. I can tell by counting them.

Q. Were they in your possession until delivered to the sheriff?

A. They were. [887]

Q. Have you examined those cartridges, Captain? A. I have looked them over.

Q. Now, will you tell the jury of what makes those cartridges are and how many of each make are contained in the envelope? A. There are four different makes. There is a Peters, a Remington,—U.M.C., and there is a Winchester, say W.R.A. [Ed. Error is corrected below.]

Q. Instead of just giving the initials will you give the full names of the makes of those cartridges? Go a little slower. A. On the **16**, Peters Cartridge Company; **3** Remington U.M.C. Cartridge Company; **7** United States Cartridge Company and **6** Winchester Cartridge Company, made by Winchester Arms Company, Repeating Arms Company, the full name.

MR. WILLIAMS. I offer these.

(32 cartridges are admitted in evidence and marked "Exhibit 31.")

MR. JEREMIAH McANARNEY. Save our exception to the admission.

THE COURT. Admitted. Just one question. When you say, Captain, the police officer handed them over to you, to Captain Sccott and Captain Scott handed them over to you, were the shells handed over to Captain Scott in your presence? ... .

THE WITNESS. They were [handed over "at the same time"].

THE COURT. All right. Admitted.

Q. What calibre are those, did you tell us? A. 32.

Q. Now, did you receive a revolver at any time? A. I did.

Q. When? A. At the same time.

Q. That is this revolver which is Exhibit 27. That is right? A. Yes. [Ed. Vanzetti's revolver.]

Q. Did you receive in connection with that revolver any revolver cartridges, lead cartridges?

A. I did.

Q. Were they in the revolver or separate? A. Separate.

Q. Were you handed those at the same time those other things were given you? A. I was.

Q. I show you these cartridges and ask you if you can identify them (handing cartridges to the witness)? A. (Witness examines cartridges.) I can identify the envelope, and the cartridges look just about the same.

Q. Were they in your possession until you turned them over to the sheriff? A. They were.

(Mr. Williams shows cartridges to counsel for the defense.)

MR. JEREMIAH McANARNEY. I assume they are.

MR. WILLIAMS. I offer these five revolver cartridges, if your Honor please.

MR. JEREMIAH McANARNEY. We object, if your Honor please.

[888]

THE COURT. Your objection goes to the competency of the evidence, I take it, rather than to any question about the identification? In other words that the pistol was the pistol found upon the person of one of the defendants at the time of his arrest?

MR. JEREMIAH McANARNEY. I do not question that, if your Honor please.

THE COURT. That is what I want to get at.

MR. JEREMIAH McANARNEY. I do not question that.

THE COURT. And there is no question about the—what they call the revolver that was found on the person of Mr. Vanzetti?

MR. JEREMIAH McANARNEY. Pardon me a moment, your Honor. As to the revolver or the pistol, there is no question there as to the identity, but as to the identity of some of these unmarked shells, I would not waive any rights there.

THE COURT. All right. Then you must bear that in mind with reference to evidence tending to prove identity. I do not know but you have.

MR. WILLIAMS. If I have not, I will try to check it up later, if your Honor please.

THE COURT. All right.

MR. WILLIAMS. This exhibit becomes Exhibit 32, five revolver cartridges.

(Five revolver cartridges admitted in evidence and marked "Exhibit 32.")

[Ed. 5 bullets from Vanzetti's gun. Sheriff gave envelope holding bullets to McAnarney, p. 774.]

Q. Will you look at those cartridges, Captain, and describe them to the jury? Go slow, ...

(Mr. Williams hands the witness a magnifying glass, who examines cartridges through same.)

THE WITNESS. There are two. Those are S. & W. cartridges, 38 calibre. **Two** of them are made by the Union Metallic Cartridge Company,—Remington Union Metallic Cartridge Company. The other **three** are made by the United States Cartridge Company... .

Q. Captain, I now show you Exhibits 19, 20, 21, 24 and 25, which are bullets testified to by physicians as being found in the body or bodies [889] of the victims of this shooting. Will you look at bullet No. 1 first and tell the jury what kind of a bullet that is, the make, ...

A. That is a full—

Q. Let me ask you first, Captain, you have examined at the request of the District Attorney those bullets before going on the stand, have you not? A. I have.

Q. And have examined them, yes. A. That (indicating) is a full metal patch bullet, 32 calibre, adapted to auto cartridges. That is, cartridges fired in an auto pistol.

Q. When you say "auto" what do you mean? A. Automatic. And my opinion is that it is Winchester make... .

Q. Will you tell the jury through what make and type of gun, in your opinion that bullet [bullet No. 1] has been fired? A. A Savage.

Q. Now, what is the basis for your opinion in that respect?

A. By measuring the width of the grooves on the bullet caused by the lands in the pistol.

Q. Now, what are the "lands" in the pistol? A. The "lands" are the raised-up places in the pistol that have grooves between them, and when a bullet is pushed in the pistol, when it goes through the pistol, it gives it a twist, holds the bullet and it is given a twist coming out of the barrel.

Q. Can you open up that pistol so that I can allow the jury to look through it and see just what you mean by referring to the raised portions of the barrel? (Witness opens up pistol.) Those raised up portions and the other lowered portions of the barrel are what is commonly referred to as the rifling? A. Yes. [890]

(Court officer leaves the room and gets magnifying glass.)

(Mr. Williams passes pistol barrel to jurors, who examine it with a magnifying glass.) ... .

Q. You say those raised portions we see in the barrel are the lands?

A. Yes.

Q. And what do those lands do to a bullet when it is pushed or fired through the barrel?

A. The lands make a groove on the bullet. It reverses where the groove is in the pistol... .

Q. Now, on a Savage what is the width of the lands?

A. It makes a groove on the bullet .035 of an inch.

Q. ... [A]nd what sort of a twist does a Savage automatic pistol give to the bullet?

A. Right-hand. In standing the bullet up, it slants to the right.

Q. Now, have you measured the width of the groove on No. 1 bullet?

A. I have.

Q. What is the width of the groove made by the lands of the barrel? A. .035 of an inch.

Q. And in which direction is the twist on the bullet? A. Right-hand.

Q. ... Is there any other gun which makes a .035 groove on a bullet and a twist to the right?

A. There is not... .

Q. How certain can you be then of your opinion that that bullet was fired from a Savage automatic 32? A. I can be as certain of that as I can of anything. [891]

[Ed. Proctor testified that bullet 2, bullet 4, bullet 5 [892] and bullet 6—were all fired by a Savage automatic pistol, 32 calibre, each one with a right-hand twist.] [893]

Q. Now, I call your attention, Captain, to Bullet No. 3, and ask you if you will look at it and tell us if you have an opinion as to the make and type of weapon from which that weapon [bullet] was fired? A. I have.

Q. And what is your opinion? A. That it is a Winchester make, W.R.A., and that it was fired by a Colt automatic revolver, 32 calibre or pistol, I mean... .

Q. What is the basis of your opinion? A. In the first place this bullet has got a left-hand twist instead of a right. In the second place, the grooves made by the pistol while passing through on this bullet are .060 of an inch... .

Q. ... .Do you know of any other automatic pistol that gives a groove of the width of .060 of an inch? A. I do not... .

MR. WILLIAMS. (To the jury) I show you bullet No. 3, gentlemen, and ask you to note the left-hand slant to those grooves, ...

Q. How do you ascertain that [Bullet 3] is a W. R. A. bullet? A. ... [I]n that particular bullet it is the "W" which is above the cannon-lure, one of the ends of the grooves that distinguishes the Winchester bullet. They put "W" on their bullets. [893]

Q. ... There is a "W" above the what? A. Above the cannon-lure. That is the ring that goes around it.

MR. KATZMANN. Exhibit number [of Bullet 3]?

MR. WILLIAMS. 18.

(Short recess.)

MR. WILLIAMS. I don't know whether you can see this, gentlemen, but you will notice the "W". You see, gentlemen, this bullet here lop-sided, so that there is more or less of a pronounced point, a sharp bend, and that "W" appears right above—... .

(The bullet is examined by the jury.)

Q. Captain, did you participate in some experiments with the Colt automatic which is in evidence, at Lowell on Saturday where there were present Captain van Amberg, representing the District Attorney, and also Mr. Burns, representing the defense? A. I did. [June 18,1921]

Q. **Mr. Burns** is the gentleman seated beside **Mr. McAnarney**?

A. Yes.

Q. What was the character of the experiments there carried on by you three gentlemen? A. We fired the automatic pistol in the case [Sacco's Colt] into sawdust, and we recovered the bullets themselves, that sprung from the pistol. I got six empty shells that I picked up that came from the pistol.

Q. How many— A. Then van Amberg fired six and Mr. Burns fired eight.

Q. And did you recover the shells from the six cartridges which you and Captain van Amberg fired? A. I did. [Ed. Proctor did no firing. See Transcript: 897.]

Q. Have you them there? A. I have.

Q. Will you produce them?

(The witness produces some shells,)

Q. (Continued) What make of cartridges did you and Captain van Amberg fire?

A. There were three W. R. A. and three Peters.

Q. When you say "W. R. A." do you mean Winchester Repeating Arms? A. Winchester.

141

Q. What kind of a bullet would you say bullet No. 3 was?
A. W. R. A. Winchester Repeating Arms Company. [894]

[Ed. Williams questions Proctor on Shell W, the spent cartridge of Bullet 3.]

Q. Now, will you examine that W.R.A., that we will call for the minute the Fraher shell [Shell W], and compare it with the **six** shells fired by you and Captain van Amberg, of which, I understand, three are W.R.A. and three are Peters, and ask you if, in your opinion, the marks on those **seven shells** are consistent with being fired from the same weapon?
A. I think so, the same make of weapon.
Q. And on what do you base that opinion? A. Well, there is a similarity between the W.R.A.
[Shell W] and the other cartridges that were fired.
Q. A similarity where? A. In the looks of the hole in the primer, which does not exist with the other three.

MR. WILLIAMS. Now, gentlemen, I wish when you pass these around you would keep these six in the right hand, and keep this, which is the so-called Fraher shell [Shell W], in the left, just keep them apart, and compare the holes made in the primer on those six Lowell shells with the one Fraher shell [Shell W] ... I will let you look at the Peters shells first in comparison with that [Shell W]. I am sorry to be so slow, if your Honor please, but I am afraid it cannot be avoided.

THE COURT. All right.

MR. WILLIAMS. ...If any of you want the microscope, I have it here.

(The jury examines the shells.)

MR. WILLIAMS. I now, gentlemen, wish to show you the so-called Fraher shell, which is a Winchester [Shell W], and at the same time to examine the three Winchesters fired at Lowell by this Colt automatic [the Sacco gun]. So there will be no confusion, I am going to ask the consent of the defendants if I may [895] have a slight scratch on the Fraher shell [W], simply for the purpose of identification.

MR. McANARNEY. That is exhibit what?

MR. WILLIAMS. That is **one of four** in Exhibit 30. Now, gentlemen, will you examine the Fraher Winchester shell [Shell W], and compare it with the three Lowell Winchester shells which, if you recall, were shot [June 18, 1921] from the Colt Automatic [the Sacco gun] in evidence? Notice the size of the hole in the primer made by the firing pin, and also notice the position of the hole in the primers of all four shells with reference to the middle of the primer.

(Mr. Williams shows the shell to the jury.)

MR. WILLIAMS. If your Honor please, I offer these six shells fired at Lowell.

MR. McANARNEY. No objection, if your Honor please... .

(The three Peters shells are placed in an envelope marked Exhibit 33, and the three Winchesters in an envelope marked Exhibit 34.)

Q. Captain Proctor, have you an opinion as to whether bullets Nos. 1, 2, 5 and 6 were fired from the same weapon? A. I have not... . [897: Proctor—"all five were fired from the same pistol."]

Q. Have you an opinion as to whether bullet 3 was fired from the Colt Automatic which is in evidence? A. I have.

Q. And what is your opinion?

A. My opinion is that it is **consistent with** being fired by that pistol. [896]

Q. How many lands are there to a Savage automatic? A. Six.

Q. And by the "lands" again you mean the raised—the ridges in the barrel? A. Yes.

Q. So, I take it, it must necessarily be that there are six grooves in the bullet? A. Yes.

Q. Caused by those lands? A. Yes... .

Q. What bullets did you take? A. One and two. [Ed. Two of the six murder bullets.]

MR. WILLIAMS. I ask you to notice the marks on those two bullets.

(Mr. Williams shows the bullets to the jury.)

Q. While the jury are examining those bullets,—Have you got the six bullets which were fired by you and Captain van Amberg at Lowell? A. I have not.

Q. Who has those? A. Van Amberg has three.

Q. ... I will introduce them when he is called. Have you any of them? A. I have three.

Q. Well, I will take the three that you have.

(The witness produces the bullets.)

Q. (Continued) Are those the three that were fired by you?

A. He fired the gun, but I stood right there and picked them up. [Ed. Proctor did no firing.]

Q. These are three what, what kind of bullets? A. Winchester.

MR. WILLIAMS. I offer these three Winchester bullets fired by Captain van Amberg at Lowell. They will be marked Exhibit 35... .
(The three bullets are placed in an envelope and marked Exhibit 35.)
[897]

Charles Van Amburgh, Sworn. June 21, 1921.

Q. (By Mr. Williams) What is your occupation or profession, Captain?
A. At present, I am an assistant in the ballistic department, Remington U. M. C. Company.
Q. And where are you located? A. In Bridgeport, Connecticut.
Q. Captain, would you give us briefly your experience in reference to firearms and ammunition for firearms, ...? A. For nine years I was connected with the Springfield Armory,—that is, eight years of it at Springfield Armory, ... one year at Frankford Arsenal, Philadelphia, ...
Q. Will you indicate ... the nature of the work which you there did, beginning with Springfield? A. The Springfield Armory, experimental work. That is, the experimental department, experimental firing with rifles, mainly military rifles and automatic pistols, machine guns. Also inspected ammunition... . [I]nspectors were frequently detailed from there to visit ammunition factories ... under contract for ammunition for the United States Government, and I at one time was detailed on such an errand. [911] One year at Frankford Arsenal, entirely in the testing of ammunition. Leaving there, I was with the New England Westinghouse Company for about two years, in the manufacture of the Russian rifle, in the test department, by the way. I was assistant proof master... . I was about one year in the employ of the Colt Patent Firearms Company in one of their branch plants,—Meriden, Connecticut, ... Then I went,—accepted a commission in the Army... .
Q. How long were you in the Army? A. One and one half years. I was instructor in small arms firing or marksmanship with rifle and pistol. Upon discharge, I went with the Remington U. M. C. Company in ballistic work, which I might explain pertains to tests of arms and ammunition, ballistic.
Q. You are still employed? A. Still employed. [912]
[Ed. Witness gave width of land and groove and weight of bullets 1, 2, 4, 5, 6: pp. 912-914.]
Q. ... Will you now take bullet number three and describe that to the jury. A. Bullet number three measures across the land of the bullet

between .107 and .108; across the groove of the bullet about .060 of an inch.

Q. ... [W]hat in general is the nature of rifling in barrels of guns, and what result does it have upon the course and flight of the bullet? A. Rifling is necessary to give rotation to the bullet; otherwise the bullet would fly out and would naturally tumble end over end. The rifling imparts rotation.... [915].

Q. Something has been said here about a twist to a bullet.

A. Twist is ... another name for spiral.

Q. Which way does the rifling of a gun twist the bullet? A. If the inclination of a rifling is to the right, that is, clockwise, ... then we speak of it being a right twist.

Q. And what mark would be made on the bullet by that right twist?

A. They will be inclined to the right, as we look at the bullet in front of us.

Q. From the base to the nose? A. From the base to the nose. And if the direction is counter-clockwise, ... we would say then our bullet would rotate to the left.

Q. Can you tell us what make that number three bullet is? A. Number three bullet, I believe, is positively identified as a Winchester Repeating Arms Company make.

Q. And what is your reason for making that positive identification?

A. There is a letter W on the bullet, which is a point which is peculiar to bullets of Winchester make,——jacketed bullets.

Q. Have you an opinion as to the type and make of weapon from which number three was fired?

A. I have.

Q. And what is your opinion? A. I believe number three bullet was fired from a Colt barrel. That is to say, Colt automatic pistol.

Q. ... [Y]ou mentioned ... where you had worked, the Colt Rapid Firearms Company, ... Is that the company that manufactures the Colt automatic? A. It is. [916]

Q. ... [W]hat is your basis for the opinion you have formed as to the type and make of weapon from which number three was fired?

A. Well, the left inclination ... . the rifling marks on our [#3] bullet indicates clearly that it was fired from a barrel having a left twist... .

Q. Are the five other bullets, ... I mean those other than number three, which I understand you have examined, from their physical appearance consistent with the fact of their having been fired from a Savage or from Savage automatic pistols? A. I would say that they are.

Q. Have you an opinion, Captain, as to whether those other five bullets, and I mean one, two, four, five and six, were fired from the same weapon? A. I believe that they were.

Q. What is the basis for your belief? A. There are peculiar markings on numbers one, two, four, five and six, which seem to occur so uniformly and on all, it inclines me to the belief strongly that they were fired from the same or through the same barrel. [917]

[Ed. After recess, testimony resumed with Mr. Moore absent, McAnarney not objecting.]

Q. Will you describe No. 3 bullet as to calibre and kind? A. No. 3 bullet, I believe, is from the 32 calibre automatic cartridge.

Q. What is the general characteristics of all those six [murder] bullets? A. They are all from 32 calibre automatic cartridges.... .

Q. Have you compared, Captain van Amburgh, No. 3 and its markings, with the markings on the six bullets which you and Captain Proctor fired from that Colt automatic at Lowell on Saturday? A. I have.

Q. Have you compared the [four] shells called the "Fraher" shells, those that are purported to have been **found in the street** in South Braintree— A. I have. [Ed. Exhibit 30.]

Q. —with the shells which you have retained from the bullets fired at Lowell?

A. Yes, sir. [918]

Q. What have you there? A. I have the four Fraher shells. [Ed. 4 shells found by Bostock.]

MR. McANARNEY. I don't hear you.

A. I have the **four Fraher shells**; I would like the six others [Lowell shells] for comparison.

Q. My question, Captain, was as to any similarity between any one of the so-called Fraher shells with the shells from the bullets fired by you and Captain Proctor at Lowell? A. There is one of these so-called Fraher shells, the one marked "W. R. A. Co." [Shell W], meaning Winchester Repeating Arms Company, and three that were fired in Lowell, W.R.A. Co., shells, a very strong similarity.

Q. Will you step down before the jury, and show what that similarity consists of?

A. Shall I explain it?

Q. Yes.... . A. The indentation is off centre slightly.

Q. Is what? A. Is off-centre slightly in all four. [Ed. Shell W and 3 Lowell Winchester shells.]

(The witness leaves the stand, and explains to the jury.)

THE WITNESS. They are about the same diameter and depth, that is the distinguishing mark. The principal distinguishing mark is the same diameter, the uniformity of diameter.

(The witness returns to the stand.)

Q. And is there any other distinguishing mark which you noticed on those four? A. There is.

Q. And what is that? A. In addition to the similarity in diameter, there is a slight set-back, so-called—A shop term, by the way—which means a slowing back of the metal around the point or end of the firing pin. That is present in the so-called Fraher shell [Shell W] and in the three Winchester shells which were fired at Lowell.

Q. ... I wish you would take the Colt and illustrate [what is meant by set-back].

A. It would be difficult to illustrate with either the pistol or the revolver.

Q. Well, illustrate with a diagram or anything, Captain, ... what a set-back is.

A. I could with a diagram, the idea, perhaps.

(Witness makes a sketch.)

Q. You may step down right in front of the jury, if you will, Captain.... (The witness leaves the stand.) [919]

THE WITNESS. A set-back on a primer is a little flowing back of the metal beyond the true surface.... that portion of it which is bearing against the **breech block**.

Q. What is the **breech block**? A. That is the point from which the firing pin protrudes.

Q. The firing pin comes through the breech block? A. It does.

Q. And strikes the cartridge? A. It does.

Q. Similar to the way my finger is now indicating?

A. Yes. The set-back takes place around the firing pin sometimes. It did in this case.

Q. And what causes the set-back? A. Largely, a little opening—In my experience, I have found it to be usually a little opening in the mouth of the firing pin hole. Do I make that clear?

Q. Is that something that occurs in all guns?

A. It is not an unusual thing, but it does not occur in all guns.

147

Q. Does it have anything to do with the Colt revolver or Colt pistol?

A. It doesn't happen in all Colt pistols.

Q. Now, how does that set-back evidence itself on the shells? A. A little ridge of metal is showing around the rim of the hole made by the end of the firing pin.

MR. WILLIAMS. Now, one I am showing is the Fraher cartridge [Shell W], and one a shell fired at Lowell, both Winchesters. Will you notice, gentlemen, the little ridge around the hole of the firing pin... .

Q. ... Have you formed an opinion, Captain, as to whether or not No. 3 bullet was fired from that particular Colt automatic? A. I have an opinion.

Q. And what is your opinion? A. **I am inclined to believe** that it was fired, No. 3 bullet was fired, from this Colt automatic pistol. [920]

Q. And when you say "this", you mean the one that you have before you? A. The one I have before me. [Ed. Colt automatic pistol taken from Sacco at Brockton police station.]

Q. Now, what is the basis for your opinion, Captain, or bases? A. My measurements of rifling marks on No. 3 bullet as compared with the width of the impressions which I have taken of No. 3 or of this particular barrel, together with the measurements of the width or dimension of rifling marks in bullets recovered from oiled sawdust in Lowell, inclines me to the belief.

Q. Now, what marks have you observed which occasioned you to have that belief?

A. You mean, in addition to the dimensions of rifling marks?

Q. Yes, I mean, are there any peculiarities or irregularities of those bullets which you have observed which assist you to form an opinion? A. There are.

Q. And will you describe them to the jury? A. There are irregularities evidently caused by similar scoring or irregular marks in rifling which appear on all bullets which I have examined that I know have been fired from this one automatic pistol which is before me.

Q. Yes. And what about No. 3? A. No. 3 bullets, I find on No. 3 bullets such evidence of scoring in the barrel. It takes on the bullets the form of a, well, a long streak bordering close on the narrow cut, the land cut, on the bullet.

Q. Is there anything in the barrel of that revolver which can be shown to the jury so they can see it which will help them to understand what you mean by irregularities caused by something in the pistol? A. I believe it can be shown to the jury.

Q. ... [S]how it, if you will, and I will manipulate any lighting apparatus which is necessary. You are at liberty to step down from the witness stand and do anything that is necessary.

(The witness leaves the stand.)

THE WITNESS. It is a difficult matter to point it out. I can indicate it.

MR. WILLIAMS. If you can tell them what you see in there, then, possibly, by looking themselves they will be able to see part at least of what you see.

THE WITNESS. Close to the land which is now on the bottom portion of the bore of the barrel, on the right side as you look in, you will see a rough track.

MR. WILLIAMS. Would a microscope assist?

THE WITNESS. It might.

MR. WILLIAMS. Mr. Katzmann suggests that the jury be allowed one by one to go to the window and look at the bullet.

THE COURT. I would suggest that the witness go to the window and see if it may be explained better at the window.

THE WITNESS. I believe the light is better. [921]

MR. WILLIAMS. You can hold it in proper position. The jury may step up one by one.

THE COURT. Explain to the jury what you have in mind, but explain it in such a way that all can hear.

MR. WILLIAMS. Did you hear, Captain, the Judge's suggestion?

(The jurors go one by one to the window to examine the barrel as shown by the witness.)

THE WITNESS. On the bottom portion of the barrel as you look into it, beside that land on the right side of it is a rough track, at the bottom of the barrel... .

THE COURT. Mr. Foreman, you might come right around and be ready, and then follow right around so you will be there.

THE WITNESS. On the bottom a rough track At the bottom of the barrel is a rough track.

(The witness returns to the witness stand.)

Q. Captain, what, in your opinion, has caused that rough track which you have just been showing? A. This appears to be what is generally known as a pit. I really believe that it is caused by allowing powder

149

fowling [sic] to stand in the barrel, and the matter of rust allowed to stand and eat its way in, and finally pits occur.

Q. What effect does it have on bullets? A. The bullet has got to drag—If it touches, expands to barrel size, it has got to drag along. It will be scored in travelling over a rough track.

Q. And have you found on those bullets you have been speaking of marks corresponding with the rough track which you have shown to the jury? A. I have.

Q. I notice that you showed to the jury what you designated as "a rough track". Is there more than one rough track in the barrel?

A. Yes. There is a general—Yes. I would say there are quite a few streaks of roughness and quite a collection of pits in there, but it seems to be more pronounced in the corner of the groove in the barrel the corner of the groove.

Q. Are there any marks upon the bullets consistent with the tracks which you have seen in the barrel? A. I know of no others, I can think of no others, that I have noticed, for the moment, other than those caused by those rough tracks in the barrel.

Q. And how many of those are there on the bullets?

A. There seems to be one which has impressed me very much, one streak along each bullet fired through this exhibit gun [Sacco's]—very pronounced. Others are not so prominent. [922]

Cross-Examination.

Q. (By Mr. McAnarney) What do you mean by "pitting"?

A. Pitting is the effect of rust.... [923]

Q. I show you, marched for identification, "15", a series of pictures....

Q. (Continued) Would you glance at those, ... A. Is there a question?

Q. Mr. Witness, those purport to be six different views of the same six bullets.

[Ed. Photos of the 6 murder bullets cited on p. 225 & transcript 1406.]

MR. KATZMANN. Mr. McAnarney, do you mean 36 pictures?

MR. McANARNEY. No, six pictures.... Each picture is a different bullet.... Six different bullets and six different pictures....

Q. You may look at the whole set, but examine 1, 3 and 4 carefully.

A. I have examined them.

Q. Now, are you able to form an opinion as to what kind of bullets those are, from what shell? A. Not what kind of bullets they are, no, sir.

Q. Or from what shell they came from? A. No sir, I wouldn't be able to form an opinion from the pictures, ... No, I can't form an opinion as to classification; I can't classify them as to calibre or anything of that sort. [925]

Q. Did you measure that automatic gun [the Sacco gun]? A. Did I measure the automatic?

Q. Yes. A. In what respect?

Q. What are the lands, the diameter? What are the diameters of the lands in that Colt automatic? A. Diameter of the lands, do I get you clearly?

Q. Well, the widths of the lands? A. The width of the lands. From measurements made, I believe the width of the lands to be about 60/1000... .

Q. Now, what instrument did you measure that with?

A. I used a scale, dividers, micrometer and depth gauges. [930]

Q. You understand I am talking about the gun? A. My understanding is, you mean the barrel.

Q. Now, what is the width of the groove? A. 107/1000 of an inch.

Q. What is the diameter of the groove? A. The diameter of the groove, .3115.

Q. What is the diameter of the lands? A. I didn't get the diameter of the lands or bore measure.

Q. Well, did you overlook that? A. I overlooked it. I didn't consider it important, because——

Q. The lands in your gun make the grooves upon the bullet, don't they? A. It makes the little groove on the bullet.

Q.... You say you overlooked it, is that right? A. I didn't measure the diameter between lands.

Q. Give us the diameter of the lands of the bullets fired at Lowell?

A. Do I understand now you mean the lands of the bullets representing the grooves in the barrel?

Q. Yes, that is right. A. I made them to be across their greatest diameter about .311.

Q. What was the width of the land? A. I made the width to be about .107.

Q. ... The test was made with the exhibit gun [Sacco's gun]?

A. Yes. [931]

Q. Do you know of any left-hand twists 32 automatic other than a Colt? A. I haven't met up with any in my experience... .

Q. Now, as to the Savage gun, do you know of any other gun the same width of land and groove as the Savage? A. I haven't observed any.

Q. Are you acquainted with the Steyr gun? A. I am not familiar with it.

Q. Are you familiar with the Bayard automatic? A. I have heard of it, but have not found any. Those are foreign guns you have mentioned.

Q. Don't you know there were a lot brought back from overseas?

A. I haven't seen any.

Q. Are you acquainted with the Stauer? A. I have not handled a 32 Stauer. [933]

Redirect Examination.

Q. (By Mr. Williams) Why could you not tell the kinds and make of bullets from the photographs which were shown to you, Mr. Van Amburgh? A. The photograph does not enable me to visualize an article... in any detail as fine as here on those bullets... .[S]mall details on [933] bullets...are sometimes not present in photographs.

Q. Do you know of any gun which combines a left twist with lands of .061 in width? A. I don't know of any. [934]

Q. Now, I find I have omitted to put in the three bullets which you shot and which I understand Captain Proctor and you have in your possession. Are these the bullets shot by you?

A. They are the three bullets fired at Lowell.

Q. Those are what make? A. Those are the Peters.

Q. Captain Proctor fired the Winchesters? A. Captain Proctor fired the Winchesters.

MR. WILLIAMS. I offer these three bullets.

[Ed. See transcript, 897. Proctor did no firing.]

THE COURT. They may be admitted. [935]

(The three Peters bullets are placed in an envelope and marked Exhibit 36.) [936]

14. CONCLUSION OF COMMONWEALTH CASE

THE COURT. I see Dr. Magrath is here. I believe he was to be asked one or two more questions.

MR. WILLIAMS. We shall not call him tonight.

THE COURT. Then, having reached the hour of five—Before the jury goes out, I would like to have the exhibits taken care of. May I ask you, Mr. District Attorney, about when will the prosecution finish its evidence, with a view of giving information to counsel for the defendants, so that they may be ready at that time.

MR. KATZMANN. Except for the matter that is involved in a private conference at the bench with your Honor, which has been ruled upon finally by your Honor, we will immediately determine, and we believe we have nothing further to offer. We will determine that by looking over our notes. We think not, but we will have to have a conference with your Honor on that matter in abeyance.

THE COURT. I suppose now is the appointed time?

MR. KATZMANN. At some cooler place.

THE COURT. Now, Mr. Williams, you may examine that later, if you please. I want to let the jurors go, and I want to hear at the bench what this question is.

MR. WILLIAMS. I was not delaying things. The Captain is simply putting the gun together.

THE COURT. Now, are the exhibits all out of the way?

MR. WILLIAMS. Yes.

THE COURT. You may go until tomorrow, gentlemen, at ten o'clock.

(The jury retires.)

THE COURT. Now, I will hear counsel.

(Conference at the bench.)

THE COURT. I asked Mr. McAnarney if he recalls anything where I admitted evidence to be introduced by the commonwealth tending to prove certain matters upon which the competency of the evidence depended. Mr. McAnarney says that he recalls nothing. I wanted to say I want to keep my word by striking out such evidence if there was any failure on the part of the commonwealth to furnish such evidence. Mr. McAnarney says he recalls nothing, but he went on to state—Go ahead, about the cap. There was evidence tending—

MR. McANARNEY. I understand your Honor has admitted the cap.

THE COURT. Do you recall anything else? [Ed. Inference shows the cap, #29, was admitted.]

MR. McANARNEY. I will have to look over my notes.

THE COURT. Suppose you look them over during the night.

(Adjourned until 10 A. M., Wednesday, June 22, 1921.) [937]

Wednesday, June 22, 1921.

THE COURT. Will you poll the jury, please?

(The jury is polled, and the defendants answer "Present.")

(Conference at bench between Court and counsel.)…

(The Court excuses the jury, and they retire to the jury room.) … .

MR. MOORE. The defendants move that the jury be instructed that all evidence that they secured by reason of the view of a certain Buick car they shall disregard as evidence, and that they further be instructed to disregard the testimony of Mr. Wind, Mr. Fuller and Officer Hill of the finding of this specific Buick … on the ground that no one of the three witnesses referred to above testified … that this was the same car as was used at Braintree on April 15th, and that no witness has definitely identified the Buick car found in the Manley woods as one and the same car that such witness saw at Braintree on April 15th, … that the first evidence of the bullet hole in the car comes after the car has been taken out of the woods … after the lapse of… one or two hours… .

THE COURT. The Court is to look up the evidence, and the defendants waive no rights because the Court did not pass on this motion at the conclusion of the evidence offered by the Commonwealth. [Ed. Motion on Buick denied on p. 2099.]

MR. MOORE. The defendants move that the Court at this time instruct the jury to disregard all evidence of Mr. and Mrs. Johnson to the effect that on May 5th they saw Boda and Orcianni or either of them at the Johnson home, and also to instruct the jury to disregard all evidence of any conversation had between either Mr. or Mrs. Johnson and Boda. [938] This conversation referred to above is intended to refer to the phrase "I will call my husband" as made by Mrs. Johnson, and the conversation between Johnson and Boda. [Ed. See similar motion denied in Plymouth trial: Appel, VI: 333. Motions such as

Moore's are routinely made at the conclusion of the prosecution's evidence.]

(Short recess.)

[Ed. Transcript does not show that the jury returned here. The jury obviously did return.]

MR. KATZMANN. (To the stenographer.) Read the stipulation to the jury about **the shells.**

(The stipulation is read as follows:

'It is agreed on behalf of the defendants Vanzetti and Sacco that of the **four shot-gun shells** found on the defendant Vanzetti at the time of his arrest, two have not been introduced in evidence because they are not in the same condition as when found on him, and this through no fault of either the Government or the defendants, and that the two shot-gun shells that are hereby admitted are subject"—)

THE COURT. All right.

MR. KATZMANN. Now, I offer these two shells which I submitted to counsel [Moore and McAnarney] and ask that they be marked as exhibits.

THE COURT. They may be.

(Two shells admitted in evidence and marked "Exhibit 37.")

[Ed. By stipulation, the two shells that had been opened by the Plymouth jury are excluded as evidence. See "The Plymouth Shell Mystery" in The Case That Will Not Die, pp. 99-115.]

MR. KATZMANN. I should like these to be shown to the jury, if your Honor please, but I will wait until this further stipulation is read:

(The stipulation is read to the jury as follows: "It is agreed there shall be no argument or claim on the part of the defendants because of the fact that the rifle found at the home of the defendant Sacco was not produced in court.") ... [939]

MR. JEREMIAH McANARNEY. I said, the jury be instructed to entirely disregard any evidence with reference to the finding of the rifle at Sacco's house, not any reference to the rifle in the case.

THE COURT. (To Mr. Katzmann) Do you object to that?

MR. KATZMANN. I do not. That is my understanding of the merits of the agreement... .

THE COURT. (To the jury) Mr. Foreman and gentlemen, it is my duty to instruct you that there was a misunderstanding in regard to the last statement or stipulation read to you by the stenographer. It was agreed and it is now agreed that so far as the finding of the rifle at the home of Sacco is concerned, you will entirely disregard it, … because, as it stands now, under the agreement, there is no evidence before you that there was a rifle found at the home of Sacco. It was agreed between counsel, … that no argument would be made because of the fact that the rifle was not produced.… . [940]

MR. KATZMANN. The Commonwealth rests, if your Honor please. [941]

[Ed. Katzmann says the Commonwealth has completed its introduction of evidence.]

INTERLUDE

Newsweek, February 5, 2007
Announces
Peter Miller's Documentary "Sacco and Vanzetti"

On p. 18 of Newsweek, February 5, 2007, appears the news item "Immigrant Injustice?" under the rubric FAST CHAT. Peter Miller, identified as a documentarian, tells Joshua Alston that Sacco and Vanzetti were "two Italian immigrants executed in 1927 for a murder they probably didn't commit."

Newsweek may or may not publish responses to this update on Sacco and Vanzetti. The content of Miller's film is not noted. Where it is viewable is not stated.

Slater & Morrill lower factory. Lola Andrews saw the bandit car in A.M. parked on Pearl Street thirty feet from the north end of the factory. Lewis Wade, looking west (toward camera), witnessed the crime as he stood near the concrete house identified in Breed's Plan. (Courtesy Massachusetts Supreme Judicial Court)

Crime scene, looking west down Pearl Street toward railroad crossing. Berardelli and Parmenter were shot by two bandits waiting for them at the pipe fence in front of the Rice & Hutchins factory on the left. Bostock witnessed shooting from the east side of the water tank, and McGlone witnessed shooting from the excavation site. (Courtesy Massachusetts Supreme Judicial Court)

157

The Escape. The bandit car, approaching the railroad tracks, was seen by Splaine, Devlin, Carrigan, Pierce, and Ferguson from the Hampton House on the right, and by Levangie at his gate tender's shack on the left. (Courtesy Massachusetts Supreme Judicial Court)

SOUTH BRAINTREE

SCALE; I IN.= 10 FT.   MAY, 1921

C. B. BREED
CIVIL ENGINEER

(SCALE OF THIS COPY I IN.= 40 FT.)

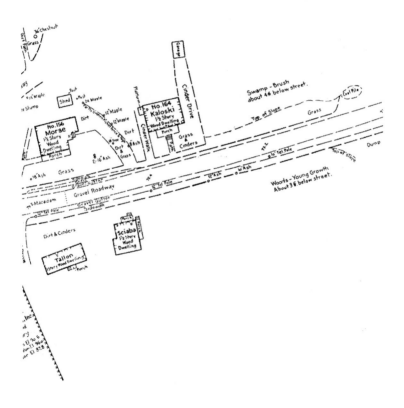

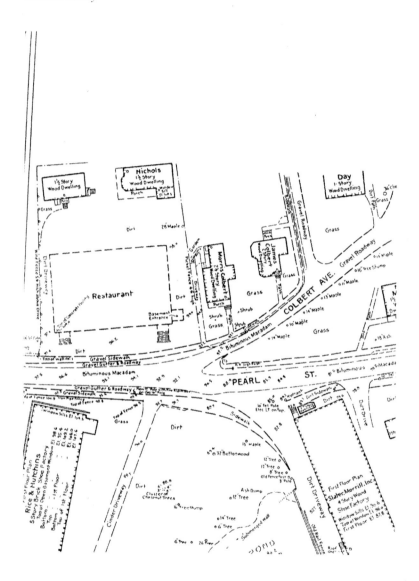

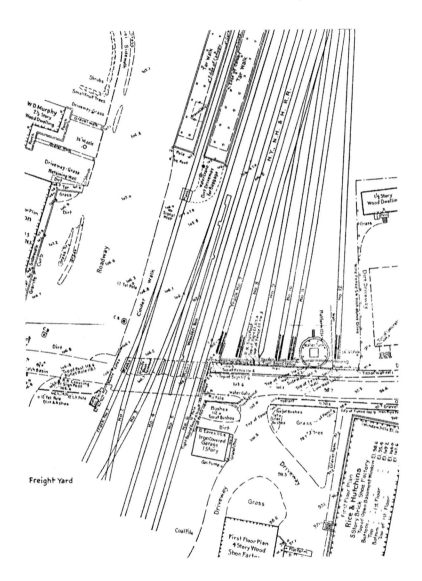

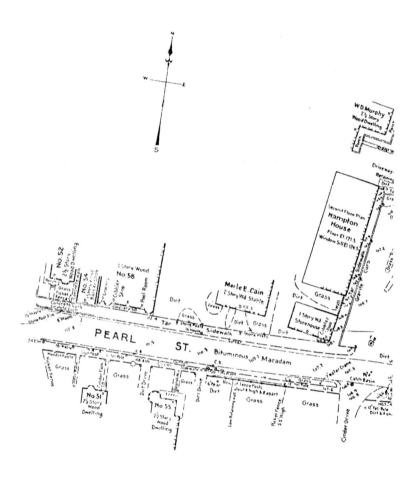

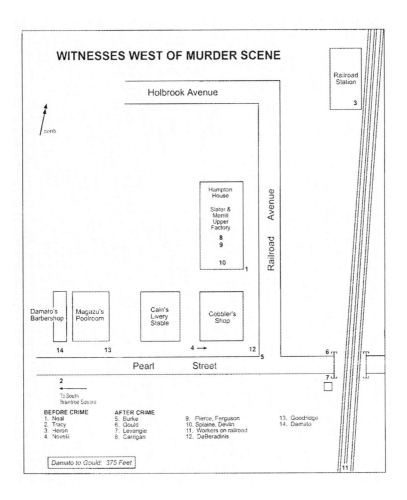

ESCAPE AND ARREST

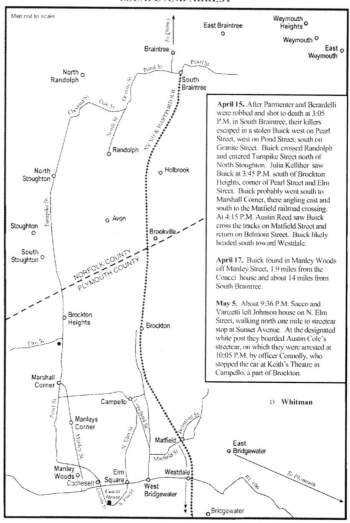

Map not to scale

April 15. After Parmenter and Berardelli were robbed and shot to death at 3:05 P.M. in South Braintree, their killers escaped in a stolen Buick west on Pearl Street, west on Pond Street, south on Granite Street. Buick crossed Randolph and entered Turnpike Street north of North Stoughton. Julia Kelliher saw Buick at 3:45 P.M. south of Brockton Heights, corner of Pearl Street and Elm Street. Buick probably went south to Marshall Corner, there angling east and south to the Matfield railroad crossing. At 4:15 P.M. Austin Reed saw Buick cross the tracks on Matfield Street and return on Belmont Street. Buick likely headed south toward Westdale.

April 17. Buick found in Manley Woods off Manley Street, 1.9 miles from the Coacci house and about 14 miles from South Braintree.

May 5. About 9:36 P.M. Sacco and Vanzetti left Johnson house on N. Elm Street, walking north one mile to streetcar stop at Sunset Avenue. At the designated white post they boarded Austin Cole's streetcar, on which they were arrested at 10:05 P.M. by officer Connolly, who stopped the car at Keith's Theatre in Campello, a part of Brockton.

GEOGRAPHY OF THE SACCO-VANZETTI CASE

Eastern Massachusetts

Boston-East Boston-Charlestown
Charlestown State Prison

Station Stops:
East Weymouth to Quincy

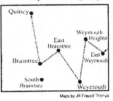

Maps by Jill Freund Thomas

Bridgewater. Attempted holdup on December 24, 1919.

South Braintree. Parmenter & Berardelli killed on April 15, 1920.

Needham. Murphy's Buick and Ellis's plates stolen here.

Lynn. Galleani published Cronaca Sovversiva here.

Norwood. Orciani worked here in a foundry with Slater.

Hopedale. Sacco worked here 1908-1909, met Boda here in 1913.

Webster. Sacco worked here six or seven months.

Milford. Sacco worked here nine years. Gatti's home. Sacco met Orciani here. Both joined Milford anarchists.

Haverhill. Sacco worked here after 1917 trip to Mexico with Boda.

Stoughton. Sacco's home. He worked at 3-K Shoe Company.

Boston. Sacco said he went here for his passport on April 15, 1920.

Hyde Park (in Boston). Sacco met Orciani here on May 4, 1920.

North Plymouth (Seaside). Vanzetti boarded with Brinis four years.

Dorchester (in Boston). Rosen lived here.

Whitman. Rosen said he spent the night here on April 15, 1920.

Cohasset. Faulkner boarded a train for Watertown, April 15, 1920.

East Weymouth, Weymouth Heights, Weymouth, East Braintree. Station stops on Faulkner's trip to Watertown.

Kingston. Vanzetti, by one theory, got on train here, April 15, 1920.

East Braintree. Prosecution said Vanzetti exited train here.

Wellesley. Boda and his brother had a store here.

Wrentham. Madeiros killed bank cashier here on November 1, 1924.

South Duxbury. Morey bought a boat here, and Corl towed it from Duxbury to Plymouth on April 17, 1920.

West Bridgewater. Ruth and Simon Johnson lived here, 1.4 miles from Coacci house, from which Boda's car was towed on April 19.

East Bridgewater. Pappi, Vanzetti's friend, lived here.

Salem, Haverhill, Everett, Bridgewater. Cities to which Vanzetti and Boda would travel to collect anarchist literature.

Brockton (Campello). Sacco and Vanzetti arrested on a streetcar, May 5, 1920. Sacco worked here in 1918.

Quincy. Home of Coacci, deported April 18, 1920.

Somerville. Home of Valdinoci, Dominick Ricci and Falzini. Falzini once lived in East Boston, where Sacco worked in 1917.

Lowell. Ballistics test at U.S. Cartridge Co. factory, 6/18/21.

Providence, R.I. The Joe Morelli gang lived here.

Seekonk. Madeiros stopped here after the Wrentham murder. In 1924 he was a bouncer at the Bluebird Inn, Seakonk.

Randolph. James F. Weeks and Madeiros lived here in 1924.

East Boston. (Across Boston Harbor). Italian Naturalization Club.

Plymouth. Vanzetti's trial for Bridgewater crime, 6/22-7/1, 1920.

Dedham. Trial of Sacco and Vanzetti held here in 1921, during which Mrs. Sacco stayed in Dedham home of Louis D. Brandeis.

Charlestown. Madeiros, Sacco, and Vanzetti executed here on August 23, 1927.

Sources: *Trial Transcript;* and Paul Avrich, Sacco and Vanzetti: The Anarchist Background

UNSIGNED LETTER FROM NEW YORK CITY
New York City, New York

September 28th, 1923.

County Prosecutor,
Norfolk County,
Dedham, Mass.

Dear Sir:

Last night's papers show that affidavits have been made in the Sacco and Vanzetti case and one of them Albert H. Hamilton who poses as a firearms expert.

Mr. Hamilton poses as an expert on seventeen different subjects, handwriting, ink analysis, firearms, powders; and others. He is an ex-druggist from Auburn, N.Y., and is anything but reliable.

Should you wish to find anything about Mr. Hamilton, just consult Mr. Albert S. Osborn, Handwriting Expert, of No. 233 Broadway and Loren C. Horton, No. 261 Broadway, also Handwriting Expert, they can give you documentary evidence that he is a faker.

The Attorney Generals Office of New York can give you a record of the Stielow case, where he testified to markings on bullets which were absolutely wrong. The case was investigated by the Attorney General after the [defendant] had had [sic] been convicted of murder first degree and on his report Stielow was released by the governor.

If you approach the above men in the right way they can give you documentary evidence that Mr. Hamilton is absolutely unreliable. Call them on the telephone or write them and they will furnish you enough to disqualify Mr. Hamilton.
Yours very truly, [NYPL confirms addresses are accurate.]
[Source: The Sacco-Vanzetti Case Papers, Reel, 21. See pp. 594, 617.]

PART II

EVIDENCE BY THE DEFENSE

INTERLUDE
VOICES OF HISTORY PROFESSORS

"If the trial had been held in an atmosphere less surcharged with anti-Redism, the outcome, at worst, might well have been only a prison term."
[Thomas A. Bailey, *The American Pageant* (1956), p. 775.]

"If the trial had been held in an atmosphere less surcharged with anti-Redism, the outcome might well have been only a prison term."
[Thomas A. Bailey,*The American Pageant* (1975), 5th edition,vol. 2, p. 814.]

"Among the undergraduate courses that I most enjoyed teaching was the introductory seminar in historical methodology, . . . My zest for this work was increased by a recollection of how revealing it had been to me as a student, particularly the process of putting a historical account together by one's self. Such an approach was much more satisfying than extracting history passively from a printed secondary (secondhand) account written by someone who perhaps had not consulted the necessary primary (eyewitness) sources or had not interpreted them correctly."
[Thomas A. Bailey, *The American Pageant Revisited: Recollections of a Stanford Historian*, (1982) p. 112. Bailey died July 26, 1983.]

"If the trial had been held in an atmosphere less charged with antiredism, the outcome might well have been only a prison term."
[David M. Kennedy, Lizabeth Cohen, Thomas A. Bailey, *The American Pageant* (12th edition (2002), p. 730. The **13th** edition (2006), p. 721, has the same sentence.]

"[A]t its best, history is a detached and disinterested weighing of all the evidence, . . ."
[Ira Berlin, "American Slavery in History and Memory and the Search for Social Justice," *Journal of American History* (March 2004), p. 1265.]

15. OPENING STATEMENT AND M.I.T. PROFESSOR

THE COURT. (To Mr. Jeremiah McAnarney.) Are you ready to open now?

MR. JEREMIAH McANARNEY. Yes.

THE COURT. (To the jury.) Mr. Foreman and gentlemen, it is my duty to make the same suggestions to you immediately preceding the opening by counsel for the defendants that I did preceding the opening by Mr. Williams, counsel for the Commonwealth. As I said to you then, and I repeat now, these are simply opening statements, sometimes called the opening arguments, but they are statements to give you an intelligent idea of the evidence that the defendants propose to introduce for your consideration, ... [Y]ou must bear in mind, ... that statements by counsel in any opening should never be considered evidence ... . It is simply statements of what counsel propose to prove, ... [K]eep your minds open.

The Commonwealth has now rested. You must keep your minds in a state of absolute impartiality. You have not heard the testimony of the defendants... [Y]ou should still keep your minds open ... with a view of deciding these cases after you have heard all the evidence, and after you have heard the arguments, and after you have heard the charge, and then you will return to your jury room... . You may proceed with the opening, please... . [941]

Opening Statement by William J. Callahan. June 22, 1921.

MR. CALLAHAN. May it please the Court, Mr. Foreman and gentlemen: You have now heard the Commonwealth's direct case... . [Y]ou have heard now substantially all the evidence which they base their proof of the allegations stated in the indictments upon which these men at bar are charged with... . [941]

We start at the opening of the defendants' case in the same legal predicament as when the Commonwealth opened their case, that is, the defendants now are innocent of this crime, and they remain so until you have determined the evidence and changed their legal category from that of innocence.

169

The presumption of law still is that they are innocent of the crimes stated in these indictments, and the burden of proof is still upon the Government, or Commonwealth, to prove to you all the allegations set out in the indictments beyond reasonable doubt.

As a matter of law, the defendants are not obliged to offer any testimony whatsoever, ... they do not sustain any burden.... . But the defendants do intend to offer themselves as witnesses, and they do intend to call other witnesses who will explain certain situations that were brought out by the Commonwealth's witnesses.

The defense will be made up of practically two parts. We shall offer witnesses that were at or near the scene of the shooting April 15 that [942] will tell you what they saw and who they saw, ... with reference to the defendants. The defendants will explain to you in person what they were doing on the day of April 15, ... not only at the time when the crime was committed—or crimes were committed—but also throughout the entire day.

The defendant Vanzetti will offer himself as a witness and tell you his experience from the time that he landed in this country, . . and his life experience of the years he remained in New York City, working around restaurants, washing dishes and maintaining himself as best he could, until some few years ago he made his home in Plymouth, Plymouth County ... [F]or a few years he worked there in a mill, doing unskilled labor. After saving a few dollars, he bought out a small fish business ... and sold fish around the streets in Plymouth with his push cart.... .

Sacco will also tell you that some few years ago,—1908, ... he landed in Boston, went to live first in Milford, Massachusetts, obtaining employment as a water boy with some contractor ... who was doing paving work in the streets of Milford.... . He worked there for nearly a year and then went to a school to learn edge-trimming, ... went to what was known then in Milford as the 3-K Shoe Factory, which is now in Stoughton, and a Mr. Kelley—not the man who testified here a few days ago, but I think his father—taught him ... the trade of shoe trimming or edge trimming.

[H]e went to Webster and worked in the shoe factory.... . Then he came back to Milford again and worked in another factory, in his trade as edge-trimmer. Then he came ... to Stoughton. I think he worked in Rice & Hutchins in South Braintree ... as edge-trimmer. Then he worked in Cambridge.... . Then he worked in Somerville and then in

Chelsea, until later he came to ... Stoughton and [worked]... for the 3-K Shoe Factory ... up to May 1st ... [1920].

He will tell you of his home conditions, of his mother passing away some time in the early part of March of last year, and the receipt of a letter from his father asking him to come home on account of his mother's [943] death, and on account of the illness of his father ... [H]e went to his employer at the 3-K Shoe Factory in Stoughton, showed the letter, ... and told his employer that he had decided to go back home, and then asked that arrangements might be made that he could go to Boston some day the latter part of the week of which April 15 fits in.

Sacco had asked him [Kelley], ... about getting away some day, ... [so that] he might go in to Boston and make application and obtain his passport, and that he was told by his employer that after he had caught up his work he could so do, and he went and obtained the services of another man who he "broke in" as they say in a factory, taught or instructed or demonstrated the work; that a man and he worked together for several days until the work was caught up, which happened to be Wednesday, April 14; and that night he called the condition of his work to Mr. Kelley's attention, and Mr. Kelley said, "Very well, go tomorrow."

And he will tell you that he went in on the early train from Stoughton ... to Boston. He will tell you about going to the office of the Italian Consul, having with him a picture, himself and his wife and child, as a requirement for the application of a passport. And he will tell you his experience there in the office of the Italian Consul, in that the picture was not in right form or the right size, and that he had to go out and obtain another one, and he went back again after he had left the employ of Mr. Kelley, namely, May 2nd [May 4], when the passport [was] issued, three days before his arrest.

We will offer you in corroboration of that fact a deposition that was taken in Italy from the man whom he saw in the Italian Consul's office on the date of April 15. We will show you that that man worked in the Consul's office up until some time in that fall of 1920, when, on account of his health, he [Adrower] went back to Italy, and in that deposition, ... it will show of the visit of Sacco to his office ... Then we will show you by Sacco his time taken up in Stoughton on the 2nd, 3rd, 4th and 5th of May, up to the night of his arrest. In those two courses I have followed now, they will show what these men were

171

doing the day of April 15. They will also explain to you the reason for them having guns, and ammunition, in their possession. [944]

Now, going back to South Braintree for a moment, we will offer some 12 or 15 witnesses who were stationed . . . at certain points, and they will tell you what they saw of the shooting, what they saw of the men that did the shooting, and what they saw of the automobile and . . . the men in the automobile.

We will produce a witness [Burke] who was at or near the crossing directly opposite to the cobbling shop . . . that was within six or eight feet of the automobile when it came across the railroad crossing from the lower part of Pearl Street, a man who was in South Braintree there that day on business. He arrived at the South Braintree station some time in the neighborhood of 2:30, had some paraphernalia with him that he brought along in the train with him. He was on his way to give an exhibition in one of the schools there in glass-blowing. . . .

His partner [Pecheur] was with him. . . . He [Burke] saw the shooting, . . . [H]e got a full-face view of the automobile, and he got a full-face view of three of the occupants in the automobile, . . .

In addition to that, we will offer you a witness [Frantello] who was then in the employ of Slater & Morrill. His duties were, . . . chasing damaged shoes or lost shoes or stock shoes, some occupation . . . that took him to the lower Slater & Morril factory a part of the day. . . . [945] [A]s he walked along the sidewalk, the southerly side of Pearl Street, where the two men that you have heard described were standing against the iron fence [in front of Rice & Hutchins], . . . he noticed that they were sort of nervous, turning, and with their caps pulled down, and he got suspicious of them and he stopped and paused . . . to get a look at them, . . .

We will offer you witnesses that were working there in the excavation where they were digging the cellar. . . . We will offer you witnesses that were in the employ of the New York, New Haven and Hartford Railroad who were working on the track at the South Braintree crossing, just south of the crossing. . . . Then we will offer you witnesses who . . . are in the employ of Slater & Morrill. . . . [T]hey [witnesses one floor above Splaine and Devlin] will tell you what they saw. . . .

And I want to say to you in conclusion that when you are taking in this evidence that you will give the defendants and their witnesses the [946] same consideration, the same attention and the same patience that you have given the witnesses for the Commonwealth.

Mr. Jeremiah McAnarney Chooses Not To Make a Statement. June 22, 1921.

MR. JEREMIAH McANARNEY. Your Honor, in view of the statement of Mr. Callahan, and it is so substantially covering the whole affair, I do not think I will make any opening on behalf of the defendant Vanzetti; the two being interwoven together, it would be a good deal of repetition. Where our cases differ will be shown by the evidence. [947]
THE COURT. We will proceed with the evidence, if you please; if counsel for the defendants are now ready. [947]
[Ed. Here begins the evidence by the defense.]

Charles B. Breed, Sworn. June 22, 1921.

Q. (By Mr. Callahan) Your full name is what, sir? A. Charles B. Breed.
Q. Your occupation? A. Civil engineer.
Q. In connection with your occupation do you now occupy a position?
A. I am professor of railway and highway engineering at the Massachusetts Institute of Technology, and am in consulting engineering practice, with offices in Boston... .
Q. May I direct your attention, Professor, to this map hanging on the wall. Did you ever see that before? A. I have.
Q. Will you tell me what it is? A. It is a map or **plan** which I made, or which was made under my direction of, of Pearl Street and its vicinity where it crosses the railroad tracks of the New York, New Haven and Hartford Railroad at South Braintree. [See, here, plan in four parts.]
Q. And that plan was made at whose suggestion, by you?
A. That plan was made by me under the direction of Mr. Moore. [947]
Q. And it was made in connection with the so-called Sacco and Vanzetti cases?
A. That is correct... . [948]
Q. Now will you give me the distance to a point in the center of Pearl Street at the nearest rail of the railroad crossing to a point at the window in the Hampton House Slater & Morrill factory, that faces on the roadway parallel with the railroad crossing? A. From the center of that window to the westerly rail at the center of Pearl Street, 121 1/2 feet in a horizontal direction. Practically 122 1/2 in the inclined direction.

Q. That is, 122 1/2, that is from the window above that second story?
A. That is from the window at the second story. [950]
(The plan is admitted in evidence and marked "Exhibit 38".) [954]

Cross-Examination.

Q. (By Mr. Katzmann) Professor, I am pointing to a railroad crossing sign post on the southerly side of Pearl Street, somewhat east of the words "catch basin." I call your attention to your wording there, "top of the post 118.6", "bullet hole 118.1", … and ask you if you put that on the plan? A. I did.

Q. From whom did you obtain that information that that was **a bullet hole**?

A. From the gate tender at the crossing.

Q. What was his name? A. I don't know.

Q. What does he look like? A. Short, light weight, I think lame. [956] [Ed. The gate tender is Levangie. Because Levangie was Breed's source of information, the Court deemed the plan (admitted on p. 954) incompetent "because it is hearsay." {957} Then Katzmann accepted the plan.]

MR. KATZMANN. I desire to take the plan now as it was offered.

THE COURT. As it is?

MR. KATZMANN. Yes.

THE COURT. Very well, proceed, please. [957]

16. LOLA ANDREWS IMPEACHED

Mrs. Julia Campbell, Sworn. June 27, 1921.

Q. (By Mr. Jeremiah McAnarney) What is your full name? A. Julia A. Campbell.

Q. And you reside somewhere in the State of Maine? A. Yes, sir, in Stockton Springs, Maine.

Q. You did live in Quincy last year [in the same building with Lola Andrews]? A. Yes, sir... .

Q. On the day of April 15th, 1920, did you go to Braintree, or South Braintree, with Mrs. Andrews? A. I did... .

Q. When you got down to Slater & Morrill's factory, before you went in, did you see anything or any person outside? A. We saw a car there, and we saw a man in khaki clothes... .

Q. Where was the man? A. The man standing—

Q. Yes. A. He was standing just on the face of the building now, where there is a **cement building** there. [1308]

Q. How near was he to that concrete— A. Well, very near it. I couldn't say just exactly, but very near it. That is the man we asked.

Q. That is the man you asked? A. Yes. [The man in khaki.]

Q. Which of you, Mrs. Andrews or you, asked him anything? A. Mrs. Andrews.

Q. What did she say to that man? A. She asked him where the entrance was to that building.

Q. And what did he say? A. He told us right around there on the side... .

Q. How near was the automobile to the building, to Slater & Morrill's factory?

A. ... I didn't think it was any more than five feet away from the factory... .

Q. Did you see any man doing anything to the automobile?

A. There was a man down underneath the automobile. He never looked up at all.

Q. Did you or Mrs. Andrews speak to that man who was down under the automobile?

A. We did not.

Q. You went into the factory? A. Yes. [1309]

Q. When you and Mrs. Andrews came out of Rice & Hutchins, did either you or she speak to a man there at the automobile? A. We did not.

Q. Slater & Morrill factory [This corrects previous question.]? A. No, we did not.

Q. Did you hear Mrs. Andrews have any talk with any man who was working around an automobile that morning? A. No, sir. [1310]

Q. Are you blind? A. Well, I can't see as well as a great many, but I am not blind, sir. [1311]

Q. ... Did you notice whether there was anyone in the automobile? A. Not anyone at all when I seen it. [1312]

Cross-Examination.

Q. (By Mr. Katzmann) Has anyone visited you, Mrs. Campbell, purporting to come from the State of Massachusetts? A. Yes, sir... .

Q. Have you had more than one such visit [in connection with this case]? A. I have had two.

Q. Who has visited you, if you know? A. Mr. Reid... . [Ed. Defense investigator for Moore.]

MR. KATZMANN. I wonder, if your Honor please, if Mrs. Campbell might not better be seated?

THE COURT. Would you like to be seated?

THE WITNESS. No. I just as soon stand.

THE COURT. You may be, if you like to. [1312]

Q. Were you subsequently visited by someone who purported to represent the Commonwealth?
A. Yes, sir.

Q. Who was that? A. I can't tell you what that gentleman's name was... .

Q. ... And he talked with you in the presence of somebody else? A. Mr. William Berry.

Q. Who is William Berry? A. He is sheriff there at my town.

Q. Stockton Springs? A. Yes... .

Q. Are you quite sure you did not tell him [Mr. Berry] there were two men and you could not identify either one of them? A. Yes, I guess I did tell him that.

Q. There were two men, were there?

A. There was a man in a khaki suit and a man at the automobile... .
[1313]

Q. Which way was the automobile facing, Mrs. Campbell? A. It was facing down from the track.

Q. Back to the track? A. Yes, back to the track.

Q. Have you said it was facing towards the track? A. No, sir, I have not. I told the same story, dear man, every time, and I don't want to get into trouble.

Q. I don't want you to. A. Just as true as you live. It ain't my good will I am here.

Q. That is all right. You and I are friends, are we? So far, I mean? A. Yes.

[The witness cries, and an officer brings a glass of water.] [1315]

[Short recess.]

Q. You say it [bandit car] was facing away from the railroad track, down the hill?

A. Down the hill... .

Q. Do you remember what you said in the letter [to your son in Revere] between January 21, 1921, and the first day of February, 1921? ... . A. I told him [I wanted him to meet me] because I couldn't see to get in from the train, after dark. [1316]

Q. You are bothered with cataracts, aren't you? A. Yes.

Q. On both eyes? A. Yes... . [1317]

Q. Did you look to see if there was anybody in the rear seat?

A. Well, I do not know. No, I did not notice anybody in particular.

Q. Did you look to see? A. No, because I did not think anything about it... .

Q. You did not look? A. No, I did not... . [1322]

Q. Will you describe the man, so far as you could see him, who was bending under the automobile? A. Well, all I know, he had a cap on, and [1323] he was squinching down underneath the automobile, ...

Q. What kind of cap was it? A. He had a kind of dark cap. I couldn't tell you the color of it... .

Q. Do you remember who asked him how to get into Rice & Hutchins factory, asked anybody, I mean? A. Well, it was Mrs. Andrews that asked the man in the khaki clothes.

Q. And that is the man who was standing out in front of the automobile?

A. Yes, by **the cement house**, by those steps... . [1324]

177

Q. Was there anything, Mrs. Campbell, about this episode, looking for work and seeing the car that impressed you particularly? A. Not a thing. [1328]

Q. And you are able to tell this jury, are you, a man who was down under the side of the automobile and you went behind him; could not see his face?

A. No. His cap was drawn down, and he never looked up... .

Q. He had his head down? A. Yes, his head hung down.

Q. And you tell this jury that neither of those defendants is that man?

A. I should say they were not the man.

Q. You did not see his face? A. Well, that is all I did see.

Q. You did not see his face, did you? A. No, his head was right down there, ...

Q. Have you seen the back of the head of the defendant Sacco?

A. No, I didn't, no... .

Q. Have you compared the back of Sacco, the defendant Sacco's head, with the back of the man you saw down? A. No.

Q. How do you know he is not the man? A. Well, I don't know that he is not the man, but he don't look like the man I saw there... . [1331]

Q. Did you look at his face? A. Just looked up, yes.

Q. Did you look at his face?

THE COURT. Just answer that by yes or no, if you can.

A. Well, yes, I will say I looked, just looked up at his face.

Q. Could you see it? A. I saw the side of his face, yes... .

Q. I want to know how much you saw of him? A. I didn't see very much of him.

MR. KATZMANN. I guess that is all. [1333]

George W. Fay, Sworn. June 28, 1921.

Q. (By Mr. Jeremiah McAnarney) You are a member of the Quincy Police Department?

A. I am... .

Q. Do you know Mrs. Andrew,—Lola Andrews? A. I do.

Q. And in what way, please [was your attention called to her February last]?

A. In passing the Alhambra building one night in the middle of February. [1373]

178

Q. What happened? A. I was called in [to her apartment in the Alhambra]... .

Q. And what did she say? A. She said that when she came home ... she went up into the apartments, went into the toilet and as she stepped into the toilet she was grabbed by a man and forced down onto her knees... .

Q. Now, tell us the questions you asked her and the answers she gave. A. I asked her if the man who assaulted her, if she thought that [1374] he was one of the men she saw at Braintree on the day of the shooting, and she said that she could not tell because she did not see the faces of the Braintree men... . [1375]

Harry Kurlansky, Sworn. June 28, 1921.

Q. (By Mr. Jeremiah McAnarney) Are you in business in Quincy?
A. Yes, sir.

Q. Where is your place of business? A. 1466 Hancock Street, Quincy... .

Q. Do you know Mrs. Lola Andrews? A. Yes, sir.

Q. How long have you known her?

A. I have known Mrs. Lola Andrews for the last seven or eight years.

Q. Sometime in February of this year did you have a talk with her?

A. Yes. I was right on my doorstep and Lola Andrews went by. [1377]

Q. Now, tell us what was said. A. ... She says, "The Government took me down and want me to recognize those men," she says, "... I have never seen them and I can't recognize them... ." [1378]

Cross-Examination

Q. (By Mr. Katzmann) Did she tell you that any ... police officer urged upon her to say anything she did not know? A. She did not mention any police officer or no,—anybody. She simply say the "Government." [1381]

THE COURT. Mr. Witness, ... Did you attempt to find out who this person was who represented the Government who was trying to get her to ... state that which was false? ...

THE WITNESS. I don't think of anything like that just simply what she tell you. [1383]

179

[Ed. Alfred N. Labrecque, newspaper reporter, gave testimony on his interview of Andrews regarding an alleged assault on her in mid-February 1921. Andrews told Labrecque she "did not see the faces of the men in Braintree." {1377} Lena Allen, Andrews' neighbor, testified Andrews' reputation for truth was bad. {1601} Katzmann asked Allen: "Are you an enemy of hers?" Allen responded: "Well, yes."] [1603]

Ranney's Letter to Charles Van Amburgh

June 25, 1927

Capt. Charles J. Van Amburgh,
Department of Public Safety,
State House,
Boston, Mass.

Dear Captain:-

I am particularly anxious to have you send copies of the shell photographs to Major Calvin H. Goddard, 4 East 28th Street, New York City, as soon as possible, my reason being that the Governor apparently refuses to give any credence to this vital and important evidence in the Sacco-Vanzetti case. I am doing my best to place this before him. If he persistently refuses and should pardon these criminals, I am preparing to help Goddard throw out to the public through the New York World this evidence which Goddard says not only from the shell evidence but the bullet evidence is positive proof that Sacco at least committed this crime. To this end I trust you will co-operate with us by letting him have these photographs at your very earliest convenience.

I may add that through recent tests made at the request of the New York World on the bullet and shells [June 3], Goddard is positive that our constant contentions are absolutely sound and correct.

    With kind regards, I remain
     Yours very truly,
     Assistant District-Attorney (Dudley P. Ranney)

[Source: The Sacco-Vanzetti Case Papers, Reel 21. See pp. 311, 478, 594.]

17. EYEWITNESSES ON PEARL STREET

Mrs. Jennie Novelli, Sworn. June 25, 1921.

Q. (By Mr.McAnarney) What is your name? A. Mrs. Jennie Novelli.

Q. You at present are a nurse? A. I am.

Q. Do you recall the day of this shooting? A. I do.

Q. Whether or not you had occasion on that day to be down in the vicinity of Rice & Hutchins' factory? A. I was going to ... call on a friend by the name of Mrs. Knipps, Colbert Avenue... . [1221]

Q. At about what time of the day was it that you turned down into Pearl Street from Washington Street [on April 15]? A. About ten minutes of three... .

Q. Then, at a point 150 or 200 feet down Pearl Street your attention was attracted to an automobile? A. Yes, sir.

Q. What kind of a car was it? A. It was a large car, the top was up, and it was painted dark.

Q. ... [W]as the automobile going in the same direction you were going, or in a different direction? A. It was going alongside of me.

Q. How fast was the automobile travelling at that time? A. Not any faster than I was walking.

Q. Did you observe the persons on the front seat of the automobile?

A. I observed the man to the right more than I did the driver, because I thought I knew this man.

Q. ... Was the car going faster than you, or how was it? A. It was going for some distance alongside of me, and when I got to the cobbler's shop on the corner near the Hampton House, it got a little ahead of me, it paused, and then went over the tracks... . [1222]

Q. Now, will you kindly describe the appearance of the driver, ...? A. I only saw the back of the driver. From what I saw of his hair, it was light, and the complexion was much fairer than the other man's... .

Q. ... Now, kindly describe the appearance of the man seated to the driver's right.

A. He was a young man, about the age of 30, and he had dark hair, and he had a dark complexion. He looked like a man that has to shave about every day, ...

Q. Where was the automobile when you last saw it? A. It was down the road past the shop.

Q. Past which shop? A. Past the factory, past Slater's... .

Q. ... How far below that factory was the automobile when you last saw it?

A. Well, it was a little past Tallons house. [Ed. See east section of Breed's Plan.]

Q. ... What was the automobile doing when you last saw it?

A. It was then getting ready to turn around... .

Q. And what happened, so far as your attention was called to this shooting? A. I saw some men running past the house. ... [1223] I went out and asked a man what was the trouble... .

Q. Where did you go? A. I ran right up to the road where the man was lying on the ground... .

Q. I call your attention to the Rice & Hutchins factory on one side, and here we have a gravel sidewalk, gravel gutter and roadway, macadam, gravel sidewalk. Here is where the men were digging? A. Yes, sir.

Q. ... [W]here was the man you saw lying on the ground? A. Well, he was in the road near the sidewalk, near Rice & Hutchins factory, about halfway between the buildings.

Q. What, if anything, did you do? A. I stepped into the crowd, and I asked the men to pick him up—

MR. KATZMANN. One moment, please.

THE COURT. That is not competent... .

Q. ... You may tell us what you did, not what you said, but what you did.

A. I was in Mr. Colbert's house. The doctor asked me to please wash off—

MR. KATZMANN. One moment.

THE COURT. You can't tell the conversation.

THE WITNESS. I just washed him off, washed his face off... .

Q. Was the man alive then? A. No, sir.

Q. Well, did you see another man? A. I did.

Q. Where did you see the other man? A. He was lying on the couch in the sitting room.

Q. Was he alive? A. Yes, sir... .

Q. Which one was alive, Parmenter or Berardelli? A. Mr. Parmenter. [1224]

Q. I ask you now if either of the men in the dock were either of the men you saw in that automobile? A. No, sir, they were not... . [1226]

Jennie Novelli, (Continued). June 27, 1921.
Cross-Examination.

Q. (By Mr. Katzmann) Mrs. Novelli, are your glasses reading glasses or distance glasses?

A. I can see at a distance and also reading and sewing.... . [1229]

Q. You did say Saturday you saw the back of the head of the light haired man? A. I did.

Q. That you looked at the man more than at the driver, the man who sat at the right of the driver, you said that? A. I did.

Q. Did you see any more than, at most, a profile of that man?

A. Yes; I had a good look at his face.

Q. How could you see his face if you could see only the back of the head of the driver?

A. Because he was sitting sideways; he was turned facing the driver... . [1232]

THE COURT. Did you say how many persons were in this car that you saw?

THE WITNESS. There were two in the car. I had a good look at one of them.

THE COURT. There were two in that car?

THE WITNESS. Two in the front seat.

THE COURT. Whether there were any in the back seat——

THE WITNESS. There wasn't any.

THE COURT. Nobody in the back seat?

THE WITNESS. No, there wasn't any.... . [1236]

[The witness is seated.]

Q. Do you know Mr. Hellier? A. Yes, sir, I do... .

Q. Who is he? A. He is a State detective for the Pinkerton Detective Agency.

Q. Well, he is a Pinkerton detective? A. Yes, sir... .

Q. Do you remember saying to Mr. Hellier that Sacco's photograph greatly resembled the man you saw in the bandits' car, but you couldn't be positive as you only saw a side view of the man? A. No, sir, I don't remember. [1238]

Q. Let me read it to you again. After seeing three photos, did you say, on May 8, 1920, to Mr. Hellier, that Sacco's photo greatly resembled the man you saw in the bandits' car, but you couldn't be positive as you only saw a side view of the man? Did you say that to Mr. Hellier?

A. No, sir.

Q. You are sure of that? A. I am sure. [1239]

Mr. Albert Frantello, Sworn. June 23, 1921.

Q. (By Mr. Callahan) What was your occupation April 15 last year?

A. Cripple chaser, Slater & Morill Shoe Factory... .

Q. Did you go to the Hampton House Slater & Morrill factory on that day? A. I did.

Q. What place did you leave to go to the Hampton House Slater & Morrill Factory?

A. The lower factory.

Q. Do you recall about what time it was that day that you left the lower factory ...?

A. Between five minutes of three and three o'clock... .

Q. Did you notice anybody on Pearl Street as you went up by the Rice & Hutchins factory?

A. Yes, sir.

Q. Where were they situated?

A. Two men leaning against the railing of the Rice & Hutchins factory. [1007]

Q. The railing right outside the factory? A. Yes... . [1008]

Q. Was there anything else about them [besides the fact that the "dark complexioned fellow...needed a shave"] that attracted your attention particularly?

A. The first fellow was criticising the fellow that was further away from me.

MR. KATZMANN. What was that?

THE WITNESS. The first fellow was criticising the other fellow. That is what made me pause.

Q. Can you tell me what language they were using? A. Speaking in the American language.

Q. Speaking in the American language. How near were you to them when they were talking?

A. I could have touched them.

Q. Did you walk along right by them or did you stop? A. I paused and looked at them. [1010]

Q. Which one ... did you ... observe when you paused ...? A. The dark complexioned fellow.

Q. Can you give me the proportion of the time of your pause that you used in observing the dark-complected man in comparison with the time you used in observing the light-complected man? A. I paused about a second altogether.

Q. Can you tell me from you[r] seeing these two men at South Braintree as you described, whether or not either of the two men in the cage or the dock, were either one of those two men?

A. Neither of them... .

Q... . Were you interviewed by anybody with reference to the shooting? ... A. I was.

Q. When ...? A. First I was taken up to the Town Hall in South Braintree. [1011]

The Court. Put on the record the name of the officer.

Mr. Callahan. Mr Brouillard, the State police officer.[1013]

Cross-Examination.

Q. (By Mr. Katzmann) When was it that you went over to the Town Hall in Braintree? A. About a week after the shooting.

Q. And how many times have you talked with State Officer Brouillard? Stand up, will you please, Mr. Brouillard? (Officer Brouillard stands up.)

Q. I mean this gentleman now standing up. Haven't you talked with him more than once? A. Twice.

Q. Twice. When was the last time? . . . A. I would say two or three weeks after the murder. [1014]

Q. When was the first time? . . . A. I would say it was about two weeks after the murder.

Q. Was there a stenographer present at the occasion of your second talk with him? A. I don't recall. I think my statement was taken.

Q. Do you recall that that [second] interview with Officer Brouillard was on Friday, February 4, 1921? A. I do not recall whether it was or not. [1015]

Q. ... Whom did you see at the Braintree Town Hall? Did you see these two defendants?

A. I did not.

Q. Whom did you see, if you saw any prisoner?

A. I do not know his name.

Q. What does he look like?

A. He was kind of a tall fellow, with short mustache, khaki shirt. [1015]

Q. How many times did you see that man whom you say you saw in the Braintree Town Hall at the court house here? A. I think I have seen him every day.

Q. Every day. Talked with him, have you? A. Talked to him once or twice... .

Q. Have you seen him [Orciani] out in front driving a Ford automobile? A. I have.

Q. With the top up and the curtains open? A. Yes, sir.

Q. That is where you have seen him most of the time? A. That is where I think I have seen him outside. [1016]

Q. When you went up to go from the Pearl Street factory to the Hampton House, no shooting had occurred at that time, had it? A. No, sir... .

Q. And it was a pleasant day? A. It was... .

Q. Nothing to disturb you? A. No, sir... .

Q. And I suppose it is not an uncommon sight to see men sitting around on Rice & Hutchins' fence, is it? A. It is not uncommon.

Q. No. And it is not uncommon to see men sitting around there in working clothes, is it?

A. It is not. [1017]

Q. Have you a good memory? A. As far as I know I have.

Q. Well, now, Mr. Witness, you come down with me, please.

(Witness leaves stand and goes in front of jury rail with Mr. Katzmann.)

Q. Just come down here. I am going to stop opposite to these jurymen. I am going to give you one second to look at them. Then I am going to ask you to take the stand and describe them. You did not have that warning in advance when you talked with these two people,—when you looked at these two people? A. No.

Q. Well, I am going to give it to you. Now, walk along with me, pause here (witness does so), and give me a description of those two jurymen. Take the stand, please.

(Witness returns to the witness stand.) [1018]

THE COURT. ... Do you know the two [jurymen] the District Attorney had in mind?

THE WITNESS. I think it was the two in the middle.

MR. KATZMANN. Yes, that is the two you paused at… .

Q. Will you describe those two men [of the jury] to me? A. I can.

Q. Do it, please. A. Both are sitting down.

Q. Yes. A. Blue suits.

Q. Yes. A. Hats off.

Q. Yes. A. The first one is kind of bald up here (indicating).

Q. Yes. A. Has a watch chain on.

Q. Yes. A. And a mustache.

Q. And a mustache. Now, will you take a look at him, please. Do you see any mustache on either of those men? A. I don't see any.

Q. And you had just as long an opportunity to look at those two men, didn't you, as you had at the two men on the fence? [Ed. McAnarney objected and question was rephrased.]

Q. Pardon me. Answer that question. Did you have as long a time to look at those two jurymen as … at the two on the fence? A. I think I had a longer time on the two men at the fence… .

Q. Where is the watch chain on this No.1 you were talking about? Do you see any? A. No, sir.

Q. And it was wrong when you said he had a mustache, wasn't it?

A. It is now. [1019]

Q. … And what you saw were two men in shabby clothes, with caps, sitting out there [on the fence]? A. That was what attracted my attention that made me pause to look at them… .

Q. Did you form any impression in your mind as to their nationality at that time?

A. I couldn't say what the nationality was, because he spoke in American… .

Q. Do you know what nationality is meant by the term "wop", the colloquial term "wop"?

A. Certainly.

Q. What nationality? A. Italian.

Q. Yes. Have you ever stated to any person that they were of that nationality? A. Never.

Q. Did you so state to Officer Brouillard? A. I do not recall whether I did or not. [1020]

Q. You are of Italian descent yourself, are you not? A. I am.

Q. And I suppose that naturally you associate with a good many Italians? A. I do… .

Q. Now, ... these two men you have described, would you or would you not say that they were Italians or Italian descent? A. Well, to me, they did not look like an Italian... .

Q. All right. Do you remember Officer Brouillard on February 4, 1921, asking you:

"Q. Where did you see them? A. On the rail in front of Rice & Hutchins."

Does that recall some questions on the subject matter of Officer Brouillard's talk with you on February 4th last? A. That is where I saw them. [1024]

Q. ... Did you say anything about either one being a regular "wop", did you? A. I did not say.

Q. You did not state it, in response to that question: "What kind of fellows were they?"

"A. One fellow looked like a regular wop. The other looked just the same."

You did not say that to Officer Brouillard, did you? A. [No response audible to stenographer.]

Q. Did you say one looked like a regular wop and the other looked just the same? Did you say that, sir? A. [Witness hesitates.] I think I did say something like that.

Q. You know you did, don't you, Mr. Frantello? A. I do now.

Q. And that is true, isn't it? A. That is.

Q. You know they were both Italians whom you saw on that fence, don't you?

A. They were not both Italians... .

Q. Wait a minute. Wasn't one of those men an Italian, in your opinion?

A. Well, judging from what I know of Italians, he looked like one, but he wasn't... . [1025]

Q. If in Officer Brouillard's talk to you, you told him you couldn't tell whether they were talking in English, you said something that was untrue, if you said it? A. If I said that, it was untrue.

MR. KATZMANN. That is all. [1034]

Henry Cerro, Sworn. June 24, 1921.

[The witness is sworn through an interpreter, but the examination is in English.]

THE COURT. Do I understand he can get along without an interpreter?

MR. CALLAHAN. He can talk some, but I don't know how well. See how well we can get along.

Q. (By Mr. Callahan) What is your name? A. Henry Cerro.

Q. What is your occupation? A. Granite cutter... .

Q. Where were you working April 15th last year? A. South Braintree.

Q. Where? A. What they call Rice & Hutchins' factory, and Company, right across from the factory in an excavation... .

Q. What were you doing? A. I was loading a wagon with a shovel.

Q. Is that where they were building the restaurant?

A. That is what they said they were going to do... .

Q. You were working about there on April 15th?

A. Yes, sir. A little after three o'clock. [1105]

Q. Did you see the shooting that afternoon?

A. Well, yes. When I saw a few groups of men somewhere, four or five men tied together... .

Q. Did you see more than one shoot?

A. One. The most attention I paid to him. I took it serious then... .

Q. First of all, will you describe to the jury the man you saw do the shooting ...?

A. Gentlemen of the jury, the man that I seen with my eyes doing the shooting was a man that looked to me taller than I am, kind of slim, lighter complexion.

MR. KATZMANN. What is that?

A. Taller than I am, slim build, overcoat on, that is, with his coat turned up, with a soft hat. That is about the description I could get out of him,—smooth face... .

Q. How tall are you?

A. Oh, I am about—I don't know—somewhere five and seven or five five. [1106]

Q. Taller than you. How did he [the shooter] compare in weight with you?

A. Oh, he would weigh probably about 180.

Q. Have you told me what his complexion was? A. Light complexion... .

Q. What space of time were they there while you were looking at them? A. Why, I wouldn't think it would take them only just as long as you could press a button and go... . [1107]

189

Q. Did you see the man fall in the street after he was shot?

A. In the street towards us, almost across the sidewalk.... [1108]

Q. Did you see anybody else do any shooting? A. No, sir.... [1109]

Q. Now, are you able to say that man you saw do the shooting was either one of these two men in the cage? A. These two men in the cage?

Q. Yes. A. No, sir, I do not.

Q. What do you mean by that? A. They are not the men. [1110]

Cross-Examination.

Q. (By Mr. Katzmann) Do you know how long a second is, Mr. Cerro?

A. Well, a second is very short.... [1110]

Q. And do you know which of the two, the paymaster or the guard was the one who came across the street and dropped on the sidewalk where you have indicated?

A. The paymaster had a mustache on him.

Q. The paymaster had a mustache? A. Yes.

Q. Was it the paymaster dropped on the sidewalk? A. Yes.

Q. And he, you say, was shot at by the light-haired man? A. Yes

MR. KATZMANN. That is all. [1112].

[Ed. Three other workers at the excavation site for the restaurant— **Emielio Falcone**, sworn June 23 [1076]; **Pedro Iscorla**, sworn June 24 [1095]; and **Sibriano Gudierres**, sworn June 24 [1112]—testified that they were close enough to the shooting to identify physical features of the bandits. The three workers testified that the bandits in the car were not the defendants. See "Summary" by Fraenkel, The Sacco-Vanzetti Case, p. 307.]

18. LOUIS PELSER IMPEACHED

William Brenner, Sworn. June 24, 1921.

Q. (By Mr. Callahan) What is your occupation? A. Shoe cutter.

Q. Where were you employed April 15 of last year? A. That was the time of the—

Q. That was the day of the shooting. A. Rice & Hutchins.

Q. I call your attention to Exhibit 7. Can you point out on that picture at what window you were working? A. Why, the window that was up about three or four inches. There was a window there that would not shut... .

MR. KATZMANN. Keep your voice up.

MR CALLAHAN. Don't go too fast.

MR. KATZMANN. These gentlemen up here want to hear.

THE WITNESS. I looked out the window Pelser looked out.

MR. KATZMANN. I ask that may be stricken from the record.

THE COURT. It may be... . [1122]

Q. You were working at that window, which is one of the three center windows in the Rice & Hutchins factory, facing Pearl Street? A. Yes, sir... .

Q. Did you know a man whose name is Pelzer? A. Yes, sir.

Q. Where, with reference to your place of work, was he working that afternoon, April 15 of last year? A. ... [H]e was working on the same bench with me, on the same aisle [line].

Q. How many benches away from where you were working, would you say?

A. Why, two or three boards... .

THE COURT. What is that?

THE WITNESS. Cutting boards... .

Q. Where did you see him [Pelser]? A. Why, I seen him in the crowd. He was the one, they claim he was the one who got the number of the car. [1123]

Q. Not what they claim. Where did you see him? A. Why, I see him up in the corner,—corner of the building. Show me a picture and I will show you where.

Q. You saw him where? A. At the corner there,—at the corner of,— facing Pearl Street... .

Q. Did you look out the window while the shooting was going on? A. No, sir.

Q. Did you see anybody look out of a window on the Pearl Street side of the Rice & Hutchins factory while the shooting was going on?

A. Well, I can answer that. All I heard, the shots, I looked through the crack myself. I was the first one that looked through **the crack**... .

Q. ... Was there an open space [an "open space" Brenner mentioned when asked to repeat]?

A. Yes, sir. That window was broken and you could not shut it. It was about—

Q. Will you point out on Exhibit 7 where that window was broken and there was a hole or space, that you mentioned? A. It was the next window from where I was working. [1124]

Q. How much open space, would you say, there was there? A. About three or four inches... .

Q. Did you look out of that open space? A. Yes, sir... .

Q. While the shooting was going on? A. When I heard the shots.

Q. What did you see? A. Why, I see a man sinking,—sinking... .

Q. How long were you there at that open space looking out? A. Why, just for about a minute or so. Then I had this fellow working right aside of me. I drew his attention. He jumped on the bench and opened the window.

Q. Who was that? A. Peter.

Q. Peter who? A. Peter McCullum.

Q. Peter McCullum. You say Peter McCullum opened the same window you were at?

A. Yes, that I looked through the crack... .

Q. Did you see Pelzer near that window? A. No. [1125]

Q. Did you look out the window when he [McCullum] opened it? A. I did not get a chance. I noticed the body sinking, and I happened to look and he opened it again and he hollered, "Duck", something like that. I did not see anything after that.

MR. KATZMANN. I didn't get that.

THE WITNESS. ... As he opened the window, all I noticed was this Berardelli sinking and he opened the window again, and this Peter McCallan [sic] that opened the window, he hollered out for us, for me to duck or for the rest of the fellows and I ducked after that and I don't know what happened.

Q. Was there anybody else other than you and Peter looking out that window? A. No, sir.

Q. When, with reference to that time, was it that you saw Pelzer in the corner that you have described? A. Oh, long after the thing happened. About—that is, when the auto, after the auto was out of sight... .

Q. Did you see the auto going up the street? A. I saw the auto ... crossing the railroad track.

Q. And from what window were you looking when you saw the auto crossing the railroad track? A. I was at the window facing the yard. On that scene I can show it to you... .

Q. Will you point with a pencil [on Exhibit 6]? A. Right there (indicating).

MR. CALLAHAN. (To the jury) The witness points to a window on the second floor on the westerly side of Rice & Hutchins factory, one near to Pearl Street. [1126]

Q. ... Who was there looking out the window, if anybody? A. Oh, there was quite a crowd there.

Q. Was Pelzer there? A. Yes, sir.

Q. Looking out the window with you? A. Not looking out the window. He was there.

Q. Near the window?

A. Right there, around somewhere around the window. I couldn't say just where.

Q. ... Are you certain that Pelzer was not at the window that McCullum opened?

A. Yes, sir. [1127]

Cross-Examination.

Q. (By Mr. Katzmann) If there were a number plate there on the rear of the car, could you have read the numbers from that window? A. I don't know.

Q. What is your best judgment? ... A. No, I don't think I could... .

Q. Is there a bench, a workbench in front of the—they are in groups of three, is it? A. Yes.

Q. And on the photograph indicated you were at the west window of the middle trio? A. Yes... .

Q. Do all three open and shut in the trio in that middle group?

A. ... Do you mean all these three here?

Q. Yes. A. The center window of the three does not open or shut.

Q. Do the other two on either side open and shut? A. Yes, sir. [1128]

Q. Did you see him [Berardelli] when he was sinking put his arm up like that (indicating)?

A. No, sir... .

Q. Did you see another man right aside of him shooting at him?

A. No.

Q. Was there another man right there? A. No, sir.

Q. Was he alone? A. Yes, sir.

Q. Was there anybody just outside him on the outside of the gutter in the street?

A. None that—I didn't see anybody.

Q. You were looking, weren't you? A. I just saw Berardelli... .

Q. Did Pelzer work to your [right], as you looked out the window—

A. To my right. [1129]

Q. Then you were in the center between McCallan [sic], is it?

A. Peter McCallan [sic], yes... .

Q. How far away from you was Pelzer? A. Why, I should say about where that fellow is sitting there, that corner there, inside... .

Q. This gentleman here? A. Something like that.

Q. Then Mr. Pelzer was in front of another window, wasn't he?

A. Yes. [1130]

AFTERNOON SESSION

William Brenner [Continued].
Cross-Examination Resumed.

Q. (By Mr. Katzmann) Where was Mr. Pelser when Peter McCullum raised the window in front of which you were? A. I don't know... . [1137]

Q. Where was he when you came to the window, if you went to the window? A. I don't know.

Q. How many men were at the window? A. Oh, there was fifteen, I guess.

Q. There were fifteen men at that window?

A. It is a glass wall, practically, and it is small windows that open in the center... .

Q. Show me the window at which you say fifteen men were.

MR. KATZMANN. May we have some light, Mr. Sheriff, please?

A. That window there [indicating] this corner window. It is practically all glass there. [1142]

Q. ... Who were the fifteen men ... looking through that west window? A. I don't know.

Q. Was Pelser there? A. No, sir... .

Q. Haven't you said so this morning? A. No, sir.

Q. Did you see Pelser in that corner of the building as the automobile went over the crossing? A. No, sir.

Q. Haven't you said this morning on direct examination that when you got to that window he was in that corner? No, sir.

MR. KATZMANN. That is all. [1143]

Peter McCullum, Sworn. June 24, 1921.

Q. (By Mr. Callahan) Where were you employed April 15th, last year? A. Shoe cutter.

Q. Where? A. In Rice & Hutchins factory.

Q. The floor above the basement? A. Yes, sir. [1149]

Q. Did you open a window that afternoon that faced out on to Pearl Street? A. Did I open a window? . [See Ehrmann, The Case, p. 224: The window was opaque to shut off sun's glare.]

Q. Yes. A. Yes, sir.

Q. Either the fifth or sixth window from the northwest corner of the factory?

A. Yes, sir. I believe it was the fifth... . [1150]

Q. Can you point out on the map for me the window that he [Pelser] was working at, ...?

A. I think it was this one here, sir (indicating).

Q. Well now, pointing here—I don't get you. That is the third—

A. Third from the [easterly] end of the building... .

Q. How soon before you opened the window did you see Pelser?

A. Oh, I didn't say nothing maybe for an hour and a half after I closed it... .

Q. Before you opened it? A. Before I opened it?

Q. Yes. Before you opened it, how long did you see him at his work?

A. I imagine I must have seen him just before the thing happened. [1151]

Q. Was there anybody else near the window when you opened it? A. I didn't see anybody.

Q. What did you see out in the street, ... when you opened the window? A. Why, I saw one man.

Q. What was he doing? A. Why, it seems he was pushing some money into the car, or the box they had got away with, and he pushed it into the car.

Q, You saw an automobile, too? A. Yes, sir.

Q. This one man you saw was . . . putting something into the car? A. Putting something into the car.

Q. Is that all you saw? A. That is all.

Q. Did you see any gun? A. One gun, sir.

Q. Where was the gun? A. It seemed in the man's left hand.

Q. Was it a gun or revolver type, which? A. Revolver type, I should say.

Q. Did you notice anything else about the man other than he had a gun in his hand?

A. Bare-headed... .

Q. Can you give me his complexion? A. ... [H]e might have been— kind of a dark man.

Q. Mustache, or not? A. I figured he was clean shaven.

Q. How tall was he? A. 5 feet 7 or 8, I should imagine. [1152]

Q. When you put the window down, what did you do? A. What did I do?

Q. Yes. A. I went down with it... .

Q. You jumped down to the floor? A. Yes, sir.

Q. Did you see Pelser at all then, ...? A. I seen him after the thing was all over, ...

Q. Where did you see him? A. It seems he came over to talk to us like. [1153]

Q. Where did you see him? A. When he came down and started to talk to me at my board. [1154]

Cross-Examination.

Q. (By Mr. Katzmann) ... Pelser worked, I think you said, down in front of the **seventh** window? You didn't say seventh, but it would be, wouldn't it (indicating plan). A. Yes, sir.

Q. That would be, as one looked out, the **left-hand window of the last trio**? A. Yes, sir.

Q. They are in groups of three, aren't they? A. I believe they are, sir.

Q. That window is a window that opens, referring to the one where you worked?

A. It opens just the same as mine. [1155]

Q. Was it open three or four inches that afternoon at the time of the shooting?

A. Which window, sir?

Q. The one where Pelser worked? A. I don't believe so.

Q. Do you know? A. I don't know for sure.

Q. Did you look at it? A. No, sir... .

Q. You have no knowledge of it? A. I have no knowledge of it.

Q. Was the next one to the right of it, the eighth, open three or four inches?

A. I have no knowledge.

Q. You have no knowledge of the eighth window?

A. No, I have no knowledge of the eighth window... .

Q. Have you any knowledge as to whether it was open or not? A. No, I have not. [1156]

Q. This man [you saw] had no hat on? A. This man had no hat on...

Q. Did you get any view of the gun that you saw in his left hand?

A. It looked like a white gun...

Q. What did he have, if he had anything, in his right hand?

A. I don't know, He seemed to be pushing something.

Q. Did you get any impression that it was a box?

A. It might have been a box, I don't know for sure, sir. [1157]

Q. Did he do anything with respect to the automobile?

A. It seemed this box was being pushed into the automobile.

Q. He was putting something in? A. Yes, sir... .

Q. Well, what portion of the automobile was he putting that something in? A. What end of the automobile, do you mean, sir?

Q. Yes. A. It seems the rear.

Q. The rear door leading to the rear seat? A. Yes, sir. . . . .

Q. You sensed personal danger, didn't you? A. Yes, sir.

Q. Immediately when you closed it you didn't look around to see where Pelser was? A. No, sir.

Q. Or where Mr. Brenner was? A. No, sir.

Q. You wanted to duck to cover? A. Yes, sir.

197

Q. And you ducked to cover? A. Yes, sir.

Q. Under your bench? A. I don't know whether it was under my bench.

Q. Don't know where you went? A. No, sir.

Q. You were excited, weren't you? A. Certainly. [1158]

Q. ... Has your attention ever been called to Pelser's position, before you took the stand?

A. Talking with Mr. Moore. [Ed. Chief defense counsel.]

Q. When was that? A. This morning.

Q. Was that the first time since April 15th, 1920, that your attention has been called to Pelser's position at the moment of the shooting?

A. Mr. Callahan last Monday, ... asked me something.

Q. I suppose you told Mr Callahan you didn't know, just as you told on the stand?

A. Yes, sir. [1161]

[Ed. On June 30, defense witness William Gibson Foley testified to what he saw from his truck at the dump eastward on Pearl Street: "As they done the shooting these two men grabbed a large black box, one on each end. Both had a gun in their hands, firing at the same time,—— put it into the Buick car."] [1593]

Redirect Examination.

Q. (Br Mr. McAnarney) Did you see others duck, too? A. No, I did not, sir. [1162]

Recross Examination.

Q. (By Mr. Katzmann) Did the gun you saw in the left hand of this man look like either of those (indicating)? A. Seemed as if it was more the color of this (indicating). [1163]

Dominic Constantino, Sworn. June 24, 1921.

Q. (By Mr. Callahan) Where were you employed April 15th of last year?

A. In Rice & Hutchins.

Q. Did you see any of the shooting? A. No. [1166]

Q. Do you know where Brenner worked? A. He worked two windows from Peter McCullum.

Q.... That would be the **fourth window** on the Pearl Sreeet side of the factory from the northwest corner? A. Yes.

Q. ... Can you show me on the plan where Pelser works?

A. He works the next window to Brenner, about here [indicating].

Q. One, two, three, four, five, six, seven, eight. The eighth window from the northwest corner of the factory. Anybody else work on that line? A. No, sir.... [1167]

Q. Did you see Pelser get under the bench? A. Yes.

Q. What bench did you see Pelser get under? A. His own place.... [1168]

Q. What did you hear Pelser say? A. Well, I heard him say that he did not see anybody. [1172]

Cross-Examination.

Q. (By Mr. Katzmann) Did you hear somebody say from that crowd [around you] that the number was put down on a board? A. I saw Pelser write the number on the board....

Q. Whose bench was that he wrote it on? A. It was, I think it was McCullum's bench....

Q. I am showing the window [in question] facing the railroad.

A. Well, I was there.

Q. Isn't that the window they looked out? A. No.

Q. Which window was it? A. The corner window.

Q. This window [indicating]? A. Yes.

Q. Is that the window that McCullum looked out? A. No.

Q. Is that the window that Brenner looked out? A. No.

Q. Well, who did look out that window? A. Pelser.

Q. Pelser? When? A. After the automobile started speeding away. [1178]

Q. Were you watching to see who was at any other window? A. No. [1179]

Q. ... Has anybody ever asked you where Pelser was when the shooting was going on? A. No.

Q. Nobody? A. Nobody.

Q. So that before you took the stand nobody had asked you that?

A. Well—

Q. Well, that can be answered yes or no. A. Yes.

Q. Then will you so answer it? A. I volunteered myself... .

Q. To whom did you volunteer it? A. I went to see a member of the committee.

Q. What committee? A. The defense committee [formed by Felicani].

Q. And you weren't interested in this case, were you?

A. I did, after I read the Pelser testimony. [1180]

Mrs. Barbara Liscomb, Sworn. June 24, 1921.

Q. (By Mr. Jeremiah McAnarney) Did you work at Rice & Hutchins' factory last year? A. Yes.

Q. Were you there working the day of the shooting? A. Yes, sir.

Q. In what room did you work? A. In the treeing room [third floor]. [1190]

Q. What did you do when you heard that ["a man had been shot"]?

A. I ... went to the window, which was opened [second window facing Pearl Street].

Q. And when you looked out that window, what did you see? A. I saw two men lying on the ground, and one man, a short dark man, standing on the ground facing me, with his head up, holding a revolver in his hands.

Q. Did you get a clear view of his features and his face? A. Yes, sir, I would always remember his face.

Q. Did he have a revolver, this man you saw? A. Yes, sir.

Q. And what did he do with it?

A. He was ... pointing it ... toward the window which I was looking out of.

Q. What did you do then? A. I sort of fainted away.

Q. Were you later taken, either by the officers or by some one in the factory, to see some men?

A. Yes, sir.

Q. Where, first? A. I was taken first to Braintree.

Q. How soon was that after the shooting? A. Well, I really do not know, but I think it was about four or five days after, this last time... .

Q. Are either of the men in the dock the man you saw pointing the revolver at your window?

A. No, sir.

Cross-Examination.

Q. (By Mr. Katzmann) Did you say that, Mrs. Liscomb, four or five days after the shooting you went to Braintree? A. Yes, sir, South Braintree, Town Hall.

Q. Did you see anybody there? A. Yes, sir.

Q. In the way of a prisoner. A. I saw a man. [1191]

Q. Yes. A. Who I saw this morning. I do not remember his name.

Q. Yes. Where did you see him here this morning? A. I saw him in this [back] room out there.

Q. Will you describe him? A. He was medium height and dark, dark hair, dark eyes... .

Q. ... Did anybody call him "Ricardo"? A. I don't remember.

Q. Did anybody call him "Orciani"? A. No, I really couldn't remember the name... .

Q. You cannot tell this jury whether he had a moustache or not?

A. No, I cannot remember... .

Q. And that was four or five days after the shooting, wasn't it [that you saw a man at the Braintree Town Hall]? A. If I remember right, yes, sir.

Q. Well, do you remember right? A. I cannot tell you exactly to the date.

Q. Well, it wasn't three weeks after the shooting? A. No, sir. [1192]

Q. How long did you say you were at that window?

A. I might have been there possibly two seconds. [1194]

Q. Where was either of the two men who were laying on the ground?

A. One man was lying in the gutter; the other was lying near a pair of horses and team.

Q. Across the street? A. Yes... .

Q. As you looked out the window, and saw a man lying in the gutter——

A. Yes.

Q. Did you look to your right to see that man or to your left? A. I looked to my left.

Q. You looked to your left. He was up the hill, wasn't he? A. Yes.

Q. You say "up the hill," beyond the corner of the building, perhaps?

A. Perhaps.

Q. How far up beyond the corner of the building? A. I couldn't tell you that. [1195]

201

Q. What was the man doing ... out in the street? A. He was standing facing me, holding the revolver.

Q. Pointing it up at you? A. Pointed at the window I was standing at.

Q. Did he have a hat on? A. No, he had a cap on.

Q. He had a cap on? A. Yes.

Q. Sure of that? A. I am... .

Q. Did you see anybody other than the two men who were prostrate on the ground and the man with the revolver? A. I saw a man with a wagon and two horses. [1196]

Mrs. Barbara Liscomb.
Cross-Examination Resumed.
Saturday, June 25, 1921.

Q. (By Mr. Katzmann) Can you see at one glance,—could you see the body up here of one man and the body over here of another man in one glance? A. No.

Q. Then you did have to turn your head, didn't you? A. Yes, sir. [1200]

Q. And when you said yesterday afternoon you looked to your left and saw one body and to your right across the street and saw the other, you meant it, didn't you?

A. I admit I said it, but I made a mistake. [1201]

19. THE ESCAPING BANDIT CAR AGAIN

Nicolo Gatti, Sworn. June 25, 1921.

[The clerk starts to administer the oath to the witness through the interpreter.]

THE COURT. Wait a minute, Mr. Interpreter. He seemed as though he understood you.

THE INTERPRETER. No, he don't understand, "I understand very little."

MR. JEREMIAH McANARNEY. I could not carry on an intelligent conversation with this man. I just interrogated him this morning.

THE COURT. Go ahead.

[The witness is sworn through the Interpreter.]

[The testimony of the witness is given through the Interpreter.] [1209]

Q. (By Mr. McAnarney) April 15th, last year, who were you working for? A. I was working for the railroad ...

Q. Where were you working ...? A. I was working right back of the gate, behind of the gate.

Q. How near were you working to the gateman's shanty?

A. Why, about twenty-five or thirty feet away from him.

Q. Did you hear any shots? A. Yes, sir.

Q. When you heard the shots what did you do? A. I ran right away.

Q. Ran where to? A. Toward the factory, where I heard the reports.

Q. You did not run away from the shots? A. No, sir.

Q. ... When you ran towards where you heard the shots, where did you stop? A. I stopped between the shanty and the factory, about halfway between. [Ed. Witness points on photograph.]

MR. JEREMIAH McANARNEY. ... [Indicating on the map.] Apparently, if your Honor please, for the purposes of the plan, the witness went over to the building called the "iron covered garage, one story," marked on **the plan**, the building directly across the tracks from the shanty; ... [1210]

Q. When you got over there near this building, what did you see?

A. I stopped sudden, because the automobile [bandit car] was coming.

Q. As the automobile came up to you, what did any one in the automobile do, if anything?

A. Well, there were two in the front of the automobile and one of the two had the gun like that [indicating].

Q. What, if anything, did they do with the gun? A. He fired a shot.

Q. In what direction did he fire? A. Towards,—he fired at my direction, almost to the gate.

Q. Calling your attention to the photograph, there is a gate over near the building where you stood? A. I was between the two gates... .

Q. How many men did you see in the auto? A. I saw three distinctly.

Q. ... [H]ow many men were in the automobile? A. Four or five. No more than five. [1211]

Q. ... Now, give us the best description you can of the man that was sitting beside the driver?

A. The man that was sitting aside of the driver, he was somewhat round face, thick-set fellow, and somewhat brown color.

Q. Do you remember if he had anything on his head? A. Yes, he had a cap... .

Q. Have you known Nicola Sacco? A. Yes.

Q. When did you first know Nicola Sacco? A. I have known him between 1912 and 1913.

Q. Where was he living when you knew him? A. At Milford. [Last saw him eight years ago.]

Q. Was Nicola Sacco any of the men you saw in the automobile?
A. No, sir.

Q. Was the other defendant in the dock either of the men you saw in the automobile? A. No, sir. [1212]

Cross-Examination.

Q. (By Mr. Katzmann) Well, there are six tracks here south of the crossing. Which one of those six were you working on? A. I was working on the second track from the—

Q. How long have you been in this country? A. Twenty-one years.

Q. You speak English all right, don't you? A. No, I don't. I do not speak English... .

Q. Did you say you ran over in front of this building, across the track?
A. Yes, I crossed the tracks. [1213]

Q. ... [Y]ou ran up the street and came out at the garage. That is right?
A. Yes, sir.

Q. You said "right" before I put the question, didn't you? You understood my English, didn't you? You didn't? What did you say "right" for? A. I understand some words in English... .

Q. But you were out in the street, were you?

A. In the middle of the tracks, in the railroad tracks... .

Q. You understand that, do you? A. Well, there is two gates. I was in the centre, between the two gates. [1214]

Q. How far to your left was it [the bandit car]?

A. Well, passed,—when the automobile passed me, four or five feet... .

Q. You stood right in the centre of the crossing? A. Yes... .

Q. Did it [bandit car] touch you? A. No, sir.

Q. Did it go over you? A. What do you mean, over me? ...

Q. Do you want me to answer that? A. I was standing there as the automobile went by. [1215]

Q. Did you see anything in the back curtain? A. I didn't see anything.

Q. Did you see any glass as shown in defendants' Exhibit A? A. I saw that glass.

Q. Was it in there in the back of the curtain? A. Yes, the glass was in it. [1217]

Q. How long did you know the defendant Sacco? A. I knew him from 1912 up to 1913.

Q. Did you live near him in Milford? A. No, sir,—about a half hour's walk.

Q. Did you go to see him at all? A. No, sir. I have seen him on the street.

Q. How did you know it was Sacco? A. Well, I have met him several times on the street, and because, you know the Italians, they all talk together, and I had seen him on the street, we met on the street, and I knew him.

Q. Did you ever meet Ricardo Orcianni? A. No, sir... .

Q. Did you know that Ricardo ever lived in Milford?

[Ed. McAnarney objected, then withdrew his objection after Katzmann cited Kelley's testimony.]

Q. Did you know that Orcianni ever lived in Milford? A. No, sir.

Q. Have you met Orcianni since you have been in attendance on the court? A. I don't know him.

Q. How long have you been waiting in attendance on this court?

A. Two days.

Q. Where have you been [where in the court house]? A. Do you mean in those two days?

Q. Yes. A. In the back room.

Q. Did you see a man with a little black mustache in there?

A. I didn't pay any attention. [1219]

[Ed. On June 27, six more workers for the New York, New Haven & Hartford Railroad Company were sworn—**Dominick DiBona** [1242], **Cesidio Magnerelli** [1252], **Donato DiBona** [1258], **Fortinato Antonello** [1267], **Antonio Frabizio** [1272], and **Tobia DiBona** [1273]. Frabizio was excused, and the other five testified that the men they saw in the bandit car were not the defendants. An eighth railroad worker, **Joseph Cellucci** [1571], sworn on June 30, testified that the men he saw in the bandit car were neither Sacco nor Vanzetti.]

Daniel Joseph O'Neil, Sworn. June 28, 1921.

Q. (By Mr. Callahan) Where do you live? A. South Braintree.

Q. What is your business, your occupation? A. I just got through school. [Business school]

Q. Where were you [April 15, 1920]? A. South Braintree depot.

Q. What were you doing there? A. I just got off the 2:29 out of Boston.

Q. … Where did you go when you left the train? A. I was sitting in the taxi… .

Q. While you were sitting there, was your attention called to something?

A. There was shooting… .

Q. What did you do … when you heard the shots? A. I looked in the direction from which I heard the shots, and I seen a woman standing near the crossing, and she hollered that somebody was shot, and I immediately ran in that direction… .

Q. Where did you stop, if you did stop? A. I stopped a ways near a signal up the other side of the crossing [by a wooden box]. [1390]

Q. Where was it [the bandit car] when you first saw it? A. Just coming from behind that fence that runs up to the end of the crossing just mounting the raiload crossing.

Q. Did you see anybody in the automobile?

A. I saw one man standing on the running board. [1391]

Q. ... Will you tell the jury what you saw him do? A. ... I seen this man reach out there to turn some knob that opens the door or unbuckle the fastening that held the curtain down, ... and he came right out on the running board of the side of the car, this man, with a gun in his hand, and he walked along that running board, and before the car had got over the other side of the crossing that man was sitting in the front seat of that same car, with the gun still in his hand, and sort of leaning out of the door, and he pointed at the cobbler as the cobbler stuck his head out ... of the door of the cobbler shop, ...

Q. ... Now, will you describe that man to the jury? A. ... dark hair, cleanly shaven, broad shoulders and held himself erect and square, of light complexion, ... He wore a blue suit and no hat, and his hair was thick but straight and combed back straight over his head. [1392]

Q. Will you say that man in that automobile on April 15, last year, was either of those two men sitting in the dock? A. No, sir. [1393]

Cross-Examination.

Q. (By Mr. Katzmann) How old are you, Mr. O'Neil? A. I will be 19 October11th of this year.

Q. I believe that you have fixed the point from which you said you saw the automobile crossing the tracks as at the end of the box, wooden box between tracks 4 and 5 **north** of it?

A. Yes, sir.

[Witness leaves witness stand.] [1393] [Ed. O'Neil looks at Breed's Plan, Exhibit 38.]

Q. [T]his scale ... is 10 feet to the inch. So ... you ... would be between 155 and 170 feet from the automobile. Is that right? A. I don't know. I don't know just how far it is... . [1394]

[Witness returns to witness stand.]

Q. And the door was behind him [the bandit] when he moved forward on the running-board. Is that correct? A. ... I didn't take no particular notice of the door, but as I seen the door there was a clear space for him to come out, ... nothing in his way at all.

Q. When he got out, was there any door in front of him across the running-board? A. No... .

Q. Are you aware of the fact that on a Buick car the rear door opens from the back and does open forward and comes out 11 1/2 inches from the outer edge of the running board?

A. It may be. It may come out on a Buick. [1395]

Winfred H. Pierce, Sworn. June 23, 1921.

Q. (By Mr. Callahan) Where were you employed April 15, last year?
A. Slater, Morrill Company.
Q. In the factory? A. In the so-called Hampton House. ...
Q. Which floor of that factory? A. The third floor.
Q. In what part of the third floor...? A. The third window from the Pearl Street end.
Q. On the right-hand side as you faced out of the window?
A. As I faced the railroad track.... southerly side of the window facing east. [1040]
Q. How many shots did you hear fired?
A. That is impossible for me to state, but I should think eight or ten. [1041]
Q. Now, will you tell the jury what you observed with reference to the automobile and the occupants, ... A. I noticed the auto as it came on to the crossing, and it seems there was a man climbing from the rear to the front.... [1042]
Q. Will you describe that man to the jury? A. ... Seeing that man starting over, ... just getting another view of him, a very short view, ... he would weight from 175 to [1043] 180 pounds. I don't know whether he was a short or medium height man, ... No hat on....
Q. Can you describe the man further? A. Well, he had what appeared to me four or five days' growth of beard, ... a man, ... 42, 3 or 4 years old.
Q. Did he wear a mustache? A. He did not, he was so-called smooth-shaven.
Q. What would you say of the man you saw in the automobile, ... was he either one of the two defendants in the dock or cage?
A. I don't think that it was, but I am not positive, but I don't think so. [1044]

Cross-Examination.

Q. (By Mr. Katzmann) How long was he [man you saw in the car] in your view?

A.... . I don't believe that the car could go over ten feet before it would be lost from my view... .

Q. That man ["leaning out" of the car] had no hat on, did he? A. He did not. [1048]

Q. And you don't say, do you, Mr. Pierce, that the defendant Sacco is not the man?

A. I don't think so.

Q. You cannot honestly say that he is not the man, that he is not the one and the same man that was leaning over with his arm extended?

A. No, I cannot... . [1049]

Q. Do you remember attending an inquest at the Quincy court? A. I do, well.

Q. On Saturday, April 17th, you were asked some questions there?

A. I was. [1055]

Q. Do you remember at the inquest this question and answer was asked of you and you answered as follows:

"Q. Could you get a good look at him, his face?"——referring to the man who was firing?

"A. I did and I didn't. All that I noticed was that he was a dark man."

Did you make that answer at Quincy some two days after the shooting?

A. I stated there that he was a dark man.

Q. Just a minute. A. And had apparently a beard on. [1056]

Mr. Lawrence Dubois Ferguson, Sworn. June 23, 1921.

Q. (By Mr. Callahan) Where were you employed April 15th of last year? A. Slater & Morrill, South Braintree.

Q. On what floor? A. Formerly the Hampton House... It is the floor just above the office, ...

[1065]

Q. Did you ... see anybody in the automobile? A. ... I thought I saw somebody climbing or starting to climb from the rear of the car over into the front... . [1068]

Q. ... [A]re you able to say that that man was either of these two defendants?

A. Not positively. but I don't——

Q. What is your best impression? A. I don't believe it was. [1070]

Cross-Examination.

Q. (By Mr. Katzmann) It may not have been and it may have been.
A. Yes. [1070]

Frank J. Burke, Sworn. June 22, 1921.

Q. (By Mr. Callahan) Where do you live? A. Hotel Norris, Brockton.
Q. And what is your business? A. Giving glass-blowing exhibitions.
Q. Do you recall the day of April 15th, last year? A. Yes, sir.
Q. Were you in South Braintree that day? A. Yes, sir.
Q. What time did you arrive in South Braintree? A. I left on a train which left somewhere about half past two in the afternoon. [969]
Q. Anybody with you? A. My partner, Augustus Pecheur. [970]
[Ed. Hearing shots after leaving Officer Harry Schwartz, Burke walked toward R.R. crossing.]
Q. How near did you go to **the westerly rail** of the railroad crossing before you came to a stop? A. Probably **60 feet**. [971]
Q. Now, when you got to the point near the railroad crossing and as you have testified stopped, will you tell me what you observed? A. As I said, I seen an automobile coming slowly up the incline toward the railroad track. Just at that time two men run in a diagonal direction and jumped on the running-board of that car and got into the back part of the car... .
Q. Have you told me now all you observed while you were standing at that point as the car came up the hill? A. As the car approached the crossing, ... one of the men who was in the back of the car started to climb over the back seat into the front seat with the driver... .
Q. How near did the car get to you when this man had got seated in the front seat?
A. Probably within ten feet, ...[972]
Q. What [did you observe him doing]? A. After he got seated in the front seat, he faced toward me... [H]e leaned ... forward, grabbed hold of the door, ... and poked a gun, a revolver, at me, and snapped it, and said, "Get out of the way, you son of a B."
Q. Using the English language? A. Fully... .
Q. Did he have any head covering? A. A cap... . [973]

Q. ... [A]re you able to say whether or not those men [you saw in the bandit car] were either of the two defendants in the dock? A. I would say they were not.... .

Q. What did you do after [the car got out of sight and your talk with Officer Harry Schwartz]? A. [W]atched him...[try] to start his car.

Q. What did you do then? A. [Phoned Brockton Enterprise from American Railways Express].

Q. Did you later after that day learn of the arrest of the two defendants? A. Yes, sir.

Q. When? A. About two weeks after, I should judge. I was off on the road and came home.

Q. You were away on the road [when defendants were arrested]? A. Yes, sir. [977]

[Ed. Burke said he knew "all the police officers in Brockton well, being years ago connected with the police department." This was stricken.] [978]

Q. You spent four or five minutes at the different cells with the defendants, ..?

A. Probably four or five minutes all together [at cells in the Brockton police station]. [979]

Cross-Examination.

Q. (By Mr. Katzmann) ... On which side of the car did those two men get in, the left or the right? A. On the south side.... .

Q. In which direction was the car traveling? A. Towards me.

Q. By point of the compass? A. Traveling west.

Q. They got in on the north side? A. On the north side. Yes.... .

Q. From which side of the car? A. From the north side of the street.

Q. That is the same side as the tank is situated on? This side, the north side of Pearl Street, there is a tank? A. That is on the south side of Pearl Street, isn't it?

Q. Well, what do you say? A. I say it is on the south side.

Q. What does that [indicating] say? Don't you see that? Can't you see that? A. Yes.

Q. What does it say? A. "North."

Q. Yes. Then, what side of the street is it on? A. It is on the north.

Q. Then you needed to change your answer, didn't you, that they got in from the other side?

A. Yes. [980]

Q. Are you familiar with a Buick car? A. No, sir. [Ed. See reference to photograph, p. 976.]

Q. How could you tell it was a Buick?

A. Well, I saw one this morning. I rode over in it and noticed the name plate on it... .

Q. Whose Buick was it you rode over in this morning? A. [Witness hesitates.] Lawyer Callahan's...

Q. Was it a Hudson or a Buick?

A. I believe it is a Hudson, now that you call my attention to it. [982]

Q. Do you know Mr. Woodbury [investigator for Moore]? A. Yes, sir. I met him. [983]

Q. How many times in all have you talked with him about it [the case]?

A. Oh, perhaps a half dozen. [984]

Q. Have you been in the employ of the defense securing evidence in this case?

A. No, sir, I have not.

Q. ... [Y]ou talked with Mr. Woodbury on five other occasions when there were others present talking about the case? A. Yes, I said that, for there were ... others present, ...

Q. How many times all together did you go to Mr. Moore's office [in Boston]?

A. I probably have been there seven or eight times all together... . [985]

Q. What was the occasion of your going to Mr. Moore's office a dozen times or more to tell your story? A. Several reasons... .

Q. Then you went in on some other business? A. Yes, I went in on other business. [997]

Mr. Augustus Pecheur, Sworn. June 23, 1921. Corroborative Witness.

Q. (By Mr. Callahan) You reside where? A. Somerville.

Q. What is your business? A. Glass worker.

Q. Was he [Mr. Burke] at one time a partner of yours? A. Yes.

Q. Were you in South Braintree on that day [April 15, 1920]? A. Yes, sir.

Q. Who was with you. A. Mr. Burke... .

Q. Do you know whether you arrived at South Braintree that day before the shooting happened?

A. Oh, yes, a long time.

Q. When you got to South Braintree that day, where did you go?

A. I stayed right on the platform. [1000]

Q. Later on did you hear of the arrest of the two defendants? A. Yes.

Q. Where were you when you heard of their arrest? A. Well, I was in Harmony Hall there.

Q. Harmony Hall in Brockton? A. I think it is the Knights of Pythias hall.

Q. Do you recall the day of their arrest or the night of their arrest?

A. Well, no, I did not hear until the next morning... .

Q. Did you see Burke that next morning? A. Oh, yes.

Q. Did you know of him going to the Brockton police station?

A. Yes, I went with him... .

Q. Can you tell me when it was with reference to the night of the arrest of the defendants [May 5] that you and Burke went to the police station in Brockton? A. The next morning. [1001]

Cross-Examination.

Q. (By Mr. Katzmann) How long before you heard the shooting was it that you arrived in South Braintree that afternoon? A. Oh, I had been there quite a while on the platform. [1002]

Q. How long is it in your judgment you and Burke were in South Braintree before you heard the shots ...? A. Well, I couldn't tell that... . [1003]

Q. You and he were then giving an exhibition, weren't you? A. No, not the——that is Burke's home town.

Q. Weren't you giving a glass-blowing exhibition there? A. We were going away from Brockton. We were working school exhibitions every night. We came back to Brockton.

Q. Then you were not off on the road when you heard that [of the arrest]? You and he were right in Brockton? A. Yes, right in Brockton... .

Q. Did you hear of the arrest the same night it was made?

A. No, I did not hear of it until the next morning.

Q. ... Hearing of the arrest the night before, you hearing of it the next morning, what did you and Burke do? A. Right after we had breakfast, Burke says to me—

Q. ... What did you do? A. After,—I went over to the [police] station wih Burke.

Q. The same morning you heard of it [May 6]? A. Yes. [1004]

Peter Magazu, Sworn. June 28, 1921.

Q. (By Mr. Callahan) What is your name? A. Peter Magazu.

Q. What was your occupation on April 15, 1920 of last year?

A. At that time I was running a **pool room and a shoe store** in the same building.

Q. What was the location of it? A. On 56 and 58 Pearl Street.

Q. South Braintree? A. South Braintree. [1355]

Q. Were you in your store on the afternoon of April 15 of last year? A. Yes, sir.

Q. Do you recall anybody being in the store there with you? A. Well, part of the afternoon I had a man named Goodridge... .

Q. Do you recall the shooting? A. No, I didn't hear no shooting.

Q. Do you recall it happened that day? A. Yes.

Q. Did you see any of it? A. No.

Q. Do you recall hearing the automobile go by your store? A. Seen the automobile went by the corner after he called my attention.

Q. What corner did you see the automobile go by? A. Corner of **Pearl and Hancock** street.

Q. Previous to your seeing the automobile go around the corner did you have a talk,—did you see Goodridge? A. Yes, he was playing [pool] with me.

Q. What happened while he was playing with you? A. I had a customer came in the other store, in the shoe store. I had a door between those two stores, so I left him in the pool room... .

Q. Door between. A. Connected, yes. While I showed the customer a pair of shoes, he comes right in and says, "My God, something wrong about down the street." I says, "What?" He says, "I think they kill the paymaster and get the payroll." I says, "Did you see the men?" He says, "I seen the men, they pointed with a gun." I says, "How do the men look like?" He says, "Young man with light hair, light complexion and wore an army shirt." [1356]

Q. Did he say anything further about it to you?

A. He says, "This job wasn't pulled by any foreign people."

Q. Was that conversation he had with you in your store? A. In the shoe store.

Q. What did you do? A. We walk outside and see the automobile went by the corner. [1357]

Cross-Examination.

Q. (By Mr. Katzmann) How long were you in the other side of the partition?

A. About three or four minutes, no more, no longer.

Q. When did you have this talk you spoke of with Goodridge, before or after you went out on the sidewalk? A. That is when we were coming into the store, the time he came into the store.

Q. Was it before or after you went out on the sidewalk? A. No, before.

Q. That you had the talk? A. Before we went to the sidewalk.

Q. Before the automobile had gone by the store? A. No. The automobile was gone by already.

Q. Was it then that Goodridge said to you that the paymaster had been shot and the money, the payroll taken? A. Yes... .

Q. No. Wait a minute. Did he tell you that about the paymaster being killed and the money box taken——was gone——before you went out to the street? A. Yes. [1357]

Q. Could you see anybody lying in across the street at the restaurant?

. A. Yes, could see some one.

Q. You could see right behind this fence (indicating), could you?

A. Yes.

Q. And through the water tank? A. Yes.

Q. Would you say that water tank was in line with where Berardelli's body lay?

A. It was on the other side of the street... .

Q. Did you see anybody come up and talk to Goodridge? A. No. [1359]

215

Nicola Damato, Sworn. June 29, 1921.

Q. (By Mr. Callahan) What is your name? A. Nicola Damato.

Q. What is your business? A. Barber, at 54 Pearl Street, South Braintree.

Q. Were you at or near your shop last year, April 15th? A. ... Yes, sir. [1487]

Q. Do you know Mr. Goodridge, Carl Goodridge? A. Very well I know him, yes. [1488]

Q. Did he come into your barber shop? A. Yes, sir.

Q. Often? How often? A. No often, but he was get a haircut pretty near once a month, but I was going in his place... .

Q. What kind of place did he have? A. He was manager of a talking machine place... .

Q. Near your barber shop? A. No, no. About pretty near ten minutes away... .

Q. Did you have a talk with him about the shooting? A. Oh, yes, the first day it happened.

Q. You mean the day it happened? A. The day... .

Q. Tell me, will you, what he said to you about the shooting?

MR. KATZMANN. One moment, if your Honor please.

THE COURT. That may be. It may be competent and may not be. [1489] The only thing you can use him on with reference to Goodridge is the contradiction of certain questions that were asked.

Q. Have you heard him say this: that he was in the pool room and he did not see anybody in the automobile and if he was outside he could have seen them? A. Yes.

Q. How many times have you heard him say that? A. Every time.

Q. How many times? A. Well, I don't remember exactly. Maybe four or five times. Every time we meet one another. [1490]

AFTERNOON SESSION.

Nicola Damato, Resumed.
Cross-Examination.

Q. (By Mr. Katzmann) Do you know Peter Magazu? A. Yes, sir.

Q. Is his pool room near your barber shop? A. Well, two stores ... from my barber shop.

Q. Did you talk with Peter after the shooting about Goodridge?

A. After the shooting?

Q. Yes; about Goodridge, what Goodridge knew about the shooting?

A. Yes, we were talking when we read in the paper, when we were reading the [Boston] Globe.

Q. When was that? A. I do not remember the day. After he was in on the witness stand.

Q. Did Peter tell you that Goodridge came out of the—off the sidewalk back into his shop, and he told him about what had happened?

A. Magazu told me nothing.

Q. ... Didn't Magazu tell you at any time that he saw Goodridge come off the sidewalk and come back into the shoeshop where he was fitting a pair of shoes to a lady?

A. He never told me that. [1493]

Q. He did not tell you anything about it, and you know Peter well, don't you? A. Yes, sir.

Q. Peter is a truthful man, isn't he? A. Yes, sir

MR. KATZMANN. That is all. [1494]

[Ed. Olaf Olsen testified {1484} bandit car met him 150 feet from the drug store. At the Quincy inquest he testified {1487} the gunman in the front seat "had a cap pulled down too far."]

Elmer O. Chase, Sworn. June 27, 1921.

Q. (By Mr. Callahan) Employed where?

A. South Braintree Cooperative Association. I drive a truck for them.

Q. Where is the South Braintree Cooperative store, Mr. Chase?

A. That is on Hancock Street, near Pearl. [1339]

Q. Where were you ... in the afternoon of April 15 of last year?

A. I was at the store, with the truck.

Q. How near was the [bandit] car to you when it passed you?

217

A. I should say from eight, six to eight feet. [1340]

Q. Can you describe to the jury the other man [beside the driver] you saw? A. The other man was … a … dark-complexioned man. He stood on one knee looking back … through the car.

Q. Did you get a view of his face …? A. Yes. I had a pretty good look at him… . He was kind of heavy featured man, with long, dark hair. He was bare-headed. His hair was blowing. [1341]

Q. Did you notice anything with reference to the back of the automobile?

A. The back window was out.

Q. Were either of the two men you saw in that automobile … either of those those two men sitting in the dock?

A. No, they are not those men. [1342]

Cross-Examination.

Q. (By Mr. Katzmann) Any trouble with your eyes?

A. Well, I have had trouble with my eyes. [1342]

Q. Were you shown any picture by Chief Stewart? A. Yes.

Q. Were you shown a picture that purported to be a picture of [1343] defendant Sacco?

A. I do not think he told me who they were. He asked me if it looked like any of those… .

Q. Do you remember pointing to a picture and saying:

"A. This fellow's haircut would make me think of the man I saw kneeling on the seat. His hair was blowing and it seemed to me kind of kinky. He was dark." Did you say that? A. I think I did. [1344]

Albert Frank Farmer, Sworn. June 27, 1921.

Q. (By Mr. Callahan) Where do you live? A. Randolph, Massachusetts.

Q. What street? A. Orchard Street… .

Q. Was your attention called to an automobile that afternoon [April 15]?

A. Yes, sir. I saw an automobile coming down Oak Street. [1334]

Q. What kind of looking automobile was it? A. A dark colored one, what I call black.

Q. The size of the car? A. Well, what they call a seven-passenger car.

Q. What else did you notice about the car? A. That there was five men in it.

Q. What else? A. Two on the front seat and three on the rear. [1335]

Q. How old a man [was the man next to the driver]? A. I suppose about 28.

Q. ... What time in the afternoon was it? A. About 20 minutes past 3:00.

Q. Was it on Oak Street you saw this automobile or on Orchard Street? A. I was on Orchard Street. They were on **Oak Street** at first. [See map: Escape and Arrest.]

Q. Did the automobile go on Orchard Street?

A. On Orchard Street ... when they went by us. [1336]

Cross-Examination.

Q. (By Mr. Katzmann) They kept on toward Randolph? A. Yes. [1337]

[Ed. Bandit car was sighted by **Buckley** at 3:10 (561); **Baker**, "around three," (563); **Desmond** at 3:12 (1389); **Chisholm** at 3:30 (567); **Hewins** (Appel,V: 5378s); **Wilson O. Dorr** (cited in James M. Hayes's testimony) at 3:30 (1366); **Lloyd** at 3:30 (588).]

McAnarney Reads a Letter to the Court.

Mr. Jeremiah McAnarney. By agreement of counsel it is agreed that this letter may be read into the records and its contents as given received as evidence. (Reading.)

"New York, New Haven & Hartford Railroad,

"Central New England Railway Company,

"New Haven, June 27, 1921.

"Mr. J. J. McAnarney,
Dedham Court House,
Dedham, Mass.

"Dear Sir:

"Your inquiry of even date regarding make-up of Train 5108, Plymouth to Boston, April 15, 1920: According to our records this train consisted of the following equipment: Type; baggage and mail, number 2741. Length over buffers, 62 feet, 11 inches. Smoker number 1183; length over buffers, 68 feet, five inches."

Then follows three coaches and the respective numbers and length over buffers given, which isn't material.

"Train was handled by engine 323. Smoker 1183 is a full length wooden vestibule smoker. Pintsch gas lighted with seating capacity of 77. Train was handled by H. L. McNaught.

"Yours truly,

"E. J. Mather,

"Passenger Assistant."

(This letter dated June 27, 1921, from E. J. Mather to J. J. McAnarney, admitted in evidence and marked "Exhibit E.") [1350]

20. LEVANGIE IMPEACHED

Henry McCarthy, Sworn. July 11, 1921.

Q. (By Jeremiah McAnarney) You live in Stoughton? A. Yes, sir.

Q. By whom are you employed? A. New York, New Haven & Hartford Railroad.

Q. As what? A. Fireman, locomotive fireman.

Q. On the 15th day of April, last year, 1920, on what route were you firing?

A. I was firing on the 3:07 out of Boston to Stoughton, by the way of South Braintree.

Q. About what time did your train get to South Braintree? A. At 3:46.

Q. Did you make any stop there at South Braintree? A. Yes, sir, we stopped to take water and stayed there half an hour, twenty-four minutes... .

Q. Did you get off your engine? A. After I took water, yes.

Q. ... Where did you go? A. I went over to the crossing tender... .

Q. Did you have a conversation with him? A. Yes. [1999]

Q. Who was this man you talked with? A. Levangie. That is all I know, is the last name... .

Q. Now, will you please tell us what was said by Levangie or you in connection with this matter? A. After I took water I went down there. I had seen the crowd down there between Slater & Morrill's. I asked him what was going on.

THE COURT. Asked who?

THE WITNESS. Levangie. And he was at the gate. The gates were up. He says, "There was a shooting affair going on." I says, "Some one shot?" I says, "Who?" "Some one, a fellow got murdered." I said, "Who did it?" He said he did not know. He said there was some fellows went by in an automobile and he heard the shots, and he started to put down the gates, and as he started to put them down one of them pointed a gun at him and he left the gates alone and ducked in the shanty. I asked him if he knew them. He said, no, he did not. I asked him if he would know them again if he saw them. He said, "No." He said all he could see was the gun and he ducked. [2000]

221

Cross-Examination.

Q. (By Mr. Katzmann) Have you told this story to anybody before you took the stand today?
A. To-day?
Q. Yes. A. I told them in a barber shop in Stoughton a week ago Thursday night.
Q. Whose barber shop? A. Harris, in Stoughton. I was reading the newspaper and I was reading Levangie's story, and I said he told me a different one, and some one picked me up. I do not know who it was.
Q. Was that the first time, when you read Levangie, the newspaper account of Levangie's testimony in this trial, that the matter had been called to your attention? A. Yes, sir... .
Q. How long were you talking with Levangie? A. Oh, about seven or eight minutes.
Q. What did you do with the rest of the time [of your stop]? A. I went back on the engine.
Q. Did you talk with your engineer about it? A. No, sir.
Q. Did you talk with the station agent about it? A. No, sir. [2001]
Q. What made you ask him [Levangie] if he knew these men?
A. Why, just a matter of course, if they ever should get caught could identify them, I suppose. That is the only thing... .
Q. That when the gun was pointed at him he ducked, I think you said, into the shanty? A. Yes.
Q. Didn't he tell you that the gates were down when the automobile approached from the east side? A. No, sir.
Q. Didn't he say anything about raising the gates? A. He said he started to put them down... .
Q. Didn't say they were down? A. No.
Q. Did he say anything to you about hearing the tap signal from the train coming in on the Brockton line? A. No.
Q. Did he tell you what the color of the car was? A. No, sir.
Q. Or say anything about the curtains? A. No, sir.
Q. He told you he did not know any of these men? A. Yes. [2002]
Q. And he had already told you he ran into the shanty? A. He ducked into the shanty.
Q. His back was turned? A. Yes... .
Q. You assumed he immediately turned his back, didn't you?
A. Why, he says yes.

Q. Yet you asked him if he would know these men again? A. Yes.
MR. KATZMANN. That is all. [2003]

Edward Carter, Sworn. June 22, 1921.

Q. (By Mr. Callahan) Where were you employed April 15 of last year?
A. Slater & Morrill's shoe factory.
Q. The lower one on Pearl Street? A. The lower one on Pearl Street. [964]
(The fans are adjusted for the jury.)
Q. Did you have any talk with any one that afternoon with reference to the shooting with a man on the street near the shooting about an automobile? A. Why, I had a talk with the gate-tender.
Q. Who was the gate-tender? A. Michael Levangie.
Q. How long had you known him that day? A.... Oh, about 15 years.
Q. Did he say anything to you with reference to men in an automobile?
A. ... I asked him ... if he saw the driver of the car, and he said Yes. I asked what he looked like, and he said he was a light man. That is all the talk I had with him.
Q. A light man? A. A light-complected man. [965]

Cross-Examination.

Q. (By Mr. Katzmann) ... You asked one question of Mr. Levangie, didn't you? A. Yes, sir.
Q. And you asked him if he saw the driver of the car? A. Yes, sir.
Q. And he said he was a light-complected man? A. Yes, sir.
Q. That is all you asked him? A. Yes, sir.
Q. And that is all he said? A. That is all to me.
MR. KATZMANN. That is all. [969]

MR. JEREMIAH McANARNEY. If your honor please, ... We have agreed here and now I will state ... that it may be entered in the record that the transcript of the evidence which I have of the hearing in the lower court [preliminary hearing on May 26 at the Quincy Court], and which they have of the hearing at the inquest [April 17, 1920], is a correct transcript of the evidence given at both of those hearings.

[1404-1405] [Ed. For comment on this stipulation of June 28, 1921, see Ehrmann, The Case That Will Not Die, p. 181.]

INTERMISSION
(Bricolage)

"Art historians have no less an obligation than other scholars to get their facts straight, and especially to avoid misrepresentations that have had such a pernicious impact."
[Eric Foner, "Not Illiterate." *New York Review of Books*, November 19, 1998, p. 78. See Foner, p. 559.]

"In coming years, one hopes, new evidence will be discovered and deeper meaning obtained. In the end, however, we may never succeed in resolving the controversy. As the bigrapher of the Lowells remarked, immortality would almost be desirable so as to get at 'the truth' of the Sacco-Vanzetti case."
[Paul Avrich, *Sacco and Vanzetti: The Anarchist Background*, p. 6.]

"The [1927 Fuller's] commission's findings and [James E.] Starrs' presentation of them [in the *Journal of Forensic Sciences* (April and July 1986)] are hardly indisputable. But they do pose a challenge to straightforward assertions of Sacco's innocence--an issue that by this point will probably never be satisfactorily resolved."
[Michael M. Topp, *The Sacco and Vanzetti Case: A Brief History with Documents*, p. 194.]

Edwin M. Borchard

"Albert H. Hamilton, an expert for the state, said that the four bullets taken from the bodies of Phelps and his housekeeper, had been fired from the revolver owned by Stielow. . . . The experts, Mr. Bond, and the Governor [of New York] concluded that the trial testimony of Mr. Hamilton that the death bullets had come from the Stielow pistol was clearly erroneous. . . . It appeared, moreover, that the Stielow revolver had not been fired for some years."
[Edwin M. Borchard, "Stielow and Green," *Convicting the Innocent: Errors of Criminal Justice* , pp. 246, 252.] See p. xxxviii, p. 464, and p. 617.

21. DEFENSE'S BALLISTICS EXPERTS

James E. Burns, Sworn. June 28, 1921.

Q. (By Mr. Jeremiah McAnarney) What is your full name? A. James E. Burns.

Q. What is your present occupation? A. Ballistic engineer, United States Cartridge Company.

Q. How long have you been working for the United States Cartridge Company in that capacity?

A. Thirty years.

Q. What has been your experience with ... firearms? ... A. Why, with different—all makes of ammunition... .

Q. Now, have you had outside experience other than working for the company? A. Why, naturally I am, I like shooting and I have followed the rifle game in the militia. I have been in the militia eighteen years, followed the rifle game, shot on the Massachusetts team and won distinguished marksmanship in the United States with the rifle; with the shotgun, an expert, and shot on the Eastern team against the West in 1893 and beat them. Pistol,—I won the championship of Massachusetts. [1405]

Q. You have made a study of the bullets that were found in connection with this case, have you not? A. Yes, sir... .

MR. JEREMIAH McANARNEY. Let me have the revolvers please, the revolver and the pistol.

THE COURT. The sheriff has gone into town... . [Ed. Expected back at 3:00 P. M.]

Q. What bullets did you examine? A. I examined six bullets.

Q. I call the witness' attention to "Identification 15". What is that?

A. That is **a photograph of the six bullets** that were called the murder bullets.

[Ed. Burns' photographs of the 6 murder bullets labeled "Exhibit H" and "Exhibit I" on p.1426.]

Q. The bullets that were taken from the body of the men? A. From the body of the men, as I understood.

Q. ... Now, will you turn to your notes and describe what those bullets are? A. Bullet scratched number "I" on base, made by the Peters Cartridge Company; weight was 72.3 grains; lands .040 wide. The diameter of the lands 297 to 302 1/2. That is, thousandths of an inch. The grooves—

MR. KATZMANN. Wait a minute.

THE WITNESS. That is, the imprint that the lands made on the bullet. You might call it the groove on the bullet. We don't. We call it the [1406] land mark on the bullet. The groove, the width was 125. The diameter was .3075. The length of the bullet was .465. There were six grooves and lands on the bullet. Fifty-seven knurl marks in the cannon lure.

MR. KATZMANN. I did not get it.

THE WITNESS. Fifty-seven knurl marks in the cannon lure. The cannon lure was .035 of an inch wide.

[Ed. Burns stated photographs show the six murder bullets from many perspectives—1407.]

Q. So that the photographs you have there show the **photographs of the six bullets** that were taken from the body of the deceased. A. Yes, sir.

Q. And shows them so that you get an exposure of every land and every groove of every bullet?

A. Yes, sir.

Q. ... Now, will you give us No. II. A. No. II bullet, U. M. C. bullet, manufactured by the Remington Union Metallic Cartridge Company. The weight is 70.6 grains. The width of the lands, .040. Diameter of the lands .305, .302 and .302; taken in three measurements. The width of the grooves is .125. The diameter was 309, 310 and 310, measuring at 3 points. The length of the bullet was .449 of an inch, six lands. There was no cannon lure or no knurling,—smooth bullet... .

Q. All right. Keep right on. I want them complete. A. No. III? No. III was a Winchester bullet. The top of the lands,—the top of one of the lands was a part of the "W" shot. That is the trademark that the Winchester Company uses on their bullets.

Q. That identifies that as a Winchester bullet? A. That identifies that as a Winchester bullet, and also the weight identifies it. If you notice the Winchester bullets, that is the heaviest one of the lot. The Winchester bullet is 74 grains. They won't go far from 74 grains. The lands at the base, .050. At the top, that is up here (indicating) where it starts in to rifling, .060. Deformed,—you could not get a diameter, but the two diameters given were .302 and .330 of an inch.

Q. No. III, calling your attention to the twist of the bullet shown on these photographs, and I ask you how the twist on No. III compares with the others shown? A. No. III bullet has got a left-hand twist. All the others are right.

Q. From what gun may No. III be fired, or gun or guns? A. It could be fired from a Colt; fired from a Bayard.

Q. Is there any difference in the measurements of the lands and grooves of a Bayard 32 automatic and a Colt 32 automatic? A. There is.

Q. Give us the difference... A. The **Bayard is .040 wide**; the **Colt is 50**. That is the width of the lands... . [1408]

Q. I interrupted you. I beg your pardon. You complete bullet No. III. A. The width of the grooves, .105 of an inch. It is deformed. I could not get the diameter. The length is .462. Six lands and grooves. Fifty-four knurl marks. Cannon lures, .047 wide.

Q. By "knurl marks" you mean the indentations? A. The indentations of the knurl, tool marks on the bullet.

Q. The knurling marks, meaning those little indentations that appear there where the shell is pressed onto the lead? ... Give us No. 4 now. A. No. 4 bullet, made by the Peters Cartridge Company. The weight is 72 1/2 grains. The lands is .040 wide. The diameter is 299, 300 and 302, measured in three points.

Q. Repeat IIII slowly. A. The diameter of the lands is 299, 300 and 302. Grooves, the width, 120. Diameter, 308, 308, 305, measured at three points.

Q. 308, 308, 305. Does that finish it? A. No. The length is .467. Six lands and grooves. Fifty-seven knurl marks.

Q. Now, take up the next bullet, please. A. And the cannon lures, .035 wide. The next bullet, No. 5. Made by the Peters Cartridge Company. Weight, 72.1 grains. Lands, .040. Diameter of the lands, 302, 300, 303. Grooves, widths, 125, 308, 308, 309. I didn't take the——

MR. KATZMANN. That is the diameter, isn't it?

THE WITNESS. Diameter, yes, sir.

MR. KATZMANN. You did not so state.

THE WITNESS. Cannon lures, .035 wide, six lands and six grooves. Bullet marked "X" on the base.

Q. What is that, No. 6? A. No. 6, do you wish to call it? It is marked "X" on the base. Weighs 70 grains. Lands .040 wide. Diameter, 3023, 3035. Grooves, widths, 125 by 308, 308, measured in two places. The length of the bullet was .443 of an inch. All six lands and six grooves,—in fact, all these pistols are. No cannon lure.

MR. KATZMANN. What is the make?

THE WITNESS. What, sir?

Q. What is the make? A. Union Metallic Cartridge Company, Remington UMC.

Q. That completes this list of bullets? A. That completes that list, yes, sir.

Q. And those which you have already said shows a complete view of all the marks, lands and grooves? A. Yes. I forgot to ask,—to add, those two bullets [in photograph] are taken three diameters, so they are **three times the length of the original bullet**.... [1409]

Q. For a minute I call your attention to bullet No. III, which has a left twist. That is a 32 Winchester bullet, is it? A. Yes, sir.

Q. And I was interrogating you when I switched away from it as to what gun that bullet could be fired from? A. Well, it has the characteristics of a Colt, but I wouldn't swear that it was a Colt because,—it is deformed....

Q. Tell us about how much deformity there is in that bullet. A. The lead to the rifling is corroded, showed it was corroded and fouled.

Q. Have you anything to show what the leads represent, Mr. Burns? A. I think I let you take it.

Q. Well, it is lost, then.... Explain as well as you can without it.

A. Why, it is impossible to make a true print of the lands any wider than it is, so there is a strip there. I withdraw that. There is no indications of it, but there was a fouling, corroded fouling there that made an imperfect mark at the point of the lands; and as the bullet travelled up, that gave a false impression of the true lands, ... Well, ... I will give it to you whether it goes over your head or not.

Q. All right... Try and not be too technical.... A. Yes. As the bullet enters the rifling, the average pressure, gas pressure is, breech pressure is 12,000 pounds per square inch.... That maximum pressure takes place just as the bullet is getting into the gun, into the rifling, just after it gets out of the lead, which I will explain, ...

Q. (Mr. McAnarney hands paper to witness) What have you here?

MR. JEREMIAH McANARNEY. I will show it to Mr. Katzmann.

THE WITNESS. As the bullet gets into the lead——

MR. KATZMANN. Wait just a minute.

MR. JEREMIAH McANARNEY. That your Honor may follow us,

(Mr. McAnarney hands paper to the Court).

Q. Now, you take that (indicating) and turn toward the jury and try to explain what you mean by the "leads".... A. (Witness leaves witness stand and goes to the jury) Here is a so-called **blueprint** of the chamber and bore of a Colt rifle.

Q. Turn it up so they may see it... A. This (indicating) is the throat. Here (indicating) is the chamber, comes to here (indicating). The chamber ends right there [1410] (indicating). This little taper that comes up in here (indicating) is called the throat. This taper here (indicating) is the bore or lands, and that is what we call the "lead". That is the little taper that comes from here (indicating) and in this case here (indicating). Here you are. Here (indicating) are the figures of the true gun, what it should be. "D" is the lead, .013 of an inch taper. "C" is the throat, .050 of an inch, from here to here (indicating), so it is .063 of an inch from the mouth of the shell into the true rifle....

Q. Now, you spoke of an imperfect land on bullet No. III. How does that imperfect land manifest itself on bullet No. III so that it may be seen? A. Yes, particularly in No. II.

MR. KATZMANN. Well, wait a minute.

THE WITNESS. No. III, No. IIII is not clear.

MR. JEREMIAH McANARNEY. Do you wish to object to something?

MR. KATZMANN. I thought he changed to bullet No. II,—**picture No. II**.

THE WITNESS. Picture,—six views of all the lands.

Q. Now, tell us how it manifests itself? A. Visible to the eye right there (indicating).

Q. Now, in what way is it visible to the eye?

A. Wider at the top by .010 of an inch than it is at the bottom.

Q. What does the fact that that groove in the bullet is wider at the top than it is at the bottom indicate? A. It indicates that the lead was corroded and fouled. What I mean by "fouling" perhaps might be metal fouling. Invariably, it is metal fouling. If a gun is corroded there, this jacket—which is soft, it is only .013 of an inch thick, thirteen to fourteen thousandths of an inch thick at the base or throughout the whole bearing—of course would collect metal fouling... [1411]

Q. Assuming that the lead of the gun that fired bullet No. III had been clean and normal would you have found such irregularity as exists in bullet III on **this photograph**?

229

A. I have never found it.

Q. Have you some bullets that have been fired from the—we will call it the so-called Sacco gun? A. Yes, sir.

Q. Will you produce those bullets? A. (Witness does so.)

MR. JEREMIAH McANARNEY. I am calling the Colt automatic, for the purpose of designation on the record, the Sacco gun.

Q. How many bullets have you that were fired from the so-called Sacco gun?

A. I had eight to start.

Q. How many have you lost? A. Two. [Ed. Burns test fired at Lowell on June 18, 1921.]

Q. Well, you have six with you. All right. Now, do those [six test] bullets that you have there show the irregularity that is shown on bullet No. III in these **photographs**? A. No, sir.

Q. How are the lands and grooves on those bullets, whether regular or not?

A. Regular, clean-cut.

MR. JEREMIAH McANARNEY. (To the jury) Now, gentlemen, you may pass those [Lowell bullets] among you. Wouldn't the [magnifying] glass help out better with this? [1412]

THE WITNESS. Yes... .

[Short recess.]

MR. JEREMIAH McANARNEY. Now, let me see some of these bullets. Mr. Katzmann and if the Court please, I am now showing to the jury some bullets that came from the alleged Sacco gun, with a glass.

MR. KATZMANN. Are those the ones he fired at Lowell? ...

THE WITNESS. (Examining with glass). Yes, sir... .

MR. JEREMIAH McANARNEY. (To the jury) Well, gentlemen, here are two more [Lowell bullets] he says are from the Sacco gun. You may use those and pass them along. While the others are going along, I call your ... attention to this **photo** of No. III, which seems to be a remarkably good one. So that the jury may understand, I would like to state No. III is supposed to be the fatal bullet that was found in the body of Berardelli. III is the same bullet in each... .

Q. Well, having in mind the appearance of No. III on the **photograph** there, bullet No. III, and having in mind the grooves made on the

[1413] bullets fired from the Colt automatic [at Lowell] and designated as the Sacco gun, have you an opinion as to whether the so-called fatal bullet No. III was fired from the Sacco gun? A. I have.

Q. Was it fired from the Sacco gun? A. Not in my opinion, no.

Q. What is the ground and base of your opinion, and on what do you base that opinion? A. On the 11 bullets that I examined that were fired from the Sacco gun. It doesn't compare with it at all.

Q. In what way does it not compare with it? A. It shows a clean-cut lead all the way through, the same diameter, the same width at the top as it does at the bottom, practically no difference.

Q. What does the fact that the groove is clean-cut all the way through coming from the Sacco gun indicate with reference to the rifling of that gun, the condition of the rifling? A. Clean lead... .

Q. ... [W]as that [Bullet 3] fired from a gun that had a clean lead? A. It was not.

Q. Any other reason that you have from the appearance of the bullet that would indicate that it was not fired from the Sacco gun? A. That is all. The main point. The bullet is deformed so you could not get any connecting links as to diameter. Those were wiped out.

Q. The bullet was somewhat deformed? A. The **photograph** does not show the deformation... .

THE COURT. Is there any way of reaching the sheriff?

THE WITNESS. Starting with No. I, turn the bullet around. Six——

THE COURT. Any way of reaching the sheriff?

A VOICE. Telephone his home.

THE COURT. See if you can get him. It seems to me probably both sides will want **the bullets and pistols that he has now locked up here**, so it is quite advisable that he be reached some way. Now, you may proceed, please... . [1414]

Q. Now, I am going to divert for a few minutes, and I call your attention to the Exhibit 27, that is what? A. Harrington & Richardson... .

Q. I call your attention to that gun (indicating). What kind of a gun is it, the one to your left hand? A. Harrington & Richardson 38 revolver. She is 38 Smith & Wesson cartridge... .

Q. Have you at my request examined that gun [Vanzetti's gun] with reference to the hammer in that gun being a new hammer or not? A. Yes, sir.

231

Q. Is that a new hammer? A. In my opinion it is not any newer than the rest of the gun... .

Q. Can you tell us why you say it is not a new hammer? A. Well worn down where the double acting sear——[1417]

Q. ... [H]ow old a gun is that? A. Well, that gun is sixteen years old... .

THE COURT. Where did you say this gun was made?

THE WITNESS. In Worcester (showing to the Court).

MR. JEREMIAH McANARNEY. I am returning this gun **to the sheriff**... . [1419]

Q. ... I call your attention to Bullet No. III. I have here the Government exhibit, bullet III, and whether or not that is the bullet that you have photographed there on the—— A. Yes, sir, that is the bullet.

MR. JEREMIAH McANARNEY. I am now calling the expert's attention to the Government's Exhibit 18, marked on the envelope, "Bullet III." [Ed. McAnarney hands Bullet 3 to Burns.]

Q. I understand your answer to be that that is the bullet shown as No. 3 on the set of photographs, "Defendant's for Identification No. 15"?

A. Yes, sir.

Q. May I ask you, after you have examined that, is there anything you wish to say about that in particular? A. Not any more, only it shows here (indicating), of course, the deformity where it has been deformed by striking some object, which did not show so plain in the **photograph**.

MR. JEREMIAH McANARNEY. (To the jury) You may have in mind, gentlemen, this: The No. III bullet which shows a little out of true where the Medical Examiner testified it came up against the side of the pelvic [1421] bone, that is the bullet that is shown in 3 that you have seen (showing to the jury). That is the same bullet that was shown the first day. I am putting this No. III bullet **back in the envelope** that it was in, and returning it to the sheriff's desk.

MR. KATZMANN. Those which are exhibits should stay here. Those are exhibits, are they not, and should stay here?

MR. JEREMIAH McANARNEY. They have been shown to the jury. I am going to put them in as exhibits... . No objection being offered, I will ask those be introduced as exhibits. Six bullets fired from the so-called Sacco gun at Lowell in the presence of experts representing the Government and the defendants.

(Six bullets fired from so-called Sacco gun at Lowell admitted in evidence and marked "Exhibit F.")...

Q. From what gun could the bullets other than the one [Bullet 3] that might have been fired from a Colt, from what gun or guns could they be fired? A. From a Steyer or a Walther.

Q. From how many different guns could the other bullets found in the body of the men who was [were] shot,—from how many different guns could those [five] bullets have been fired?

A. Five different guns.

Q. Name the guns. A. Colt, Bayard, Savage, Steyer and Walther... .

Q. I guess you did not understand my question. I was speaking of the other bullets, eliminating No. III. A. Oh—

Q. Eliminating the Colt, from what other guns...could those other bullets have been fired?

A. Savage, Steyer and Walther, made in Germany... . [1422]

Q. And you give as your judgment that bullet No. III, alleged as the fatal bullet, was fired from a Colt or could have been fired from a Bayard possibly? A. Yes, sir... .

Q. Well, what is your belief on that [which gun fired Bullet 3]? A. It shows indications of [1426] a Colt. Still, I believe it could be fired from a Bayard... . [1427]

Cross Examination.

Q. (By Mr. Katzmann) Mr. Burns, how many bullets at Lowell did you fire through the Sacco gun? A. Eight. [1427]

Q. What manufacture of cartridge did you fire through the Sacco gun at Lowell? A. "U. S."

Q. What manufacture of cartridge is it your opinion No. III bullet was fired from?

A. Winchester.

Q. Was there any reason why you should not have fired eight Winchesters through that Sacco gun? A. Yes, sir.

Q. What was the reason? A. Because our bullet represented that bullet nearer than the present Winchester bullet that we could buy.

Q. Did you make any effort to procure a Winchester bullet?

A. Yes, sir.

Q. Was that the only reason? A. Yes, sir.

Q. Is there any difference in size between a Winchester 32 and a United States 32?

A. Which Winchester do you mean?

Q. The Winchester of the type that was taken from the body of Alessandro Berardelli?

A. It is practically the same as ours, with the exception of a grain, 1-1/10 grains in weight.

Q. Is there any other exception? A. That is all.

Q. Any difference in the length? A. That would make it slightly longer.

Q. Then there is that difference, isn't there? A. Yes, slightly.

Q. Is there any difference in the contour of the nose of the bullet?

A. Very slightly. [1428]

Q. Do you now say that bullet No. III was fired by a Bayard? A. Not positively.

Q. And do you now say that bullet III was not fired by a Colt 32 automatic?

A. It could have been fired in both.

Q. Do you say that bullet III was not fired by a Colt 32? A. I will not, sir.... [1430]

Q. Did you have opportunity to go to the Winchester factory and seek to obtain any bullets of the same make, same characteristics as bullet No. 3? A. I did not.

Q. Did you make any efforts to find such bullets? A. Only all through New England here. That is as far as I could go, between here and Lowell, and around with an automobile, in the time that I had.

Q. Where is the Winchester bullet manufactured? A. New Haven, Connecticut. [1435]

Q. Did you go down there [to the Winchester factory]? A. No, sir.

Q. Did you write to them? A. No, sir. [1436]

Q. Are the physical properties of bullet No. III ... different from or the same as the physical properties of the eight United States bullets which you fired through the Sacco gun?

A. Can I answer that in my own way? ... . [Ed. Brief exchange between Katzmann and Burns.]

Q. Answer it, if you please, your own way. A. ... [T]his No. III bullet was a hollow base bullet. ... It is not of recent manufacture.... The latest manufacture of this cartridge has got a smooth bullet. Undoubtedly Mr. Van Amburg had the same trouble in getting it, because I noticed he had the smooth bullet and I had the same.... Now, this bullet of ours is the nearest thing I could get to this Winchester bullet [Bullet 3], ... [1437]

[Ed. Burns refers to the lack of success both he and Van Amburgh had in finding Winchester bullets that matched the manufacturing date and type of Winchester bullet (Bullet 3) which Dr. Magrath took from the body of Berardelli. Both experts test fired bullets with the Sacco gun at Lowell on Saturday, June 18, 1921, to make comparative studies of bullets and shells.]

Q. Do you say bullet No. III was not fired through the Sacco gun?
A. I do not. [1438]

Wednesday, June 29, 1921.
James E. Burns, Cross-Examination, Resumed.

MR. KATZMANN. If your Honor please, it is agreed between counsel that Exhibit 37, two shot-gun shells, contain buckshot.

[Ed. Shells found on Vanzetti. See stipulation in transcript, p. 939.]

MR. JEREMIAH McANARNEY. You may ask him if it did, rather than open it... .

Q. (By Mr. Katzmann) What was the size of those shells, Mr. Burns?
A. 12 gauge.

Q. I did not mean the shells. I meant the shots in them. A. Double 00 buck.

Q. How large would that be? A. About 310.

Q. As big as an ordinary pea? A. Oh, larger.... A little larger. [1444]

Q. Is there a land on bullet No. III between the grooves? A. This (indicating) is the lands. The groove on the bullet is the lands.

Q. Yes. The groove on the bullet made by the lands of the barrel?
A. Made by the lands of the barrel...

Q. ... What is the width of that same portion caused by the groove on the barrel of bullet No. III? A. The width of the groove is 105.

Q. And the width of a groove on a Bayard is 120, isn't it? A. 120... .

Q. When you said the width of the groove was 105, did you mean that is what you found on bullet No. 3? A. Yes, sir.

Q. Yes. That corresponds to the groove space in the barrel of the firearm that discharged it?
A. Yes, sir. [1447]

Redirect Examination.

Q. (By Mr. Jeremiah McAnarney) Speaking of the bullets that you used in your test with the other experts at Lowell, why did you use the bullet that you used? A. Because it had more of the same contour, same effect as the Winchester bullet that was used, or No III bullet.... [1459]

Q. ... I believe you stated yesterday it was practically impossible to get a bullet like that bullet No. III; they are not made now, those? A. To the best of my knowledge they are not made now.

Q. And you said you went between Boston and Lowell way. Lowell is your home? A. Yes.

Q. You live that way? A. Yes.

Q. In your search for bullets you took that course? A. I took that course, yes, sir.

Q. I see. A. May I add to that?

Q. Yes. A. I had two assistants out looking for them. [1462]

J. Henry Fitzgerald, Sworn. June 29, 1921.

Q. (By Mr. Jeremiah McAnarney) What is your full name? A. J. Henry Fitzgerald.

Q. You reside where? A. Hartford, Connecticut.

Q. What is your present employment? A. I have charge of the testing room at Colt Patent Firearms Company of that city.

Q. Is that where this automatic pistol is made? A. At Colt's factory, yes, sir.

Q. How long have you been connected with the gun business? A. About 28 years.

Q. Prior to going with the Colt people, whom were you employed with? A. By Iver Johnson Company, in Boston.

Q. What was your work there? A. I had charge of the revolver department.

Q. How long were you in charge of the revolver department at Iver Johnson's? A. ... Somewhere five to six years. I don't exactly remember.

Q. Well, before we get into the thing too deep, I call your attention to the revolver, Exhibit 27. Directing your attention to the hammer, what have you to say, Mr. Fitzgerald, whether that is a new hammer, new in March, 1920,—what is your opinion?

A. May I look at this at the window?

MR. JEREMIAH McANARNEY. Yes.

THE COURT. Haven't you looked at it before? [1464]

THE WITNESS. Yes... .

(Witness examines revolver under light at desk.) The hammer in this revolver has every indication of being as old and used as much as any other part of the pistol.

Q. Does it bear evidence of having been used? A. You mean, has it been fired?

Q. Had the hammer been fired in use? A. In my judgment it has.

Q. What do you base that on? A. On the condition of the hammer nose... .

Q. That is all. Now, passing to other parts of the case, you have made an examination of bullet No. III? A. I have... .

Q. And have examined it? A. I have.

Q. And have examined these **six photographs of it**? A. Yes, sir.

Q. Are you able to form an opinion, ... as to whether the bullet No. III was fired from the Colt automatic now before you, Exhibit 28?

MR. KATZMANN. One moment, if your Honor, please.

THE COURT. Read the question.

(The question is read.)

MR. KATZMANN. There is nothing, if your Honor please, to indicate he ever looked at the Colt automatic, either in the preliminary question or in that question.

MR. JEREMIAH McANARNEY. Previous to that he said he had examined it.

MR. KATZMANN. Examined the bullet.

MR. JEREMIAH McANARNEY. The revolver, I thought.

(A portion of the witness' previous testimony is read.)

THE COURT. Suppose you ask him, to be quicker. [1465]

Q. However, have you examined this revolver, this pistol, they all call it? A. I have... .

Q. In substance, ... were you able to form an opinion as to whether bullet No. III was fired from Exhibit 28 [the Sacco gun]? A. I was.

Q. What is your opinion? A. My opinion is that No. III bullet was not fired from the pistol given me as Exhibit 28.

Q. [E]xplain to the jury the reasons that you have for that opinion.

A. The land marks on the No. III bullet do not correspond ... to bullets I have seen fired from this pistol.... [1466]

Cross-Examination.

Q. (By. Mr. Katzmann) How long have you been in charge of the testing room at the Colt place? A. Between three and four years... .
Q. When you were at Iver Johnson's, would you call yourself a salesman?
A. Part of the time. I had charge of the revolver department, and of course I sold pistols... .
Q. From your examination of Exhibit 27, will you say that in March, 1920, a new hammer was not put in that gun? A. I can't say what was done to the pistol in 1920.... [1469]
Q. [Katzmann asked about the indentation made on the shell by the firing pin.] I will take the Fraher Winchester [Shell W] in my left hand and the Lowell, one of the three. It [the hole] is the same in the three, isn't it? A. Not the same... . [1473]
Q. What is the standard width of a barrel groove in a Colt 32?
A. .105.
MR. KATZMANN. That is all. [1480]

SACCO-VANZETTI AND SYLVESTER G. GATES
The Times (London) Nov. 11, 1972, p. 18, column 7

A friend writes: [in response to Gates's obituary of Nov. 5].
Your description of Mr. Sylvester Gates as "a distinguished banker" was no doubt a just one; but it gives no hint of his equal distinction in several other fields. A brilliant pupil of Gilbert Murray at Oxford, Gates remained all his life a true scholar--not a pedant, not a mere retailer of classical allusions, but a discriminating critic over a wide range of ancient and modern literature. Equally brilliant at the Harvard Law School under Felix Frankfurter (to whom he gave notable assistance in his vindication of Sacco and Vanzetti), he might well, had he remained in practice at the bar, have attained to high judicial office...; in personal relations and in sorrow he was a paragon of loyalty and of courage; and on whatever he did he left the impress of a fine mind and a fastidious temper.
[Ed. See pp 413, 489, 644.]

22. THE PLYMOUTH TRAIN AGAIN

Henry L. McNaught, Sworn. June 27, 1921.

Q. (By Mr. McAnarney) What is your occupation? A. Conductor on the New Haven Railroad.

Q. And on what line were you running April 15th, 1920? A. On the Shore Road from Plymouth to Boston.... [1275]

Q. I now ask you, did you take up any tickets from Plymouth to Seaside and Kingston for any of the Braintrees on April 15th? A. Not to my recollection, no, sir. The tickets I could not vouch for. They are turned in to the company....

Q. ... Will you describe what kind of a smoker is it that is on that train?

A. Usually a long smoking car, a full car. [1276]

Q. Did you have a combination smoker and baggage on that train?

A. I can't recall that I ever had one on that train, no, sir....

Q. What time does it leave Plymouth? A. 8.14 [A.M.]. [1277]

Cross-Examination.

Q. (By Mr. Katzmann) Have you any record of mileage books used on the train that left Plymouth of April 15th? A. I have no record of it.

Q. Whether anybody rode on mileage from Plymouth to East Braintree? A. No, sir.

Q. Whether any one rode on mileage from Seaside to East Braintree, you have no knowledge?

A. No, sir.

Q. How many passengers were on your train that morning? A. That I couldn't say. We have seven or eight cars every morning. It is a heavy train....

Q. Did any one get on at East Braintree that morning? A. I couldn't say.

Q. Did any one get off at East Braintree that morning? A. I couldn't say positive.

Q. You don't say a man wearing a black mustache with a grip didn't get off at East Braintree that morning? A. I wouldn't say he did or didn't.

239

Q. You don't know anything about it? A. No, sir. [1279]

Q. Where was the smoker proper on that train that morning?
A. The second car from the engine, head end... .

Q. Who sat, if anybody sat in the seat next to the toilet on the right rear coming into East Braintree station that morning? A. I couldn't say... .

Q. You don't know anything about that, do you? A. No.

Q. How far away is the Braintree depot from East Braintree? A. It is about a mile. [1280]

Ernest Pratt, Sworn. June 27, 1921.

Q. (By Mr. McAnarney) In 1920, April 15th, you were the ticket agent at the Plymouth Station, were you? A. I was.

Q. Now, have you, at our request, looked up the records to see whether or not there was a ticket sold from Plymouth to Braintree or East Braintree on the 15th of April? A. I have.

Q. Was there such a ticket sold? A. There was not. [1283]

Cross-Examination.

Q. (By Mr. Katzmann.) Were there any tickets sold from Plymouth, on April 15th, to Quincy?
A. I couldn't answer that question.

Q. Were there any sold from Plymouth to Boston on April 15th?
A. There was.

Q. Do you know who purchased those tickets? A. I do not... .

Q. How far is the Plymouth depot from the Seaside depot?
A. Approximately two miles.

Q. And in what section of the town of Plymouth is the Seaside depot?
A. In the north end.

Q. Called North Plymouth? A. The North Plymouth post office.
[1283]

Harry C. Cash, Sworn. June 27, 1921.

Q. (By Mr. McAnarney) What is your present emploment?
A. Station Agent, Seaside.

Q. Were you station agent April 15th, 1920? A. Yes, sir.

Q. Directing your attention to April 15th, 1920, were there any tickets sold from your station to Braintree or East Braintree, April 15, 1920? A. No, sir. [1285]

Cross-Examination.

Q. (By Mr. Katzmann) If he [Vanzetti] bought the ticket the night before, you don't know whether he got on the train that morning or not? A. No, sir. [1288]

Lester S. Wilmarth, Sworn. June 27, 1921.

Q. (By Mr. McAnarney) What is your employment? A. Ticket agent and telegraph operator at Kingston.
Q. So, I take it, you were there in April, 1920? A. I was.
Q. Have you looked up your records to ascertain and inform us whether any tickets were sold from your station to East Braintree on the 15th day of April, 1920? A. I did.
Q. Was any ticket sold from your station? A. There was none to East Braintree sold on that day [1295]

Cross-Examination.

Q. (By Mr. Katzmann) Was any sold Kingston to Boston that day via the South Shore?
A. I couldn't say, because I didn't look that up.... .
Q. How many people got on the 8:22 train at Kingston via South Shore on April 15th?
A. I couldn't tell that.
Q. Did you look them over to see? A. No.... .
Q. Then you don't know whether Vanzetti got on or not at Kingston [1295] that morning?
A. Not unless he came and bought a ticket or was walking around the station in view of the ticket office.   .
Q. Did you look through the ticket office at the 8:22 at any one coach that morning?
A. I couldn't say now, because I don't remember. [1296]

Edward P. Brooks, Sworn. June 27, 1921.

Q. (By Mr. McAnarney) At the time of the shooting you were ticket agent at the East Braintree station? A. At the East Braintree station.

Q. ... The morning train that came about 8:14 ... from Plymouth via Cohasset, whether or not there are any milk cars, milk cans, on that train?

A. The train that gets to East Braintree at 9:52 carried milk.... .

Q. How many cans [sic] did that carry? A. One long smoker, American baggage car and smoker—Two cars and one baggage car. One was a smoking car and the other was a full baggage car of the American Express Company.... [1298]

Q. ... Did you see a man get off at the East Braintree station within a month or two after this shooting that attracted your attention? A. I did.

Q. Will you describe that man? A. He was a tall, thin man, and he carried a [black] bag, ...

Q. Did you see a man, that man, on the 15th day of April, 1920?

A. I don't remember that I did see him that day.

Q. Did you see a man on the 15th day of April get off that train at East Braintree?

A. [After interruption.] I do not remember whether I did or not.... . [1300]

Q. ... How soon after that [after Brooks's talk with an investigator] was it you first saw this man with the black bag? A. I don't remember. [1301]

Q. ... [H]ow many times have you seen that man [with the black bag] get off?

A. I have seen that man, say, half a dozen times within the last six months back, or year. [1302]

Cross Examination.

Q. (By Mr. Katzmann) Did a man get off the train that arrived at 9:52 at East Braintree on April 15th in the morning? A. As nearly as I remember there was.

Q. There was such a man? Can you describe him?

A. A tall, thin man, and he carried a small Boston grip bag.... .

Q. Now, I repeat the question. On April 15, 1920, did a man get off the train that was due from Plymouth at 9:54 at East Braintree?

A. Well, I can't remember... .

Q. You don't know, do you? A. I don't know, no, not for sure. [1303]

Q. But I think you told Mr. McAnarney some four or five weeks after the 15th you were talked to by somebody and that perhaps two weeks after that for the first time you saw the lanky man. You said that, didn't you? A. Yes.

Q. That is the first time you saw the tall, lanky man with the black bag; no question about it?

A. No question about it.

Q. How many cans of milk do you have to unload? A. Sixteen to eighteen cans of milk.

Q. I suppose the stop at the depot is a very brief one? A. Very... .

Q. You weren't looking around the depot to see who was getting off of that train? A. No... .

Q. Your whole attention was attracted to those cans? A. Yes... .

Q. Did baggage sometimes come in, besides? A. Yes, sir.

Q. Whose duty was it to take the baggage off? A. Mine.

Q. Was your time restricted? A. I sold tickets for that train and waited until the train drew into the station. Then I would run for the baggage car.

Q. I take it from that you would be a pretty busy man about that time? A. That is a busy time, yes, sir. Very busy train, the passengers. [1304]

Q. Did the milk cans come in the 15th of April? A. Every day, yes. [1305]

[Ed. Placido Calabro, official interpreter at the Quincy court, testified that McAnarney asked him to have a Norwood photographer take three pictures of Joseph Scavitto. See transcript, pp. 1530-1531. Picture of Joseph Scavitto marked Exhibit "L".]

Joseph Scavitto, Sworn. June 29, 1921 (through interpreter).

Q. (By Mr. McAnarney) What is your name? A. Joseph Scavitto. [1531]

Q. Were you,—April, 1920, ... at East Braintree aboard a train and did you get off at the East Braintree station? A. No, sir.

Q. Were you any time in the month of April aboard a train that came through on the South Shore? A. No, sir.

Q. By East Braintree? A. Not on that line. [1532]

243

Cross-Examination.

Q. (By Mr. Katzmann) On April 15, 1920, were you at the Matfield crossing in West Bridgewater? A. No.

Q. And on April 15, 1920, were you in the front seat of an automobile that crossed over the Pearl Street crossing at the South Braintree depot? A. No, sir.

Q. And on April 15, 1920, at some time between the hours of 11 and 12 o'clock in the forenoon, were you... the middle occupant of three occupants of the rear seat that turned south from Holbrook Avenue into South Braintree Square? A. No, sir. [1532]

Q. You came here [to the trial] just by chance? A. Yes....

Q. When did you first came [sic] here? A. Well, I came here three weeks ago Monday. Four times. [1533]

Q. Who asked you to go to Norwood and have your picture taken? A. Mr. Reid called me in. [1534]

[Ed. Reid was an investigator for Fred Moore.]

Redirect Examination.

Q. (By Mr. McAnarney) Do you remember sitting back in the court room and I walking out ... and patting you on the shoulder? A. What? ... Yes. [1534]

Recross Examination.

Q. (By Mr. Katzmann) Do you know either of these two defendants? A. I know one.

Q. Which one? A. Sacco....

Q. That is why you came out to the trial, wasn't it? A. Of course I was loafing the same time.

Q. Is he a friend of yours? A. I have spent two times with that fellow.

Q. Where was that? A. This was about three or four years ago.

Q. Where. A. Milton.

Q. What doing? A. Walking——Milton. [1535]

23. VANZETTI'S H. & R. REVOLVER

Eldridge Atwater, Sworn. June 30, 1921.

Q. (By Mr. McAnarney) What is your name? A. Eldridge Atwater.

Q. Where do you live? A. Dexter, Maine.

Q. How long have you lived there? A. All my life. That is, all but about seven or eight months.

Q. And that seven or eight months, you lived where? A. Worcester.

Q. Worcester. Are you married? A. Yes, sir.

Q. Kindly take the revolver on the stand before you and examine it. A. [Witness does so.] ...

MR. JEREMIAH McANARNEY. You may step to the window, ... and look it over carefully.

[The witness goes to window and examines the revolver and returns to witness stand.]

Q. Now, you examined the revolver when before you went on the stand, please? [Ed. The revolver is Exhibit 27. See p. 102.]

A. When before just now?

Q. Yes. Sometime last week? A. Two weeks ago Saturday, I think ...

Q. Where was the revolver when you examined it? A. ... It was in this court house, I believe. [Ed. See Palmer, p. 413.]

Q. Now, will you tell me the **history of that gun**, so far as you know, ...? [1556] A. Well, about eight years ago I was working for my father-in-law in a grocery store in Dexter, Maine. He had a revolver, .38 calibre H. & R., and I had,—at that time I was living with him over the store. I used to take the gun out hunting, out shooting at targets; fired it quite a few times.... .

THE COURT. Does he say that is the revolver that his father-in-law owned and that he shot?

Q. Is that the revolver you are speaking about? A. It is.

Q. Perhaps you might now tell us what there is about the revolver by reason of which you say that? A. Well, on right up over here, over the cylinder, the nickel was worn off along here [indicating]. Also I noticed it was worn off here [indicating].

MR. KATZMANN. Pointing to the muzzle.

THE WITNESS. On the end.

THE COURT. Just make that so the record will disclose just where "here" is on the revolver.

Q. What end? A. On the end of the barrel... .

Q. Now, perhaps you might tell us on the chamber, tell us what was on that.

A. I do not remember anything about the chamber.

Q. Well, I have got it wrong. The cylinder. I said chamber. Cylinder, you described something there... . You had your finger on it. A. The nickel over the cylinder.

Q. Oh, I see. A. I do not know the part, what it would be called, but it was worn off here [indicating].

MR. JEREMIAH McANARNEY. Well, the witness points to ... the part of the revolver immediately above the cylinder?

THE WITNESS. Yes.

Q. You mean one or both sides. Look at both sides. A. Well, I never noticed the other side, whether it was worn off or not. I noticed this side.

Q. That would be the left-hand side? A. Left-hand side, yes.

Q. Now, anything else on the gun? A. That is all on the gun that I know about. [1557]

Q. Go ahead and tell us **the history of the revolver**, so far as you know.

.THE COURT. Of course, you can't testify as to what happened since it left your possession, ... A. Well, after——that was eight years ago that I was working in the store.

Q. Yes. A. ... and five or six years ago my father-in-law died, and my mother-in-law came out to Massachusetts to visit her relations and her daughter. After she had left Maine, I don't remember just how long, I was asking my wife--

MR. KATZMANN. One moment.

Q. ... Take it where you say you left Maine, ...

A. Well, I wanted to know where the gun was, and I asked her.

MR. KATZMANN. One moment, if your Honor please... .

Q. Now, from the time that you asked her that question, did you see the gun,——have you seen this gun until you examined it here in the court house? A. No.

Q. Now, that was about how long ago? A. I should think about five years ago... .

246

Q. And it was then in the possession of whom? A. Of my mother-in-law.

Q. Very well. Where did she--did she continue to live there at Dexter, Maine? A. No, no; she came out to Massachusetts.

Q. When did she come to Massachusetts?

A. Well, I could not just say, but it was shortly after my father-in-law died. [1558] [Ed. Frank Morgridge died on Oct. 30, 1916.]

Q. ... Now, do you know anything about this case [handing case to the witness]?

A. That is just like the case that was with the gun when I had it [in Dexter, Maine].

Q. Well, is there anything on it other than what you say "it is just like it" that enables you to say anything on it either way? A. Only that it was open at this end, this lapel came down and hooked on a brass knob... .

[Revolver case admitted in evidence and marked Exhibit "M".]

Cross-Examination.

Q. (By Mr. Katzmann) Just a minute. Do you know Rexford Slater?

A. Yes. [Ed. See p. 413; and see Katzmann, p. 438.]

Q. Who is he? A. He is a brother-in-law to me... .

Q. Is Rexford Slater in the court house to-day?

A. He is out in the anteroom.

Q. Has he been summonsed here as a witness by the defense?

A. Yes, sir.

Q. Do you say, Mr. Atwater, that that leather case is the case that went with that revolver? [Ed. The "case" is the leather holster.]

A. I say that case is exactly like the case that went with the revolver.

Q. Do you say that it is the case?

A. I wouldn't say that it was the case.

Q. Then it may not be the case that went with that revolver?

A. It might not be.

Q. Do you say that that revolver, Exhibit 27, is the revolver that your father-in-law owned?

A. As far as the marks on this revolver on the end and here [indicating], I say it is. [1559]

Q. Is that your father-in-law's revolver, yes or no? A. I said as far as--

247

Q. You said that once, yes or no, is it your father-in-law's revolver?
A. Not now.
Q. Was it your father-in-law's revolver? A. Yes, sir.
Q. How do you say it was your father-in-law's revolver?
A. Because it is exactly like that one and had these two marks.
Q. Well, is there any other Harrington & Richardson .38 manufactured fifteen or sixteen years ago that is any different from that? A. I don't know about that. [1560]
Q. Do you know the number of that revolver? A. I do not.
Q. Is there any better means of identification than the number of a revolver?
A. No, I wouldn't say there was.
Q. Is there a number on that revolver? A. I should say there was.
Q. Where is it? A. [Witness examines revolver.] On the handle.
Q. What is the number? A. G-82581.
Q. Did you ever see that number before? A. I don't remember.
Q. Do you know where your father-in-law purchased the revolver?
A. No, I do not.
Q. Do you know how it came into his possession?
A. I couldn't swear how it came into his possession.
Q. Do you know what caused the nickel to become eroded from both sides of the firing end of the barrel of that revolver? A. I do not.
Q. Do you know whether or not discharging a revolver erodes the nickel from that portion of the revolver immediately above the cylinder? A. I do not.... [1561]
Q. How many times did you personally discharge this revolver when it was down in Dexter? A. I couldn't say exactly.
Q. Give us your best judgment? A. Why, I might have seventy-five or one-hundred times, or more or less. Q. Had you finished? A. Yes.
Q. Over what period were you discharging this revolver? A. How long, do you mean?
Q. Yes; this seventy-five times? A. Perhaps a year, perhaps not quite. I don't remember.
Q. And that is the sixth year preceding this time, is it? A. What, sir?
Q. Is that the sixth year preceding this present time? A. That was eight years ago when I was working there, when I fired this revolver.
Q. Then you did not see the revolver for three years prior to your mother-in-law's going to Massachusetts? A. Why, it was there at my house until she did.

Q. Did you see it? A. Yes.

Q. Did anybody else fire it off? A. I could not say as to that.

Q. Did your father-in-law use it? A. I do not think he ever fired it.

Q. Did your brother-in-law use it? A. I couldn't say.

Q. Are there any other members of the family that you know of who used it before it was taken to Massachusetts? A. No, I couldn't tell you that. I don't know. [1562]

Q. Did you ever notice on the right-hand side of the trigger end of the barrel over the cylinder that the revolver is similarly eroded?

A. I never,—I don't remember that I ever noticed that. [1564] ...

Q. When were you first interviewed, prior to two weeks ago Saturday on the subject matter of this revolver?

A. I think it was Thursday before that Saturday, the Thursday. [1565] [Ed. June 16]

Q. Was that the first time? A. That I have been, yes; that I have been interviewed.

Q Where were you interviewed? A. In Dexter.

Q. By whom? A. By Mrs. Moore. [Ed. See Palmer's letter, p. 413.]

Q. What Mrs. Moore? A. Mrs. Fred Moore, I think that is Fred Moore.

Q. Have you seen her about here since your arrival? A. Do you mean since in the court room?

Q. Any time in the court house? A. No, I have not seen her.

Q. Who told you it was Mrs. Fred Moore? A. Why, she told me herself.

Q. Did she give you any card? A. I do not think so, no, sir.

Q. Had you been interviewed before that by anybody else? A. No, sir.

Q. Do you know whether or not your brother-in-law had been interviewed?

A. You mean Slater?

Q. Yes. A. He had.

Q. Prior to your interview? A. Yes, sir. [1566]

Q. ... Mr. Atwater, will you say that [1566] there was no erosion on the Atwater revolver, in the Slater revolver,—will you say that there was no erosion on the right-hand side over the chambers?

A. What do you mean by the Slater revolver?

Q. Why, the revolver that your father-in-law, Mr. Slater, owned?

A. Mr. Mogridge.]

Q. Rexford Slater isn't the son of your father-in-law? A. No. That [Mr. Mogridge] is my father-in-law. [Ed. Defense claims Vanzetti's H. & R. revolver is the Mogridge revolver.]

Q. He married your sister? A. We married sisters... .

Q. Have you ever been in Norwood? A. Yes.

Q. When? A. Between three and four years ago.

Q. Was Mr. Slater there then? A. Yes, sir. [1567]

Q. Then you don't say this is the Mogridge revolver, do you? A. I say as far as those two markings, that is the revolver Mr. Mogridge had eight years ago. [Ed. See p. 245, where Atwater says "over the cylinder, the nickel was worn off along here."]

Q. ...[T]hey are similar to what was on the Mogridge revolver?

A. They are just like what was on the Mogridge revolver. [1568]

Rexford Slater, Sworn. July 1, 1921.

Q. (By Mr. Jeremiah McAnarney) What is your name? A. Rexford Slater. [Ed. See letter by C.C. Palmer.]

Q. Where do you live? A. Dexter, Maine.

Q. Did you live at one time in Norwood? A. I did.

Q. When? A. I left Norwood a year ago the 12th day of last April. [April 12, 1920]

Q. How long did you live in Norwood? A. Some four to five years.

Q. Prior to living there, where did you live? A. Dexter.

Q. And what was your wife's name before marriage? A. Mogridge.

Q. Do you know Mr. Atwater? A. I do.

Q. Is he a brother-in-law of yours? A. He is... .

Q. I call your attention to the revolver, Exhibit 27. Examine that as much as you wish.

A. [Witness examines revolver, breaking same open.] ...

Q. Have you ever seen that revolver before to-day? A. Yes, sir.

Q. Where? A. A week ago last Saturday, at the court house... .

Q. Where had you first seen that revolver? A. In Norwood.

Q. Norwood, Massachusetts? A. Yes.

Q. When did you first see it? A. About three years and a half ago.

Q. Where was it when you saw it? A. In my mother-in-law's possession. [1635]

Q. How did this revolver get to Norwood? A. My wife's mother brought it... .

Q. Have you used that revolver any? A. I have.

Q. Kindly tell us to what extent you have used it?

A. I fired it several times, and shot a cat with it once.

Q. While you were down in Maine, before coming up here, did you use the revolver?

A. No, sir, never saw it... .

Q. You now have the revolver with you at Norwood. What did you do with the revolver?

A. I kept it in the house most of the time. [Ed. Slater said he used gun for target shooting.]

Q. Well, I take it you haven't got it now. What did you do with it?

A. I sold it.

Q. Who did you sell it to? A. A brother workman in the shop.

Q. What was his name? A. Orciani.

Q. Do you remember his first name? A. Ricardo... .

Q. How long did you work with him, ...? ... A. [P]robably nearly a year, ...

Q. Was he in the same department you were? A. Yes.

Q. ... [D]o you know what he paid you for it? A. I do.

Q. What? A. Four dollars.

MR. JEREMIAH McANARNEY. Have you the case, Mr. Sheriff? I think that was left with the Clerk. [1636]

Q. I show you Exhibit "M". And would you examine that?

A. [Witness examines Exhibit "M".]

Q. Have you ever seen that case before? A. I have.

Q. Where? A. I owned it with this gun.

Q. Well, was it the case that came with the gun? A. It was the one that was on it when I got it.

Q. Was it on it when you sold it? A. It was.

Q. Show the jury how you identify that as the case that was on that revolver?

A. On account of this brass knob on here; also that tear on the back, and this little strap....[Ed. McAnarney shows "tear" to jury 7 times.]

Q. What is there about that revolver by which you now say it is the revolver you sold to him?

A. Well, the enamel on the gun that I sold was off from the end of the barrel; also over the cylinder.

Q. Do you mean one or both sides? A. Well, that [indicating] is the cylinder, as far as I know. Well, I never noticed only one side of the gun. I don't know. I can't remember which side it was.

Q. Did you tell us when it was you sold it to Orciani? A. I sold that in the fall of 1919. [1637]

Cross-Examination.

Q. (By Mr. Katzmann) When in the fall of 1919 did you sell that gun,—sell a gun to Mr. Orciani? A. I wouldn't be sure. It was late in the fall... .

Q. Did you own the gun? A. I did.

Q. How did you get it? A. I bought it from my mother-in-law.

Q. Bought it with the holster? A. I did.

Q. Did you sell both the gun and the holster to Orciani? A. I did. [1638] [Ed. See p. 409.]

Q. Was Mr. Mogridge your father-in-law? A. Yes.

Q. Did he own it? A. I don't know.

Q. Did you have any idea he owned the gun while he was alive? A. No, sir.

Q. Where did you see it? A. I saw it in Norwood.

Q. How much did you pay your mother-in-law for the gun? A. Four dollars... . [1639]

Q. Do you know if the gun [Exhibit 27] differs from any other gun of the H. & R. make, .38 calibre, that has been discharged as much as that has, with respect to loss of nickel at either side of the barrel? A. Why, no, I don't know.

Q. Then how can you say that [Exhibit 27] is the [Mogridge] gun? A. Well, I can say that it is the gun because it has those places gone, and I don't think another gun would.

Q. I thought you said you did not know how another gun would appear? A. I don't know for sure.

Q. Then you don't know for sure that is the gun, do you? A. Well, it looks exactly like it. [1641]

Q. Doesn't every H. & R. .38 look exactly like that? A. I don't know... .

Q. ... Are you sure that is the same gun [sure that Exhibit 27 is the Mogridge gun]? [Ed. Presumably, Slater did not respond.]

THE COURT. Answer the question. [1642]

A. I am not... .

Q. Is there any number on the holster? A. Yes, sir.

Q. What is the number that you remember? A. I don't know.

Q. Is there anything indicating the calibre of the gun to be carried in that holster?

A. Not that I ever noticed... .

Q. That indicates,—what numbers there indicate the calibre of the gun to be carried in that holster?

A. [Witness examines holster.] Why, there is none that indicates the calibre of the gun... .

Q. Do you see any number right under my finger? A. Yes, sir.

Q. What is it? A. Can't see, the way you are holding it.

Q. Well, take it so you can. A. 5121, .32, 4.

Q. What does ".32" mean to you? A. Doesn't mean anything.

Q. Doesn't mean "calibre" to you? A. Not necessarily so.

Q. Never occurred to you that indicated calibre, did it? A. No, sir... .

Q. Did you ever notice any marks inside that holster? A. No, sir.

Q. Are there any there? A. I don't know.

Q. Take a look. A. [Witness examines holster.] Marks where the gun slides in.

Q. Now, Mr. Slater, is this the rip to which you referred? A. That is.

Q. And is that the brass knob, to which you refer? A. It is. [1643]

Q. And those two features enable you to say that this is the holster you owned? A. No, sir.

Q. What other feature is there? A. This one right here [indicating].

Q. You never had a strap, did you? A. I never had a belt... .

Q. Did you ever have any belt on which you wore that holster?

A. No, sir.

Q. Is that a belt wear, in your opinion? A. I don't know.

Q. Does the belt go through that strap? A. Supposed to, supposed.

Q. Yes. Which is the upper part where the belt would come?

A. Right—

Q. Right where the tear is? A. Yes.

Q. Haven't you any opinion whether that is a belt tear or wear?

A. Might be a belt tear. [1644]

Luigi Falzini, Sworn. July 1, 1921.

[The testimony of the witness is given through Interpreter.]

Q. (By Mr. Jeremiah McAnarney) What is your name? A. Luigi Falzini.

Q. Where do you live? A. 7 North Street Court, Somerville.

Q. How long have you lived there? A. About three months.

Q. Where did you live before that? A. In Framingham.

Q. When did you come from Framingham? A. Three months ago.

Q. Did you live in Boston sometime before that? A. Yes, in East Boston.

Q. Do you know an Italian fellow named Orciani? A. Yes.

Q. You examined that revolver [indicating]? A. [Witness examines revolver.] Yes.

Q. Have you seen that revolver before? A. Yes, sir.

Q. Where? A. I had it.

Q. When did you get it? A. I bought that in October, 1919.

Q. From whom? A. From Mr. Orciani.

Q. And when did you last have it? A. February, either January or February, 1920.

Q. And to whom, or,—what did you do with it then?

A. I sold it to Mr. Vanzetti. He came to my house and I sold it to him. [1629]

Q. Where were you living then? A. 183 Leyden Street, East Boston.

Q. ... [H]ow do you know that is the revolver you had? A. I recognize from those scratches on the right-hand of the revolver, this little rust,—over here on the right-hand.

Q. What make was the revolver that you sold him? A. H.R. Army Company, I think.

Q. "H.R. Ary Company, I think"? [Sic.]

THE COURT. Everybody seems to be in doubt. I think it is fair to the witness——

Q. Ask him, H.R., what did he say after "H.R."?

THE COURT. Ask him what he said.

THE WITNESS. "H. R. Army Company."

THE INTERPRETER. H. R. Arm Company. I think that is the way.

THE WITNESS. I never examined the gun before.

Q. Point out to us the mark that you saw on the gun.

A. Right one here [indicating], and over there, a little rust... .

Q. How long have you known Vanzetti? A. About five or six years... .

Q. How do you know that is the revolver that you sold to Vanzetti?

254

A. Well, because of this scratch here and a little rust here as I pointed to.

THE COURT. For the record, have it designated just where it is on the revolver.

MR. JEREMIAH McANARNEY. A scratch above the back of the trigger, between the back of the trigger and the back of the cylinder, or back of a line drawn between those two points, and the rust on that portion of the revolver above the cylinder.

MR. WILLIAMS. On which side? [1630]

MR. KATZMANN. The right.

MR. McANARNEY. Yes, the right side. Insert there that the scratch [is] on the right side of the revolver. [1631]

Cross-Examination.

Q. (By Mr. Katzmann) How old are you? A. Thirty-three... .

Q. Where did you get acquainted with Vanzetti? A. In Boston.

Q. Whereabouts in Boston? A. Down in the North End and several other places where we met.

Q. ... How long did you own the revolver? A. A few months. Four or five months.

Q. Did you use it while you owned it, fire that off? A. No, sir.

Q. How much did Vanzetti pay for it?

A. He paid five dollars, just the same as I paid, five dollars.

Q. Was it loaded when you sold it to him? A. Yes, sir.

Q. Did you sell him any cartridges? A. No, sir.

Q. How many chambers are there in this revolver? A. Six.

Q. And there were six chambers in the revolver you owned, weren't there?

A. Well, it appears to me, yes. I never shot them.

Q. Well, you loaded them, of course? Did you load them?

A. No, sir, I did not load it. I bought it already loaded.

Q. Did you ever take it apart like that [Indicating] A. No, sir, never.

Q. Well, count the number of chambers in that revolver. A. There are five.

Q. Were there any other scratches on the revolver besides the one you pointed out?

A. I never paid any attention.

Q. How did you happen to see this scratch you pointed out to the jury?

A. Well, as I looked at the revolver and I twisted and turned it around I saw that mark.

Q. When was that? A. The time that I bought it.

Q. Did you ever look at it again to see the scratch? A. No, sir, I never. I bought it that day and I saw it then and I did not see it any more. I did not look at it any more.

Q. And you always remembered that scratch?

A. Yes, particularly a scratch there which I used it as a mark.

Q. What did you use it as a mark for? A. Well, because he [Orciani] talked about it when I bought it, and I spoke about the mark. [1631]

Q. Where were you when you bought it? A. In Orciani's house.

Q. Where is that? A. In Hyde Park. [A part of Boston.]

Q. Whereabouts in Hyde Park? A. On Hyde Park Avenue.

Q. What is the number? A. 1014... .

Q. Has Ricardo Orciani been here while you have been here? A. No, sir, I did not see him.

Q. Did you see a Ford automobile outside with a top up, five passenger, with a permanent top? A. I saw several of them.

Q. Did you see Orciani sitting out in front in any one of them?

A. When?

Q. Any day that you have been at court? A. I saw him last week, yes, sir.

Q. Where? A. Outside the court house.

Q. Are there any other rust marks on this revolver save the one you pointed out?

A. I didn't pay any attention. I don't know. [1632]

Q. ... Was there any number on the gun that you bought? A. If there was I did not observe it.

Q. Did you examine this gun this morning out here near the sheriff? A. Yes... .

Q. Did you tell Mr. McAnarney in the presence of the sheriff that there wasn't any number on this gun I hold in my hand? A. No, I did not tell him.

MR. KATZMANN. That is all. [1633]

24. VANZETTI'S ALIBI WITNESSES

Joseph Rosen, Sworn June 29, 1921.

Q. (By Mr. Callahan) What is your full name? A. My full name is Joseph Rosen.

Q. Where do you live? A. I live No.12 Fowler Street, Dorchester, Massachusetts.

Q. What is your business? A. Peddling along all over the state of Massachusetts.

Q. Peddling what? A. Woolens.

Q. Do you know where you were April 15 last year? A. Yes.

Q. Where? A. I been down in Plymouth, Massachusetts.

Q. Do you know what time you arrived at Plymouth?

A. I arrived at Plymouth ten minutes of eight.

[Ed. Rosen said he left Boston on the 6:37 train.]

Q. When you got to the Plymouth station, where did you go?

A. I went down to a little restaurant to get——

Q. Speak up loud. A. I just went down to a little restaurant to get my breakfast... .

Q. After you got your breakfast, where did you go? A. I took the street car from Plymouth to the Seaside, where they call it, North Plymouth. [1494]

Q. What did you have with you? A. I had with me a valise and a handful of men's suitings... .

Q. Do you know Vanzetti? A. Not to be speaking of.

Q. Did you see him that day? A. Yes, sir.

Q. Had you seen him before that day? A. I seen him just once before that.

Q. Once before? A. Yes.

Q. When with reference to April 15th did you see him **the first time**?

A. My best recollection, I should suggest it was ... about two months before that.

Q. Two months before that [April 15]? A. Yes.

Q. Where did you see him then? A. A street by the name, they call it Cherry Street.

Q. Where? A. In the Seaside section [North Plymouth], not in Plymouth.

Q. Did you have some business transaction with him then [two months before April 15]?

A. I sold him a piece of material in the house, in the Cherry Street house.

Q. Now, getting back to April 15th, did you see Vanzetti on April 15th? A. Yes.

Q. Where? A... . I have seen him at a street, I think they call it, it starts with "C" but I can't pronounce the full street.

Q. Castle Street? Is it Castle Street? A. It is Castle Street.... [Corner of Castle and Main.]

Q. In what town? A. In the Seaside section.

Q. What was he doing there? A. I find him in the street at that particular corner with a push cart of fish. He was selling fish. [1495]

Q. Well, when you saw Vanzetti there at the corner of Castle and Main Street?

A. I sold him a piece of material, just enough to make for himself a suit.

[Ed. After Rosen showed Vanzetti his suitings.]

Q. Did you and he go to some place? A. Yes.

Q. Where? A. He took me down just to a house, ... two blocks away from the place.

Q. Do you know what their names were [people you saw in the house]? A. No.

Q. What transpired in the house? A. I showed him a piece of material and he took it into the house to show it in the house up to a lady [Mrs. Brini] whether it was good material or not.

Q. Did Vanzetti have anything in his hand when he was in the house? A. Yes.

Q. What? A. A suitling [sic], you know, a piece of cloth, you see.

Q. Where did he get the piece of cloth? A. On the street.

Q. From whom? A. From me.

Q. What did he do with it in the house? ... A. He showed it to the lady. [1496]

Q. After the conversation [of Vanzetti and Mrs. Brini] what took place? A. Well, we came out.

Q. Who came out? A. I and Vanzetti came out ... right to the place where we started from.

Q. Where did you go? A. We went to the same place where we started, right to his push cart.

Q. What transpired there? A. We were trying to make a price on the piece of material.

Q. Did you finally sell that piece of cloth? A. Yes, sir.

Q. Can you tell me what time it was when you first met Vanzetti that day?

A. On the first day [two months before April 15] or the second day.

Q. No. The second day, April 15th, last year?

A. … [I]t was just noontime, about twelve o'clock.

Q. How do you place it noontime? A. By the whistles from the Plymouth Cordage [rope factory], they been blowing and people just going home to get their dinner… .

Q. When you came back to the fish cart, how long did you stay there with Vanzetti? A. About five minutes. [Ed. Rosen said his walk to Brini home and back to fish cart took 10 minutes.]

Q. What did you do that afternoon? A. That afternoon I took the car back, I took the car back down to Plymouth. [Streetcar.]

Q, Did you stay in Plymouth that afternoon? A. I stayed in Plymouth up to the last train.

Q. What time was that? A. Up to 6:10

Q. And you took the train from the Plymouth station? A. Yes, sir.

Q. Where did you go? A. I went to Whitman.

Q. What time did you arrive at Whitman, if you know?

A. I should suggest about ten minutes to seven… .

Q. Did you stay in Whitman over night? A. Yes, sir.

Q. Do you know where? A. I do not know just their names, but [1497] it is right across, right from the station there is kind of a lunch room and rooming house.

Q. Did you hear the name that night when you were there? A. It starts with "L", but I can't say the name.

Q. "Littlefield", or "Litchfield"? A. Something like that… .

Mr. CALLAHAN. If your Honor please, … I would like to call people that he saw in Plymouth so as to get identification. He doesn't know their names.

(A court officer brings two ladies into the court room, who come near the witness stand.)

Q. Did you ever see either of these people before? A. Yes, sir.

Q. Which one? A. I seen this lady with the young lady; seen them together.

Q. Both of them? A. Both of them together. [Ed. Mrs. A. Brini and daughter LeFavre.]

Q. Whether or not this lady is the lady whose house you went to with Vanzetti? A. Yes, sir. [1498]

Cross-Examination.

Q. (By Mr. Katzmann) How old a man are you, Mr. Rosen. A. 33.

Q. Are you married? A. Yes, sir.

Q. Any children? A. Yes, sir. [1498]

Q. How long have you lived at 212 Fowler Street, Dorchester? A. This is a mistake in the number. No.12... .

Q. What day did you move in there? A. I can't recollect.

Q. What month did you move in there? A. I should say in May.

Q. What time in May? A. 1920.

Q. What time in May, in the month of May, 1920? A. I couldn't say.

Q. Where were [you] on the 16th day of May, 1920? A. I don't know.

Q. Where were you on the 15th day of April, 1921? A. I don't know.

Q. Where were you on the 15th day of May, 1921? A. I don't know.

Q. Where were you on the 15th day of June, 1921? A. I don't know...

Q. Had you ever been in Plymouth before? A. Yes, sir.

Q. ... Before what? What are you answering? A. I have been in Plymouth, oh, about three or four times during the year. I was coming down to Plymouth for the last five years. [1499]

Q. How often have you been in Wellesley? A. Once in a while.

Q. When was the last time? A. I can't say.

Q. Was it this year or last year? A. I can't tell you.

Q. Have you ever been in Fall River? A. Yes.

Q. When was the last time? A. I can't tell you.

Q. Have you ever been in Taunton? A. Yes, sir.

Q. When was the last time? A. I can't answer.

Q. When was the last time you were in Plymouth before today? A. The last time was April 15th, 1920.

Q. You haven't been down there this year [1921]? A. No, sir.

Q. Do you keep any memorandum of the places and the times you visit them? A. No, sir.

Q. So that what you are giving as to the 15th of April, 1920, is entirely a matter of recollection? A. Because—

Q. I did not ask you the reason, Mr. Rosen. Is it entirely a matter of recollection, is the question? A. Yes, sir.... [1500]

Q. ... [B]efore the summons [to appear in Dedhan Court] was left at your house last Wednesday, had you ever told anybody before then about Vanzetti?

A. No, I did not speak to anybody.... [1502]

Q. ... When did you speak to your wife about Vanzetti?

A. ... [W]hen I seen his picture [which appeared with news item of his arrest] in the paper.

Q. When was that? A. I don't know. I can't remember it correctly, the date.

Q. What paper did you see it in [news item of Vanzetti's arrest]?

A. In the Boston paper

Q. How long was it after the day you saw Vanzetti at Plymouth?

A. It was just about ... I think two months up to ten weeks.... .

Q. ... Did you read it [the story that was with the picture]? A. Yes, I read the story. [1503]

Q.... . Are you sure it was between the middle of June and the first of July that he [Vanzetti] was arrested? A. I think it must be.

Q. Did you sell anybody else any cloth in Plymouth the day you saw him there? A. Yes, sir.

Q. Whom did you sell?

A. I sold up to a Greek ice cream parlor. I do not know his name personally. [1504]

Q. What did you sell him? A. I sold him a suit of clothes.

Q. All made up, or the suiting? A. No, just the material, the cloth.

Q. What color was it? A. Well, it was a Palm Beach piece of cloth, a very light color.... .

Q. Did you sell anybody else at Seaside? A. I sold up to a milkman in Seaside.

Q. What is his name? A. I don't know.... .

Q. Did you sell anybody else at Seaside? A. I have got to have an awful good head just to think of that. [1505]

Q. What? A. I have to have an awful good memory just to remember things, ...

Q. What time did you sell to the Greek on the day you say you sold to Vanzetti?

A. I sold him in the morning.

Q. What time in the morning? A. About quarter past ten.

Q. What time did you leave [Greek ice cream parlor]? A. I think about ten minutes after.

Q. What time did you sell the milkman? A. The milkman, I sold on the street.

Q. I did not say you didn't. I asked you the time,——what time?

A. It must have been somewheres just around eleven o'clock.

Q. How long did that sale take? A. About five minutes.

Q. Where were you in between 25 minutes past ten and eleven o'clock?

A. I went up into the Greek store, the Greek ice cream parlor store.

Q. I thought that was a ten-minute sale? A. Yes, but it take me ten minutes before I got through.

Q. That is 25 minutes past ten, isn't it?

A. It is a pretty close figure at that, because I can't give it to you to the second.

Q. Then where did you go? A. After, when I walked out from the ice cream parlor, I met the milkman on the street... .

Q. How near to the ice cream parlor? A. Oh, I should suggest about two blocks.

Q. How long did it take you to walk there? A. Not very—

Q. Two or three minutes? A. I suppose so.

Q. What time was it then?

A. It must have been somewhere around eleven o'clock when I sold the milkman... .

Q. If you finished with the Greek at 10:25 and walked two blocks, taking you two or three minutes, that would make it just eleven when you met the milkman, wouldn't it?

A. Yes, but I take—you always understand, a rest.

Q. Where did you rest? A. In the outside, anywhere I get a chance.

Q. Where did you rest that day outside? A. When I left just the Greek ice cream parlor, ... I just got a suit case and when I might get a little tired walking with the stuff along I took a rest for five minutes. I can't give you full particulars up to the second. [1506]

Q. You had been resting for ten minutes while you had been selling the Greek?

A. This is not resting... .

Q. Did it [showing the material] tire you? A. Yes, sir... . [1507]

Q. Did you meet the milkman? A. Yes, on the street.

Q. What did you say to the milkman? A. He came right in the same street I was resting.

Q. Then you did not meet him two or three blocks up, did you, from the Greek's?

A. (Witness hesitates.)

THE COURT. Can you answer the question, please?

A. Well, I should not say "Yes". I should not say "NO."

Q. In between? A. Yes.

Q. Just about. Is he a fat man, or thin man? A. Who?

Q. The milkman? A. He is a skinny fellow.

Q. A skinny fellow. Tall or short? A. Oh, just as tall as I am. Perhaps a little bit shorter. [1508]

Q. How tall are you? A. I don't know what you figure me.

Q. I am not good on figures. What do you say?

A. Well, I don't know myself. I never took pains to find out.

Q. Never measured yourself? A. No.

Q. How much do you weigh? A. 162.

Q. You weighed yourself? A. I did weigh myself once in a while.

Q. But you never measured yourself? A. Never had the occasion. Too busy.

Q. Make your own suit of clothes? A. Yes, sir.

Q. You don't know how tall you are? A. I did not ask the tailors.

Q. I thought you made your own clothes? A. Me, I am not a tailor.

Q. Didn't you just say you did? A. I make them, yes.

Q. What? A. Oh, yes, make my own clothes, but not myself. I take them into a tailor to have them made for me.

Q. What is the name of the man you sold in Plymouth that afternoon? A. I don't know.

Q. Did you sell anybody else in Plymouth that afternoon? A. I been in the chief of police's house.

Q. Did you sell him? A. I was trying to sell his wife some ladies' stuff. She was washing, I remember, that day.

Q. Yes. On a Thursday? A. I think so. She must have been doing something around the kitchen.

Q. Was she washing or not, on Thursday? A. I say she was-- [1509]

Q. You saw her over the tub, did you? A. Yes, sir, she was doing some scrubbing around.

Q. Did you talk with her? A. For a few minutes.

263

Q. Where does she live? A. She lives,--there is a bridge on the main street and you turn, I do not know just the name of the street correctly, but I can show you the house, if it is necessary.

Q. What is necessary for you is to answer the question: Where does she live? A. I do not know the name of the street.

Q. Describe where it is. . . A. It is,--I have been down in Middle Street and I got through just through the station way, through the back, I suppose up through a back street, you understand, where I came to the chief of police, right in there, but I do not know the name of the street. .

Q. How long were you at the chief's house? A. For about two minutes, something like that.

Q. Then where did you go? A. I went to . . . the next house from the chief. I made a sale over there with a lady, the next house from the Chief's house.

Q. Do you know the name? A. I did not ask her particularly, but her husband she told me was working for the Plymouth Cordage, . . .

Q. . . . What was her description? A. She is kind of a tall lady; and I sold her.

Q. Never mind what you sold. Go on and describe her. She is tall? A. Tall, a blonde, some blonde looking, not any dark lady, kind of blonde looking lady.

Q. How old a person would you say she was? A. Well, I don't know. . . . I should think between 38 and 40 years. [1510]

Q. Did you say you met Vanzetti once before that day [April 15, 1920]?

A. About two months before.

Q. What month was it? A. I don't know... .

Q. What time of the day? A. Well, I should say it was in the afternoon.

Q. What time in the afternoon? A. Well, about two o'clock.

Q. Where? A. In his house on Cherry Street. [This is two months before April 15, 1920.]

Q. Was it the Brini house? A. I do not know the name. [1512]

Q. Did you sell anybody else in Plymouth on that occasion [first trip]? A. I sold it to the same lady.

Q. What lady? A. Sold to the same lady just in the Cherry Street house.... [1513]

Q. Where were you two weeks ago today? A. I don't know. [1515]

(Short Recess.)

Q. When was it you first talked with either of these two ladies that were brought into the court room? A. April 15th, 1920.

Q. Have you talked with them since that date? Have you seen them since that date?

A. Well, I seen them after that, oh, yes, I believe.

Q. Where? A. Up in Plymouth,—I mean on the Seaside... .

Q. When after April 15th? A. Well, I should say just about in two months after, something like that. I had an occasion I should come back to Plymouth and I should do a little more business.

Q. Was he [Vanzetti] under arrest then? A. Yes... .

Q. Have you seen the milkman to whom you referred since that date [April 15, 1920]?

A. I seen him, yes, several times in the street... .

Q. Have you ever been up to his house?

A. Yes; oh, yes, a couple of times; sold him some more stuff. [1516]

Q. Just one other question. How many times have you been down to Plymouth, if you have been to Plymouth, since the 15th of April?

A. Well, I usually come down between seven and eight times a year.

Q. I am not asking you what you usually do, but how many times, if you have been to Plymouth, since the day you say you saw Vanzetti. How many times since then have you been to Plymouth? A. Well, up to a year just expired, up to 1921, the year just expired I think it must have been between about eight or nine times, rather, eight or nine times, rather... .

Q. Since you saw Vanzetti at Plymouth, that was the last time you saw him at Plymouth, wasn't it? A. I call Plymouth and Seaside together; just Plymouth to me.

Q. You saw him in Seaside? A. Yes.

Q. All right. Since that time how many times have you been in Plymouth?

A. Several times. I can't give it you up to the figure. Any time I get a chance I go to Plymouth.

Q. And not at all in the year 1921? A. Well, 1921, no.

MR. KATZMANN. That's all. [1517]

[In Redirect Examination, Rosen testified his wife paid their poll tax on April 15, 1920. A receipt verified this date, and Rosen's "full payment of 1918 poll tax and costs" was admitted as Exhibit K. [1519] In Recross Examination, Rosen could not remember getting a "notice of an overdue poll tax."] [1520]

Miss Lillian Shuler, Sworn. June 29, 1921. Corroborative Witness.

Q. (By Mr. Callahan) What is your name? A. Lillian Shuler. [1520]

Q. Where do you live? A. Whitman.

Q. What was your occupation April 15th of last year? A. I was a waitress.

Q. Where were you employed? A. Littlefield's.

Q. Littlefield's what? A. Littlefield's restaurant and rooming house.

Q. Where? A. Whitman. [Ed. Whitman is 19 miles from Plymouth.]

Q. Do you know what your hours of work were? A. Four [in the afternoon]... until midnight.

Q. Were you working April 15, 1920? A. Yes, sir.

Q. Did you ever see this book before? A. A good many times.

Q. Will you state what it is? A. That was a book we kept memorandums of money paid out in a day, and renting rooms, and things like that.

Q. You made your own personal memorandum in the book?

A. Yes, and then Littlefield took it at night when he came down, and put it in his book.

Q. Will you turn to the page there dated April 15, 1920? A. [Witness does so.]

Q. State whether or not the record shows a room being rented that night. A. Yes, sir... .

Q. Do you recall, Miss Shuler, renting a room April 15, 1920? A. No, I could not. [1521]

Q. Well, did you rent a room April 15, 1920?

A. Well, by this book I did. That is the only way I can remember it... .

Q. Can you tell me whether or not you rented more than one room or not that day? A. One room.

MR. CALLAHAN. One room. Your witness.

MR. KATZMANN. No questions. [1522]

Mrs. Alphonsine Brini. Sworn June 29, 1921.

[The oath is administered to the witness through the interpreter, Mr. Ross.]

Q. (By Mr. Callahan) What is your name? A. Alphonsine Brini.

Q. Where do you reside? A. I live No. 5 Cherry Court, North Plymouth.

Q. Do you know Mr. Vanzetti? A. Yes, sir.

Q. How long have you known him? A. About eight years.

Q. Do you know the man that you saw on the stand here a few moments ago? A. Yes.

Q. When did you see him before? A. I saw him in my house.

Q. When? A. On the 15th day of April.

Q. What year? A. 1920.

Q. ... Who was with that man when you saw him at your house, if anybody? A. Mr. Vanzetti. [1522]

Q. What time in the day was it? A. It was ... between half past eleven and twelve o'clock.

Q. What did ... Mr. Vanzetti do when he came into your house? A. He showed me a piece of cloth.

Q. Who was in the house there at that time? A. My daughter.... .

Q. Let me go back a moment. Had you ever seen this man [Rosen] that you saw on the witness stand here a moment ago before that day [April 15]? A. I do not recall that I have seen him. It looks, it appears to me that was the first time I ever saw him.

Q. Now, what time was it that day when you **first saw Vanzetti** that same day [April 15, 1920]? A. Between half past ten and eleven o'clock.

Q. Where did you see him? A. I saw him in the house of the owner of the house where I live [home of Mrs. Eva Forni, her landlady, 80 to 90 feet distant], with the fish.... .

Q. Did you examine the cloth Vanzetti gave you? A. Yes.

Q. What color cloth was it? A. Dark blue. Woolen, dark blue, men's suit.

Q. Do you recollect noticing anything else about it? A. As I looked at the cloth I do not remember whether it is one or two small holes in the middle of that piece of cloth.

Q. How do you recall it was the 15th of April of last year? A. I remember because it was,—that was my first week that I came home from the hospital. [1523]

Cross-Examination.

Q. (By Mr. Katzmann) Did Vanzetti ever live with you at your house?
A. Yes.
Q. How long? A. Four years.
Q. When did he leave your house? A. A little over four years ago.... .
Q. Don't you live at Cherry Street?
A. Now I live in Cherry Court. At that time I lived in Suosso's Lane.
Q. On April 15, 1920, you lived in Suosso's Lane? A. Yes, sir. [1524]
Q. Is there anything about the fact that there is two holes in a piece of cloth that enables you to fixe [sic] any date? A. Well, I remember that I saw the cloth and I saw the holes. [1525]
Q. What is it about the holes in the cloth that fixes the date or helps you to fix the date?
A. I remember that was the 15th day of April because the day before, on the 14th, my illness was getting worse.
MR. KATZMANN. I ask that be stricken out, if your Honor please, as not being responsive.
THE COURT. That may be. Just tell her, Mr. Interpreter, to pay attention to the question.... .
Q. Mrs. Brini, is there anything about the fact of your seeing two holes in a piece of cloth that enables you to say it was on a date certain because you saw those holes? A. Why, yes. I remember that that morning I had a visit from a person that came up to visit me in regard to my sickness that very morning.... .
Q. Did you ever see Rosen before the day [April 15] that Vanzetti came up there with the cloth? A. I cannot say. I may have, but I think that was the first time.
Q. Did he ever sell you cloth? Did he sell you a piece of cloth two months before? A. No, sir.
Q. Did you ever buy any cloth from Rosen yourself? A. No, sir.
[1526]

Miss LeFavre Brini, Sworn. June 30, 1921.

Q. (By Mr. Callahan.) Do you recall the day of April 15th last year?
A. Yes.
Q. Where were you? A. I was working until twelve o'clock that morning... .
Q. Do you know Mr. Vanzetti? A. Yes.
Q. Do you recall seeing him on the day of April 15th last year?
A. Yes, I do.
Q. When? What time of the day? A. About ten, half past ten, I should think. [1537]
Q. What was he doing at your house? A. He brought me fish.
Q. Do you know where your mother was at that time? A. No, I don't.
Q. And who was there when he brought you the fish? A. I was there alone.
Q. Did you later that day see him again...? A. Yes, I did.
Q. Where was he? A. In my house again with another man.
Q. What time of day was it? A. About noontime.
Q. Who was the other man that was with him? A. I don't know him. He was a peddler.
Q. What did you see Vanzetti do when he came in the house with the peddler? A. I saw him hand some cloth to my mother.
Q. How do you recall this being April 15th of last year? A. Because it was just one week after I left my work to take care of my mother, who came home from the hospital.
Q. Is there any other reason?
A. Because that morning my father called the nurse for my mother.
Q. Is there any other reason that you remember it was April 15th [1538] that you saw Vanzetti at your home? A. Because the day before the 15th my mother was sick and called the doctor. [1539]

Cross-Examination.

Q. (By Mr. Katzmann) How old are you, Miss Brini? A. Fifteen.
Q. And you are the daughter of Alphonsin [sic] Brini? A. Yes... .
Q. ... On that day when you saw the cloth, did you say, "I will remember this day because it is the day my father is telephoning to the

Cordage nurse"? A. No, I did not say that then. There was no use of saying it. [1539]

Q. Was it of the slightest consequence what day you saw the piece of cloth? A. No... . [1540]

Q. ... How many times, Miss Brini, would you say you talked over with your mother about what you and she were going to say about where he [Vanzetti] was on the 15th of April?

A. [Witness hesitates.]

Q. Can't you answer that? A. It is impossible to answer that question.

Q. Well, Miss Brini, is it impossible because you have talked it over so many times with your mother? A. [Witness hesitates.]

MR. KATZMANN. Well, I won't press it... .

Q... . I am asking you if you said to Mr. Callahan before this jury when he first asked you about the 15th of April, did you say, "I was working until twelve o'clock that morning"? Did you?

A. That was a mistake. [1543]

Q. Was your mother out of the house between ten and half past ten that morning? A. Yes... .

Q. Where was she? A. She was in Mrs. Forrini's house... .

Q. Who is Mrs. Forrni? A. The landlady... .

Q. Is it true you did not know where your mother was at that time?

A. Yes.

Q. Well, is it true you knew at that time she [Mrs. Brini] was at Mrs. Forrni's?

A. I know she was at Mrs. Forrni's because I went there.

Q. If you knew she was at Mrs. Fornni's, why did you tell Mr. Callahan and the jury you did not know where your mother was? Why did you say that? [Witness hesitates.]

Q. Well, I will pass to the next question. How long have you known Mr. Vanzetti to have lived at your house? A. About seven or eight years.

Q. Is he like a relative of yours, so friendly with your family? A. Yes. [1544]

Q. ... Is there any other date you could give me with certainty as to Mr. Vanzetti's whereabouts except this date?

THE COURT. This date he means of April 15th... .

MR. CALLAHAN. I think she gave another date to you.

MR. KATZMANN. She is answering.

MR. CALLAHAN. I pray your Honor's judgment.

THE COURT. She may answer it if she can.
[Witness hesitates.]
THE WITNESS. I don't know. [1545]

Mrs. Alphonsine Brini, Resumed. June 30, 1921.

MR. JEREMIAH McANARNEY. If your Honor please, it is agreed bu counsel for the Commonwealth and counsel for the defendant as follows: that the witness—I will change that to "this"—... .
MR. KATZMANN. I would like to have that read as finally agreed. [Ed. First reading rejected.]
[The agreement is read as follows:—
    "It is agreed by counsel for the Commonwealth and counsel for the defendant as follows: that this witness, Alphonsin Brini has, in another case, testified on behalf of the defendant Vanzetti as to his whereabouts different from the place set forth in that case."]
THE COURT. Now, you are through with the witness?
MR. KATZMANN. Yes.
THE COURT. She is excused. Have you sent for another witness?
MR. CALLAHAN. No. We are discussing about the daughter, whom we suspended with.
MR KATZMANN. In view of that agreement made of the matter as a matter of evidence, I don't care for the daughter to remain. [1555]

Ella M. Urquhart, Sworn. June 30, 1921. Corroborative Witness.

Q. (By Mr. Callahan) What is your present occupation?
A. Nurse for the Plymouth Cordage Company.
Q. What was your occupation April 15th last year? A. The same.
Q. What are your particular duties at the Cordage Company? A. We tend to any emergency, accidents in the mill, and we also visit in the families, in their homes.
Q. Whether or not there are other nurses there at the Cordage?
A. There are two other nurses.
Q. Who keeps the records? A. No one in particular.
Q. Have you the records of that department with you of the Cordage Company?
A. Yes, sir, of the month of April, 1920... . [1581]

Q. Do you recall having a telephone call on the morning of April 15th of last year from Dr. Shurtleff?

MR. KATZMANN. One moment.

THE COURT. You may answer.

A. No, I do not know when the telephone call came.

MR. KATZMANN. Can't hear you, please.

THE WITNESS. He called us to go to the case.

Q. Just a moment. Do you recall, madam, of having a telephone call from Dr. Shurtleff? A. Yes.

Q. Did you have the call? A. I do not know.

MR. KATZMANN. I ask the preceding answer be stricken out, if your Honor please.

THE COURT. Why should it not be?

MR. CALLAHAN. It should be.

THE COURT. It may be.

Q. Do you know Mrs. Brini? A. No.

Q. Did you ever attend her? A. No, not that I remember of.

THE COURT. Allow me to suggest, Mr. Callahan, in order to get the evidence in that I think you have in mind, if it is competent, is to have the nurse [who attended Mrs. Brini.]

MR. CALLAHAN. I do not know whether we can get her or not. That is my difficulty. [1584]

Q. In consequence of the telephone call was anything done by you or anybody else in your department, if you know? A. The nurse visited Mrs. Brini.

THE COURT. I can't hear.

MR. KATZMANN. I ask that be stricken out, if your Honor please.

THE COURT. I do not believe anybody heard it. I did not,

MR. KATZMANN. I heard it. I ask it be stricken out.

THE COURT. Now, let me hear it. Then I will determine whether it should be stricken out.

[The answer is read.]

THE COURT. Well, do you mean that you know that of your own knowledge...?

THE WITNESS. I have the record here. That is all I know of.

THE COURT. That is not according to my view of the law, if you will pardon me. It is not competent testimony. Do you still say you know nothing about it except what somebody told you?

THE WITNESS. That is all I know, except referring to this.

MR. KATZMANN. Then I ask it be stricken out.
THE COURT. It may be.
MR. CALLAHAN. That is all.
MR. KATZMANN. No questions. [1585]

Gertrude Mary Matthews, Sworn. July 1, 1921. Corroborative Witness.

Q. (By Mr. Callahan) What was your occupation April 15th of last year, or during the month of April of last year? A. Nurse at the Plymouth Cordage Company.
Q. Do you know Mrs. Brini, in Plymouth? A. Yes.
Q. Did you call on her sometime during the year of 1920? A. Yes.
Q. Can you tell me the month of the year? A. April.
Q. Do you recall whether you made one or more calls at her home?
A. Yes, I made several.
Q. And can you tell me whether or not those several calls you made were during the month of April, 1920? A. Yes.
Q. What did you do for her? A. I did an abdominal dressing.
Q. Can you tell me from your own recollection as to the dates that you made those calls?
A. Well, probably between the 15th and the 25th of the month.
Q. Do you recall specifically the date that you made the call? A. No.
Q. Did you recall the date you made the first call at her home? A. No.
MR. CALLAHAN. That is all.
MR. KATZMANN. No questions. [1634]

Angel Guidobone, Sworn. June 30, 1921.

Q. (By Mr. Callahan) Where do you live? A. Suosso's Lane, Plymouth, No. 10.
Q. Do you know Mr. Vanzetti? A. Yes, I know him.
Q. How long? A. About six years and a half or more.
Q. Do you recall seeing him on the day of April 15th last year?
A. Yes, I remember.
Q. Where was he when you saw him? A. I saw him in the Court, about quarter past twelve, while I was coming home from my work.
THE INTERPRETER. In this Lane. He calls it the Court.

273

Q. In what Lane? A. Suosso's Lane. That is where I live. I saw him on the corner of that lane.

Q. What was he doing? A. He was selling fish, and he give me some fish in my hand... .

Q. Do you recall what kind of fish it was? A.... . Codfish.

Q. What time was it? A. I saw him on the 15th day of April, about thirteen minutes past twelve or quarter past twelve; well, I was going to my dinner.

Q. How do you fix the date as being April 15th that you saw him there?

A. Well, I have a mark here [pointing on his right side]. I had appendicitis. I had an operation.

Q. When did you have the operation? A. I had it on the 19th day of April. [1587]

Cross-Examination.

Q. (By Mr. Katzmann) I take it, Mr. Guidobone, that the fact you were operated on on April 19th makes you remember you bought some fish on the 15th. Is that it? A. Yes.

Q. And that is the only thing that makes you remember it?

A. Well, the operation and that, because I was very careful what I was eating.

Q. Do you think the codfish caused the appendicitis? A. No, no, no.

Q. What is the connection between the operation on the 19th and your buying codfish on the 15th? A. It had nothing to do with it with me.

Q. How long were you troubled with the pain that resulted in the operation?

A. Oh, over a year before. I did not have the courage to do it.

Q. Then you had the pain for quite some time, didn't you?

A. Yes, I had it over one year and I was afraid to go and have the operation.

Q. Did you have a pain on the 15th? A. No, sir. I did not. On the 17th, I did.

Q. ... [W]hat was the last date before the 17th you had a pain?

A. Well, there were other days, different days, that I had pains, but I do not remember now what days.

Q. But you remember codfish on the 15th day, is that right?

A. Yes. [1588]

Melvin Corl, Sworn. June 30, 1921.

Q. (By Mr. Callahan) Where do you live? A. 18 Atlantic Street, Plymouth.

Q. What is your occupation? A. Fisherman.

Q. Do you recall where you were April 15th, last year? A. At the shore, painting my boat... .

Q. Do you know Mr. Vanzetti? A. Yes, sir ... since about 1915.

Q. You had business transactions with him? A. During the fall of 1919.

Q. What were they? A. Selling him fish. [1548]

Q. Do you recall seeing him on the 15th of April, last year? A. I do.

Q. Where was he and where were you when you saw him?

A. I was painting my boat and he came down the shore and stopped and talked with me.

Q. What time of day was it that he was talking with you? A. Around 2 o'clock he arrived there.

Q. How long did he remain talking with you? A. About one hour and a half, I should say.

Q. How do you fix it as being the 15th of April?

A. He came along and he said he was going to Mr. Sampson's to look for a job.

MR. KATZMANN. I object.

Q. You can't tell what he said to you. A. On account of painting my boat, and I was going to put it in the following day, but it was not completed and I put it in on the 17th, my wife's birthday.

Q. Whether or not that was the first day you had started painting your boat?

A. No, I was painting,——I had been working on it practically the whole week.

Q. When did you put the boat in the water? A. April 17.

Q. Does that date mean anything to you?

A. It was my wife's birthday; and I also towed a boat from Duxbury on that date... .

Q. Do you recall anybody else being there while you and Vanzetti were having a talk?

A. Yes, sir. Mr. Jesse.

Q. And do you recall overhearing a conversation between Mr. Vanzetti and Mr. Jesse?

A. Yes, sir.

Q. Was it about an automobile? A. It was. [1549]

Cross-Examination.

Q. (By Mr. Katzmann) Mr. Vanzetti was a customer of yours, wasn't he? A. Yes, sir. [1549]

Q. Were there any other men there any other time you were painting your boat in the week you were at it? A. Yes. There was men going up and down... .

Q. Do you know how long any of those men stayed talking? A. No, I could not tell the length of time.

Q. What day did any particular one of them other than Vanzetti stop at the boat while you were painting? A. Mr. Jesse. He came out there.

Q. Mr. Jesse was there all the time, wasn't he? A. Not in the yard. He was in his shop.

Q. He was in the shop. I am talking in my question about anybody except Vanzetti or Jesse?

A. Mr. Holmes of the lumber yard.

Q. What day did he call? A. I could not say the date.

Q. What time of day did he call? A. That would be apt to happen many times... .

Q. What time did he call? A. I could not say the time.

Q. Any other man? A. I can't remember of any one particular... .

Q. Where were you 21 days ago to day?

A. I could not say just now... . [1551]

Q. What day of the week did the 17th day of April, 1920, fall on?

A. On Saturday... .

Q. ... How do you remember it was the 17th that fell on a Saturday?

A. On account of my wife's birthday and going to Duxbury.

Q. On what day of the week did your wife's birthday fall, April 17, 1921? A. Monday. [1553]

Q. Are you sure? A. I am not exactly sure... .

Q. You think April 17, 1921, fell on Monday, do you? A. Sunday or Monday. I could not say which. [1554]

Frank Jesse, Sworn. June 30, 1921.

Q. (By Mr. Callahan) Where do you live? A. I live in Prince Street, Plymouth.

Q. What is your occupation or business? A. Boat builder.... .

Q. Do you know Mr. Vanzetti? A. Yes, sir.

Q. How long have you known him? A. I know him five or seven or eight years. [1585]

Q. Do you know Mr. Corl? A. Yes, sir.... .

Q. Do you recall seeing him painting his boat last year? A. Yes, sir.

Q. Where was he when he was painting his boat? A. Right in my yard.

Q. Do you recall seeing Vanzetti there? A. Yes, sir.

Q. At some time when he was painting the boat? A. Yes, sir.... .

Q. Do you recall that Vanzetti was talking to Corl? A. Yes, sir, he was.

Q. Did you have a conversation with Vanzetti? A. Yes, sir.

Q. Was that conversation with reference to an automobile? A. Yes, sir.

Q. Do you recall the date? A. I couldn't remember, sir.

Q. Can you give me the season of the year? A. I could not remember.

Q. Haven't got any idea what time of the year it was? A. Well, it was in the spring.

Q. In the spring, but you haven't any idea of the month or the day of the month?

A. I couldn't remember, sir.... .

MR. CALLAHAN. That is all.

MR. KATZMANN. No questions. [1586]

Mrs. Melvin Corl, Sworn. July 1, 1921. Corroborative Witness.

Q. (By Mr. Callahan) What is your full name? A. Mrs. Melvin Corl.

Q. Where do you live? A. 18 Atlantic Street, Plymouth.

Q. Are you the wife of Melvin Corl? A. I am.

Q. What day of the year does your birthday fall on? A. The 17th of April.

Q. Do you recall anything your husband was doing during the week of April 17, 1920?

MR. KATZMANN. One moment, if your Honor please.

277

THE COURT. Her husband has been a witness.

MR. KATZMANN. Yes. He is not a defendant here. I will state, if your Honor please, her husband is not a defendant.

THE COURT. That is all true, but he is here. I suppose it is corrobo-
[1670] rative. That is the purpose of it, to a certain extent. He mentioned something about—

MR. KATZMANN. He mentioned she had a birthday that year.

THE COURT. I suppose that is the purpose of it. You may inquire.

Q. Will you answer? A. Answer your question now?

Q. Yes. A. He was getting his boat painted and ready to put in the water.

Q. Did you see the boat painted?

A. Why, I saw it one evening, not while he was painting it, but during that process... .

Q. Did you see the boat during the week of April 17, 1920? A. I did.

Q. What is your best recollection as to the date?

A. A couple of nights or so before the 17th of April. [1671]

Cross-Examination.

Q. (By Mr. Katzmann) How far do you live from where you saw the boat, Mrs. Corl?

A. Well, it takes me about five minutes to walk down to there from the house.

Q. You said you saw the boat a couple of nights or so before your birthday? A. Yes, sir.

Q. What night was it you saw it? A. It was not the night before.

Q. That wouldn't be a couple of nights, would it? A. No, sir.

Q. What night was it? A. It was about Thursday night.

Q. Why didn't you say a couple of nights before? A. I did.

Q. Didn't you say a couple of nights or so? A. Yes, I did.

Q. May it have been Wednesday night? A. I do not think it was Wednesday night. [1672]

Q. ... Where were you two nights before the 17th of April, 1921?

A. At home.

Q. ... [W]hat day of the week did the 17th of April fall on?

A. The 17th of April, my birthday this year, I believe, was Sunday.

Q. Yes. Where were you Friday, the 15th of April?

A. The 15th of April, at home, or at the pictures.

Q. At home or at the pictures. Which was it? A. I can't be positive as to the dates.

Q. Can't be positive of that date [April 15, 1921], can you? A. No. [1673]

Redirect Examination.

Q. (By Mr. Callahan) What did he tell you about the Duxbury tow? A. That he had to go to Duxbury Saturday afternoon to tow a boat from Duxbury to Plymouth for Mr. Morey. [1674]

Joseph Morey, Sworn. July 1, 1921. Corroborative Witness.

Q. (By Mr. Callahan) Where do you live? A. 11 Castle Street, Plymouth, Mass.

Q. What is your occupation? A. Cloth inspector.

Q. Where? A. Puritan Mills.

Q. Do you know a Mr. Corl? A. Yes sir, I do.

Q. Did you have some transaction with him? A. Yes, sir.

Q. Sometime last year? A. Yes.

Q. When was it? A. April 17th, Saturday. [1674]

Q. What was the transaction?

A. He towed a boat I bought over at South Duxbury into Plymouth for me.

Q. Who did you buy the boat from? A. Charles F. May, South Duxbury.

Q. How much did you pay for it? A. $75.

Q. Did Corl tow the boat for you?

A. Yes, sir, he towed it for me down to Frank Jesse's boat yard.

Q. Do you recall the condition of Mr. Corl's boat? A. It was newly painted. [1675]

Cross-Examination.

Q. (By Mr. Katzmann) How old are you? A. Twenty-two years old.

Q. Did you get a receipt when you bought the boat? A. No. One of my partners had the receipt.

Q. Where is your partner? A. He lives at Plymouth.... .

Q. You don't know whether it [purchase of boat] was Monday or Tuesday or Wednesday? A. No.

Q. Or Thursday? A. Haven't any idea.

Q. Or Friday? A. I don't remember.

Q. What day did you take it out? A. It was sold there. I did not take it out at all.

Q. What day did you sell it? A. I do not know the date. It was sometime in May... .

Q. Are you on the water a good deal yourself? A. No, not a bit.

Q. How many days elapsed between the time you bought the boat and the time of day it was sold?

A. Well, I could not give the exact number of days, but it was less than a week.

Q. Can't you tell the day? A. Can't tell the day. I didn't take any notice of it. [1675]

Q. ... How soon after the date the boat was towed was your attention first called to the date when you were asked to recall when the date was? A. I couldn't answer that question... .

Q. Has your attention ever been called since the day the boat was towed to the date?

A. No, sir, it hasn't, not until this morning.

Q. Not until this morning? A. Never looked back.

Q. Never looked back. Who called your attention to it this morning?

A. I was talking with Mrs. Corl on our way up... .

Q. Is that the first time in fourteen months your attention has been atracted [sic] to the date? A. Yes, sir. We had a disagreement with the partnership, and I sold it and I never thought any more about it after that.

Q. I am asking you if that was the first time you were asked to bring your memory back to some transaction in April, 1920? A. Yes.

Q. Did you remember it right off? A. No, I did not.

Q. Did somebody tell you what it was? A. Yes.

Q. Who told you? A. Mrs. Corl and I talked it over.

MR. KATZMANN. That is all.

THE WITNESS. And decided that was the date.

Q. You decided that that was the day? A. We weren't sure of it.

Q. You weren't sure? A. She wasn't sure.

Q. She wasn't sure? A. Yes.

MR. KATZMANN. That is all. [1676]

[Ed. See alibi witnesses Carbone, 1624-1625 and Bova, 1626.]

25. TESTIMONY OF BARTOLOMEO VANZETTI

Bartolomeo Vanzetti, Sworn. July 5, 1921.

MR. JEREMIAH McANARNEY. Now, before I ask you any question, I want to say this to you: if any time you do not understand the question, you please say so, because we are going to try and go along in English, and we would all like you to tell us when you do not understand the question or any word in the question, and if you make an answer and use the word and you think you have not used the right word, if you will tell us the Court will gladly let you explain it or make it right.

THE WITNESS. Yes, sir.

MR. JEREMIAH McANARNEY. You do as well as you can and perhaps we can go all through your examination without any interpreter. Now, it is important to you, and I thank the Court for allowing me to say this to you, when you haven't understood, and so you must tell us if you do not understand.

THE COURT. And this applies to not only what Mr. McAnarney may ask you, but also to what may be asked of you in cross-examination by [1689] the District Attorney. You have a right to understand the question before you answer.

Q. (By Mr. Jeremiah McAnarney) Now what is your full name?

A. Bartolomeo Vanzetti.

Q. And Mr. Vanzetti, where were you born? A. I born in Italy.

Q. What town and province? A. Town of Villeefalletto [Villafalletto]; province of Cuneo; region of Piedmont.

Q. How old are you? A. I am thirty-three years old. [1690] ...

[Ed. Vanzetti testified that he came to New York in 1908 {1691} and came to Plymouth in 1913. Here he worked about eighteen months for a Mr. Stone {1693} and approximately eighteen months for the Cordage Company of Plymouth. {1694} He held many jobs as an unskilled laborer. He first peddled fish in the spring of 1919 and returned to peddling fish in the fall of 1919 {1696}. In March 1920 he "started to peddle fish" again. {1698} He received a shipment of 488 pounds of fish by American Railway on April 8, 1920. {1699} His last day of peddling fish was April 15. {1700} On April 16 he dug clams.

{1703} McAnarney questioned Vanzetti about his activities on April 15, 1920.]

Q. Continue, now. On the 15th, where did you peddle? A. On the 15th, I have a few, not very many, fish in the morning of the 15th, and I peddled in Cherry Street, Standish Avenue and Cherry Court, down Suosso's Lane, ... Castle Street is the last place I sell fish on the day of the 15th.

Q. Now tell us anything else that you did on the day of the 15th.

A. ... Almost on the corner of Castle Street I met this man [Rosen] that go around with cloths... .

Q. Did you do anything with him? A. Yes. He stopped me. He says something to me.

Q. Very good... . Did you do anything? A. Yes, I buy a piece of cloth from him.

Q. Yes. Now, what was done with the cloth? A. He sold me a piece of cloth and I told him I don't know nothing about the cloth.

MR. KATZMANN. One moment... .

THE COURT. In consequence of that, what did you do?

Q. Good. A. I bring him [Rosen] to the Brini house. I knew that the Brini wife was in the house, and I know she worked in the woolen mill and she know the cloth... .

Q. Did she look at the cloth? A. Yes... . [1701]

Q. [D]id you or did you not buy it? A. Not in the house of Mrs. Brini.

Q. Then you went out after she looked at the cloth, ...?

A. Yes, he went out alone and I went out a little after him.

Q. After you had got out [of the Brini house], what happened then?

A. I go around my cart, the fish cart, with the fish in, and I found that man wait for me, and he say, "If you want"—

Q. ... [D]id you, yes or no, buy the cloth? A. Yes, I buy the cloth.

Q. What did you pay for it? A. ... $12.75 or something like that... .

Q. What time in the day was that, about what time? A. Near one o'clock, about half past eleven, something like that, half past twelve, about one o'clock.

Q. Now, you say then you had your fish about all sold?

A. Yes. Then I went to Castle Street and I finished my fish.

Q. Where did you go then? A. Then I took my cart and I went ... in front of Mr. Corl's house.

Q. All right. Now, what did you do when you got down in front of Corl's house? A. I left my cart there and I went down to the shore. I have finished the fish. I went down to the shore... .

Q. ... [W]ho did you see there? A. I saw ... Mr. Corl in the boat, ... The boat was on the sand.

Q. What was he doing? A. I went there and I saw he was painting the boat... .

Q. And about how long were you there with him? A. More than an hour, anyhow.

Q. And do you remember whether any one else came while you were there near Mr. Corl while he was working on his boat ...? A. Yes, two men came... .

Q. Who were the men that came there?

A. I think it was Mr. Jesse... . [1702]

Q. Is he a man you knew? A. Yes, I know him. He is a boat builder there in Seaside.

Q. Who was the other man who came? A. The other man is Mr. Holmes, but he don't stay long. He say two or three words and then go away... .

Q. After you left Corl there at the boat, where did you go?

A. I came back and took the cart in the street, then go home.

Q. Where do you keep the fish cart ... you sell fish in? A. I keep my fish cart in the yard of Mr. Fortini, where I board... . [1703]

Q. What did you do on the afternoon of the 17th? A. I take the train. I went to Brockton.

Q. To Brockton. You took a train? A. Yes, I take a train, Plymouth to Whitman, and from Whitman to Brockton I take the electric car... .

Q. Where did you sleep that night, the night of the 17th?

A. I should say that I sleep in Boston, but I don't remember exactly... .

Q. Who did you see when you went to Boston?

A. When I went to Boston I saw many of my old friends.

Q. Yes. A. Saw Manchini.

Q. Where does he live? A. He lives in Readville... . [Ed. See Readville in Sacco's testimony.]

Q. What other man did you see, do you remember? A. I remember Felicani.

Q. Anybody else? A. I remember Colorarossi... . [1705]
[Ed. Vincenzo Colarossi. See Avrich, p. 188.]

Q. ... Who did you stay with that ... night of the 18th?

A. I sleep in the room of Colorarossi.] [1705]

Q. What did you do on the day of the 18th? A. On the day of the 18th we [Vanzetti and his friends] come down together in the street and we make breakfast in the American lunch room in I think they call Scollay Square, that Square in the bottom of Hanover Street.

Q. ... Now, where did you go? A. Then we go down toward ... North Square, and we meet many other friends, ... and ... we make dinner at the Boni restaurant.

Q. And that is where? A. Boni restaurant is in North Square.... . [16 North Square]

Q. That is an Italian restaurant? A. Yes. [Ed. Anarchist hangout in North End. Kaiser, 138.]

Q. After dinner, where did you go? A. After dinner we went to East Boston. [Avrich, p.188.]

Q. Where? A. That is Maverick Square.... .

Q. East Boston? A. Yes. [Ed. Reached by one-cent ferry across the harbor.]

Q. Where there did you go? A. We went in the hall of the Italian Naturalization Club.

Q. The rooms of the Italian Naturalization Club?

A. The rooms of the Italian Naturalization Club, in the hall.... .

Q. Is that hall there in Maverick Square? A. Yes.... [1706]

[Ed. McAnarney asked Vanzetti about his activities on Sunday, April 25. See Avrich, pp. 188-189.]

Q. ... [Y]ou ... took a train and went to Boston [Saturday]. Now where did you go in Boston, please? A. I went in East Boston, in the Italian Naturalization Club.... .

Q. What did you do the next day? A. The next day, we go around. It was on Sunday. We meet many other friends there in the North Side...

Q. Where did you spend the next night, ...?

A. Yes. We decided to send a man to New York that evening, and my friend asked—

MR. KATZMANN. One moment.

Q. You can't tell what your friend said. A. And I was the man that they decided to go.

Q. Go to New York? A. Yes.

Q. ... When did you go to New York, do you remember? A. On Sunday night.... . [April 25]

Q. ... How long did you stay in New York? A. I stayed three days... .
[1710]

Q. Now, when next did you leave Plymouth after you got back from the New York trip?

A. I left Plymouth on the evening of May 1st [Sunday].

Q. And where did you go? A. I go to Boston... .

Q. And where did you stay in Boston that night, . .?

A. ... In Colorarossi's home. [Sunday night.]

Q. And the next day. That is May 1st. Now, May 2d, where did you stay? A. May 2d?

Q. What did you do? A. I came from Boston to the Sacco house.

Q. Sacco. He lives in Stoughton? A. Yes. I mean in May 3d I came to the Sacco house. May 2d I live in Boston. I stay in Boston... .

Q. ... [H]ave you told us ... the places you went the week before May 1st...? A. ... [B]efore I went to New York when I left Plymouth on the date the 20th, I go to Readville... .

Q. To Readville. That is what I had in mind. Where did you go in Readville? A. Mr. Manchini's.

Q. [D]id you ... stay there any night? A. Yes, I stayed there three days. [1711]

Q. ... Where did you stay the night ... of May 2d?

A. ... Colorarossi's house and the room... .

Q. When had you seen Sacco before that day? We will call that May 3rd...?

A. I have seen Sacco on the Sunday before.

Q. Where did you see him? A. I seen him in the Naturalization Club. [Sunday, May 2.]

Q. Maverick Square, East Boston? A. Yes... .

Q. Did you have any conversation with Mr. Sacco with reference to his going to Italy?

A. Yes. [1712]

Q. Now [where did you stay] May 4th? A. In the Sacco house, too.

Q. Did Sacco go away to work on May 4th ...? A. No, he went to Boston on May 4th... .

Q. When he came home from Boston did any one come with him, ...?

A. He come with Orcciani.

Q. With Orcciani. How did they come to Sacco's house ...?

A. They come,—I learned after, because I was in the kitchen... .

Q. But you learned afterward they came in the motorcycle?

MR. KATZMANN. One moment, pardon me.

MR. JEREMIAH McANARNEY... . I did not want to lead him too—

[The answer is read.]

Q. Did you see a motorcycle there that evening? A. No.

Q. Do you know how he came there, how Sacco came there? A. Yes, because they speak of the motorcycle, and Orcciani got some dress like a motorcycle... .

Q. You mean clothes that they use when they ride? A. I mean clothes that the men who go on a motorcycle, something like that, use, yellow dress, yellow pants... .

Q. ... Did you have a conversation there with Orcciani and with Sacco [about] what you were going to do the next day, May 5th ...? A. Yes. [1713]

Q. May 5th, what did you do? A. May 5th? ...

Q. What did you do during the day, . .? A. We do many things. Split some wood, cut some wood.

Q. ... Did you see Mrs. Sacco doing anything? A. Oh, yes, Mrs. Sacco was preparing the stuff, clothes and everything...to be ready to go away.

Q. ... What was she doing? A. She was preparing the stuff for the trip.

Q. For what trip? A. To put in order to go to Italy... .

Q. Did any one there give you anything?

A. Yes, before we go away I take the three [shot] gun shells. [1714]

Q. How come you to get those [three]? Where were they got?

A. They got in top of the stage in the kitchen... .

Q. A shelf, we will call it? A. Yes, and it was on top of there.

Q. How come she to give them to you? ... A. Because I say, "I will bring to my friends in Plymouth." My friends, I know they go to hunt in the winter time... .

Q. What did you do with those shells?

A. I put in my pocket. I want to give to him when I reach Plymouth.

Q. ... When you were arrested, you had a revolver on you? A. Yes.

Q. Where did you carry that revolver? ...A. I carried on my... pants back pocket, ...

Q. When, about when, did you get that revolver? A. It was two or three months.

Q. And what was the occasion of your getting that revolver? A. I went to Falzini's house one day.

Q. ... But did you get a revolver at the Falzini house? A. Yes.

Q. Why did you get the revolver? A. I got the revolver because it was a very bad time, and I like to have a revolver for self-defense.

Q. How much money did you use to carry around with you? A. When I went to Boston for fish, I can carry eighty, one hundred dollars, one hundred and twenty dollars.

Q. What do you mean by "It was a bad time"?

A. Bad time, I mean it was many crimes, many holdups, many robberies... .

Q. Do you remember what you paid for the revolver? A. I think $5.

Q. ... On the afternoon of May 5th, what happened at Sacco's house? Perhaps it will be plainer to you; did anyone come there?

A. Yes.

Q. Who came? A. Orcciani came there with Mike Boda.

Q. How did they come? A. I should say they came in a motorcycle.

Q. How long did they stay there? A. I should say two hours, ... [1715]

Q. About what time did they leave the house?

A. ... I do not know, because I leave the house before them.

Q. What time did you leave the house? A. About seven o'clock, something like that.

Q. Did you leave alone, or some one with you? A. With Sacco, me and Sacco leave the house.

Q. Where did you and Sacco go? A. We went to Bridgewater [stopping first in Brockton].

Q. ... How did you go from Stoughton to Brockton ...? A. In the electric car [interurban].

Q. ... When you got to Brockton and got out of the electric car, what did you do?

A. We looked for a car to Bridgewater.

Q. You looked for a car to Bridgewater? A... . [W]e asked ... a conductor ... when the car for Bridgewater came, and he say we are to wait ... fifteen minutes ... [T]hen we went ... [to] an Italian fruit store and cigar store. We buy Italian cigars... [W]e drink a cup of coffee in the lunch room, and I take a pencil and piece of paper and I started to write... .

Q. And what did you write? A. I write public invitations for a meeting next Sunday [May 9].

Q. ... And where was that meeting to be held? A. It was to be held in one hall there in Brockton, but I do not know the name and the place of the hall... .

MR.JEREMIAH McANARNEY. Mr. Katzmann, may I ask if you have that paper that he wrote?

MR. KATZMANN. Yes, we did have it, Mr. McAnarney, and we have been searching for it. But I can give you a copy of it... . [1716]

Q. The next Sunday ["it was arranged you were to speak in Brockton"]? A. Yes.

Q. That would be May 9th. At what hour in the day were you to speak there? A. I do not remember what hour we fixed, ... I do not write the hour nor the street nor the place... .

Q. You have given that paper to Nick, ... so as to have that printed. Now, I take it from what you said you [later] got aboard a car going to West Bridgewater? A. Yes... .

Q. And you rode on,—where were you going to get off? A. In the Square, down in West Bridgewater, Elm Square.

Q. **Was it arranged** before you left home, Sacco's home, between you and Orcciani, where you were to get off that car? A. Yes.

Q. And it was at Elm Square? A. Yes. [Ed. Johnson brothers' garage was in Elm Square.]

Q. Who were to meet you there? A. Boda and Orcciani.

Q. What was the purpose of Boda and Orcciani going there? A. Go there to take the automobile.

Q. To take an automobile? A. Boda's automobile. [1718]

Q. How do you know you had got to Elm Square? A. ... I was explained that so you cannot mistake. You take a car from Brockton towards Bridgewater, first square you see. When you see the street become large and you see the light there, ... there is Elm Square... .

Q. You got off this place, Elm Square. Was there any sign there ... you could see to read?

A. Well, I saw the sign.

[Ed. Vanzetti and Sacco waited at Elm Square, as they had been instructed. When Boda and Orciani did not appear, they walked south, then north, to Ruth and Simon Johnson's house.]

Q. When you started to walk toward Brockton, what, ... did you see ...? A. ... [W]e saw the light of the motorcycle on the street. [Near Johnson house on North Elm Street.] [1719]

Q. What did you do ...? A. We walked toward it and we approached the man ... Orcciani... .

Q. Now, did you see any one at this house near which the motorcycle was standing...?

A. After a little while we seen a woman [Ruth Johnson] coming to the house.

Q. Where did she come from? A. She come toward Brockton.

Q. She come toward Brockton? Well,— A. She come from toward Brockton. [Brockton is north.]

Q. Where did she go? A. She go in the house in front of the motorcycle... .

Q. Where the motorcycle was standing in front? A. Yes.

Q. Did you see a women [sic] go out of that house before that?

A. I did not see... .

Q. Now, when you came up to Orcciani you had a talk with him?

A. Yes.

Q. Boda was not in sight then? A. No, I don't see Boda at that time.

Q. ... After you talked with Orcciani beside the motorcycle, what did you and Sacco do?

A. We stayed and entertained ourselves to talk with Orcciani. [1720]

Q. Anything else? A. Yes, and after a little while Boda come on the street.

Q. Where did he come from? A. From the house.

Q. The house near the motorcycle? A. Yes.

Q. Did you hear any talk between Boda and any one before he came out?

A. No, I don't hear no talk.

Q. Did Boda have talk with you or with Orcciani in your presence after he came out? A. Yes... .

Q. What did Boda say? A. He say that we cannot take the automobile because Mr. Johnson say that he cannot take it without having a new number... . [Ed. No 1920 license plates.]

Q. ... What were you going to get the automobile for? A. For to take out literature, books and newspapers, from the house and the homes. [Ed. Vanzetti means anarchist literature.]

Q. What house and homes did you want to take the books and literature from? A. From any house ... in five or six places, five or six towns. Three, five or six people have plenty of literature, and we want, we intend to take that out and put that in the proper place.

Q. What do you mean by a "proper place"? A. ... I mean in a place not subject to policemen go in and call for, see the literature, ... as in that time they went through in the house of many men who were active in the Radical movement and [1721] Socialist and labor movement, and go there and take letters and take books and take newspapers, and put men in jail and deported many.

MR. KATZMANN. I ask it be stricken out.

THE WITNESS. I say that in that time——

MR. KATZMANN. Wait one moment.

THE WITNESS. And deported many, many, many have been misused in jail, and so on.

Q. Where were you going that night if you could have got the automobile? A. I intended to go to Plymouth and speak to some of my friends of Plymouth who is owner of the house.

Q. And do what?

A. And if they are willing to receive such literature and newspapers in his house.

Q. ... Suppose you had got the automobile that night and you had gone down to Plymouth to these houses? What were you going to do with the papers you would pick up here? A. Before to pick the paper, I want to find the place and ask if my friend in Plymouth, if he was willing that we bring the paper in his house... .

Q. Now, whether or not this going around to get these papers was as a result of what you learned when you went to New York? A. Yes. What we read in newspapers, too... .

Q. Well, you did not get the automobile that night? A. No, we were arrested that night. [1722]

Q. Were you there [West Bridgewater] on the 14th or the 15th of April? A. Only on that day, on that 5th of May. [1723]

AFTERNOON SESSION.

July 5, 1921

Bartolomeo Vanzetti, Direct Examination, Resumed.

Q. (By Mr. Jeremiah McAnarney) While you were in the electric car before the police automobile came up [at Brockton], did you try to get your hand in your clothes to take the revolver out? A. No.

Q. Did the police officer say to you, "Don't put your hand in there or I shoot"? Did that take place? A. No, absolutely.

Q. You heard Officer Connolly, when he testified, what the language he used to you was? A. Yes.

Q. Did that take place there in that car? A. No. [1724]

Q. Now, I had asked you what you were going to do if you had got the automobile up at Elm Square that night. You have told me about going to pick up this literature, these books and tracts, ... Was there anything else you were going to do? A. Well, I was to pass in Bridgewater and if possible find Pappi. [Ed. Pappi had worked at the Cordage, Plymouth rope plant, with Vanzetti.]

Q. What for? A. To tell him we will have a meeting, ... in Brockton the next Sunday, ...

MR. KATZMANN. I did not hear that.

MR. JEREMIAH McANARNEY. I did not, either. Kindly repeat the answer.

THE WITNESS. Yes. To go to Pappi and tell to Pappi that next Sunday [May 9] we will have a speech in Brockton somewhere, in Brockton Hall... . [A]fter speaking with him we intend to go to Plymouth and speak with my friend, if he was willing to accept the literature in his house.

Q. Now, in talking to Officer Spear and to any other official, District Attorney or others, did you at any time tell them what you have now told us, that you were going to get any of this literature, or anything of that sort? A. No, I don't tell them that thing... .

Q. Why not? A. Because in that time there, there was the deportation and the reaction was more vivid than now and more mad than now... . [1726]

Q. During the year of registration, 1917 [military draft 5/18/1917], you went away? A. Yes

Q. Why did you go away? ... A. I go away for not to be a soldier... . [Vanzetti did not register.]

Q. Where did you go to? A. At first time I went to Mexico [May 1917].

Q. How long did you remain in Mexico? A. Three or four months, four or five months... . [1727]

Q. Now, ... did you ever go to the station, East Braintree, and get off there? A. Never.

Q. Did you ever ride on a South Shore train and inquire at some station along the line, Cohasset or East Weymouth ... asking a man if he could tell you where East Braintree was?

A. Absolutely not.

Q. Were you at South Braintree on the 15th day of May, 1920?

A. No.

MR. KATZMANN. April.

MR. JEREMIAH McANARNEY. April, 15th day of April, 1920.

Q. Did you take any part in any shooting or anything that occurred there? A. No, sir.

Q. On the 15th day of April, 1920? A. No, sir... . [1729]

Q. ... After your talk with the peddler [Rosen] you and the peddler went up to Mrs. Brini's?

A. Yes.

Q. And whether or not this cloth was shown to her? A. Yes, it was.

Q. Is this the piece of cloth [you bought from Rosen]? A. Yes.

Q. Whether or not that hole was in the cloth? A. Yes, it was... .

MR. JEREMIAH McANARNEY. [Showing cloth to the jury.] I do not know that you gentlemen see the hole in the material. You see it on the back... . I suppose I might offer that in evidence, if your Honor please. I am going to offer this as an exhibit, Mr. Katzmann.

MR. KATZMANN. I haven't seen it yet.

[Mr. Jeremiah McAnarney shows cloth to Mr. Katzmann.]

[The cloth is admitted in evidence and marked "Exhibit N."]

Q. ... Why did you not tell Mr. Stewart the truth that night when he arrested you and talked with you at the station? A. I don't tell the truth because I am afraid he went in that house of the people that they named and found some literature or some paper and arrested the men. [1731]

Q. ... Did you tell Mr. Katzmann the truth about Pappi...?

A. About Pappi, yes, but I don't say that I was there to take the automobile and I don't speak about the literature... . [1732]

Q. What was the purpose of the meeting that you were going to speak at on May 9th? A. The purpose ... was to help the political prisoners, but especially to help **Salsedo and Elia**... .

Q. Was Boda at any of the Boston meetings?

A. No, not at the few last meetings in Boston. I don't saw Boda.

Q. At Maverick Square? A. Yes.

Q. The last two meetings you did not see— A. Last two meetings I did not see him...

Q. ... Had you ... before the last two or three [meetings] seen Boda there?

A. Oh, yes, I seen Boda there in Boston, too.

Q. As nearly as you can to the first of May, when was it you saw Boda at any of those meetings? A. Two or three months.

Q. Two or three months. Before? A. Yes... . [1733]

Q. Mr. Witness, you saw Boda there [at Stoughton] that afternoon?

A. Yes, sir.

Q. At Sacco's house, May 5th? A. Yes, sir.

Q. ... [Y]ou had some information as to why Boda was there?

A. Previous to that day, yes.

Q. When did you get that information? A. On Sunday before. The evening or afternoon of Sunday in Boston. [May 2.]

Q. Now, where were you when you got that information? A. We were in East Boston, in that Italian Naturalization Club.

Q. What was Boda to come for May 5th, ... what purpose?

A. The purpose, to take that automobile that he has.

Q. Where was his automobile? A. I do not know at that time.

Q. Did you later learn? A. I learned when he came [to Sacco's house, May 5]. [1736]

Cross-Examination.

Q. (By Mr. Katzmann) So you left Plymouth, Mr. Vanzetti, in May, 1917, to dodge the draft, did you? A. Yes, sir... .

Q. When this country was at war, you ran away so you would not have to fight as a soldier?

A. Yes. [1737]

[Ed. Katzmann discontinued this approach after p. 1737. On p. 1738 Vanzetti denied he ever drove an "automobile truck" in his railroad work at or near Springfield, Massachusetts.]

Q. Do you remember where you were at twelve o'clock and thirteen minutes to fifteen minutes after on April 15, 1920? A. I remember where I was.

Q. Yes. Where were you? A. I was in Plymouth.

Q. Whereabouts in Plymouth? A. In near or in the Brini house at that time.

Q. Were you in the Brini house at 12.13 on that day? A. I could not say exactly. I could not say exactly how many minutes after twelve o'clock... .

Q. How long were you in the Brini house? A. ... Ten or fifteen minutes. Not fifteen minutes,—ten or twelve minutes. [1739]

[Ed. Katzmann asked Vanzetti to recall his interrogation on May 6, 1920, in the Brockton police station. Indented "Q" indicates a question from the May 6 interrogation.]

Q. Do you recall that there was a stenographer present when you talked with me? A. Yes.

Q. A man who took down what I said and what you said?
A. Yes, sir... . [1742]

Q. Do you remember my then saying [at Brockton]:

"I am the District Attorney in this district, and I wanted to ask you some questions. You do not need to answer these questions if you prefer not to"?

A. I already said that.

Q. [Reading]

"Q. "And what you may say in reply to questions might be used in court against you. You are at liberty to answer them or not, as you see fit. Are you willing to answer some questions?"

Do you remember my saying that to you? A. I already say yes... . [1743]

Q. ... When did you say, Mr. Vanzetti, that you first knew about Mr. Boda having an automobile. A. On the Sunday [May 2] previous to my arrest.

Q. ... From whom did you learn that ... Boda had an automobile?
A. From Orcciani... .

Q. Did you intend, Mr. Vanzetti, to take that literature on the night of May 5th?
A. Not that night.

Q. When did you intend to take the literature? A. When I have found in Plymouth. I intend to go in Plymouth and found a place to put this literature and then take the literature. [1744]

Q. Did you expect that Boda was coming to the Sacco house on May 5th? A. Not exactly... .

Q. Did you state to Mr. McAnarney ...that Boda's purpose was to take the automobile to take the literature? A. Yes.

Q. Doesn't that mean he was to take the literature that night?

A. No, that don't mean that necessarily, at all.

Q. Then what was your purpose and...two others besides Boda, in going down to West Bridgewater to get an automobile that was not to be used for that purpose that night?

A. ... [M]y intention is to take the automobile with Boda, because I do not know how to drive the automobile, to go to Bridgewater and if we will be able to find the party, because I do not remember the address of the party. I do not know exactly where he lived. We will tell to Pappi about telling the Italian people of Bridgewater to come in Brockton next Sunday at the speech, and after I found Pappi, and speak to Pappi, go toward Plymouth and speak with my friends if I can find some friends who want to take the responsibility of receiving such books in their house, in his house... . [1745]

Q. ——that you were going to Pappi's house, that you did not know his address——you had forgotten it——that you were going to look, and if you found Pappi you were going to ask him to spread the news of the May 9th meeting, and then you were going on to Plymouth? A. Yes, sir... .

Q. Couldn't Boda have gotten his automobile out of Johnson's garage without your help?

A. I know ... . We want to go together in Plymouth and look for the place, for the permission of a man of the house, and so with Bridgewater and Brockton and many other places and take the [anarchist] literature and bring it in Plymouth.

Q. Did you know that Boda lived in West Bridgewater at that time?

A. No.

Q. Do you know where he lived?

A. No, I do not know where he lived. I do not know where he lived, no.

Q. Then you don't know, in order to come up to Sacco's house, he had to leave a place within three quarters of a mile of where his automobile was...? A. No, I don't know that... .

Q. Couldn't you have met Boda in the morning as well as at the dark of night? A. That is not my fault, because I don't know where Boda is or [if] Orcianni lives with Boda. We went down in the afternoon. [1746]

Q. Didn't you make the arrangement with Orcciani to have Boda there at Sacco's house?

A. Not at all.

Q. Weren't you the man who spoke to him at the East Boston hall?

A. Yes, I say in the Italian Boston hall that it is better to clean up the house of the literature, ... of the more active friends. We speak about the means, about how to do, ...

Q. Mr. Vanzetti, when Mr. McAnarney was examining you this morning, do you remember that you said you took three gun shells off a shelf in the Sacco kitchen? A. Yes, sir... .

Q. Well, I will ask you now if you took four shells?

A. I don't remember. I believe that I took three shells.

Q. Do you remember this question and this answer that I asked of you at the Brockton police station: [1747]

"Q. Did you have anything else that could be shot in your pocket?"

And your answer:

"A. I have four of that thing to go hunting."

Did you say that at Brockton? A. I don't remember... .

Q. And did I then follow up with this question:

"Q. Shells, you mean? What did you take those for?"

And your reply:

"A. I took that because Nick gave it to me, gave them to me."

A. Yes... .

Q... . Did you say anything this morning about his wife giving you those shells?

A. I don't remember if his wife——...

Q. Which one [Sacco or Sacco's wife] gave you [the shells]?

A. I don't remember, I told you.

Q. Do you remember saying this morning that you—referring to the revolver which was in your possession when you were arrested—that you had it, you got that revolver two or three months before? A. Yes.

Q. That you went to the Manchini house one day and you got the revolver there... .

A. I say Falzini house.

Q. You say Falzini house? A. Falzini house.

Q. Did you get it there two or three months before? A. Yes, sir.

Q. Do you remember being shown that revolver in my presence by an officer at the Brockton police station? A. Yes.... [1748]

Q. Do you remember my asking you:

"Q. How long have you owned that revolver?"

And your answer:

"A. A long time."

A. Yes, sir.

Q. Do you remember my asking you then:

"Q. Where did you get it?"

And your reply:

"A. In Boston."

A. Yes, sir.

Q. Was that answer that you had owned the revolver a long time true? A. No, sir... .

Q. Do you remember my then asking you:

"Q. Whereabouts in Boston?"

And you said:

"A. On the north side of Boston."

Do you remember saying that? A. I have the opinion I said I buy in Hanover Street.

Q. One at a time. Did you make that answer? A. Maybe, yes.

Q. Isn't it true you did? A. I don't remember.

Q. Do you remember my then asking you:

"Q. What street and what store?"

And you replied:

"A. Well, I think, I don't know if Hanover Street or something like that."

Did you say that? A. Probably.

Q. Was it true? A. No, sir, it was not true.

Q. Do you remember my then asking you:

"Q. Well, what number Hanover Street? A. Well, I don't remember. It is a long time."

Do you remember saying that? A. Yes.

Q. Was that true? A. No, it was not true.

Q. Do you remember my then asking you:

"Q. How long ago was it?"

And your reply:

"A. About four or five years ago."
Did you say that? A. Yes, sir.
Q. Was it true? A. No, sir.... [1749]
Q. Do you remember my then asking you:
     "Q. How much did you pay for it? A. $19, or something like that.
Eighteen."
Did you say that? A. I don't remember.
Q. Will you say you did not say it? A. No, I do not say I did not say
it.
Q. If you said it, Mr. Vanzetti, was it true? A. No, sir.
Q.   Mr.   Vanzetti, is there any reason connected with collecting
literature that made you say on May 6th to me that the revolver cost
you $19, when it cost you only five, as you now say?
A. No, there is no reason.... [1750]
Q. As a matter of fact, it was Sunday morning wasn't it, when you left
Plymouth before your arrest?   A.   It was Saturday, not Sunday
morning.
Q. Was there any reason, Mr. Vanzetti, why you should deceive me on
the day you left Plymouth? A. No.
Q. That did not make any difference, did it? A. No. [1754]
Q. Do you remember my asking you at the Brockton police station:
     "Q. How long have you known Boda? A. I don't know that
name."
Did you say that to me? A. Yes, sir.
Q. Was it true? A. It was not true.... [1755]
Q. Do you remember my asking you at the Brockton police station
when you got off the car, when you were going down to look for Pappi,
your friend, somewhere down in the village:
     "Q. Did you see any sign that you and Nick looked at, any street
sign? A. No. I no observe any sign."
Did you say that to me? A. It could be....
Q. Will you say you did not [say it]? A. I don't say I did not....
Q. Do you remember my asking you if you saw an automobile, saw a
motorcycle at West Bridgewater that night? A. Yes, I remember I said
"No." [1757]
Q. Was it true you did not see a motorcycle?
A. No, it was not true....
Q. You intended to deceive myself and the officers who were present,
did you not?

A. I intend to not mention the name and the house of my friends… .

Q. Was there a single name or address I asked of you at the time I talked with you except that of Mike Boda and Pappi? A. Well,— [1758]

Q. Did you know that Mike Boda owned a Buick car, or had a Buick car, in his possession at one time? A. Not at all. I don't know [1759] nothing about the automobiles. I don't know nothing, I don't know nothing about the automobiles… .

Q. Where, Mr. Vanzetti, were you going to get the papers and the books, at what houses?

A. When we found a place to put those papers and those books… .

Q. Where were they? A. There were some in Bridgewater, some in Brockton, some in Sacco house, some in Orciani house, there are some in Haverhill, some in Salem, and many other places that I don't know, but some other man knows the other place and he will tell me… .

Q. You had never been in Bridgewater before in your life, had you?

A. Yes, I have been in Bridgewater six years and a half ago, in East Bridgewater.

Q. I am talking about Bridgewater, not East Bridgewater. Had you ever been in Bridgewater before in your life? A. No, not before my arrest. I mean in the centre of Bridgewater, I never been before my arrest. [1760]

Q. That is one place where you wanted to go and help get this literature, wasn't it, Bridgewater?

A. But I don't know if they are the same place, I am sure, but I don't know the people of Bridgewater.

Q. Then what did you go on the trip at all for? A. For to see Pappi and to tell Pappi to tell the Italians to come on Sunday at the meeting, not at the meeting, but at the speech [May 9].

Q. So that you did not,—you had no fear, did you, about telling me about this meeting at which you were going to speak when I talked with you at Brockton? You did not have any fear about telling me that, did you? A. That isn't a question of fear. That is that you found the pamphlets in Nick's pocket speaking of this meeting… .

Q. Was the time or the place [of the Sunday meeting] in that notice? A. No, sir. [1761]

July 6, 1921.
Bartolomeo Vanzetti.
Cross-Examination Resumed.

Q. (By Mr. Katzmann) How long had you known Mike Boda prior to April 15, 1920?
A. Many, three years, something like that.
Q. Where did you first get acquainted with him? A. I can't remember.
Q. ... Is that true, you can't remember the place? A. Maybe in Boston. [1762]
Q. I say, if it was in Boston, where was it in Boston?
A. Where in Boston? In the town halls where we arrange a meeting or speech... .
Q. Tell me this: what hall was it?
A. One hall is that in East Boston,—Maverick Square.
Q. Was that where you first met him? A. No, I do not think so.
Q. I am asking you, sir, where you met him first. A. In another hall in Richmond Street... .
Q. Did you ever know where Mike Boda lived? A. I hear that he live in where Orcciani lives, in the town, Hyde Park... . [Hyde Park is part of Boston.]
Q. Is Readville part of Hyde Park? A. I don't know. It is near Hyde Park. [1763]
Q. ... At whose house in Bridgewater were you going to collect literature and books? A. I do not know in what house.
Q. Can you name a single individual in Bridgewater from whom you were going to collect books and papers? A. Not now... .
Q. Did you mention Everett yesterday? A. Yes.
Q. Name an individual in Everett from whom you were going to collect papers?
A. Oreste Branci.
Q. Where did Oreste Bianci [sic] live in Everett? A. I do not remember the address. [1765]
Q. [To interpreter.] Did you make any efforts to hide or secrete any books or literature in Sacco's house before you left May 5th?
A. [Through the interpreter.] No, sir... .
Q. Did you take them out [take anarchist literature from Sacco's house]? A. No. [1766]

Q. Where were you at ten o'clock on the morning of April 14, 1920?
A. I can't tell you that place... .

Q. How many years did you live with the Brini family in North Plymouth...?
A. ... four years.

Q. Have you any more intimate friends in the world than the Brini family?
A. The Brini family is very good friends of mine... . [1769]

Q. Then on April 15, 1920, is it not the fact that the Brinis did not live on Cherry Street?
A. Yes, Brini lived in Suosso's Lane.

Q. In Suosso's Lane, and it was to the Brini house in Suosso's Lane that you said that you went with that cloth and the man [Rosen]?
A. Yes, yes.

Q. How long, Mr. Vanzetti, was Mrs. Simon Johnson in the Bartlett house on the night of May 5, 1920? A. I don't know about that... .

Q. With your motorcycle light facing toward Brockton, could you see the telephone wires going into the next house, the Bartlett house?
A. I never saw them... . [1774]

Q. Did you hear Mike Boda call out, "His wife"? A. No.

Q. Did you hear Orcciani call out, "His wife"? A. I don't hear nobody call out "His wife." ... .

Q. Were you in any hurry when you left there, Mr. Vanzetti? A. No, we weren't in a hurry... .

Q. How long have you known the defendant Sacco? A. Three or four years. [1776]

Q. Do you remember this question and this answer that I asked of you and you gave the answer at Brockton:

"Q. How did you happen to go to Stoughton to see him?" meaning Nick.

"A. Because we were very good friends, me and Nick." ... .

Q. That would be the way you did answer it [previous question]?
A. Yes.

Q. Do you remember the next question:

"Q. When? A. A year and a half." [Ed. Length of time he had known Sacco.]

A. I don't remember that I told you more short time than a year.

Q. Was that true, Mr. Vanzetti? A. It is not true.

301

Q. Was there anything about telling that untruth to me that would help conceal the addresses of any friends from whom you were going to get literature? A. Not the address, but something else.

Q. Didn't you state yesterday that your purpose in telling untruths to me was to conceal the names and addresses of friends of yours who had literature? A. Yes, but,—also the friends who; I don't tell you that because I know we went together in Mexico, because to avoid conscription or registration.

Q. Did I ask you at Brockton anything about where you were at the time of the registration under the selective service draft? A. No, you don't ask me that... .

Q. Was there a single question asked by any police officer about your evasion of the draft, when you were arrested? A. No, no, there was not.

Q. Did I ask you a single question about your evasion of the draft? A. No... . [1777]

Q. And he [Sacco] is an intimate friend of yours, isn't he? A. Yes, he is. [1784]

Q. You said yesterday, did you not, that on May 5th, Wednesday, Orcciani came to Sacco's house with Mike Boda on a motorcycle? A. Yes... .

Q. And on Tuesday, the day before, Tuesday, the 4th of May, did you see Orciani on his motorcycle at Sacco's house? A. 1st of May?

Q. 4th. One, two, three, fourth,—Tuesday? A. Yes, I saw him, yes, sir... .

Q. Do you remember this question I asked you:
  "Q. Did you see any man at all on a motorcycle?"
And your answer:
  "A. No."
A. Yes, sir... .

Q. The answer wasn't true, was it ...? A. What I say was not true, what I say.

Q. Do you remember this question:
  "Q. Monday, Tuesday, or Wednesday, was there any motorcycle at Nick's house?
  A. I don't remember a motorcycle there."
Did you make that answer? A. Possibly, yes. Possibly.

Q. If you made it, was it true? A. No, it was not true. [1786]

Q. Referring to down in front of Johnson's house, do you remember this question:

"Q. Didn't you see a man as you came along the road sitting on a motorcycle?

A. No, I don't remember."

A. Yes, sir.

Q. Did you make that answer? A. Yes... .

Q. Was it [answer] true or false? A. False.

Q. And this question:

"Q. Didn't you talk to the man who was on the motorcycle?

A. No."

Did you make that answer? A. It is possible. If you asked me that sure, I said no.

Q. If you made it, was it true or false? A. It was all false... . [1787]

Q. You know ... at one time Mike Boda lived in Hyde Park with Orcciani? A. Yes.

Q. And you knew he left Orcciani's house ... in the winter, don't you? A. No... . I don't know when Boda leave the Orcciani house... . I was one time in the Orcciani house. [1790]

Q. Did Mike Boda go to Mexico with you? A. No, he don't come with me. [See Avrich, p. 65.]

Q. He did not come. Did Orcciani? A. No.

Q. Just Sacco, of those men? A. Sacco and some other friends... . [1791]

Q. Do you know where Mike Boda is now, Mr. Vanzetti? A. No... .

Q. When was the last time prior to May 2d, that you saw Mike Boda? A. I don't remember. [1792]

Q. Give us your best recollection, whatever it may be? A. I should say it was in the fall.

Q. The fall of 1919? A. Yes. [See Boda/Buda in Avrich, p. 188.]

Q. And where was it? A. In a picnic... .

Q. Was Sacco at the picnic? A. No, I do not remember that Sacco was there at the picnic.

Q. Was Orcciani there? A. Orcciani I think was, yes. I am not sure, but I think so. Sacco, too, was there at the picnic... . [1793]

Q. Do you remember this question and this answer I asked you at Brockton, referring to the purchase of your revolver:

"Q. What name did you give when you bought it? A. I gave another name but I don't remember."

Did you say that to me at Brockton? A. Yes, sir.

Q. Was that true or false? A. It was not true.

Q. "Q. Why didn't you give your own name? A. I was scared." [Two "Q's" in transcript.]

Did you make that answer to me? A. I don't remember, but if I have gave it, it is wrote there, I made you at that time. [1797]

Q. Do you remember these following questions that were asked of you at Brockton and answers were made by you as follows:

"Q. You say, Mr. Vanzetti, that you bought the revolver that the police took from you last night about four years [ago] in Boston, and you think it was in the spring time, somewhere on Hanover Street. Now, where did you get the cartridges to go into that revolver? A. I took at that time in the same place."

Did you say that to me? A. I don't remember... .

Q. If you said it, was it true or false? A. It was false.

Q. Do you remember the next question:

"Q. One box? A. Yes."

Did you make that reply? A. Possibly. I don't remember.

Q. If you made it, was it true or false? A. Yes, it was not true.

Q. It was not true. Do you remember the question as follows:

"Q. A full box, unopened, no cartridge taken out? A. Yes, just a full box."

Did you make that reply? A. Maybe.

Q. If you made it, was it true or false? A. It was false... .

Q. All right. Do you remember this question:

"Q. Did you ever fire off any of those cartridges? A. When I buy that, yes."

Did you make that reply to me? A. I don't remember, but it can be.

Q. Will you say you did not? A. No, no.

Q. If you made it, was it true or false? A. False.

Q. Do you remember the next question:

"How many?"

referring to your firing off.

"A. I shot sometime ago on the beach or on the water."

Do you remember that? A. No.

Q. Was it true or false? A. It was false.

Q. Was that helping you to conceal the names and addresses, Mr. Vanzetti?

A. I don't say I bought that by Falzini. [Ed. Vanzetti means he was protecting Falzini.]

Q. Do you remember the next question?

"Q. Was that box when you bought it at this store on Hanover Street tightly closed or had it been opened before you got it? A. I [1799] think it was closed tight. I don't remember particularly. The box was well closed tight, never opened before."

Do you remember that answer to that question? A. No, I do not remember... .

Q. If you made it, was it true? A. No, it was not true... .

Q. Do you remember this question, Mr. Vanzetti:

"Q. Where did you get the cartridges that were in the revolver last night when the police took it from you? A. I just remained that, and I did not want to shoot when I saw there was only six cartridges left. I took the six cartridges and put them in the revolver and generally take the revolver with me when I go out, because I have money with me, and I threw the box away."

Did you make that answer, Mr. Vanzetti? A. I don't know if I say six or five.

Q. Will you say you did not say six cartridges in it? A. Not at all.

Q. You had had that revolver, you say, for two or three months in your possession before the police took it from you? A. Yes.

Q. And you did not know whether there were five or six cartridges in it? A. Maybe I know; maybe I forget at that time.

Q. Wasn't the revolver shown to you that night? A. That one? ...

Q. Yes, that one? A. I don't know for sure.

Q. [Mr. Katzmann shows revolver to the witness.]

A. [Witness examines revolver.] I cannot recognize the revolver, sir.

Q. Is that the revolver that was shown to you at the Brockton police station?

A. I cannot recognize the revolver... .

Q. Is it yours? A. I cannot recognize. I do not know the name, I do not know the number, I do not know nothing, see... .

Q. Did you notice any marks on it when you had it? A. I did not know it, don't know, no marks.

Q. Mr. Vanzetti, did you, on May 6th, know whether it was five or six chambers? A. I don't know if I know or not on the May 6th... . [1800]

Q. Those five cartridges [found in Vanzetti's .38 H. & R.] never came out of the same new box, did they, Mr. Vanzetti? A. Never came out from—

Q. —the same new box, unopened box? A. I don't say that.

Q. You did say it at Brockton, didn't you? A. Brockton?

Q. You did say it at Brockton, didn't you? A. Maybe I say in Brockton. [1801]

Q. Do you think attempting to deceive the District Attorney who was questioning you at that time as to the kind of box that those cartridges came in helped you to conceal any names and addresses of your friends? A. No.

Q. Mr. Vanzetti, do you remember this question and this answer at the Brockton police station that I made of you, and which you gave in reply:

"Q. Well, do you remember the holiday we had in April, the 19th of April, they call it Patriots' Day, the middle of April? A. Yes, I heard that before, but I did not remember that was in April."

Do you remember saying that to me in Brockton? A. What holiday?

Q. The 19th of April? A. What holiday it is? ...

Q. Patriots' Day. A. Oh, patriotics day.

Q. Yes, do you remember my asking you that question ...? A. No, I don't; I don't remember.

Q. Will you say you did not make that reply to that question? A. No, I don't say that I didn't... .

Q. Do you remember this question and this answer:

"Q. You don't know where you were the Thursday before that Monday, do you?

A. No." [Ed. Thursday would be April 15, 1920.]

Do you remember that answer to that question? A. Oh, yes, I answered some other thing no, that I don't remember in that time, but I remember it now, not only this.

Q. On May 6th, 1920? A. Yes.

Q. You did not remember where you were on the 15th of April, did you? A. More probable, yes.

Q. But after waiting months and months and months you then remembered, did you?

A. Not months and months and months, but three or four weeks after I see that I have to be careful and to remember well if I want to save my life. [1802]

Redirect Examination.

THE WITNESS. Please give me some water?
MR. JEREMIAH McANARNEY. Yes.
[The witness is given a drink of water.] [1806]

Q. (By Mr. Jeremiah McAnarney) Any one time you mentioned that you were afraid, what did you mean by that? A. I mean that I was afraid, for I know that my friends there in New York have jumped down from the jail in the street and killed himself. The papers say that he jump down, but we don't know.

Q. You now allude to who? Who is that man? A. **Salsedo.** [See Avrich, p. 183.]

Q. When did you learn of Salsedo's death? A. On the day, in the day, fourth, 4th of May.

Q. Fourth of May. Now, you were appointed, you say, by a committee, to go to New York? A. Yes, sir... [1808]

Q. After you got back from New York, did you explain to your friends what you had learned? A. A few days after, yes. [1810]

Q. What did you hear in New York? What did you learn? A. I learned that most probably for the May 1st there will be many arrest of Radicals and I was set wise if I have literature and correspondence, something, papers in the home, to bring away, and to tell to my friends to clean [1810] them up the house, because the literature will not be found if the policemen go to the house. [Ed. Anarchist literature.]

Q. And it was in consequence of that that you were there that night, May 5th, to get this car?

A. Yes, not only for that, not necessarily for that,—we want to go to Bridgewater to speak to Pappi for the conference, for the speech, to.

Q. Well, the two things? A. The principal purpose is to go to Plymouth, suggest a place where we can put the literature and then bring around the literature to that place.

Q. Now, assuming you had got the Boda car as you had planned, were you going to Plymouth that night? A. Yes... .

Q. So that at the time, then, that night, May 5th, you had not arranged with any one to receive or to keep or to hide this literature? A. No, we don't know yet on that night nor if we take the literature out where we are to put it. We don't agree yet on the place. We don't know yet the place. [1811]

307

Recross Examination.

Q. (By Mr. Katzmann) Mr. Vanzetti, have you ever ridden in a Buick automobile?

A. I should say no.... .

Q. First day of April, 1920, were you riding in a Buick automobile in the city of Brockton? You shake your head. Does that mean "No"?

A. I mean no because I never rode in Brockton in an automobile, in Brockton.

MR. KATZMANN. That is all. [1812]

[Ed. After Vanzetti left the witness stand, the defense recalled Simon E. Johnson. In cross-examination, Johnson testified he received a telephone call from Mike Boda on April 30, 1920.]

Q. (By Mr. Katzmann) And what was that telephone message you got [from Boda]?

MR. JEREMIAH McANARNEY. I object.

THE COURT. On what ground is that competent?

MR. KATZMANN. If your honor please, it now appears from the defendant Vanzetti that he went down there May 5th to get the car for a specific purpose. I propose to show that is not the fact,——the result of conversation he said he had with Mike Boda or with Orcciani on Sunday, May 2d, they went to get the car. If permitted, I propose to show there was a different arrangement made by Boda himself, and made on April 30th. [1815]

[Ed. McAnarney's objection was sustained in a "Conference at bench between Court and Counsel." In the afternoon session, July 6, 1921, the jury was taken outside for a view of Boda's Overland.] [1816-1817.]

26. VANZETTI'S NEW YORK TRIP

Walter Nelles, Sworn. July 9, 1921.

[Ed. Nelles is listed as Counsel, ACLU, in NECLC letter of Feb. 19, 1921, by Anna N. Davis. See pp.459-460.]

Q. (By Jeremiah McAnarney) What is your name? A. Walter Nelles.

Q. Your home is New York City? A. Yes, sir. [1981]

Q. You are an attorney by profession? A. Yes... .

Q. Sometime in 1920 were you retained to represent a party named Salsedo? A. I was... .

Q. When were you consulted with reference to Salsedo?

A. About a week before his death. In the latter part of April, 1920.

Q. On what day did his death occur? A. The 3d of May.

Q. And you had not seen him personally? A. I never saw him... .

Q. I see. And in what way were you consulted and by whom, I mean?

A. Luigi Quintiliano. [Ed. Transcript shows Quintilino on p. 2047.]

Q. Who was Luigi Quintiliano?

A. He came to me on behalf of the Italian Workers' Defense Committee.

Q. Of New York City? A. Yes... .

[The Jury retire from the court room and return after brief conference at the bench.]

Q. Now, I will ask you if, during those consultations, you advised him [Quintilino] about disposing of literature, Socialistic or Radicalist literature? A. Yes.

Q. When was that? A. In the week preceding the 3d of May. [1982]

Q. How many times did Quintiliano consult with you?

A. He had consulted with me on a great many occasions.

Q. I mean with reference to this disposing of literature? A. That was not the primary object of any consultation. That was a matter which came up in the course of his consultation with reference to my appearance for **Salsedo and Elia.**

Q. I mean, was there more than one conversation with reference to the literature?

A. No. [1983]

Cross-Examination.

Q. (By Mr. Katzmann) Mr. Nelles, did you ever consult with or talk with the defendant Vanzetti? A. I think not.

Q. And have you any definite recollection of the date when you had the conversation with Quintiliano of which you have just spoken?

A. Only that it was within a very few days of the death of Salsedo, which took place on the 3d of May.

Q. Can you thereby approximate the date any closer than to say a few days?

A. Only within a week....

Q. I suppose, like most good lawyers, you keep some memoranda of the times that you are consulted by clients? A. I am sorry to say that I don't, because I did not at that time.

Q. So that you have no means of refreshing your recollection? A. No.

Q. As to the exact date when you talked with Quintiliano? A. No....

MR. KATZMANN. I think that is all. [1983]

Louis Quintilino, Sworn. July 11, 1921.

Q. (By Mr. McAnarney) What is your full name? A. Louis Quintilino.

Q. You live where? A. In New York. [2047]

Q. Do you know Attorney Nelles? A. Yes, I know him very well....

Q. In April, 1920, did you employ him as attorney?

A. Yes. Well, I employed him as attorney of our committee.

Q. For what? A. For Italian Defense Committee....

Q. Did you in April see Mr. Vanzetti?

A. I saw Vanzetti April 27th or 28th. I think it was on two days.

Q. Where did you see him? I mean, in New York? A. I met him in New York in my office.

Q. In what way did you say you represented these societies,—did you?

A. Yes. I am the secretary of that society....

THE COURT. Secretary of what?

THE WITNESS. The Italian Defense Committee.

Q. That was in the defense of Salsedo?

A. Salsedo and the whole Italian political prisoners. [2048]

Q. You have answered me that you conferred with Mr. Vanzetti in regard to Salsedo and Elia, as to what Attorney Nelles said. Now, I ask you if you informed Mr. Vanzetti with reference to what Attorney Nelles had said about the literature? A. Yes, I did.... .

Q. Did you have a conversation with him about his representing a committee in Boston? A. Yes.

MR. JEREMIAH McANARNEY. That is all.

MR. KATZMANN. No questions. [2049]

[Ed. Andrea Salsedo, typesetter, and Roberto Elia, compositor, were arrested and detained by the Department of Justice after the bombing of Attorney General Mitchell Palmer's home in Washington, D.C., on June 2, 1919. See Avrich, pp. 182-185.]

Ranney's Letter to Abbott Lawrence Lowell: July 6, 1927
(The Sacco-Vanzetti Case Papers: Reel 21)

Dear Sir:

This morning Mr. Thompson advanced certain arguments in regard to . . . the proper construction of the word "consistent". I have had in my possession for a short time the testimony of . . . Mr. Proctor given in the case of Commonwealth v Ismaiel, in Essex County, in 1915, and I forward to you the original of this paper given . . . by James Lynch, an official stenographer in the Superior Court in Essex County. We believe that Mr. Thompson's contentions [transcript, 3699-3701] are met by this excerpt from Proctor's testimony, since he [Proctor] was using this word "consistent" at that time which was six years before the [Dedham] trial of the cases under consideration.

About a month ago one Major Calvin H. Goddard, of New York City, was introduced to me by Mr. William H. Crawford, a reporter . . . for the New York World. He desired to investigate the evidence of the bullets and shells and I was glad to give him the opportunity to do so. The investigation was conducted at Dedham on June 3rd, in the presence of representatives of the Commonwealth and of the defendants. The results of this investigation have been forwarded to Governor Fuller. I request that you read Major Goddard's report and make the fullest inquiry into the matters therein presented. . . . I consider his report to be of the greatest significance in the establishment of the truth, and trust that you will advise me . . . of the procedure which you desire adopted in satisfying yourselves of the accuracy and merit of his work. He . . . has told me that he has repeatedly tried to arrange an interview with the Governor.

Yours very respectfully, Assistant-District-Attorney. [Ed. See pp. 180, 594.]

INTERLUDE

Dudley P. Ranney's Letter to Frank N. Nay
(The Sacco-Vanzetti Case Papers: Reel 21)

July 14, 1927.

Mr. Frank N. Nay,
Box 67,
Stonington, Conn.

My dear Mr. Nay:

I was glad to receive your letter of July 11th, referring to one Albert H. Hamilton.

On the very day that your letter arrived, I cross-examined this gentleman who appeared before the Commission appointed by Governor Fuller to consider the Sacco-Vanzetti Case. The previous day he was annihilated by the Commission itself, so there was little left for me to do.

I merely had him admit that he only had a public school education, and yet for forty-one years had testified as an expert in a large variety of subjects, all of which require a technical education, and even that he had testified on medical subjects when he admitted that he was not a doctor.

I was aware that the gentlemen of the Commission raised their eyebrows very slightly, but it signified to me that they did not look very favorably upon this obvious quack and fraud.

I cannot thank you enough for your public spirit in assisting the Commonwealth in curbing any further attacks by him on its good reputation.

With kindest regards, I am --   Dudley P. Ranney
[Ed. Nay was a Boston attorney. See Hamilton, p. 464; and Ranney, p. 594.]

27. THE KELLEYS

Michael F. Kelley, Sworn. June 30, 1921.

[Ed. Michael Kelley is the father of George, Leon, and Margaret.]

Q. (By Jeremiah McAnarney) What is your full name?

A. Michael F. Kelley.

Q. What is your business? A. Shoe manufacturer.... .

Q. You are now at Stoughton? A. Yes.... .

Q. You are one of the firm of the 3-K? A. I am the owner; the 3-K is a trade name.... .

Q. How long have you known the defendant Nicola Sacco?

A. About twelve years, twelve or thirteen years.

Q. ... How did you get acquainted with him? A. When I was the superintendent of the Milford Shoe factory he applied there for a position, ...

Q. Did he go to work at the Milford shoe?

A. He came there to learn edge trimming.... . We taught him edge-trimming. [1604]

Q. When next did you come in personal contact with him? A. He came into my factory at Stoughton I think about three years ago, ... I remembered his face, ... not ... his name.... .

Q. In what capacity did he come to work there for you at Stoughton? A. As an edge-trimmer.... .

Q. Where did he live? A. He lived in a house that I owned, directly back of where I live. [1605]

Q. What have you to say with reference to his reputation for being a peaceful and law-abiding citizen?

THE COURT. He may answer.

A. I have to say this: I never saw a man that was more attentive to his family.

MR. KATZMANN. One moment.

THE COURT. Mr. Kelley, you pay attention to the question, will you, please, and answer that and nothing else.

THE WITNESS. I did not understand it.... .

[The question is read.]

THE COURT. That means whether it is good or bad.

THE WITNESS. It is the best,—good.... .

313

Q. How steady did he work? A. Every day.

Q. Did he occupy any position of responsibility or trust there with you...?

A.... In reference to his night watchman's work there? [See Appel, V: 5232-5233.]

Q. Yes. A. Yes, he had keys to our factory and the whole thing was in his hands there in the evening after everybody had gone home. [1606]

Q. ... Whether or not you saw a letter during March or April purporting to have come from Italy? A. Yes, sir.

Q. Will you describe the appearance of that letter? A. I did not read the letter... . I am sure Mr. Sacco showed me the letter and if,——it had,——the mourning stripe,——I think it was a letter that showed it was a letter that was usually sent out at any death in the family... . [H]e showed it to me, and said his mother died. I did not read the whole letter... . [1607]

Q. Did you know anything about his carrying a revolver as watchman? A. Yes, sir.

Q. ... Did Sacco, when he went on, have a revolver ...? A. Yes, I had purchased one for the use of the watchman, and if the watchman did not have one, why, we used that one that I purchased. [1608]

Cross-Examination.

Q. (By Mr. Katzmann) Do you remember seeing a letter that had the black outline that we use in mourning correspondence? A. Yes, sir.

Q. Did you see more than one? A. One letter, that is all.

Q. Do you remember when you saw that letter? A. I cannot say... .

Q. How long before that [May 5, 1920] was it that you saw that letter? A. I couldn't say as to that.

Q. Can't you give me any idea as to the number of days? A. No, sir. ...

Q. Nothing of the sort? A.... . I remember seeing that letter. He ... took it out of his inside pocket and said, "Here is a letter, my mother has died." I could not tell you the date. I know it was long before that time [May 5], because after that he began to get ready to go to Italy.

Q. What sort of revolver did you purchase for your night watchman? A. We purchased,——I purchased a .22 automatic revolver.

Q. It wasn't a Colt .32 was it? A. No, sir. Colt .22. [1609]

Q. Colt .22. Was Sacco the watchman for whom you purchased it?

A. No.

Q. Was it a predecessor of his? A. Yes.

Q. Did you know Sacco had a gun of his own? A. Yes, sir.

Q. And that was a Colt .32 wasn't it? A. I never saw it... .

Q. Did he tell you [he] had a gun of his own? A. Yes. He said he had a gun and—

Q. ... Then he did not need to take your .22 automatic, did he?

A. No, sir, he did not. [1610]

Redirect Examination

Q. (By Jeremiah McAnarney) What was said? A. ... [W]hen he said he had a gun of his own, I asked him if he got a permit from Vansent of Stoughton to carry it. [1610]

Leon Kelley, Sworn. June 30, 1921.

Q. (By Mr. Jeremiah McAnarney) You are the son of Mr. Kelley, the preceding witness?

A. Yes, sir.

Q. You work there with your father [and George and Margaret] in the business? A. Yes... .

Q. What are your duties in the factory? A. Office manager... .

Q. Do you know what the defendant Sacco's reputation for being a peaceful and law-abiding citizen is? A. Why, I never seen anything wrong while I was there.

MR. KATZMANN. I ask that be stricken out.

MR. JEREMIAH McANARNEY. That is hardly a technical answer.

THE COURT. That may be stricken out. [1611]

Q. And personally do you know anything about his carrying a revolver there, or pistol?

A. No, sir... .

MR. KATZMANN. No questions. [1612]

Margaret J. Kelley, Sworn. June 30, 1921.

Q. (By Mr. Jeremiah McAnarney) Are you employed at the 3-K shoe factory? A. Yes, sir.

Q. What are your duties? A. Secretary and pay-mistress.

Q. Have you examined the books and have you with you here any data showing the work of Nicola Sacco? A. I have examined the books and taken off the weeks since he worked in here at the factory. [1612]

Q. Using that to refresh your recollection, when did he begin to work at your factory?

A. November 9, 1918... .

Q. Well, what was his average weekly pay? A. Well, I will pick up January 3d. It was $52.22.

The 10th, $73.54. [1613]

Q. ... You live with your father and mother? A. Yes, sir.

Q. In the house right where Nicola's house was, right back of that?

A. Yes.

Cross-Examination.

Q. (By Mr. Katzmann) Did the defendant Sacco work on April 15th, 1920? A. That I can't answer. Sacco is a piece hand. If he was a day hand, I could, but being a piece hand, I could not tell whether a party in the factory was out or not... .

Q. You have a pay roll record, then? A. Yes.

Q. That is all you have? A. Yes, sir.

Q. For the piece hands? A. Yes.

Q. Will you give me what amount of money the defendant Sacco received for the week ending November 1, 1919? ... A. Do you want the amount of it?

Q. Yes, please. A. $78.28. [1614]

Q. What was due [on work] for the week ending December 13th?

A. There wasn't any.

Q. He did not work one week, then?

A. There must have been a week out.

Q. How about the week of December 20th?

A. He wasn't on the pay roll.

Q. Isn't it fair to say he did not work that week? A. Yes, sir.

Q. How about the week ending December 27th?

A. Not on the pay roll.

Q. Then he did not work then, did he? A. No, sir. [1615]

[Ed. On June 30, the defense called Plymouth police officer Joseph W. Shilling [1618], who testified that Vanzetti had a good reputation "for being a law-abiding, peaceful citizen." Katzmann said to Callahan: "Step up to the bench." On July 1, Katzmann read this.]

MR. KATZMANN. If your Honor please, I desire to read to the jury, after the [June 30] conference that was had with counsel for the defendants the following agreement:

The Commonwealth assents to the request of both of the defendants that all evidence heretofore offered in the course of this trial to the effect that either or both of said defendants bore the reputation of being peaceful and law-abiding citizens be stricken from the record of this trial, and that such evidence heretofore offered be entirely disregarded by the jury, so that as a result of striking the same from the record there is no evidence before the jury that either or both of said defendants bore the reputation of being a peaceful and law-abiding citizen. [1629]

[Stipulation: Katzmann could not mention Vanzetti's Plymouth trial, and the defense could not use testimony on the good character of either defendant. For Thompson's analysis, see Appel, V: 5301-5302. For Katzmann's explanation before Fuller's committee, see Appel, V: 5080-5081. For Ehrmann's analysis, see The Case That Will Not Die, pp. 393-395.]

Financial Report of The Sacco-Vanzetti Defense Committee
Aldino Felicani, Treasurer

Disbursements, May 31, 1921
Orciani, salary	132.30

Disbursements, June 30, 1921
Orciani, salary	167.18
automobile expenses	252.96
Orciani, traveling expenses	39.86

July 1, 1921 C. Affe
general expenses	6.00

[Ed. See p. 409 and p. 413.]

Russell's Note on Deposition of Adrower
(See p. 319)

The written cross-interrogatory contained the by-now-familiar Katzmann hurdles. Adrower had stated [in Rome] that between a hundred fifty and two hundred people a day came to the consulate to inquire about passports. He was asked [in Katzmann's prepared questions for the Rome deposition] to give the name of each person he talked with [at the Italian Consulate in Boston] on April 17, 19, 21, 24, 29, and May 2, 3, and 4. He could not remember their names. He was then asked [in questions submitted by Katzmann] to describe every person with whom he talked on those days. "I cannot describe them in detail," he admitted.

Source: Francis Russell, Tragedy in Dedham, pp. 173-174. Russell got his information from Sacco-Vanzetti Case Records, 1920-1928: Finding Aid, Harvard Law School Library. See Source 1. Scroll to Box 4-30.

[Ed. Transcript of the record has three items at the bottom of p. 1628.]

Giuseppe Andrower.

[The deposition of Giuseppe Andrower is read to the jury by Mr. Williams.

Editorial Note: This deposition is printed as an appendix, pp. 2266a-2266f.

[Ed. Transcript of the Record has two statements below at the top of p. 1629.]

Interrogatories Nos. 27, 35, 36 and 37 are excluded.]
[Cross-interrogatories propounded by the Commonwealth are read.]

[Ed. The last item means the jury heard Katzmann's challenges that Andrower had to respond to in Rome. But Appel did not print these cross-interrogatories by the Commonwealth in the appendix, 2266a-2266f. Appel chose to exclude Katzmann's questions to Adrower about persons Adrower talked to in the Italian Consulate on April 15, 1920.]

28. SACCO'S ALIBI WITNESSES

[Ed. Sacco's first alibi witness, Giuseppe Adrower, left the United States for Italy on May 22, 1920. His testimony is in the form of a deposition taken in Rome. The deposition appears in the <u>Transcript of the Record</u>, 2266a-2266f. Katzmann read the agreement reached on this deposition.]

MR. KATZMANN. ... I agree that the reading of the direct interrogatories and the cross-interrogatories and the answers thereto and the redirect interrogatories and the answers thereto in case No. 5546 is identical with those in case No. 5545, and that I agree that if they were re-read again in the second case the questions and the answers in each case would be identical. I mean ... that the reading of one applies to both cases without re-reading the same thing over.

THE COURT. The reading of one shall be evidence in both cases.

MR. KATZMANN. That is it.

THE COURT. ... Suppose, Mr. Callahan, you read the interrogatories, and let Mr. Williams read the answers.... . Have you the answers, Mr. Williams?

MR. WILLIAMS. I have, right here.

THE COURT. All right. [1628] [Ed. Deposition is read on July 1, 1921.]

APPENDIX
Deposition of Giueseppe [sic] Andrower
[Ed. Transcript omits Katzmann's questions.]

The deposition of Giuseppe Adrower taken before James M. Bowcock, Vice Consul of the United States of America and Commissioner at the City of Rome, Kingdom of Italy, on the eleventh day of May, 1921, pursuant to a commission to take depositions duly and regularly issued under an order of this Court by R. B. Worthington, Clerk of the Superior Court of Norfolk County, on the thirteenth day of April, 1921. "Q. What is your full name? [Read by Callahan.] A. Giuseppe Adrower. [Read by Williams.]

Q. Where were you residing during the month of April, 1920?

A. In Somerville, Massachusetts.

Q. By whom were you employed during the month of April, 1920?

319

A. By the Italian Consulate, Boston, Massachusetts... . At 142 Berkeley Street.

Q. ... [S]tate if there were any regular office hours maintained by said Consulate ... A. There were regular hours. Every day the office was opened at ten o'clock A. M. and closed at three o'clock P. M. with the exception of Saturdays. [Ed. Saturday hours 10:00 A. M. to 12 Noon.]

Q. ... [S]tate whether, in the ordinary course of your routine duties, you had to do with the advising...of people who desired to procure passports for Italy. A. Yes, I did. [2266a]

Q. ... State whether ... in the ... performance of your duties, you had occasion to advise persons who contemplated going to Italy, of the necessity, ... to furnish photographs of themselves, to be used in connection with such passports. A. Yes, I did.

Q. Annexed to these interrogatories is a sheet of paper marked 'A', upon which is printed across the top, 'R Consolato D'Italia' and on the 3rd line there is printed 'Foglio Di Via'... . [S]tate whether or not you have ever seen a paper identical with this blank form. A. Yes, I have.

Q. ... [S]tate for what purpose said form was used. A. This paper called Foglio di Via was used in place of a passport by all Italian subjects returning to Italy who did not have regular Italian passports or did not want to go to the expense of procuring a regular passport... .

Q. Annexed to these interrogatories is a photograph marked 'B'. Please examine the same and state whether or not you have ever seen said photograph before. A. Yes, I have seen the photograph marked Exhibit 'B'. [2266b] [See transcript, p.1981.]

Q. Did you see the photograph, herein referred to, and marked 'B', on the 15th day of April 1920? A. Yes, I did,

Q. ... [P]lease state all the facts and circumstances surrounding and incidental to your first seeing the photograph herein referred to, marked 'B' giving your best recollection of every act and thing done by the person that presented said photograph to you, and by yourself.

A. Early in April Mr. Sacco came to the Royal Italian Consulate for information how to get a passport for Italy. I gave him the information and told him that he should bring two photographs, one to be attached to the passport and the other for the records of the office. He then left and on April 15th, 1920, as I have stated before, he returned with a photograph the same as exhibit 'B'. I told him that this photograph was too large for use on a foglio di via or an Italian passport. He left saying that he would return with smaller photographs but I never saw him again.

Q.... . [S]tate how, and in what manner and why you are able, if you are able, to identify the date when you first saw said photograph marked 'B'. A. April 15th, 1920, was a very quiet day in the Royal Italian Consulate and since such a large photograph had never been before presented for use on a passport I took it in and showed it to the Secretary of the Consulate. We laughed and talked over the incident. I remember observing the date in the office of the Secretary on a large pad calendar while we were discussing the photograph. The hour was around two or a quarter after two as I remember about a half an hour later I locked the door of the office for the day.

Q. ... [S]tate fully how you are able to fix said date, ... A. This day made a special impression upon me as there was much less business than on the previous and following days. There were only about thirty or forty people in the office applying for passports that day and we usually had about two hundred.

Q. ... [S]tate ... what the man whose likeness appears in the photograph said to you at the time, and in [2266c] connection with the photograph. A. Mr. Sacco objected ... to the expense of having other photographs made and asked if I could not cut the pictures down to suit the forms... .

"Q. ... state your best recollection with reference to whom he desired to obtain the passports for. A. He wanted a passport for himself, his wife, and his boy.

Q. ... [S]tate when, and by whom, you were first interviewed with reference to the photograph marked 'B', ... A. The photograph was showed to me again by Professor Guadagni who asked me if it was true that Mr. Sacco had come to the Consulate with the photograph on April 15th, 1920, and asked for a passport. When Professor Guadagni came to see me he asked me first if I remembered that Mr. Sacco had applied for a passport on April 15th, 1920, to which I answered that I did not remember who Mr. Sacco was. Professor Guadagni then asked me if I would remember the photograph... .

"Q. ... [P]lease state for what [2266d] reason you left the employ of the Royal Italian Consulate, in the City of Boston, Massachusetts, U.S.A., if you have left said employ. A. I left the employ of the Royal Italian Consulate at Boston, Massachusetts, for reasons of health.

Q. State the date when you left the United States of America.

A. I left the United States of America from New York on May 22nd, 1920.

Q. State whether you are or not, in any wise related to Nicola Sacco. A. No, I am not.

Q. State whether or not you ever knew, ... Nicola Sacco previous to April 15, 1920. A. I saw him for the first time when he appeared at the Royal Italian Consulate during the first week of April, 1920, requesting information... .

Q. State whether or not there are any political or social affiliations ... of any kind, to the best of your knowledge between yourself and Nicola Sacco. A. No, there are none.

Q. State whether or not there are any political affiliations or social connections ... between yourself and Felice Guadagni. A. No, there are none... . [2266e]

(signed) Giuseppe Adrower" [2266f]

[Ed. Eight more alibi witnesses for Sacco are arranged by the chronology of April 15, 1920. Four of these testified after testimony of Sacco, who took the witness stand on July 6.]

Dominick Ricci, Sworn. July 1, 1921.

Q. (By Mr. Callahan) What is your name? A. Dominick Ricci.

Q. ... Where do you live? A. 44 Brookline Street, Needham.

Q. What is your occupation? A. My occupation is carpenter... .

Q. Do you know the defendant Nicola Sacco? A. Yes

Q. How long have you known him? A. I know him from about two years ago... .

Q. Where did you meet him? A. I met him in to a picnic in Milford once.

Q. Were you in Stoughton April 15th of last year? A. Yes, sir.

Q. Did you see Sacco on that day? A. Yes, sir, I did.

Q. Where? A. I saw Sacco on the platform station of Stoughton... .

Q. What time did you see him there?

A. It was between quarter past seven and twenty minutes of eight.

Q. Morning or afternoon? A. Morning.

Q. Did you have a conversation with him about a passport? A. Yes, sir. [1679]

Q. Did you see [him] take the train? A. No, sir... .

Q. Where did you go from the station?

A. From the station I took my right way to go up to the job... .

Q. Where was that? A. That was in Park Street, South Stoughton... .

Q. What kind of work were you doing on the day of April 15th last year? A. April 15th last year I remember that we were putting ceadar [sic] (beaver) boards on the ceiling of the piazza.

Q. When next did you see Sacco after leaving him at the Stoughton station that morning of the 15th of April? A. The next time I seen Sacco was in the morning after April 15th. [1680]

Q. Where did you see him next morning? A. I seen him in Kelley's factory, 3-K shoe factory.

Q. What were you doing there? A. I just went over there to read the paper and pass time until my time was ready to call work... .

Q. Did you have a conversation with Sacco [April 16] about a holdup in South Braintree?

A. Yes, sir.

Q. Did you have a talk with Sacco about a murder in South Braintree? A. Yes, sir. [1681]

Cross-Examination.

Q. (By Mr. Katzmann) How long were you working on that house where you were putting the beaver board on the piazza ceiling?

A. I worked there all day.

Q. What day? A. April 15th.

Q. What other day? A. Other day was April 16th.

Q. What other day? A. April 19th,—18th, 17th, 18th, and going right along.

Q. Did you work on the 18th, too? A. Yes, I did. [April 18 fell on Sunday.]

Q. Did you work on the 25th [Sunday]? A. Yes, sir.

Q. Did you work on the 2nd of May [Sunday] there? A. Yes, I did. [1682]

[Ed. Katzmann gave dates of 33 Sundays following May 2. Ricci said he worked on all of them.]

MR. KATZMANN. I have got to the end of my calendar. You worked every Sunday, didn't you, from then on. That is all. [1683]

Angelo Monello, Sworn. July 1, 1921.

Q. (By Mr. Callahan) What is your name? A. Angelo Monello.

Q. Where do you live? A. 137 Devon Street, Roxbury.

Q. What is your business? A. Contractor.

Q. Do you know Nicola Sacco? A. Yes.

Q. How long have you known him? A. A couple of months ... . I mean fourteen months. [1667]

Q. Where did you meet him? A. I met him on Hanover Street, in Boston.

Q. For the first time? A. No, The first time I met him in East Boston... .

Q. On what occasion did you meet him in East Boston? A. It was dramatic people there, at Maverick Square Hall. He was ... introduced to me by a nephew of mine. ...

Q. Did you later again see him? A. I seen him later, on the 15th of April.

Q. What year? A. Last year.

Q. Where did you see him? A. I saw him down on Hanover Street; I saw him on Hanover Street.

Q. In what town, where? A. Boston.

Q. What time of day did you see him? A. About eleven o'clock.

Q. Who was with him? A. Nobody... .

Q. How long were you with him? A. I walked with him down Hanover Street to the corner of Prince and Hanover Street... . [Ed. Talking with him "all the time" while they walked.]

Q. How do you fix it it was the 15th of April last year you met him at Hanover Street?

A. How I fix it?

Q. Yes. A. Of course, you know the next Sunday, April 18th, was a play by a great artist from New York. His name is Mimi Aguglia.

Q. What nationality, do you say? A. Italian. [1668]

Q. And you were going to say where the play was. A. The play at Tremont Theatre, "Madame X."

Q. Did you talk with Sacco about that play? A. Yes, I just——

MR. KATZMANN. One moment. One moment.

THE COURT. Did you have any conversation with him about the play?

THE WITNESS. Yes.

324

Cross-Examination.

Q. (By Mr. Katzmann) How long have you been a contractor?

A. About thirteen years... .

Q. Did you enjoy the play? A. Enjoy the play?

Q. Yes. A. Sure, yes... .

Q. Went to see the play, how many went with you?

A. Oh, it was a lot of people, was crowded there.

Q. I don't mean in the whole crowd. They weren't all with you, were they? A. I was alone.

Q. You were alone. Sacco wasn't with you? A. Oh.

Q. And did you talk with anybody on the 14th of April about the play?

A. On the 14th?

Q. Yes. A. I talked every day, because I am an amateur myself.

Q. I see, you are an amateur actor? A. Yes.

Q. Who did you talk with on the 14th about the play?

A. On the 14th, I talked with a man I meets. I belong to the dramatic club.

Q. Who was it you talked with? A. Which man I talked with?

Q. On the 14th day of April, 1920? A. On the 14th?

Q. Yes. A. I could not remember which man I was talking with on the 14th. [1669]

Q. Who was it you talked to on the 16th about the play? A. I don't remember... .

Q. On the 19th? A. I don't remember... .

Q. On the 21st? A. I don't remember... .

Q. On the 4th day of April? A. I don't remember. [Same answer for April 1, 8, 9, 17, 28.]

MR. KATZMANN. That is all. [1670]

[Ed. In redirect examination, Monello testified he talked with Sacco on April 15 about a passport and the consul's office.] [1670]

Felice Guadenagi, Sworn. July 9, 1921.

Q. (By Mr. Jeremiah McAnarney) What is your business? ... A. Journalist and literature.

Q. When did you first meet Nicola Sacco?

A. I met Nicola Sacco in some hall where I was speaking, in Boston... . Two years ago... .

325

Q. How often have you seen him before 1920? A. I can't say, but ten or twelve times.

Q. In April, 1920, did you see Nicola Sacco? A. Yes, sir.

Q. On what day did you see him? A. April 15th... .

Q. Where at? What hour did you see him? A. I seen him in the step door of Boni's restaurant in North Square at half past eleven... . [16 North Square]

Q. Did you and he do anything there? A. Oh, we ate together in Boni's restaurant... .

Q. And did any one come in there while you were dining? A. Coming in?

Q. Yes. A. Mr. Williams.

Q. Who is Mr. Williams? A. He is advertising agent for papers. [1991]

Q. What time did he [Sacco] have his dinner and what time did he go away? A. As soon as we came in the restaurant we called for dinner, and about half past one we go out... .

Q. What time did he leave? A. Who, Sacco?

Q. Yes. A. Half past one, about half past one. [1992]

Q. Did you see him again that day? A. Yes.

Q. About what hour? A. About three, three o'clock.

Q. Where were you when you saw him? A. In Joe Giordano's coffee house.

Q. Where is that? A. In North Street... . [37 North Square]

Q. Now, how is it, Mr. Guadenagi, that you say that you saw him on the 15th day of April; how do you know that? A. I first recollect that it was the 15th, because in that day I had some discussion about a banquet which was given to Mr. Williams, the editor of the Boston Transcript, and I had some discussion about that banquet with Bosco first and Professor Dentamore afterwards in the coffee house. I was invited to that banquet.

Q. When was the banquet to be? A. The night of the 15th. [1993]

Q. Did you have a conversation with one of the officials at the Italian consulate? A. Yes.

Q. Would you tell us when that was?

A. It was four days, four or five days after the arrest of Sacco.

Q. And with whom did you talk? A. Mrs. Sacco came up to me and remembered—

Q. ... Mrs. Sacco came to you, did she? A. Yes.

Q. Very well. Now, did you go to the Italian consulate? A. Yes.

Q. And when did you talk with her...? A. I talked with Melano Rossi, who was acting consul.

Q. ... [D]id you talk with any one else there?

A. Yes.... We were talking with Mr. Silvio Vidale, who is now vice-consul.

Q. Did you talk with any one else there? A. Yes. With Mr. Joseph Andrower.

Q. ... Do you know what he did at the consulate? A. Andrower?

Q. Yes, Andrower. A. He was employed in the Italian consulate....

Q. ... Was there any talk [with Sacco] about the passport at the coffee house? A. Yes. [1994]

Q. Was there any talk about the passport at the [Boni] restaurant ...? A. Yes.

Q. And in your talk with Andrower was the matter of when Sacco was there [at the Italian consulate] spoken about? A. Yes. [1995]

Cross-Examination.

Q. (By Mr. Katzmann) Are you a member of the Defense Committee? A. Yes, sir.

Q. And when you talked with Andrower after Sacco's arrest, did you bring with you a photograph of Sacco? A. Yes, sir.

Q. And did you show that photograph to Andrower? A. Yes....

Q. ... Did you first show him [Andrower] the photograph [before you talked]? A. Yes.

Q. What day was it you were at the Brockton police station? A. Two or three days after.

Q. What day? A. What day?

Q. Yes. A. I think it was Thursday or Friday.... [1995]

Q. What time was it you walked into the [Brockton police] station?

A. I don't take my watch to see.

Q. Did you take out your watch when you met Sacco at the restaurant?

A. Yes, because I went from the office and I wanted to know what time I go out of the office.

Q. Did you want to know on the day you saw Sacco in Boston what time it was you met him ...?

A. Yes, because I went from the office.

327

Q. Well, you go from the office every day, don't you, Mr. Guadenagi?
A. Yes... .
Q. What time did you leave your office on the day you met him?
A. Half past twelve, half past twelve. [1996]
Q. What kind of hat did he [Sacco] have on? A. Derby hat.
Q. He always wears a derby, doesn't he, when you see him in town?
A. Well, I have seen him in town; he always wore a derby hat.
Q. Yes. What time before the day he was talking about passports was it you had seen the defendant Sacco? A. I can't say when, but sometime before. He was in the hall at East Boston.
Q. What was the date? A. We have every week there a meeting, Saturday and Sunday.
Q. What Saturday or what Sunday is it you had seen him? A. I don't remember. ...
Q. Why, this [April 15, 1920] is the only date you can remember, isn't it? A. Oh, yes... .
Q. Of what importance was the day [April 15] to you before he was arrested?
A. The day before he was arrested? No, sir.
MR. KATZMANN. That is all.
MR. MOORE. That isn't the question. He did not understand that question.
THE WITNESS. Get an interpreter... . [1997]
MR. KATZMANN. All right. Mr. Ross, please.
THE WITNESS. You mean the day, the 15th?
Q. Yes. I mean the day you say was the 15th. A. [Through the interpreter.] Yes, it interested me because that day I was invited to a banquet.
Q. What had that to do with Sacco? A. Because at the time that Sacco came in I was talking about this banquet in the restaurant, in the coffee house... .
Q. ... [W]hat day did you receive the invitation [to the banquet]? A. About a week ago.
Q. No, not about. What day? A. What day?
Q. Yes. A. I don't think it is necessary to fix the day when I received——
Q. I did not ask you whether you thought it was necessary. I asked you what day it was?
A. I can't fix the date. [1998]

John D. Williams, Sworn. July 1, 1921.

Q. (By Mr. Jeremiah McAnarney) What is your business?

A. Advertising agent.

Q. Advertising what particular goods?

A. We specialize in foreign language newspapers, general advertising.

Q. Have you ever met Nicola Sacco? A. Once.

Q. How long ago was that? When was it? A. It was on the 15th day of April, 1920.

Q. Where were you when you met him? A. Boni's restaurant, North Square.

Q. What time of day was it?

A. I should say between 1:15 and 1:30... .

Q. When you went in there, who did you see?

A. Professor Guadenagi and a stranger, who I found out afterwards was Mr. Sacco.

Q. Were you introduced to Mr. Sacco? A. I was, yes, sir.

Q. How long did you remain in his company? A. About ten or fifteen minutes... .

Q. When was your attention first called after that meeting, April 15, 1920, to the man Sacco?

A. Felicani, who is the compositor on the Italian paper, La Notizia. [The News.]

Q. You say he called your attention to it? A. Yes, he did... . [1645]

Q. ... [W]hat effort have you made [after Felicani spoke to you], if any, to ascertain if it was really the 15th day of April that you saw the man Sacco? A. ... During the time when help was so hard to get, it was my custom to make the rounds of the North End candy factories and the big manufactories there every Thursday for help wanted advertising for Saturday and Sunday of that week, ... I made my rounds that day. That was the Thursday, and when this was called to my attention I looked back at my advertising book to see the—... .

Q. You looked at your advertising book?

THE COURT. Have you that book with you?

THE WITNESS. No, sir, I haven't... . [1646]

Q. ... After looking at the book, what did you look at, what did you do? A. I was treating at the time with Dr. Gibbs, and I recalled at the same day I took dinner there I made a visit to him, and I went to his office.... [1647]

[Ed. Williams produced a transcript of an advertisement for the Washington Knitting Mills he obtained on April 15, 1920. See pp. 1647-1648.]

Cross-Examination.

Q. (By Mr. Katzmann)   Do you solicit advertising for Jewish newspapers? A. Yes, sir.

Q. And in what other language are the newspapers printed for which you solicit advertising?

A. Italian, Polish, Armenian, Greek, Lithuanian, French, German... .

Q. Do you know of any other activities of Mr. Felicani during the past winter?

A. I believe he was connected with the defense here... .

Q. Didn't you know he was treasurer of the defense committee?

A. I did not.

Q. Is Professor Guadenagi connected with the defense committee?

A. I couldn't answer. I don't know.

Q. Isn't Felicani the real editor of La Notizia? A. No... .

Q. Are you a personal friend of his? A. I know him casually. That is all. He worked there.

Q. How long a period have you known him casually? A. I was [1650] business manager for the paper [La Notizia] when he came there to work, and I think he has worked there for about a year and a half, ...

Q. For what paper were you soliciting advertisements from the Washington Knitting Mills on the 15th day of— A. I got that for the La Notizia [a daily paper].

Q. That is the paper Felicani is connected with? A. Yes, sir. [1651]

Q. How frequently in the month of March and April and May, 1920, did you visit Dr. Gibbs?

A. I should say an average of once a week... .

Q. When was the visit [to Dr. Gibbs], Mr. Williams, next immediately prior to April 15th?

A. I couldn't answer that. His records would show... .

Q. What advertisements did you solicit on April 14, 1920?

A. I can't remember. I can tell you from my records. [1652]

Q. Is there any connection in your mind between the Washington Knitting Company, Knitting Mills "ad," and the defendant Nicola Sacco?

A. You mean that they have any relationship to each other?

Q. Yes. A. None whatever I know of.... .

Q. Did you go looking for the,—to see what "ad," if any, you secured on the 15th of April?

A. Naturally, for I consulted my records, Mr. Katzmann.

Q. Were you asked to consult your records? A. Certainly.... .

Q. Sacco was an utter stranger to you? A. Yes, sir, absolutely. [1653]

Q. Did you meet Guadenagi in Boni's restaurant on any other occasion other than the day in April? A. Yes.

Q. When? A. Many times.

Q. When? A. I can't recall the exact date. He worked on the paper. We used to go there.... .

Q. Have you met him during the past winter in Boni's restaurant?

A. I don't think so. [1654]

Q. When Felicani spoke to you, did he call your attention to the date, April 15th? A. Yes.... .

Q. They [Then] you went and looked at that "ad"? A. I went first and looked at my order book and then the files and looked at this "ad," yes, sir. [1655]

Dr. Howard A. Gibbs, Sworn. July 1, 1921. Corroborative Witness.

Q. (By Mr. Jeremiah McAnarney) What is your name?

A. Howard A. Gibbs.

Q. What is your profession? A. I am a physician.

Q. Where is your place of business?

A. On Boylston Street, Boston.... .

Q. Did you have a patient named John D. Williams? A. I did.

Q. For what were you treating him?

A. ... I treated him for intestinal trouble and asthmatic trouble and lumbago, I think.... .

Q. Kindly turn to your card records.... . [A]re you able to say whether or not you treated him during the month of April, 1920? A. I did, yes.

Q. On what day or days? A. I have it here on one day, the 15th of April, 1920.

Q. Did you treat him on any other day in April, 1920, ...? A. I did not, no. [1661]

Cross-Examination.

Q. (By Mr. Katzmann) Doctor, ... when was the next visit prior to that?

A. The next visit prior?

Q. To the 15th of April? A. On the 31st day of March.

Q. When prior to that? A. On the 29th day of March.

Q. When prior to that? A. On the 18th day of March.

Q. And prior to that? A. 17th.

Q. Now, following the 15th of April, 1920, when was the next subsequent visit?

A. The 7th day of May.

Q. And after that? A. On the 26th day of June.

Q. And after that? A. On the 29th day of June.

Q. And the next one? A. On the 30th of June.

Q. Were these treatments for asthma?

A... . I judged from the type of the treatment they were, but I couldn't say positively.

Q. Was the treatment on the 15th day of April for asthma?

A. It is treatment I usually use for asthma, yes.

Q. Has Mr. Williams seen your records? A. He has seen them once. [1661]

Q. When? A. I can't say exactly. It was sometime, I think, during April or May of this year [1921].

Q. Did he call and ask to see your record? A. He did.

MR. KATZMANN. That is all, sir. [1662]

Albert Bosco, Sworn. July 1, 1921.

Q. (By Mr. Jeremiah McAnarney) Where do you live?

A. 284 Sumner Street, East Boston... .

THE COURT. I guess we better have Mr. Ross.

[The witness's testimony is given through the interpreter.]

Q. What is your occupation? A. I do writing for the La Notizia.

Q. In what capacity are you employed? A. Well, I am one of the editors of the paper.

332

Q. That is an Italian newspaper, I should assume? A. Yes.

Q. Is it published daily? A. Yes, sir.

Q. What is the amount of its circulation? A. About 20,000 copies a day.

Q. Now, have you ever met Nicola Sacco? A. Twice.

Q. When was the first time you met him? A. The 15th day of April, last year.

Q. Where was it you met him? A. I met him in Mr. Boni's restaurant, 16 North Square... .

Q. Were you in the restaurant first or did Sacco come in first?

A. I was sitting down when Sacco came in.

Q. Did any one come in with him?

A. Guadenagi, Professor Guadenagi. [1662]

Q. Was there anything that transpired on the day of your meeting Sacco that enabled you to in any way to check that date up?

A. Yes, sir. [1663]

Q. What was it? A. Well, from the conversation that I had with Mr. Guadenagi that we were giving a banquet to the director of,—Mr. Williams.

Q. Who is Mr. Williams? A. He is the director of the Transcript.

Q. Boston Transcript? A. Yes, sir, the Boston Transcript.

Q. What were you giving to him? A. A banquet.

Q. When was that banquet held? A. The evening of the 15th.

Q. Well, how do you know that it was the 15th day of April that you saw Sacco? A. When I saw the picture in the paper and Mr. Guadenagi spoke to me about it. I went and looked back to the paper and I discovered that that was the evening of the banquet. [1664]

Cross-Examination.

Q. (By Mr. Katzmann) Did you have anything to do with the preparations for the banquet?

A. No, sir.

Q. Was that something that Guadenagi was doing?

A. No, he was invited... .

Q. What is Mr. Felicani's connection with the La Notizia?

A. He is the compositor... .

Q. Did the [Sacco-Vanzetti] defense committee have an office in the same building with La Notizia [at 34 Battery Street]? A. Upstairs, yes, sir.

Q. And how often did they, the defense committee, meet since last September?

MR. JEREMIAH McANARNEY. How is that of any importance?
THE COURT To show this man's interest and bias. [1664] [Ed. Question is ruled competent.]

Q. Is Professor Guadenagi a member of that committee?
A. I think so, but I don't know. I think he is. [1665]

Q. ... How many times have you seen Felice Guadenagi in the building at 34 Battery Street since last September?
A. Very few times... .

Q. A dozen times? A. Three or four times.

Q. Is Mr. Felicani connected with that committee? A. Yes, sir

Q. In what capacity? A. I think he is a secretary. I don't know.

Q. Do you know whether he is likewise the treasurer? A. Yes, yes. [1666]

Q. Do you know Fred H. Moore [chief defense counsel]?
A. Yes, sir... .

Q. Have you ever seen him with Mr. Felicani? A. Outside of the building of the La Notizia. [1667]

Antonio Dentamore, Sworn. July 11, 1921.

Q. (By Mr. Jeremiah McAnarney) You reside in Boston? A. Yes.

Q. What is your work?

A. I am foreign exchange man in the Haymarket National Bank.

Q. Now, sometime in April [1920] did you meet Nicola Sacco?
A. Yes, sir.

Q. When and where? A. April 15th, about quarter of three, in the coffee house, Giordani.

Q. When you met him was he alone or [was] some one with him?

A. Well, Mr. Guadenagi introduced him to me.

Q. ... How long were you in Sacco's company [in the coffee house]?

A. Oh, about twenty minutes. I am not sure. No more than that.

Q. In that conversation, as a fact, was mention made of passports?

A. Yes.

Q. Or the consul's office? A. Yes.

Q. Now, when next after that three o'clock, April 15th ... was it that the matter of Sacco was brought to your attention? A. About May 17th,—May 7... .

Q. And in what way was it called then to your attention? A. By Mr. Felicani. [2024]

Q. In what way are you enabled to tell this jury ... that you met Sacco on the15th day of April? A. I know because that day I went to the banquet in honor of Editor Williams of the Boston Transcript.

Q. Commander— A. An Italian decoration given by the ... king to Mr. Williams for the attitude of his newspaper during the war, in favor of Italy... .

Q. Where was that banquet held? A. At the Italian Friars Convent in the North End.

Q. What hour in the day was the banquet held? A. April 15th.

Q. What hour? A. About noontime... . At noon.

Q. So that you had been to the banquet when you met Sacco? A. Yes, sir.

Q. Who up to the time of this introduction was a stranger to you?

A. Yes. [2025]

Cross-Examination.

Q. (By Mr. Katzmann) Have you given all the reasons, Mr. Dentamore, why you recall the date April 15th? A. Well, not all. There is another reason.

Q. What is the other reason?

A. Well, about an argument I had with Mr. Guadenagi about that banquet. [2025]

Q. What time did you have the argument with Guadenagi? A. In Giordani's coffee house.

Q. At what hour? A. What hour? It was about quarter of three, ten minutes of three.

Q. Are you sure of the time, that it was quarter to ten minutes of three? A. Yes.

Q. And that the defendant Sacco was there then? A. He came afterwards.

Q. What time did he come? A. Very few minutes after.

Q. Did you not say, Mr. Dentamore, in your direct examination that you met Sacco in Giordani's coffee house about three o'clock, quarter of three? A. Well, about.

Q. How elastic is "about quarter to three...?" A. Well, about from five to ten minutes.

Q. Then it was between what hour that you fix it? You mean what time?

A. About, I should say, I meant about ten minutes of three... .

Q. When did you receive,—did you have an invitation to that banquet? A. Yes.

Q. When did you receive it? A. About a week before.

Q. Well, exactly on what day? A. Well, I can't remember.

Q. What did you do the next day after you received the banquet invitation?

A. The next day. At that time I was the editor of the Italian newspaper.

Q. What paper? A. La Notizia.

Q. When did you sever your connection with La Notizia? A. Last August.

Q. What did you do on the next day after you received the invitation?

A. Just my routine work.

Q. Who did you speak to on that day? A. Not a particular man... .

Q. Was there anybody with you at ten minutes of three on the day after you received the invitation to the banquet? A. I was in the office. [2026]

Q. Well, the defendant Sacco was no particular friend of yours, was he?

A. He wasn't a particular friend, but—

Q. You never met him before, had you? A. No... .

Q. Where were you,—with whom were you talking, if anybody, at ten minutes to three twenty-two days ago from today? A. I can't say that.

Q. Twenty-one days ago? A. I can't say that.

Q. Twenty days ago? A. I am not a fortune teller... . [2027]

Q. Are you connected with this Defense Committee? A. No ...

Q. Do you ever eat in the Boni restaurant? A. No.

Q. Have you never eaten there? A. Never? Sometimes.

Q. And when is the last time you ate there? A. Oh, about a year ago. [2028]

[Ed. The Court ruled (2032) that Dentamore could not testify he had asked Sacco, in Giordani's coffee house, to convey—assuming Sacco's

336

return to Italy—best wishes to Leone Mucci, member of the Chamber of Deputies in Italy, and tell Mucci that he [Dentamore] and Sacco had met in Boston on April 15, 1920. See Transcript, 4341.]

Carlos M. Affe, Sworn. July 11, 1921.

[The witness's testimony is given through interpreter.]

Q. (By Mr. Jeremiah McAnarney) What is your name?

A. Carlos M. Affe.

Q. Where do you live? A. 153 Marion Street, East Boston.

Q. What is your business? A. I buy fruits and grocery.

Q. What business were you in in April, 1920? A. The same business.

Q. Did you know Nicola Sacco? A. Perfectly.

Q. When did you first get acquainted with him?

A. I think that I have seen him the first time at Boni's restaurant.

Q. About when was that? A. I believe the first part, the beginning of March.

Q. Did you ever sell him any goods? A. Yes, sir.

Q. When? A. The 20th day of March [in 1920]. [2033]

Q. Where were you or where was he when you made that sale?

A. I think that was 180 North Street.

Q. Have you a record of what you sold him? A. Yes, sir. [Witness produces book.]

Q. How much did the bill of goods amount to? A. The bill was $15.67, but I got $15.50.

Q. How many times did you sell him goods? A. The only time... .

Q. Were you introduced to him there or how did you come to know him? A. I was introduced to him.

Q. Did he pay cash for those goods that day or not? A. He did not.

Q. When were the goods paid for. A. The 15th day of April [1920].

Q. What time in the day? A. After dinner, after the middle of the day.

Q. Are you able to say what part of the afternoon it was?

A. I believe that it was between three and four o'clock, something like that.

Q. Where is the store from which those goods were purchased?

A. That store was not mine, but I used to call there. That is where my headquarters were... . 180 North Street. [2034]

Cross-Examination.

Q. (By Mr. Katzmann) Mr. Affe, have you any store of your own, any place of business of your own? A. Not now. I had it before.

Q. Did you have a place of business in April, 1920? A. I did not have any business at that time, but I was going to this store, was trying to buy... .

Q. How did you conduct your grocery and fruit business at that time, March, 1920? A. I would go outside to buy the fruits and I sell it to my customers and the clients, to my clients.

Q. How did you bring it to your clients?

A. It all depends on quantity. I might bring it with my hands or send it by express.

Q. Where would you buy this stuff? A. I would buy it from all the wholesalers in Boston. [2034]

Q. Is this place at 180 North Street a wholesale place?

A. There is wholesale cigars and retail cigars.

Q. Well, what you sold him was groceries, wasn't it? A. Yes, sir.

Q. This was a cigar store you met him in?

A. Well, no, I think that I met him in Boni's restaurant... .

Q. And the place where the sale was made was in a cigar store?

A. I believe so.

Q. And it was all groceries? A. Grocery stuff... .

Q. Where did you buy the groceries you sold to Sacco on the 20th of March? A. I think I bought some from Majoli and Salini, Fulton Street. The macaroni, I think that I bought at 141 Richmond Street... .

Q. Did Sacco go around with you or stay at the cigar store?

A. No. He gave me the order in the Boni restaurant.

Q. What did you mean by saying first it was made at 180 North Street?

A. I said that I lived at 180 North Street. I did not tell you the sale was made over there.

Q. Didn't you state to Mr. McAnarney, "Where was the store where the goods were purchased?" Didn't you say that store, "was not mine. It was my headquarters. It was at 180 North Street." Didn't you say that to Mr. McAnarney? A. Yes, I was there every day.

Q. Did you say to Mr. McAnarney you made the sale to Sacco at 180 North Street?

A. I don't believe I told you that. It is impossible that I could give him that stuff there.

Q. How many customers have you? A. I got several of them.

Q. How many? A. Hundreds. [2035]

Q. How many hundreds? A. About one hundred.

Q. About one hundred. Do you sell for cash or on credit?

A. Sometimes cash and sometimes on credit.

Q. Do you keep a set of books? A. No, sir. I sell small sales... .

Q. Well, when you make sales on credit, whatever the amount, do you keep it in a book any place, the date and the amount? A. Yes, on credit I do. Sometimes I mark it on a book and sometimes I do not put any date, because I remember in my mind. I carry it in my mind.

Q. Did you carry this in your mind? Yes or no? A. [The witness talks to the interpreter.]

Q. Did you carry this in your mind, yes or no, sir? A. I carried it in my brains. And until I discovered this book, I could not tell, I could not tell, I could not say yes or no.

Q. When did you discover that book? A. Two or three weeks ago. [2036]

Q. Have you ever had any other customers who made first purchases from you on credit?

A. Oh, several of them.

Q. In those cases did you put down the date of credit and the date of payment?

A. Sometimes I did. Sometimes I did not, some, yes, some I did not...
.

Q. Have you the book in which you made those entries here? A. Yes, sir.

Q. I would like to see it, please. A. [Witness hands book to Mr. Katzmann.]

Q. Where is the entry to which you refer to here?

A. [Witness points out.] Right here. And that [indicating] is another one.

Q. Show me the whole of the entry that relates to this transaction. Is this it [indicating]?

A. Yes.

[Mr. Katzmann shows entry to the jury.] ...

Q. Is this the book in which you kept the entries of all of your hundreds of customers to whom you sold on credit? A. No, I got several.

Q. Well, where are the other books along about March, 1920?

A. Well, some one I got it at home. I think I got it at home. Some one I threw away. [2037]

Q. I show you entry on this page, "165 North Warren Avenue, Brockton, Massachusetts." What does that show? A. Nine head of cheese, Reggino cheese. I think one head of cheese.

Q. What does the rest of it say? A. "Reggino, 17 pounds, 14.90"

Q. What does it say underneath there? A. "Paid."

Q. Was that a credit transaction to somebody who lived at 165 North Warren Avenue, Brockton?

A. That I cannot remember.

Q. Is there anything about any date in connection with that transaction? A. I don't believe so.

Q. Is there anything about the date you sold the cheese? A. No, sir.

Q. Is there anything in that entry about the date the payment was made? A. No, sir.

Q. Do you know to whom you made that sale? A. To whom I sold it, I don't remember any more.

Q. And you don't remember whether it was cash or ... credit?

A. I don't remember... .

MR. KATZMANN. I desire to show that entry. [Showing entry to the jury.] [2038]

AFTERNOON SESSION.
Carlos M. Affe,
Cross-Examination, Resumed.

Q. (By Mr. Katzmann) Did you write in the,—on the 20th of March— the merchandise you sold Sacco in the book here? Is that your writing there [indicating]? A. Yes, sir... .

Q. Then everything that is on that page beginning, "Marcho 20, 1920," is in your handwriting?

A. Yes, sir.

MR. KATZMANN. I ask that that page be marked in some way, if your Honor please, by the stenographer so as to indicate what page it is. There are several pages.

[The stenographer writes his name on page indicated.]

[The page is shown to the jury.] ... . [The page is shown to the Court by Mr. Katzmann.]

Q. Have you a pencil in your pocket? A. Yes, sir.

Q. Will you take that piece of paper in front of you and will you write for me on each line what I give you, please, writing out in Italian, "March 20, 1920." A. [Witness does so.]

Q. Next line, "N. Sacco, Stoughton." A. [Witness does so.]

Q. Next line, "15 pounds Pasta." A. [Witness does so.]

Q. When I said "fifteen," I meant the figures "15," not the word "fifteen." Then write, "10 cents." "10" on the rest of that line, wait a minute. Is that "10" or "12" there [indicating]? A. "12."

Q. All right. Write that, Mr. Affe. "$1.80." "5 pounds lard, 24—— $1.20." A. Yes. [Witness does so.]

Q. "6 cans Salcina, 72 cents." A. [Witness does so.]

Q. "3 pounds of cheese, $3." A. [Witness does so.]

Q. "5-7/16 Salami, 4.45." A. What is the amount?

Q. "4.45." A. [Witness does so.]

Q. "1 gallon of olive oil, 4.50." A. [Witness does so.] How is it written over there?

Q. "Gls." for gallons; "olio d'oliva." A. How much?

Q. 4.50. Then draw a line. A. [Witness does so.]

Q. Put underneath it "$15.67." A. 67?

Q. $15.67. A. [Witness does so.] [2039]

Q. Next line, "Paid the 15 April." A. [Witness does so.] ... .

MR. KATZMANN. I offer this, if your Honor please, as a standard of this man's writing.

[Standard of witness Affe's writing admitted in evidence and marked "Exhibit 39."]

Q. I show you in this book of yours a page which says, "A. Monello, 137 Devon Street. Telephone, R. O. tel. Rox. 288-W." Did you write that in there? A. Yes, sir... .

Q. When did he [Monello] give you the address of his house? A. He knows it. He remembers it.

Q. Well, do you remember it? A. No, sir.

Q. And is he the Angelo Monello who testified here in this court in this trial? A. I don't know.

Q. Have you ever been out to his house? A. Yes, I was to his house because four years ago we were together in business, four or five years ago. [2040]

James Matthews Hayes, Sworn. July 11, 1921.

Q. (By Mr. Jeremiah McAnarney) What is your full name? A. James Matthews Hayes.

Q. You live at Stoughton? A. Yes.... Thirty-three years.

Q. At one time did you hold some position there in the town of Stoughton?

A. I held the position of highway surveyor for three years... .

Q. Were you and your wife seated in the court room here one day in the early part of last week?

A. Yes, sir.

Q. Did I ask you to step out in the anteroom, that I would like to talk with you? A. Yes, sir... .

Q. Well, I don't know that it is competent what our conversation was, but I had a conversation with you? A. Yes, sir.

Q. As a result of that conversation did you go back home and make an investigation with reference to trying to find out if you could place yourself on the 15th of April, 1920?

A. Yes, sir. [2014]

Q. What investigation did you make? A. I found that on the 15th of April I had gone to Boston.

Q. Tell us now how you remember that you went to Boston on the 15th of April?

A. I remembered that by a perusal of my time books and by other incidents that happened previous to that.

Q. ...What first set you on the track?

A. Well, I see by my time book I had received some money the 15th from my brother.

Q. Have you got your time book with you? A. Yes, sir.

Q. You may confer, look at that, if it refreshes your recollection.

A. And another thing, the 11th day of April, one of my children had a birthday... .

Q. On the 11th of April, one of your children had a birthday? A. Yes, sir. And of course I remembered giving the child a little time. The next day, Monday, I worked in the forenoon ... at Meade's factory. At noontime, coming home from my father's place I ... strained my instep, which made it impossible for me to ... do my work for a couple of days.

342

Q. Now what did you do? A. I had my Ford automobile, so the rear end was grinding, … needed taking down … and I took that down, that rear end down.

Q. When did you take that down? A. I took that down Tuesday and Wednesday and a couple hours Thursday morning, and then I needed some things, grease, and one thing and another, a grease gun in order to put that back again. And, another thing, previous to that I had joined what they call the Montgomery-Brooks, taking some profit-sharing stock in that Montgomery-Brooks concern, and the 27th day of March I had paid, that is, the 25th day of March I had paid $126 on that, and before I paid any more I made up my mind I would go and look the concern over and see whether it was worth going through with it or whether I would drop it. So I took the day off. However, I could not work very well at my own work, and also was to make some of these purchases, and I … took a little after twelve train and went into Boston, and I went down to this Montgomery-Brooks place and bought the stuff… .

Q. What time did you come out from Boston? Strike that out. About what time did you arrive in Stoughton…? A. Between five and six.

Q. That is on the 15th day of April? A. Yes, sir. [2015]

Q. Did you know Sacco?

A. No, I never knew Sacco. Never met him… .

Q. Whether Sacco was on that train or not you don't know.

A. I don't know. [2016]

Cross-Examination.

Q. (By Mr. Katzmann) How many days, Mr. Hayes, have you been in attendance in the course of this trial? A. The day that Mr. McAnarney called me out of this court room, that was the fourth day I attended this trial. …

Q. Were you here during the process of the drawing of the jury?

A. Yes, sir… .

Q. What was the occasion of your visiting the court then?

A. The occasion of my visiting that day was to see Mr. Woodbury.

Q. Who is Mr. Woodbury? A. Mr. Woodbury is connected with the defense.

Q. In what way? A. He is an investigator [for Fred Moore].

Q. And did you come [to court] to impart information to Mr. Woodbury?

A. Yes, sir. It was previously arranged... .

Q.... Are you a little hard of hearing?

A. I got hit with an iron bar a year ago last April in the ear, and I am at times hard of hearing.

Q. Get that on the 15th day of April?

A. Got that on the 19th day of April.

Q. 1920 or 1921? A. 1920. [2016]

Q. That [injury] did not help you fix the date?

A. It could have if I had thought of it, but I had not thought of it... .

Q. And did the fact that you had bought Montgomery-Brooks stock on the 25th of March help you fix the 15th day of April? A. Yes, sir. [2017]

Q. What did you do on the 26th of March? A. I couldn't tell you.

[Ed. Hayes gave the same answer for March 27, 28, 29, 30, 31.]

Q. There isn't anything in your book, is there, about going to Boston on the 15th day of April? A. No, but there is things that would call my attention to going.

Q. When next did you go to Boston after the 15th of April, 1920?

A. I have not had occasion to look it up. [2018]

[Ed. In Recross examination, Hayes testified he went in October 1920 to Wilson O. Dorr's house in Stoughton, before Dorr testified, to accommodate Woodbury. In second Redirect examination, Hayes testified Woodbury asked him for assistance because of Hayes's "knowledge of streets as highway surveyor." {2020} Hayes is the ninth alibi witness for Sacco. Sacco's Recall (2021) necessitates the return of Hayes on p. 2023.]

29. TESTIMONY OF NICOLA SACCO
(GEORGE KELLEY RECALLED)

Nicola Sacco, Sworn. July 6, 1921.

THE COURT. Let me suggest, Mr. Sacco, to you, the same as I did to Mr. Vanzetti, if you do not understand any questions put to you either by Mr. Moore or by,—either in direct examination or by Mr. Katzmann in cross-examination, it is your right to say so and have the questions put so that you may understand each one and all. You may proceed, Mr. Moore.

Q. (By Mr. Moore) Mr. Sacco, state your name in full, please.

A. Nicola Sacco.

Q. Where were you born?

A. Toremaggione, Italy. [Ed. Torremaggiore.]

Q. What year were you born? A. 1891. [1817]

Q. ... What was the occasion for your coming here [to the United States]? Who did you come with? A... . [M]y brother—who is Sabeno—he was in army three years and ... when he came back from the army, he desired to come to this country, so I was crazy to come to this country because **I was liked a free country**, call a free country, I desire to come with him... .

Q. You and your brother Sabeno, where did you go? A. We got a steamboat to Naples to Boston the last of April... . We reach Boston at twelve of April, 12th of April, 1908... .

Q. What kind of work did you take up first [at Milford]

A. Water boy... . [1818]

Q. Now, how long did you work in the foundry at Hopedale? A. I should say about a year, ...

Q. Where did you learn edge trimming?

A. Michael Kelly [sic] 3-K... [Ed. Michael Kelley's Milford factory.]

Q. After you had learned the trade, Mr. Sacco, what did you do then?

A. After three months, I got a job in Webster [Massachusetts]... .

Q. And that was at edge trimming? A. Yes, sir... .

Q. ... [W]hat [work] did you do [after you worked six or seven months at Webster]?

A. I left the job at Webster. I took a job at Milford Shoe Company, Milford. [1819]

Q. Well, now, assuming that registration [for the draft] was on June the 5th, 1917, how long before that date was it that you left the Milford Shoe Company? A. Sometime, a week before.

Q. ... Then, from 1910 until the last week in April—in May 1917—during all of that period did you work for the Milford Shoe Company? A. Yes sir, right along.

Q. What did you do in June of 1917? A. I left Milford... .

Q. How long were you away from Milford?

A. ... [A]bout three months and a half or four months.

Q. Were you outside of the state of Massachusetts during that period of time? A. Outside of this country, the United States.

[Sacco went to Mexico with Vanzetti and Boda and other anarchists.]

Q. What month, if you know, did you come back? A. Sometime the last of September [1917].

Q. Where did you go to work [after returning from Mexico]?

A. Cambridge, in a candy factory.

Q. What name had you been using since you left Milford in April, in May of 1917?

THE COURT. Does it appear he used any other name than his own?

Q. Yes. Had you, I am asking you? A. Yes. Nicola Mosmacotelli, my mother's second name. [1820]

Q. How did you get that name? A. Well, to not get in trouble by registration [military draft].

Q. ... What company did you work for next [after working "seven or eight days" for Victoria Shoe Company in East Boston]? A. Rice & Hutchins' shoe factory.

Q. What? A. Rice & Hutchins' shoe factory, South Braintree... .

Q. About what date was that? A. I should say the last of October... .

Q. Last of October of 1917? A. Yes, sir... .

Q. How long were you there? A. Seven or eight days, no more... .

Q. Then where did you go? A. I go straight to Haverhill. [1821]

Q. Now, when did you go to work for Mr. Kelley at the 3-K shoe at Stoughton?

A. It began in November of 1918... .

Q. And where were you working at the time that you went to work for the 3-K?

A. I was working, E. Taylor Shoe Company in Brockton... .

Q. How many different companies had you worked for during the period after leaving Rice & Hutchins and going to Milford or going to the 3-K? A. I see. I should say about six.... .

[Ed. Sacco mentioned Fred Field, Brockton. Sacco had carried "iron in South Boston, too."]

Q. Did you work all the time from that through to the time of your—of May the 1st of 1920? A. No. I was sick sometimes.

Q. When, if you remember?

A. 1919, three weeks before Christmas, sick about three or four weeks, anyway.... .

Q. You were sick for some three or four weeks?

A. Three weeks, sure.

Q. In December of 1919? A. Yes.... . [1822]

Q. Mr. Sacco, where were you on April 15th, Mr. Sacco? A. I was in Boston.

Q.... . Or, first, I will ask you what you went to Boston for? A. To get my passport.

Q. Now, at any previous time before that time, had you made any effort to get a passport? A. Yes, I did.

Q. How long before? A. Sometime in the middle of March, I should say the middle or last of March.... .

Q. Did you make an application for a passport? A. I went to see why I could not get my passport, what way I could get it.... . I did not know what way I could get information.

Q. What time did you leave Stoughton that day [April 15, 1920]?

A. I leave Stoughton on the 8:56 train.... .

Q. And where did you go on arrival in Boston? A. I left the South Station. I went in the North End. I went buy a paper, La Notizia [The News].... . [1823]

Q. What did you do then [after walking to Hanover Street in the North End]?

A. I turned a corner on Hanover Street.... . I met a friend.... . Angelo Monello.

Q. And did you have a talk with him? A. Yes.

Q. Then where did you go? A. We walked until Washington Street, and I go back again, so I stopped in the stores and been looking at a straw hat, some suits,—a price, you know. Then I go back. I have my mind to go in the afternoon and get my passport. I say probably I go to get my dinner first, so I have a little time and I go there, so I went to Boni's restaurant.

Q. And who did you see there?

A. I met Mr.—Professor Guadenagi... . [Ed. Outside.]

Q. Now, do you remember who else you met there, if any one?

A. Yes. Mr. Williams.

Q. Any one else? A. Mr. Bosco.

Q. ... Well, how long were you in the restaurant? A. [A]bout an hour and fifteen minutes, ...

Q. ... At what hour did you leave there? A. Twenty minutes past one; twenty minutes past one.

Q. Where did you go then? A. I went right straight to the consul's,— Italian consul.

Q. About what hour, if you know, Mr. Sacco, did you get to the Italian consul? A. It was about two o'clock. [1824] ... . [Ed. Consulate at 142 Berkeley St., not far from the North End.]

Q. Now, what did you say [to the clerk] and what did he say? A. I said, "I like to get my passport for my whole family." He asked me,— he said, "You bring the picture?" I said, "Yes," so I gave it to him, see, a big picture. He says, "Well, I am sorry. This picture is too big." "Well," I says, "can you cut, and make him small?" "No," he said, "the picture we cannot use, because it goes too big." I says, "Can you cut?" He says, "No, no use, because got to make a photograph just for the purpose for the passport, small, very small,"—so I did.

Q. Now, I call your attention to the photograph marked "B" attached to the depositions in this case.

MR. MOORE. You gentlemen have seen this, I believe.

MR. KATZMANN. Yes.

Q. Is that a duplicate of the photograph that you showed the gentleman there that day? [Ed. See Adrower deposition, p. 321.]

A. Yes, sir.

MR. MOORE. [Showing picture to the jury.] I imagine you gentlemen have all seen this.

Q. How long were you in the consulate, ..? A. Ten or fifteen minutes, ... about ten minutes.

Q. Then what did you do? A. I go back to buy my stuff, groceries, so before I got my groceries, I went to get coffee in a coffee store in the North End near the Boni restaurant.

Q. About what time did you get to the cafe, or coffee house?

A. It was a little before three o'clock.

Q. How long were you in there, if you remember? ... .

A. About twenty minutes,—twenty.

Q. Twenty minutes. And did you see any one while you were there?

A. Yes.

Q. Who? A. Professor Guadenagi.

Q. Any one else, if you know? A. Yes. Professor Dentamore.

Q. Then where did you go? A. I went to buy grocery.

Q. Do you remember where? A. Yes. I do not remember the name of the store, but I remember the street, the same street in the North End, about fifteen minutes,—about ... one hundred steps from the cafe. [1825]

Q. Do you know about what hour you left for Stoughton that night, that afternoon?

A. I should say about twenty minutes past four... .

Q. Now, that afternoon or that day in Boston, do you remember any other particular thing or special thing that occurred during this morning or afternoon? A. In the afternoon, yes.

Q. What? A. I met Afa and pay him $15 for bill.

Q. Are you sure about any of these spellings, or are you just spelling by ear?

A. I know him sure. I think Afa is the way you spell it. I don't know for sure.

Q. At any time, Mr. Sacco, on April 15, 1920, were you at South Braintree, Massachusetts?

A. No, sir. [1826] [Ed. Sacco repeated "No, sir" here and on p. 1864.]

Q. Did you see Mr. Vanzetti at any time on or about April 15, 1920?

A. No, sir.

Q. When was the first time that you saw him ... near that period of time?

A. The 25th of April. [Ed. 1920 is specified in next answer.]

Q. What was the occasion of your meeting him at that time?

A. Naturalization Club in Maverick Square, East Boston... .

Q. And did you know that Mr. Vanzetti was going to be there?

A. No, I never,—was not sure he would be there. [1827]

Q. Did you attend another meeting at a later date, Mr. Sacco? A. Yes, sir.

Q. Where at? A. The 2d of May, the same place... .

Q. On the meeting of May 2d, was Mr. Vanzetti present? A. Sure.

349

Q. Did you hear him at that time make any statement of where he had been and what he had done, since you last saw him? A. Yes.

Q. What did he say?

MR. KATZMANN. I object.

THE COURT. Excluded. [1829] [Ed. Court ruled it hearsay at this juncture.]

Q. Mr. Sacco, had you seen Mr. Vanzetti between April 25th and May 2d? A. Yes.

Q. You had seen him between those dates? A. No.

Q. You had not seen him? A. No, no.

Q. Did you see him at any place other than the meeting of the night of May 2d? Did you see him at any other time that day except at the meeting at Maverick Hall? A. No, sir.

Q. When did you see him again? A. May 3d. [Monday]

Q. Where at? A. Over to my house.

Q. What hour? A. I was in the factory all the morning. I came back from the factory about twelve o'clock, so he was already over to the house. [1830]

Q. Where were you on May 4th? A. I went in Boston.

Q. What for? A. To get my passports.

Q. Did you obtain them? Did you get your passport? A. Yes, sir.

Q. When you left your home was Mr. Vanzetti there or not?

A. Sure, he was home.

Q. Was he there when you returned or not? A. Yes... .

Q. Where did you go, direct to Stoughton?

A. No. When I go to Boston I got a train. When I come back I went the Elevated.

Q. Where did you go when you came back on the Elevated?

A. When I came back on the Elevated, I went to see Orcciani. [1832]

Q. Where at? A. At Hyde Park [part of Boston], I think, between Hyde Park and Readville.

Q. Did you see him? A. Yes. He was come down to the work. I met him on the road.

Q. ... What did you do? Where did you go? A. In his house... .

Q. Then where did you go? A. Over to my house... .

Q. Who was with you? A. Orcciani.

Q. How did you come there? A. On a motorcycle. [On May 4]

Q. Was it at that time that you introduced Mr. Kelley to Mr. Orcciani, as has been referred to?

A. Yes, sir... .

Q. Now, Mr. Sacco, going back for the minute, when did you quit work for Mr. Kelley, the 3-K Shoe Company? A. The 1st of May. [1833]

Q. Now, on May 5th, were you home all of that day? A. Yes.

Q. Who was present at your house? A. Mr. Vanzetti.

Q. Did any one else come in later? A. Yes.

Q. If so, when, what hour? A. I should say about half past four... .

Q. Who? A. Orcciani and Boda.

Q. How long had you known Mr. Orcciani?

A. I know Orcciani for seven years, seven years anyway.

Q. Where had you met him, if you know? A. Milford.

Q. He lived there when you lived there? A. Yes. [See Avrich, p. 27.]

Q. Where had you last seen Orcciani previous to May 5th, or May 4th, ...? A. May 2d.

Q. Where at? A. In East Boston, in the hall.

Q. ... [W]hat was he there for, if you know? A. I do not know what he was over there for... .

Q. On the evening or afternoon of May 5th or when you say that Boda was there— A. Yes.

Q. That is Michael Boda that has been referred to. How long had you known him?

A. I should say about three years before I got arrested.

Q. Where had you met him, if you know? A. I think I did meet him the first time in Boston, on Richmond Street. They used to have a Socialist hall once before the war. That is where I met. Some friends make me shake hands with him... . [1834]

Q. Now, on the afternoon or evening of May 5th, what was the occasion, if you know, for Orcciani and Boda being at your house? A. Yes.

Q. What was it? A. We are to go and get the automobile.

Q. To get whose automobile? A. Boda's automobile... .

Q. What for? What was the purpose? A. Well, we are to get the books.

Q. What? A. The prints of those out of the houses of the friends. [Anarchist literature.]

MR. KATZMANN. Louder, please.

THE WITNESS. We decided in the meeting in Boston [May 2] to get those books and papers, because in New York there was somebody said

351

they were trying to arrest all the Socialists and the Radicals and we were afraid to get all the people arrested, so we were advised by some friends and we find out and Vanzetti take the responsibility to go over to the friends to get the books out and get in no trouble. The literature, I mean, the Socialist literature.

Q. What hour did you leave your house? A. May 5th? Twenty minutes past seven... .

Q. How did you go? Where did you go first? A. By car. [Streetcar.]

Q. Where to? A. To Brockton.

Q. Who? A. Me and Vanzetti.

Q. How did Orciani and Boda go, if you know?

A. I think they went on the motorcycle, but they went afterwards, I suppose. [1835]

Q. What did you do on arrival at Brockton?

A. We got off the car at Brockton on Main Street, to get the Bridgewater car.

Q. What did you do in Brockton? A. So we lost the car.

Q. What? A. We lost [missed] the car for Bridgewater... .

Q. Then what did you do while you waited? A. We walked to School Street in Brockton and Vanzetti want to buy some cigars. He went in Italian stores,—a fruit store. He buy a couple of cigars there, so then we ... went in the lunch cart. We took coffee. After ... [w]e take a walk.

Q. What did you do in the cigar store? A. When we took in the lunch cart, I mean the coffee, Vanzetti was write, copying, was write a manifest, a bill, handbill for the conference.

Q. What do you mean by a "conference," Mr. Sacco? A. Call the people to hear a conference.

Q. To be held when? A. I do not remember the day exactly, but ... the hall was already hired by a friend from Brockton. It was Clark Hall. I do not know if it was on the 9th or 10th. I forget. [1836]

Q. Now, where did you go on the street car? You took a car to Bridgewater, did you? A. Yes.

Q. Where did you get off that car? A. We got off at Elm Square.

Q. How do you know you got off at Elm Square? A. Well, Mr. Moore, I do not know if I did ... but I am sure after I got off the car I saw the sign over there on the post ... **I sure remember I read Elm Square.**

Q. When you got off the car, where did you go?

A. We remained there for a couple of minutes, three or four minutes.

Q. What did you do then? A. We did walking, up the car track, going to Bridgewater.

Q. Had you been down there at that point before? A. No, sir.

Q. When you got off the car, which direction did you go…?

A. To Bridgewater the first time we stopped there.

Q. Well, why did you go that way? A. Well, we thought we could meet the friends by that road.

Q. Then how far did you go? A. We walked, I should say, about ten or fifteen minutes.

Q. Then what did you do? A. I think we reach the Square over there, some Square there.

Q. Then what did you do? A. Then we go back again.

Q. Where did you go then? A. Elm Square again. [To Simon Johnson's garage.] [1837]

[Ed. After three more questions, Sacco testified he saw the light of a motorcycle.]

Q. What did you do when you saw the lights of the motorcycle?

A. Well, we passed the bridge. I went in near the car to see who it was, to find out.

[Ed. Car is Orciani's motorcycle near R. R. bridge described by Ruth & Simon Johnson.]

Q. To see what? A. Who is near the car. I crossed the road. I went near the car to find out who it was standing near the car, so I see Orcciani and I speak to him…. [1838]

Q. Who else did you see? A. I saw Boda near the house, the little house…. [Johnson house]

Q. What happened after that or while you were there? A. Between us we have a conversation, me and Vanzetti with Orcciani. I could see by the door,—Mike Boda was standing on the door, outside. But … I could not recognize the other man who was talking…. He [Boda] could not get no car because he have no number, no number plates, so after a little while Boda came back, because Orcciani told us, he says, "I don't know." … .

Q. Did you see any one other than Mr. Vanzetti, Orcciani, Boda and yourself there; …

A. Yes, sir.

Q. Who?

A. I saw a woman come by from Brockton, coming from the little house, going in that house.

Q. Go in what house? A. I guess it is her house... little house near the bridge, ... [1840]

Q. Do you know whether she came from Brockton or not? A. No, I can't say. I couldn't say if she came from the house or Brockton,— from some other house. I saw she come, anyway.

Q. Where did you then go? A. ... I took a car. I went home. I mean, I took a car, me and Vanzetti. We got arrested in Brockton.

Q. Now, at the time that you were arrested in Brockton on the street car, did you or Vanzetti, either one of you, reach for or attempt to get ahold of any weapon, any gun? A. No, sir. [1841]

Q. Going back for the minute, Mr. Sacco, as you left the Johnson house going walking down the car line— A. Yes.

Q. —did you speak to some one? A. Yes, sir.

Q. Who was that, if you know? A. A woman... .

Q. What did you say to her? A. I asked where ... was the stop to where we could get the car. She said, "The white post, right here... ." [Ed. Designated stop of streetcar.]

Q. You have heard the testimony of a witness, Mr. Cole, here, to the effect that on April 15th, or April 14th—he is not certain—he had seen you taking a car at this point? ... [Ed. Debate by lawyers.]

MR. MOORE. The testimony of Mr. Cole is that on the night of May 5th they took the car at Sunset Avenue.

THE COURT. Yes, exactly.

MR. MOORE. And that on the night of April 14th or 15th, they had taken the car at the same point. [1842]

Q. Mr. Sacco, had you on April 14th or 15th or any date taken a car anywhere near or about this point? A. No, sir. [1843]

Q. You, I believe, have stated that you told him [Michael Stewart] you went there [West Bridgewater] to see Pappi with Vanzetti? A. Yes.

Q. You actually went there [West Bridgewater] to get an automobile? A. Yes.

Q. Mr. Sacco, ... the following day you had a conversation with Mr. Katzmann. Is that correct? A. The night after [arrest].

Q. May 6th? A. Yes... .

Q. During the entire conversation was there a **stenographer** present, as you recollect it?

A. I should say yes... .

Q. Were all the questions and answers taken through an interpreter, or was it direct, without an interpreter? A. Well, sometimes I could not answer and **the interpreter** explained... .

Q. Were you told that you were charged with any crime? A. No... .

Q. And during this entire period of time, nothing was said with reference to any particular crime committed at any particular place? A. No, sir.

Q. What did you think you were being held for, then, by Mr. Katzmann?

A. I did not know, I did not know myself. [1846]

Q. Now, Mr. Sacco, on the night of May 5th, you went to the,——with Boda, Orcciani and Vanzetti, to the Johnson house. Why, for what purpose and reason? A. To get the automobile.

Q. Why did you want an automobile? A. To get the literature. [Ed. Anarchist literature.]

Q. When had you decided to get the literature? A. I could not say, because I was just in his company that night. I was to go back to the old country. [This was stricken out.]

Q. When had you decided to get this literature? What date had you decided to get it?

A. I suppose they will get it if they have a chance; **the same night,** some house. [1847]

Q. Now, Mr. Sacco, what was the decision reached, if any, on May 2d with reference to the taking care of or moving of this literature you have referred to? A. Taking care?

Q. What decision was reached? How were you going to do it?

A. Well, I suppose we take—[1849]

Q. Not what you supposed. What did you discuss as to method of doing it on May 2d?

A. The best way to take by automobile, could run more fast, could get more fast, could hide more fast. It could go, and some have a little education, you know, to find where you could put so well some place to hide, see; to learn where nobody could know anything. That is all.

Q. Who had an automobile? A. Well, I don't know who had it, because we have been talking about finding somebody who could have it, who could offer himself.

Q. Who did? A. Well, Orcciani says he knows Boda, he has an automobile. "I will ask him if he wants to come. I think he won't refuse to do such work, because he is a Socialist himself. He is an active Socialist." ... .

Q. When were you to see about whether the car would be usable or "get-atable"? When were you to find out about the car?

A. Well, we were waiting for the answer. Orcciani was to get the answer.

Q. Waiting for the answer? A. Yes.

Q. Who was to get the answer? A. Orcciani.

Q. Did he deliver the answer? A. Yes, sir.

Q. When? A. May 4th when I go back to Boston I went over to his house. He told me, so I told him Vanzetti was over to my house, so he came with me together to have a conversation in my house... .

Q. By the way, Mr. Sacco, there has been introduced in evidence here a cap that is marked Exhibit 29. Is that your cap? A. [Witness examines cap.] I never wear black much. Always a gray cap; always wear gray cap. Always I like gray cap.

MR. MOORE. That is not an answer to my question. [1850]

MR. KATZMANN. I ask that answer be stricken out. The question is, is it your cap, not what color he wears.

THE WITNESS. No, sir.

THE COURT. The other answer may be stricken out.

Q. Do you know anything about that cap? A. No, sir, never saw it. [Ed. This is Exhibit 29.]

Q. Did you ever have a cap of any color made in that form with the fur lining?

A. Never in my life.

Q. See if this is your size. A. [Witness puts cap on head.] The way I look. Could not go in. My size is 7 1/8.

THE COURT. Put that on again, please.

[The witness places cap on head again.]

THE COURT. That is all... .

[Ed. Exhibit 29 is the cap which Fred Loring testified "was about 18 inches from Berardelli's body."]

Q. Mr. Sacco, do you know anything about that cap [indicating]?

A. That is my cap.

Q. When did you buy that? A. I buy that sometime last March.

[Ed. Moore has a third cap, not #29.]

Q. Last March? A. In 1920.

Q. Did you have another cap that you used ... another cap in addition to that one? A. Certainly.

Q. What kind of a cap?

A. Just the same. A little more white,—gray... .

Q. Do you know where the **other hat** of yours is? A. Sure.

Q. Where? A. The police took from my house. I heard that by my wife. [1851]

[Ed. The "other hat" is the **Guerin cap** taken from Sacco's home by Lt. Guerin. See Rebuttal.]

MR. MOORE. We ask this [#O below] be marked at this time as defendant's exhibit and make a request also at this time, your Honor, the cap, if any of the Government officers have the cap that we understand was taken in the Sacco home May 6th, ...

THE COURT. Why haven't you asked the District Attorney privately if he has or anybody representing him?

MR. KATZMANN. No trouble about it, your Honor. We have the cap [Guerin cap], we have had the witness here all day yesterday, waiting for Sacco to be on the stand. We do not think he [Guerin] is here to-day, but we will introduce it [cap] before he [Sacco] gets off the stand... .

MR. MOORE. Is the cap here in court? It is in your room, is it?

MR. KATZMANN. No. It is in the possession of the officer who took it, whom we had here yesterday for the purpose... .

[Cap admitted in evidence and marked "Exhibit O."][1852]

[Ed. Appel identifies Exhibit O as "cap of Sacco." The Loring cap is Exhibit 29; the Guerin cap is identified as both #27 and #43. Fraenkel, p. 379, says a cap "had been purchased by counsel to serve as a basis for comparison." See Appel, IV: 4331. Sacco tried on Guerin cap, #27, on p. 1928.]

Q. Did you go in front of any Judge on May 6th? A. May 6th? I think I made a mistake. I guess we went on Saturday or Friday, No, on Saturday.

Q. You were arrested on Wednesday, May 5th, weren't you?

A. Yes. We went in court Saturday morning. [May 8]

Q. On May 6th, were there people brought in who looked you over? A. Yes. [1853]

Q. Where at? A. Up to the police station in Brockton.

Q. How many people were brought in to look you over that day, if you know, approximately?

A. Oh, I couldn't say how many there was, Mr. Moore, but I know there was more than thirty, I should say twenty-five or thirty.... [1854]

[Adjourned to Thursday, July 7, 1921, at 9:30 a.m.] [1856]

Thursday, July 7, 1921.
Nicola Sacco.
Direct Examination, Resumed.

Q. (By Mr. Moore) Mr. Sacco, what did you intend to do on arrival at West Bridgewater or at Elm Square that night? A. We went there to get the automobile.

Q. Then what were you going to do? Tell us what did you intend to do? A. Well, if we get the automobile, Vanzetti and Boda will go to Plymouth. Before they go to Plymouth, they are to go and see Pappi in Bridgewater, West Bridgewater,—I do not know where it is—and I will come back with Orcciani, with me to Brockton to see the friends, my friends, and try to find out when we can print those handbills, print, have the bills for Sunday, and another thing, I will advise the same thing to my friends to be preparing, letter and paper, everything in a valise, so next day the friend will come around and take the literature and bring it away. Then after I go back to my house,—Orcciani bring me to my house... .

Q. Now, Mr. Sacco, ... you stated yesterday that on May 4th you had secured your Foglio di Via from the Italian consulate. Is that [indicating] the paper you were given at that time?

A. Yes, sir... .

MR. MOORE. The passport paper is offered as an exhibit at this time. [1857]

[Foglio di Via issued to defendant Sacco is offered in evidence and marked "Exhibit P."]

Q. Mr. Sacco, how did it happen that you were carrying on the evening of May 5th a revolver or a pistol? A. Well, to use like that. My wife used to clean the house, get ready, because we are to go Saturday to New York to get the steamboat, and she ... cleaned the bureau, and because the revolver, the pistol and bullets—

MR. KATZMANN. I will have to ask him to repeat... .

358

Q. Start again. Repeat that entire answer loud and full. A. May 5th, always to start from May 2d. My wife started ... to get ready, so May 5th she cleaned the bureau, and the pistol was closed with a key, because I was afraid that sometime my boy could go after it, so she cleaned the bureau and she pulled out the bullets and the pistol, and then she ask me, she said, "What are you going to do, Nick, with this?"
MR. KATZMANN. One moment.

Q. Not what she said to you, but what you did. A. So I took that sometime in the afternoon, about half past three, ... I said, "Well, I go to shoot in the woods, me and Vanzetti." So I did. I took it in my pocket. I put the revolver over here [indicating] and the bullets in my pocket, in my pocket back. Well, we started to talk in the afternoon, me and Vanzetti, and half past four Orcciani and Boda came over to the house, so we started an argument and I forgot about to go in the woods shooting, so it was still left in my pocket.

Q. Where did the shells that you had in your pocket ... when you were arrested, where had you gotten those?

A. I bought. I bought that on Hanover Street.

THE COURT. Boston?

THE WITNESS. Yes, Boston.

Q. Have you any idea how long you had had them? A. ... I bought sometime in 1917 or 1918, ... I can't remember the date, but I buy that sometime in the war times when the bullets were very scarce and you could not buy it. [1858]

Q. Did you speak to Mr. Kelley about leaving his employ and going to Italy? A. Yes, sir. [1859]

Q. Then when you went to the 3-K, in addition to the regular work as a piece worker, did you do anything else? A. Yes.

Q. What? A. I used to light the steam heat in the shop in the winter time, the fireman, and assist watch the shop... .

Q. How did you get into the shop? A. By the key.

Q. Did you always carry a key to the shop? A. Yes, sir... .

Q. Mr. Sacco, does this savings account deposit book appearing in the name of Rose Sacco, account No. 78320, represent the deposits and the bank balance from your earnings or your joint earnings? A. Yes... .

[Bank Book No. 78320 admitted in evidence and marked "Exhibit Q."]
[1860]

Q. What did you do when these various people were in the room [crime witnesses brought to Brockton police station]? A. The first time I walked a couple of steps... .Then I walked a couple of steps like that [indi-{1861} cating] in this way... . They make me just to shoot, wait for somebody to hold up money, with a dirty cap on my head... . [1862]

Q. There has been some testimony here with reference to some **shotgun** shells. What is the history of those shells, Mr. Sacco?

A. The history of those shells,—one of the friends of mine, sometime in 1919 or 1918, I can't remember exactly,—

Q. 1919 or 1918... . A. Yes. So he came over with his wife—his wife was sick—to pass a couple of days with me to my house. He was going to Italy, the whole family ... He bring a gun, and at the same time he bring a box of shells, and we went in the woods that day, me, him and his wife, playing and shooting in the wood,—mostly destroyed moths, but there was left in the box **about three**. So the three were always in my house. The 5th of May, when Vanzetti came over, he went to drink water and he saw those three shells. My wife was cleaning over there.

Q. Where were they?

A. On a shelf near where they put the glass, ... [1863]

Q. Mr. Sacco, you know Mr. Dominick Ricci? A. Yes, sir. [1864]

Direct Examination by Mr. Jeremiah McAnarney.

Q. Now, when you were interrogated by Stewart, did you tell Stewart the truth? A. No, sir.

Q. When you were interrogated by the District Attorney, did you tell him the truth, or did you lie to him? A. I did not tell him the truth... .

Q. Why not? A. Well, because I was,—I wouldn't give him all that work we had done.

Q. What is that? A. All the work we had done to get the literature, not to name my friends to get them in trouble. [1866] [Ed. McAnarney asked for privilege of recalling Sacco to the stand.]

Cross-Examination.

Q. (By Mr. Katzmann) Did you say yesterday you love a free country?
A. Yes, sir.
Q. Did you love this country in the month of May, 1917?
A. I did not say,—I don't want to say I did not love this country.
[1867]
[Ed. This topic takes up the first 14 pages of Katzmann's cross examination, pp. 1867-1881.]
Q. Did you have some circulars and books in your house on May 5th?
A. Yes... .
Q. Printed in this country or in Italy?
A. I couldn't say, but the most they are printed in Europe... .
Q. Papers? A. You mean I could say the paper I get every day?
[1881]
Q. Yes, please. A. I will. I used to get Le Mortello. [The Hammer—martello]
Q. Where is that printed? A. In New York City. [Ed. Carlo Tresca's newspaper.]
Q. In English or Italian? A. In Italian.
Q. What other paper? Is that a daily? A. No, weekly.
Q. Weekly. A. Every 15 days.
Q. Fortnightly? A. Yes. I used,—before the war, I used to get a Cronaca Soverseva.
[Ed. Galleani edited <u>Cronaca Sovversiva</u>, Subversive Chronicle. See Avrich, <u>Sacco and Vanzetti: The Anarchist Background</u>, p. 28.]
Q. Printed where? A. Lynn. [1882]
Q. Were they Socialist papers? A. Yes, sir.
Q. They anarchistic papers?
MR. JEREMIAH McANARNEY. I object. [1883]
THE COURT. What is the objection to that? As I understand it, the papers, under your theory, were of such a character that he was going to collect them and dispose of them some way.
MR. JEREMIAH McANARNEY. The objection is that the question is incompetent, immaterial and irrelevant at the present state of the record.
THE COURT. I will admit it on the ground that I have already stated... .
MR. JEREMIAH McANARNEY. Save an exception.

THE COURT. Certainly.

Q. Were they anarchistic? A. Some of them: …

Q. How many [books in your house were "anarchistic"]? A. You want me to name those books?

Q. No. I want the number, not the name.

A. I never counted them… .

Q. Two dozen? A. More.

Q. Three dozen? A. Yes, I guess so.

Q. That is about right? A. Yes.

Q. What size books were they? A. Some sizes four or five hundred pages. Some size two hundred. Some size one hundred. Some size two thousand. Some size four thousand. Many size.

Q. Could you have carried those books out of your house yourself unassisted in two or three or four trips in your arms? A. No, sir.

Q. How many trips would it take you? A. I should say a dozen.

Q. A dozen… . You were home Monday afternoon, May 3d, weren't you? A. Yes… .

Q. You talked with Vanzetti on Sunday, May 2d? A. Yes.

Q. You had heard this terrible report from New York, hadn't you? A. Yes.

Q. Did you make any move Monday afternoon to take any of those things out of your house?

A. No. [1884]

Q. Tuesday night? A. No.

Q. All day long Wednesday? A. No.

Q. Did you know Fruzetti, of Bridgewater, who was deported you said? A. Yes. [1885]

Q. Were you afraid of deportation … on May 5th? A. Yes, sir. [Objection sustained.] [1886]

Q. Who was the other man that you said was deported from Bridgewater?

A… . I am sure there is another man been deported, but I do not know the name.

Q. See if I can refresh your recollection. Was it Ferruccio Coacci?

A. He is one. There is another one. [1889] [Ed. Coacci was deported on April 18, 1920.]

Q. Did you come to a realization over night last night that Vanzetti had said you were not going to get books that night and that yesterday you

said you were? Did you think that over during the night? A. I says if
we had the time, if they had that time early.

Q. No, pardon me. Last night when you left this court room, and
before you came back this morning, did you realize you had said one
thing and in that regard Vanzetti said another? Did you realize that
Vanzetti said you were not going to collect that night and that you said
you were going to collect in the auto? Did you think that over last
night?

MR. JEREMIAH McANARNEY. Do you claim Vanzetti said that
he, Sacco, was going to collect, or that he, Vanzetti, was? Your
question is to him, "Did you?"

MR. KATZMANN. I claim that Vanzetti said they were not going to
collect any books or periodicals that night. This man said yesterday
they were. [Ed. Short dispute about phrasing.]

Q. Didn't he say that he intended—that he had not—that he was going
to make inquiry at Plymouth the next day and that it was not their
intention to collect until he found a place to hide the books. Didn't
Vanzetti say that?

A. Probably I mistake or probably Vanzetti is right. [1892]

Q. Did you ever see that gun, that revolver, Exhibit 27, prior to the 5th
day of May, 1920?

A. No, sir.

Q. Did you take that revolver off the person of Alessandro Berardelli
when he lay down on the sidewalk in front of the Rice & Hutchins
building? A. No, sir... .

Q. Did you know Alessandro Berardelli? A. No, sir.

Q. When did you first hear of him? A. The 16th, the morning.

Q. The morning of the 16th? A. Or 17th, I mean, exactly. [April]

Q. Do you remember my asking you on the evening of May 6th:

"Q. Do you know Alessandro Berardelli?"

And your reply:

"A. No; who is this Berardelli?" ... .

Q. You knew who he was on the 16th or 17th of April, didn't you?

A. Probably I forgot.

Q. Did I ask you on May 6th if you knew who he was, and did you
make that reply?

A. No, sir. You did not ask me.

Q. Do you say, Mr. Sacco, that I did not ask you this question: [1893]

"Q. Do you know Berardelli? A. No. Who is this Berardelli."

363

Did you make that answer to that question on **the night of May 6th** to me in the Brockton police station? A. I don't remember.

Q. Will you say that you did not? A. Probably I did, but I don't remember.

Q. When I was asking you that question, Mr. Sacco, you knew who Berardelli was, didn't you?

A. No, sir.

Q. I thought you had said this morning, within three minutes, that you read and knew who Berardelli was on the 16th or 17th of April, 1920?

A. I could not remember. [Ed. McAnarney asked for repeat of question.]

Q. On the 16th or the 17th day of April, 1920, did you learn that a man named Berardelli, from reading the newspapers did you learn a man named Berardelli had been shot at South Braintree? A. Yes, sir.

MR. KATZMANN. May I have those three shotgun shells?

Q. I show you Exhibit 37. Do you know what kind of game is shot with buck shot? A. I can't understand nothing about those.

Q. You say a friend and his wife came over to see you one day and he brought a shotgun? A. Yes.

Q. And he brought a box of cartridges? A. Yes, sir.

Q. And that there was some cartridges left when Vanzetti came to your house in May? A. Yes.

Q. But that before that you had been out shooting with that shotgun with this friend and his wife? A. The day he was over to the house... .

Q. What were you shooting at with shells like that? A. I did not shoot. He shot... .

Q. How big was the bird he was shooting with that kind of cartridge? A. I don't know. [1894]

Q. Is Exhibit 28 your gun? A. Well, it looks like it is a Colt.

Q. It is a Colt, .32, isn't it? A. Yes. It looks like mine.

Q. And are the **32 cartridges** making up Exhibit 31 the cartridges that were in your automatic and your pocket ["When you were arrested"]? A. Yes, sir.

Q. And you bought them all in one box, didn't you? A. Yes.

Q. It was a new box, wasn't it? A. No, sir.

Q. Was it opened when you bought it? A. I think so.

Q. Have you learned since I talked with you on May 6th that there are sixteen Peters, three Remingtons, seven United States, and six

Winchester cartridges in it? Have you learned that since you talked with me? A. I don't remember exactly.

Q. Did you tell me the truth on May 6th as to where you got those cartridges? A. No, sir... .

Q. You now say these 32 cartridges did not all come out of the same box?

A. Yes, come out of the same box. Not box,—open box.

Q. Open box? A. Yes.

Q. Not a new box? A. No.

Q. Where did you buy that gun? A. When I buy it?

Q. Where? A. Milford.

Q. In Milford. When, in Milford? A. In 1917 [in a "public store"]. [1895]

Q. And you went right in a store openly and bought it, didn't you?
A. Yes.

Q. There was nothing to conceal about that transaction, was there?
A. No, sir... .

Q. ... What is the reason you did not tell me the truth about it when I asked you at the Brockton police station? A. Probably I did not remember at the time... .

Q. Then if you did not remember and it was an open purchase in a store, why did you tell me an untruth about it? A. Well, I thought I buy in Boston.

Q. You thought you bought it in Boston? A. Yes.

Q. You just told me you did not remember that night when I asked you where you bought it. Well, let us see. Do you remember my asking you this question:

"Q. How long have you owned this automatic gun, revolver?
A. About two years."

Did you make that reply? A. Yes.

Q. Do you remember this next question:

"Q. Where did you get it? A. Boston."

Do you remember that reply? A. Yes.

Q. Was that statement you made true? A. No, sir.

Q. Did you know it was untrue when you made it to me? A. Yes, sir.

Q. Then it wasn't because you had forgotten, was it? A. [Witness hesitates.]

Q. Was it, Mr. Sacco? A. No, sir.

Q. Why did you falsify to me about such an innocent transaction as that?

A. Do you want me to answer that? [1896]

Q. I want you to answer it ... A. Because ... men could get one year imprisonment for that.

Q. You thought you could escape one year imprisonment when they found a revolver on you by saying you bought it in Boston instead of Milford. Do you mean that, Mr. Sacco?

A. Well, I don't think I did remember at that time... .

Q. Do you remember my then asking you:

"Q. Whereabouts in Boston?

And your reply:

"A. On Hanover Street, where they sell revolvers."

Did you say that to me? A. Yes. [1897]

Q. Was anybody forcing you to answer those questions?

A. There must be... .

Q. Do you remember my saying:

"My name, Mr. Sacco, is Mr. Katzmann, and I am the District Attorney in this district. You are under arrest, and you are not under obligation to speak or answer any questions that I ask you at all. I should like to ask you some questions, perhaps a good many. You may answer them or you may refuse to answer them and it is entirely your right to refuse. It is for you to decide. Whatever you may say may be used in court against you, but you are under no obligation whatever to answer any questions that I or anybody else here may ask you. Has the interpreter fully explained to you what I have said?"

Did I say that to you before I asked you more than, yes, the two questions?—[1] "Do you speak English? A. A little." [2]—"Would you like an interpreter? A. Yes, I would like,"—and then I started the question: "Mr. Minini is the interpreter," and said that to you. Isn't that true?

A. I remember that... . [N. B. Editor numbered and bracketed the two questions of May 6.]

Q. Did I say that in substance to you? A. Probably you did say, but I don't remember. [1898]

Q. Do you remember my then asking you:

"Q. What name did you give when you bought it [Colt .32]? A. I know I did not give my name, but I do not remember the name."

Did you say that? A. Yes, sir... . [1899]

Q.   Since you have owned that automatic, how many boxes of cartridges have you bought?

A. Two, I guess.

Q. Two. Do you remember my asking you then:

   "Q. Did you buy a new box of cartridges? A. Yes, a new box"

Did you say that? A. Yes.

Q. Was that true? A. No, sir.

Q. And why didn't you tell me the truth about that?

A. [Witness hesitates.] Probably I did not remember at that time... .

Q. Mr. Sacco, isn't the real reason why you now say it was not a new box because since May 6th you found out there was four different kinds of cartridges in the 32 of them...?

A. No. [1900]

Q. Do you remember my asking you then:

   "Q. An unopened box? A. It was a brand new box."

Did you tell me that? A. Probably I did. I don't remember.

Q. Was it true? A. It was not true, if I did... .

Q. Do you remember my asking you:

   "Q. Where did you buy the box that the cartridges came from that were in the gun when you were arrested? A. I don't remember."

Do you remember saying that? A. Yes.

Q. Was that true, that you did not remember? A. It was not true.

Q. You knew that that was on Hanover Street, didn't you? A. Yes... .

Q. If you told me the truth about that box, would it have helped to give us the names and addresses of the friends of yours who had the literature? A. No, sir. [1901]

Q. Did you buy a secondhand box of cartridges on Hanover Street?

A. No secondhand. But it was at the time of the war. You could not buy any cartridges if you paid $10 a box, so I just see,——I don't know, he took and mixed together and give me a box.

Q. Why didn't you tell me that that night [May 6]?

A. I don't know if I did remember at that time... .

Q. And you remember I asked you if it was a new box, don't you?

A. Yes.

Q. And an unopened box? A. Yes.

Q. And you could not remember that it was not, and you told me what was untrue, didn't you?

A. It was not true... . It was not true.

Q. It was not true. I have asked you why you told me that [May 6 statement: "a new box"]. Can you answer that question? A. I don't see the way I could answer... .

Q. Where did you carry the gun when that day you went out or you were going to go out and do some shooting in the woods with it? A. I put it over here [indicating].

Q. Did you go out of that house not knowing you had the gun in [1902] your pants,—the waistband in your pants? A. Well, I know I have it when I was going to shoot. Then I forgot.

Q. Yes. But did you have it in the waistband of your trousers when you sat down to supper? A. Yes. In the night.

Q. Yes. And then did you get up and go out to take the car [streetcar]? A. Yes.

Q. Didn't you know you had it in the waistband of your trousers, then? A. I forget... .

Q. Are you telling this jury that you were not aware of the fact when you left your house on May 5th that you had this gun tucked in here? Are you telling them that? A. Yes.

Q. Did not perceive the weight of it? A. No, sir. [1903]

Q. Did not notice it? A. No.

Q. Did not notice 22 extra cartridges in your pocket? A. No. [1904]

AFTERNOON SESSION. July 7, 1921.

THE COURT. Will the defendant Sacco please return to the witness stand.

Nicola Sacco,
Cross-Examination, Resumed.

Q. (By Mr. Katzmann) Under what name did you work at Rice & Hutchins' factory after you returned [from Mexico in September 1917]? A. Nicola Mosmacotelli. [1904]

Q. You saw Mrs. Ruth Johnson on the stand here, did you not and you now know her by name and by sight? A. Yes.

Q. On the night that I talked with you at Brockton, was she brought into the room where you and I were? A. Yes... . [1905]

Q.... . [D]id I ask you about that lady at the police station? A. Yes. [1907]

Q. And did you know when I was asking you that I was referring to the lady who walked by the motorcycle [near the Johnson house]? A. Yes.

Q. Did you tell me the truth about it? A. No, sir... .

Q. Then when I asked you this question, ... and I will ask you to tell me whether I did, ...

"Q. Didn't you see this lady and walk along the street and walk back when she walked back last night?"

Did I ask you that question? A. Yes.

Q. Did you say,

"A. No, sir, we walk about an hour and we did not see anything?"

Did you tell me that? A. Yes, sir.

Q. That was false, wasn't it? A. Yes, it was false.

Q. Do you remember this question: ...

"Q. This woman that was sitting in here [Brockton police station] says you followed her across the street last night when she went to a neighbor's house and that you walked up and down and that she knows you. Why don't you tell the truth?"

Did I ask you that question? A. Yes.

Q. Did you say, "That is not true"? A. Yes.

Q. It was true, wasn't it? A. **It was not true I followed her**... . [1908]

Q. Do you remember my asking you this question:

"Q. This woman never saw you before. Why should she lie about you?"

and your answer,

"A. Well, maybe somebody else and she wants to blame me."

Was it somebody,—did you make that answer? A. Yes, I did.

Q. Was it somebody else that was there or was it yourself? A. That was myself... .

Q. Did you say yesterday that on the 4th of May, Tuesday, when you came out with your passport, that you went to Orcciani's house? A. Yes.

Q. And that you went there for the purpose of getting a message from Boda? A. Yes.

Q. About his car? A. Yes.

Q. It is a fact, isn't it, that you knew Boda for three years before you were arrested, that is true, that you knew him well? A. Not very much.

Q. Where did he live May 5, 1920? A. I don't know.

Q. Are you certain you did not know? A. Well, why, I hear he was living with Coacci. [1909]

Q. Then my question is, the night that you were arrested did you then know that night where Boda lived? A. No, sir.... .

Q. Had you known before that night that at one time he lived in Hyde Park with Orcciani?

A. No, sir.

Q. Had you been to Orcciani's house before May 4th? A. No.

Q. That was the first time? A. Yes.

Q. How did you know where to go? A. He been telling me lots of times he live between Hyde Park and Readville, River Street. [Ed. Hyde Park, 1.2 miles n/e of Readville, is part of Boston.]

Q. You don't mean that, do you? A. Yes... .

Q. Do you remember my asking you at Brockton on May 6th:
    "Q. Did you ever go to Ricardo's house in Hyde Park?"
You know who Ricardo is? A. Yes. [1910]

Q. That is Orcciani? A. Yes... .

Q. Do you remember your answer? A. Yes.

Q. What was it? A. "Yes."

Q. You told me you had been? A. Yes.

Q. Didn't I say,—didn't you reply to that question:
    "Q. Did you ever go to Ricardo's house in Hyde Park? A. No."
Didn't you say that to me? A. If I say, it was false.

Q. Did you say it? A. Probably I did.

Q. And that was another falsehood, wasn't it? A. Yes.

Q. You knew that we had Orcciani under arrest right then and there, didn't you? A. Yes, sir.

Q. Could falsifying about whether you had been to his house help him at all then? A. Sure.

Q. How? A. Because he had literature just as much as I had... .

Q. But we had him there [at Brockton police station], didn't we?

A. Yes.

Q. ... Didn't you talk with him before you talked with me down in the cell room?

A. No, sir. I says some words, I says, that is all... .

Q. Didn't he tell you we had gotten [arrested] him that day out of the foundry in Norwood?

A. I do not remember if he did tell me... .

Q. And before you ever saw me upstairs, hadn't you been looked over by thirty or thirty-five people, as you said yesterday? A. One day.

Q. That day before you saw me [May 6, before Katzmann saw Sacco that night]? A. Yes.

Q. And you did not know what we had you there for? A. No... .

Q. Didn't have any idea when I asked you if you knew Berardelli, and you said: "No. Who is this Berardelli?" A. Well, fellows read one day the paper. He could not remember. [1911]

Q. Did I ask you if you ever worked in Braintree? A. I think you did.

Q. Did you forget about that, Mr. Sacco? A. No... .

Q. Did you falsify about it? A. Yes.

Q. Why, Mr. Sacco? A. Because I am not registered. I am a slacker. Then, another thing, I don't want you to find that literature and then I won't be in trouble, that is all.

Q. Are you telling this jury you falsified about ever working in Braintree because you were a slacker? A. Yes, sir. [1912]

Q. Did I ask you anything about socialistic or anarchistic literature? A. No, sir... .

Q. Did Mr. Kelley, father of the Kelley boys, ... come to see you at the Brockton police station on the day of May 6th? A. Yes, sir.

Q. Did you then know what you were under arrest for? A. No, sir. [1913]

Q. Did he [Kelley] ask you what you were being held for? A. I guess, "I am surprised, Nick, you been here." That is all.

Q. Did you tell him ... that you were charged with being a murderer? A. No, sir.

Q. You are sure of that? A. I am very sure.

Q. If Mr. Kelley walked out on the street and said anything about your being charged with that, he did not get it from you? A. No, sir... .

Q. What time did you go to the lower court the first time you went there after your arrest?

A. I think about ten o'clock.

Q. Wasn't it May 6th? A. Was it May 6th? I forget.

Q. Don't you know what you were there charged with the first day?

A. Yes.

Q. What? A. For the revolver.

Q. What did you say when you were asked as to whether you were guilty of carrying a revolver without a license?

A. I said I was guilty... . [1914]

Q. Didn't you then say to the Judge? "I did not know I had to have a license to carry a revolver"? A. I don't remember that.... .

Q. If you did say it, was it true? A. Not true. [1915]

Q. Do you remember my asking you at Brockton if you knew Mike Boda? A. Yes.

Q. Do you remember saying:

"A. No, sir, I never heard of him."

A. Yes, sir. [Ed. Sacco's next answer: "I don't even think it is an Italian name."] [1916]

Q. Have you been sick very much since you worked for the 3-K?

A. About three or four weeks.

Q. All at one time? A. Yes, right along.

Q. Christmas, 1919? A. Yes.... . [1919]

Q. You said this morning in your direct examination, ... that they [witnesses at Brockton jail] made you stoop down and point and,—as if pointing a revolver? A. Yes. [Ed. See p. 360 in this book.]

Q. Did you think that had anything to do with collecting [anarchist] books? A. No, sir.

Q. Or papers? A. No, sir.

Q. Or Radicalism? A. No, sir.... . [1922]

[Short Recess.]

Q. I show you a cap. Will you look it over, please, and tell me if you know whose cap that is?

MR. MOORE. May—

[Mr. Moore confers with the Court.] [1927]

THE COURT. You may answer the question.

Q. It is all right now. A. It looks like my cap.

[Ed. Lt. Guerin took this cap from Sacco's house on May 6. See Moore's protest, p. 2093.]

Q. Yes. Did you have such a cap as that in your house at the time of your arrest?

A. Yes, sir, something like.... .

Q. Isn't it your cap? A. I think it is my cap, yes.... .

Q. Will you try that cap on, please, and watch yourself when you put it on, just how you put it on? A. [Witness does so.]

Q. Will you turn around so the jury can see, all the way, please?

A. [Witness does so.]

Q. The other side, this side. Is there anything you want to say? Did I catch you as wanting to say something? ... A. I don't know. That cap looks too dirty to me because I never wear dirty cap. I think I always have fifty cents to buy a cap, ... I always keep clean cap ... It look to me pretty dirty and too dark. Mine I think was little more light, little more gray... .

Q. Put it on again and keep it buttoned, will you, please? A. Sure. [Doing so.]

Q. On pretty hard? A. No, well, all right.

Q. All right. Now, will you try— A. Not very loose.

Q. Not very loose? A. No.

Q. Will you try Exhibit 29 on, and use the same amount of force [1928] in putting it on that you used in putting that [Guerin] hat on? A. Yes. [Doing so.] Can't go in...

[Ed. Exhibit 29 is the Loring cap.]

Q. Try and pull it down in back and see if it can't go in? A. Oh, but it is too tight.

Q. What is the difference in size between those two hats? A. I don't know, but it looks that is tight to me... .

MR. KATZMANN. I will offer this hat. I can't offer it now, but I ask it be marked for identification.

[Cap marked "Exhibit 27 for identification."] [Ed. This is the Guerin cap, the lining of which had a hole in it. Three times (1929) Sacco denied knowledge of this hole.] [1929] [See Fraenkel, p. 383.]

Q. Did you tell the officers [at Brockton police station] you[r] real purpose of the going to West Bridgewater was to see Pappi? A. Yes.

Q. That he was a friend of Vanzetti's?

THE COURT. Did you say that to the officers?

THE WITNESS. That is what he [Vanzetti, presumably] told me.

Q. Did you have any intention of seeing Pappi that night? A. Me?

Q. Yes. A. No, sir.

Q. That was an utter falsehood, wasn't it? A. Yes.

[The last three questions and answers are read.] [1930] [Ed. Brackets, at left, in Transcript.]

Q. Do you know how far the Coacci house is from Elm Square? A. No, sir.

Q. Did Boda tell you when he came to your house in the afternoon of May 5th where he had come from? A. No, sir.

Q. Did he come in Orcciani's motorcycle to your house?

A. Yes, sir.... [1931]

Q. Had you ever tried it on [Loring cap] before you tried it on when the jury was here?

A. No, sir... .[1932]

Q. All right. You are sure? A. Yes. I think I did try. I was sitting over there with Vanzetti.

Q. And **the jury was not in** here then, were they? A. No, sir... .

Q. Have your lawyers had, to your knowledge, in this court room any letter that you received from your father announcing your mother's death? A. Yes.

Q. What was the date of that letter? A. I don't remember the date, the day when it came.

Q. No. What was the date that it was written? A. Printed?

Q. Yes. A. It reached my house, you mean?

Q. No, no. What was the day your father said he was writing it? What date did he put on that letter? A. Oh, I could not remember, Mr. Katzmann, but I think he wrote me after a couple of days my mother died. My mother died on the 7th of March. I think he wrote me a couple of days after. I got one from my brother Sabeno. He wrote me, I guess, the same night the funeral of my mother.

Q. Then I suppose you got those letters about the same time, didn't you?

A. Yes, I think I got my father's letter pretty near a week later... .

Q. When do you say your father's letter came? A. I should say sometime the last March.

Q.... You mean a year ago last March? A. Yes.

Q. What time in that March [1920]? A. 23d or 24th.

Q. 23d or 24th. Are you pretty sure of that? A. No, I wouldn't say sure. [1933]

Q. In what studio did you have the picture taken that was attached to the Andrower deposition? A. Brockton... .

[Ed. See Adrower on Foglio Di Via and see Moore in Reply to Rebuttal.]

Q. ... When did you have those pictures taken, near what time?

A. Before my mother died. I guess sometime in March.

Q. What did you have them taken for? A. To send to my mother, because she was very sick.

Q. Where did you have the pictures taken that were on the Foglio di via? A. Stoughton.

Q. When? A. After the 15th of April, when I come back from Boston.

Q. What is the photographer's name? A. I do not know his name. He got a studio ... on the top of the Brockton market, on South Stoughton Place... .

Q. See if I read it right. "Neville"—N-e-v-i-l-l-e, photographer, 63 Main Street, Richmond Building, Brockton, Massachusetts." A. Yes. [1934]

["The large photograph that he [Sacco] had said he carried with him {to the Italian consulate} had been taken by a Brockton photographer named Neville." Ehrmann, The Case That Will Not Die, p. 363]

Q. How many times in all did you go to the consul's office in Boston about your passport in 1920? A. Three times... .

[Ed. See Sacco's testimony below on the **second time**, April 15.]

Q. When were they? A. I do not remember the first time, the day, but there was something the last of March or beginning of April. I wouldn't say yes, because Mr. Kelley said the 8th of April.

Q. Never mind what Mr. Kelley says. What would you say?

A. I do not member. I think it [first visit] was sometime in the **last of March**. [1935]

Q. ... When did you get them in the house, I mean the Brockton picture, the big one?

A. Yes. The beginning of March, I guess... .

Q. Was it before your mother died? A. Yes... .

Q. Are you certain of it? A. Well, of course, I don't know my mother was died the 7th of March, because I was in this country and my mother died in Italy. I waited for the answer to my letter. Probably my mother is died when I have that photograph all ready to send; was dead already, probably. [1936]

Q. Now, the **first** visit in to the consul's office, they said you would need a photograph? A. Yes.

Q. Did they tell you how large the photograph was [on the first visit]? A. No.

Q. Did they tell you where it was to go? A. No. [1938]

Q. Hadn't you ever seen a passport when you came in 1908? A. Yes.

Q. Didn't you know the size of the photograph that was attached to that?

A. I didn't see no photograph on my passport... .

Q. Didn't they tell you, Sacco, the **first time** you went in that it would have to be a photograph that would go in the corner of that Foglio di Via? A. No, they did not... .

Q. They did not say a word to you about the size? A. No, sir... .

Q. At the consul's office they let you come in and go away without giving you any information as to the size of the photograph? A. Yes, sir.

Q. [D]id you go for information the **second time**? A. No, sir. I brought in the [See "big picture" on p. 348.] photograph.

Q. What train do you say you took to go in that day [April 15, 1920]? A. I think it was about 8:46 or 8:56.

Q. What time did that train get to Boston? A. ... [A]bout twenty-five minutes to ten. [1939]

Q. Why didn't you go up to the consul's office in the morning and take the noon train out?

A. Well, I think to pass all day when I been in Boston. I think better stay here... .

Q ... [D]id you tell George Kelley the next morning that there was such a crowd in there you could not get your passport and the place closed and you missed the noon train for that reason? A. Yes, I did. [See George Kelley, p. 128.]

Q. That was another falsehood, wasn't it? A. That was an excuse.

Q. It was a falsehood, wasn't it? A. Yes... . [1942]

Q. You said yesterday, didn't you, Mr. Sacco, to your counsel, or to [1944] your counsel's questions, that when you talked with me ... that night, the night you talked with me there was no talk between us about any particular crime. Is that right? A. Yes... . [1945]

Q. Do you remember my then asking you this question:

"Q. Did you ever hear about anything happening in Braintree in the last month?"

And your answer:

"A. "Yes."

A. I don't know if I did say that... .

Q. Do you remember after I said:

"Q. Did you hear anything about what happened in Braintree?"

I then said "What?" And you said:

"I read there was bandits robbing money."

Do you remember that answer? A. Yes, I do.

Q. That is true, isn't it? A. Yes... .

Q. Do you remember my asking then:
   "Q. Where?"
And you said:
   "A. In the Boston Post."
A. Well, probably I did, but I wouldn't say it was Boston Post or
Boston Globe.
Q. Do you remember my then asking you:
   "Q. Where did they rob the money?"
And your answer:
   "A. Over near Rice & Hutchins. I don't read English very good,
but there was bandits in Braintree, and I think it was at Rice &
Hutchins."
Did you say that? A. I think I did.
Q. We were not talking about any crime when you and I talked
together? Do you still say that?
A. I remember you asked me if I did work in April 15th... . [1946]
Q. What did you think the thirty people or so were looking at you for?
A. I was thinking they were looking for some crime, now, anyway.
Q. Some crime? A. Sure.
Q. And wasn't this the only crime I talked with you about, what
happened at Rice & Hutchins the month before? A. No. You asked
me if I was working in,—you asked me some other questions.
I don't remember now. I don't remember... .
Q. And do you remember the next question:
   "Q. Were you working the day before you read it in the papers?"
And you said, and your answer:
   "A. I think I did."
Did you say that? A. Yes, sir.
Q. And do you remember the next question:
   "Q. Well, do you know?"
And your answer:
   "A. Sure." [1947]
Q. Will you say you did not say it ["Sure"]? A. Probably I did... .
Q. And do you remember the next question, after you had said "Sure."
   "Q. Worked all day? A. Yes, sir."
Did you make that answer to me? A. Well, I did, I guess.
Q. And it was true, was it? A. No, sir.
Q. It was false? A. It was false if I did say it.

Q. And why did you tell me that falsehood, Mr. Sacco? A. Well, of course, I never remember...

Q. If you were in Boston on the 15th day of April, getting your passports, why didn't you tell me that the night I talked with you at Brockton? A. If I could remember I would tell you it right off... . [1948]

Q. You don't get it yet. When I asked you the question:

"Q. Did you ever hear anything about anything happening in Braintree in the last month?"

That means April? A. Yes.

Q. Did you reply, "Yes"? A. Yes.

Q. You knew what I meant, then, didn't you? A. Well, yes.

Q. You knew I was talking about the South Braintree murder, didn't you? A. Yes.

THE COURT. We will stop here until to-morrow morning. [1949]

July 8, 1921.

THE COURT. ... Let Mr. Sacco return to the stand, please. [1949]

Nicola Sacco,
Cross-Examination, Resumed.

THE WITNESS. Oh, excuse me, I like to say, Judge, to get the interpreter. I have been thinking yesterday I did make some mistake. I understand wrong. I think I would like to have the interpreter if I could... .

THE COURT. Why didn't you tell me so yesterday?

THE WITNESS. I been thinking over last night. I did answer something wrong. Probably I did not understand something.

THE COURT. The only thing I regret,—I told you at the beginning if there was any question you did not understand, to let me know and I would see that you did understand. I regret that you did not. Let Mr. Ross come forward... .

[The following testimony is given through interpreter.] ... [1950]

Q. (By Mr. Katzmann) If you told me you worked the day before you read it [item on Braintree crime] in the paper were you telling me the truth? A. I told you a lie. [1954]

378

Q. All right. Have you just said before we started this discussion about an interpreter that I did not ask you this question:

"Q. Did you ever take a whole day off in April to look for your passport all day?

A. I don't recall. [1956]

[Ed. Debate on competence of interpreter Mr. Ross is on p. 1957.]

THE COURT. Put the question so that he may understand it.

Q. If you made this answer [to the question: Did you ever take a whole day off in April to get your passport …?], was it true:

"A. I think either Tuesday or Wednesday."

If you made that answer, was it true, "I think either Tuesday or Wednesday"? [1958]

MR. JEREMIAH McANARNEY. Mr. Ross, will you ask the defendant to speak loud so we can hear him?

MR. ROSS. Yes.

THE WITNESS. You said Tuesday or Wednesday?

Q. Yes. I ask if you said that to me? A. I don't remember that I said either of those days, but I remember that I said to you that that week I was out all day.

Q. What week? A. Well, I mean the week between the 15th day of April and the 18th.

Q. Did I then ask you:

"Q. Is that true, Mr. Sacco?"

That is the date you and I were talking about, the date between the 15th and the 18th of April. Is that was [what] you said to me? A. I don't remember if I said it that way to you. I said that I was out twice, but as to you asked me if I was out a full day, I don't remember if you asked me that.

Q. Do you remember my asking you this question:

"Q. What Tuesday or Wednesday in April?"

A. I don't remember if you said that.

Q. Do you say I did not? A. Perhaps you said it… .

Q. Did you make this reply, if I asked you such question? Put that to him and I will give you the question.

[The interpreter talks to the witness.]

Q. "A. Well, I don't remember. Either the 5th or the 8th or 10th. I don't remember, I can't say for sure."

That is only part of the answer. That is only part of the answer. And was this the remainder of the answer?

379

THE COURT. What was the answer to that part?

MR. KATZMANN. All right. It was only part of the question. It was so long I did not suppose Mr. Ross could carry it. What is the answer so far?

THE WITNESS. Perhaps I have said it, but I don't remember it.

Q. And did you make in answer the following reply?

"A. This was in April I lost a day to fill out the income tax and I don't remember, but I can tell it from the factory the day I was out a full day."

A. No, I did not say that. I never answered, I never gave you that answer.... [1959]

Q.... . Did you tell me it was the beginning of the month of April?

A. Yes.

Q. And that that was the only day you were out a full day. Did you tell me that? A. No, sir.

Q. You are sure of that, are you?

A. I am sure. I am sure, because at that time I was not away all day.

Q. Did you shave this morning? A. Yes, sir.

Q. Have you shaved every day since this trial opened? A. Yes, sir.

MR. KATZMANN. That is all, sir. [1961]

Redirect Examination.

Q. (By Mr. Moore) Mr. Sacco, in the questioning of yourself by Mr. Katzmann at the police station in Brockton, with reference to whether or not you were working on April 15th, did you refer at that time to the matter of passports? A. Yes, at that time. If I told him I was out of the factory all day, that was for the reason that I went out to get my passport. I told him that I was out several days. Pardon me, several times,——regarding looking for my passport.

Q. Well, ... did you, at that time, Mr. Sacco, give Mr. Katzmann a definite date as to when you were out? A. No, sir, I did not. I could not remember.

Q. Why didn't you give him a definite date? A. Because I did not remember. [1961]

Q. Mr. Sacco, on April 15th or any time during the month of April, or in the month of May, or any time did you ever visit the home of ... this man that has been referred to here as Boda?

A. Never.

Q. Now, did you know at any time the place or town where this man Boda lived?

A. Never, I never did for certain. [1963]

Q. Now, Mr. Sacco, your mother died on what date? A. The 7th day of March.

Q. What was the first you learned,—when was the first that you learned of her death?

A. The first letter I received from my brother Sabeno the 23d or 24th of March.

Q. When was the next word that you received? A. After I received a letter from my father the beginning of April that my mother was dead. [1964]

Q. ... The letter sent immediately after the death of your mother and that you have referred to as around March 23d or 24th, what was done with that letter, if you know?

A. Well, I sent those letters to Mr. Callahan. I did not send them, but, as I understand, my wife, she sent them to Mr. Callahan.... .

Q. Mr. Sacco, did you show Mr. Kelley a letter? A. Yes. [1965]

Q. Who was that letter from? A. That came from my father.

Q. The first letter announcing the death of your mother came from whom? A. From my brother Sabeno.

Q. The second letter came from whom? A. The second letter that I got said my mother was dead came from my father. It was a black letter.... . [Ed. In a black band to signify mourning.]

Q. What letter was it, the first or the second letter, that you showed to Mr. Kelley announcing the death of your mother? A. That is the one from my father, the second letter. [1966]

Recross-Examination.

Q. (By Mr. Katzmann) Did you see a black bordered letter handed to George T. Kelley in his cross-examination? [Ed. See Recross (omitted by editor), pp. 872-873] A. You mean the son or the father?

Q. The son, George? A. I think so. I think yes.

Q. Did you recognize it from the black border? A. I think so.

Q. Was that the letter from your father? A. Yes, sir.

Q. The letter announcing your mother's death? A. Yes.

Q. Where is that letter? A. The first letter?

381

Q. No, the letter from your father, the black letter? A. My wife, she does not remember, she is not sure whether she gave it to Mr. Callahan [1969] the first lawyer, or not. She looked for it in the house. She could not find it.

MR. KATZMANN. I ask that be stricken out, if your Honor please. I am not talking about that letter.

THE COURT. That may be stricken out.

Q. Where is the black bordered letter ... shown to George Kelley when he was on the stand in this court room?

A. ... I know that my lawyer, Mr. Moore, had the letter but I don't know other than that... .

[Ed. Fraenkel, p. 72: "The original letter from his father announcing his mother's death had apparently been lost and was not produced."]

Q. You mean the letter ... shown to George Kelley ... from your father announcing your mother's death? A. That cannot be the first one.

Q. Why can't it be the first one? A. Because the date is pretty late... .

Q. Referring to the letter that was shown to Mr. Kelley in the court [1970] room, did you make your first visit to the [Italian] consul's before or after you got that letter?

A. The first visit was before that letter.

Q. How long before? A. I don't remember if it was between the last part of March and the first part of April.

Q. No. That does not answer the question. How long was it before you got that letter that you first went to the consul's office? A. I don't remember.

MR. KATZMANN. That is all... .

MR. JEREMIAH McANARNEY. ... I have a motion to present to the Court which may entail some discussion, and ... whether you wish me to make it in the presence of the jury or not.

[The jury retire from the court room.]

THE COURT. May I see the motion, please? Is it in writing?

[Mr. McAnarney hands motion to the Clerk, who hands it to the Court.]

MR. JEREMIAH McANARNEY. I have shown it to Mr. Katzmann, if your Honor please. That I offer if your Honor please.

[The Clerk puts filing stamp on motion.]

MR. JEREMIAH McANARNEY. [Reading.]

"COMMOMWEALTH vs. NICOLA SACCO.
COMMONWEALTH vs. BARTOLOMEO VANZETTI.

Now comes the defendant Vanzetti and renews his motion previously filed for a severance and separate trial in the above indictments and proceedings.

By his attorneys,
J. J. McANARNEY.
THOMAS McANARNEY."

THE COURT. I will hear you, Mr. McAnarney.

MR. JEREMIAH McANARNEY. At the onset, at the beginning of these [1971] cases, as counsel for the defendant Vanzetti I was apprehensive and fearful of what might transpire during this case were it tried in conjunction with the indictment against Nicola Sacco, and meeting that situation we filed a motion for severance and separate trial. At that time, in the informal discussion before your Honor, mention was made that if at any time during the trial things should occur we could renew the motion. It now seems to me ... fitting in view of all the evidence on this record ... that the motion be granted for a severance of these cases, and I now offer that motion.

THE COURT. Won't you tell me wherein there is anything that is prejudicial to the defendant Vanzetti if they are tried together and proper instructions are given to the jury?

MR. JEREMIAH McANARNEY. I do not feel,—in fact, reversing that, I do feel that it would be absolutely impossible under the most careful and earnest instructions that your Honor could give this jury to eliminate from their minds what has transpired up to the present time.

THE COURT. It may be possible that I ought not to have asked you that question. I will have you come to the desk, and counsel may come to the bench.

[Conference at bench between Court and counsel.
[Noon recess.]

[Ed. Vanzetti's illness announced at start of afternoon session, July 8.]
[Adjourned to Saturday, July 9, 1921, at 9:30 a.m.] [1972]

Saturday, July 9, 1921.
Nicola Sacco,
Redirect Examination, Resumed.

Q. (By Mr. Moore) Mr. Sacco, on May 5th and previous thereto, had you had books in your house?
A. Yes, sir. [Ed. These are books on anarchism.]
Q. I call your attention to these books individually and ask you if that [indicating] was in your house ... previous to May 5th and on the date of May 5th? A. Yes.
[Ed. Same question and same answer on two more books.]
MR. MOORE. I ask these all be marked for identification.... .
[Three books are marked, "Exhibit 28 for identification," "Exhibit 29 for identification," and "Exhibit 30 for identification."] [1973]

Nicola Sacco.

Redirect Examination.

MR. JEREMIAH McANARNEY. While the witness is on the stand, if your Honor please, I desire to offer a copy of the record of the court in Quincy, relative——
(Mr. McAnarney shows record to Mr. Katzmann and the Court.)
wherein it appears that Nicola Sacco was charged on a complaint made out the 11th day of May, 1920, charging him with the assault and intent to murder at Braintree, April 15th.
(The record is admitted in evidence and marked "Exhibit R.")
THE COURT. All you gave me was assault with intent to murder.
MR. JEREMIAH McANARNEY. I did not go into detail. I will give it.
THE COURT. I mean, assault with intent to murder whom?
MR. JEREMIAH McANARNEY. Alessandro Berardelli.... . I will read it.
THE COURT. That was all I wanted.... . [1974]
Q. (By Mr. Jeremiah McAnarney) Who in your family first informed you of your mother's death? A. My brother Sabeno.
Q. And when did that letter arrive in Stoughton? I mean, about when?
A. The best that I could tell, it was between the last part of March and the first part of April.

Q. Was that letter a letter in a white envelope or did it have the black mourning on it?

A. It was in mourning,—black.

Q. When did you **next** receive a letter from your folks after that letter?

A. I do not remember the date or the day exactly, but to the best of my memory it was the last part of April.... .

Q. Which letter of the two did you show to Mr. Kelley? A. It was [1975] the first letter that I received, and receiving that letter I was unable to work for a half day. I was disabled.... .

MR. JEREMIAH McANARNEY. I am going to offer the letter and the translation I will offer later as quick as it is typewritten, and I formally offer this as a piece of evidence.

THE COURT. All right.

MR. KATZMANN. May I see it?

(Mr. McAnarney shows letter to Mr. Katzmann.)

(Letter from Sabeno Sacco to Nicola Sacco, with black bordered envelope, admitted in evidence and marked "Exhibit S".) [1976]

Q. While you were seated in the dock the other day, did you call my attention to something?

A. Yes, sir.

Q. Did you point out a man to me who was seated on the front row?

A. Yes, sir.

Q. And did you tell me you thought that man was a man who came on the train from Boston with you on the 15th day of April? [1977]

[Ed. After a dispute, Sacco answered "Yes, sir" on p. 1978. McAnarney's last three questions on July 9 prepare jury for testimony of James Hayes (alibi witness #9) on July 11. Court gave McAnarney right to recall Sacco "when Mr. Hayes arrives."] [1979]

George T. Kelley, Recalled. July 11, 1921.

[Ed. Kelley's Recall precedes testimony of Hayes, p. 2014, and Affe, p. 2033.]

Q. (By Mr. Jeremiah McAnarney) Mr. Kelley, I show you Exhibit 29 in the record and Exhibit 27, and ask you to examine both caps and see which appears more like the cap which you saw in your factory as being the one that Sacco used to wear, ...? A. [Witness examines cap, hanging one of the caps on a hook on the door and leaves the witness stand to look at it.]

Q. Which cap appears more like the one you saw Sacco have? A. If this cap here [indicating] was just a shade dirtier, I should say that would look more like it than it would be by hanging that one up there and looking at it. The cap I had reference to wasn't as dark as this particular cap [indicating], and this one [indicating] is just a hair lighter, and I would say offhand, that it looked, to the best of my recollection now, this one [indicating] is my idea of a salt and pepper if it was a little bit soiled. You understand?

Q. You think Nick's hat was somewhat soiled? A. I was of the [2003] opinion it had been used a little bit more than that. That is, through natural wear... .

Q. Take it as it is. A. I would give that cap there [indicating] the preference.

MR. JEREMIAH McANARNEY. The witness indicates cap Exhibit 27. [Ed. The Guerin cap marked Exhibit 27 on p. 1929] [2004]

Q. Don't answer this question if it is objected to. Did you have a...conversation with Sacco wherein you informed him that his activities were being investigated [by authorities]?

MR. KATZMANN. To that I object... .

Q. You may answer that yes or no. A. Yes. [2006]

Cross-Examination.

Q. (By Mr. Katzmann)... [Y]ou and Mr. Sacco, during the two or three years that he lived near the 3-K factory, were intimate friends, were you not? A. Yes, sir.

Q. Is it not the fact that you were over in his house a great many times? A. I don't understand what you mean by "a great many." ... .

Q. Frequently? A. Frequently, yes.

Q. Is it the fact frequently he had been in your house? A. Yes.

Q. And you were fond of him, weren't you, as man to man? A. Yes, sir... .

Q. Is Exhibit 27 for identification salt and pepper? A. No, sir.

Q. Is Exhibit 29 salt and pepper? A. No, sir. [2007]

Redirect Examination.

Q. (By Mr. Jeremiah McAnarney) Taking the two caps, … is there any explanation you want to make …? A. Either one of those caps does not come up to my idea of salt and pepper, …

Q. Kindly explain what you mean. A. The cap I had reference to as salt and pepper in my testimony was a heavier, fuzzier material with black, white, green set right out there prominent, and soiled, dark in color from being soiled. [2008]

Recross-Examination.

Q. (By Mr. Katzmann) Mr. Kelley, do you remember a week or so before the opening of the trial, having a conversation with Officers Stewart and Brouillard? A. Yes. [2009]

Q. And at the time did they ask you to describe Sacco's cap without showing you a cap? A. Yes.

Q. Then after you had described a cap which you had seen the defendant Sacco wear, did they produce that dark cap? A. Yes, sir.

Q. Did you then say to them, "Well, I described it pretty well, didn't I?" A. Yes, sir.

MR. KATZMANN. [To the jury.] I just want you gentlemen to hear this question. I don't want to speak it out loud. The reason will be obvious.

Q. Did you then say to them,—did they say to you,"Is that Sacco's cap?" referring to the dark cap? A. Yes.

Q. Did you then say, "I have my opinion about the cap, but I don't want to get a bomb up my ass." Did you then say that? "I have my opinion about the cap, but I don't want to [get a] bomb up my ass." Did you then say that to those officers? A. I might have… .

MR. JEREMIAH McANARNEY. That question is objected to, if your Honor please.

THE COURT. Yes.

MR. JEREMIAH McANARNEY. And exception noted.

Q. Didn't you, Mr. Kelley? A. Sometime during the conversation, but not then.

Q. Sometime during the conversation? A. Yes, sir.

Q. They asked you to give a definite answer, "Is it or is it not his cap?" A. Yes, they asked me.

Q. Didn't you reply on each occasion, "I have my opinion about the cap, but I don't want to get a bomb up my ass"? A. That part I can't remember.
Q. Do you say you did not say that? A. I said the last part there. I might have said it when they drove off, but not at the time when they showed me the cap.
Q. Was that in reference to the cap? A. Yes.
Q. When you made the remark? A. Yes, surely. [2010]

Nicola Sacco, Recalled. July 11, 1921.

[The testimony is given through the interpreter.]
[Ed. Testimony of Hayes concludes on p. 2021, the page on which Sacco's Recall begins.]
Q. (By Mr. Jeremiah McAnarney) Mr. Sacco, where did you see this man [Mr. Hayes]?
A.... I remember that I have seen him the 15th day of April in Boston.
Q. Well, where did you see him? A. I saw him on the train coming home to my house. [2021]

Recross-Examination.

Q. (By Mr. Katzmann) What car [of the train] did you ride out in?
A. I don't remember....
Q. On what side of the coach did you sit?
A. I remember that I sat on my right, as you go to Stoughton.
Q. ... [H]ow far from the front or how far from the rear. Locate the seat. A. About the centre.
Q. Where did this man [Hayes] sit you are now speaking of?
A. On the left, right aside of me.
Q. On the aisle side of the seat? That is, next to the aisle? A. Near the aisle, on the side.
Q. And where were you sitting? Next to the aisle or next to the window in your seat?
A. I was sitting near the aisle. [2022]
Q. Was there any particular occasion for you to look at the man who was seated at your left on this particular trip? A. Nothing, no occasion, well—

MR. JEREMIAH McANARNEY. Mr. Sacco, will you please talk louder. We cannot hear you.

THE WITNESS. No, there wasn't any occasion, but he got off at the same place where I did, and I noticed his face and I remember faces.

Q. Was there anybody else who got off at the Stoughton depot besides yourself?

A. Yes, sir, there were others.

Q. How many? A. I don't remember.

Q. Describe what any other person looked like who got off at the Stoughton station that day.

A. I cannot do it, because I don't remember.

MR. KATZMANN. That is all.

MR. JEREMIAH McANARNEY. That is all. Tell the officer to bring Mr. Hayes back for one question. [2023]

James Matthew Hayes,
Cross-Examination, Resumed.

Q. (By Mr. Katzmann) … Do you remember, Mr. Hayes, in what coach you came out?

A. It seems to me I came out along in the middle of the train… .

Q. And whereabouts in the car? A. About midway in the car.

Q. And on which side of the seat? A. On the inside of the seat.

Q. That is, next to the window or next to the aisle? A. Next to the aisle.

Q. Have you talked this over with Mr. Sacco before he took the stand? A. No, sir.

Q. Or his counsel? A. No, sir.

Q. Has anybody asked you before I asked you in which part of the coach you were seated?

A. No. [2023]

Q. Was there anybody seated opposite to you? A. Yes, sir.

Q. Who was it? A. I don't know.

Q. Did you look at him? A. No, sir.

Q. Was it a man or a woman?

A. I don't know that. I know that the seats opposite me were full. I have that recollection… .

Q. Did he [Mr. Woodbury] know you by name? [Ed. Woodbury an investigator for Fred Moore.]

389

A. No, sir. Yes, he did know me by name. That is, he asked me if I was Hayes.

Q. Had you ever met him before? A. Never saw the man before.

MR. KATZMANN. I think that is all.... [2024]

MR. JEREMIAH McANARNEY. At this time I want to state that by agreement with the District Attorney it is agreed to go into the record and may be considered as evidence that the party mentioned as Coacci, with whom there is some evidence that Boda at one time boarded, was taken on deportation process on the 16th. On the 17th was taken to New York, and on the 18th was put aboard a boat under the deportation order. That is 1920, the year.... [2032]

[Conference at the bench between Court and counsel.]

MR. JEREMIAH McANARNEY. It is further agreed, gentlemen, and may appear on the record in connection with the agreement of Mr. Coacci, that Coacci's family, to wit, his wife, and the personal effects of the house, were moved from the place in West Bridgewater where he had resided to some place in Boston.

MR. KATZMANN. State that place.

MR. JEREMIAH McANARNEY. I don't know where.

MR. KATZMANN. Corner of Lincoln and Elm Streets.

MR. JEREMIAH McANARNEY. Yes, moved from where he lived in West Bridgewater, and Mr. Katzmann says corner of Lincoln and Elm streets, to some place in Boston.

MR. KATZMANN. Lincoln and South Elm.

MR. JEREMIAH McANARNEY: Lincoln and South Elm. [By old map, in or near Cochesett.]

MR. KATZMANN. West Bridgewater. [2033] [Ed. See map: Escape and Arrest.]

30. FINAL WITNESSES

Mrs. Rose Sacco, Sworn. July 11, 1921.

Q. (By Mr. Jeremiah McAnarney) What is your name? A. Rose Sacco.

Q. And you are the wife of Nicola Sacco? A. Yes. [2052]

Q. ... When is it, Mrs. Sacco, if you recall, that your husband got word of his mother's death? A. Sometimes in the last of March and the beginning of April, something like that, ...

Q. Who wrote that letter? A. His brother. [2053]

Q. You said that before this [word of his mother's death] some arrangement had been made about going to Italy. A. Yes.

Q. Well, I will try to get along without an interpreter. Had your husband been to Boston to do anything about going to Italy? A. Yes.

Q. When did he go first? A. Oh, I do not remember just now. I can't remember how long he went.

Q. When you said something had been done before this letter was received, what did you mean? What had been done? A. Well, he wanted to inform himself at the consul's about going to Italy. Is that what you mean?

Q. Yes. A. Have I answered right? Sometimes I don't understand.

Q. Had anything been done about a photograph?

A. I remember he brought **the large picture** and the **consul** said it was too large... .

Q. And he came back [home] with the large picture? A. Yes.

Q. When did he go,—when did he take the large picture, as you say, go with it and come back? When was that? A. That was on the day of the 15th of April.

Q. How do you place that?

A. I remember that because I had company that day in the house from Milford. [Ed. Guests were Henry Iacovelli and wife: 2064]

Q. ... When was the next letter received after the one written by his brother?

A. I don't remember. I can't remember. [2054]

Q. Now, after your husband came home from Boston with the large photograph, was there anything else done about photographs? A. We had some more small ones taken... .

391

Q. Repeat that, please. A. After, we had some more small ones taken in Stoughton.

Q. And how many did you have taken? A. I think a half dozen.

Q. Do you know anything about your husband taking one of those or some of them to Boston?

A. Yes.

Q. Do you know when he did that? A. ... [D]uring the beginning of May, May 4th. [2055]

Q. Had you and your husband made up your mind when you were going to leave Stoughton?

A. Yes.

Q. What day were you going?

A. Let us see. The passport was taken May 4th. Well, right after the passport.

Q. I mean, had any day been decided on? A. It was, I think, the day after. Yes, the day after he was arrested [May 6] we thought we were going to leave the house. [2057]

Q. Now, did your husband have some of this Socialistic, Radical newspapers and books in the house? A. I beg your pardon?

Q. Did your husband have some literature in the house, books and papers? A. Yes, yes... .

Q. Now, there has been some,—the other day there was some literature brought into the court room as your husband's? A. Yes. [2061]

[Mr. McAnarney shows bank book to the Court.]

MR. JEREMIAH McANARNEY. [To the jury.] This, Mr. Foreman and gentlemen, is the bank book, deposits beginning 1918, and running down to various sums so that down to May 1st it is about $1500... .

THE COURT. The maximum sum, I take it, give that.

MR. JEREMIAH McANARNEY. Yes. The amount on deposit May 1st was $1508.92. [2063]

Q. You say Exhibit 27 [Guerin cap] looks more like your husband's cap? A. Yes.

Q. Did your husband ever wear a cap like that, "29", this cap...?

A. My husband never wore caps with anything around for his ears, never, because he never liked it and ... besides that, never, he never wore them because he don't look good in them, positively... .

[Ed. "29" is cap found near body of Berardelli. On p. 2064 McAnarney notes: "three caps marked "Exhibit 29," "Exhibit 44," and "Exhibit 27."]

Q. Did you ever see a mark like this [indicating], you might or might not, but did you ever see a hole like that [indicating] in your husband's cap? A. Not that I remember. I never seen holes in my husband's cap like that. [2065] [Ed. Rose Sacco refers to "Exhibit 27."]

Cross-Examination.

Q. (By Mr. Katzmann) Mrs. Sacco, I show you **the large picture** that is attached to the deposition and marked "B." Do you remember [2065] when you and your husband and your son went to the photographer's to have that picture taken? A. Yes.

Q. When was it, please? A. I could not say sure, but sometimes in March.

Q. Well? A. Late in February or sometimes early in March. That is what I remember. [2066]

Q. —did you say that your husband had made up his mind to go to Italy before he had heard from his brother that his mother was dead? A. I told you we had the idea to go to Italy from a long, long time ago. That is why we were saving our money, because we wanted to go across in the old country, but since the mother died, we hurried more because he was sorry about his mother died without seeing him.... . [2067]

Q. Did you give Sabeno's letter announcing the death to Mr. Callahan? A. Sure I did.

Q. What was the date of that letter that Sabeno wrote it over in Italy? A. The mother died on the 7th.

Q. No. What is the date of the letter from Sabeno? A. The mother died on the 7th of March, and I suppose Sabeno write the letter a few days after or probably the day after the mother died. It reached here sometime the 23d or 24th of March.

Q. Then, I take it, you and your husband were in a hurry to get over to Italy? A. Positive.

Q. And he went right in town to see about the passports, didn't he? A. Yes.

Q. Went the next day after he got the letter? A. Oh, no, no. You mean when I received the letter that the mother was dead?

Q. From Sabeno, yes. A. No, he did not go right after.

Q. How soon? A. A little, a few days, a little while after.

Q. What do you mean, Mrs. Sacco, by "a little while?" How many days?

A. About thirteen or fourteen days afterwards.

Q. Was that the day that he took **that large picture** in that I showed you?

A. I don't think he said like that, not exactly that. I says, I don't think he asked that question.

Q. I think you wanted an interpreter?

A. I can't explain myself better, but I understand more than I can explain.

Q. I see. Here is the question. You said thirteen or fourteen days after Sabeno's letter he went into Boston, didn't you? A. Yes... .

Q. Did he take that picture ["that large picture"] with him that day?

A. Sure, he did.

MR. KATZMANN. That is all. [2068]

THE WITNESS. I beg your pardon. You say thirteen or fourteen days after. I would say if it was in the end of March and my husband went on the 15th, well, that is the day my man went to the consul, and I am positive, because I went myself and asked him... .

Q. Why did you say thirteen or fourteen days if you did not mean it?

A. Well, you count up from the 23d or 24th of March, and going to the 15th, I says thirteen or fourteen days, and I don't think it is much different, because it is over a year he is in prison and I don't remember everything.

MR. KATZMANN. That is all. [2069]

Edward Maertens, Sworn. July 9, 1921.

Q. (By Jeremiah McAnarney) What nationality are you?

A. Belgian... .

Q. Your business? A. Oh, photographer.

Q. Where do you carry on the business of photography?

A. In Stoughton,—Monks Block... .

Q. What have you in your hand now?

A. This is a photographic plate... .

Q. That is a print from that plate? A. From that plate.

MR. JEREMIAH McANARNEY. Before I discuss it any further, I want to have this marked for identification.

[Photograph marked "Exhibit 42 for identification."]

[Plate marked "Exhibit 43 for identification."]

[Mr. McAnarney shows photograph and plate to the Court and to Mr. Katzmann.]

Q. When were these taken, Mr. Martens [sic]? A. I can't tell sure the date, you know... .

Q. Tell us the best you can. A. The nearest I can say about when that photograph is made must be between April and the first of May... .

THE COURT. What time in April?

[The answer is read.]

THE COURT. What does he mean by that?

THE WITNESS. And the reason why I think it must be made about that time is because I know I got recollection about that a certain soldier [1979] came back in my studio to have his pictures, and it was during April and I had to make it for the town hall from Stoughton, for a record, and now because that picture is made only for passport and they tell me in advance that it was going to be used as passports I never record the plates and put them in a box with plates. It usually takes me three or four weeks to have a box of plates, you know, about twelve bad plates, and I fill them all in one box. Now, I found a plate of that soldier in the same box with them together with the girl who came at the same time with Mrs. Sacco, and I put them all in one box, so that is why I think it must be made in that month.

Q. Did you send the pictures to them or did they come and get them? A. They came after them.

Q. Who got them? A. I guess Mr. Sacco,—Mrs. Sacco herself.

Q. Did you know her before she came to have the photograph taken? A. No, I never saw her before.

Q. And if I understand you, when they tell you that the picture is made for a passport, you do not record? A. I don't ... because ... when they go back to the old country I never see them any more again and [I have] no use to save them.

Q. You mean save the record or the plate? You did save the plate? A. No, I did not save the plate. But I stored them in the bad plates ready to be sold to any one, junkman or somebody who makes picture frames, to sell them as old glass... .

Q. Do you know how many they ordered? A. I guess they must have surely three, but I can't tell sure, but they need three surely at that time, ... three copies, you know... .

Q. When they come to have a photograph for a passport you know they are not coming back, and no more business to you? A. No.

Q. So you don't register their name? A. That just to make three pictures and they are gone and I never see them no more. [1980]

Cross-Examination.

Q. (By Mr. Katzmann) What size plate was Exhibit 42 made on?
A. What size? A. 5 by 7. That is the original plate... .
[Ed. "A" appears two times here.]

Q. Have you any smaller size, referring to the plate? A. No, I have none... .

Q. ... Were you told what size of plate to make, what size? A. Yes, and I said 5 by 7.

Q. That was your smallest? A. That is the smallest, yes. It is what I always use for ordinary photographs even cheap or costly, you know, the size is big... . [T]he smallest plate I ever use.

MR. KATZMANN. I see. I think that is all.

THE COURT. That is all.

MR. JEREMIAH McANARNEY. If your honor please, by agreement of counsel it was agreed that order No. 2348 was on March 21st or 20th. The date is not quite clear.

MR. KATZMANN. I think Mr. Callahan and I ascertained it was the 21st.

MR. JEREMIAH McANARNEY. All right, March 21st, 1920, "Mr. Nicola Sacco, To some pictures, 7 by 9, $4 paid," and the address, "694 Park Street, post office, South Stoughton, delivered April 5, 1920."

MR. KATZMANN. No, April 3d.

MR. JEREMIAH McANARNEY. April 3d.

MR. KATZMANN. Mr. Callahan and I went over that.

MR. JEREMIAH McANARNEY. It could be taken for 3 or 5. It is agreed it is April 3, 1920. Balance paid, $17, and I am told that refers to the large photographs that were shown in evidence to the jury, the date being delivered April 3, 1920; and it is appropriately suggested that this refers to the photograph which is shown on the **deposition of Andrower**, the assistant consul. [1981]

["Sacco had a proper passport photograph taken by Edward Maertens of Stoughton." Ehrmann, The Case That Will Not Die, p. 364.]

Edward B. Haywood, Recalled. July 11, 1921.

Q. (By Jeremiah McAnarney) Mr. Haywood, [Hayward on p. 96] could you tell us approximately the distance from the place where the car was found in the Manley woods to the Matfield station, taking the route that we took that day? A. Yes. The distances are marked right on the map in pencil, from point to point... .
Q. From the cart path on Manley Street to the Matfield station?
A. 4-9/10 miles.
Q. 4.9? A. Yes. [2071]

Cross-Examination.

Q. (By Mr. Katzmann) How far is the entrance to that path from the railroad crossing, just roughly? A. 4/10 of a mile. [2072]
[Ed. R.R. crossing mentioned in H. P. Williams's pre-tour statement.]

Redirect Examination.

Q. (By Mr. McAnarney) What is the distance from Elm Square to the Coacci house?
A. South Elm Street?
Q. Yes. A. It is 1.15 miles... .

Recross Examination.

Q. (By Mr. Katzmann) How far is the junction of Sunset Avenue from the railroad bridge at which the Johnson house is? A. I should say it was about a mile.
[Ed. Sacco and Vanzetti walked this route to board a streetcar on May 5.]

Redirect Examination.

Q. (By Mr. McAnarney) While you are there, from the Coacci house to where the car was found, what is the distance? A. A mile and 9/10ths. [See map: Escape and Arrest.]

Recross Examination.

Q. (By Mr. Katzmann) Mr. Haywood, is there a street at the Manley railroad crossing? Is there a way of getting to Plymouth from there?
A. Why, the only way would be to take this street to East Bridgewater and then take Plymouth Road.
Q. How far is the crossing from the centre of East Bridgewater?
A. Why, I should say about two miles.
Q. And from East Bridgewater is there a direct route to Plymouth?
A. Yes. [2073]

MR. JEREMIAH McANARNEY. ... [S]ubject to anything that is omitted in the nature of checking up, the defendants rest.... [2074]
THE COURT. With that one **exception**, do I understand that the defendants rest?
MR. JEREMIAH McANARNEY. Yes, if your Honor please.
THE COURT. The rebuttal, please. [2077]

[Ed. McAnarney asked for an **exception** (see **The Court**) when he concluded his examination of Henry Iacovelli, the edge trimmer chosen to replace Sacco upon Sacco's anticipated return to Italy. Katzmann did not cross-examine Iacovelli, either on June 30 {1627} or in recall on July 12 {2077}.]

INTERMISSION

"Once ensconced in a textbook, misinformation becomes effectively permanent, because textbooks copy from previous texts."
Stephen Jay Gould, "This View of Life," Natural History (March 2000), p. 46. See p. 631 in this book. See also p. 168 in this book.

31. REBUTTAL

"After the defense rests its case, the prosecution may call rebuttal witnesses, with the intention of either discrediting the testimony of a previous witness or discrediting the witness her- or himself... . In general, evidence may be presented in rebuttal that could not have been used during the prosecution's main case... ."
David W. Neubauer, America's Courts and the Criminal Justice System, West/Wadsworth, 6th ed., p. 353. See Crime & Punishment: The Multimedia Simulation of Criminal Sentencing, the compact disc in the front of the Neubauer text.

MR. KATZMANN. If your Honor please, in beginning the rebuttal of the Commonwealth, I state that by counsel's agreement for the Commonwealth and the defendants, it is agreed that we need,—the Commonwealth need not recall Simon Johnson to testify again, but that if he were recalled he would testify now in rebuttal, he would give the same testimony that he gave in direct evidence as to the conversation that he had with Mike Boda at West Bridgewater on the night of May 5th in respect to the number plates, ... that this agreement is for the purpose of avoiding the necessity of recalling him technically to testify again. [2078]
MR. JEREMIAH McANARNEY. And to be subject to the defendants' same exception.
[Ed. Moore had moved, p. 938, that Simon Johnson's conversation with Boda be stricken. Motion was denied. See motion to strike Johnson's conversation in Plymouth trial, Appel, VI: 333.]

Angelo Ricci, Sworn. July 12, 1921.

Q. (By Mr. Katzmann) What is your business? A. Railroad foreman.
Q. Section gang foreman? A. Section gang foreman, yes.
Q. What was your occupation, what was your job April 15, 1920?

A. Yes.

Q. Was it the same? A. Yes.

Q. Were you at work that day? A. Up to the freight house, behind the station on south... .

Q. ... How far **south** of the railroad crossing, the Pearl Street crossing, is the freight house? A. Well, ... about five hundred feet.

Q. Were you in charge of the section gang that day? A. Yes, sir.

Q. That afternoon? A. Yes. [2078]

Q. Did you hear any sound of shooting that afternoon?

A. Oh, I hear, yes.

Q. Did you go up to the crossing? A. No.

Q. Did any of the men in the gang go up to the crossing? A. No.

Q. Did you see the [bandit] automobile go over the crossing? A. Yes, I saw it.

Q. How far away were you at that moment? A. Well, 140 feet [south].

Q. Were any of your section hands, workers, as near to the crossing as you were when the automobile was going over the crossing? A. All the hands were in the way I work, about 140 feet. [2079]

Mrs. Mary Gaines, Sworn. July 12, 1921.

Q. (By Mr. Katzmann) Where do you live, Mrs. Gaines? A. I live 198 School Street, Quincy...

Q. Do you know Mrs. Lola Andrews? A. Yes, sir, I do.

Q. Do you know Mrs. Julia Campbell? A. Yes, sir.

Q. Do you know Mrs. Campbell's sister? A. Yes, sir.

Q. ... [D]id you learn about the shooting at South Braintree sometime shortly after?

A. Well, I happened to be at Mrs. Campbell's sister's.

Q. Before you happened to be at Mrs. Campbell's sister's had you read in the paper?

A. Well, yes, I seen it in the papers.

Q. How soon after that were you at ... Mrs. Campbell's sister's?

A. ... that same week, ...

Q. During the same week? A. Yes.

Q. ... Who were the people in the room, please? A. My husband.

Q. Yes. A. And Miss Lola, Miss Andrews, and Miss Campbell was there.

Q. Who was Mrs. Campbell? A. That is Mrs. Lancaster's sister.

Q. Is her name Julia? A. Yes... .

Q. Was there some talk with regard to the shooting that night?

A. I heard Mrs. Andrews speaking about it, yes.

Q. What did Mrs. Andrews say? A. Well, Mrs. Andrews says—

[Ed. After McAnarney objected and was overruled, Katzmann made this statement.]

MR. KATZMANN. I will say to your Honor that there was no conversation by Mrs. Campbell at this time that she called there. The purpose of [2085] introducing this is to show that the statement that Mrs. Andrews made about making inquiry of the man under the car is not one of recent contrivance and that she there, at that time, made the statement within a week of the shooting. I assume that the argument will be that Mrs. Andrews' statement on the stand about inquiring the way to the Rice & Hutchins factory and the man who was under the car is one of recent contrivance, and I offer this testimony to rebut it.

THE COURT. Do you make that claim? Will you argue that? Of course, it is open to you if you see fit. It is legitimate argument.

MR. JEREMIAH McANARNEY. I propose to argue everything that is legitimate.

THE COURT. Well, then, that is one of the things.

MR. JEREMIAH McANARNEY. Not leaving anything.

THE COURT. That is one of the things, then, I take it, you reserve the right to argue, that this is a recent contrivance on the part of Mrs. Andrews or the result of recent contrivance. Now, under that theory the Commonwealth would have a right to show that immediately following the shooting she made a statement which was consistent with the testimony that she has given in court.

MR. JEREMIAH McANARNEY. If your Honor will save my rights there.

THE COURT. With that understanding and with that right on your part open to you, it seems to me that I am obliged, under the decisions, to admit it... .

Q. ... [D]id Mrs. Andrews that evening make any statement about her being at South Braintree on the day of the shooting? A. Yes, sir... .

Q. Just what she said. A. Yes. And she walks over and she asks, she seen this man underneath the automobile, and she taps this man on the shoulder and asks him to please direct her to the Rice & Hutchins shoe shop, and he got up and directed her to it... . [2086]

Q. Where was Mrs. Campbell when Mrs. Andrews made that statement? A. She was sitting right in the room there, right near us. She never said a word, never answered.

Cross-Examination.

Q. (By Mr. Jeremiah McAnarney) Are you any relation to Mrs. Andrews? A. No, sir, ...

Q. Do you remember of her being to your house any in the last year? A. Not that I remember of.... [2087]

THE COURT. [To the jury.] Perhaps, gentlemen, I might explain to you now ... why this woman's testimony was admitted. It is contrary ... to what is recognized as a general rule of law that hearsay testimony is not competent. Whenever a witness takes the stand and the testimony is of such a character that counsel on the other side might claim that such testimony was the result of recent contrivance or a recent concealment of the facts, then under those circumstances it is competent, as in this case, for the Commonwealth to meet that theory by showing that the witness had made statements before that time consistent with the witness's testimony on the stand. This now leaves open to the defendants to argue that question, that Mrs. Andrews' testimony was of recent contrivance. To meet that issue the Commonwealth has offered this testimony. Its probative effect rests exclusively with you. [2089]

Henry Hellyer, Sworn. July 12, 1921.

Q. (By Mr. Katzmann) Mr. Hellyer, what is your name, full name? A. Henry Hellyer.

Q. What is your occupation? A. An operator for the Pinkerton National Detective Agency....

Q. Did you make any investigation following the shooting at Braintree personally? A. I did.

Q. And in the course of those investigations, by the way, were they made in behalf of the Pinkerton people? A. Travellers' Insurance Company.

Q. Travellers' Insurance Company, who insured— A. The pay roll.

Q. —The pay roll of Slater & Morrill. And you personally went out? A. Yes, sir.

Q. Did you on the 8th day of May interview Mrs. Jennie Novelli? A. Yes.

Q. Where did you interview her? A. 27 Chestnut Street, Quincy.

Q. Had you previously interviewed her? A. I did.

Q. And as a result of that,—that was when, the first interview?

A. The 17th of April.

Q. And the second one? A. The 8th of May.

Q. As a result of that first interview, what did you do?

A. I displayed three photographs. [2089]

Q. Have you those photographs with you? A. Yes, sir.

Q. Among them was a photograph of the defendant Sacco?

A. Yes, sir.

Q. Produce that one alone, if you please. A. [Witness does so.]

Q. Did you exhibit that photograph to her? A. I did.

   [Mr. Katzmann shows photograph to counsel for the defendants.]

Q. You say that you showed Mrs. Novelli the picture I just handed you? A. Yes, sir... .

Q. On being shown that photograph, did Mrs. Novelli say that it **greatly** resembled the man that she saw in the bandits' car?

A. She did... .

Q. Did she describe more than one man at the April 17th interview?

A. I think she described two. I can find out.

Q. Yes. A. [The witness examines notes.] She described two.

Q. And where were the two men seated whom she described to you on the 17th of April?

A. Both in the driver's seat.

Q. You mean in the front seat? A. In the front seat.

Q. What description did she give of the man who was at the wheel?

A. "Twenty-five to thirty years, five feet eight inches tall, medium build, brown hair, fair complexion and smooth shaven. Wore a cap, but cannot recollect what else he wore."

Q. Did she describe the man who sat to his right? A. She did.

Q. What description did she give of that man? A. "Twenty-seven years, five feet seven inches, tall, slim build, black hair, black eyes, dark complexion, thin features, wide mouth, smooth shaven, but appeared to be a man who could grow heavy beard from the dark stubble shown on his face."

Q. Is the photograph which I have in my hand, Mr. Hellyer, the photograph which you showed Mrs. Novelli? A. Yes, sir. [2090]

MR. KATZMANN. I offer it, if your Honor please.

MR. JEREMIAH McANARNEY. To that we object and your Honor will save my rights.

THE COURT. Certainly.

[Photograph of defendant Sacco shown Mrs. Novelli by Mr. Hellyer admitted in evidence and marked "Exhibit 42."]

[Mr. Katzmann shows Exhibit 42 to the jury.]

MR. KATZMANN. That is all. You may inquire.

MR. JEREMIAH McANARNEY. No questions, if your Honor please. [2091]

Lieut. Daniel T. Guerin, Recalled. July 12, 1921.

[Ed. Guerin's testimony in the Commonwealth's evidence, pp. 802-805, is omitted.]

Q. (By Mr.Katzmann) And you are a lieutenant in the Brockton police department? A. I am.

Q. And did you go to the house of the defendant Sacco? A. I did.

Q. And when did you go with respect to the 15th of April,—the 5th of May, I should say?

A. The following day, the 6th.

Q. Did you there obtain a cap? A. I did. [2092]

Q. I show you Exhibit 27 for **identification** and ask you if that is the cap that you obtained?

A. That is the cap. [Ed. This exhibit should not be confused with Exhibit 27, Vanzetti's gun.]

Q. Where did you obtain it? A. In the kitchen of the defendant's home... .

MR. KATZMANN. I offer the cap, if your Honor please.

MR. MOORE. The defendant objects.

THE COURT. I will hear you on your objection. Both sides used this cap and asked, I don't know how many questions on it. That gives either side the right to offer it.

MR. MOORE. That has been true. It has. After the method that was sent in originally, we had to use it in order to safeguard our rights. But without arguing, my objection simply goes to the question of the unlawful seizure. [Ed. Moore said seizure violated the Fourth Amendment.]

THE COURT. I will admit it.

MR. MOORE. Simply presenting the unlawful search and seizure question?

MR. JEREMIAH McANARNEY. Your Honor reserves my rights?

THE COURT. Yes.

Q. Lieutenant, do you know Ricardo Orcciani? A. I do... .

THE COURT. Let me be sure. This is the same cap that counsel for both defendants have inquired in regard to or particularly counsel for the defendant Sacco?

MR. MOORE. Your Honor, this is the cap that came into this record ... when the defendant Sacco was on the witness stand and the Commonwealth's counsel ... asked the defendant Sacco [p. 1928] to put the cap on... . [2093]

Q. Lieutenant, you stated you know Orcciani? A. Yes.

THE COURT. At present it may stand. [Ed. The "it" means the Guerin cap, a delayed ruling.]

[Cap obtained by Lieutenant Guerin in defendant Sacco's home, admitted in evidence and marked "Exhibit 43"]

Q. Was Mr. Orcciani brought to Brockton police station on May 6th, the day after the two defendants were arrested? A. Yes, sir. I said May 5th—I meant May 6th... .

Q. How long did he remain in custody? A. The following Thursday, I believe.

Q. In that period was he brought to the town hall in Braintree? A. He was... .

Q. Was Orcciani brought,—was the man Orcciani brought to the town hall in Braintree within one week of April 15,1920? A. Within one week? [2094]

Q. Of April 15, 1920? A. No, sir, he was not.

MR. JEREMIAH McANARNEY. I object to that.

MR. KATZMANN. That is offered for the purpose of contradicting Barbara Liscomb, if your Honor please.

THE COURT. That is what I supposed.

MR. JEREMIAH McANARNEY. Will your Honor save an exception to that.

THE COURT. Certainly... .

Q. Lieutenant, were you at the Brockton police station on the night of May 5th? A. No, sir, I was not.

MR. KATZMANN. You were not. That is all.

MR. JEREMIAH McANARNEY. No questions. [2095]

[Ed. Guerin's testimony in rebuttal has more significance than his testimony—omitted—in the Commonwealth's presentation of evidence. Jury saw Buick July 12, and Katzmann said its opened door "would impede the progress of a person coming from the opened rear door along the running-board into the front seat." {2101} On July 12, 1921, the Court ruled on Moore's June 22 motion on the Buick.]

THE COURT. Then I will pass upon that. What was your motion, to strike all the evidence with reference to the Buick car, was it not?

MR. MOORE. Yes, sir. [Ed. June 22 motion (p. 938) is repeated by Moore (p. 2097).]

THE COURT. Your motion is denied and exception saved. [2099]

Frank W. Hawley, Sworn. July 12, 1921.

Q. (By Mr. Katzmann) What was your occupation in the month of April, 1920? A. Salesman.

Q. Were you in the city of Brockton on Thursday, the 1st day of April, 1920? A. Yes, sir.

Q. Did you see an automobile that day, a Buick automobile that day? A. Yes, sir.

Q. At what hour? A. It was about ten minutes past three, I should say.

Q. In the afternoon? A. Yes.

Q. Where? A. It was down in School Street; going from City Hall you cross Montello Street. Between there and the railroad track.

Q. Were you afoot or in an automobile yourself?

A. In an automobile... .

Q. Did you stop it [the Buick]? A. Well, I started to turn around to go to Whitman, so I was headed up to the curbstone. That car had to stop on account of my turning around.

Q. Was there any conversation between you and any occupant of [2101] that car?

A. The driver stuck his head out and asked me if that was the road to Whitman... .

Q. How near were you to the occupants of the front seat of the car?

A. When it started I don't think the front of their car was more than a foot from mine... .

Q. ... What kind of Buick car was it?

A. Why, two seated car, closed car. I mean open car, with the top on.

Q. How were the curtains that day? A. The curtains were up on the back seat. The side of each back seat, but it was flopping down from the top on my side.

Q. Did you see the occupants of that car, or any of them?

A. Well, I could get a good look at two of them in the front seat.

Q. Do you know how many occupants there were in the rear?

A. Three.... [2102]

Q. The question, Mr. Hawley, which you are to answer, is this: Do you see in the court room the man who was seated on that day in Brockton at the right of the driver? A. Yes, sir... .

Q. Where is he?

MR. JEREMIAH McANARNEY. Exception, if your Honor please.

THE COURT. Yes.

Q. Where is he? A. On the left in the cage... .

THE COURT. Supposing you make your record complete on that.

MR. KATZMANN. I beg your pardon. Is it agreed that the defendant Vanzetti sits at the left of the cage, of the witness facing him?

MR. JEREMIAH McANARNEY. Yes... .

THE COURT. The witness identifies Vanzetti.

MR. KATZMANN. Vanzetti. [2103]

Cross-Examination.

Q. (By Mr. Jeremiah McAnarney) How long have you been a salesman?

A. Well, for a good many years... .

Q. You live in Brockton? A. Yes, sir.

Q. At one time a special police officer? A. Yes, sir.

Q. How many years were you a special police offecer? A. Well, I guess I have been special police officer and constable for about eighteen or nineteen years.

Q. ... When did you cease to be a special police officer? A. Why, I could not say in regard to that. I have been a constable ever since.

Q. You are a constable now? A. Yes, sir... .

Q. What time in the day is it that you saw the man you call Vanzetti in a Buick car?

A. About ten minutes past three in the afternoon. [2104]

[Ed. After Stewart testified in rebuttal {2110-2117}, Judge Thayer read to the jury: It is agreed that counsel will not argue nor claim that Chief Stewart should have arrested **Boda at the time he saw him on April 20th at the Coacci house**. See Chronology, p. xl.] [2117]

AFTERNOON SESSION. July 12, 1921.

MR. KATZMANN. If your Honor please, as in the case of the inquest testimony, by agreement with counsel I shall read certain questions that were denied by the defendants as having been made at the Brockton police station, and it is agreed that this is a correct transcript of what was said by the defendants there, the defendants waiving no rights otherwise to object. This question was put to Mr. Vanzetti: ...

"Q. You don't know where you were the Thursday [April 15,1920] before that Monday [Patriots' Day, 19th of April], do you? A. No." ...
Of the defendant Sacco, the following questions:

"Q. Did you ever take a whole day off in April to look for your passports all day?
A. Yes, I did.

Q. What day? A. I think either Tuesday or Wednesday.

Q. What Tuesday or Wednesday in April? A. Well, I don't remember. Either the 5th or 8th of April, or the 10th, I don't remember. I can't say for sure. This was in April I lost a day to fill out the income tax, and I do not remember, but I can tell it from the factory the day I was out a full day." [2117]
And this question:

"Q. Do you know Berardelli? A. No. Who is this Berardelli?"
And these questions and these answers: ....

"Q. Where [did you read about the robbery/murder]? A. In the Boston Post.

Q. Where did they rob the money? A. Over near Rice & Hutchins. I don't read English very well, but there was bandits in Braintree, and I think it was at Rice & Hutchins.... .

Q. Were you working the day before you read it [robbery and murder on April 15, 1920] in the paper? A. I think I did.

Q. Well, do you know? A. Sure.

Q. Worked all day? A. Yes, sir." .... .

MR. KATZMANN. The Commonwealth has nothing further to offer in rebuttal.

THE COURT. Have you anything in reply to it, gentlemen? [2118]

32. ATWATER TELLS HIS DEDHAM TRIAL
STORY
Dexter Man Took Part in Famous Case

Dexter--Quite possibly Elbridge Atwater of Dexter is the only living person in this state to have testified at the much publicized Sacco-Vanzetti trial.

Atwater, who is a retired foundry worker at the Fayscott Landis Machine Cohporation [sic] of Dexter, once owned the revolver with which the two men were accused of killing the paymaster and guard of a South Braintree, Mass., shoe factory.

After the death of Atwater's father-in-law, Frank Morgridge, Mrs. Morgridge went to visit a daughter and son-in-law, the late Rexford Slater at Norwood, Mass. When she unpacked her trunk, the Harrington and Richardson revolver was at the bottom, so she gave it to Mr. Slater. He in turn sold it to a man named Oceana [Orciani], who figured in the trial. Oceana allegedly sold the weapon to one of the two accused men. Both Oceana and the wife of the defense lawyer came to Dexter and finally persuaded Mr. Slater and Mr. Atwater, who had handled his father-in-law's revolver many times, to go to Massachusetts three times: first to identify the revolver, next to testify at the trial and the third time . . .

[Source of this truncated news item is The Eastern Gazette, March 5, 1964. Above the headline is a photo of Elbridge Atwater, beneath which is this caption:
"**RECALLS TRIAL**--Elbridge Atwater of Dexter relaxes with his dog Trixie while he relates his part in the noted Sacco-Vanzetti case."
Slater died on March 5, 1960. Abbie Morgridge Cruise, who, according to Slater's testimony (transcript, 1635), traveled to Norwood about January 1, 1918, died on March 15, 1942. See transcript, 1566. And see Palmer on p. 413. Editor received this 1964 news item from local historian Frank Spizuoco of Ripley, Maine. Dexter Historical Society e-mailed editor (July 25, 2005): "There were very few Italians ever in Dexter. Some passed through working on the railroad in the 1880s and there was a man who had a restaurant in the 20s."]

33. REPLY TO REBUTTAL

[Ed. In the defense's reply to the Commonwealth's rebuttal, Moore read to the jury excerpts from the deposition of Giuseppe Adrower, pp. 2118-2119.]

THE COURT. [To Mr. Moore.] You may make the statement that has been agreed upon, to the jury.

MR. MOORE. If your honor please, by agreement with Mr. Katzmann, the following is a translation of the circular found on the person of the defendant Sacco at the time of arrest. There is one word, gentlemen, that I will use in a triplicate sense. [2119]

"Fellow workers, you have fought all the wars. You have worked for all the capitalists."

By agreement of the interpreter, it is agreed that the word "padrone", the original Italian "padrone" word, is subject to also the interpretation of "owners" and "employers," making it read:

"You have fought all the wars. You have worked for all the capitalists," or, "all the owners," or "all the employers." "You have wandered over all the countries. Have you harvested the fruits of your labors, the price of your victories? Does the past comfort you? Does the present smile on you? Does the future promise you anything? Have you found a piece of land where you can live like a human being and die like a human being? On these questions, on this argument, and on this theme the struggle for existence, Bartolomeo Vanzetti will speak. Hour"—blank—"day"—blank—"hall"—blank. "Admission free. Freedom of discussion to all. Take the ladies with you." [2120]

The following, gentlemen, is agreed to be the translation of the Exhibit "P", which is what we have seen fit to call the passport paper, but which officially is not. Photograph in the corner and seal.

"**ITALIAN CONSULATE,**
Boston, Massachusetts.

"Foglio di Via"—(described as passpaper).

"This pass paper is given to Sacco, Nicola, son of Michele, who has certified to have lost his regular passport and to have been born in 1891 at Torremaggiore. Good only for passage back to native land. Boston, Massachusetts, May 4, 1920.

Description, hair, brown (chestnut). Color, natural, eyes, brown. Marks, none. Acting Royal Consul. (Signed) H. Mellano Rossi.

The above will be accompanied by his wife Rosa Zambelli, twenty-five years old, and his son Dante, seven years old. Signature. Seal of the Italian Consul. (Signed) Nicola Sacco. No. 6949. Registered"—something—I don't know what the words are. They are evidently registration numbers, I take it. This [indicating] is an exact copy of the original, and this, so far as I know, is a registration number on some official document itself. [Ed. Photocopy of Sacco's passport in Avrich, p. 85.]

THE COURT. Are those books all in the Italian language?

MR. MOORE. Yes, your honor.

THE COURT. They may be admitted. I don't know what good they may do the jury.

Give them a number of books and then a number of pamphlets. Mark the books Exhibit—four books, are they not? [Ed. Anarchist literature from Sacco's home. See Moore, p. 1973.]

MR. MOORE. Four bound volumes, your Honor. [2120]

[The books and pamphlets are admitted in evidence and marked "AA", "BB", "CC", "DD", "EE", "FF", "GG", "HH", "II", "JJ", "KK", "LL", "MM", "NN", "OO", and "PP".]

THE COURT. Is there anything further, gentlemen, for the consideration of the jury?

MR. KATZMANN. Nothing, if your Honor please, on the part of the Commonwealth... .

THE COURT. Do you think we better take the time to have any interpretations made of simply the titles, ... [T]he District Attorney is entitled to have interpretation of some of the contents in the book.

MR. MOORE. Well, in some degree the titles speak for themselves. We will rest.

THE COURT. What say you, Mr. McAnarney, so far as the defendant Vanzetti is concerned? ... .

MR. JEREMIAH McANARNEY. If your Honor please, the defendant Vanzetti rests.

MR. MOORE. The same.

THE COURT. Well, gentlemen, the book of fate in these cases has been closed... . [2121]

I must again suggest to you to still keep your minds open. The evidence has simply closed now. You have not heard the arguments of counsel and you should hear the arguments of both counsel, and during all that time keep your minds open, impartial... . [K]eep your minds open in that state of impartiality because you have not heard the Charge of the Court. You must hear what the law is of the Commonwealth in order that you may apply the law to established facts found by you to be true, ... [2122]

[Adjourned to Wednesday, July 12, 1921, at 9 o'clock.] [Ed. Transcript error: July 13.]

Introducing New Evidence

The next page has new evidence, a letter the editor discovered in 2005. This primary source, hitherto unpublished, may prove to be useful to historians. "Primary sources," says historian Jules R. Benjamin, "can be newspaper accounts, diaries, notebooks, letters, minutes, interviews, and any other works written by persons who claim firsthand knowledge of an event." See Benjamin's A Student's Guide to History, 9th edition, p. 13. Pages 14-17 also offer excellent advice.

A newspaper account of the letter writer, C. C. Palmer, is in the Bangor Daily Commercial, Thursday, Dec. 29, 1927. Its headline reads: **C.C. Palmer, Widely Known Reporter, Dead**. The December 29 account offers this opinion: "As a newspaper man, Mr. Palmer was accurate, trustworthy and conscientious. His work with the state police was always efficient."

Palmer's Phone Call to Katzmann

Dexter, Maine

COLLECT   June 21

District Attorney,

Will come to Dedham if necessary, upon telegraphic request, but require 24 hours notice. Message to this town will reach me at any time. Parties mentioned in letter have returned home but will return to Dedham later.

(Received over telephone 9.15 A. M. June 22)

C. C. Palmer.

34. PALMER'S LETTER TO KATZMANN

Dexter, Me. June 17, 1921.

District Attorney,
Dedham, Mass.

Dear Sir-:
I am taking this opportunity to give you a bit of information
which, perhaps, may prove of some benefit to you in the trial of the
Italians for murder in which you are now engaged.

Rexford Slater and Elbridge Atwater of this town left this
noon for Boston to be in readiness to tesify in the defense of Sacco and
Vanzetti. Slater, it seems, last year was employed in a foundry at
Norwood, Mass. and working in the same shop with him was an Italian
[Ricardo Orciani] to whom he sold a revolver and as I understand it, the
contention of the defense will be that this revolver was later sold to
Vanzetti. The purpose of placing Slater and Atwater on the stand will
be to identify this revolver. Atwater, who is Slater's brother-in-law
was in Norwood at the time and knew something regarding the transfer
of the weapon.

Several weeks ago an Italian came to this town and, as I
understand it, endeavored to get these men to go to Dedham to testify.
They refused and several days ago Mrs. Fred H. Moore, wife of one of
the attorneys for the defense, came here and labored with them until
they agreed to go to Dedham.

My purpose in writing you is to inform you that Slater told me
to-day that he would be unable to identify the revolver which he sold
the Italian. . . .

Yours truly,

Signed   C. C. Palmer

[Source: Sacco-Vanzetti Case Papers, Reel 21. Charles C. Palmer of
Dexter was appointed Automobile Inspector for the Maine State Police
on May 2, 1921. See on p. 412 the Dedham record of Palmer's Phone
Call to Katzmann, a document on Reel 21. Palmer's "Parties" are Slater
and Atwater. See Slater, p. 409.]

35. CLOSING ARGUMENTS

"After the prosecution and defense have rested (that is, completed the introduction of evidence), each side has the opportunity to make a closing argument to the jury. **Closing arguments** allow each side to sum up the facts in its favor and indicate why it believes a verdict of guilty or not guilty is in order. The prosecutor goes first, carefully taking what appeared during the trial to be isolated or unimportant matters and tying them together into a coherent pattern. The prosecutor calls upon the jurors to do their duty and punish the defendant, who has committed the crime. The defense attorney goes next, highlighting the evidence favorable to the defendant, criticizing the witnesses for the state, and showing why they should not be believed. The defense also calls upon the jurors to do their sworn duty and return a not guilty verdict. Because the prosecutor bears the burden of proof, he or she has the opportunity to make one last statement to the jury, refuting the defense arguments.

In closing arguments to the jury, lawyers muster all the art, craft, and guile of their profession... ."

David W. Neubauer, America's Courts and the Criminal Justice System, West/Wadsworth, 6th ed., pp. 353, 355. Boldface is by Professor Neubauer. Procedure in Massachusetts in 1921 differed from this account of 1999. Note: "to do their duty" and "to do their sworn duty."

Note: Complete summations by Frederick H. Moore, Jeremiah J. McAnarney, and Frederick G. Katzmann can be seen at the web site Famous Trials by Doug Linder (2004), UMKC School of Law.

July 13, 1921.
ARGUMENT OF MR. MOORE TO THE JURY

There is no penalty too great for the man that pulled the trigger that killed Mr. Berardelli or Mr. Parmenter or either of them. [2123] ...

But what is the issue? The mere fact that an atrocious and vicious crime is committed should be no cause nor no reason for visiting the penalty for that crime upon any man other than the guilty man. [2124]

The primary issue and the only issue here is the issue of identification. The one issue is, Has the Commonwealth proved beyond reasonable doubt that the defendant Sacco fired the fatal shot that caused the death of one or the other of these men? Or did the defendant Sacco aid or abet or contribute in any wise to that crime? [2125]

[T]he Commonwealth ... called Neal upon the issue of the identification of the car.... [2125] Neal says ... that morning ... it was newly varnished, a brand new car... Mr. Neal ... five hours later, ... says that as he looked out of this window over here (indicating)—a distance that you can compute—says that he recognized the car because he saw the varnish underneath the dust on the car.... . Human credulity [in Neal's testimony is] stretched to the utmost, gentlemen.... . [2126]

Mr. McAnarney will take care of Vanzetti, but the cases of these men are so intermingled that I may ... advert for just one minute to Faulkner.... . [Y]et this man Faulkner, ... this man Faulkner did not see a single man on that train that he knew and he had ridden the train every day for years.... . Vanzetti [by Commonwealth theory] had to get from Plymouth somehow up to East Braintree on a train. He got onto it, but the ticket agent at Plymouth, at Kingston, at Seaside and at East Braintree, none of them saw him. There is no registration of tickets bought on the train. Something wrong, gentlemen.... . [2127] Ah, again they say the car this Buick car, drove over the road that we all traveled from East Braintree to South Braintree, or, at least, that is the inference... Where is the testimony, gentlemen, that the car ever went over that road? ... . [2128]

Now, you remember Bostock... He says he saw two men standing in front of Rice & Hutchins, two men standing there.... . [I]s it significant at all in this case that Mr. Bostock, a plain, solid, substantial type of American citizenship, that Bostock refused to make an

415

identification? ... Bostock at the time of the shooting had just as good vision as did this man Wade. [2128]

Now, our friend Wade ... makes a partial identification, yet he was farther removed than was Mr. Bostock... . Wade ... says that he identified these men at a distance that he placed, in response to Mr. McAnarney's question, as from 72 to 73 steps.... . [2129]

You remember the man who was working here in the yards who knew Sacco, from Milford, intimately, lived in the same block with him; ... He [Gatti] has known Nick, known Sacco, for five years in Milford. His reputation for truth and integrity and veracity is not attacked. So far as this record shows, this man's reputation is as clean as any one's is clean. He says it was not Sacco. [2131]

Miss Splaine is in this factory building of the Hampton House, second floor. Miss Splaine did not know Sacco, never had seen him before... . Only saw him at best for a matter of seconds, [2131] ... . Gentlemen, that description [Splaine's description of Sacco] is built bone and sinew, from top to bottom, not from what she saw from the window but from what she saw in the Brockton police station. [2133]

Mrs. Lola Andrews ... made some rather unpleasant remarks with reference to my having offered her a trip to Maine ... [2135] [I]f she interpreted something that I said to her in the manner that she wants you to believe, ... why didn't your witness seek the district attorney's office of this county? ... You remember the confusion of the witness. You remember the uncertainty. I say to you that her testimony brands itself as manifestly false upon its face. Something wrong!

Ah, but you need not take my word. When you come to consider her, remember the testimony of Mrs. Campbell, who was with her, ... [2136]

Ah, but we come now to the rebuttal. This young woman [Gaines] who took the witness stand yesterday morning. I have forgotten her name. Pathetic, tragic little figure here that took the witness stand to do what? To corroborate Mrs. Andrews. [2136]

You gentlemen are just as good judges of human character, many of you a thousand-fold better judges of human character than am I. Many of you have had a breadth [2136] of human experience and human conduct that dwarfs anything that I have had, but I will ask you, gentlemen, would you want to send a man to the chair on the testimony of the little girl that went on the stand yesterday? ... This woman [Gaines] ... comes to attack the credibility of Mrs. Campbell, ... of

Officer Fay, ... of LaBrecque, ... of Harry Kurlansky, ... of Miss Allen.

Gentlemen, ... even though we had not offered a single witness against Lola Andrews, she killed herself on the witness stand by her own personality, ... [2137]

Gentlemen, remember you are judges of human credibility. You are the ones to determine how much faith and credit you are going to give to the testimony of witnesses. [2137]

Now we come to Goodridge ... who says he identified Sacco. You remember that he never saw Sacco until sometime in September when Sacco was arraigned in court, ... [H]ow Goodridge happened to be in this court room at that time does not appear ... . Hans Berhsin could not identify any one, but this man Goodridge ah, positive, certain, definite, unequivocal. [2137]

I pass on to Louis Pelzer, the man up in the Rice & Hutchins factory who looked out through the crack in the window and saw Berardelli falling, and with the divided attention upon the one side he fastened his eyes down here on Sacco and fixed him in his mind forever as the guilty murderer. Over here with his other eye he fixed it on the number of the car, and that number of the car remained forever fixed in his mind, bullets flying in all directions...[2137] He says he did not want to be called as a witness and that was the reason he gave this statement to Mr. Reid. Yet what had he done at that very time? He had given the automobile number, he says, to the Government, and he was the only witness that had it, and ... he knew that the Commonwealth was bound to call him. He had nothing to gain by telling us this story, unless he was filled with malice and prejudice and ill will... . [2138] When Mr. Reid talked with Mr. Pelzer, Pelzer was not working. Ah, but a few months later he got a job at Rice & Hutchins, ... [2138] To what extent ... did the ... economic need of a job mold Pelzer's mind into saying what they need. [2139]

But my attitude is here, that so far as the trial of this issue is concerned, the attitude of the district attorney's office has been one of unfailing courtesy and unfailing fairness, but the ancestry of some of this testimony, for which the district's office is not responsible, may be subject to serious question. I refer to Pelzer. [2139]

Brenner, McCallum [sic] and Constantino ... who were working right alongside of Pelzer, they all give the unequivocal contradiction to Pelzer's testimony, that Pelzer did not see the number of the car from

417

out of this window at all, facing on Pearl Street. He saw the number of the car from out of this window (indicating) facing up Pearl Street as the car disappeared. Pelzer did not see a thing out of the window on Pearl Street except possibly the falling body of Berardelli through the crack in the window. [2139]

Burke was right down there eight feet from the car, rushed to the telephone and put the call into the Brockton Enterprise, ... [2140]

[T]he Court will instruct you...that circumstantial evidence is a proper matter for a jury to consider. **Circumstances may point to guilty many times even stronger than the human eye itself as a matter of direct testimony**.... [2140]

Sacco when taken into custody did say that he did intend to go with his friend Vanzetti to see Vanzetti's friend Pappi that night.... It is admitted that that is a false statement of fact. I should say it is only partly true. They did intend to see Pappi, but they did also intend to do something else, namely, to get the Overland car. [2142]

Now, I am not going to pretend to you gentlemen that all that Sacco said to Mr. Katzmann was predicated upon the fear that he was going to get in trouble over selective service or over his war attitude or anything of that kind. That is not my position. I am explaining solely and exclusively the Johnson episode on that issue. Inso- [2144] far as Sacco's other statements, to wit, the most flagrant example, "Did you work on April 15th?" there is a pure matter of recollection. It is manifest from the record that Sacco did his best to tell Mr. Katzmann all the truth as he was best able to recollect it.... I do not believe there is a man in this [jury] box but what if he came to any one of us of counsel in connection with a small sized petty civil matter and we began to check you back on your dates that you would have an awful lot of trouble to tell where you were 30 days, 60 days or 90 days back. It is a hard job, gentlemen and remember that that boy was under arrest at that time. Is it any wonder that he was uncertain? [2145]

Why, gentlemen, what have you got to do in this case in order to return a verdict? You have got to say that the whole Kelley family lied. You have got to say that some 20 odd witnesses called in connection with various phases of the movement of the defendant are all liars, unequivocal, unmitigated, unfaltering liars, and on top of that you have got to say that we of counsel had aided, abetted, advised, encouraged this perjury.... [2145]

Bosco, Dentamore, Williams, Affe, Kelley, Mr. Hayes all have told you the movements of Sacco on April 15th. You have got to say that they have all committed perjury... . [2147]

Gentlemen, if the time has come when a microscope must be used to determine whether a human life is going to continue to function or not and when the users of the microscope themselves can't agree, when experts called by the Commonwealth and experts called by the defense are sharply defined in their disagreements, then I take it that ordinary men such as you and I should well hesitate to take a human life. [2147]

The man that committed that crime must go to the chair... . If that boy committed this crime, there is no penalty too severe to visit upon him .

You are the responsible men. You are the judges of the facts. The Court gives you the law, but you and you only can pronounce the verdict upon facts, ... [Y]ou are duty bound to give it [the verdict] in accordance with the facts as you believe them to have been found on the witness stand. I thank you. [2148]

ARGUMENT OF JEREMIAH J. McANARNEY, ESQ.

You are 12 men, and it will be foolish for me for one minute to think that the consensus of you 12 men, your minds acting together, is not far [2148] superior to mine... [2149]

You cannot kick a ball around 5 or 6 weeks but what it will get its level. You cannot play with this case as a case of a murder at Braintree for 5 or 6 weeks and conceal the true issue in this case... . You would not kill a dog on that identification at Braintree. [2149]

She [Splaine] says she sees this man; he is leaning out of the car...If his body obscures the driver, how did she see the hand leaning one-third of the way along on the seat, only that she is mistaken. [2151]

You take Miss Devlin, "it was a tall man, a stout, large man" that she saw... . They [witnesses like Devlin at the Brockton police station] are brought up, ... they are packed up there ... [t]o pick out a man. What man? This man, the man they got down in the room [cell]. That may be ... their conception of a fair way to identify a man [no police line-up]. [2151]

That McGlone, ... There is nothing yellow in that young fellow... . [I]sn't that the man to say if these were the men he wouldn't have

419

known it when we are under the cloud—not under cloud, but when the government is carrying the burden of proving beyond reasonable doubt that these are the men and such a man as that [McGlone] says he can't identify them, what does it mean...? [2152]

Bostock says—and what do you say of Bostock? Was there anything weak looking about that man? He was right there, he saw them. He was within 50 or 60 feet of them.... He could have touched the automobile if he wanted to. Are these the men? What do you say about that? Doesn't that, if we stop right there, or if we went a thousand times beyond there, wouldn't these two men be two men— English speaking men—wouldn't that prove to you that these [defendants] were not the men...? [2152]

Well, gentlemen, we slip along this identification. We pick them as we get them. Unfortunately there were Spaniards and Italians there .... It is the first time in ... my experience as a lawyer was a race indicted as they are in this case .... Is it to be presumed because an Italian is an Italian that he is a murderer, that he will shield a murderer...? [2152]

She [Mrs. Liscomb] told you ... that that face [she saw] wasn't the face of Sacco.... [2153]

And Chase, the man that worked on the corner ... heard the car whirl around the corner.... He tells the state officer that man he saw had hair nothing like the defendant Sacco. [2154]

[I]t isn't one reflection on this district attorney, who, outside of the fact that he wants to win this case—and I want to win it also—is as good a friend as I have got, and he or Mr. Williams or any other man there, I have got to go before those men, I have got to contest them, with them other cases and before this court—one of the most learned judges we have, whose brains and whose ability is acknowledged by the bar, by the judges of the supreme and superior court and every court in this land. [2154]

[W]e have got to produce the evidence that will show these men are innocent. The government is producing evidence that will show them guilty.... [2155]

But, gentlemen, I want to say I am not going to stay a great while at Braintree. They came and went. Beridinis [sic], that Italian fellow... . He can't give us a very intelligent description of what the men looked like.... We have a man also who was a rather cool, calculating fellow, that Goodridge that follows him.... [B]ut when that man Goodridge came here it turned out he was up here on business of his own with his attorney here on the September [court] term.... [2155]

This, gentlemen, was a hold-up job, pure and simple. Going back. The men planned to get away after they got this money. All right. How were they? They would park a car somewhere, wouldn't they? They wouldn't undertake during a period of two or three days in the car they were exhibiting themselves from 9 o'clock until 3 o'clock right in the heart of the ... town of South Braintree where everyone saw it. [2156] .... That Sacco, known as he was—on their own evidence— **who is within 15 feet of the windows of the Rice & Hutchins factory,** right there for hours, standing up in front of the drug store on the corner, the best place he could expose himself, in the depot, where that big man, [Heron] ... said he saw him, where every one saw him, knowing that he was known, knowing that he had worked there, ... Gentlemen, does that [behavior] appeal to you as the ordinary human reasoning? [2157]

And gentlemen, when you weigh this case and any part of this case, it isn't what witnesses say, it isn't what attorneys argue, but you take what the ordinary human mind would probably do under the same circumstances, and you have got a pretty fair rule to get the answer. Take what the ordinary man would do under those circumstances. [2157]

If he [Sacco] now got that money and got into his car by the taking of those two lives away, he knew that the limb of the law of the United States was against him, and he wouldn't be—it is foolish to say he would take a chance and he would go back to the factory. These men are brighter than that. They don't understand our language very well, but when you strip those men from their broken English, you have got more than the ordinary type of fellow. [2157]

The poise of Vanzetti as he spoke on that stand, courteously and gently to the district attorney, ... his poise was simply wonderful. [2157]

Now, Sacco has met with the situation, sickness at home. What was his home? His mother had died, and he has told you he had some letters. He showed to Kelley the letter that came to him about the first. Kelley says so ... [H]e was going home, and that he hurried up then. [2158] .... Was he the type of man who would be out doing a hold-up job, he with his father ill, with his mother dead, and the people at home advising him to come home to his father? [2159]

George Kelley, when last on the stand gave some evidence which was not interesting. It was that rear end collision that he might get in certain conditions... . Don't you feel that Kelley, as he first said, he trusted this fellow with the keys of the place...? [2159]

There is going to be into this case **the question of conscious guilt**... . [2159] [I]t is going to be said that their actions up there at West Bridgewater, their conduct ... indicated that they were guilty of some crime... . Is it a crime because Williams, ... the man on the financial paper or some paper in Boston, that he comes here when he knows this man [Sacco] was there? Is that a crime? The dinner—he is the only one apparently in the group that went to the dinner. The dinner was spoken of by Quadagnia [sic] and by Williams and by somebody else. I think Quadagnia [Guadenagi] said the dinner was in the evening. That isn't true, because the dinner was at noon, because this ... last man, and he is a clean cut type of man—his position shows it—he [Dentamore] said he had just come from the dinner to Editor Williams of the Boston Transcript. [2160]

There have been men here ... who know that that meeting on the 25th of April was held. Those men know that at that meeting the situation in New York was discussed. Those men know that Vanzetti was appointed a committee to go over there in regard to this Salsedo who met his death on the 4th, 3rd or 4th of May. [2160]

There are many human beings in this state ... who know that is the truth, who know that Vanzetti went out to do that which he says he went to do, know that they arranged to get this car, know that just what he was doing was what you would expect him to do, to slip around and get hold of that [anarchist] literature and put it out of the way. [2161]

Gentlemen, this is no myth. You have got Coacci deported on the 16th day, taken in custody, taken to—on the train on the 17th and put aboard boat on the 18th... . Is it nothing that Boda was last seen there on the **20th** and the chief of police talked to him? Note the question of the district attorney to Sacco, "Do you mean to tell this jury that Boda, living in Bridgewater, came from Bridgewater down to Stoughton and went from Stoughton back to Bridgewater to get his Overland car?" ... Boda was living in Boston at that time. The Coacci house was cleaned out. Boda beat the authorities to it. Get aboard and exit Boda; and we care not for Boda only he had that Overland car and we were going to use it that night. [2161]

Yes, we have got officer Connolly here. On the words, the wonderful words of that man Connolly we are going to have the question of **conscious guilt** worked out.... On the witness stand there he was going along mildly, had a quiet tone of voice, and when he got to the question what he did, Connolly began to smile.... Connolly was there then listening to the sweetest music of his young life, the sound of Connolly's voice when he was telling you what he did... He sees poor Sacco there [in the police car] and he [2162] reaches to put his hand under his overcoat, and that smile came on again. [McAnarney cites Connolly's testimony.] [2162]

Ruth Johnson—she testified to seeing these men. She testified they were up there. She went up [to the Bartlett house] and they followed her.... Now, gentlemen, bear in mind that Mrs. Johnson said that—told about the light playing and the light waving with his hand and these men acting suspiciously. Where she got that inspiration, I don't know. [2163]

These men lied. They lied and lied when they were arrested.... A man is arrested, but that is different from being convicted. He [Katzmann] said, "They had Orcciani. You knew that. Why did you lie that you did not know Orcciani?"

They were informed with knowledge of what had transpired in New York. They knew their position exactly without any question. They knew they were amenable to something [possessing anarchist literature]. [2164]

We have had experts on revolvers, and we have had Mr. Colt here. You get an answer here, a little bit with Levangie.... Levangie at that time saw the man. He may be the connecting link against Vanzetti. Levangie said and pointed to Vanzetti in that box, "There is the man who was driving the car over there." He yellowed right down to his shoes [see Transcript pp. 419-425] when he said that after what he had told me.... [2166]

I will take the Colt revolver. We had Van Amburgh. I will call him the "circles" man... And he says that the bullet 3, the one the doctors say killed Berardelli came from the Colt revolver that was found on Sacco. That is a fearful statement to make.... [2166]

[H]ere is Vanzetti, gentlemen.... Take the revolver, the H. & R. revolver. What have we done? We have gone back and faithfully brought that revolver from Maine.... Atwater, the first gentleman who took the stand, a stately man, and he answered like a man, and he never lost his dignity. He knew that H. & R. revolver, how it was come by. He knew it was in the family of the brother-in-law and testified to it. Orcciani got it. Orcciani sold it to the Italian fellow [Falzini], and the Italian fellow sold it to Vanzetti, a clean, straight transaction. [2168]

May I see that please, the revolver? And the holster——the stitching on it.... Gentlemen, give us credit for something. There was numbers on the bottom of that revolver. If falsehood was going to help us win this case and if we were going to stoop to falsehood, gentlemen, we would have done it a thousand times. What would we have had to have done? There is your number right there on the bottom, G-82, 581.... If we wanted to deceive, if we wanted to tell an untruth to escape death, we could do it, gentlemen, but that table [of defense counsel] has not stooped to that and never will while I am conducting a case. There is proof of our honesty. ... [N]otice on it [holster] a tear. [2168]

He [Slater] made a stitch right on there [holster]. Those fellows [witnesses on Vanzetti's revolver] come up here under summons as well as Slater in that room for a week, but for what? To tell the truth for two unfortunate men, and they are branded as falsifiers, they too, go in with all the others, that men may escape their just deserts. [2169]

What is the meaning of this Iver-Johnson matter? What does it mean? Their last man [James H. Jones] says there is no record of the revolver being taken out. Mrs. Berardelli says that that revolver had a broken spring. Here is the joke. Why ask a man up there about a hammer? [2169]

Vanzetti discarding a powerful Savage revolver with which **they say he was shooting**, going in and getting and carrying around this branded gun in his pocket to help identify him? An old obsolete revolver16 or18 years old, and giving away a good one that was a gun. Gentlemen, it is easy or hard, just as you want to take it. You saw them. [2169] You saw the second Iver-Johnson man say that the Berardelli revolver was a 32.... This is a 38; and that other little fellow [Falzini] who sold it to Vanzetti, didn't know whether there was 5 or 6 chambers. I bet there are some fellows on this panel [jury] have a revolver and don't know whether there are five or six chambers in it. [2170]

How about Hayes? ... Hasn't he produced here his book? ... When that man says he went to Boston and came out about that time...No, no, he didn't see Sacco, but Sacco picked him out and said he saw him. Give Hayes credit for telling the truth, because were he disposed to help us, all he had to do was say "Yes, I saw Sacco on that train." Please let the truth come in, even though it comes through our side of the case, and we gave you the truth there. [2170]

There is one thing you want to bear in mind. Please don't construe the ordinary man by an Italian. If you go out and flock a dozen Italians together, the chances are you will get a gun or two, anyway. You could handle one hundred—fifty other men and you won't find a revolver. [2170]

Sacco says he went the last week in March to get information in regard to a passport. He learned some things. He took the big photograph in on the 15th. Those show one thing or the other, they are telling the truth or not. Take it as you will. If all the men have lied about the 15th, it may be so. Believe it if you will.

She [Mrs. Sacco] said they were cleaning house, that they came there, that they talked about getting the [anarchist] literature away, that they took those shells out, Vanzetti took the shells, ... and said he would sell them for propaganda. [2170]

They have got to get **conscious guilt** into this case because that identification will not stand ... the acid test of truth. Vanzetti ... did not have Alvin [sic] Fuller, ... down there on this case to come in and testify to you. He has only got the poor people he traveled with and who know him, joking with the Jewish fellow, who sold him cloth. But the more my brother [Katzmann] pricked that fellow [Rosen], the more he began to ring true. He was funny as could be, but as he came along he told enough. **He pretty near made an iron proof safe there**. Did Vanzetti buy of him or did he not? [2171]

Vanzetti, 11 years down there in Plymouth... . Is he intelligent? Would he be bobbing up and down at every station to see where East Braintree was? [2171]

This man who was on the train, Parkhurst [Faulkner], though he picked this fellow out as the fellow, Vanzetti as the fellow he saw get on the train he don't know who was sitting beside him... [2172]

Now, the fellow who was here yesterday [Affe]. May I have the signatures, the grocery book? ... There was some other papers with that. They are all together. Now, you have seen that. I have not even looked at this. I have not compared it at all. You can look at it. You compare the entries. [2172]

Mr. Cole has testified. Cole picked out that fellow... . Cole says they were up there twice... . We get back to another man, [Austin

Reed]. He says these fellows in this car, 40 feet from the railroad track or about there, that the car stopped. He was down there with his stop sign. These, gentlemen, are the men who committed the murder... . What did they do? Pull their heads down on their shoulders? No. Vanzetti sticks his head out and yells at this fellow and wants to know what he is stopping him for. How foolish that is. Didn't he know there were trains went up in front by him and knows? He did not have to ask him why he was holding him up. Take your own common reasoning, and if you come to a crossing and there is a flag man expecting a train comes out in front of the gates, tell me whether you will ask that fellow why he is holding you up, and you never committed a murder and ... shouts at him again. [2173]

Mrs. Andrews takes the stand again [after a recess: see transcript, p. 357], and she then says that this she thinks is the face that she pointed out to Mr. Moore as one that was there... . What she had for dinner was more than milk... . [2174]

But going back to my client, Vanzetti, all there is against Vanzetti is what? That he happened to be alive at this time, that is about all. [2174]

But you gentlemen, you are here today, and may you live long, and I know that your decision when you make it in this case will be such that your feeling ever afterwards will be that you did right, that you did right in this case. [2174]

The only issue here is the identification, and when I say to you what I have said, I have passed the details of this identification, because no human mind can come to anything other than utter confusion as to that identification in every part of it. If it leaves anything with you, it leaves the biggest, most wholesome reasonable doubt that ever was, and no man would want a friend of his convicted on that identification. [2175]

But unfortunately they were laying **a trap for Coacci and Boda**, and when that trap was sprung, Vanzetti and Sacco unfortunately were in it. That was the unfortunate thing for those two. Coacci was wanted, and he got it pretty quick, in his line. Boda was wanted when they were ready on him. [2175]

I will say to you I did not want a man sitting upon the panel whose face I did not like. I am throwing no bouquets to you. We had a very funny experience here, Mr. Katzmann and I. He has been, as he always has been, a perfect gentleman. [2175]

There are men, 12, on this panel. You may be friends of mine. You may be friends of Mr. Katzmann... . Be that as it may, we have selected you as being 12 men we are satisfied to look you in the eye and ... feel there is no antagonism. That is a wonderful thing. [2175]

I want them [Sacco and Vanzetti] to know that we have done—that everything has been done as Massachusetts takes pride in doing, granting to any man, however lowly his station, the fullest rights to our Massachusetts Commonwealth laws. . . Those are the parts we play. And no man sympathizes any more with you when you walk from this room than I do. I know every one of you want to do what is right... . Those two human beings in that dock want you to do what is right. [2176]

I expect on that evidence that you will say that the evidence does not prove beyond a reasonable doubt that those men were there. There can be no gainsaying that. Human logic doesn't stop, human reasoning doesn't fail because these two radicals are on trial. [2176]

[A]ll this camouflage about the Berardelli gun is simply to put that gun into the possession of Vanzetti, and **if that is Berardelli's gun**, of course he is guilty, ... [2178]

This case has no parallel in the history of Massachusetts criminal jurisdiction... . I thank every man of you from the bottom of my heart for the consideration you have given this case, and I want every man, too, of this panel to treat these two defendants as if they were your own individual brother. Take that as the test [when making your judgment]... . I thank you, gentlemen. [2179]

ARGUMENT OF THE DISTRICT ATTORNEY, FREDERICK G. KATZMANN, ESQ.
AFTERNOON SESSION

I have listened to the arguments of learned counsel through a long morning, and I have wondered why it was that the tremendous force of personality and argument exhibited by both counsel has been directed almost entirely, gentlemen of the jury, to the defense of the defendant Sacco and almost not an appreciable portion of either argument devoted to the defense of the defendant Vanzetti. [2181]

Is it, gentlemen of the jury, that neither counsel who have argued to you have confidence in the alibi of the defendant Vanzetti, and that it is hopeless in their opinion, and that all their tremendous effort and intelligence must be directed to pulling out a verdict in favor of the defendant Sacco if they can, and that the alibi of the defendant Vanzetti does not satisfy these two gentlemen themselves? [2181]

It is akin, ... to the opening made by [the] other learned, skillful and experienced counsel. He [Callahan] never whispered a word to you, gentlemen, when he opened this case, as to where Vanzetti was on April 15th. And ... he never even suggested on the day that he opened this case for the defense, that they were prepared [2181] to admit that the defendants, Sacco and Vanzetti, were down in West Bridgewater at Simon Johnson's house on the night of May 5th, ... I won't overlook that, gentlemen, because it is of tremendous probative force. The acts of counsel, gentlemen, bind the defendants themselves. [2182]

The Commonwealth demands that if you are satisfied beyond a reasonable doubt that these defendants, either one of them or both of them acting jointly, took the lives or assisted in taking the lives of Alessandro Berardelli and Frederick A. Parmenter, that you find them guilty of the full offense; and if we failed to satisfy you beyond a reasonable doubt, that you acquit them. [2182]

My brother McAnarney said in his argument this morning, that the defendant Vanzetti would be foolish to take up a 38 calibre Harrington & Richardson revolver in place of a Savage automatic... . We say in Plain English that on the evidence we have proven to you beyond any reasonable doubt that the defendant Sacco fire[d] a bullet from a Colt automatic that killed Alessandro Berardelli; that **some other person** whose name we do not know and who is not under arrest, in custody or upon his trial, **killed** the man **Frederick A. Parmenter** with a Savage automatic, and that that was **not** the defendant **Vanzetti**. [2183]

Who it was that with a Savage automatic fired three bullets from a Savage automatic into Berardelli and two into Parmenter, we do not know and we have offered no evidence on, except that there was such a man... . [2183]

That we do say to you is that we expect you find upon all the evidence that the 28 [sic] Harrington & Richardson revolver that was found upon the defendant Vanzetti was the 38 Harrington & Richardson revolver that poor Berardelli tried to draw from his pocket to defend himself... . [2183]

There were six bullets and every one of them were automatic bullets, and the Harrington & Richardson cannot fire an automatic bullet. We offered that evidence, gentlemen, to show you that some person took that revolver off the person of the dying Berardelli... . [2183]

He [McCullum] says that when he raised the window in the middle trio and looked out from the second floor, he saw a man whom we have shown and will argue was Sacco, with a gun answering the description, a bright nickel gun, gentlemen of the jury, in the left hand of the man putting in the auto a money box. And that is from ... the defendant's own witness, Peter McCullum. [2184]

[T]he assailant of Berardelli ... had to use his right hand to put the box into the automobile. In his left hand he had neither the time nor the opportunity to dispose of the gun that he had just taken from the dying Berardelli. We say that man is the defendant Sacco. [2184]

[F]or days they have been devoting their utmost effort to satisfy you that it was from **consciousness of guilt** of a trivial offense and not consciousness of guilt of the commission of this tremendous and atrocious crime of taking the lives of two innocent men... . [2185]

Do you remember Frantonelli's [Frantello's] testimony? ... [Y]ou will remember the discussion ... between his examiner, myself, and Frantonelli, as to the nationality of these two men. Nationality is not an issue in this case, gentlemen, except as a means of identification... . He said that he passed men on the fence ... [while] going from the lower to the upper factory.

He said one was dark complected, shabbily dressed and needed a shave, and he said that one week later he was taken to the town hall in Braintree to see a man there under arrest, and you gentlemen know ... that the only man taken under arrest in connection with this crime to the Braintree town hall was a man who has never yet, gentlemen, stepped a foot inside this Court room, Ricardo Orcciani. [2187]

He was arrested May 6th, the day after these defendants were arrested, and he still remains, ... a mystery to you 12 men. You have heard of his being out in front of this court house during this trial ... Orcciani, the associate of these [2187] two defendants at the Simon Johnson house, at the Sacco house, a friend of Boda and a friend of both these defendants, never for some reason, gentlemen, has been permitted by the defense to take the stand. [2188]

Frantello, ... in describing to you gentlemen, that these two men who were at the fence were English speaking men and not "wops" as the Commonwealth claimed he said when interviewed by them, ... [H]e is the star witness produced by the defense to show that neither Sacco nor Vanzetti—and we do not claim Vanzetti was sitting on the fence on all our own evidence—... but we say and ask you to find Sacco was one of those two men and Frantonelli is the only witness produced to show you that it [he] was not. [2188]

And they produced one Frank Burke from Brockton, one of their early witnesses, ... and he tripped himself up and contradicted himself so many times in the course of his testimony that ... it is idle for me to go over it step by step... . You remember ... that Burke said that he was away [from home] when he learned of the arrest of these defendants. And again the next witness, Pecheur, tripped him on that, because he said they were up in Harmony Hall, the Knights of Pythias hall up to Brockton, ... the next morning when they learned of the arrest. [2190] This man Burke [is one] who talked with Mr. Woodbury of the defense six or seven times ... and who had been to the office of Mr. Moore from seven to eight times.... . [2191]

I want to discuss the manner in which an alibi may be put together, ... Take Rosen, take Mrs. Brini—Mrs. Brini, a convenient witness for this defendant Vanzetti... . Mrs. Brini, in whose husband's home the defendant Vanzetti lived the first four years that he ever lived in Plymouth [1913-1917] and whose daughter Lefavre, the little 16 year old girl said of Vanzetti that he was the most intimate friend and was like one of the family.... . Mrs. Brini, it is agreed in another cause when another date was alleged, testified to the whereabouts of this same Vanzetti on that other date there involved, a stock, convenient and ready witness as well as friend of the defendant Vanzetti. Mr. Corl, Mrs. Corl, young Morey. That is all. [2192]

And for Sacco, Bosco, Guadenagi, John D. Williams, Dentamore, Affe, and finally rest yesterday. And how are those alibis put together? [2192]

Guidobone is typical of the manner—each and every witness save Affe, the travelling grocery man—his manner of fixing the date of it is typical of that of every other witness for the defense in this case. Guidobone says [2192] to you under his oath to you 12 men of common sense and intelligence, "I remember I had a cod fish put in my hand at 12:10 o'clock on April 15 because on the 19th day of April I was operated on for appendicitis." [2193]

The witness Corl says, and his wife and Morey—until he spilled and destroyed the whole of the Corl evidence by the last remarks he made on the stand—that during the whole of the week that ended April 17, Saturday, Corl was painting a boat, and because on the 17th it was his wife's birthday and that he put the boat into the water and towed a boat from South Duxbury over to Plymouth, he remembers what he was doing on the 15th... . He was painting that boat, Monday, Tuesday, Wednesday, Thursday and Friday, and what he said happened could have happened as well on the 14th or the 13th or the 12th as on the 15th, ... [2193]

Why, gentlemen, I once knew of a preposterous story ... told by a man ... being caught out in a fog when he was leading his cow out from pasture not 500 feet distant from his barn. He said the fog set in so suddenly and terrifically and remained so long it was a week before he could find the barn. He became lost. And his listener refused to accept that story and doubted its veracity, and the teller of it indignantly replied, "If you don't believe me, you walk over there and I will show you the barn." [2193]

Gentlemen, if you do not believe that I had a cod fish placed in my hands at 12:13 on the fifteenth because of this appendicitis operation on the 19th, would it have added any verity to the story, any convincing quality that would have warranted merit if Guidobone had bared his side and shown you the scar. "Gentlemen, if you do not believe I had the cod fish on the 15th at 12:13 and was operated on on the 19th, look at the scar, that proves it." [2193]

Would it have added to the convincing quality of the stories of any [2193] of these alibi witnesses, ... if Dentamore produced the menu, if there were a printed one that was given to the guests at the Williams banquet on the 15th, and said, "If you don't believe that I met Sacco at quarter of three in the Giordani coffee house after the banquet was over, look and see, we had olives and we had chicken, and here is the menu to prove it." [2194]

What in logic, gentlemen, is the connection between any of these things that they say helps to mark the time...? Corl says he remembers it was the 15th he saw him in part because he was painting the boat that week, and in part because his wife's birthday fell on the17th. [2194]

If there was any actual connection between the indisputable events upon which they predicate their recollection! Do you suppose that there wasn't a banquet to Mr. Williams of the Transcript on the 15th? You know better. You know there was such a banquet. Do you suppose Guidobone did not go to the hospital and was operated on for appendicitis...? [T]he Commonwealth has never taken a move to dispute it. Of course it is true. That is fixed. They start with something fixed. Do you suppose ... Corl did not paint his boat that week? Of course he painted his boat that week. It is a probable fact, undisputable. He starts with that. [2194]

Lastly, do you suppose ... John D. Williams did not insert an ad which he secured for La Notizia ... on some Thursday in April. When he was asked by Guadenagi and when he was asked by Felicani to fix the date when he had met the defendant Sacco—... and the date that he had to fix it upon was the 15th day of April, what would he do, what would you do if you had records like his? You would go and see what business you did that day. Then you would start with that. [2194]

Rosen ... described the selling of the cloth to the defendant Vanzetti [on April 15]. Well, that should be examined in exactly the same light that you would examine the [2195] cow and barn, the appendicitis and the fish, the wife's birthday and the boat and the banquet to John D. Williams [Editor Williams], which indisputably fell upon that date. [2196]

There was no connection between any of those things nor any more connection than the Rosen testimony. An itinerant pedlar [sic] he went all over the Commonwealth of Massachusetts selling goods, ... and he could not tell you with accuracy the number of times or the date that he had visited any other place, and he said in direct examination ... that April 15, 1920, was the last time he had been to Plymouth. Then in the next breath he said he had been down to Plymouth several times. He could not give you the date of any other time he was there, and what was there extraordinary about that? A visit to Plymouth in his usual course. He made three or four of them a year. He had been down two months before, he said, and he said he sold cloth to the same woman to whose house he went with Vanzetti on the 15th, two months before. That lady was Mrs. Brini, and she took the stand and she said she had never seen Joseph Rosen before the 15th of April. [2196]

Think of it, gentlemen! A man who came down at the expense that would be involved to earn his living in Plymouth selling cloth sitting down when he had just started to work and just got up from the only customer he had got that day going around the corner of the street and sitting down to use up time so as to make it come out right with blowing whistles at 12 o'clock. And you are expected to believe his testimony, ... Why, gentlemen, they brought the cloth here with the hole in it.... . The minute you saw the hole in the blue piece of cloth you instantly knew that Mrs. Brini, Lefavre Brini, the daughter, and Joe Rosen were all right because there was the hole in the cloth. [2196]

That is the alibi defense in this case. I have not begun to do it justice, and the only way that justice could be done to it in its full absurdity and [2196] utter lack of convincing qualities would be to read every word of it and you would be here very likely until Labor Day. [2197]

What is the connection and what is the importance of the [2197] West Bridgewater trip? ... [I]t affords to you ... evidence ... that the actions of those two defendants that night showed **consciousness of the guilt** of the commission of those two murders... . [W]hat is the explanation of the ... conduct ... by the defendants that night?... "Yes," in effect they said, "We acted suspiciously ... because we were conscious of our guilt in another regard. We were conscious that we were guilty of a federal offense...that was of a Radical or Anarchistic or Socialistic nature. And we were also conscious of our guilt because of the fact that we had evaded the draft and that was why we did what we did. That is why we went away and that is why later on to the officers of the Commonwealth we denied that we had been there." [2198]

Well, now, let us examine that just a little closer. Does it strike you quite as being the truth? The defendant Vanzetti says that on April 25th, Sunday night, he took a train from Boston to New York, that he went over there in the interests of some people in whom his organization had an interest, with whom we have no concern, ... That issue is not being tried here. Neither is Radicalism being tried here. This is a charge of murder and it is nothing else, ... [2198]

And Vanzetti says he returned to Plymouth on April 29th, ... and in explaining his ... conduct, or their joint course of conduct in running away from the Johnson house—because that is what they did, gentlemen, they ran away... . [H]e was in Plymouth on the afternoon of the 29th of April, the 30th of April and the 1st day of May until he departed for Boston in the afternoon or evening and he says in later explaining his monumental falsehoods to me on everything I asked him about the Johnson episode and in explaining it on the stand, "Why, we weren't going to get the literature that night. We were going to get the Boda automobile and Boda and I were going on to Plymouth and Orcciani and Sacco were going back home." [2199]

In the next, witness Sacco himself, we have the testimony that they were going to get literature that night.... . He had previously said the day before when I was examining him that they were going to get the literature that night, but it was the next morning that he came back, after an absence from his examiner of some 10 or 12 hours, that he changed his story and said they were not going to get literature but they were going to warn friends in Brockton. [2199]

Vanzetti, loafing around there from Monday afternoon to Wednesday night, the man who came back from New York with the terrible report, frightened to death, wanted to go notify people in Bridgewater, Brockton, Everett and Salem to be sure to get this stuff out of their house and Vanzetti was going to provide a hiding place, as he said, with some house owner down in Plymouth. Vanzetti goes over to New York for that information. He was so frightened, gentlemen, when he was down in Plymouth on the ... 29th and 30th of April and 1st of May, he never made a move to ask an individual to hide it ... . April 29th, April 30th, May 1st, May 2nd, May 3rd, May 4th, May 5th. Seven days gone by, frightened out of his life for fear of deportation, and he never asked an individual. [2200]

Sacco, frightened so he could not tell the truth, and he never made a move from May 2d, when he went home from that Sunday meeting and heard this awful report by Vanzetti, to protect his own home and take it out.... . That is their explanation! ... They ask you to swallow that.... . He was so afraid of deportation he says he was going Saturday the 11th ... when he had been wanting to go [to Italy]for months, he falsified to the authorities because he would be taken back there free of charge. That is their defense. [2200]

She [Ruth Johnson] went in [to the Bartlett house]to telephone for Warren Lawton of the police department of West Bridgewater in consequence of **a prearranged plan** when the authorities were looking for Mike Boda and for nobody else. She said that these defendants followed up on the street railway side of the track and waited outside until she came out 10 minutes later, and then accompanied her back and came over to the motor cycle, ... [2201]

They both stubbornly resist any suggestion that she is right that they followed her up, and they have good cause for resisting that assertion, because it shows you, gentlemen, that their story could not possibly be true on **consciousness of guilt** for a slacker job, ... [T]hey could not possibly explain that [following Ruth Johnson] on the basis of [collecting] literature ... . [2201]

[T]hese men who had not gotten the automobile, who ... did not have a single scrap of Socialistic, Anarchistic ... literature ... in their physical possession, who were simply men who were on foot out there that night.... What was there for them to be afraid of? ... They had no literature.... But they had arsenals upon them. [2203]

Maybe, gentlemen, you think that is the way men would be armed who were going on an innocent trip, ... at night time after closing hours of the garage and when the men [sic] who ran it was in bed, going to make a social trip down to see Pappi, the friend of Vanzetti, and he did not know where he lived, save that it was in East Bridgewater, gentlemen. [2204]

Sacco ... denied that he was armed, ... would have you believe, gentlemen, that he took the revolver,——think of it, gentlemen, going out in the woods to fire off the 32 cartridges to get rid of them because they were going next day, and tucked it in the waist band of his trousers and sat down to his supper and never knew it was in there and did not know there was 22 cartridges in his pocket, ... [2205]

[A]nd you will remember that he had said in direct examination that I never asked him about any particular crime in the interview I had with him! [Ed. Katzmann cites transcript, 1945-1946.] [2206]

"A. No, who is Berardelli? [See p. 1945.]

Q. Well, don't you read the papers? A. Yes, every morning I read the paper, Boston Post. [See. p. 1945.]

Q. Did you ever work in Braintree? A. No.

Q. Did you ever look for work in Braintree? A. No.

Q. Do you know what happened in Braintree last month?" I was talking in May, and that meant April, 1920. A. Yes.

Q. What was it? A. I read in the paper about bandits over there in front of Rice & Hutchins, robbing money. [See p. 1946.]

And he said 30 or 35 people came over and made him assume a posture, first facing them, then side to them, then turn around for them, and finally Sacco says, "Mary Splaine made me get down and point as if I was shooting, and I did not know that they were asking me about my whereabouts on the day of those bandit murders." [See p. 1922.]

Well, gentlemen, on top of these other fabrications perhaps you believe that. [2207]

I suggest common sense and logic must force you to find that this is a suspicious alibi that Sacco has built up around himself about being into Boni's restaurant and meeting people, talking with them, ... who are friends and associates of his, some of them associated with his very defense here now, and Williams associated in a business way with those friends, ... [A]nd he admits that he lied to his friend George Kelley—that he was falsifying again from consciousness of guilt of the crime that had happened but the day before. [2209]

He has falsified to you before your very faces. When Exhibit 43, his own cap that Lieut. Guerin says he got out of his own house was produced and shown to him before Lieut. Guerin testified he would not admit, gentlemen, that his own cap was his. [Moore interrupted and asked for a retraction of the last statement or for a reading of the record.] [2209] ... [A]nd will you ever forget, gentlemen, the amount of time that he took on the stand examining that [Guerin]] cap, ... [2210]

Then came the episode of trying the [Loring] cap on. Not his first trial of the cap, gentlemen, since it had been first produced in evidence, ... because it was tried on in your absence early one evening when we were out. You went out for recess. It was first handed to him, and properly so, by his counsel. He tried it on. Then he put it on his head, and it rested there, and then he pulled it down, and I submit to you gentlemen that that dark hat, which is the hat of the man who killed Alessandro Berardelli—because the man who killed Alessandro Berardelli went away bareheaded in that automobile—fits the head of the defendant Sacco exactly the same as does the hat that on the testimony of Guerin you would be warranted and should find is his hat... . Some one of you who wears a 7 1/8, if that is the size of those caps, try them both on. There is the acid test for you, gentlemen. [2210]

Pelzer ... got the number [of the bandit car] from the front end, 49783, ... His identification on the stand in direct examination of the defendant Sacco was positive. [2212]

There is Mr. Tracy, to whom the defendants have not referred in long argument. There is Harry Dolbeare ... Austin Reed ... Austin Cole. [2215]

They find fault, gentlemen, with Levangie, they say that Levangie is wrong in saying that Vanzetti was driving that car. I agree with them, ... but he saw the face of Vanzetti in that car, ... And can't you reconcile it with ... the probability that at that time Vanzetti was directly behind the driver.... If you recall the [bullet] hole in the sign board ... not far from his shanty, will you have any difficulty in dealing with the testimony of Levangie? [2215]

Mary Splaine ... Frances Devlin ... [are] young ladies who could have no enmity against the defendant Sacco. [2217]

Goodridge, when he saw the defendant Sacco, ... said that he was the man he saw on the right side of the car pointing the revolver at him.... [T]here is Tracy, who owned the drug-store building. He did not care much about people leaning up against it and he went down twice within a few minutes on a couple of errands just before noon time, went over to the jail, ... saw and recognized the defendant Sacco.... Austin Reed ... saw them just before the turning point in the flight of the car.... [2218]

I cannot recall ... that ever before I have laid eye or given ear to so convincing a witness as Lola Andrews. [2219]

I ask you to find, gentlemen, as to that Scavitto picture, Mr. Cole, the street railway conductor, on whose car these two defendants got the night of their arrest, ... said, "as I did not get a side view of him, Vanzetti, I would not say he is the man, but he looks like the man." [2221]

... McAnarney picked out Scavitto in the rear seat [of the court room] and rushed him out in the back and somebody conveniently lost good old Scavitto's straw hat and put on one [for the trial exhibit photograph] that looked, well, more like somebody else's hat, and then conveniently restored his straw hat when he came back there, and that is Scavitto.

Mr. McAnarney would have failed ... in this photographic effort of his if Cole did not state that he [Scavitto] looked like Vanzetti. He does look like Vanzetti. That is what McAnarney had his picture taken for. [2221]

Where was the [bandit] car found April 17th? In the [Manley] wood in West Bridgewater near the poor farm not far from Elm Square, a mile or two, where these defendants were on the night of May 5th.... Is there any association geographically there, gentlemen? [2223]

Then, gentlemen, this left handed twist bullet, No. 3, was fired by a Colt 32. Was it fired by this Colt 32? ... I say heaven speed the day when proof in any important case is dependent upon the magnifying glass and the scientist and is less dependent upon the untrained witness

437

without the microscope. Those things can't be wrong in the hands of a skilled user of a microscope.... [2224]

[T]here is [sic] lies the skill and the value of James E. Burns to his defense. He knew that bullet No. 3, the fatal bullet, was a Winchester. He used seven United States Bullets, and he gave as the reason the fact that the bullet no. 3, was of old manufacture by the Remington (Repeating) Arms, the Winchester (Repeating) Remington, and that he could not procure one just like it, and that the nearest to it [for test firing on June 18, 1921] was the United States bullet. [2226]

[S]omebody representing the defense, ... argued that man, Faulkner, [had] been coming on that train for months. That is not the fact.... He had ... injured a thumb or some portion of the hand and had been receiving hospital treatment at the Watertown Arsenal and was on his way that morning. He had been there several times before. [2228]

[T]hey produced this man Brooks to tell about a man getting off there [East Braintree] with a regularity, and they are trying to make you believe that a man who has been getting off within four to six weeks after the 15th of April with some regularity three or four or five times would have to ask where the East Braintree station was. [2228]

[T]hey produced the photograph of a man ... the defense considered to be a double of Vanzetti, ... and asked John Faulkner if this was the man he saw get of [sic] the train at East Braintree, and he said, "I wouldn't say," ... but on looking at the defendant in the dock, not looking at any picture of a man with a straw hat, not a man with a slouch hat, a man with a straw hat, ... if they wanted him [Faulkner] to recognize his face they ... should have got a picture of his face and his face only— [2229]

Now, passing hastily on to the question of the 38 revolver, I told you in the beginning the theory of the Commonwealth as to how it came into the possession of the defendant Vanzetti. The theory we say is supported amply by evidence. To controvert that they bring two men from the State of Maine who tell you they remember that gun substantially by the fact that the muzzle end, the end that would be fouler anyway, from the discharging, the bright nickel is worn off and right over the firing chamber. [2229]

One man said he saw it worn off on one side, and it is worn off on both sides, and then they produce a man, Falzini. Are you satisfied with the quality of that testimony? And don't forget what Vanzetti said. He said he bought it four or five years before somewhere in Boston and paid $16 or $17 for a $5 gun. [2229]

And is there any significance, gentlemen, in the fact that Falzini, the East Boston man last October, to whom Orcciani, the elusive Orcciani who has not been produced, is alleged to have sold it after buying it from a man in Norwood [Slater], Falzini says "that was a six-cylinder gun I had," and this revolver is a five cylinder. Is there any significance to the fact, gentlemen, that Vanzetti himself, when he was in the Brockton police station said it was a six-cylinder revolver? What does that mean, gentlemen? [2229]

Fitzmeyer the gunsmith ... said it was a new hammer put in that gun. Who knows more about it, the man who put the hammer in or James E. Burns; an expert user of fire arms, . .? [2230]

Now, as to the note book and the standard of writing of the itinerant grocery man Affe, who says on the 15th of April he received a payment of $15.50 and he wrote it in a book. The whole book is in evidence, gentlemen. Look through it.... . [2231] I say that Affe never wrote it, ... Look through it.... . Look at the very few times he wrote any dates. [2232]

Why didn't you bring Orcciani into this court room and why didn't you permit Orcciani to testify, ... He has been within the control of this defense. He had been outside the court room, as witnesses have testified, and he is not produced. What is the reason?

The Commonwealth has a right to draw the inference that if produced he would give testimony that is not helpful to the defendants. [2233] [Ed. Moore interrupted Katzmann again.]

MR. KATZMANN. I want to say with the utmost good nature, gentlemen, when I listened to four hours of argument ... on behalf of the defendants ... I never arose from my chair to interrupt in argument... . I have quoted you the evidence when they have interrupted before and I will quote it to you again. [2234]

[T]he deponent Andrower over Italy says in the early part of April he [Sacco] was there at 11 o'clock in the forenoon.

Mind you, he has 150 or 200 applications for passport a day, or they had in the consul's office, and that the 15th was a very slack day and that he remembered that Sacco was in on that day because when he came in with the family photograph of large size, taking it into the secretary to the consul, they looked at it and laughed, Andrower says, and expects 12 men in the county of Norfolk to believe it. "I remember the day because I happened to look at a calendar pad on the desk of the secretary." ... Well, maybe you believe that, gentlemen. Maybe you have grown up to years of discretion and you accept that. That is his testimony. [2235]

It is my duty as a public prosecutor to see that the constitutional guarantee to you, to your fellows, and to your families and friends within this district is upheld, to the end that your lives and your property and your safety may be assured. If I fail in the prosecution of my duty to use every honorable, every reasonable effort to keep that guarantee under the constitution, then I am an inefficient public servant. [2236]

If the Commonwealth has satisfied you beyond a reasonable doubt that they are guilty, the Commonwealth expects you to say so like men of honor and like men of courage. And the Commonwealth expects you to say they are not guilty if it has failed to satisfy you in accordance with the requirements of law.... They have had their day in court, and the Commonwealth has had its day in court. Both parties desire a final decision on this accusation. [2236]

A jury must decide the facts judicially.... Leave any consideration of sympathy for Mrs. Berardelli or sympathy for Mrs. Parmenter out of the case. Leave any sympathy for Mrs. Sacco or her boy out of this case...[H]e [Sacco] did not have sympathy for Mrs. Berardelli and Mrs. Parmenter, and he should have none extended to him.

The question is one of fact, gentlemen, arrived at under the rules of law.... [2236]

You are not taking away the lives of the defendants by finding them guilty of a murder of which they are guilty. The law takes their lives away and not you. It is for you to say if they are guilty and you are done. You pronounce no sentence of death ... . You are the consultants here, gentlemen, the twelve of you, and the parties come to you and ask you to find what the truth is on the two issues of guilt or innocence. Gentlemen of the jury, do your duty. Do it like men. Stand together you men of Norfolk. [2237]

THIRTY-SEVENTH DAY.
Dedham, Massachusetts, July14, 1921.

[Ed. Now, defense motions are made. Moore speaks to jury.]

MR. THOMAS McANARNEY. Motion for severance filed in behalf of the defendant Vanzetti July 8th, withdrawn, without prejudice to the original motion or without waiver of any private rights. [See p. 1972: "[We] filed a motion for severance and separate trial." Court denied defense motions for separate trials on June 6 (p. 50) and June 7 (p. 93).]

MR. JEREMIAH McANARNEY. Motions filed in behalf of the defendant Vanzetti that a verdict be directed for Vanzetti in both cases, which were filed at the close of the argument of the District Attorney, wherein counsel for the defendant Vanzetti states that the District Attorney disclaimed that the defendant Vanzetti was driving the automobile as it came over the crossing immediately following the shooting that day.

MR. MOORE. On behalf of the defendant Sacco, the defendant's counsel moves as follows: Now comes the defendant Sacco and moves that the Court order the jury upon all the evidence to return a verdict of not guilty as to said Sacco in each case, No. 5545 and 5546.

THE COURT. This Motion in behalf of the defendant Sacco was made after the conclusion of the arguments.

MR. MOORE. That is agreed, your Honor, but may I ask this: Let that be filed as at the conclusion of the evidence.

THE COURT. You may poll the jury, please, Mr. Clerk.

(The jury are polled and both defendants answer "Present.")

THE COURT. Do you desire, Mr. Moore, to make some statement to the jury in regard to the evidence? If you do, you may do so now.

MR. MOORE. If your honor please, just one matter that Mr. Katzmann and myself have agreed may be read. It is very short, with reference to the revolver matter:

"Q. Have you a distinct recollection of anything on that revolver? A. No, sir, not one particularity. I could not tell it if I saw it again.

Q. And that is the only time you saw it? A. Yes, sir. I have seen it a number of times in his possession.

Q. But you could not tell it again? A. No, sir.

Q. And you do not know whether this is the revolver? A. No, sir."

This is from the evidence of Mr. Bostock. [2238]

441

36. CHARGE TO THE JURY

Jury Instructions

"Although the jury is the sole judge of the facts of the case, the judge alone determines the law. Therefore, the court instructs the jury as to the meaning of the law applicable to the facts of the case. These **jury instructions** begin with discussions of general legal principles (innocent until proven guilty, guilty beyond a reasonable doubt, and so forth). They follow with specific instructions on the elements of the crime in the case and what specific actions the government must prove before there can be a conviction.... . Finally, the judge instructs the jury on possible verdicts in the case and provides a written form for each verdict of guilty and not guilty... ."

David W. Neubauer, America's Courts and the Criminal Justice System, West/Wadsworth, 6th ed., p. 356. Boldface is by Neubauer.

JUDGE WEBSTER THAYER

The defendants, Nicola Sacco and Bartolomeo Vanzetti, stand before the bar charged under separate indictments with the murder of Frederick A. Parmenter and Alessandro Berardelli, on the 15th day of April, 1920. The agency employed in causing the alleged murder was a pistol.

Murder in the first degree is the gravest offense known to the law. This is so because of the statutory penalty of death. The severity of the penalty is demanded, not in the spirit of revenge or of vengeance, but [2239] rather as punishment for the crime committed, and for the following reasons: first, because the life of a human being has been taken, and secondly, because the law seeks to protect and make safer the lives of all the people of the Commonwealth by deterring and preventing the further commission of similar crimes. [2240]

Let your eyes be blinded to every ray of sympathy or prejudice but let them ever be willing to receive the beautiful sunshine of truth, of reason and sound judgment, and let your ears be deaf to every sound of

442

public opinion or public clamor, if there be any, either in favor of or against these defendants. [2241]

I therefore beseech you not to allow the fact that the defendants are Italians to influence or prejudice you in the least degree. They are entitled, under the law, to the same rights and consideration as though their ancestors came over in the Mayflower.

Guilt or innocence, gentlemen, of crime, do not depend upon the place of one's birth. [2241]

The law says that no inference of guilt shall be drawn from the fact that indictments have been found against these defendants. The Constitution of the United States and of this Commonwealth require an indictment by a Grand Jury before there can be a trial upon the merits; for until an indictment shall have been found, no person can ever be put to the expense, embarrassment or humiliation of a trial, for a right granted by law should never be the cause of an inference or bias or prejudice whatsoever. [2242]

The Commonwealth must prove beyond reasonable doubt every fact or element necessary to prove the crime of murder.... [Y]ou must thoroughly understand that it means the doubt of a reasonable man who is earnestly seeking the truth. It does not mean the doubt of a man who is earnestly looking for doubts. [2243]

The law does not require proof so positive, so unerring and convincing that amounts to a mathematical or absolute certainty. You might obtain proof of that character in the exact sciences, but not in human investigations. For, you must remember, gentlemen, that we are involved in human investigations, in which all the evidence must be considered and weighed and determined by jurors who are human beings. You must, then, see that we are not dealing with absolute certainties, because God has never yet endowed man with sufficient power of intelligence and reason to reduce the results of human investigations to absolute certainty. Crime could be proven with difficulty if the law required proof to this extent, and practically never in those cases that are dependent for their proof upon circumstantial evidence. [2243]

If, then, reasonable doubt does not require absolute proof, certainty of proof, it becomes my duty to explain to you as intelligently as I can what degree of certainty it requires. Inasmuch as I have told you we are [2343] dealing with human investigation, you must, then, see that it requires reasonable and moral certainty as distinguished from absolute certainty. Therefore, whenever the proof satisfies a jury to a reasonable and moral certainty, then proof beyond a reasonable doubt has been established. This is so because proof to a moral and reasonable certainty is, as a matter of law, proof beyond reasonable doubt. [2244]

Let us now consider the substantive law of murder. I have already told you that at common law there was only one degree of murder. By our statutes there are two degrees of murder, the first and the second. I shall now read to you this statute and I trust you will give me the strictest attention while I am so reading. I will read from General Laws, Chapter 265, Section 1.

"Murder committed with deliberately premeditated malice aforethought or with extreme atrocity or cruelty or in the commission or attempted commission of a crime punishable with death or imprisonment for life is murder in the first degree. Murder which does not appear in the first degree is murder in the second degree. The degree of murder shall be determined by the jury." [2245]

You see, under this statute murder in the first degree may be committed in one of three different ways. First, with deliberately premedi- [2245] tated malice aforethought; or, second, with extreme atrocity or cruelty; or third, in the commission or attempted commission of a crime punishable with death or imprisonment for life. [2246]

The Commonwealth relies only upon the first and third ways, namely, murder committed with deliberately premeditated malice aforethought, and third, in the commission or attempted commission of a crime punishable with death or imprisonment for life. The second form, which refers to murder committed with extreme atrocity or cruelty, you will entirely disregard and dismiss from further consideration. [2246]

"Murder" is the unlawful taking of a life of a human being with malice aforethought... . "Malice" means something more than ill-will, hatred, malevolence or a wicked or cruel heart against a certain individual or class of individuals... . If a person intentionally injures another without justification or excuse, such intention, in the eyes of the law, is malice. The question of malice, therefore, you must determine, is: Did the defendants at the time of the alleged homicide intend, without justification or excuse, to take the life of Frederick A. Parmenter and Alessandro Berardelli or to put their lives in jeopardy? If they did, the law says that such intention is malice. [2246]

444

The law says that every person intends the natural, reasonable and probable consequences of his own acts. To apply this principal [sic] of law to the facts in these cases, you should first determine if the defendants caused by the use of a pistol the death of the deceased. The Commomwealth claims they did. Did the defendants know at the time of the shooting, if they did the shooting, that a pistol was a deadly weapon? From their knowledge of the use of a pistol, if one was used by them or either of them, did they expect naturally death to follow or that human life would be put in jeopardy by its use? If they did, that is, as a matter of law, malice. [2247]

"Aforethought" means to think before. To think before what? To think before the alleged shot or shots were fired... . The thought or intention to kill, as a matter of law, must precede the killing. There must be, however, gentlemen, some intervals of time between the intention to kill or the act of killing, but, as a matter of law it is sufficient if the intention preceded the actual shooting even though the interval consumed only seconds. [2247]

Let me recapitulate,—if the defendants, before the fatal shots were fired, if they were fired by them, by either of them or by one of their co-conspirators, intended to kill the deceased or to do either of them great bodily injury and such intention was preceded by and was the result of a premeditated design and a fixed and a wicked purpose to kill in order to accomplish the robbery, then your verdict should be guilty of murder in the first degree. [2249]

Now, motive does not constitute any part of the proof of the crime itself, for a person may be convicted of the commission of a crime without any evidence whatsoever that tends to prove motive. [2249]

Now, we will take up the second form by which murder in the first degree may be committed under the statute ... [L]et me read to you from General Laws, Chapter 265, Section 17:

"Whoever, being armed with a dangerous weapon, assaults, robs, steals and takes from a person money or other property which may be the subject of larceny, with intent, if resisted, to kill or maim the person robbed, or, being so armed, wounds or strikes the person robbed, shall be punished by confinement in the State Prison for life." [2250]

In conclusion, therefore, upon the subject of murder in the first degree, I say to you that if you are satisfied beyond reasonable doubt that murder has been committed by these defendants either, first, by reason of their having acted with deliberately premeditated malice aforethought or, without such deliberate premeditation, they committed murder in the commission or attempted commission of a crime punishable with imprisonment in State Prison for life, then such defendants who committed such murder are guilty of murder in the first degree. [2251]

On the other hand, if you are not satisfied that they committed either form of murder, then you should return a verdict of not guilty. [2251]

The Commonwealth claims that these defendants were two of a party of five who killed the deceased. The defendants deny it. What is the fact? As I have told you, the Commonwealth must satisfy you of that fact beyond reasonable doubt. The defendants are under no obligation to satisfy you who did commit the murders, ... If the Commonwealth has failed to so satisfy you, that is the end of these cases and you will return verdicts of not guilty. This is so because **the identity of the defendants is one of the essential facts to be established by the Commonwealth**. On the other hand, if the Commonwealth has so satisfied you, you will return a verdict of guilty against both defendants or either of them that you so find to be guilty. [2251]

It has been said that circumstantial evidence alone should never be sufficient to establish the guilt of any defend-[2251] ant in any criminal case. Such a statement, gentlemen, is the result of ignorance rather than sound reason or mature judgment, for it has been truly said that crime would go unpunished to a very large extent without the aid of circumstantial evidence.... [2252]

Therefore, in the eyes of the law there is no important distinction between circumstantial evidence and any other kind of evidence. It is the degree of proof that the evidence establishes; for, no matter what the evidence may be, it is necessary that that evidence should satisfy you of the guilt of these defendants so that you cannot come to any other reasonable conclusion than that they are guilty.... [If] it ... has not satisfied you, then they are not guilty. [2252]

Now, how are you going to determine wherein lies the truth? You must **use your best judgment and common sense**, your knowledge of human beings and human conduct, your ability to dissect and analyze evidence so that you can separate truth from falsehood and actualities from things imaginary. You should carry also in your minds the fairness and impartiality of each of the witnesses upon both sides, their desire and willingness to tell the truth, their interest, if any, in these cases, their power of vision, their freedom from nervous strain or excitement, their bias or prejudice, their opportunities for observation, the duration of such observation, their reasons for making such observations, and their intellectual qualifications which would enable them to ... reliably reproduce for your consideration what, in fact and in truth, they did or they did not see. [2253]

Now, the Commonwealth claims ... that the fatal Winchester bullet, marked Exhibit 3, [Bullet 3] which killed Berardelli, was fired through the barrel of the Colt automatic pistol found upon the defendant Sacco at the time of his arrest. If that is true, that is evidence tending to corroborate the testimony of the witnesses of the Commonwealth that the defendant Sacco was at South Braintree on the 15th day of April, 1920, and it was his pistol that fired the bullet that caused the death of Berardelli. To this effect the Commonwealth introduced the testimony of two experts, Messrs. Proctor and Van Amburg. And on the other hand, the defendants offered testimony of two experts, Messrs. Burns and Fitzgerald, to the effect that the Sacco pistol did not fire the bullet that caused the death of Berardelli. [2254]

Now, gentlemen, what is the fact, for you must determine this question of fact. [2254]

Berardelli had a revolver ... [A]bout three weeks before his death, in company with his wife, [he] left said revolver with the Iver Johnson Company of Boston.... [A]ccording to the foreman of the repair shop of Iver Johnson Company a new spring and hammer were put into an H. & R. revolver that had a repair tag number upon it of 94765, which number was given to the repair job by the person who took the revolver from Berardelli.... [O]n the Saturday night previous to the shooting some witness testified that a revolver in the hands of Berardelli,—he saw in the hands of Berardelli, was something similar to the one he had previously seen with Berardelli.... [2255]

You must remember now, on the other hand, the defendants have offered testimony tending to prove that said revolver never was the property of Berardelli, but having passed through several hands it became the property of the defendant Vanzetti, and that, according to the testimony of the two experts, the said Messrs. Burns and Fitzgerald, no new spring and hammer were put into said revolver by the employees of said Iver Johnson Company.... . **What is the truth?** [2255]

Third, that there is evidence tending to prove that a cap was found [2255] near the body of Berardelli... . Now, the Commonwealth claims that if this cap belonged to Sacco it could not have been found near the dead body of Berardelli unless the defendant Sacco lost it at the time of said shooting... . On the other hand, you should remember that the defendant Sacco and his wife both have testified that said cap never belonged to the defendant, that he never owned it, ... Again, gentlemen, you have another controverted question of fact. What is the truth? [2256]

[T]hese defendants are being tried for the murders of Berardelli and Parmenter, and for nothing else. [2257]

Episode at the Johnson House

Were there telephone wires connected with the Bartlett house that could be seen from the street? ... The defendants say ... that they did not follow Mrs. Johnson over to the Bartlett house... The Commonwealth claims that they left because of a consciousness of what happened at the Bartlett place. The defendants say no, they left because there were no number plates which they could put upon the Overland car. ... [2258]

Now, then, the question you must determine is this: Did the defendants, in company with Orciani and Boda, leave the Johnson house because the automobile had no 1920 number plate on it or, because they were conscious of or became suspicious of what Mrs. Johnson did in the Bartlett house? If they left because they had no 1920 number plates upon the automobile, then you may say there was no consciousness of guilt in consequence of their sudden departure, but if they left because they were consciously guilty of what was being done by Mrs. Johnson in the Bartlett house, then you may say that is evidence tending to prove consciousness of guilt on their part. [2259]

[S]uch consciousness of guilt, if you find such consciousness of guilt, **must relate to the murders of Berardelli and Parmenter** and not to the fact that they and their friends were slackers.... . [2259]

There are two pieces of testimony to which I should call your attention. One is the testimony of Chief Stewart, as to a conversation between him [2260] and the two defendants immediately following the arrest; and the other is the statement of both defendants [to] District Attorney Katzmann on May 6th, 1920, at the Brockton police station.

What I told you during the trial I now repeat: That the statements made by one of the defendants can be used only against him and not against the other. [2261]

[T]he law protects persons who are under arrest from making any statement to police officers or to third persons. Therefore, under our laws silence by a person under arrest cannot be taken as an admisssion against him, although he may be questioned by a police officer or such third person, but if he sees fit to voluntarily talk and during such talk makes an admission, such admissions may be used against him at the trial. The officer is under no obligation, as a matter of law, to warn a person of his rights who is under arrest. [The Miranda ruling in 1966 changed this.] The law does, however, require that such statement made by a defendant shall be voluntarily and freely made. That is, they should be made without coercion, threats, duress, intimidation, inducement, or offer or hope of reward. [2261]

Now, the law says that intentional false statements, deception and concealment of truth are evidences of consciousness of guilt and can be used against a defendant when, and only when, such consciousness relates to the crime charged in the indictment. That false statements were made by both of these defendants is admitted. This being true, you must deter- [2261] mine their purpose, object and intent in making them. Did they know that Berardelli and Parmenter had been murdered? Did they realize and appreciate that they were being held in connection with these murders? Did they make false statements for the purpose of taking away suspicions from them of these murders? Did they knowingly make false statements as to their whereabouts on the day of the murders for the purpose of deceiving both Chief Stewart and District Attorney Katzmann and eventually for the ultimate purpose of establishing their innocence of the crimes charged? [2262]

Now, in answer to this claim of the Commonwealth,—and I have only stated the claim of the Commonwealth,—the defendants say that although said statements were false, yet they were not made for the purpose of deceiving Chief Stewart or District Attorney Katzmann in regard to any fact whatsoever that had any relationship to the murders of Berardelli and Parmenter, because they said they had no knowledge whatsoever at that time of the murders of Berardelli and Parmenter. But they ... say that they made them [false statements] to protect themselves and their friends from some kind of punishment, either by way of deportation because they were radicals, or because of their activities in the radical movement, or because of radical literature that they then had possession of. [2262]

Again, you have another controverted question of fact, **the truth** of which you must determine. [2262]

An alibi is always a question of fact. Therefore, all testimony which tends to show that the defendants were in another place at the time the murders were committed tends also to rebut the evidence that they were present at the time and place the murders were committed. If the evidence of an alibi rebuts evidence of the Commonwealth to such an extent that it leaves reasonable doubt in your minds as to the commission of the murders charged against these defendants then you will return a verdict of not guilty. [2263]

On the other hand, if you find that the defendants or either of them committed the murders and the Commonwealth has satisfied you of such fact beyond reaonable doubt from all the evidence in these cases, including the evidence of an alibi, then you will return a verdict of guilty against both defendants or against such defendants as you may find guilty of such murders. [2263]

I have now finished my charge.... I have tried to preside over the trial of these cases in a spirit of absolute fairness and impartiality to both sides. If I have failed in any respect you must not, gentlemen, in any manner fail in yours. I therefore now commit into [2263] your sacred keeping the decision of these cases.... [T]ake them with you into yonder jury room.... Reflect long and well so that when you return your verdict shall stand forth before the world as your judgment of truth and justice. Gentlemen, be just and fear not.... [2264]

(Conference at bench between Court and counsel.)

THE COURT. (To the jury) You may go out a few minutes, gentlemen.

(The jury retire from the court room.)

MR. THOMAS McANARNEY. Now comes the defendant Sacco and moves that the Court, on all the evidence, order the jury to return a verdict of not guilty as to the defendant Sacco in cases 5545 and 5546. This applies to motion previously overruled by the judge in the lobby, where it was on a single sheet of paper.

[Ed. A motion such as Thomas McAnarney's is routinely made by defense counsel.]

THE COURT. (To the court officers.) Ask the jury to come back, please.

(The jury return to court room.)

THE COURT. I said in my charge that a new hammer and spring were put on the Berardelli revolver at the Iver Johnson place.... I was in error in that statement. The record shows there was only a new hammer put upon the revolver at the Iver Johnson place.

I also find I made this statement, and that was that the Saturday night previous to the murder one Bostock saw a revolver with Berardelli that was similar to the Berardelli revolver. It has been suggested that that is not consistent with the record. I am going to direct your attention to the record on that question that Mr. Moore read to you this morning. You remember the first thing he did he read to you a record of the evidence on that question and therefore you must be governed by that and not what I said. And let me also say what I think I said during the charge; You must remember this evidence. It is what you say the evidence is. It is not what I say it is. It is not what counsel say it is. It is what you say it is.... [A]nd if there is any other question that may come up, no matter whether the statement be by the Court or by counsel, you will, of course, be governed not by any of those statements, but by what you remember, what you say the evidence is, because that is the question which is exclusively within your province.

Now, is there anything else, Mr. McAnarney?

MR. JEREMIAH McANARNEY. I wish to call the jury's attention to one thing, and I think that is all.

THE COURT. All right. [2264]

MR. JEREMIAH McANARNEY. Mr. Foreman and gentlemen of the jury: It is agreed that all evidence obtained by the jury on the view at the Coacci barn or shed be entirely disregarded....

THE COURT. (To the jury) You may go, gentlemen, until half past two. [2265]

AFTERNOON SESSION.

THE COURT. Now, as I understand, gentlemen, you have agreed on the exhibits that are to go to the jury room. I want that you should be very careful to see that nothing goes excepting that which has been introduced in evidence and nothing should go excepting after there has been a thorough and careful examination by counsel for both defendants.

MR. KATZMANN. The suggestion counsel make in regard to that is the jury retire and counsel will confer and check up everything.

THE COURT. Is that agreeable to all the counsel on both sides?

MR. JEREMIAH McANARNEY. Yes, to save time.

THE COURT. That may be done. You may, therefore, gentlemen, now retire to your room with a view of reaching a verdict in these cases.

(The jury retire from the court room.)

THE COURT. If the jury should call for a magnifying glass, the one that was used during the trial by counsel and by the jury, the Court in its discretion allows the same to be sent to the jury, over the objection of the defendants. To this order of the Court, if it should be made, the defendant duly except.

(The jury later sent for the magnifying glass, and the Court ordered it sent out, to which counsel for the defendants objected and exception duly noted.) [2265]

Rep. Cella's Hearing in Boston, April 2, 1959
Gardner Auditorium, Massachusetts State House

Harvard historian Arthur M. Schlesinger, Sr. addressed the Joint Judiciary Committee of the Massachusetts Legislature: " . . . I think even more interesting is the fact that the Dictionary of American Biography, which is a twenty-volume compilation, written by scholars all over the country, and contains sketches of American figures from Colonial times to the present, in this sketch on Sacco-Vanzetti, which is a very condensed and objective sketch, it ends up by saying that the verdict in the case left misgivings in many minds, both in this country and abroad.

. . . Now the only reason I mentioned this [book on Sacco and Vanzetti by Felix Frankfurter] is the fact that this book was reprinted in 1954 with the consent of the author; that is, it was reprinted after Frankfurter had been fifteen years a member of the United States Supreme Court.

In other words, he in no sense has repudiated anything he said in his book, after the passage of a considerable number of years, . . . Justice Frankfurter is regarded as one of the conservative members of the High Court."

[Source: Hearing before Joint Judiciary Committee, pp. 111-112. See p. 584.]

37. THE VERDICT

EVENING SESSION.

THE COURT. Poll the jury, Mr. Clerk.

(The jury are polled and both defendants answer "Present".

THE COURT. If the jury is agreed, you may please take the verdict.

CLERK WORTHINGTON. Gentlemen of the jury, have you agreed upon your verdict? [2265]

THE FOREMAN. We have.

CLERK WORTHINGTON. Nicola Sacco.

DEFENDANT SACCO. Present.

(Defendant Sacco stands up.)

CLERK WORTHINGTON. Hold up your right hand. Mr. Foreman, look upon the prisoner. Prisoner, look upon the Foreman. What say you, Mr. Foreman, is the prisoner at the bar guilty or not guilty?

THE FOREMAN. Guilty.

CLERK WORTHINGTON. Guilty of murder?

THE FOREMAN. Murder.

CLERK WORTHINGTON. In the first degree?

THE FOREMAN. In the first degree.

CLERK WORTHINGTON. Upon each indictment?

THE FOREMAN. Yes, sir.

CLERK WORTHINGTON. Bartolomeo Vanzetti. Hold up your right hand. Look upon the Foreman. Mr. Foreman, look upon the prisoner. What say you, Mr. Foreman, is Bartolomeo guilty or not guilty of murder?

THE FOREMAN. Guilty.

CLERK WORTHINGTON. In the first degree, upon each indictment?

THE FOREMAN. In the first degree.

CLERK WORTHINGTON. Hearken to your verdicts as the Court has recorded them. You, gentlemen, upon your oath, say that Nicola Sacco and Bartolomeo Vanzetti is each guilty of murder in the first degree upon each indictment. So say you, Mr. Foreman. So, gentlemen, you all say.

THE JURY. We do, we do, we do.

THE COURT. (To the jury) I can add nothing to what I said this morning, gentlemen, except again to express to you the gratitude of the Commonwealth for the service that you have rendered. You may now go to your homes, from which you have been absent for nearly seven weeks. The Court will now adjourn.

DEFENDANT SACCO. They kill an innocent men [sic]. They kill two innocent men.

THE COURT. (After conferring with counsel). The time is extended until whatever time he wants, to which extension the District Attorney gives his consent,—November 1st.

(The Court is adjourned.) [2266]

[Ed. The Court ruled that the **Bill of exceptions** shall have been completed for review by the Supreme Judicial Court for the Commonwealth by November 1, 1921. Motion of defense counsel was granted, and the time to file the Bill of exceptions was extended to February 25, 1922. See Transcript of the Record, 5540.]

CORRESPONDENCE, 07/12/05: Reference.Desk@maine.gov

Mr. Newby:

The following is a partial quotation from the "Journal and Register of the Executive Council of the State of Maine-1921", p. 160:

"May 6, 1921
173 Ordered:

That the Secretary of State be authorized to employ in the Automobile Department as Automobile Inspectors:

Coburn C. Palmer of Dexter at $28.00 per week beginning May 2, 1921

With the understanding that the said inspectors give their full time to the work and have no other employment."

Two other folks were named, but I've omitted them . . . [F]rom 1920-22, the State Highway Commission hired uniformed inspectors.
Hope this will be helpful!
Sincerely,
Emily A. Schroeder, Reference Services, Maine State Library [See p. 413.]

PART III

DOCUMENTS IN THE SACCO-VANZETTI CASE

1920 to 2006

A representative selection

Showing all degrees of reliability

38. FIRE IN DEXTER, MAINE

[Primary Source #1]
The Eastern Gazette, Thursday, February 5, 1914

CAT GAVE ALARM
Occupants of Burned Morgridge Building Owe Their Lives to Pussy.
HAD NARROW ESCAPE
Bad Fire Early Sunday Morning Which Destroyed Building and Contents.

That the early morning fire in the grocery store of Frank Morgridge on Liberty street did not cause [loss] of life is probably due to the fact that a pet cat, smelling the smoke and instinctively seeking human aid, awoke one of the family. At a little before three o'clock Sunday morning Amos Morgridge, whose room is over the Morgridge store … was awakened by a pet coon cat scratching at his face to find that the room was filled with smoke from the fire that was fiercely raging below. With difficulty he aroused the rest of the family in time for them to make their escape.

In an adjoining room were Elbridge Atwater and his wife and the room was filled with smoke so that Mr. Atwater was obliged to carry his wife to a place of safety. A moment after they got out the room was filled with flame. Mr. and Mrs. George Weymouth, who occupied appartments [sic] in the rear of those of the Morgridge family also had a narrow escape and lost all of their household goods.

The fire had evidently been burning some time before it was discovered as the store on the first floor was a seething mass of flames….[3]

[Primary Source #2]
Bangor Daily News, February 2, 1914

CLOSE CALL OF A DEXTER FAMILY
Fire Destroys Building Owned by F.M. Morgridge—Cat Saves One.
(Special to the Bangor Daily News)

DEXTER, Feb. 1–An entire family escaped only in its night clothes, and one member of another family came very near smothering in a fire which early Sunday morning gutted the two-story wooden building owned by F.M. Morgridge….[2]

[Ed. Transcript does not mention this fire.]

39. A Letter from the Secretary of
JUSTICE OLIVER WENDELL HOLMES

1720 Eye Street, N. W.
WASHINGTON, D. C.

October 29, 1934

Dear Mr. Ehrmann:

Mr. Justice Holmes has asked me to write to you to thank you for your kindness in sending him a copy of your book. His delay in answering you was deliberate rather than negligent as he wished to read the book before replying. "The Untried Case" was finished yesterday.

The Justice, as you may possibly have heard, is, as he admits, inordinately fond of detective stories. He wished me to say that in years of reading thrillers he has come across no such engrossing a tale as your search for evidence against the Morelli gang.

As a documentary account of the Sacco-Vanzetti case in one of its manifold phases, the Justice wants to tell you that he feels the book is essential for any understanding of that cause celebre in which he has always shown the keenest interest.

He deeply appreciated your inscription on the flyleaf. Again thanking you for him, I am

Sincerely,
/s/ James Henry Rowe, Jr.
(Secretary to Mr. Justice Holmes)

[Ed. Source: Book jacket of The Untried Case: The Sacco-Vanzetti Case and the Morelli Gang (1960). Ehrmann gave copies of his books on Sacco and Vanzetti to Judge Charles E. Wyzanski. Rowe wrote this letter in 1960 text, not Howe. See online: Oral History Interview with James H. Rowe: Truman Presidential Museum & History, items 85-88. Note Rowe's view of Holmes.]

457

40. FIRST GENERATION CRITICS

BOSTON HERALD, MONDAY, MAY 3, 1920.
SUICIDE BARES BOMB ARRESTS
Salsedo Gave Names of All Terrorist Plotters Before Taking Death Leap
[Special Dispatch To The Herald]

NEW YORK, May 3. When Andrea Salsedo, Sicilian Anarchist, jumped 14 floors to his death at dawn today in Park row, he disclosed that government sleuths, working day and night for months, had solved the mystery of the attempt to kill Atty.-General Palmer and prominent men in seven cities last June, and that the principals in an anarchistic plot against government and officials, who fled abroad, were being sought by the secret police of five countries.

Salsedo and Roberto Elia, another Italian, printed the pink "Fighting Anarchist" circulars found with the fragments of a man's body on the doorstep of Mr. Palmer's house... . [A]s secret service agents ascertained and through the disclosures of Salsedo and Elia, it was the Galleani group [whose members included Sacco and Vanzetti] that staged the death conspiracy. [Ed. See p. xxxviii, p. 422, and p. 601.]

"Both men," declared Lamb [George Lamb, division superintendent of the department of justice], "were directly concerned in the bomb outrages that stirred the country last June... ."

At the time of the explosions there were found, at every place where the bombs were placed, a circular printed on pink paper. It bore the caption 'Plain Words' and was signed 'The Fighting Anarchists.' One of the statements in it was: 'There will have to be bloodshed; we will not dodge. There will have to be murder. We will kill because it is necessary... . We will destroy to rid the world of tyrranical institutions.'

"Salsedo admitted that he had printed 'Plain Words,'" [said Lamb].... .

The whole case was built up from the fragments of wearing apparel found scattered in front of the attorney-general's home in Washington... . Even the dead assassin [blown to bits by the bomb he carried] was thus identified as a missing radical. [1] [See Avrich, <u>Sacco and Vanzetti: The Anarchist Background</u>, pp. 60-187.]

**John N. Beffel."Eels and the Electric Chair." The New Republic.
Dec. 29, 1920.**

So said Vanzetti [of his emigrating friend], to me in [Charlestown] prison "I bought his little store [cart, knives and scales] and became a fish-vendor for love of independence."

Vanzetti was a friend of Andrea Salsedo, the Italian who was imprisoned secretly by the Department of Justice for many weeks, and who plunged to his death from the fourteenth story of the Park Row building in New York on May 3rd, two days after Attorney General Palmer's predicted date for a revolution. Vanzetti had gone to [128] New York a few days before, and endeavored to aid Salsedo... .

Nine witnesses of good repute took oath that Vanzetti sold eels to them in Plymouth at a time which completely precluded his being in Bridgewater when the hold-up was attempted [December 24, 1919]. Yet the jury convicted... . Examination of the court record convinces me that the defense of Vanzetti was badly handled; his attorneys, for instance, would not let Vanzetti take the witness stand [at his Plymouth trial, June 22-July 1] in his own defense unless he would agree to conceal that he held radical beliefs about the economic conflict. He refused to make that pledge; he is a philosophical anarchist, and wanted to explain why... .

If the defense can convince the next jury that Vanzetti was selling eels on the morning of December 24th, it will go a long way toward wrecking the prosecution's charge that he had a part in the payroll murder of April 15th, for its evidence in that case is no more tangible than that used in the trial for the Bridgewater attack. [129]

[Beffel was a radical journalist.]

[Ed. The N.E.C.L.C. and A.C.L.U. mail an official letter.]
New England Civil Liberties Committee
Affiliated with
AMERICAN CIVIL LIBERTIES UNION
138 W. 13th Street, New York City
44 Edgehill Road
Brookline, Mass.
February 19, 1921

To American Friends of Justice:

A fair trial for every man accused of crime:—That has been an article in the political creed of every English-speaking freeman since the days of Magna Carta. But today we know that political maxims do not execute themselves; they must be enforced by those who believe in them; and a fair trial is not secured by merely giving a prisoner his day in court; it involves investigation of evidence, summoning of witnesses, fees for capable lawyers.

We need your help to secure a fair trial for Nicola Sacco and Bartolomeo Vanzetti, who are accused of murder in connection with a hold-up at South Braintree last April. Their case has been carefully investigated by our legal advisory committee, which reports that the evidence against them is unsubstantial and that the real reason for the prosecution seems to be that Sacco and Vanzetti are "foreigners" and are active and influential radicals. The same conclusion has been reached by the American Civil Liberties Union, the Workers' Defense Union, the New Republic, the Nation and other organizations; and the Italian Government has made the case the subject of diplomatic inquiry.

. . . .

That a charge so unfounded should be pressed so earnestly proves the seriousness of the situation to the victims. They must be ready to meet the accusation fully ... and they need funds for every step.

Will you help with a prompt and liberal subscription. Checks may be sent to me at 44 Edgehill Road, Brookline.

(Signed) Anna N. Davis
Secretary-Treasurer

[Excerpted from R.H. Montgomery, Sacco-Vanzetti: The Murder and the Myth, pp. 61-63, with permission of the A.C.L.U. and Devon-Adair.]

Bartolomeo Vanzetti. "WHY I DID NOT TESTIFY." Background of the Plymouth Trial. 1926

I was willing to take the stand [at Plymouth], but Mr. Vahey opposed and resisted it until I accepted his will.... He asked me how I would explain from the stand the meaning of Socialism, or Communism, or Bolshevism, if I was requested by the district attorney to do so. At such a query, I would begin an explanation on those subjects, and Mr. Vahey would cut it off at its very beginning. "Hush,

if you will tell such things to the ignorant, conservative jurors, they will send you to State prison right away." I contend that that was ... but an excuse to hinder me from testifying... . [34] Hence, I am compelled to say that I failed to testify in my behalf because my lawyer prevented it—and that I believe that he did so because he feared that I might have convinced the jury of my innocence, and because he knew that a defendant's refusal to take the stand, is considered by the jury as a symptom of guilt. [35]
[See Pernicone's biography of Vanzetti in <u>American National Biography (ANB)</u>, vol. 19.]

Felix Frankfurter. <u>The Case of Sacco and Vanzetti</u>. March 1927.

Prefatory Note—February 15, 1927
There are no legal mysteries about the case which a layman cannot penetrate. [Prefatory Note.]
My aim is to give in brief compass an accurate re´sume´ of the facts of the case from its earliest stages to its present posture... . The necessary selection of material has been guided by canons of relevance and fairness familiar to every lawyer called upon to make a disinterested summary of the record of a protracted trial... . [3]
At the time of the Braintree holdup the police were investigating a similar crime in the neighboring town of Bridgewater. In both cases a gang was involved. In both they made off in a car. In both eyewitnesses believed the criminals to be Italians. In the Bridgewater holdup the car had left the scene in the direction of Cochesett. Chief Stewart of Bridgewater was therefore, at the time of the Braintree murders, on the trail of an Italian owning or driving a car in Cochesett. He found his man in one Boda, whose car was then in a garage awaiting repairs. Stewart instructed the garage proprietor, Johnson, to telephone to the police when anyone came to fetch it. Pursuing this theory, Stewart found that Boda had been living in **Cochesett** with a radical named Coacci. Now on April 16, 1920, which was the day after the Braintree murders, Stewart, at the instance of the Department of Justice, then engaged in the [4] rounding-up of Reds, had been to the house of Coacci to see why he had failed to appear at a hearing regarding his deportation. He found Coacci packing a trunk and apparently very anxious to get back to Italy as soon as possible. At the time (April 16), Coacci's trunk and his haste to depart for Italy were

not connected in Chief Stewart's mind with the Braintree affair. But when later the tracks of a smaller car were found near the murder car, he surmised that this car was Boda's. And when he discovered that Boda had once been living with Coacci, he connected Coacci's packing, his eagerness to depart, his actual departure, with the Braintree murders, and assumed that the trunk contained the booty.

Stewart continued to work on his theory, which centred around Boda: that whosoever called for Boda's car at Johnson's garage would be suspect of the Braintree crime. On the night of May 5, Boda and three other Italians did in fact call.

To explain how they came to do so let us recall here the proceedings for the wholesale deportation of Reds under Attorney-General Palmer in the spring of 1920. In particular the case of one Salsedo must be borne in mind—a radical who was held incommunicado in a [5] room in the New York offices of the Department of Justice on the fourteenth floor of a Park Row building. Boda and his companions were friends of Salsedo. On May 4 they learned that Salsedo had been found dead on the sidewalk outside the Park Row building, and, already frightened by the Red raids, bestirred themselves to "hide the literature and notify the friends against the federal police." For this purpose an automobile was needed and they turned to Boda. Such were the circumstances under which the four Italians appeared on the evening of May 5 at the Johnson garage. Two of them were Sacco and Vanzetti. Mrs. Johnson telephoned the police. The car was not available and the Italians left, Sacco and Vanzetti to board a street car for Brockton, Boda and the fourth member, Orciani, on a motor cycle. Sacco and Vanzetti were arrested on the street car, Orciani was arrested the next day, and Boda was never heard of again.

Stewart at once sought to apply his theory of the commission of the two "jobs" by one gang. The theory, however, broke down. Orciani had been at work on the days of both crimes, so he was let go. [6]

Frankfurter's footnote on the Bridgewater crime.

More than twenty people swore to having seen Vanzetti in Plymouth on December 24, among them those who remembered buying eels from him for the Christmas Eve feasts. Of course all these witnesses were Italians. The circumstances of the trial are sufficiently revealed by the fact that Vanzetti, protesting innocence, was not allowed by his counsel to take the witness stand for fear his radical opinions would be brought out and tell against him disastrously. [7]

Frankfurter's opinion on Vanzetti's alibi for the South Braintree crime.

The alibi for Vanzetti was overwhelming... . Thirteen witnesses either testified directly that Vanzetti was in Plymouth selling fish on the day of the murder, or furnished corroboration of such testimony. [30]

What, then, was the evidence against them? [36]

1. Sacco and Vanzetti, as we have seen, were two of four Italians who called for Boda's car at Johnson's garage on the evening of May 5. It will be remembered that in pursuance of a prearranged plan Mrs. Johnson, under pretext of having to fetch some milk, went to a neighbor's house to telephone the police. Mrs. Johnson testified that the two defendants followed her to the house on the opposite side of the street and when, after telephoning, she reappeared they followed her back... . [36]

3. ... The other evidence from which "consciousness of guilt" was drawn the two Italians admitted. Sacco and Vanzetti acknowledged that they behaved in the way described by Mrs. Johnson, and freely conceded that when questioned at the police station they told lies. What was their explanation of this conduct? To exculpate themselves of the crime of murder they had to disclose elaborately their guilt of radicalism. [40]

In order to meet the significance which the prosecution attached to the incidents at the Johnson house and those following, it became necessary for the defendants to advertise to the jury their offensive views, and thereby to excite the deepest prejudices of a Norfolk County jury, picked for its respectability and sitting in judgment upon two men of alien blood and abhorrent philosophy. [40]

Up to the time that Sacco and Vanzetti testified to their radical activities, their pacifism and their flight to Mexico to escape the draft, the trial was a trial for murder and banditry; with the cross-examination of Sacco and Vanzetti patriotism and radicalism became the dominant emotional issues... . Outside the courtroom the Red hysteria was rampant; it was allowed to dominate within. [46]

By systematic exploitation of the defendants' alien blood, their imperfect knowledge of English, their unpopular social views, and their

463

opposition to the war, the District Attorney invoked against them a riot of political passion and patriotic sentiment; and the trial judge connived at—one had almost written, cooperated in—the process. [59]

But recently facts have been disclosed, and not denied by the prosecution, to show that the case against Sacco and Vanzetti for murder was part of a collusive effort between the District Attorney and agents of the Department of Justice to rid the country of these Italians because of their Red activities. [68]

3. <u>Hamilton motion</u>. Hamilton, an expert of fifteen years' experience in the microscopic examination of exhibits in criminal cases … from Maine to Arizona, gave in the form of an affidavit the result of his examination under a compound microscope of the bullet taken from Berardelli's body … [74] In his opinion minute comparison of the scratches on the bullet and the grooves inside the barrel of Sacco's pistol conclusively disproved the claim of the Commonwealth that it was from Sacco's pistol that the fatal bullet was fired. [75] [See p. 312.]

4. <u>Gould motion</u>. Gould, who was in the business of selling razor paste to employees of factories, gave an affidavit to the following effect. He arrived in South Braintree on April 15, 1920, at about 3:00 P.M.... . [S]uddenly the shooting began. An automobile passed him within five feet; he saw a man with a revolver in his hand … and that man pointed a revolver at him and fired, the bullet passing through his overcoat. Gould had thus a better view of the man alleged to be Sacco than any witness on either side. He gave his name and address to the police, but was never called upon to testify. [75]

The reader has now had placed before him fairly, it is hoped, however briefly, the means of forming a judgment. Let him judge for himself! [91]

Hitherto the defense has maintained that the circumstances of the case all pointed away from Sacco and Vanzetti. But the deaths of Parmenter and Berardelli remained unexplained. Now the defense has adduced new proof, not only that Sacco and Vanzetti did <u>not</u> commit the murders, but also, positively, that a well-known gang of professional criminals <u>did</u> commit them. Hitherto a new trial has been pressed because of the character of the original trial. Now a new trial has been demanded because an impressive body of evidence tends to establish the guilt of others. [92]

[T]he Madeiros confession [of the South Braintree crime] … was only the starting point which [92] enabled the defense to draw the network of independent evidence around the Morelli gang of Providence. [93]

He [Madeiros] already had a criminal record and was associated with a gang of Italians engaged in robbing freight cars.... [I]n a saloon in Providence, some members of the gang invited him to join them in a pay-roll robbery at South Braintree.... [O]n April 15, 1920, the plan was carried into execution. In the party, besides Madeiros, were three Italians and a "kind of [93] a slim fellow with light hair," who drove the car.... [T]hey adopted the familiar device of using two cars. They started out in a Hudson, driving to some woods near Randolph. They then exchanged the Hudson for a Buick brought them by another member of the gang. In the Buick they proceeded to South Braintree, arriving there about noon. When the time came the actual shooting was done by the oldest of the Italians, a man about forty, and one other. The rest of the party remained near by in the automobile. As the crime was being committed they drove up, took aboard the murderers and the money, and made off. They drove back to the Randolph woods, exchanged the Buick again for the Hudson, and returned to Providence. [94]

A man who seeks to relieve another of guilt while himself about to undergo the penalty of death does not carry conviction. The circumstances of Madeiros's confession, however, free it from the usual suspicion and furnish assurances of its trustworthiness. Far from having nothing to lose by making the confession, Madeiros stood to jeopardize his life. [98]

Every reasonable probability points away from Sacco and Vanzetti; every reasonable probability points toward the Morelli gang. [101]   [Ed. Frankfurter calls Vanzetti "a dreamy fish peddler."]

Frankfurter's statement on Thayer's denial of Motion 6.
(based on Madeiros' affidavit)

[S]pace permits only a few summary observations.... I assert with deep regret, but without the slightest fear of disproof, that certainly in modern times Judge Thayer's opinion stands unmatched, happily, for discrepancies between what the record discloses and what the opinion conveys. His 25,000-word document cannot accurately be described otherwise than as a farrago of misquotations, misrepresentations, suppressions, and mutilations. The disinterested inquirer could not possibly derive from it a true knowledge of the new evidence that was

465

submitted to him as the basis for a new trial. The opinion is literally honeycombed with demonstrable errors, ... [104]
[Frankfurter, Professor of Law at Harvard Law School, helped Croly, Lippmann, and Learned Hand found The New Republic. He was one of the founders of the American Civil Liberties Union in 1920.]

Reviews of The Case of Sacco and Vanzetti

Morris L. Ernst. Review of The Case of Sacco and Vanzetti. Yale Law Journal. June 1927. #1

In this case of Sacco-Vanzetti, the prosecutor—with what is the approval of Massachusetts' highest court—withheld important evidence tending to prove innocence. Read the exciting story [Frankfurter tells] of Gould (page 75) whose testimony was known to authorities, but who was never called as a witness, presumably because he would have helped prove the innocence of the condemned men. [1193]
[Lamson (Roger Baldwin, 172) says Ernst was "the ACLU's eminent, and with Arthur Garfield Hays, most durable lawyer." Ernst wrote "Sacco-Vanzetti case" for Encyclopaedia Britannica.]

George W. Stumberg. "Book Reviews." Texas Law Review. June 1927. #2

It is of course impossible to judge the merits of a claim of innocence by an examination of only part of the evidence available. Hence a reader of Mr. Frankfurter's book could hardly expect it to convince him that Sacco and Vanzetti are innocent. While Mr. Frankfurter attempts to make his discussion impartial, it is apparent that he is a partisan. [450]
[Stumberg, Professor of Law at the University of Texas, 1925-1964, held law degrees from Columbia (1912) and Yale (1924).]

Andrew R. Sherriff. "Book Reviews." Illinois Law Review. December 1927. #3

There is a notable absence of any intention [by Frankfurter] to marshal the evidence in support of the verdict, which would be indispensable to a fair process of treatment. On the contrary, the facts supporting the verdict are minimized and impaired by the argument; while every shred of evidence or circumstance to discredit the verdict is cleverly utilized, ... [462] [Frankfurter's] book would not necessarily persuade an experienced lawyer that the verdict should have been judicially set aside, ... [463]

As a brief or argument for the defendants, or as a means of public agitation, the book is great. [463] ... . His little book ... establishes a memorable instance of indiscretion, of misapplied talent and misdirected zeal, of academic naivety. [465]
[Sherriff was a member of the Illinois Bar.]

Frankfurter replies to Sherriff in <u>Illinois Law Review</u>.

I wrote what I wrote as a matter of history, and in order to educate public understanding... . It cannot be that it is right for an influential bar association [of Massachusetts] to approve of a judge [Thayer] whose conduct is under criticism, but not right for a disinterested lawyer-teacher [Frankfurter] to analyze the work of such a judge in the light of the record. [467] [Ed. See p. xxxviii and p. 457.]

Morris L. Ernst. "Deception According to Law." <u>The Nation</u>. June 1, 1927.

"The attorney who prosecuted Sacco and Vanzetti suppressed information and evidence in his possession tending to affirm the innocence of the defendants... . The jury never heard of it [Gould affidavit], and when the defendants' attorneys objected to this suppression the highest court of Massachusetts declared: 'A prosecuting official is violating no canon of legal ethics in presenting evidence which tends to show guilt while failing to call witnesses in whom he has no confidence, or whose testimony contradicts what he is trying to prove.'"
... "[T]his reasoning seems to me clearly unethical, ..." [602]
["50" words by Ernst and '39' words by Chief Justice Rugg. See 'Rugg' in Appel, V: 4883. See "Address by Morris Ernst, Esq." in pp. 94-110 in <u>Hearing before Joint Judiciary Committee of the Massachusetts Legislature on the Sacco-Vanzetti Case</u>. 1959.]

Bruce Bliven. "In Dedham Jail: A Visit to Sacco and Vanzetti." The New Republic. June 22, 1927.

Well, perhaps Sacco and Vanzetti were members of the band which did that deed [murders at South Braintree], though I know what I am talking about when I say that the chances against it are a thousand to one [120]... . Their political faith is philosophical anarchism. [121] [ANB: Bliven was "managing editor of the liberal New Republic."]

John Dos Passos. Facing the Chair. 1927

Carlos Affe, East Boston grocer, testified that between 3 and 4 o'clock on April 15 he was paid by Sacco for an order of groceries purchased at an earlier date. He exhibited a notebook of the transaction. [110]

[Dos Passos visited Vanzetti and Sacco in prison. He helped found the New Masses in 1926. In 1927 he was arrested during a Sacco-Vanzetti protest at Boston and put in a jail cell with the communist author Michael Gold. In 1936 he honored Sacco and Vanzetti in The Big Money, last volume of his trilogy U.S.A. Later he turned rightward and defended Senator Joseph McCarthy's investigation of communists in the U. S. government.]

REPORT TO GOV. FULLER BY GRANT, LOWELL, STRATTON, JULY 27, 1927.

YOUR EXCELLENCY:

Starting on the investigation with which you have charged us, with almost no knowledge of the evidence in the case of the Commonwealth vs. Sacco and Vanzetti, we have felt that our first duty was to read the full stenographic report of the trial; then the various affidavits and documents bearing upon the motions for a new trial; and, thereafter, to seek and hear such information as might throw light upon the report to be made to you. In doing this we have felt that our investigation had better be wholly independent of yours; ... [Appel, V: 5378i]

There had been presented by the Government a certain amount of evidence of identification, and other circumstances tending to connect the prisoners with the murder, of such a character that—together with their being armed to the teeth and the falsehoods they stated when arrested—would in the case of New England Yankees, almost certainly have resulted in a verdict of murder in the first degree,—a result which the evidence for the alibis was not likely to overcome. [5378j]

They [Dedham jury] state that the Judge tried the case fairly; that they perceived no bias; ... [5378k] It may be added that the Committee talked with the ten available members of the jury—one, the foreman, being dead, and another out of reach in Florida.... . Each of them felt sure that the fact that the accused were foreigners and radicals had no effect upon his opinion.... . [5378l]

[W]e are forced to conclude that the Judge was indiscreet in conversation with outsiders during the trial. He ought not to have talked about the case off the bench, and doing so was a grave breach of official decorum... . [W]e believe that such indiscretions in conversation did not affect his conduct at the trial or the opinions of the jury, ... [5378l]

In one of the motions for a new trial, Mr. Thompson, now counsel for the defense, contended that between the District Attorney and officers of the United States Secret Service engaged in investigating radical movements there had been collusion for the purpose either of deporting these defendants as radicals or of convicting them of murder, ... and that the files of the Federal Department of Justice contain material tending to [5378l] show the innocence of Sacco and Vanzetti... . but none of these affidavits [submitted by Thompson] states or implies that there is anything in those files which would help to show that the defendants are not guilty. For the Government to suppress evidence of innocence would be monstrous, and to make such a charge without evidence to support it is wrong. [5378m]

Before the Committee Mr. Thompson suggested that the fatal bullet shown at the trial as the one taken from Berardelli's body, and which caused his death, was not genuine; that the police had substituted it for another, in order by a false exhibit to convict these men; but in this case, again, he offered no credible evidence for the suspicion. Such an accusation, devoid of proof, may be dismissed without further comment, save that the case of the defendants must be rather desperate on its merits when counsel feel it necessary to resort to a charge of this kind ... . [5378m] To summarize, therefore, what has been said: The Committee have seen no evidence sufficient to make them believe that the trial was unfair. [5378n]

Madeiros ... confesses to being present [in the bandit car in South Braintree], ... [H]e says that he, as a youth of eighteen, was induced to go with the others without knowing where he was going, or what was to be done, save that there was to be a hold-up which would not involve killing; ... His ignorance of what happened is extraordinary, and much of it cannot be attributed to a desire to shield his associates, ... This is true of his inability to recollect the position of the buildings, and whether one or more men were killed... . To the Committee he said that the shooting brought on an epileptic fit which showed itself by a failure of memory; ... [5378s]

Even without considering the contradictory evidence it does not seem to the Committee that these affidavits [of Motion 6] to corroborate a worthless confession are of such weight as to deserve serious attention. [5378t]

The case has been popularly discussed as if it were one turning mainly upon identification by eyewitnesses. That, of course, is a part, but only a part, of the evidence. As with the Bertillon measurements or with finger prints, no one measure or line has by itself much significance, yet together they may produce a perfect identification; so a number of circumstances—no one of them conclusive—may together make a proof clear beyond reasonable doubt. [5378w]

Then there is the fact that a pistol that Berardelli had been in the habit of carrying, and which there is no sufficient reason to suppose was not in his possession at the time of the murder, disappeared and a pistol of the same kind was found in the possession of Vanzetti when he and Sacco were arrested together, and of which no satisfactory explanation is given. It is difficult to suppose that Berardelli was not carrying his pistol at the time he was guarding the paymaster with his pay-roll, and no pistol was found upon his person after his death. It is natural also, if the bandits saw his pistol they should carry it off for fear of someone shooting at them as they escaped. [5378w]

[W]e can be sure that the shot was fired by the kind of pistol in the possession of Sacco. Then again, the fatal bullet found in Berardelli's body was of a type no longer manufactured and so obsolete that the [5378w] defendants' expert witness, Burns, testified that, with the help of two assistants, he was unable to find such bullets for purposes of experiment; yet the same obsolete type of cartridges was found in Sacco's pockets on his arrest... . Such a coincidence of the fatal bullet and those found on Sacco would, if accidental, certainly be extraordinary.... . [5378x]

On these grounds the Committee are of opinion that Sacco was guilty beyond reasonable doubt of the murder at South Braintree. In reaching this conclusion they are aware that it involves a disbelief in the evidence of his alibi at Boston, but in view of all the evidence they do not believe he was there that day. [5378y]

The evidence against Vanzetti is somewhat different. His association with Sacco tends to show that he belonged to the same group.... . His falsehoods and his armed condition have a weight similar to that in the case of Sacco.... . [5378y]

The alibi of Vanzetti is decidedly weak. One of the witnesses, Rosen, seems to the Committee to have been shown by the cross-examination to be lying at the trial; another, Mrs. Brini, had sworn to an alibi for him in the Bridgewater case, and two more of the witnesses did not seem certain of the date until they had talked it over. Under these circumstances, if he was with Sacco, [5378y] or in the bandits' car, ... he was undoubtedly guilty; ... On the whole, we are of opinion that Vanzetti also was guilty beyond reasonable doubt. [5378z]

It has been urged that a crime of this kind must have been committed by professionals, and it is for well-known criminal gangs one must look; but to the Committee both this crime and the one at Bridgewater do not seem to bear the marks of professionals, but of men inexpert in such crimes. [5378z] [Ed. Signed by Robert Grant, A. Lawrence Lowell, S. W. Stratton.] [On Aug. 7, 1927, the Boston Herald published this report by Fuller's Advisory Committee.]

DECISION
of
GOV. ALVAN T. FULLER
IN THE MATTER OF

THE APPEAL OF BARTOLOMEO VANZETTI AND NICOLA SACCO
FROM SENTENCE OF DEATH IMPOSED UNDER THE LAWS OF THE COMMONWEALTH   [5378a]

[Ed. Fuller's Decision starts on p. 472.]

Richard Newby

Boston, Massachusetts, August 3, 1927.

I realized at the outset that there were many sober-minded and conscientious men and women who were genuinely troubled about the guilt or innocence of the accused and the fairness of their trial.... I believed that I could best reassure these honest doubters by having a committee conduct an investigation entirely independent of my own, their report to be made to me and to be of help in reaching correct conclusions.... For this committee I desired men who were not only well and favorably known for their achieve-[5378c] ments in their own lines, but men whose reputations for intelligence, open-mindedness, intellectual honesty and good judgment were above approach. I asked to serve on that committee President Abbott Lawrence Lowell of Harvard University, former Judge Robert Grant, and President Samuel W. Stratton of Massachusetts Institute of Technology.... They ... labored continuously during much of June and through July, holding their sessions independently, and arrived unanimously at a conclusion which is wholly in accord with mine. [5378d]

I have consulted with every member of the jury now alive, eleven in number. They considered the judge fair.... I find the jurors were thoroughly honest men and that they were reluctant to find these men guilty but were forced to do so by the evidence. I can see no warrant for the assertion that the jury trial [at Dedham] was unfair. [5378e]

The next question is whether newly discovered evidence was of sufficient merit to warrant a new trial.

After the verdict against these men, their counsel filed and argued before Judge Thayer seven distinct supplementary motions for a new trial, six of them on the ground of newly discovered evidence, all of which were denied. I have examined all of these motions and read the affidavits in support of them to see whether they presented any valid reason for granting the accused men a new trial. I am convinced that they do not and I am further convinced that the presiding judge gave no evidence of bias in denying them all and refusing a new trial. The Supreme Judicial Court for the Commonwealth, which had before it appeals on four of the motions and ... read the same affidavits which were submitted to Judge Thayer, declined to [5378e] sustain the contentions of counsel for the accused. [5378f]

I give no weight to the Madeiros confession... In his testimony to me he could not recall the details or describe the neighborhood.... I am

not impressed with his knowledge of the South Braintree murders.
[5378f]

The next question, and the most vital question of all, is that of the
guilt or innocence of the accused. In this connection I reviewed the
Bridgewater attempted holdup for which Vanzetti had previously been
tried before another jury and found guilty. At this trial Vanzetti did not
take the witness stand in his own defense. He waived the privilege of
telling his own story to the jury, and did not subject himself to cross-
examination. Investigating this case, I talked to the counsel for
Vanzetti at the Plymouth trial, the jurymen, the trial witnesses, new
witnesses, present counsel and Vanzetti [5378f]... I believe with the
jury that Vanzetti was guilty and that his [Plymouth] trial was fair... .
[A]s noted above, ... Vanzetti did not testify.

As the result of my study of the record and my personal
investigation of the case, including my interviews with a large number
of witnesses, I believe, with the jury, that Sacco and Vanzetti were
guilty and that the [Dedham] trial was fair. [5378g]

[T]here was a feeling ... that the various delays that had dragged
this case through the courts for six years were evidence that a doubt
existed as to the guilt of these two men. The feeling was not justified.
The persistent, determined efforts of an attorney of extraordinary
versatility and energy, the judge's illness, the election efforts of three
District Attorneys, and dilatoriness ... are the principal causes of delay.
[5378h]

... I find no sufficient justification for executive intervention... . I
furthermore believe that there was no justifiable reason for giving them
a new trial. [5378h]

[The Boston Herald (and NY Times) published Fuller's Decision on
August 4, 1927.]

BRIDGEPORT POST. THURSDAY, AUG. 4, 1927.
BRIDGEPORT MAN THINKS SHELL PHOTOS BEAT SACCO-VANZETTI

[James E.] Burns did everything that he could consistently do upon
the witness stand at the [Dedham] trial six years ago to save the
accused, truthfully answering questions that were put to him by
attorneys for the defense and by the prosecution. Certain facts relative
to the bullets and shells which figured as evidence in the case ...

473

appeared to convincingly prove that the missile which killed the Braintree paymaster Parmenter [Berardelli] was fired from the revolver later found in the possession of Sacco. By [But] the prosecution, either through ignorance or neglect, failed at the trial to bring out some of these facts. The prosecution did not question Burns [expert witness for defense] relative to file markings on the shells... .

[C]ounsel for the defense carefully kept away from this line of testimony [on Shell W], confining their questions to the markings on the bullet [Bullet 3].

A few days ago Mr. Burns [was] summoned to appear before Governor Fuller. "I was in an unenviable position," said Burns today. "I had appeared as a witness for the defense in the original trial, and I had answered the questions that were put to me. Yet, I knew that in one of the attempts to secure a new trial, counsel for the defense had called in another ballistic witness [Albert Hamilton] who had seen fit to introduce a series of photomicrographs (enlarged photographs showing microscopic details), ... Instead of helping the case for the accused, these photomicrographs of the shells involved in the case, only helped the prosecution... ."

When Governor Fuller questioned Mr. Burns relative to the markings on the shells, the Bridgeport ballistic expert saw that there was no use attempting to lie to the governor upon this point. The photographs spoke for themselves. [1]

[This news item is cited in the <u>Boston Evening Transcript</u>, August 10, 1927, p. 16.]

Heywood Broun. "Sacco and Vanzetti." <u>New York World</u>. Aug. 5, 1927.

"It is not every prisoner who has a president of Harvard University throw on the switch for him." [1]

[Broun was a respected journalist of liberal persuasion.]

BOSTON EVENING TRANSCRIPT. TUESDAY, AUG. 9, 1927.
How the Sacco Bullet Was "Fingerprinted"
How the Sacco Bullet Was Tested at Dedham June 3, 1927
Maj. Goddard's Report to Gov. Fuller and His Commission, Which
Convinced an "Expert" for the Defence

474

"I submit below my report of the tests conducted by me on the afternoon of June 3, 1927, in the courthouse at Dedham, Mass., upon certain bullets and shells which figure as exhibits in the case of the Commonwealth vs. Sacco and Vanzetti. In these tests _____, an expert representing the defense, checked on my findings by personal observations through the instruments employed, manipulating the apparatus as he saw fit... .

"Many tests were made, and the findings in substance were:

"1.—That 'Fraher Shell No. 3' was fired in the Sacco pistol and could have been fired in no other.

"2.—That the so-called 'fatal' bullet, being one of four from the body of one Berardelli, was fired through the Sacco pistol and could have been fired through no other... .

"While the defense expert is in no way collaborating with me in this report, I am satisfied from his expressions at the time of the test, that he concurs with me in my findings with respect to Fraher Shell No. 3, and also with regard to the fatal bullet, subject ... to the qualification that he is unwilling to commit himself to a formal opinion until he has had an opportunity to examine the exhibit bullets once more, after they have been ... cleaned."

... I conducted the tests outlined for the simple reason that I knew that the comparison microscope would reveal, with mechanical accuracy, and in a manner which no human opinion could refute, the facts of the case... . I ... offered to conduct the tests as an impartial observer, not in the employ of the State or the defence, directly or indirectly. I received no compensation of any kind from anyone for what I did, nor do I expect to. I saw to it that both sides were represented, and that the only expert present who represented either side (_____ for the defence) had ample opportunity to repeat at his own convenience each test which I undertook.

Yours very truly,

Calvin H. Goddard [10]

ILLUSTRATIONS.

1—The Comparison Micrometer, by Which Scientific Identification of Bullets and Shells Irrefutably Supplants Opinions of Experts. It reveals the Tell-tale "Fingerprints" of Barrels on Bullets and Breech Blocks on Shells. The Bullets May Be Seen just Below the Two Microscopes—the "Fatal" Bullet Under the One, the "Test" Bullet Under the Other. By a Series of Prisms, These When Looked at Through the Eye-piece at the Top, Come Together as in Figure 2 and Figure 5, Proving in the Former by the Matching or "Fusing" of the lines That They Are from the Same "Gun" or by Failing to Do so as in Figure 5 That They Are Not.

2—The Fusion of a "Fatal" Bullet and Bullet from Suspected Gun as in Sacco's Case, Showing Positive Identification by Markings That Fatal Bullet at Upper Half and Test Bullet Below Dividing Line, Came From Same Gun.

3—A Breech Block of a Gun, Showing Rough Surface Left by Casting the Lines of Which Become Imprinted on Shells, Permitting Positive Identification.

4—The Shell Found at the Scene of the South Braintree Crime Showing Breech Block Markings Which Were the Same as on Shells Fired in Tests from Sacco Gun.

5—Fusion of Two Bullets, as Shown by Instrument, Which Never Could Have Been Fired from Same Gun as the Markings Nowhere Correspond. [10]

After a verbal controversy with Mr. Thompson, the defense expert who had been involved in the tests wrote to him and severed all connection with the defense, stating that after the tests he had grave doubts as to the present truth of his affidavits of 1923. [6]

[Ed. Defense expert is Professor Gill, who "asked that for obvious reasons he be left in the background of this article."] [10]

[Wendell D. Howie, reporter for the Transcript, and correspondent for the State House.]

BOSTON EVENING TRANSCRIPT. WEDNESDAY, AUGUST 10, 1927.
Facts on Sacco Shells Confirmed by Expert

In yesterday's special article on the Sacco shells and bullets it was stated that one of the defense experts [Professor Gill] withdrew from the case following the so-called Goddard tests. It develops that a second defense expert, who testified at the trial in 1921, declares that he told the "truth" when questioned by Governor Fuller concerning the shells in the course of the review, and tacitly admitted that the fatal shell and the test shells fired in the Sacco gun had identical markings.

James E Burns, expert of the Remington Arms—U. M. C. Company, Bridgeport, Conn., is the defense witness in question. He states not only that he was in an awkward position under all the circumstances but that "I could only answer the governor's questions truthfully." He does not for a moment imply that he was untruthful at the trial, but points out that only certain questions were put to him which did not bring out the complete facts. [1] Wendell D. Howie.

BOSTON EVENING TRANSCRIPT. WEDNESDAY, AUGUST 10, 1927.
"Exceptions Noted" to Major Goddard's Ballistic Experiments
By William G. Thompson, former counsel for the defendants

[A]bout noon on Friday, June 3, ... Professor Gill telephoned me that he and Major Goddard were going out to Dedham at 2 o'clock to experiment with the bullet and shell. He did not tell me that Mr. Ranney and a stenographer were to be present... . Having a court engagement I could not go myself... . There were present also [besides Mr. Ehrmann] Mr. Buxton and Mr. Carens of the Boston Herald... .

Mr. Ehrmann reported also that Professor Gill, whose remarks were taken down by a stenographer, after witnessing the experiments, expressed doubt as to the correctness of his former view. This led to an exchange of letters between Professor Gill and myself [Thompson], to which it is unnecessary for present purposes to refer further... .

Mr. Goddard asked me if I would consent to further experimentation by him in the presence of other experts. This I declined with emphasis, stating that I felt that there had been a lack of frankness, and an attempt to take advantage of me in the making of the experiment; and also that I would not co-operate with anyone who denounced as crooks experts in whom I had confidence. [New York reporter had called Turner's photographs valueless and had spoken in derision of Hamilton.] ... We [Ehrmann and Thompson] felt justified in arguing that there was a reasonable doubt as to the genuineness of these two exhibits. [16]

[The Boston Evening Transcript summarized Thompson's allegation that Bullet 3 and Shell W may not have been genuine trial exhibits. Thompson gave a similar statement to NY Times, 8/11/1927: 2. See

Transcript of the Record, 5038, 5186-5187, 5314, 5320. District Attorney Ranney responded on pp. 5188, 5339.]

"Goddard Defends Sacco Bullet Test." New York Times. Aug. 12, 1927.

... Major Goddard said that his services were first offered to the defense committee, but that Mr. Thompson rejected the photographic evidence on the bullet when he saw that its presentation might be detrimental to his clients' interest. [2]

Dudley P. Ranney's Letter to Governor Fuller
(The Sacco-Vanzetti Case Papers: Reel 21)

Plymouth,
June 8, 1927.

His Excellency Alvan T. Fuller,
Governor of Massachusetts,
State House,
Boston, Massachusetts.

Your Excellency:

I have this morning received from Major Calvin H. Goddard, of New York, the enclosed communication. I take the liberty of forwarding it directly to you for your consideration. It needs no comment on our part.

Major Goddard's examination of the shells and bullets was entirely unsolicited on our part; - we merely consented to his request that he be allowed to make this experiment.
Respectfully yours,
Ass't District Attorney. (Dudley P. Ranney)
[Ed. See Ranney's letter to Charles Van Amburgh on p. 180. See p. 594.]

Walter Lippmann. "Doubt That Will Not Down." New York World. Aug. 19, 1927.

... The Sacco-Vanzetti case is clouded and obscure. It is full of doubt. The fairness of the trial raises doubt. The evidence raises doubt. The inadequate review of the evidence raises doubt. The Governor's inquiry has not appeased these doubts. The report of his Advisory Committee has not settled these doubts. Everywhere there is doubt so deep, so pervasive, so unsettling, that it cannot be denied and it cannot be ignored. No man, we submit, should be put to death where so much doubt exists.

The real solution of this case would be a new trial before a new judge under new conditions. Fervently we hope that the Supreme Judicial Court [240] of Massachusetts will decide that under the law such a new trial can be held. But if it does not, then to the Governor, to his Council and to his friends of justice in Massachusetts we make this plea: Stay the execution. Wait. The honor of an American Commonwealth is in your hands. [241]

[Lippmann's editorial excerpted from abbreviated reprint in Edward P. J. Corbett, Classical Rhetoric for the Modern Student, Oxford Univ. Press, pp, 235-241.] [Ed. Corbett finds (p. 387) "such a moving eloquence" in the "most memorable statement" Vanzetti made to Phil Stong. No change in Corbett's 4th edition.]

Michael E. Parrish. Felix Frankfurter and His Times. 1982

He [Frankfurter] advised Ehrmann on how to present the defense's case before the advisory committee. [189] [Parrish's note #360 on p. 306: Frankfurter to Ehrmann, July 14, 1927, Box 2, Herbert Ehrmann Papers, Harvard Law School. Editor **breaks** chronology.]

Walter Lippmann's editorial attack on the commonwealth's case that appeared in the New York World sprang almost entirely from Frankfurter's efforts, and he made a similar but futile attempt to persuade the leaders of the New York Times. [193]

[Parrish cites the wiretap logs on Frankfurter. Parrish, a student of Alexander Bickel, is Professor of History, Univ. of California, San Diego. See his entries on Felix Frankfurter and Charles E. Wyzanski, Jr. in American National Biography, 1999.]

Upton Sinclair Letter to Robert Minor, Feb. 8, 1928

Robert Minor,
New York City.

My dear Bob:

Here is the strictly confidential problem which is agitating me in connection with "Boston".

When I went East I expected to find that the anarchists knew all about a lot of bombing, and at first I attributed all the sense of mystery and secrecy to that, but gradually I became convinced . . . that Sacco and Vanzetti had at least known about the holdup. I found several Socialists who believed that they were guilty, but I did not think seriously about the possibility until I met an Italian radical connected with the committee and entirely in touch with the situation from the beginning, who warned me not to write the story, because I would make a fool of myself. I got him to talk to me in strict confidence, and what I find is that the Italian radicals believe that Sacco was guilty and Vanzetti knew it. It is this talk, pretty general among the radicals, which caused the stiffness of attitude on the part of Thayer and Fuller. And their spys [spies for Thayer and Fuller], of course, brought them everything. On the last day Fuller said to some labor men, "I know they are guilty, so I don't care whether they had a fair trial or not."

I left Boston feeling that I did not really know, and that I could write my book on the basis of certainty that they did not have a fair trial. But in Denver I met Fred Moore, and he told me the whole story. He told me how he framed the witnesses and what the other side had done, and he gave me permission to tell everything as it really happened, provided I would make it plain that it is the universal custom in big criminal trials. In other words, I am free to tell the truth, which is, of course, all I ever thought of doing. Moore is absolutely certain that Sacco was guilty. He is not certain about Vanzetti, but thinks he was. I do not think so. . . .

Now I had gone to Boston with all the publicity my publishers could get, and I had signed a contract with the Bookman to furnish them with a novel, telling the truth about the Sacco-Vanzetti case [serialized in February 1928]. If I quit on the job, there could be only one possible explanation. It would have been the same thing as admitting that I was afraid to tell the truth. The problem I am now confronting is how I am going to handle this story and what is going to be the effect upon the movement. It is absolutely impossible to keep it quiet always. Too many people know it and it is spreading all the time. It seemed to me that you who were an anarchist and advocated violence, and are now a Communist and have changed to that extent, are the best person to advise me about the matter. How much shall I tell? . . . My wife is absolutely certain that if I tell what I believe, I will be called a traitor to the movement, and may not live to finish the book.. . . . It sems to me that you, as a Communist, will probably feel that this individual anarchist violence ought to be repudiated rather than hushed up. It seems to me that the movement has to work in daylight. . . Of course, the next big case may be a frame-up, and my telling the truth about the Sacco-Vanzetti case will make things harder for the victims. But surely the movement cannot go on blindly believing in the anarchists as pacifists. They are now posing as that, and have earnestly implored me to represent them that way in my book. You will see in the March installment of the Bookman that I have declined to do so, and have portrayed Vanzetti as a militant, as he actually was.

. . . I am asking you to consider it absolutely confidential to you and Lydia, because

. . . some anarchist might think it his duty to keep me from finishing the book, and I do want to finish it!

[Sinclair Mss., Courtesy The Lilly Library, Indiana University, Bloomington, IN.] [Ed. See Sinclair's letter. p. 634.]

[Ed. Next, see excerpts from Sinclair's novel "Boston".]

Upton Sinclair. Boston: A Documentary Novel of the Sacco-Vanzetti Case, November 1928 (Bentley edition, 1978)

[In Boston, Sinclair builds his plot-line around Cornelia Thornwell (an imagined character), widow of ex-Governor Josiah Quincy Thornwell. Cornelia becomes a runaway grandmother who takes a job with the Plymouth Cordage Company, boarding with the Brini family in Suosso's Lane, North Plymouth. Another boarder, Vanzetti, speaks his anarchist views to a sympathetic Cornelia, who sees Galleani in the Brini home during the Cordage strike in 1916. Excerpts are the words of the **Narrator** unless otherwise indicated.]

Narrator. And then, that evening, he [Vanzetti] turned up at the Brini home with a gun! He, the apostle of brotherhood—the tenderhearted one who had refused to let a sick kitten be killed—he was getting ready to kill policemen! To be sure it was not a very efficient weapon, a five-chambered revolver of an old type, much rusted... . Galleani ... came to the Brini home the afternoon of the meeting [of strike leaders], so Cornelia got a good look at him: [76] [Ed. Galleani's visit is historic fact.]

Henry Cabot Winters, conservative lawyer, is Cornelia's son-in-law. Henry had been shocked by the Wall Street "bomb explosion." Five days after the indictment of Sacco and Vanzetti a wagonload of explo- [283] sives had gone off in front of the building of J. P. Morgan and Company in New York, and thirty-three persons had been blown to fragments. The newspapers were certain that this was the work of anarchists, and the Boston Traveler had come out with a full-page article, to the effect that the crime had been traced to the Galleani group, a vengeance for the arrest of the bandits, Sacco and Vanzetti. [284]

[See Avrich, Sacco and Vanzetti: The Anarchist Background, pp. 205, 245, on Wall Street bomb; and see Russell, Sacco & Vanzetti: The Case Resolved, p. 105.]

Lee Swenson was of Swedish descent, and came originally from Minnesota. He had been in practically every big criminal case which involved labor during the past fifteen or twenty years. As a cub reporter he had helped to get evidence for Moyer and Haywood in Idaho; he had helped defend the McNamaras in Los Angeles and Tom Mooney in San Francisco, and several groups of the I.W.W. in Chicago. [288] [See Felix (Protest, p. 23) on the fictional Swenson.]

Swenson speaks to Cornelia. Orciani has been driving me about, looking for evidence, ... [293] [Ed. Orciani did chauffeur Fred Moore during the Dedham trial.] I could name several laws of your great Commonwealth we broke in putting that job across—[295] [Ed. Swenson, an ill-disguised Fred Moore, refers to Moore's legal work that helped to exonerate two men charged with murder in the Lawrence textile strike of 1912.]

Another lawyer had come, a friend of Swenson's from the west; Fred Moore, an Irishman, but a radical, and Swenson's aide in many a fight. [348]

Swenson urges Cornelia to commit perjury. Nonna ... why don't you let me fix you up a story, about how you went down to Plymouth on April fifteenth of last year, and spent the day with the

Brinis, and had lunch with Bart, and later walked on the beach and saw him digging clams? That's the way to win this case, Nonna; ... [359]

Narrator. As a matter of fact it would have been easy for the prosecution to have verified Rosen's story if it had cared to, for he said he had sold cloth to many persons in Plymouth that day, including the wife of the chief of police. [411]

Sinclair judges jury. Never in a thousand years could they [jury] be made to realize that of the five identification witnesses upon whom the case against Sacco rested, one was a many times convicted crook, one a hysterical prostitute, one a half wit, one a disordered fantast, and one a feeble victim of police pressure. [411]

Task of the jury. The total amount of testimony was thirty-five hundred typewritten pages, more than a million words. To study them, and analyze their meaning and relationships, to digest and evaluate them, would occupy a brilliant legal mind several months; and here were two real estate men, two machinists, a grocer, a mason, a stock-keeper, a clothing salesman, a mill-operative, a shoemaker, a last-maker and a farmer. They could not assimilate the evidence... They must make some sort of guess; ... [436]

Dedham jury again. The twelve good Yankees and true would be arguing; now and then they would take a ballot; they would question the ones who disagreed, find out what was troubling them, argue again, cite this detail and that, seeking to change the doubters—but which way? [441]

Henry Cabot Winters to Cornelia. Did you ever see a book called 'Faccia a Faccia col Nemico'—that is to say, 'Face to Face with the Enemy'?" And Henry held up a thick book, bound in red covers. [456] Henry ... was turning over the pages of the red-bound book. He got up and came over and laid it on the arm of the Morris chair in which his mother-in-law sat. "Look at that!" he said. "A diagram of one of the bombs used by the assassins... ."

Cornelia replies: "My guess about the matter would be this, Henry: that Vanzetti was the despair of this group—he could not follow along."

Henry speaks: "Here is 'Fight for your Lives.' Here is the leaflet, 'Plain Words'—an outrageous thing, widely circulated. [458] I am told that the men's own lawyers know they were hiding dynamite—the men have admitted it." [459]

The imaginary Cornelia hears Gov. Fuller allude to mystery witnesses.

"I have sources of information, Mrs. Thornwell, which I am not at liberty to reveal. You should find out what the Italian colony thinks about this case."

"Governor, what are you saying? Some one has come and whispered into your ear, and you have been willing to believe it!"

"You cannot expect witnesses to tell all they know in the face of such peril as has been created in this community, Mrs. Thornwell." [667]

Climactic Scene on August 22, 1927

Cornelia: "Henry, did you find out what is that 'confidential information' that Mr. Lowell and the Governor are talking about?" . . .
Henry: "The story runs something like this, Mother: one of the Italian anarchists got drunk and talked, and admitted that Sacco had been in the bandit car at South Braintree." [713]
Cornelia: " . . . We have to assume that some government spy got the anarchist drunk, and then the anarchist comrade talked, and the spy told the Governor about it."
Cornelia speaks in 'cold fury': "Our dignity requires us to assume that the spy talked to some police official, whose business it is to know spies." [714] [See book by Anthony Arthur, Radical Innocent, p. 219.]

F. R. Bellamy. "The Truth About the Bridgewater Hold-Up." Outlook and Independent. Oct. 31, 1928.

At the moment of their arrest, they said they were calling for their friend's car at Johnson's garage in order to use it to transport literature. [1053] [See Fraenkel's book, p. 199.]

The Outlook ... objected to the payment of any money for such evidence [to Frank Silva] on the ground that it would prejudice the facts so obtained.... . With the help of one James Mede of Boston ... former friend of Frank Silva and the man in whose cigar store the Bridgewater crime had been ... planned, satisfactory arrangements were agreed upon. The money to be paid to Silva for his facts was deposited in the Corn Exchange Bank in New York City to the account of James Mede and the Publisher of the Outlook, with the understanding that if the affidavit which Silva gave was susceptible of proof, ... the money would be paid him after thirty days. [1054]

Frank Silva, who had been one of the gangsters who committed the crime [at Bridgewater], gave The Outlook the facts contained in the sworn statement printed in this issue... . [A]ll important statements made to The Outlook's investigation have been checked, and in all vital particulars corroborated. Only one conclusion ... is possible: Vanzetti was not present at the commission of the Bridgewater crime and had no ... knowledge of it whatever. [1054]

[In 1929-1960 <u>Encyclopaedia Britannica</u> cited this Oct. 31 article in <u>The Outlook</u>.]

[R. M. Lovett]. "Vanzetti Was Innocent." <u>The New Republic</u>. November 7, 1928.

Bartolomeo Vanzetti was innocent of at least one of the two crimes for which he was tried and found guilty. This fact is shown, in a manner to satisfy any reasonable human being, by the investigation conducted over a period of months by The Outlook, of New York, the results of which were made public on Monday of this week. The Outlook publishes an affidavit from one of the men who participated in the crime [Frank Silva], ...[317]

[Lovett was on the Editorial Board of <u>The New Republic</u>. See his editorial in <u>Unity</u>, 1937.]

Fred R. Brine. "Contradicts Story Clearing Vanzetti in Bridgewater Crime." <u>Boston Herald</u>. Jan. 13, 1929.

A story purporting to prove the innocence of Bartolomeo Vanzetti in connection with the attempted Bridgewater hold-up, published in the October 31, 1928, issue of the Outlook and Independent, has been contradicted by an affidavit which has been in the possession of the Massachusetts authorities since December, 1922, and which is published here for the first time.

The story is told by the same person—Frank Silva, alias Paul Martini—first to former Asst. Atty.-Gen. Albert Hurwitz, and later for the benefit of the Outlook. The substance of the Outlook affidavit is contradicted in the main and almost its entirety... . [H]e [Silva] said "no, sir" to the question, "Were you ever in Bridgewater yourself?"

Another affidavit, made by Jacob Lubin, a confederate of Silva in a New York mail robbery, discloses a frame-up that was in the making to have Silva assume partial blame for the attempted Bridgewater job. [1] [Brine was a staff writer.]

Book Reviews. "Boston by Upton Sinclair." The Road to Freedom. April 1929.

In the December issue of Road to Freedom, Hippolyte Havel [Czech anarchist] presented a cursory sketch of this latest work by Upton Sinclair. But this is a book that deserves more ... critical treatment from the anarchists.... . Sinclair believes that he is eminently fitted to write a history of the Sacco-Vanzetti case. His book proves him to be singularly unfitted, for as a historian, he is not in possession of all the facts and as a supporter of the State he is out of sympathy with the aims of the anarchists.... .

Lee Swenson, another mythical character [in Boston], suggests to Cordelia that they frame up a story for the jury in which the runaway grandmother would swear to a falsehood. [Ed. Reviewer makes fun of Sinclair's fictional creations.] By blowing into the ribs of Moore [see Felix, p. 23], once attorney in the case, Sinclair creates Swenson. Only a very gullible person could be fooled by the subterfuge.... . [6]

Upton Sinclair. "Sinclair Protests." The Road to Freedom. June 1929.

It is a fact that Sacco was a "Militant Anarchist", and gloried in the fact, despite the advice of many of his more cautious friends. That is one of the facts which I had to deal with in "Boston". [6]

[Hippolyte Havel, editor of this anarchist journal, replied (p. 7): "Of course, Sacco was a militant." See pp. 480, 503, 634.]

H. L. Mencken. No Title. Lantern. August 1929.

The Sacco-Vanzetti case, though it has got more notice than the others, is but one of a long series of gross perversions of justice in America. The Mooney-Billings case and the Centralia case are still being fought out, and a new atrocity of precisely the same sort seems to be in preparation at Gastonia, N.C.... . All of these cases show the same elements. First a man suspected of subversive opinions is harassed and prosecuted by the police. Then, failing to shake him, they accuse him of some overt crime, and proceed to manufacture evidence against him. Then he is convicted by a jury of frightened half-wits, carefully hand-picked for the purpose, with a complaisant judge roaring at him from the bench... . The victim is railroaded to the tune of patriotic hosannahs. The newspapers approve, often with vast gloating. The rev. clergy are discreetly silent. [5] [Ed. Mencken "thought the defendants guilty." See William Manchester, DISTURBER OF THE PEACE, p. 213. Mencken edited The American Mercury. Aldino Felicani and Gardner Jackson published Lantern.]

Walter Lippmann. No Title. Lantern. August 1929.

If Sacco and Vanzetti were professional bandits, then historians and biographers who attempt to deduce character from personal documents might as well shut up shop. By every test that I know of for judging character, these are the letters [The Letters of Sacco and Vanzetti] of innocent men... I am deeply interested in the Sacco-Vanzetti case, and firmly convinced that it is not closed. [5]

[Ronald Steel (Walter Lippmann and the American Century, p. 233) said Lippmann wrote this "in a promotion blurb for Frankfurter's book." Lippmann was chief editorial writer of the New York World, and a founder of The New Republic.]

Edmund Wilson. No Title. Lantern. August 1929.

The execution of Sacco and Vanzetti was one of the most conspicuous and terrible triumphs of ... stupidity and cowardice of the American capitalist mob... . Our worst characteristic today is intellectual and moral cowardice. [5]

[Wilson, a Marxist who visited Lenin's tomb, was an associate editor of The New Republic, 1926 to 1931. Wilson voted for the Communist candidate, William Z. Foster, in the 1932 presidential election. See Harvard Freshman Seminar 46k (2004) in ADDENDA.]

Richard Newby

Osmond K. Fraenkel. <u>The Sacco-Vanzetti Case</u>. 1931

Although it is not definitely known when Sacco and Vanzetti first met, the time must have antedated the war, for, in 1917, it was together they fled the draft. Both men belonged at the time to the Galleani group of philosophical anarchists, and both had been suspected by the United States Department of Justice of violation of the Selective Service Act and of holding views which made them liable to deportation. [5]

Portrait of Mike Boda. Just what this man's occupation was remains uncertain. Himself perhaps not a radical, he was the friend of radicals, at a time when to be such in one's associations and a foreigner besides, constituted strong grounds for suspicion. [10]

It will be observed that in this opening address counsel for the defendants referred to witnesses who were going to contradict prosecution witnesses as to the presence of the defendants at the place of the crime and to the alibis, but that there was no discussion of any other contentions of the defense. Mr. Callahan said nothing either as to the cap the prosecution claimed had been Sacco's, or as to the revolver belonging to Vanzetti. He said nothing as to how the defense intended to meet the contention that Sacco's gun had fired the fatal bullet. He was silent about explanations the defendants might offer of suspicious acts and falsehoods and made no answer to the charge of guilty consciousness. Why defendants' counsel failed to discuss these points and to prepare the minds of the jurors for the evidence they intended to develop does not appear. [66]

The <u>Outlook and Independent</u> ... published ... articles and an editorial which dealt with the Bridgewater case. Unfortunately, **insufficient care was taken by the editors to verify all their statements of fact.** One instance of this ... follows. The introductory editorial states that "at the moment of their arrest, they said they were calling for their friend's car at Johnson's garage in order to use it to transport literature." Had the defendants indeed on their arrest made any such explanation, their radicalism might have been kept out of the Braintree case, since there would then have been no lies to explain away. [199]

AUGUSTUS PECHEUR, a partner of Burke's, corroborated his presence in South Braintree on the day of the crime, but differed from him on some details of their visit. Burke said he had been there only a short time before the shooting [970]; Pecheur that it was about an hour and a half [1000,02]. Pecheur had heard the shooting but not seen the escaping car. [301] [Ed. This is Fraenkel's full analysis of Pecheur. Fraenkel cites pages in transcript.]

The Supreme Judicial Court made no express reference to the subject of consciousness of guilt. Twice in its opinion it stated that Mrs. Johnson had telephoned the police on account of the actions of the defendants, once asserting that her suspicions had been aroused [4315, 4336]. These statements are, of course, misleading, because Mrs. Johnson actually went out to telephone in accordance with a prearranged plan, and before she had noticed the defendants at all. [463]

[Fraenkel, counsel for ACLU, is the author of "Sacco-Vanzetti Case" in Encyclopedia Americana, 1950-2005.]

Sylvester G. Gates. "A Formidable Shadow." Rev. of The Sacco-Vanzetti Case. The New Republic. December 9, 1931.

([W]ith the exception of Dean Wigmore, ...) no responsible and independent lawyer has attempted anything like a detailed defense of the conviction. Mr. Fraenkel's 550 pages are as fair, accurate and well balanced an account of the case as it is possible to make... . The authorities, judicial and executive alike, remained obdurate to the end, inflicting on the two men that irrevocable sentence which has made Vanzetti in his prophetic words "a vanquished man but a formidable shadow." [103] [Gates quotes from Vanzetti's letter, Nov. 18, 1926. Gates, Frankfurter's pupil, wrote the 3-column biography of Sacco and Vanzetti for the Dictionary of American Biography. See Gates, 311.]

Frederick L. Allen. Only Yesterday. 1931

Vanzetti in particular was clearly a remarkable man—an intellectual of noble character, a philosophical anarchist of a type which it seemed impossible to associate with a pay-roll murder. [85]

[Allen was a staff member of the Atlantic Monthly, The Century, and an editor of Harper's.]

Edward Holton James. "New Light Coming on the Sacco-Vanzetti Case." Unity. August 15, 1932.

[Ed. E. H. James, wealthy nephew of Henry and William James, took Dante Sacco, Sacco's son, with him to Italy in 1932. Buda, exiled on the island of Ponza, kissed Dante's cheeks (327). Leaving Ponza, Dante and James went to Fano, where James questioned Orciani, who was frightened when James appeared at his house in December 1927, thinking Katzmann had sent James to arrest him.]

There is only one man in the world that he [Orciani] is really afraid of, and that is Katzmann. When I asked him why he had disappeared from Boston after having helped Moore all through the Dedham trial, he answered: I thought that Katzmann might change his mind about me and arrest me again. I went to New York City and lived there till February, 1922, when I came to Italy.

James's conclusion. We have, therefore, the history of Buda and Orciani, driven away from the United States by a reign of terror and by a conspiracy of forces which was too powerful for them to battle against... . Sacco and Vanzetti were therefore deprived of the testimony of these two important witnesses at the time of the trial. [329] [Ed. See p. 409.]

[See Avrich, pp. 207-210, on Buda's (Boda's) life in Italy.]

Herbert B. Ehrmann. The Untried Case: The Sacco -Vanzetti Case and the Morelli Gang 1933

The evidence we had gathered was destined never to be presented before a jury. Of course, the jury which convicted Sacco and Vanzetti in 1921 had no knowledge of the facts incriminating the Morelli gang... . Few people to-day know the chain of circumstances linking the Morellis to the South Braintree killings. As will be seen, Governor Fuller took no interest in it, the committee which he appointed misunderstood and omitted much of it, the Supreme Judicial Court of Massachusetts ruled that it had no power to determine the question. There was, in fact, only one judicial hearing—if it may be called that—at which the evidence supporting the Madeiros-Morelli theory was considered at length. This was the hearing at Dedham in September, 1926, upon our motion for a new trial based upon the newly discovered evidence [motion 6]. The denial of this motion effactually ended all real hope of saving Sacco and Vanzetti. Also, it shut off forever any official investigation into the possible guilt of the Morellis. [149] [Ehrmann helped Frankfurter in Cleveland crime study in 1922.]

E. M. Morgan. Rev. of The Untried Case. Harvard Law Review. Jan. 1934.

[Ed. Ehrmann argues that the Morellis were the South Braintree murderers. Morgan reviews The Untried Case.]

Beginning with a wholly worthless story from an utterly untrustworthy source, our investigator [Ehrmann] turns up clue after clue and fact after fact until he is transformed from an honest doubter into an enthusiastic convert... .

Are these officers of the government madmen? Or has our investigator put his case too enthusiastically? Let us look beyond his book. Sacco and Vanzetti had a long and expensive trial. No lawyer has seriously asserted that the evidence against them was insufficient to justify submitting the issue of their guilt to the jury. It convinced the jury, the trial judge, the Governor, and the members of the Lowell Committee; and it would be rash to condemn all of these as totally unreasonable, ... If the accused were alive today and were to be tried again, and the witnesses who then appeared for the state, buttressed by those who have since been discovered, were to testify, the case would again have to be submitted to a jury; and if a verdict of guilt were returned, it could not be set aside as contrary to the weight of the evidence, at least as against Sacco.

Sacco had been employed in the Rice and Hutchins factory for seven days in 1917. He was not at his usual place of work in Brockton on April 15. He lied to his employer to account for his absence from work on the afternoon of April 15. When arrested he gave an inaccurate statement as to his whereabouts on April 15, and told a number of deliberate lies upon material matters including an assertion that he had never been in South Braintree. [538]

Until the hearing before the Lowell Committee there was no suggestion that Exhibit 18 was not the fatal bullet, and there has not yet been disclosed anything that could reasonably be dignified as evidence to support any such suggestion.

If the comparison microscope shows as to the bullets what Colonel Goddard insists that it does, and if the photographs show as to the shells what they appear to show and what the Gunthers assert, then the balance of probability that they were fired from the same pistol is so heavy as to leave no room for a reasonable doubt. [539]

Notwithstanding possible inherent verities discoverable in it [Madeiros' confession] by a skilled analyst, it would be almost presumptuous to ask that without corroboration it be given very serious consideration. Madeiros was an epileptic and a liar, who in the course of a short career had been a bouncer in a house of ill-fame, a rumrunner, a smuggler, a crook, a thief, a robber, and a murderer. At the time of the confession he was in jail after conviction of murder, awaiting the result of an appeal to the Supreme Judicial Court. His conviction was later reversed on the sheerest of technicalities; and this confession was not used, or any investigation as to its truth made, until after he had been convicted a second time. [544]

Mr. Ehrmann's publishers advertise his book as furnishing proof of the innocence of Sacco and Vanzetti and of the guilt of the Morelli gang. Of course it does nothing of the kind. [546]
[Morgan was Bussey Professor of Law and Frankfurter's colleague at Harvard Law School.]

Jack D. Gunther and C. O. Gunther. The Identification of Firearms. 1935

[Ed. See photos of comparison microscope on pages 21-22.]

He [Burns] contended that bullet III might have been fired from a Bayard despite his measurements of 0.050 inch for the Colt land width, 0.040 for the Bayard, and 0.050 to 0.060 inch for the width of the land mark on the fatal bullet No. III, ... [201]

Gill's credibility is seriously weakened by his assertion, "I am absolutely convinced from my own measurements that the so-called mortal bullet never passed through the Sacco gun," in the face of his admission of lacking skill and experience in this line... . Hamilton's testimony forces the conclusion that he was trifling with the truth. [228]
[Ed. See Gunthers' footnote #25, and see New York Herald-Tribune, March 11, 1934, "Strewl Defense Expert {Hamilton} Admits Deceiving State," p. 9, columns 4-6.]

Nils Ekman of Bridgeport, Connecticut, at the request of Van Amburgh, took photographs of the mortal bullet and one test bullet [post trial]. [237]   Hamilton attempted to attack the Ekman photographs, which the photographer testified were of <u>approximately</u> 13 diameters' magnification... . This was another of Hamilton's silly attempts to cloud the issue by adding to the already existing confusion on measurements. Hamilton measured the photographs in hundredths of an inch, and therefore his division by 13, which was only approximate, would not produce results accurate to ten thousandths of an inch, as he would like one to infer. [241]

Hamilton was guilty of using all possible arguments in his client's behalf whether founded in fact or in fiction, and his testimony creates a suspicion of charlatanism. [244] [Ed. Jack D. Gunther, Member of the New York State Bar; Charles O. Gunther, M.E., Professor of Mathematics, Stevens Institute of Technology, Lieutenant Colonel, Ordnance Department, The Army of the United States.]

Malcolm Cowley. "Echoes of a Crime." <u>The New Republic</u>. August 28, 1935.

An important ... feature of the Sacco-Vanzetti case is its effect on ... the American intelligentsia... . The intelligentsia can be defined as the part of the population that tries to think for itself, ... [T]here was the situation of two men tried unjustly and sentenced to death, the old story of innocence endangered... . It was the intelligentsia rather than the labor unions that conducted their defense... . [T]he intellectuals for once assumed most of the responsibility [for defense of Sacco and Vanzetti] ... [79] [Ed. Cowley, a Stalinist in the 1930s, was literary editor of <u>The New Republic</u> from 1929 to 1944. See Tanenhaus, <u>Whittaker Chambers</u>, p.166.]

Eugene Lyons. <u>Assignment in Utopia</u>. 1937

He [Fred Moore] had given me explicit instructions to arouse all of Italy to the significance of the Massachusetts murder case. [22]

Lyons finds Coacci in Italy. Sacco-Vanzetti matters also sent me into the Marchesan hills, ... I tracked down an anarchist deportee from Massachusetts [Coacci], ... The man's shelves were lined with brochures on the home manufacture of bombs and he professed himself a terrorist of the Galleani school. So deep, however, had the fear of American law and police entered his heart that it needed a week of pleading and threatening and pressure by Merlino, the grand old man of the anarcho-syndicalist movement, to bring this terrorist to the point of signing an innocuous affidavit in support of Sacco's alibi. [24]

The arrest of Nicola Sacco and Bartolomeo Vanzetti on May 5, 1920, was not mentioned outside the local press. Their conviction on July 14, 1921, rated exactly seven and a half inches on an inside page of the New York Times. Their execution six years later, on August 23, 1927, received five full pages in the same newspaper, ... [30]
[Lyons, a radical journalist, wrote articles for the Defense Committee. He became a Senior Editor for Reader's Digest. His ironic title signals his disillusionment with the Soviet Union.]

Robert M. Lovett. "Sacco-Vanzetti—After Ten Years." Unity. August 16, 1937.

The publication of the entire record of the case in several volumes, ... has convinced educated opinion of the innocence of these victims. In addition, the enterprise of the Outlook brought to light the true story of the Bridgewater hold-up, for which Vanzetti was falsely convicted...
. [T]he sober second thought of mankind, ... has all but unanimously convicted the Commonwealth of Massachusetts of the crime of shedding innocent blood... Governor Fuller ... was a man of large ambition, of little education, and almost no common sense. [220]
[Lovett, an editor of The New Republic in 1921, chaired the Sacco-Vanzetti National League.]

William Allen White. Forty Years on Main Street. 1937

I am now satisfied that Sacco and Vanzetti were innocent of the crime for which they were convicted. Their execution was a crime for which America lost prestige in the eyes of millions all over the world. [184] [Ed. White was called the Sage of Emporia. In 1927 he said Sacco and Vanzetti were "probably guilty."]

George Seldes. You Can't Do That. 1938

And nothing can repair the injustice done to Sacco and Vanzetti. Here judicial injustice goes so far as to refuse to arrest the real murderers since the proof that innocent men were murdered by the law would further add to the contempt of honest men for the courts which condemned the fish peddler and the shoemaker, two real libertarians.

[53] [Ed. Seldes published 21 books. When he died at age 104, the AP called him an "award-winning journalist and media watchdog."]

Michael A. Musmanno. After Twelve Years. 1939

Summary.

Vanzetti could not testify at his Plymouth trial. Vanzetti's lawyer, John P. Vahey, advised him to stay off the witness stand. About his innocence Vanzetti could not speak to the Plymouth jury. [80]

Honest people free of prejudice got proof that Vanzetti did not participate in the holdup at Bridgewater. What really occurred at Bridgewater on December 24, 1919, was published in the Outlook and Independent on October 31, 1928. The large headline declared Vanzetti innocent. The published story was authentic. Frank Silva confessed he and others tried to rob the payroll truck. Silva is really Paul Martini, who led the would-be robbers. The blueprint of the crime was drawn up by James Mede, whose affidavit is in the Outlook and Independent. [82]

The numerical opposition—and this means witnesses—in the 1921 trial was 55 versus 99. In football parlance, this would suggest the Commonwealth was outscored by 44 points. This is a comparative point on the matter of truth. [169]

Albert H. Hamilton, the expert in firearms, had worked in criminology for 37 years by the time he reached age 62. Assignment in 164 homicide cases took this "criminologist" to all corners of the United States. Statistically, he was a Government man in 147.6 of these cases. Qualified he truly was to answer factual questions on guns and bullets. [176]

In the principles of anarchism they expressed a strong faith. In their anarchist creed was no clause which countenanced violence. Each considered himself a "philosophical" anarchist. On one occasion Vanzetti wrote: "On principle we abhor violence, deeming it the worst form of coercion and authority." A respect for property and individuals was as firmly declared by Sacco. Not once was Sacco tempted to use force or contemplate destruction of human beings. [178]

In the 52-day period from July 1, 1927, through August 21, Musmanno talked to Sacco and Vanzetti in the Charlestown State Prison at least 21 times, perhaps as many as 28 times. (By car the prison can be reached in 15 minutes.) Yes, Mrs. Sacco paid more visits to the prisoners than Musmanno. But Musmanno was No. 2 in prison visits "with these two." [278]

To Hanover Street, friends of Sacco and Vanzetti came to await the decision of Governor Fuller [Aug. 3]. It was arranged that Musmanno would telephone the headquarters there when the decision was announced. Seated on a box at the Sacco-Vanzetti headquarters was courageous Felix Frankfurter, whose feet banged the box. [281-282]

Thompson stepped down as chief counsel for Sacco and Vanzetti. Arthur D. Hill replaced him. On August 5 Herbert B. Ehrmann, Francis D. Sayre, Frankfurter, and Musmanno talked with Hill in his office. Two more men, Elias Field and Richard C. Evarts, soon joined the legal team. (Sayre married President Wilson's daughter.) All were esteemed for ability and reputation. [291]

[Ed. On August 4, 1927, Thompson and Ehrmann resigned as defense counsel. At Frankfurter's request, Arthur Hill took over defense. Appel, VI: 479.]

World support for Sacco and Vanzetti comes not from Communists but from moderate citizens who fear God and demand fairness, H. G. Wells being one such citizen. Another moderate is Arnold Bennett. [328]

Musmanno recounts his plea with Attorney General Reading on August 22, 1927.

The eleven eyewitnesses for the prosecution [Andrews, Tracy, Heron, Pelser, Splaine, Devlin, Goodridge, Faulkner, Levangie, Reed, Dolbeare] all equivocated at the trial. They could not have succeeded if the law had been upheld. The 105 defense witnesses were "forthright." They lost because the Judge violated the Constitutional rights of the defendants. [371]

[See Musmanno's reviews of Montgomery (p. 515), Russell (p. 526), and Felix (p. 549).]

Bennett Cerf. "Trade Winds." The Saturday Review. December 11, 1943.

STIRRING UP of the Frank lynching inevitably calls to mind that other classic miscarriage of justice—The Sacco-Vanzetti case—an indelible blot on the integrity of the law in the State of Massachusetts. [Cerf charged the Commonwealth of Massachusetts with] "putting innocent men to death." [19]
[Cerf was an editor of The Saturday Review. See "The Leo Frank Case Reconsidered," Journal of American History 79 (Dec. 1991): 917-948. Boldface is by Cerf.]

Charles J. Van Amburgh. "Common Sources of Error in the Examination and Interpretation of Ballistics Evidence." Boston University Law Review. (April 1946).

It is well at this point to consider the collateral interest of the medical examiner and the ballistic operator. The latter should never stumble into the medical field by attempting to testify about bullet wounds except so far as to note their location and general surface appearance. His is purely an exterior problem. By the same token **the medico should stay out of ballistics.** There is opportunity for some mutual assistance. Better for the medical man to simply report that he has recovered so many bullets, wads, or shot pellets, leaving their classification to someone better versed in that subject. [230]
    Van Amburgh's footnote. At the inquest held April 17, 1920 (Re: Sacco-Vanzetti case) the medical examiner, testifying about the autopsies, described six bullets as "identical". He made some further references to pistols and revolvers. Attorney Herbert B. Ehrmann, representing the defence before Governor Alvan T. Fuller's Committee in August, 1927, argued that this testimony [transcript: 5038, 5187, 5320] disagreed with the description by experts of bullets offered at the trial; therefore, there must have been a substitution of bullets after the inquest. [230]
[Van Amburgh was ballistics expert witness for the Commonwealth at the Dedham trial. In 1985 Kaiser quoted from pp. 240-241 in this B.U.L.R. article.]

Louis Joughin and Edmund M. Morgan. The Legacy of Sacco & Vanzetti. 1948

INTRODUCTION by A. M. Schlesinger

This book, an arresting and cogent evaluation of the legal, social, and literary aspects of the case, will make clear to a generation fresh to the facts why the interest was so intense, as well as why historical scholars and textbooks writers have deemed the affair sufficiently important to include it in general works on American history.

Professor Morgan, one of America's foremost authorities on the law of evidence, carefully examines the legal record, including the repeated attempts through six years to secure a retrial or executive clemency. [xi]

Professor Joughin, a student of literature and its social implications, then shows how society—in Massachusetts, in the country at large, in other lands—rendered its own verdict on the case. [xii.] [Schlesinger is Professor Emeritus in the Humanities at the Graduate Center of the City University of New York.]

Morgan. There was perhaps an unnecessary delay in bringing the men to trial, but the more than three hundred entries indicate clearly that responsibility for the length of the controversy rests chiefly upon the defense attorneys; they chose to fight vigorously, and to present every discoverable additional fact and argument; if they had not done so, the end would have come much sooner. [4]

These interrogations [of defendants by Stewart, May 5, and by Katzmann, May 6] were, in large part, introduced as testimony in the trials. It was made clear by cross-examination, and often by admission of the defendants, that they had given inexact, incorrect, and deliberately false answers to Stewart and Katzmann. They explained their lies by saying that they were afraid of expos-[8]ing their friends and themselves to prosecution as radicals; the prosecution attacked this excuse as inadequate to explain all of the lies; the further defense was offered that those lies which did not relate to the issue of radicalism were in fact innocent errors, and that those errors arose through indifference to the events of April 15, the day of the murders. The answers and manner of Sacco and Vanzetti at these preliminary questionings furnish important evidence as to their consciousness of guilt. Were they afraid, and if so of what? [9]

Vanzetti's Plymouth trial. Weak as the prosecution may have been, it succeeded in getting a conviction; it was opposed by an unconvincing defense. Vanzetti's lawyers offered an alibi intended to show that he was going about his usual routine of peddling fish. All sixteen of the witnesses called were Italians, and they spoke through an interpreter to a Yankee jury. Some were confused, others were abnormally exact and helpful.... . Vanzetti did not testify. [10]

This statement [confession by Madeiros], coming from a man of the worst possible sort of reputation and criminal record, was naturally suspect, even though it virtually assured his eventual execution. [19]

[T]his cross-examination [of Beltrando Brini], taken alone, tends strongly to show that a group of Italians had framed an alibi for Vanzetti and had coached this bright youngster to tell his story with details which would tie in with the incidents related by other witnesses.

Katzmann's cross-examination of the defendant's witnesses was severe; [46] ... It ... could not with any show of reason be called misconduct. [47]

... Vanzetti makes statements concerning both this trial [at Plymouth] and the trial of himself and Sacco at Dedham which are not sustained by the printed [48] record. He attributes low motives to witnesses against him and virtue to all who favored him. His readiness to ascribe corruption to all who did not support him seriously impairs the value of all his assertions about the Plymouth trial. [49]

The defendant's failure to take the stand [at Plymouth] coupled with the impeachment of his alibi witnesses explains and justifies the verdict. [55]

There is nothing to support a charge of unfairness or prejudice on the part of the trial judge [at the Plymouth trial]. [56]

The Dedham Trial. After such a trial and such a summing-up the verdict of the jury is not astonishing. But to account for the verdict is not to say that the defendants were fairly tried. The reader puts down the story of the trial with the feeling of one who has witnessed a game between contestants of unequal ability. [107]

Did Hamilton actually try to walk off with pistols that had been on file in the clerk's office and had just been used as exhibits at the hearing [Appel, IV: 3732bb-3732tt]? If not, why did the judge have occasion to order the pistols to be delivered into the custody of the clerk? [173]

499

It was Moore who had used such stupid and questionable methods to obtain from Andrews and Goodridge a repudiation of their evidence at the trial. It was this same Moore who had hired Hamilton and asked the court to rely upon his testimony on the most crucial issue in the case. Was this **switching of the barrels** just another manifestation of Moore's unethical conduct, this time in co-operation with an unscrupulous expert? [174]

[I]t should be noted that a subsequent study of the ballistic testimony and exhibits, as they appeared in the public record, by disinterested competent **experts** resulted in the conclusions (a) that the expert evidence at the trial was worthless and misleading, (b) that Hamilton's expert testimony created a suspicion of charlatanism and of trifling with the truth, and (c) that a comparison of the engravings made by the breechblock of Sacco's pistol on the test shell with those made by the breechblock of the pistol that fired the Fraher shell furnished most persuasive evidence that the two shells were fired in the same pistol. [175]

[Ed. Morgan's **experts** are J.D. Gunther and C.O. Gunther. Endnote on p. 537 reads: "The conclusion (c) ... is not in the text of the book but was expressed by the authors [Gunthers] in a communication to the writer."]

The Sacco-Vanzetti case continues to be of vital legal signifi-[196] cance because it is among the most important of those litigations which have left us with unresolved doubts. [197] [End of Morgan's section.]

Joughin. It would be hard to imagine a more unfortunate coincidence than the indictment of Vanzetti for murder on September 11, 1920, and the Wall Street explosion of September 16. Thirty-three persons were killed. [216] [See Avrich (pp. 205, 245) on Wall Street bomb.]

The filed correspondence of the American Civil Liberties Union contains a letter from its Director of that time in which he says:

Director: The Civil Liberties Union has been connected with the Sacco and Vanzetti matter, but has hidden its participation under various false fronts. We are at present instigating a nation-wide movement among lawyers in the various university faculties to join as signatories ... for a review of the case de novo. This work is being done behind the name of a group of lawyers at Columbia. Karl Llewellyn is the chief promoter. [255]

The Governor conducted his personal investigation in strict secrecy; it is hard to see how he could have done otherwise; if he had thrown the door open, he would have needed the complete paraphernalia of a court of law... . **He talked to Rose Sacco** and told her that attorney Vahey had given him assurance of his desire that Vanzetti take the stand at the Plymouth trial—and that Vanzetti had refused. [300] [See NYT: 7/28/27/8. Fuller had "a full hour" w/Vahey.]

The Committee [Fuller's] must have known of matters which never became part of the official record: the Goddard ballistic test of June 3, Vahey's private communication to the Governor on the failure of Vanzetti to testify at Plymouth, and the nebulous rumors that someone in the Italian colony had finally implicated Vanzetti. [304] [See Boston, p. 667.]

In the same year [1935], True Detective Mysteries ran a series of articles entitled "The Hidden Drama of Sacco and Vanzetti" ... a collaboration between ... Fred H. Thompson and Charles J. Van Amburg, ... Apart from thrills, there is some error and a modicum of new information. [352]

Most terrible of all is the fact that the term "anarchist" has been misunderstood; holders of that philosophy are fundamentally believers in the natural goodnes of man. Sacco and Vanzetti were such men and had nothing to do with the bomb-throwing minority which has discredited their system of thought. [379]

There are, unquestionably, elements of proof against them, but there is a greater weight in their favor... . The present judgment of history is that the two men were unjustly sent to death. [512]

[Joughin taught at New York's School for Social Research, and Morgan was Royall Professor of Law at Harvard University.]

Sunday Standard-Times. New Bedford, Mass. Nov. 12, 1950.
Jurors Unshaken in Verdict. Sacco and Vanzetti Guilty.

Pair's Political Beliefs Had No Bearing on Decision, Say 7, Unswayed by 29-Year Propaganda Barrage

Here is what the seven known survivors of the Sacco-Vanzetti jury told The Standard-Times about their memorable verdict.

THE VERDICT OF GUILTY was in accordance with the evidence, was a just verdict, and they would vote the same way today.

Richard Newby

THE TRIAL JUDGE was eminently fair, indicated no inkling of prejudice, if he had any, to the jury, and his memory has been inexcusably sullied by defenders of Sacco and Vanzetti.

THE SO-CALLED RADICALISM of the defendants played absolutely no part in the verdict. In fact the jury is astounded still at the charge to the contrary, and amazed the trial ever became a worldwide cause celebre on that basis.

From children of the four jurors known to be dead, it was learned that their juror-parents shared the sentiments of the survivors... [T]he other juror, if he is living, cannot be located. [12]

AUTHORS NEVER MET JURORS

In 1949, author Philip Duffield Stong wrote in The Aspirin Age of the Sacco-Vanzetti case. His comment on the jury: "A dozen Yankees who had decided on the guilt of the accused before they took their seats."

According to the surviving jurors, Stong is a liar. Before making his incredibly sweeping statement, did Stong take the trouble to meet any of the jurors? He did not.

Does the Sacco-Vanzetti jury fit the condemnation of it by Supreme Court Justice Felix Frankfurter? The latter, in 1921 a Harvard Law School professor, long was articulate in the Sacco-Vanzetti cause. He has written magazine articles alleging a miscarriage of justice by the jury, and also a book... .

In his book, "Case of Sacco and Vanzetti," Frankfurter wrote there was no wonder the jury voted for conviction, with its "solidarity against the alien, the indignation against the two draft-dodgers." They had been inflamed by a "riot of political passion and patriotic sentiment," he wrote.

Justice Frankfurter is, more than anybody else, responsible for the widely-accepted belief Sacco and Vanzetti were convicted as radicals, not murderers. He never met or talked to the jurors he said were unfit. He has never tried to... . No juror ever met either author of "The Legacy" [Joughin and Morgan]. ... They damned the jurymen and let it go at that.

Most articulate survival of the tribunal is Mr. Dever. His memory is astounding. Perhaps the fact he became a lawyer after the trial served to impress the details of the case in his mind. [12]

John Dever's Statement to <u>Standard-Times</u> Staff Writer

"When we first left the courtroom for deliberations, I had the feeling that most everybody felt Sacco and Vanzetti were guilty. But I clung to the theory I began the trial with, that we should give them every opportunity. So I suggested, after a brief spell, that we have an informal ballot, nothing binding, just something to get a sample of opinion. My hope was that the ballot would inspire a thorough review of what we had heard and seen.

"Well, that informal ballot was 10-2 for conviction with me one of the two. And just what I hoped would transpire, did. We started discussing things, reviewed the very important evidence about the bullets and everybody had a chance to speak his piece.

"There never was any argument, though. We just were convinced Sacco and Vanzetti had done what the prosecution had charged them with." [12] [See <u>Boston</u>, pp. 436, 441.]

"As I say, I was a defendants' man," Mr. Dever continued, "and if the judge was prejudiced against the men, he did not give any indication to us."

"I remember in Barre, my birthplace, there was a wonderful statue to Robert Burns of pure marble from the quarries there. It was carved by an Italian. I was brought up near that statue and I acquired a respect for anyone who could create a marvelous work of art like that with his hands. I admired Italians then, I did during the trial and still do. It is nonsense to say we were prejudiced against Sacco and Vanzetti because they were Italian immigrants." [13] [Edward B. Simmons, staff writer.]

Upton Sinclair. "The Fishpeddler and the Shoemaker." <u>Institute of Social Studies Bulletin</u> II. 1953.

… While I was in Boston on account of my novel "Oil!" a lawyer named Fred D. Moore came to see me… He had been for seven years the faithful and tireless attorney for Sacco and Vanzetti, accused of murder in connection with an attempt at payroll robbery. Moore now attempted a kidnapping; he told me he just wouldn't take no for an answer, I absolutely had to get into his car and be driven to Charlestown jail to meet Bartolomeo Vanzetti… . But Fred kidnapped me and I went, and there met a gentle, sad-eyed dreamer, an Italian

503

who seven years previously had been a poor "wop" peddling fish, but who had educated himself in prison and [23] now spoke like a foreign philosopher and saint.

I went back to California and read the news of how he and his friend Sacco the shoeworker had been electrocuted by the great state of Massachusetts.... I decided to put this story into a novel, and returned to Boston to gather the material. I spent several weeks at the task, interviewing scores of people about the case and visiting all the scenes involved. [24]

Fred Moore had moved to Denver, and I arranged to meet him there.... I had the story completely formed in my mind, and you may imagine my consternation when I found myself seated in a little hotel room with the man who had given his time and thought to the case for seven years, and heard him say that he had come reluctantly to the conclusion that Sacco was guilty of the crime for which he had died and that possibly Vanzetti also was guilty....

I pressed him with questions: "Did Sacco or Vanzetti ever admit to you by the slightest hint that they were guilty?" He answered, "No." I asked him: "Did any of his friends ever admit it?" Again he answered, "No." Fred was a criminal lawyer, and I remember one of his statements about his profession. He said: "There is no criminal lawyer who has attained to fame in America except by inventing alibis and hiring witnesses. There is no other way to be a great criminal lawyer in America." [24]

[Sinclair, who published <u>Boston</u> in 1928, was a socialist author and reformer. See. p. 480.]

Francis Russell. "The Tragedy in Dedham: A retrospect of the Sacco-Vanzetti trial." <u>Antioch Review</u> 15 (Winter 1955).

... [T]he two men were innocent.... Two men were executed for a crime they did not commit. [393]
[Russell amended his judgment on the Sacco-Vanzetti case in 1962, in 1986, and later.]

Robert P. Weeks. <u>Commonwealth vs. Sacco and Vanzetti.</u> 1958

FOREWORD. The choice of the selections that make up this collection is, of course, mine. While reading and re-reading the 6,000-page <u>Transcript of the Record</u>, I pieced together those segments of it that **I thought gave the most responsible and readable account of the trial** and subsequent legal proceedings.... . In making my selections from the <u>Transcript of the Record</u>, and from the books, pamphlets, and periodical materials that I consulted, I [v] was greatly helped by two superb studies of the case: Osmond K. Fraenkel's <u>The Sacco-Vanzetti Case</u> and G. Louis Joughin's and Edmund M. Morgan's <u>The Legacy of Sacco and Vanzetti</u>. I am indebted also to John Dos Passos who brought certain useful materials to my attention. [vi]

[Weeks selects testimony by 37 witnesses: Bostock, Splaine, Pelser, Andrews, Campbell, Fay, Kurlansky, Faulkner, Dolbeare, Levangie, McCarthy, Reed, R. Johnson, S. Johnson, Connolly, Spear, Stewart, Loring, G. Kelley, Sacco, Mrs. Sacco, Mrs. Berardelli, Wadsworth, Fitzmeyer, Burns, Proctor, Van Amburgh, Fitzgerald, Burke, Liscomb, Vanzetti, Guidobone, Nelles, Andrower, Guadenagi, Dentamore, Hayes.]
[Weeks was professor of English, Univ. of Michigan. <u>Encyclopaedia Britannica</u> cited his book, 1961-1973.]

Richard Newby

Frankfurter's Oxford Letter to Borchard

18, Norham Gardens
Oxford
xi. 9. 33.

Dear Eddie:

I assume that thorough craftsman that you are, and equally
devoted to an idea even after you have done yeoman's work to it, you
are still interested in cases of innocent convictions, particularly for
misidentification. So I send you the enclosed.

It's not a very sweet world at present, is it? But I hope all
goes well with you.

It's good to get away for a time and see oneself and one's
country in perspective. And of course Oxford is hospitality itself.

With warm regards,

Very cordially yours,

F.F.

Professor E. M. Borchard
Enc.

[Source: Edwin Montefiore Borchard Papers, Manuscripts and
Archives, Yale University Library. Frankfurter was visiting lecturer at
Oxford, 1933-1934. See Robert M. Mennel and Christine L.
Compston, Holmes and Frankfurter: Their Correspondence, 1912-
1934, p. 274. See in the Mennel and Compston book Frankfurter's
letters to Holmes from Oxford (May 7, 1934) and from Cambridge
(Oct. 8, 1934), pp. 176-177. Frankfurter tells how he chose James
Henry Rowe, Jr. to be Justice Holmes's last secretary. (See Mennel's
reference to Frankfurter's forcefulness, p. xxxi, lines 12-20). See
Mennel, pp. 216-217, for Holmes's words to Frankfurter on Sacco and
Vanzetti. See Rowe's (not Howe's) letter to Ehrmann, October 29,
1934, on p. 457 in this book.

41. SECOND GENERATION CRITICS

Robert H. Montgomery. <u>Sacco-Vanzetti: The Murder and the Myth</u>. 1960

Because of the great and continuing influence upon the world of the belief that Massachusetts executed two innocent men because of their radical opinions, the [Sacco-Vanzetti] case remains an event of importance with which historians must deal... .

I am not young enough to believe that telling the truth about the case will demolish a myth so dear to the credulous who have deified Vanzetti and so valuable to the powerful influences here and abroad who still use it for propaganda and mass agitation.

Yet the truth should be told, and by one who lived in Massachusetts at the time, knew many of the principal actors and after thirty years had the time and inclination to examine the whole record and all the documents and to consider every criticism of the trial and the conviction. [Preface, v]

In the Plymouth trial, Vanzetti did not take the stand. This was his right, and the jury was told that they must not infer guilt from his failure to testify. This counsel of perfection the jury may have followed—the Commonwealth's case was strong enough and the defense weak enough to justify the verdict without benefit of the inference—but it is surely common sense for us to infer that a defendant who does not take the stand in his own behalf has no confidence in his innocence... . [29]

But he did not take the stand and an excuse had to be found. The first version came from his own lips in the in-[29]terview upon which John Nicholas Beffel based his article "Eels and the Electric Chair," published in the <u>New Republic</u> of December 29, 1920:

Beffel: ... his attorneys, for instance, would not let Vanzetti take the witness stand in his own defense unless he would agree to conceal that he held radical beliefs about the economic conflict. He refused to make that pledge; he is a philosophical anarchist, and wanted to explain why. But the attorneys kept him from testifying, and thus the jury never heard Vanzetti's own story... . Other attorneys, who are not afraid to let Vanzetti express his real philosophical opinions before the world, have now taken charge of his defense... .

Montgomery: But this [by Beffel] was too foolish even for the mythmakers, and by 1927 the exact opposite had become the authorized version. Says Frankfurter:

Frankfurter: The circumstances of the trial are sufficiently revealed by the fact that Vanzetti, protesting innocence, was not allowed by his counsel to take the witness stand for fear his radical opinions would be brought out and tell against him disastrously.

Montgomery's Correspondence with Frankfurter: Their War of Letters

This statement interested me so much that I initiated a correspondence with Frankfurter [Associate Justice of the U. S. Supreme Court]. In my first letter, dated February 4, 1958, I quoted the foregoing sentence from his footnote and asked him if he would please tell me the source of the information upon which he based the statement.

Under date of February 20, 1958, I had in reply a letter of which I quote the opening sentences:

Frankfurter: Perhaps you will not charge me with crass immodesty if in reply to your inquiry of February 4 I vouch to warranty President Lowell for the accuracy of what I wrote in "The Case of Sacco and Vanzetti." In the fall of 1927, President Lowell said to Norman Hapgood, a Harvard friend, "Wigmore was a fool! Wigmore was a fool to enter into controversy with Frankfurter. He should have known that Frankfurter would be accurate." Now, of course, such a general statement does not give you chapter and verse for [30] the accuracy of what I said about the Bridgewater trial. I do not know whether in the great mass of my materials touching the case I would find a reference to the source of my statement. I cannot possibly undertake to go through those materials; it would involve an amount of time that is not at my disposal. But I have not the slightest doubt that what you quote as the reason given by me for Vahey's advice to Vanzetti not to take the stand in the Bridgewater trial was a fact, the truth of which I had ascertained at the time on unimpeachable evidence.

Montgomery: This [reply by Frankfurter] did not satisfy me. President Lowell may have told Norman Hapgood that Wigmore could expect accuracy when Frankfurter quoted a record, but that remark did not seem to me to establish an infallibility which would make a

Frankfurter assertion conclusive proof of a fact without production of the evidence upon which he relied. So, in search of that evidence, I wrote a letter of considerable length in which I argued the improbability of a Massachusetts lawyer advising Vanzetti to keep off the stand because of his radical opinions. A Massachusetts lawyer, I wrote, would have known, on the authority of the cases collected in Jones v. Commonwealth, 327 Mass. 491, that Vanzetti's radical opinions could not have been introduced by cross-examination or otherwise unless he himself introduced them, as he did in the Dedham trial. A Massachusetts lawyer would have known that in a serious case a defendant who does not take the stand has little if any chance of acquittal.... My letter ended with the following paragraph:

Under these circumstances it seems inconceivable that Vahey would have advised Vanzetti to keep off the stand for the reason that you give, but if there is an unimpeachable source for your statement I cannot urge you too strongly to find it. [End of Montgomery's letter.]

Montgomery: But Frankfurter had tired of our correspondence. His next letter read:

Frankfurter: This is in acknowledgment of your letter of February 25. [31]

Since Dean Wigmore published his two blasts immediately after what I wrote on the Sacco and Vanzetti case, I deemed it, of course, my duty to vindicate what I had written. Since then, and particularly since coming on the Court, I have steadfastly refused to enter upon any discussion about my book or otherwise to express comment on the case. I must adhere to that policy and leave my book to whatever fate may befall it at the hands of future commentators. Perhaps I may be allowed to add that no one was better placed than President Lowell to attest to the accuracy of what I wrote.

Montgomery: While I quite agreed that no one was better placed than President Lowell to attest to Frankfurter's accuracy, I could not give his [Lowell's] remark to Norman Hapgood the sweeping consequence that Frankfurter claimed for it. Rather I was inclined to limit that remark to its context [See Frankfurter's dispute with John H. Wigmore, dean of the Northwestern University Law School, Boston Herald (4/26/27).] and to find Lowell's appraisal of Frankfurter's accuracy about matters of fact in the following passage in a letter to Chief Justice William Howard Taft written by President Lowell on November 1, 1927:

509

Lowell's Letter to Taft: We [the Governor's Advisory Committee] certainly started with no prejudice against Sacco and Vanzetti. Indeed, all I had read was Frankfurter's article in the Atlantic, which, though partisan argument, I supposed stated the facts correctly; and that naturally left the impression that something was wrong with the trial; but on reading all the facts, none of us had the least question about the men's guilt. The proof seemed to be conclusive. On the other hand, there was gross misstatement in the propaganda in their favor.... . [Citation is to H. A. Yeomans, pp. 494-495. See Yeomans in Bibliography (1948).]

Montgomery: So, still in search of evidence, I sent the correspondence to James M. Graham, who was with Vahey in the Plymouth trial and was also Sacco's attorney at the time. On March 13, 1958, he wrote me this letter:

Graham's Letter to Montgomery. I have your letter of March 7th, enclosing some correspondence in reference to the Sacco-Vanzetti case, and I am directing my attention particularly to the footnote referred to in your letter to Justice Frankfurter, dated [32] February 4, 1958, in which it is said [by Frankfurter] that Vanzetti, protesting his innocence, was not allowed by his counsel to take the witness stand, for his radical opinions would be brought out and held against him disastrously.

There were only three people who ever knew whether Vanzetti's failure to take the stand in the Bridgewater trial was on the advice of counsel or his own decision. They were Mr. Vanzetti, Mr. John P. Vahey, and myself. We spent considerable time with him at the Plymouth County Jail as the case was drawing to a close when it had to be decided whether he would take the stand or not.... .

After a lengthy discussion with Mr. Vanzetti, at either his suggestion, or with his approval, I went to the Dedham House of Correction and talked with Sacco [Graham represented Sacco], and then came back to Plymouth and met with Vahey and Vanzetti in the Jail, and the three of us, for a considerable time, discussed the question of Vanzetti taking the stand. He was carefully and thoroughly advised as to the evidence that had gone in as to what inference the Jury might draw if he failed to take the stand despite what the Judge would tell them in his charge, and as to what information might be elicited from him if he did take the stand.

... I do recall very distinctly because of the impression it made on me, the fact that toward the very end of the discussion, Mr. Vahey said to Vanzetti, in substance, "I can advise you as to what the District Attorney may inquire about and the effect of your failure to take the stand, but you are the one who has got to make the decision as to whether you will testify or not."

After I came back from Dedham and reported my conversation with Sacco to Vanzetti, and the case was further discussed, he said, in substance, "I don't think I can improve upon the alibi which has been established. I had better not take the stand."

[33] [End of Graham's letter.]

Montgomery: Hoping that this would surely settle the question, I sent Frankfurter a copy of Graham's letter and a letter of my own in which I asked Frankfurter to permit me to include a correction of his footnote in my book.

But my hopes were ill founded. All I got was the following letter, dated March 25, 1958:

Frankfurter: You ask me to permit you to include the following sentence in your projected book: "Mr. Justice Frankfurter authorizes me to say that he was in error in stating that Vanzetti, protesting innocence, was not allowed by his counsel to take the stand because his radical opinions would have been brought out and told against him disastrously. He has learned that the decision not to take the stand was made by Vanzetti himself after discussion with his counsel and that his radical opinion had nothing to do with it and formed no part of the discussion."

Under no circumstances can I authorize you to make any such statement on my behalf. My article in the Atlantic Monthly and its slight enlargement in book form, published early in 1927, was, as I have already stated to you, the product of the most minute care for securing accuracy. President Lowell surely had the amplest means and reason for testing the accuracy of what I wrote, and I have already told you that he attested to my accuracy in emphatic language... . My book was written more than thirty years ago and is, for purposes of this case, a historic document. As such, it must, of course, share the fate of all historic documents, namely, be subject to the scrutiny and the reexamination of others. But since I have no doubt whatever that the statement which you now call in question I took great pains to verify at the time, of course I cannot say that I was in error.

I do not mean to question the good faith of Mr. Graham. [34] I do say that the time for Mr. Vahey or Mr. Graham to have challenged the accuracy of my statement was at the time that I made it and not for Mr. Graham to do so more than thirty years later. Let me say again that I do not of course question the good faith of Mr. Graham, but we all know how treacherous even the most honest memory can be. [End of Frankfurter's letter.]

Montgomery: In my next letter I was rather free in telling Mr. Justice Frankfurter what his duty was, but I thought it was unfair to Vahey and Graham, and even to me as an author seeking the truth about an important fact, for Frankfurter to take advantage of the prestige his book enjoyed as a historic document written by a law professor who had become a Justice of the Supreme Court and been honored throughout the academic world for his scholarly achievements. Should he not acknowledge his error or furnish the "unimpeachable evidence"? Noblesse oblige, quoth I.

But this appeal also failed and the reader must choose between the ipse dixit of the infallible Frankfurter on the one hand and Graham's letter and all the probabilities on the other. Frankfurter's final letter reads as follows:

Frankfurter: Since you make free to tell others of their duty, your letter of March 31 leads me to say that I assume that in case you will ever be publishing anything pertaining to the Bridgewater trial and, in connection with it, publish Mr. Graham's recent letter to you, you will also publish, and in full, my letter to you under date of March 25 in regard to the matter. [End of exchange.]

Montgomery: In the Atlantic Monthly for February 1928 there is an article by William G. Thompson entitled "Vanzetti's Last Statement, Monday, August 22, 1927." In the article, Thompson, who became defense attorney for Sacco and Vanzetti in 1924, tells of his interview with Vanzetti during the evening before the execution:

Thompson: I had heard that the Governor had said that if Vanzetti would release his counsel in the Bridgewater case from their obligation not to disclose what he had said to them the public would be satisfied that he was guilty of that crime, and also of the South Braintree crime.... I then asked Vanzetti if he had at any time said anything [35] to Mr. Vahey or Mr. Graham which would warrant the inference that he was guilty of either crime. With great emphasis and obvious sincerity he answered "no." ... I asked Vanzetti whether he would authorize me to waive his privilege so far as Vahey and Graham were concerned. He readily assented to this, but imposed the condition that they should make whatever statement they saw fit to make in the presence of myself [Thompson] or some other friend ...

Montgomery. It nowhere appears that this offer to waive the privilege was ever communicated to Vahey or Graham, and in fact Graham did not know about it until I told him in 1958. [36]

It is unfortunate that Wigmore did not know enough about the case to mention other significant omissions [Frankfurter omitted dispute on Sacco's cap in Atlantic Monthly.] made in the Frankfurter article and book, the most significant being his failure to make any mention of the obsolete-bullet evidence. [99]

Thompson's argument that Gould had been suppressed by the Commonwealth was a curious one. The affidavits [of Motion 2] show that Moore and [investigator] Reid knew of Gould before the trial, that Burke knew his permanent address, and that his name had appeared in the Boston Post.... . But, be that as it may, it is obvious that Gould's two stories were fabrications, either one of which would have been shattered in cross-examination. [171]

Hamilton was already thoroughly discredited as an expert and as a truthful witness.... . The substitute-barrel proceedings were not included in the Holt Transcript, ... [204]

Montgomery's complaint. Frankfurter and the Atlantic should not have concealed from the public his close association with the defense. Whether he was, in the strict sense of the word, counsel for the defense or not, he should not have been represented by the Atlantic as a disinterested lawyer making a complete, accurate and impartial survey of a case then pending before the Supreme Judicial Court.... .

The book has done incalculable harm because of a plausi-[294] bility gained from misstatements, artful distortion, and deliberate suppression... . Certainly the book was the basis for the faith of intellectuals, academicians, and clergy who could not but be impressed by what seemed on its surface to be an impartial and accurate survey by a professor of law at Harvard. [295] [Montgomery, Boston attorney, is identified as an archconservative lawyer and friend of Judge Webster Thayer by Professor Nunzio Pernicone, History Department, Drexel University. Montgomery is one of Pernicone's four "revisionists" of the Sacco-Vanzetti case. See Pernicone, p. 562. See Montgomery's papers at the Boston Athenaeum.]

513

Reviews of <u>Sacco-Vanzetti: The Murder and the Myth</u>

William A. Rusher. "The Bullets and the Guns." <u>National Review</u>. September 24, 1960. #1

The cause of the defendants was swiftly taken over by well-meaning civil libertarians, passionate cranks, cynical opportunists and (deadly ally!) the Communists. From a thousand printing presses there poured forth a swelling stream of propaganda: it was no longer Sacco and Vanzetti who were on trial; it was entrenched wealth—Brahminism—the old order—Anglo-Saxon "justice"! The dying hand of a Puritan oligarchy was trying to plunge a legal dagger into the hearts of two hapless, idealistic, proletarian immigrants. [184]
[Rusher was publisher of <u>National Review</u>.]

James Rorty. 'This Is Our Agony…' <u>The New Leader</u>. September 26, 1960. #2

I, who 35 years ago marched in a protest parade before the Massachusetts State house and subsequently denounced Massachusetts justice in an extremely bad poem … believed those denials [of guilt made by Sacco and Vanzetti]…

These doubts were renewed when, after reading Robert Montgomery's honest and able reappraisal of the court record, I re-read the letters and speeches of Sacco and Vanzetti assembled in 1928… . [12]

What one concludes from the book is that Sacco and Vanzetti were in all probability guilty, and that certainly, in view of the numerous appeals and the hearings by the Governor and the Lowell Committee, the full resources of Massachusetts justice were expended in their behalf. But there remains that inextinguishable doubt. [13]
[N. Y. Times obit., 2/26/1973, states Rorty was "one of the first editors of <u>The New Masses</u>, a radical literary and political magazine."]

William F. Buckley, Jr. "Sacco-Vanzetti Again." <u>American Legion Magazine</u> (October 1960). #3

I say we will not, in all likelihood, ever know for sure whether it was Sacco and Vanzetti who did the murder. [48]

"Sacco-Vanzetti, the Murder and the Myth," by Robert H. Montgomery ... is a detailed, minute investigation of the case by a no-nonsense Boston lawyer who firmly believes in their guilt. Scheduled to appear soon is another book by Francis Russell, who as firmly believes in their innocence, but who is outraged by the lengths to which Sacco-Vanzetti defenders have gone; who believes, indeed, that Sacco and Vanzetti were fairly tried, ... [49]
[Buckley is Editor-at-Large, National Review.]

Michael A. Musmanno. "Book Review." University of Pittsburgh Law Review (March 1961). #4

"Sacco-Vanzetti: The Murder and the Myth" by Robert H. Montgomery is a fascinating book. What makes it particularly fascinating is the fact that the author, without any obviously studied purpose, has put together the most disorganized volume on a serious subject that I have ever encountered. The book lacks pattern, continuity, organization, system and order. [651]

Sacco outlined in detail just where he was and what he did on April 15th. His alibi was supported by ten witnesses. The Commonwealth did not present a single witness to attack the alibi evidence presented by Sacco and his witnesses. [665]

Vanzetti's alibi was supported by six witnesses. The Commonwealth called not a single witness to refute their testimony. [666]

Vahey committed another almost unforgiveable error in advising Vanzetti at the Plymouth trial not to take the stand, ... [670]

And then, of course, there was the confession of Celestino F. Madeiros, one of the bandits in the South Braintree murder, who excluded Sacco and Vanzetti from participation in the crime. [672]

Governor Fuller ... was utterly unequipped intellectually to understand the record or appraise the significance of the evidence. [673]
[Musmanno, Associate Justice of the Supreme Court of Pennsylvania.]

Tom O'Connor. "The Origin of the Sacco-Vanzetti Case."
Vanderbilt Law Review (June 1961). #5

For the first time in the thirty-three years since Sacco and Vanzetti were executed ... there has appeared an apologia for the Commonwealth of Massachusetts. The author [of the apologia] is Robert H. Montgomery, a Harvard Law School graduate (1912) and a corporation lawyer in Boston for nearly fifty years. [987]

It is simply preposterous to say that radicalism played no part in the alleged "consciousness of guilt" displayed by Sacco and Vanzetti; ... [989]

However adept Attorney Montgomery may be in his handling of this or that phase of the case, in suppressing and distorting information, so that the unwary, the uninformed, runs the risk of being taken in, what is lacking in this pretentious book is the answer to a simple, yet all-important, question—a question that, it seems, only the ignorant would ask, namely: Why were Sacco and Vanzetti arrested in the first place?

It is a curious circumstance that the reader will not only look in vain for the answer in the book under review; he can wade through the entire six volumes of the transcript of the record of the case, and, indeed, most of the numerous books and articles written about the case, and still fail to find the answer to this question. [991]

The existence of this [Pinkerton] report, covering the period, December 24, 1919 to January 8, 1920, was unknown until the writer [O'Connor] discovered it in September 1926.

Incidentally, the Pinkerton report on South Braintree, covering the period from April 15 to May 13, 1920, was likewise buried for years, its existence unknown to the defense, until sometime in May, 1926, when the writer alerted [defense attorney] Thompson as to its existence, ... [992]

The car [Boda's] had, on April 19, been towed down to the Elm Square Garage of Simon Johnson, by Samuel Johnson, Simon's brother. After being informed of this, Stewart made preparations to apprehend Boda and whoever should appear with him to pick up the car, when repaired.

When Boda and Orciani, on Orciani's motor-cycle, along with Sacco and Vanzetti, who had come by streetcar, appeared at the Johnson garage and, finding it closed, next at the Johnson house, on the night of May 5, 1920, they stepped into Chief Stewart's preparations. Since all four were anarchists, Stewart felt his theory had been confirmed... . [T]he great Sacco-Vanzetti case had its origin in this fantastic theory [that Coacci and other anarchists had committed the Bridgewater crime and the South Braintree crime]. [994]

It would matter not in the least were both the Silva (Martini) confession as to Bridgewater and the Madeiros confession as to South Braintree to be proved false. The Sacco-Vanzetti case reminds one of a mighty cataract that roars along, carrying in its wake all kinds of debris. In another sense it might be said to have evolved into a permanent work of art. [997]

In 1924 Capt. Van Amburgh, in the case of <u>State v. Israel</u>, was discredited as a ballistics expert. [1001]

The Pinkerton report on South Braintree ... presents a totally different version of what some of the witnesses said, within a few days following the shooting, from their testimony at the trial. Its revelations concerning Mary E. Splaine destroy her testimony. [1003]

[T]he greatest single contribution yet made toward the education of the public concerning the Sacco-Vanzetti case was the massive work of Joughin and Morgan... . Known only to scholars and specialists in the years immediately following its publication, the book gradually reached a wider audience and in time came to be recognized as the **definitive work on the Sacco-Vanzetti case**. It is likely to remain so. This book has educated a generation of college teachers and students, law professors, writers, and social historians. [1006]

[In the 1920s O'Connor "was a reporter for the State House News Service in Massachusetts..." In 1961 he was "Secretary of the Committee for the Vindication of Sacco and Vanzetti."]

William J. Hughes, Jr. "Book Reviews" <u>The Georgetown Law Journal</u> (Summer 1961). #6
Summary.

Defenders of Sacco and Vanzetti have used the Big Lie. Gullible college professors were fooled by this technique. The case shows that "spurious erudition" can delude the public. [787]

This disputed case is really two cases, the first case being the Bridgewater crime. Vanzetti had no defense at his Plymouth trial unless an alibi can be termed a defense. The alibi had holes in it.

Contrary to mythmakers, Vanzetti, not his lawyers, made the decision to stay off the witness stand. The myth of innocence is not truth. [See footnote #8 in Hughes]. [787]

At Dedham, Sacco and Vanzetti relied upon an alibi for their "principal defense."

The reviewer finds both alibis unconvincing. Frankfurter is wrong to call Vanzetti's alibi "overwhelming." Frankfurter's claim that "thirteen witnesses either testified directly that Vanzetti was in Plymouth selling fish on the day of the murder, or furnished corroboration of such testimony" [See Frankfurter's book, p. 30] contradicts the transcript. To tell the truth, four witnesses, not thirteen, "testified directly" to Vanzetti's presence at Plymouth, and each one of these four fails in truthfulness. Defense attorneys, knowing the alibi to be weak, slighted it in closing arguments. [792]

Defendants' radicalism is brought into trial to rebut "consciousness of guilt."

[Hughes cites Transcript, 5057: "There would be no explanations by which to justify the lies that they gave to the district attorney." Thomas McAnarney said this to Fuller's committee, 07/13/1927.]

Frankfurter was naive to accept this argument [in boldface]. Lies about guns and bullets connect to murder, not to radical philosophy. [794]

Frankfurter's claim of accuracy is hard to explain. Justice Frankfurter lost perspective in the heated debate. His fight for social justice has won him respect. [796]

Montgomery crushed supporters of Madeiros and the Morelli hypothesis, that "boldest canard." Yet, Sacco-Vanzetti partisans will still honor Motion 6. In footnote #60, Hughes says Morgan, in his introduction to the second edition of The Untried Case (1960), "vainly argues for the Morelli hypothesis." [798]

Frankfurter's attack on Thayer's denial of Motion 6 is intemperate and unjustified. [798] Frankfurter claims Thayer's opinion has "misquotations, misrepresentations, suppressions, and...is literally honeycombed with demonstrable errors," but he fails to give examples of these flaws to support his broad accusation. [799]

[Ed. Read Hughes' full review. Scrutinize all reviews.]

[Hughes, Professor of Law, Georgetown University Law Center.]

Malcolm P. Sharp. "Book Review." <u>University of Chicago Law Review</u> (Winter 1961). #7

... The reader ... should be careful about accepting Mr. Montgomery's effort to distinguish between the various kinds of lies told by Sacco and Vanzetti on their arrest. He should firmly remember the reasons for any fear felt on arrest by Italian [403] anarchists in May of 1920. [404]

My own recollections of the feeling ... in 1927 lead me to appreciate Mr. Thompson's position [on Goddard's qualifications in ballistics]. What turned out to be concededly a mistake about a supposed fatal bullet in 1926 in an ordinary Cleveland murder case had invalidated the supposed effect of Mr. Goddard's evidence there. Mr. Thompson seems justified in his insistence that an adequate and reliable account should be given of the custody of both shell and bullet between the arrests in 1920 and the final proceedings in 1927 before either should be taken finally to be what it was thought to be. [405]

Madeiros, the Morellis, Mancini, and Benkoski are not only figures in a drama, not only a not improbable explanation of the crime [at South Braintree], ...They are also a reminder of the usual problems of the police and the prosecuting officials and a challenge to the benevolent though doubtless somewhat ambivalent anarchism expresssed by Sacco and Vanzetti and those philosophers whose teaching had influenced them. The violence in the world, including murder, robbery, racial clashes, and wars, seems to be a part of the human condition... . There is a charm about philosophical anarchism, particularly for anyone who has felt the poetical fascination of the Sermon on the Mount. The Christian anarchism expressed there and its variants make their contribution to human life. Nevertheless, it is ironical that the Morellis and their friends present so sharp a challenge to the often attractive expressions of anarchist philosophy which we find in the letters of Sacco and Vanzetti. [410]

On our assumption of guilt, he [Vanzetti] must be supposed to have tried to conceal or minimize the elements of violence in his thought as well as his practice. [412]

[Sharp, Professor of Law, Univ. of Chicago, reviewed both Montgomery's book and Ehrmann's <u>The Untried Case</u> (2nd edition, 1960).]

Robert E. Knowlton. "Book Reviews." Rutgers Law Review (Winter 1961). #8

Mr. Montgomery's book creates almost insurmountable problems for the reviewer. Dogged perseverance is required to force oneself to read through the conglomerate of fact, unwarranted inferences, and personal vindictiveness of the author... . To comment upon the inadequacies of the factual presentation, the demonstrations of bad taste, and the irritations stemming from the use of value-charged labels would require volumes. The book does not merit such an extravagant use of paper or such an imposition upon the patience of the readers of the review. [370]

There is reason to believe that this book [**The Untried Case**] was reissued [in 1960] for the purpose of setting the record straight after Mr. Montgomery's onslaught. [371]

The question of whether Sacco and Vanzetti actually committed the murders will probably never be answered. ... Of course, the ultimate issue of guilt is known in few, if any, criminal trials, and yet society, if not the convicted men, accepts the jury's verdict. [371]

[Knowlton, Professor of Law, Rutgers, The State University, reviewed both Montgomery's book and the 1960 edition of The Untried Case.]

James Grossman. "The Sacco-Vanzetti Case Reconsidered." Commentary (January 1962). #9

Editor summarizes book review by Grossman.

Those who would canonize Sacco and Vanzetti misread their letters, some of which take an unsaintly turn. In one letter Vanzetti praised the anarchist who killed Sadi Carnot. [31]

We should judge Sacco as one case and Vanzetti as a second case. Separate them. [31]

Even if we concede that the Dedham trial was unfair—and Judge Thayer's prejudice is noted on p. 31—it does not follow that Sacco and Vanzetti were innocent victims, incapable of killing at South Braintree. Sacco and Vanzetti constitute an American historical question. [32]

Though Montgomery is wrong to exonerate Thayer, he presents facts of impressive strength against Sacco. Sacco murdered at South Braintree (Hypothesis 1). If he did not murder, then the prosecution presumably presented a false bullet and false shell at the joint trial (Hypothesis 2). Which hypothesis is correct? [32]

The hypothesis Herbert Ehrmann builds to convict the Joe Moelli gang of the South Braintree crime is clever. (Footnote on p. 36 identifies Ehrmann's 1933 book: The Untried Case.) Grossman calls Ehrmann's hypothesis a "superstructure" (with no foundation), and he uses the term "brilliant" to modify superstructure. Yet Ehrmann fails in his aim to convict Joe Morelli and Madeiros of the South Braintree crime. If bullet and shell studies made after the trial are genuine, they seem to inculpate Sacco and exculpate Ehrmann's hypothetical murderer, Joe Morelli. Besides, Ehrmann's portrait of the convicted murderer Madeiros is a romantic distortion. Of Madeiros, Grossman simply writes: "his crimes." [36]

Albert Hamilton, assigned to do ballistic tests by the defense in 1923, unwittingly confirmed the trial verdict against Sacco with his photomicrographs. [36] The disinterested Gunthers, father and son, published an "authoritative book" in 1935, (The Identification of Firearms ...). Their book shows in one blended portrait that the image imprinted on Shell W found at the crime site matches the image made on a test shell. Such is the distinctive nature of breechblock engravings on shells. [37]

Grossman says the ballistics study made with a comparison microscope by Major Calvin H. Goddard on June 3, 1927, is valid. He notes that Professor Gill of MIT, following this test, would no longer support William G. Thompson, who, in the summer of 1927, alleged— Ehrmann concurring—that Bullet 3 and Shell W were false trial exhibits. Grossman calls this co-authored allegation of 1927 "a desperate theory." [37]

In 1927 Ranney asked Fuller's Advisory Committee to call Dr. Magrath to answer Ehrmann's allegation that the marks on Bullet 3 are different from the marks pathologist Magrath put on the other 5 murder bullets. Despite this plea, Magrath was not called. [37]

The confession by Madeiros may have been motivated by resentment. [39]

Goddard's test was carefully monitored by Gill and others. (See footnote, p. 39.)

Galleani, leader to Sacco and Vanzetti, justified acts of violence, praised Ravachol. [40]

Vanzetti's letters "seem" to prove innocence. Vanzetti had "credible witnesses" and a "plausible" alibi for both the Bridgewater and South Braintree crimes. [43]

Grossman suggests liberals have misread human nature. He recalls the heinous deeds of Conrad's idealistic Kurtz, and says a murderous Sacco confirms the insight of Henry James on the difference between surface "nobleness" and hideous evil beneath. We feel betrayal.

[Footnote says New York lawyer Grossman published an article in Commentary (Dec. 1953). Grossman declared Alger Hiss guilty. Grossman published in Partisan Review and Kenyon Review. He is Pernicone's fourth "revisionist."]

Harlow F. Lenon. "Book Reviews." Oregon Law Review (April 1962). #10

[Ed. Lenon, like Knowlton and Sharp, reviewed both Montgomery's book and Ehrmann's 1960 edition of the 1933 book, The Untried Case.]

Montgomery is a paleolithic conservatine. For him, the accused were direct-actionist radicals, murdering for profit or for their cause, perjuring with an ineptitude that is obvious to all except Frankfurter, John Dewey, Arthur Schlesinger, Jr., Osmond Fraenkel, and a host of spongy-minded liberals.

He so little concers himself with the atmosphere of the period and the ideology of the accused that, without some outside knowledge of the Palmer "red raids" and the personal background of both defendants, his treatment of the "aftermath" of agitation would be incomprehensible. His emphasis is so faulty that he can, with wonderful irresponsibility, defame Frankfurter as narrow, inaccurate, and insincere, Schlesinger as a loose scholar, the American Civil Liberties Union as a Communist front, and Herbert Ehrmann as gullible, slightly simple, and rather choked with his own eloquence. [269]

[I]t must be acknowledged that little of his [Thayer's] prejudice was conveyed to the jury during the actual trial. [270] [Lenon was a member of the Oregon State Bar.]

Max Eastman. "Is This the Truth About Sacco and Vanzetti?" The National Review. Oct. 21. 1961.

A "Profile" of Tresca and his career that I wrote for The New Yorker in 1934 had brought me very close to him. I felt close enough to ask him one day, when whispers had reached me concerning Upton Sinclair's distressing experience in Boston: "Carlo, would you feel free to tell me the truth about Sacco and Vanzetti?" He answered: "Sacco was guilty but Vanzetti was not... ." [T]hat quick and simple answer from such a source settled the question for me. I believe it. [264]
[In 1912 Eastman founded The Masses, a radical monthly, and edited it. See Carlo Tresca in research Topic #44.]

Francis Russell. "Sacco Guilty, Vanzetti Innocent?" American Heritage. June 1962.

When a few years ago I wrote an article, "Tragedy in Dedham" (American Heritage, October, 1958), I was convinced that the two men were innocent, ... But after the ballistics tests of 1961 I felt that, at least in the case of Sacco, I could no longer hold to my opinion [of innocent]... . Whatever my altered views about Sacco, I still continue to feel that Vanzetti was innocent... . [T]he most that can be said against Vanzetti is that he must have known who did commit the Braintree crime. [111]

Francis Russell. Tragedy in Dedham: The Story of the Sacco-Vanzetti Case 1962

Moore's initial objective was to expand the case beyond the parochial limits of Norfolk County... . He was lawyer, detective, fundraiser, and propagandist combined... . Moore's temporary [Boston] office in the Olympian Building at 3 Tremont Row [was] echoing with talk and typewriters ... In one corner the blond Lithuanian stenographer hammered away at the keys. Opposite her John Nicholas Beffel, a freelance socialist journalist from New York, sat chain-smoking and preparing press releases in English. Art Shields, sent on by Elizabeth Gurley Flynn, assisted him. Frank Lopez, a young Spanish anarchist, ... preserved somehow by Moore from a deportation order, got out

523

propaganda for the Spanish-speaking world. Felicani and the [Sacco-Vanzetti Defense] committee, from an upstairs room on Battery Street, took care of the Italian publicity. [113]

For the Communists the Sacco-Vanzetti case was an issue ripe for manipulation. By exploiting it, the Party hoped to confirm its pose as the champion of the oppressed and for the first time develop into an American mass movement. [332]

The appearance of Felix Frankfurter's article, "The Case of Sacco and Vanzetti," in the March issue of the <u>Atlantic Monthly</u> initiated the final world-shaking stage of the case. The <u>Atlantic</u> still remained the voice of conservative intellectual America.... For most of those who read it, Frankfurter's attack was **their factual introduction to the background of a case they had heard about only vaguely.** [352]

With the appearance of the <u>Atlantic</u> article, Frankfurter became the moving spirit of the Sacco-Vanzetti defense. Even Thompson turned to him. His were the final decisions as to tactics and action. [353]

When it turned to the ballistics evidence, the Lowell Committee was undoubtedly greatly influenced by the findings of Major Calvin Goddard, a New York expert who came to Boston at the end of May [1927] ... bringing with him a comparison microscope and offering to make what he maintained would be conclusive tests on the shells and bullets offered in evidence at Dedham. He was accompanied by William Crawford, a reporter from the New York World, . . .

With Gill, Ranney, and Ehrmann present, as well as a stenographer and Frank Buxton and Thomas Carens of the <u>Herald</u>, Goddard examined the evidence in the clerk of courts' office at Dedham on the afternoon of June 3. Comparing Bullet III with a test bullet fired from Sacco's pistol, he suggested that Gill make the same comparison. "Well, what do you know about that?" Gill muttered to himself as he looked into the microscope. Goddard's conclusion was that the mortal bullet taken from Berardelli's body had been fired through Sacco's pistol and could have been fired through no other. [376]

Soon after the tests, Gill told Thompson that he now doubted his original findings and wished to sever all connection with the case. His disavowal was followed by one from James Burns, another of the defense experts, who had recently become convinced, after studying [376] certain microphotographs made earlier for Captain Charles Van Amburgh, that the Fraher shell had been fired in Sacco's gun. [377]

[There was] the bombing on August 15 [1927] of the East Milton home of Dedham juror Lewis McHardy... . If before the blowing up of the McHardy house there had been the slightest chance of a commutation of sentence for Sacco and Vanzetti, afterward there was none.

Footnote: The same bombing pattern was followed five years later when Judge Thayer's house in Worcester was partially destroyed [Sept. 27, 1932]. Executioner Elliott's New York house was also bombed some time after the executions [May 17, 1928]. [426]

There was no formal [funeral] service. Mary Donovan read five bitter paragraphs by Gardner Jackson, scarcely able to control her voice as she spoke the words over the coffins:

You, Sacco and Vanzetti, are the victims of the crassest plutocracy the world has known since ancient Rome... . And now Massachusetts and America have killed you—murdered you because you were Italian anarchists.... In your martyrdom we will fight on and conquer. [460]

Many times postponed, they [ballistics tests] were finally conducted in the laboratory of the Massachusetts State Police on October 11, 1961, by Jac Weller, the honorary curator of the West Point Museum, and Colonel Frank Jury, a former head of the Firearms Laboratory of the New Jersey State Police.

The one certain method of determining whether two bullets passed through the same gun barrel is examination with a comparison microscope, which brings the bullets together in one fused image. If the striations match, the conclusion is that both bullets were fired from the same weapon. [Ed. Photos of shells, bullets and composite photo of Shell W/test shell, p. 208.]

Using a comparison microscope and bullets they themselves had just fired from Sacco's pistol, Weller and Jury determined beyond dispute that Bullet III had been fired from that pistol.... As for the four shells that Bostock had picked up and given to Fraher, three had been fired in an unknown gun. Weller and Jury agreed, after comparing the breechblock markings of Shell W with those of a newly fired test shell, that Shell W had unquestionably been fired in Sacco's pistol. Thus, the comparison microscope findings of 1961 confirmed the tests made by Major Goddard in 1927. [464]

The cumulative evidence is overwhelming that the Colt automatic found on Sacco the night of his arrest was one of the two pistols used to kill Berardelli. Even if one accepts the possibility that someone other than Sacco fired the Colt, Sacco knew who that someone was.

Vanzetti's innocence is, at least for me, confirmed by my talks with [Beltrando] Brini and by Tresca's admission to Eastman, as well as by the contradictions to the court testimony brought out in the Pinkerton reports. [466] [See Russell's 1986 book on Sacco-Vanzetti.]

Reviews of Tragedy in Dedham
Justice Michael A. Musmanno. Kansas Law Review (May 1963). #1

I would say that, following the execution of the men ... at least ninety-five per cent of the pronouncements on the case, ... have advanced the theme that Sacco and Vanzetti were innocent or that they were denied a fair trial and therefore not proved guilty. Among those who have so declared themselves have been such respected, historical, literary, and world authoritative figures as Justice Felix Frankfurter of the United States Supreme Court; Joseph B. Ely, Governor of Massachusetts; Joseph Walker, Speaker of the Massachusetts House of Representatives; United States Senator Robert M. LaFollette; William Allen White, famous newspaper editor; John Dewey, illustrious educator and philosopher; Alf Landon, once Republican candidate for the presidency; Walter Lippmann, distinguished writer and analyst of world events; Richard Washburn Child, former United States Ambassador to Italy; the world-famous authors H. G. Wells, John Galsworthy, Arnold Bennett, Romain Rolland, and George Bernard Shaw; Maximilian Harden, eminent scholar; Albert Einstein, genius mathematician; Mme. Curie, [481] renowned scientist; Edna St. Vincent Millay, great American poet; Ramsey Macdonald, prime minister of England; Bishop William F. Anderson of the Southern New England Methodist Conference; and Harvard Professor Edmund M. Morgan, one of America's foremost authorities on the law of evidence, ... [482]

So universally accepted has been the conclusion that the execution of Sacco and Vanzetti was a gross miscarriage of justice that in 1959 Representative Alexander J. Cella of Medford introduced in the Massachusetts House of Representatives a resolution calling for a recommendation that the Governor of Massachusetts grant a posthumous pardon to Nicola Sacco and Bartolomeo Vanzetti. [482]

I am satisfied that Katzmann was thoroughly aware of the innocence of Sacco and Vanzetti long before the end of the case.... . I spoke to Katzmann several years after the executions... . His comments were only fragmentary, but, listening or talking, he never looked me in the eye. [488]

Vanzetti's alibi [at Plymouth] ... was absolutely bullet-proof. No one proved that the sixteen witnesses who bought fish or saw Vanzetti on that memorable day of December 24, 1919, had lied.

Russell's book is a labyrinth of confusion, contradiction and cryptology. [492] ... For many years Russell believed Sacco and Vanzetti innocent and so stated publicly and forcibly. [493]

Katzmann's May 6 questions. The men, having no direct knowledge of the crimes and not realizing they were being interrogated about a possible complicity, gave haphazard and guessing answers as to their whereabouts on the not specified dates of the crimes. [494]

Robert H. Montgomery, a Boston lawyer, who wrote a book on the case, informed me that Russell misquoted him and misrepresented him in his (Russell's) book. [497]

I spoke to Lowell at length a decade or more following the executions and it was evident to me that he was greatly disturbed as to whether he had not failed in an obvious duty. [499]

Nine witnesses supported Vanzetti's testimony about his presence in Plymouth on the fateful April 15, 1920. [501]

If Sacco, like an honest working man, was paying his just debts at Affe's at the time he and others so testified, it was impossible for him to have participated in the bloody slaughter on the streets of South Braintree... [H]e [Russell] does not attempt to explain what happens to the alibi evidence. He does not say that eleven persons perjured themselves.... [503]

The South Braintree robbery-murder was a highly professional job: it was scouted, planned, and executed with scientific precision. There was no intimation that Sacco or Vanzetti had ever had any training in banditry.

On November 18, 1925, Celestino F. Madeiros, a professional criminal, confessed to participating in the South Braintree robbery.... . [I]t became abundantly clear that the persons responsible for the South Braintree murders were the Morelli gang of Providence. [513]

I ... spoke to Madeiros a number of times while he occupied one of the death cells next to Sacco and Vanzetti in the Charlestown state

prison and if, as a man of the law now for some forty years, I can judge credibility, I feel certain, … that Madeiros was telling the truth about Sacco and Vanzetti. [514]
[Musmanno, Associate Justice, Supreme Court of Pennsylvania, was a volunteer counsel for Sacco and Vanzetti in April-August, 1927.]

Roger N. Baldwin, "Four Decades of Doubt." <u>Saturday Review</u>. September 8, 1962. #2

Francis Russell's justification [for his book] lies in his quest to resolve his doubts regarding their innocence or guilt. A writer and critic who lives in the Massachusetts county where the trial took place, he was impelled by youthful memories of his acceptance of their guilt, and his subsequent doubts, to undertake an eight years' task of interviewing and research. [56]

There can be no doubt of the scrupulous care with which he examined the voluminous evidence, the conflicting claims and explanations, and tracked down every living person who had anything to do with the case… . Moreover, he records his investigations so skilfully that "Tragedy in Dedham" is as engrossing as a first-class detective story. [56]

On this dubious evidence of a test forty years later of a bullet not impounded [1961 test], plus some quoted personal opinion, Russell rests a shaky case for Sacco's involvement, a case weakened by his own reference to "Sacco, whatever his guilt." [56]

These conclusions are the sum of Russell's painstaking researches: that one innocent man was executed along with one who may have been guilty or at worst had guilty knowledge. What an indictment of justice! [56]

Many people Russell interviewed advised him to let the case alone after all these years. He should have. He adds nothing substantial to what was known. Doubts he sought to resolve remain, even for him… . [C]onflicting social forces … drove Massachusetts after six long years to an execution not only indefensible by American concepts of justice but so embedded in class prejudice and fear of alien radicals that it will endure as a classic … indictment of society itself. [56] [Baldwin was founding member and first Executive Director of the ACLU. R. M. Lovett called him "pope of the liberals." He visited Sacco and Vanzetti in prison.]

Louis Joughin. "Reviews of Books." <u>American Historical Review</u>
(January 1963). #3

[See Joughin's entry on Sacco-Vanzetti in <u>Collier's Encyclopedia</u>.]

An example of the author's freedom from bias can be found in his fair handling of the testimony of the witness Pelser whose only skill was repeated lying, compounding falsehood to the point of madness. New information is fairly accumulated: of seventeen significant new factual points, seven are neutral with respect to the issue of guilt, two might be introduced in evidence against the defendants, and eight in support of their innocence. Russell's field work was not guided by prejudgment. A further indication of freedom from bias is the author's evenhanded disposition of cynical attack. The following suffer derogation: the jury system, the Sacco-Vanzetti jury, Ripley, the jury foreman (because he was "slightly senile"), Katzmann, the prosecutor, Governor Fuller, and the members of the 1959 Joint Judiciary Committee of the Massachusetts legislature—... [488]

The first reason for calling the book useless is that it can be read meaningfully only by the half-dozen persons who know the Sacco-Vanzetti case and its literature practically "by heart." <u>Tragedy in Dedham</u> has no references in the text to any documents. There is simply no support; nothing can be checked. Consider ... important new evidence which is forced to stand entirely upon assertion: ... expert **Gill's reaction** to expert Goddard's posttrial ballistic tests; ... [488]

The new material cannot be received as more than allegation for a further... reason—the serious errors that exist in the testable parts of the book. Looking only to fact: Salsedo was perhaps or probably a suicide, but not so proved; Bostock did not hand the recovered shells to Fraher; Van Amburgh was not "certain" that a bullet had been fired from Sacco's gun (and Russell contradicts himself at another place); the Joint Judicial Committee did not refuse to consider granting a pardon in 1959 because it knew it could not do so. [488]

The author is much more interested in the matter of proving guilt or innocence than in the issue that has chiefly engaged historians: the nature of the failure by law and society properly to administer justice... . Space forbids discussion of the new ballistic evidence resulting from tests conducted in 1961 under bizarre and possibly illegal circumstances by experts already committed to a view of guilt. [489]

This book does not meet the standards of a civilized society for the analysis and judgment of a decision by which men have condemned other men to die. [489]
[Joughin wrote pages 201-514 of The Legacy of Sacco and Vanzetti.]

Edward Dumbauld. "Book Reviews." New England Quarterly (March 1963). #4

Having done jury duty in the very courtroom where Sacco and Vanzetti were tried, the author studied the records of the trial, interviewed parties having knowledge of the case, and even persuaded the State Police to permit tests to be made on October 11, 1961, by outside experts which proved that the bullet from the victim's body had been fired from Sacco's pistol. This confirmed a test made for the Lowell committee by a New York expert in 1927. (At that time defense attorney Thompson charged that Captain William Proctor, who never believed that the right culprits had been apprehended, had substituted a fake bullet for the murder bullet; but this appears improbable. [87]

The author also brings out the fact that the first defense attorney (Fred Moore) was a bohemian-type barrister from California who thought "that this backwater New England affair could be his big case, the culmination of his career." He made a "production" of the case and turned it into a symbol of the "class struggle." [87] [Dumbauld served as U.S. District judge for the Western Division of Pennsylvania.]

Alfred P. Klausler. "Still No Proof." The Christian Century. September 26, 1962. #5

Surely any morally sensitive American who recalls the Sacco-Vanzetti case does so with heartache. When Francis Russell began his research he learned that many of the people who had been involved in the case were still living, and that most of them still had strong feelings one way or the other concerning the two philosophical anarchists.... . [1168]

It is easy for Russell to write that Sacco and Vanzetti were figures out of Greek tragedy: the doomed king's son becomes in modern dress two Italian workmen. This is a cavalier way to write off the life of a man such as Vanzetti, a man who could write: Tank to you from the bottom of my earth for your confidence in my innocence; I am so. I did not splittel a drop of blood, or still a cent in all my life... . [Ed. Letter to Mrs. Evans, July 22, 1921. See Polenberg, Letters, p. 81.]

Russell's is an able, though partisan, reconstruction of the tragic events. [1168] [Ed. Klaussler was a Century editor at large.]

A. J. Ayer. "Books in General." New Statesman. 5 July 1963. #6

Both men were active anarchists of an idealistic kind, ... Vanzetti in particular, an autodidact with a remarkable literary gift, as the letters which he wrote from prison were to show, appeared a man of great sweetness and nobility of character. [15]

That Vanzetti was innocent is hardly to be questioned. There was never any serious evidence against him, and the crime was entirely foreign to his character.

[T]he bullet that was tested in 1961 may well have been introduced by the police. Mr. Russell gives reasons for thinking that the bullet was not substituted before the trial but does not consider the possibility that it was substituted by Van Amburgh afterwards. [16]

[Alfred Jules Ayer, Wykeham Professor of Logic, 1959-78, had a long career at Oxford University. He was visiting professor at NYU, Harvard, and Columbia.]

"The Case Reversed." The Economist. August 3, 1963. #7

The ways in which the author builds up his evidence, his obvious objectivity about the law and its servants, his judicious assessment of roles and personalities, his impartial weighing of factors in prosecution, defence and public agitation—all of this, plus a limpid style and professional expertness in deploying the results of his research, make his book the definitive work on an international cause celebre... . Mr. Russell has produced an exemplary work, ... Everyone interested in political, mass emotional, historical causes should read it. [445] [Author unknown.]

David Felix. **Protest: Sacco-Vanzetti and the Intellectuals**. 1965

Felix Frankfurter, then a Harvard Law School professor, was a leading member of the Sacco-Vanzetti Defense Committee and the author of the most authoritative article on the case. Walter Lippmann, Broun's superior as editor of the New York Evening World, would write the most widely influential articles in the form of World editorials. And long before 1927 Roger N. Baldwin, executive director of the American Civil Liberties Union, was contributing the A.C.L.U. resources to the cause.

Many of the brightest names of the twenties gave their support [13] in one form or another. There were women like Dorothy Parker, Edna St. Vincent Millay, and the suffragette, Ruth Hale, who was Broun's wife. There were ministers like John Haynes Holmes of New York's Community Church and Rabbi Stephen Wise, professors like Robert Morss Lovett, Arthur M. Schlesinger, and Samuel Eliot Morison, the literary historian Van Wyck Brooks, and the philosopher John Dewey. In the summer of 1927 they would rouse the world for Sacco and Vanzetti. [14]

Moore was an idealist, but one after his own fashion.... . [Eugene] Lyons told me: "Moore had no conscience once he decided his client was [22] innocent. He would stop at nothing, frame evidence, suborn witnesses, have his people work on witnesses who had seen the wrong things—I pity anyone he went after." [23]

Moore's skills won the admiration of Upton Sinclair, who described them under a thin fictional veil in his novel, Boston, the most explicit fictional treatment of the case. Sinclair obviously approved of what Moore did ... . [He] created one Lee Swenson as the man who carries out the questionable acts of the real Moore and later inserted a pale character named Moore who does nothing untoward in the novel...Swenson is a good journalistic likeness of Moore. [23]

Moore's ... labor connections, his I.W.W. associates, and his Boston anarchists gave him real and even frightening power. This was evident in the case of George T. Kelley, superintendent of the plant where Sacco had worked, who tried to back out of a statement that tended to incriminate Sacco. [23]

It [radicalism] was the central element in the logic of the defense case... . [24] Moore would rub in radicalism. He would make the issue of radicalism so clear and hard that Massachusetts justice would be forced to retreat from its prejudices in the face of national opinion.... Moore almost succeeded. He gave four years of his life to the attempt. Through his failure, he lifted the Sacco-Vanzetti case into American history. [25]

Katzmann had a simple hypothesis: The group [Sacco, Vanzetti, Boda, Orciani] wanted the [Boda] automobile to attempt a third holdup. That explained the late hour, the arms, the departure from the garage without the car—fear that Ruth Johnson was calling the police. [84]

Katzmann counterattacked powerfully [to Sacco's trial speech attacking capitalism], but he was careful to avoid making an issue of radicalism itself.... . Thus the prosecutor defined Sacco's refusal to register for the draft as the ingratitude of an immigrant who took his good wages and ran out when the country might have needed him.... . Yet Katzmann did not linger on the issue. The weight of his cross-examination, except for these few minutes, rested stolidly on the facts of the crime. [95]

Did Gould witness the crime? Gould, himself an I.W.W. member, was an old friend of Burke, Moore's I.W.W. assistant. Indeed, Burke had located Gould for his chief, according to the affidavit material. Furthermore, Gould describes that moment of the shooting which had been Burke's subject for his testimony at the trial. It would be an extraordinary coincidence for two friends to experience the same part of the climactic action, each remaining unaware of the other's presence. Additionally, the date of the affidavit indicates that Gould took his time about reporting what he saw. [112]

Augustus H. Gill [in 1923], Professor of Technical Chemical Analysis of Massachusetts Institute of Technology, ... measured the markings—their length, width and relative position—on the bullets. Both men [Hamilton and Gill] concluded that the markings on the test bullets were different from those on the fatal bullet. Thus, they argued ... the fatal bullet did not come from the Sacco weapon. Their statements, accompanied by lists of figures going to four decimal places, appear well taken at first view. Yet no ballistics expert would accept them today. According to an authoritative handbook, Firearms Investigation, Identification, and Evidence (1957) by Hatcher, Jury, and Weller: "Minute measurements of crime bullets and arms have been found to be of little practical significance."

No one expert agreed with the others. Indeed, one of the experts disagreed with himself. This was Gill, who recorded three [122] sets of figures, each set different. Furthermore, all of Gill's measurements differed from those of Hamilton... . At the trial Van Amburgh had placed the greater emphasis on simple recognition. You look at the bullets in question through a microscope and decide whether or not the markings are alike... . Every firearm will have markings in its barrel which are different from the markings on every other weapon—and these give the distinctive markings to the bullets. There are two reasons for the differences: the inner surface of the barrel is distinctively striated with tool scratches in the manufacturing; and rusting, pitting, and other accidents of use also leave their markings. [123]

Goddard's Comparison Microscope. It functions with one eyepiece for the two microscope barrels, focusing on two objects but showing only one in the eyepiece. The image of this one object is actually a union of halves of the two objects being viewed—the left side of one bullet and the right side of the other, or top half of one and bottom half of the other. The observer can be sure that two bullets came from the same weapon if there is no break in the one object being viewed, if the markings are continuous and consistent. If that one object studied in the single eyepiece juxtaposes two different patterns of markings which stop abruptly at the invisible line of jointure, then the observer can be sure that the bullets had been fired from different weapons. [124] [Ed. Photos of comparison microscope in Gunthers' book, pp. 21-22.]

Goddard test 1927 ... [A] test was held in Dedham courthouse on June 3, ... Despite the defense's reluctance, it was represented by Herbert B. Ehrmann, associate defense counsel, and also by Professor Gill. [125]

The first public announcement of the experiment was made two months later by the Boston Transcript of August 8 [Aug. 9]. According to the Transcript, Ehrmann had been unable to articulate any objection to Goddard's report, although he refused to sign it... . Later, Gill quarreled with Thompson, broke off with the defense, and said he doubted the "present truth" of his earlier ballistics conclusions. James Burns, one of the two trial defense experts, also accepted the Goddard test findings. [126]

Bullet 3 and Shell W. Could the exhibits have been switched in the course of the years? To this, any answer but a negative would suggest an action by the authorities that would have been as monstrous as it would have been difficult. The bullets and shells had been scratched with identifying marks immediately after the South Braintree murders, and these marks as well as the other characteristics appear in all the photographs. Although Thompson brought up the matter during the final review in 1927, it was clearly a last-minute argument of desperation when all else seemed to be failing and no responsible friend of the defense took it seriously. [127]

All the responsible tests are unequivocal: Sacco's pistol killed Berardelli. Despite his imagination and power Fred Moore had to fail on the ballistics issue. [128]

Medeiros did not make any official statement until after his second trial on May 17, 1926, when he was quickly convicted for the second time. It was only on May 29, twelve days later, that he signed the confession affidavit. [136] Inasmuch as he was facing the electric chair, he had nothing to lose and a life to gain. [137]

The idealists Sacco and Vanzetti had associates—Boda, Orciani, and Coacci—of nonidealistic, surely doubtful, and possibly criminal character; these five men are a much more logical staffing for the holdup gang than the distant Morellis. [141]

Sacco's alibis were furnished by friends and associates.... . Sacco had worked at the Rice & Hutchins plant.... . Boda had worked at the plant of the L. Q. White Company, whose payroll was the objective of the Bridgewater holdup. According to Chief Stewart, Coacci had worked at both of the victim plants and up to the same date relative to the holdups, that is, until the Monday before each attack.... . Vanzetti's alibis were furnished by friends and associates. [142]

The desperate nature of the defense case is suggested by the unscrupulous acts of Moore: intimidation of witnesses, use of such charlatans as Hamilton, etc. [143]

[T]he Red raids ... were ordered from Washington to stop the sufficiently real anarchist bomb attacks. [151]

In 1950 Edward B. Simmons, a reporter for the New Bedford Standard-Times, interviewed seven of the eight jurors then alive.... . According to Simmons, who told me ... all the jurors denied having been influenced by the anarchism or foreign origins of the accused. Of the jurors the most articulate was John F. Dever, now dead, who became a lawyer some time after his service in the trial, ... The verdict, he [Dever] said, resulted from a study of all the hard evidence:

"Various pieces fitted into chains of evidence, which to my mind, not having a weak link, were pretty strong... ." [153]

In my own pursuit of the jury question I spoke with Harry E. King, ... whose comments to me accorded with what he told Simmons... . King faced the prejudice issue squarely: ... "The jury didn't consider it [radicalism], didn't mention it when we discussed the evidence. We were asked about everything twice since then—by the Governor and the Advisory Committee. I didn't change my opinion—the other jurors didn't. I've got a clear conscience on that." [154]

Of the post-trial evidence, the Medeiros confession was the most important. Frankfurter discusses it at length in his book, but we have seen how badly it withstood a serious testing. Frankfurter also places emphasis on the affidavit of Gould, the I.W.W. razor-paste salesman, ... [157]

Thus he [Frankfurter] refers to Sacco as "in continuous employment" when Sacco was not at work on the South Braintree crime day and lacked pay records (they had disappeared) to prove he had worked on the day of the Bridgewater holdup. [159]

Repeated examination has not been able to substantiate the charge that Sacco and Vanzetti were betrayed in the courts. [160]

It was the Sacco-Vanzetti case that permitted the intellectuals to crystallize their general protest around a hard, definable issue. [163]

In December 1912 Max Eastman took over The Masses, announcing his purpose by a masthead that read "a revolutionary and not a reform magazine." ... Eastman believed The Masses was an important connection between the intellectuals and the working class. [167]

In October 1921, three months after the Dedham trial and at the most inappropriate time, the Third International stirred up demonstrations in France, Switzerland, [168] Spain, Portugal, Sweden, and Norway... . The Communists in Europe, less concerned with the details of control or cooperation, found the cause [Sacco-Vanzetti case] a superb vehicle for their purposes. Was this not a perfect example of oppression in the most capitalistic of nations? [169]

Presently, the Communist demands were being supported by scores of internationally distinguished names, including John Galsworthy and H. G. Wells (Bernard Shaw typically refused his sympathy while condemning American justice); Romain Rolland, Henri Barbusse, and fourteen other leading French writers, ... Thomas

Mann, Fritz Kreisler, Albert Einstein, and Paul Loebe, president of the German Reichstag—and Benito Mussolini. Ramsay MacDonald, the Labor Party leader and past and future prime minister, commented: "The whole affair is too terrible." [170]

In the United States a few pioneer intellectuals, Felix Frankfurter and his associates of the American Civil Liberties Union among them, had actually taken over the leadership of the defense. [171]

Thompson's Medeiros motion and Frankfurter's persuasions combined to achieve the first great public relations feat of the new efforts. Three days after Thayer denied the motion, on October 26, 1926, the Herald carried an editorial backing the defense on every point. The editorial demanded a review of the case and summarized all the major Frankfurter arguments which would appear a few months later in the Atlantic. Written by F. Lauriston Bullard, the Herald's chief editorial writer, it was a striking indication of the new power and respectability of the cause. [173]

Taking the Bullard editorial and the Frankfurter article as points of departure, the intellectuals organized one of the greatest public relations campaigns in American history. [174]

Walter Lippmann, the editor of the New York Evening World, had worked with Frankfurter as early as 1914, when the two men had joined in the founding of the New Republic, for which Frankfurter acted as legal advisor. [176]

Justice Oliver Wendell Holmes and Harold Laski Trade Letters. Citation is to Holmes-Laski Letters, vol. 2, pp. 900-999.

Felix: On November 21, 1926, attempting to provoke his Socrates [Holmes] into agreement, Laski wrote [to Holmes]: [Ed. Note that David Felix is made the interlocutor.]

Laski: "I had a long note from Felix Frankfurter yesterday, full of his crime survey of Boston and the incredible Sacco-Vanzetti case. I hope that the latter is settled, for, otherwise, the working classes will disbelieve in Massachusetts justice."

Felix: When Holmes failed to react, Laski returned to the charge … on March 20, 1927:

Laski: "But I read Felix's [Frankfurter's] little book on Sacco and Vanzetti and thought it a neat, surgical job."

Felix: On August 9, after the Advisory Committee decision, Laski returned to the subject with somewhat less restraint:

Laski: "I agree [222] fully with all that Felix [Frankfurter] says of Lowell in this case. Loyalty to his class [the values of an old New England family] has transcended his ideas of logic and of justice."

Felix: Holmes responded in his next letter, dated August 18, with an instructive rendering of the effects of the intellectuals' activities:

Holmes: "... but the result has been already some letters telling me that I am a monster of injustice in various forms of words [Holmes declined to issue a writ of <u>habeas corpus</u>.] from men who evidently don't know anything about the matter but who have the customary willingness to impute evil for any result that they don't like" ... .

Felix: Laski, functionally irresponsible as a European observer, was essentially no liberal but an idealist and a dogmatist of the Left: he could be intolerant for the sake of his vision of a better world... . Laski ... on August 19, ... revealed his European assumption that Frankfurter was the final authority on the case:

Laski: "... This case has stirred Europe as nothing since the Dreyfus case has done. And to me, at this instance, and with the reliance I have on the substantial accuracy of Felix's picture [Frankfurter's book], it seems that it is indeed another Dreyfus case."

Felix: In his next letter, dated August 24, Holmes made two illuminating points. The first is relevant to the civil rights issues of our [223] time:

Holmes: "I cannot but ask myself why there is so much greater interest in red than black. A thousand-fold worse cases of negroes come up from time to time, but the world does not worry over them..."

[Ed. See pp. 974-975 on violence in <u>Holmes-Laski Letters.</u>]

Felix: Holmes then got to the intellectuals:

Holmes: "But I see no ... reasons for the world outside the United States taking up the matter and I think your public and literary men had better have kept their gentle mouths shut... ."

Felix: In a letter of September 1 the great liberal [Holmes] returned to the intellectuals:

Holmes: "It isn't a matter of reason, but simply shrieking because the world is not the kind of world they want——" ...

Felix: Near the end of November he [Holmes] made his last judgment on the intellectuals:

Holmes: "I had a letter from A. Hill saying that Frankfurter will write nothing more about Sacco and Vanzetti for a year. I hope it will be longer than that, as I think all those who were interested in that side seem to have got hysterical and to have lost their sense of proportion." [224] [End of exchange, November 23, 1927, p. 999.]

About Sacco and Vanzetti, however, they [intellectuals] would maintain the old simplicities. Virtually all comments on the case in serious historical and cultural studies as well as in reference works define it as judicial murder or, at the mildest, as a miscarriage of justice. One can find such notes in the <u>Dictionary of American Biography</u>; F. L. Allen, <u>Only Yesterday</u>; Alfred Kazin, <u>On Native Grounds</u>, J. J. Hoffman, <u>The Twenties</u>; Edmund Wilson, <u>The American Earthquake</u>; Cleveland Amory, <u>The Proper Bostonians</u>; and Arthur M. Schlesinger, Jr., <u>The Crisis of the Old Order</u>. [244]

The Sacco-Vanzetti legend has been enormously valuable as a vehicle of protest and an inspiration to the intellectuals. In view of all this, we might be sorry for knowing what we do about the facts of the case. For, knowing them, we cannot live with the legend today. [David Felix, Professor of History Emeritus, CUNY.] [Ed. See Online: Truman Library, James H. Rowe Oral History Interview, #'s 85-88.]

Reviews of <u>Protest: Sacco-Vanzetti and the Intellectuals</u>
David Cort. "The intellectual mob for the defense." <u>Commonweal</u>. March 18, 1966. #1

[Ed. Cort reviews both <u>Protest</u> and Betty Schechter's <u>The Dreyfus Affair</u>.]

The Dreyfus Case in France ... and the Sacco-Vanzetti Case in Massachusetts ... should long ago have been bracketed as a single two-part study of justice versus mass-thinking. [700]

Sacco and Vanzetti were guilty, yet their mistaken defenders prepared America for a philosophy of social mercy. Dreyfus was innocent, yet his defenders failed to break the back of either anti-Semitism or military justice in France. The mobs were wrong in both cases but in America at least a decent heritage was left. [700]

The memory of the Dreyfus Case, ... inspired the innocent idealists who made the Sacco-Vanzetti Case their cause.... The Paris mob rioted as violently for Sacco-Vanzetti as it had against Dreyfus a generation earlier. In America the liberals, Heywood Broun, [700] Dos

Passos, Walter Lippmann, Dorothy Parker, John Dewey, discovered the cause seven years late. Just as the cry of "Guilty!" had swept France, now the cry of "Innocent!" swept the intellectuals' ivory towers. [701]

The Frankfurter brief [his article in the Atlantic Monthly] became the basic truth of the Sacco-Vanzetti case, and none of the newcomers to the cause felt any need to go any deeper. On this assurance, H. G. Wells was able to state flatly that Sacco and Vanzetti could not have been anywhere near South Braintree on that day. The whole intellectual world "knew" that the two Italians were more innocent than themselves: ... [701]

The guilty Sacco and Vanzetti bloomed in jail, received a train of sycophants and dressed like Boston bankers. Their casual jargon became Holy Writ. But Vanzetti's most glorious statement, in all that towering moraine of Vanzettiana, is now definitely proved to have been the transliteration of a professional writer, Phil Stong. [701]

[Cort, assistant foreign news editor at Time, later foreign news editor at Life, called Max Eastman "the many splendored communist" in The Glossy Rats.]

Alexander M. Bickel. "Sacco-Vanzetti and the Intellectuals." The New Republic. April 2, 1966. #2

The defense and the late Justice Frankfurter in his 1927 book explained the "suspicious conduct" [of Sacco and Vanzetti at the Johnson house on May 5] by recalling the raids, summary deportations and other persecutions to which alien anarchists like Sacco and Vanzetti were subject in this year of the reign of Attorney General A. Mitchell Palmer. To their certain knowledge, friends and associates of theirs were being arrested, grilled, deported. When they themselves were arrested, the first line of questioning addressed to them concerned their beliefs and associations. If their conduct was suspicious, it was as likely as not because they were conscious ... of a "guilt" far removed from the events at South Braintree. [23]

On this aspect of the case, Mr. Felix's essential reply is to insinuate that perhaps we are being unjust to A. Mitchell Palmer. Attorney General Palmer, he says at one point, "obliged to do something about the anarchist bombings, countered with the Red raids." Palmer's purpose, he continues—and why would anyone object to it?—"was to prevent future bombings by arresting and deporting radical aliens."

Later on, Mr. Felix adds: "As an official action, whatever injustices they caused, the raids were neither lawless nor hysterical... ."

We come thus to the ballistics evidence, ... [23] Van Amburgh testified that he was "inclined to believe" that the fatal bullet was fired from Sacco's gun... . That Van Amburgh was thoroughly entitled to harbor his reservations was demonstrated ... later ... in Bridgeport, when his ballistics methods in another capital case were discredited, ... [24]

[Bickel, law professor at Yale Law School, was a law clerk to Justice Frankfurter.]

Robert J. Clements. "Knights-Errant in Error?" New York Times Book Review. Jan. 30, 1966. #3

David Felix's volume is an unintentional ironic commentary on Julien Benda's famous "Treason of the Intellectuals" of 1927, the very year when Nicola Sacco and Bartolomeo Vanzetti were executed in Massachusetts. Benda accused intellectuals of renouncing the quest for justice and truth only to become enmeshed in political passions and party lines. [3]

Edna St. Vincent Millay, Maxwell Anderson, John Dos Passos, Heywood Broun and all the others emerge not only as misguided idealists, but as character assassins themselves of those executors of the law pictorially libeled by Ben Shahn. When Felix shows how even their solon, Justice Frankfurter, based his book, "The Case of Sacco and Vanzetti," not upon the official court record available to him but on the various defense briefs, one understands Justice Holmes's tongue-in-cheek comment on Felix Frankfurter's version: "I appreciate what I believe was the generous knight-errantry of Felix [Frankfurter] in writing the book." [3]

No one has been able to refute the proof of the Goddard Comparison Microscope (evidence retested and confirmed in 1962) that "the 'fatal bullet' in Berardelli's body was fired through the Sacco pistol and could have been fired by no other." [3]

Now that science (in the form of ballistics) seems to have given the lie to a whole generation of intellectuals, why should not one of them write a novel on the case, admitting the guilt of Sacco at least? [31]

[Ed. Clements proposes a scene for Cornelia Thornwell in a rewrite of Sinclair's Boston, suggesting Dos Passos might do the rewriting—"For the rebellious Dos Passos of the twenties has evolved to conservative positions."]

Sample of Clements' satire of Sinclair. She [Cornelia] realises that over seven years in prison the two have told their story so often that they have come to believe it as fact. Tiring of the attempts of intellectuals to vilify American justice, she walks out on a cocktail party given by Heywood Broun, Walter Lippmann and Phil Stong. [31] **End of satire sample.**

Truth is helpless against the stereotype, even though the evidence against Sacco is incontrovertible and that against his inseparable associate Vanzetti is most damaging. [31] [Clements, "director of comparative literature at NYU, has long been a student of this episode in American history." In the Columbia University Forum, Fall 1961, Clements said he was "prejudiced in favor of Italians (and currently President of the American Association of Teachers of Italian)."]

Louis Joughin. Rev. of Protest. The Journal of American History (June 1966). #4

Were Sacco and Vanzetti guilty? Felix believes they were although he expresses liking for the men. This book does not attempt full study of the evidence; rather the author selects those elements which he believes significant, emphasizes the aspects of each element which would support a verdict of guilt and de-emphasizes or neglects the aspects which would constitute insufficiency of proof. He makes no distinction between the evidential weight of evidence tested by cross-examination at the trial, untested evidence which has the lesser but considerable weight of affidavit status, and what two precommitted "experts" did in 1961 with the hapless physical ballistics evidence which had been unlawfully secluded for many years by a ... discredited prosecution witness at the 1921 trial.

Did the men receive a fair or adequate trial? Felix says they did. He pays no attention to the almost universal legal opinion, best represented by the work of the late E. M. Morgan, that the trial constituted a grave miscarriage of justice. [156]

Were the posttrial motions and appeals proper in scope and judgment? Felix, to this reviewer, fails to engage with the serious issues involved here; his treatment is fragmentary and astigmatic; he does little justice to the responsible actions taken and no justice to the irresponsible ones. For example: he notes that in 1927 the governor had the constant assistance of the state attorney general, but does not mention the fact that within less than a [156] year that lawyer became the first elected official of Massachusetts ever to be impeached; he washes out the all-important Red Raids of 1920 as irrelevant and suggests that fairness smiled upon the land; and he passes off as of minor importance the fact that a prosecution witness of 1920 [sic] four years later made affidavit virtually confessing perjury—and this was the head of the Massachusetts State Police [Proctor]. [157]

[Joughin wrote pp. 201-514 of The Legacy of Sacco and Vanzetti, and he wrote the entry on the Sacco-Vanzetti case in Collier's Encyclopedia.]

Philip R. Toomin. Review of Protest. De Paul Law Review (Spring-Summer 1966). #5

Yet, in the retrospect of history, they [protests of the 1960s] seem pallid when contrasted with the mob violence which, forty years ago, well nigh thwarted the efforts of the State of Massachusetts to bring to a final conclusion its prosecution of two anarchists convicted of murder. [516]

In "Protest," a well documented book concerning the Sacco-Vanzetti trial ... the author...enables us to appraise the questionable methods used by the defense to obtain hearing after fruitless hearing for some six years, and to organize mass protest against imposition of the extreme penalty. [516]

Then followed motions for new trial, based upon alleged discovery of new evidence, upon alleged perjury by State's witnesses and upon alleged errors during the trial. Some of the affidavits of recanting witnesses were, in turn, shown to have been obtained by duress, by financial offers or other improper [516] means. No charge of prejudice of the trial judge was made until the case reached the Supreme Judicial Court of Massachusetts, some two years after the trial. The reviewing Court found no merit in the point, or in any other advanced by the defense. [517]

At this point in the narration, the case changes from criminal jurisprudence into a vehicle of propaganda to convince the toiling masses throughout the world that two innocent radicals had been unjustly convicted by American capitalist justice for a crime which workingmen could not possibly have committed, namely, the crime of armed robbery and murder of other workingmen. The Communist Party joined the defense committee, and between them and the crowd of liberal sympathizers, a drum-fire of pamphlets and periodicals appeared, which turned the country into angry protestants on the one hand, and on the other into stubborn supporters of the rightness of the verdict. [517]

Of more than passing interest are the recounting of efforts to obtain the sympathetic interest of members of the United States Supreme Court and of their steadfast refusal to allow a foothold for further attack. [517]

[Toomin, member of the Illinois Bar, LL.B., Univ of Chicago, 1926.]

Louis B. Schwartz. Review of Protest. University of Pennsylvania Law Review (June 1966). #6

The theses of David Felix' book include the following propositions: The evidence was convincing of Sacco's guilt and persuasive of Vanzetti's. They had a fair trial despite the fact that the trial judge, Webster Thayer, was a political reactionary. The liberals of the Twenties came (belatedly) to the support of these alien defendants because the liberals themselves felt alienated in the Harding-Coolidge society, and found identity in the role of protestants. The innocence of Sacco and Vanzetti was elevated to the status of an article of faith, and Vanzetti to the role of saint in a secular hagiography created by American writers of the Thirties. [1260]

More than one of my liberal friends find Felix' theses so repellent that they refuse to read the book; and some of the reviews—e.g., that of Pro-[1260] fessor Bickel of Yale Law School in the New Republic— have a quality of anguished defensiveness about the sacred "myth," as Felix characterizes the Sacco-Vanzetti case. [1261]

At the subsequent murder trial [Dedham], it was the defense, not the prosecution, which made an issue of the defendants' politics. This was partly because the defense had to explain away some very damaging facts: that the defendants were heavily armed when arrested, and that they gave a demonstrably false explanation for their possession of the weapons. [1262]

The defense lawyers petitioned Mr. Justice Holmes of the United States Supreme Court to stay execution. He had power to do so while the Court was on vacation, but declined, saying:

I do not consider that I am at liberty to deal with this case differently from the way in which I should treat one that excited no public interest and that was less powerfully presented. I cannot say that I have a doubt and therefore must deny the stay. [1263]

[Schwartz, Professor of Law, Univ. of Pennsylvania. See Holmes in Transcript of the Record, 5517, from which Schwartz quotes.]

Osmond K. Fraenkel. Review of Protest. American Historical Review (April 1966). #7

Mr. Felix' thesis is that the intellectuals were wrong about the case, but that the case was right for them: wrong, because he believes the legal proceedings were fair and the defendants guilty; right, because the case proved a rallying point that gave the intellectuals needed cohesion and valuable experience.... For a reader unfamiliar with the case the book is a colorful presentation and discusses all the contentions, but he should be on his guard about the author's conclusions. [1093]

In reaching these conclusions, Felix gives the prosecution the benefit of every [1093] doubt and accepts ballistic tests never subjected to cross-examination. His method is, perhaps, best illustrated by his treatment of the Proctor episode which had aroused Felix Frankfurter's indignation.... After the trial Proctor gave the defense an affidavit in which he stated that he had "repeatedly" told the district attorney and his assistant that he could find no evidence that the bullet had in fact been fired by the Sacco pistol and that it had been arranged that he would not be asked that question. The affidavits of the prosecutors did no more than deny that this subject had been discussed "repeatedly." But one of them admitted that Proctor had told him that he could not tell through which pistol the bullet had been fired. That information was, of course, not transmitted to the defense at the trial. The defense had not cross-examined, fearful that they might have elicited more harmful testimony.

Felix rejects the recent theory that only Sacco was guilty because in his view Vanzetti was the more dominant character and his expressions were more violent than Sacco's. [1094]

545

[Fraenkel, author of "Sacco-Vanzetti Case" in Encyclopedia Americana, was ACLU counsel.]

John Hove. Review of Protest. North Dakota Law Review (January 1966). #8

... On the book jacket, Mr. Felix is identified as a liberal intellectual and a specialist in intellectual history with a B. A. from Trinity College and a M. A. from the University of Chicago. His former experience as a news service correspondent in Paris and a U.S. government information officer in Vienna obtrudes in his style which will undoubtedly annoy a lawyer expecting a professional review of the evidence as recorded in the official transcript of the trial.

Whatever the limitations of the book may be, it is a provocative work in that it **contradicts the popular view of the Sacco-Vanzetti case** and insofar as the charges made by the defenders became a condemnation of American society and particularly of judicial procedures in the United States, it is a book that neither students of American culture nor the legal profession will want to ignore. [254]

[Hove, Chairman, Department of English, North Dakota State University.]

Willard D. Lorensen. Review of Protest. West Virginia Law Review (Feb. 1966). #9

... With all the temerity of a fellow first-grader about to leak the news that there is no Santa Claus, Felix debunks the widely accepted version of the Sacco and Vanzetti case as a myth. The myth, he contends, is the product of an intellectual reaction to the case that was short on facts and long on sentimentality. The point of the book is of peculiar interest to the legal profession ... because an assault on the position of the late Supreme Court Justice Felix Frankfurter is crucial to Felix's theory. [222]

Frankfurter's major contribution to the Sacco-Vanzetti legend was a long article published in the prestigious Atlantic Monthly in March 1927 which **seemed to clinch the case for the intellectual community**. [224]

By avoiding "wearisome" detail he [Felix] gives the impression of subduing not only the Frankfurter criticism but of neutralizing other censures as well. But closer examination will show that his glib, once-over-lightly mode of attack fails miserably to dent the wearisome, detailed and more carefully argued critique of Frankfurter... . Frankfurter's classic indictment of the Sacco-Vanzetti trial [Frankfurter's book] escapes unscathed. [224]

What is even more shocking, though it is not expressly stated in the book, is that by necessary implication Felix must brand Frankfurter either a liar or a dupe. Frankfurter, in the introductory paragraph of his Atlantic Monthly article said: "The aim of this paper is to give in the briefest compass an accurate resume of the facts ... ." This assertion of an impartial review was expanded when the material was put in book form to read as follows: "Obviously, to tell the story within limited space requires drastic compression. The necessary selection of material has been guided by cannons [sic] of relevance and fairness familiar to every lawyer called upon to make a disinterested summary of a protracted trial... ." Frankly, Frankfurter is much more convincing on the point than Felix. There really is not much of a contest. [226] [Lorensen, Professor of Law, West Virginia University.]

Review of Protest. "Booknotes." UCLA Law Review (March 1966). #10

Not a lawyer but an intellectual historian, Mr. Felix took it upon himself to re-examine the trial record, the appeals, the commentaries, and the general climate of the trial to verify the decisions on the legal issues involved and to ascertain whether there was prejudice in the proceedings... . Mr. Felix concluded that the verdict was supported by the evidence and was rendered in a climate which was not prejudicial. Unhappily, Mr. [926] Felix substantiated the determinations made in his "dispassionate inquiry" by presenting only one side on many of the critical issues involved in the trial and overlooking much of the evidence against the verdict. On many of these issues, a comparison of Mr. Felix's presentation with the earlier one by then Professor Felix Frankfurter reveals the former's incompleteness. [927]

Felix does not mention that on cross-examination Pelser admitted that immediately after Sacco's arrest he was unable to make any identification. [927]

The book's treatment of the confession by Celestino F. Madeiros demonstrates a similar carelessness. A young man with a criminal record, Madeiros was confined in the same prison as Sacco [927] following the latter's conviction. While his appeal was pending from a conviction of murder committed in an attempted bank robbery, he sent Sacco a note in which he confessed his participation in the Braintree crime and exonerated Sacco and Vanzetti.... Mr. Felix gives little credence to the confession, emphasizing its factual flaws and its selfish motivation. 928] [Author unknown.]

"Martyrs or Murderers?" Times Literary Supplement. Nov. 25, 1965. #11

Mr. Felix remembers the bomb outrages in Wall Street and elsewhere. These people [Wobblies] remembered Bisbee and Centralia, not to speak of Ferrer and Malatesta. For Sacco and Vanzetti (and many others) the class character of American justice was an axiom that no worker of good faith could doubt. But, of course, Mr. Felix is entitled to point out that the "good character" of Sacco and Vanzetti did not necessarily prove that they were incapable of "propaganda by the deed" [violence] or of collecting necessary party funds by violence. (The degree of violence attributed to the two is a little harder to accept.) But a rising statesman of this time, J. V. Stalin, had begun his career by ideological bank robberies, the Russian equivalent of carrying a local primary, and although Sacco and Vanzetti **were not** Communists, they were "radicals". [1058]

It is Mr. Felix's belief that Vanzetti's famous declaration was really the work of Mr. Phil Stong (best known as the author of the best-seller, State Fair). [1058] [Author unknown.]

Jay M. Hollander. Review of Protest. New England Quarterly (June 1966). #12

Assuming that the author is correct in his conclusion that most intellectuals of the period were liberals, does it necessarily follow that all of the liberals and others who supported Sacco and Vanzetti were intellectuals? ... . It is likely that the case would never have received the attention which it ultimately did without the initial efforts of a relatively small group of publicists. By the time a defense rally could draw a crowd of over ten thousand people, however, the intellectuals as a class appear to be part of a larger ferment. [243]

For a work with pretensions of breaking fresh ground, Protest is woefully devoid of documentation.... . Very little consideration is given to the continuing interest (of intellectuals?) in the case almost forty years after the execution of Sacco and Vanzetti. [244]
[Hollander, J.D., Harvard University.]

Michael A. Musmanno. Review of Protest. Annals of the American Academy of Political and Social Science (July 1966). #13

Editor's summary of Musmanno's main points.
The Dedham jury made the wrong decision. [165]
Mr. Felix's book Protest adds nothing to the historical debate. A new justification for the guilty verdict is not to be found in this book. Felix has no "angle" on this, no clue. Still, Felix finds the prosecution witnesses credible.
The case is beyond Felix's understanding, intelligent and persistent though Mr. Felix seems to be. The cap evidence, "a crucial item," gets no serious consideration from Felix. President Lowell blundered when he claimed that "deceptiveness" best characterized two defense witnesses [Bosco and Guadenagi]. As in the cap topic, Felix is much too casual about Lowell, and he fails to say that Lowell apologized! Error had to be charged to Lowell on this Bosco-Guadenagi episode.
The Murder and the Myth, a book by Robert H. Montgomery, wins the prize for worthlessness. No book on the case is worse. Now Felix's book is added to the Sacco-Vanzetti library, second in worthlessness to Montgomery's book when measured by standards of factual knowledge, reflective power, and openmindedness. "Predetermined" describes Felix's approach in this book. [166]
[Musmanno, Justice, Supreme Court of Pennsylvania, was counsel for Sacco and Vanzetti in 1927.]

Wm. J. Hughes, Jr. Review of Protest. Washburn Law Journal (Fall 1966). #14

This carefully written book is an effort on the part of Mr. Felix to explain the enigma of the Intellectuals' crusade on behalf of Sacco and Vanzetti. As the author shows, the trial record proved the defendants overwhelmingly guilty and showed too that they got a fair trial. [213]

After Judge Thayer had charged the jury the Boston Herald reported: "Judge Thayer received the acknowledgement of the lawyers for the defense and prosecution for fairness and impartiality in the able way he had tried the case."

In contrast there is Professor (later Justice) Frankfurter's oft-quoted statement:

By systematic exploitation of the defendants' alien blood, their imperfect knowledge of English, their unpopular social views, and their opposition to war, the District Attorney invoked against them a riot of passion and patriotic sentiment; and the trial judge connived at—one had almost written, cooperated in-the process.

[Ed. Hughes has quoted from p. 59 in Frankfurter's book.]

Hughes: There is no basis for this disreputable tirade. [213] The dubious honor ... of giving impetus to the liberal myth [of innocence] goes to Professor Frankfurter of Harvard, a member of the National Committee of the Civil Liberties Union who has been active for the defense from March 1921 if not before. It was Frankfurter's article in the Atlantic Monthly for March 1927 which first popularized the case and later led to the standard liberal propaganda that the two anarchists had been railroaded. [215]

As Mr. Felix's book shows, the Frankfurter article made in its day an immense stir. Its invective carried conviction—indeed. A. Lawrence Lowell, President of Harvard, was almost convinced by it— until as a member of Governor Fuller's Advisory Committee he reviewed the case... . [T]he Frankfurter book ... became the bible of the Intellectuals. [215]

Frankfurter had on his side Professor Edwin [sic] M. Morgan of Harvard who should have known better. Morgan was an expert on the law of Evidence and unlike Frankfurter was used to reading trial transcripts. Compared to Frankfurter, Morgan was almost judicial. [215]

Mr. Felix makes a manful effort to explain how the Intellectuals fell for the defense propaganda. [216]

Had they [Sacco and Vanzetti] lived in the present their petition would probably have been granted by the Warren Court, (with four dissents, of course). And ... the present [Warren] court would probably have reversed the conviction. Thus all would have been merry ... in liberal circles, except ... for the widows and orphans of the deceased

Parmenter and Berardelli. [218] [Hughes, Professor of Law, Georgetown Law Center, Washington, D.C.]

Andrew Kopkind. "Causes Ce´le`bres." New Statesman. 9 September 1966. #15

[Ed. Kopkind reviews both Protest and Invitation to an Inquest. In Invitation to an Inquest Walter and Miriam Schneir find Julius and Ethel Rosenberg innocent...]

The liberal litany, if not the canon, demands repetition of two responses on suitable ritual occasions: Nicola Sacco and Bartolomeo Vanzetti were certainly innocent; Julius and Ethel Rosenberg were probably guilty—but should not have been executed. It is doubtful that definitive proof will ever be found in either case. [358]

The appeals are to history, and history is as corrupt a judge as ever wore a black robe and sat in a courtroom... . David Felix seeks to establish that Sacco, at least, was guilty of the murder of a paymaster and a guard.... . [358]

At this late date, it is much more difficult to make a case for the guilt of Sacco and Vanzetti than for the innocence of the Rosenbergs. [358] [See the Schneirs in The Venona Secrets by Romerstein/Breindel.]
[Kopkind, associate editor of The New Republic.]

William Henry Chamberlin. "Myths Die Hard." National Review. July 26, 1966. #16

... Myths die hard. But David Felix, in a calm, persuasive book based on thorough research, places a large charge of dynamite in the legend that [734] two innocent men of foreign origin and idealistic views were deprived of legal rights and railroaded to death on a charge without factual foundation.

He shows conclusively that there was no element of lynch law in the trial or in the protracted hearing of the appeals. It was the defense, not the prosecution, that dragged in the foreign origin and radical views of the defendants. There was no clamor in Boston or other Massachusetts newspapers to "hang them after a fair trial." The press was very moderate; the strongly charged emotional appeals came from the sympathizers with the defendants. [735]

The evidence on which the conviction was based was strong. When Sacco and Vanzetti were arrested they were not carrying harmless anarchist literature, as inaccurately stated by Arthur Schlesinger Jr. in his Crisis of the Old Order, but a pistol, a revolver and a quantity of ammunition.

Critics of the verdict have made much of Judge Thayer's alleged use of the term "anarchistic bastards" in referring to the defendants outside the courtroom.... That the Judge erred in expressing judgment outside the courtroom seems undeniable. But there is no indication that this affected his conduct of the trial ... or his charge to the jury.

[H]e [Felix] writes with no trace of the passion which the case stirred up at the time when it was running its course. [735]
[Chamberlin, Moscow correspondent for the Christian Science Monitor from 1922 to 1934, left the Soviet Union, for which he at first held great hope, bitterly disillusioned.]

Francis Russell. 'Innocence and betrayal'—was it a myth? Christian Science Monitor. March 10, 1966. #17

It is just a few years short of half a century since the South Braintree murders for which Sacco and Vanzetti were tried and executed, yet the case has remained for the intellectuals an emotional symbol of what Edna St. Vincent Millay called "justice denied...." It is a pity that David Felix's "Protest" comes as a somewhat belated postscript to the recent revival of interest, for it is one of the important books written about the case. [11]
[Russell, who studied the Sacco-Vanzetti case for almost three decades, was cited by Encyclopaedia Britannica in 1991, three years after Richard Newby challenged Britannica's editors. See p. 604.]

Alexander M. Bickel. Correspondence. The New Republic. May 7,1966. #18

Bickel's response to a TNR letter. I cannot be absolutely certain that Sacco was innocent. I say only that aside from the ballistics tests, there is no evidence of guilt that is even persuasive, and that the ballistics tests—all of them, on both sides—are not conclusive. [37]

David Felix. Correspondence. The New Republic. June 4,1966.
#19

[Ed. Now Felix responds to Bickel.]

Alexander M. Bickel, the reviewer of my book, ... made no effort to evaluate Protest; he is trying to pound it to death under leaden legal mysteries. The New Republic was closely associated with the Sacco-Vanzetti defense. The tone of the review makes one feel that the magazine is straining to safeguard its ideological investment in the Sacco-Vanzetti legend—at whatever violence to its normal canons of fairness... .

The reviewer is continuing a deceptive legal game when he uses the Frankfurter and Morgan books as authoritative sources. In Protest I illustrated how Felix Frankfurter marshaled his arguments to win his case. One example is his discussion of Judge Thayer's jury charge. Refusing to quote the charge at any length, he simply repeated the words of a defense brief. The brief itself had altered the sense of the charge by tearing part of one sentence out of context and introducing it in a misleading way. This is typical of the Frankfurter book throughout. [37]

Professor Edmund M. Morgan, a Harvard Law School colleague of Frankfurter, was another Sacco-Vanzetti legal partisan, no more interested in objectives than was Frankfurter. Yet his book made damaging admissions about the grave weaknesses in the defense case which the reviewer [Bickel] has carefully ignored. [37]

Herbert B. Ehrmann. The Case That Will Not Die: Commonwealth vs. Sacco and Vanzetti. 1969

THE BUICK. Paul McDonald, who used to deliver milk to the [Coacci] house, did not recognize any of the operative's photos. He had never seen a Buick car. [70] [Ed. Italics by Ehrmann. Operative is Pinkerton detective Henry Hellyer.]

Chapter 15: The Migratory Revolver. The mere possession of the Harrington and Richardson revolver was not evidence that Vanzetti was present at the scene. The bullets extracted from the bodies of the dead men were the steel-jacketed type fired from automatic pistols, not the lead slugs discharged through revolvers. The exploded shells strewn in Pearl Street had been ejected by automatics, not revolvers. The bullets and shells were all of .32 caliber, whereas Vanzetti's revolver was .38 caliber. Something more was needed to turn the revolver into evidence against Vanzetti. [223]

In his opening, Mr. Williams seemed to recognize the fact that Vanzetti's revolver was not proof that he was involved in the South Braintree affair. As the trial started, he indicated that the prosecution intended to rely solely on the eyewitness identification previously discussed in Chapter 12. Mr. Williams's only reference to Vanzetti's revolver was that "Vanzetti [when arrested] had on him a loaded .38 Harrington and Richardson revolver. There were no extra cartridges for the revolver found on Vanzetti." [223]

Before the trial was over, however, the prosecution had evolved a theory which, if sound, would have made Vanzetti's revolver direct and irrefutable proof of complicity in the crime. When Berardelli's body was picked up, no weapon was found in his hand or pocket. It was known that at times he had carried a Harrington and Richardson revolver, probably of .38 caliber. Vanzetti's gun was also a .38 Harrington and Richardson revolver. This apparent coincidence probably suggested a new and startling hypothesis, namely, that Vanzetti's revolver was actually the Berardelli weapon and had been stolen from him by his murderer as he lay dying on the ground. [223]

Vanzetti's revolver had been in the prosecution's possession for fourteen months. It therefore comes as something of a shock to learn that the district attorney did not evolve this idea until the trial was well along. This strange tardiness would be understandable if it were based on new evidence suddenly discovered during the trial. There was no new evidence. Apparently someone for the Commonwealth thought up the idea during the trial and thereafter the prosecution scrounged around for evidence to support it. This process of seeking to confirm a preconception has by now become familiar. [223]

The prosecution never produced the serial number of the gun alleged to [223] have been carried by Berardelli, although the guard was a special policeman of the town of Braintree, ...

There is nothing intrinsically implausible about the theory that the gunman who killed Berardelli might have robbed him of his revolver. This would have been a sensible precaution. (It seems irrational, however, to suppose that one of the murderers would carry around in his pocket for weeks telltale evidence of his guilt. This would have been an especially mad act on Vanzetti's part, because he was even then momentarily fearing apprehension by the police as an anarchist.)

The chief difficulty with the government's hypothesis is that there was no credible evidence to support it—either that any bandit took Berardelli's weapon from him, or that the guard was carrying his gun at the time of the robbery, or that Vanzetti's revolver was Berardelli's. [224] [Ed. Ehrmann italicized last 29 words.]

Rexford Slater came down from Dexter, Maine, to testify that Exhiibit 27 [Vanzetti's H & R revolver] had belonged to his mother-in-law, Mrs. Mogridge, about three and a half years earlier. She had sold it to him when they both lived in Norwood, Massachusetts, for four dollars. He later sold it to Ricardo Orciani. [245]

Eldridge Atwater also came down from Dexter, Maine, to testify that he [245] had fired the gun when it belonged to his father-in-law, Mr. Mogridge. The last time he had seen the revolver it was in the possession of Mrs. Mogridge, following the death of her husband. [246]

The defense did not produce Orciani to confirm Falzini's statement that he had bought the revolver from him. . . . Orciani had been around the courthouse for some time and had been Mr. Moore's chauffeur. . . . At any rate, Orciani did not take the stand, and like Boda, disappeared from the view of the authorities. [246]

Therefore, the most troubling question that the Sacco-Vanzetti case asks of us is not what kind of men the accused were. This question . . . may help to clear the names of the dead men, as Vanzetti requested. [545]
[Ed. Ehrmann aided Frankfurter in the 1921 Cleveland Crime Survey.]

Francis Russell. Tragedy in Dedham: The Story of the Sacco-Vanzetti Case. 50th Anniversary Edition 1971

According to the dogma, Sacco and Vanzetti were two philosophical anarchists done to death for their political beliefs by fearful and corrupt "hangmen in frockcoats." Arrested in a period of wild anti-Red hysteria, they were executed for a murder that they not only did not commit, but of which they had no knowledge. The police who arrested them knew they were innocent. So did the prosecution. [Foreword, xi]
[Here, Russell recites the dogma of the defendants' innocence.]

R. S. Calese. "John Nicholas Beffel, Radical Journalist: 1887-1973."
Industrial Worker (Oct. 1973).

By 1915 he [Beffel] had stopped working for the "bourgeois" press and begun reporting for the New York Call, the official paper of the Socialist Party. He also reported for the Federated Press, the radical counterpart of the AP and UPI, ... All his life he was a major publicity man for the non-Communist Left—the socialists, anarchists, and "Wobblies".

The first case he covered along these lines was the well-known Everett Massacre November 5th, 1916, ... The defense attorney was Fred H. Moore, who later defended Sacco and Vanzetti and was Beffel's roommate when Beffel covered the [Dedham] trial... .

Probably John would want his epitaph to read: "Defender of Sacco and Vanzetti". Certainly he was as loyal to their memory as anyone, including even Aldino Felicani, and it was his own article "Eels and the Electric Chair" in that same New Republic ... which first "alerted liberal thinkers in general" to that famous case.

John covered the case in situ [Dedham] for the Federated Press, ... He also handled their publicity, ... Interestingly, it was John who was highly instrumental in getting the transcript of the trial republished by Paul Appel, ...

[Ed. Beffel is mentioned in Appel's PUBLISHER'S ACKNOWLEDGEMENTS, I: ix.]

Beffel was also a close friend and comrade of William D. Haywood, Ralph Chaplin, and Eugene Victor Debs. (Chaplin wrote the radical song "Solidarity Forever" and both Debs and Haywood were founders of the IWW.)

John was a close friend and associate of Carlo Tresca, ... [5]
[Robert Calese, Emeritus Librarian, New York Public Library System.]
[Ed. Beffel's obituary in the NY Times, Feb. 26, 1973, states: "Beffel was one of the first editors of The New Masses, a radical literary and political magazine. He worked closely with Communist party members as allies in the radical movement." See Beffel's fund-raising letter of 11 May 1921 bearing a 3-line heading: SACCO-VANZETTI DEFENSE COMMITTEE; Aldino Felicani, Treasurer; 32-34 Battery Street, Boston, Mass. Beffel urges: "[S]end the defense at least $10 at once."

42. THIRD GENERATION CRITICS

Roberta S. Feuerlicht. <u>Justice Crucified: the story of Sacco and Vanzetti</u>. 1977

I don't believe the story of Sacco and Vanzetti begins in 1920, the year of the major raids and the year they were arrested.... . I believe that their story begins in 1620, with the coming of the Pilgrims or, to be more precise, in 1630, when the great Puritan migration to Massachusetts really began; that the story of Sacco and Vanzetti is the story of every unwanted immigrant and dissenter in American history. [Foreword, ix]

All [Boda, Orciani, Sacco, Vanzetti] were headed for Simon Johnson's garage to pick up Boda's Overland so it could be used to gather the incriminating literature. As Sacco explained at the trial, "The best way to take by automobile, could run more fast, could get more fast, could hide more fast." [152]

Many persons, willingly or unwillingly, contributed to the fate of Sacco and Vanzetti; their own contribution was to carry [153] weapons. **If they had not been armed**, there would have been no question of a gun taken from a dying guard, of whose bullet killed him, of contradicting the claim they had gone to Mexico because they were pacifists. [154]

Bridgewater crime. Katzmann knew Vanzetti had an excellent alibi for his whereabouts on the day of the Bridgewater crime, but he also knew the alibi had a fatal flaw: Vanzetti's witnesses were Italian. [160] He [Vanzetti] had an exceptionally strong alibi for the morning of December 24, and many witnesses to confirm it. [170]

The record [trial transcript] has convinced ... two of the outstanding legal scholars of the period, Supreme Court Justice Louis Brandeis and Professor Felix Frankfurter, that they were innocent. [203]

Vanzetti had not testified at the Plymouth trial for fear his views would be held against him; in the end his silence was held against him.... . Vanzetti testified first [at the Dedham trial]. His alibi for April 15 was so feeble it had to be true; any story invented for or by him would have been more convincing. [223] He was a speaker, writer, and thinker of limited ability and unlimited prolixity: ... [340]

In addition to the three questions asked by Lowell and Fuller, at least one other should be considered: Who killed Sacco and Vanzetti? There are such **obvious villains** as Thayer, Katzmann, Chief Stewart, and the justices of the supreme judicial court, but the list of those who contributed to the crime [of judicial murder] ... is painfully long. It includes various parties to the prosecution, those who tampered with the evidence, witnesses who lied, ... [430]

Justice Louis Brandeis, who believed in their innocence, would not grant Sacco and Vanzetti a stay of execution so the Supreme Court could hear their case. In the end, the fate of Sacco and Vanzetti was left to two Brahmins. Either Lowell or Holmes might have saved them, but Lowell chose to prove them guilty beyond the prosecution's doubt, and Holmes chose to dismiss those who begged for justice as ignorant of the law. Not only did the Puritan legacy kill Sacco and Vanzetti, but their ultimate executioners [Lowell and Holmes] were its two most prominent legatees. [431]

[Feuerlicht published Oliver Wendell Holmes, Gandhi, America's Reign of Terror, Joe McCarthy and McCarthyism, and The Fate of the Jews.]

Katherine Anne Porter. The Never-Ending Wrong. 1977

They were put to death in the electric chair at Charlestown Prison at midnight on the 23rd of August, 1927, a desolate dark midnight, ... I was one of the many hundreds who stood in anxious vigil watching the light in the prison tower, ... it was a moment of strange heartbreak. [8]

My group [in the Sacco-Vanzetti demonstration at Boston] was headed by Rosa Baron, a dry, fanatical little woman ... who talked an almost impenetrable jargon of [communist] party dogma. [17] [Ed. See Baron, NY Times, 8/11/27/2.]

I still hoped the lives of Sacco and Vanzetti might be saved and that they would be granted another trial. "Saved," she said, ringing a change on her favorite answer to po-[18]litical illiteracy, "who wants them saved? What earthly good would they do for us alive?"

I was another of those bourgeois liberals who got in the way of serious business, yet we were needed, by the thousands if possible, for this agitation must be made to appear to be a spontaneous uprising of the American people, ...

Lenin ... had only harsh words for those "weak sisters" who flew off the "locomotive of history" every time it rounded a sharp curve. [19]

I flew off Lenin's locomotive and his vision of history in a wide arc in Boston, Massachusetts, on August 21, 1927, ...[20]

AFTERWORD

[T]he [1969] book by Herbert B. Ehrmann, ... I feel, tells the full story of the case.

Also, I have read since I finished my story "The Never-Ending Wrong," the article by Francis Russell in the National Review, page 887 of August 17, 1973, ...

It is proven by testimony that he [Vanzetti] was innocent of murder. He was selling eels on that day, for Christmas. [58]

My point is this: Sacco was guilty if you like; some minor points make it reasonable, though barely reasonable, to believe it. [59]
[Porter was an American writer of fiction.]

Eric Foner. "Sacco and Vanzetti: The Men and the Symbols." The Nation. August 20, 1977.

"The evidence against Vanzetti was absurdly thin.... The defense produced thirteen witnesses, all Italian, to testify that Vanzetti had been selling fish on the day of the [South Braintree] crime." [136]
[Foner is DeWitt Clinton Professor of History, Columbia University; member of the Editorial Advisory Board, American National Biography; Advisory Editor, Encyclopedia Americana.]

Proclamation by Governor Michael S. Dukakis. August 23, 1977.

I, Michael S. Dukakis, Governor of the Commonwealth of Massachusetts, ... do hereby proclaim Tuesday, August 23, 1977, "NICOLA SACCO AND BARTOLOMEO VANZETTI MEMORIAL DAY"; and declare further, that any stigma and disgrace should be forever removed from the names of Nicola Sacco and Bartolomeo Vanzetti, ... [Proclamation is in Kaiser's Postmortem, Introduction, pp. 3-4, and in the Bentley edition of Boston, pp. 797-799.]
[Ed. See Felix on Brogan's "atonement": TLS, 5/31/1985, p. 654.]

Nunzio Pernicone. "Introductory Remarks." <u>Sacco-Vanzetti:</u> <u>Developments and Reconsiderations—1979.</u>

[M]any liberal historians who have studied the case, while arguing vehemently that these men were innocent and unfairly tried, are disturbed—almost embarrassed—by the fact that Sacco and Vanzetti were anarchists. They don't know what to do with this problem. Consequently, they call them "philosophical anarchists," a term in the liberal lexicon which is a euphemism for harmless utopians whom nobody need take seriously. What our speakers today [Oct. 27] will prove beyond any doubt is that these men were not philosophical anarchists; they were genuine, militant revolutionaries. [60] [Pernicone, Assistant Professor of history at the Univ. of Illinois, presented a conference paper at the Boston Public Library when it accepted Felicani's Collection of Sacco-Vanzetti materials. He is now Professor of History, Drexel University.]

Robert D'Attilio, "<u>La Salute 'e in Voi</u>: the Anarchist Dimension." <u>Developments</u> and <u>Reconsiderations—1979.</u>

Anarchist Literature. (Galleani's estimate of <u>Cronaca</u>'s circulation is borne out by its subscription list which had also fallen into the hands of the Department of Justice. It has about 3,200 names. Two addresses show that it dates from before May 1917: Ferdinando Sacco [later Nicola], 76 Hayward Street, Milford, and Bartolomeo Vanzetti, Suosso's Lane, Plymouth). While not an insignificant movement, <u>Cronaca Sovversiva</u> was clearly not of the size and scope of the IWW. Why, then, did this band of some five thousand beggars demand so much attention from the authorities? [81]

The answer to this question is <u>La Salute 'e in Voi</u> (Health is within you), a pamphlet published by <u>Cronaca Sovversiva</u>. At first, in 1906, it was quietly listed on the back page among the many other titles of the Library of the Social Studies Group. Later it would be more prominently displayed with the terse and somewhat recondite description, "an indispensable pamphlet for those comrades who love self-instruction." <u>La Salute 'e in Voi</u>, at 25¢ the most expensive pamphlet printed by <u>Cronaca Sovversiva</u>, was a manual for making bombs and would become the great unmentioned fact of the Sacco-

Vanzetti case, unmentioned by the two adversaries who knew of it, the anarchists and the authorities.

The tall, oblong pamphlet of forty-eight pages, written in a very clear, elementary Italian, refers to certain materials in Italian terms, with costs in Italian lire. This makes it likely that it is, or was derived from, the explosives manual written by Ettore Molinari, fervent anarchist, renowned chemist (trained in Switzerland and Germany, later Professor of Chemistry at the Politecnico in Milano), and a friend of Luigi Galleani. [81] [Authorities suspected] that Carlo Valdinoci, a former editorial associate of Galleani on Cronaca Sovversiva, a comrade of Sacco and Vanzetti, who had been with them in Mexico, was the man killed at Palmer's house. . . . [[I]t [is] a fair assumption that he was the man involved. [84]

On April 25 anarchist comrades in the Boston area—Sacco, Vanzetti and his new friend, Aldino Felicani, among them—met at the hall of Il Gruppo Autonomo di East Boston in Maverick Square to rally help for **Salsedo and Elia**... . [T]hey sent Vanzetti to New York City to find out what was happening. Vanzetti went to see Carlo Tresca, good friend of Aldino Felicani and editor of the anarchist journal, Il Martello (The Hammer)... . Tresca did ... urge Vanzetti ... to get rid of any radical literature...in their possession; more raids were anticipated, and it was best to be cautious in these dangerous times. [85]

Riccardo Orciani—A friend of Sacco's from Milford... . His name appeared in Cronaca Sovversiva both as a subscriber and a donor. [86].

The police chief, Michael Stewart, who set the trap [which closed on May 5] and first questioned Sacco and Vanzetti, had been the one who had arrested Feruccio Coacci in the anti-Cronaca Sovversiva drive of 1918. [86]

In a search of Vanzetti's room after his arrest, the police found two unopened registered letters of Carlo Tresca, sent from New York City the day after Salsedo's death. [86]

... [T]he explosion [on Wall Street] has never been clearly proven to be a bombing; ... no substantial evidence was ever produced publicly by any authorities to indicate why the so-called Galleani "gang" was suspected. [87]

[D'Attilio, Avrich wrote in The New Republic, is "perhaps the leading authority of the case." For another opinion on the Wall Street explosion, see Avrich, Sacco and Vanzetti: The Anarchist Background, 205-207, 245. See p. 134 in Newby's 2007 book.]

Nunzio Pernicone. "Carlo Tresca and the Sacco-Vanzetti Case."
The Journal of American History (December 1979).

[Ed. See Pernicone's revisionists—Montgomery, Grossman, Russell,
Felix—in footnote #3, p. 535, in the December article.]

The belief that racial bigotry and political intolerance sealed the
fate of Sacco and Vanzetti has been shared by most students of the case
since 1927, when Felix Frankfurter wrote his brilliant analysis of the
trial and appeals. For more than thirty years, in fact, the **liberal** or pro-
Sacco-and-Vanzetti **interpretation went unchallenged.** [535]

[T]raditionalists ... reject the findings of the revisionist school, ...
[536]

Russell attributed maximum importance to Tresca's alleged
statement [to Eastman] because, like Eastman, he believed the ebullient
Italian [Tresca] to have been the highest authority on the anarchist
movement in general and the Sacco-Vanzetti case in particular. [537]

The only feature of the Eastman-Russell portrait of Tresca that
bears a perfect resemblance to reality is that of Tresca as the man to
whom all anarchists (Galleanisti included) went for help whenever they
were in trouble with the authorities. Tresca was the great fixer of the
Italian radical movement, the man who had the best connections with
lawyers, politicians, and other influential Americans. [540]

To argue that Tresca could not have known the truth about Sacco
and Vanzetti is just as arbitrary and erroneous as to insist that he had to
know the [541] innermost secrets of the case. [542]

[Roger] Baldwin, ... revealed that, . . [Fred] Moore told him and
Elizabeth Glendower Evans that he suspected the reliability of Sacco's
alibi witnesses. [544]

Pernicone's Footnote. Roger Baldwin interview by Pernicone,
June 6, 1973 (conducted together with Robert D'Attilio). One key
member of the defense committee, Gardner Jackson, accused Roger
Baldwin of having been one of the first persons to spread doubts about
Sacco's innocence in the 1920s. [544]

Although documentation is scarce, there no longer can be any
doubt that Tresca actually made the statements attributed to him by
Eastman, Thomas, Roche, and perhaps a few others. [Ed. Footnote 46
asks for documentation that Tresca made allegation to Levine and
Rorty.] [545]

This analysis of Tresca and the Sacco-Vanzetti case must ... abandon the enticing realm of hypothesis for the more prosaic confines of empirical fact... . [A]ll the historian can say for certain is that on several occasions between 1941 and 1943, ... Tresca declared that Sacco was really guilty of the crime for which he and an innocent Vanzetti had been condemned.... . [547]

Thus, for revisionists to go on building a capital case against Sacco on the basis of such evidence would constitute a serious **misuse of the historian's craft**, and would lend credence to charges that they are the architects of a reconviction process intended to destroy the legend of Sacco and Vanzetti. [547]

[Pernicone, Professor of History, Drexel University, calls himself a Traditionalist.]

Ronald Steel. Walter Lippmann and the American Century. 1980
Why Lippmann Shifted His Editorial Opinion

Naturally it was assumed that the [New York] World, having proclaimed the bias of the judge and the need for a new trial, would condemn the Lowell report. It did not. Writing the lead editorial himself, Lippmann described the report as marked by "fairness, consideration, shrewdness and coolness," and declared that the case against Sacco and Vanzetti had been "plausibly and comprehensively stated." Since there were no grounds for a new trial, the only thing left, he concluded, was for the governor to commute the sentence to life imprisonment.

[Note #16 on p. 615 cites NYW 8/8/27.] [229]

Lippmann's logic may have been impeccable. But when Felix Frankfurter read his endorsement of the Lowell report, he exploded. Having managed to secure one of the three existing copies of the report, he took the first train to New York and marched into Lippmann's office with the offending document in hand. Together they went over the report point by point, with Frankfurter demonstrating that the Lowell committee could not possibly have read the trial testimony. The World must condemn the report. At first Lippmann resisted, arguing that the governor had committed himself to the report and that the only hope for saving the men lay in an appeal for mercy. Finally, however, he backed down under the combined weight of Frankfurter's aggressiveness, the evidence, and the misgivings of his own editorial team. Four days after endorsing the Lowell report, the <u>World</u> reversed itself. "Because the whole testimony before the committee was not public," Lippman wrote, "the chain of reasoning which led to the committee's conclusion was not perfectly evident ... multitudes of open-minded men remain unconvinced." Without disputing the integrity of the committee, Lippmann demanded that it show why the judge's prejudice should not require a new trial. [Note #17 on p. 615 cites <u>NYW</u> 8/12/27.] [229]

Steel quotes from Lippmann's post-execution letter to Judge Learned Hand.

You know that I was never convinced that they were innocent. [233]
[Steel, Professor of International Relations at the University of Southern California, University Park Campus, Los Angeles.]

Kenneth S. Lynn, "Versions of Walter Lippmann." <u>Commentary</u> (October 1980).
Summary.

Lippmann tried to be an independent writer on the Sacco-Vanzetti case in 1927. He would find facts without help from the Frankfurter-Broun duo. (Lynn calls Frankfurter and Heywood, the "wolfpack" leaders of liberal persuasion.) Liberals made a personal attack on members of Fuller's advisory committee after the committee recommended no change in the Dedham jury verdict. Lippmann judged this committee to be fair and considerate. Lippmann was brave. Lippmann disagreed with the "liberal intelligentsia" argument which deemed Sacco and Vanzetti as harmless as Jesus Christ. [69]

Steel lags behind in Sacco-Vanzetti scholarship. Lynn states consensus No. 1: A new trial for Sacco and Vanzetti was justified. Lynn states consensus No. 2: Sacco and Vanzetti were executed because they were guilty. Lynn tacks on the academic "probably" to both #1 and #2.

Lynn says Lippmann's 1927 opinions are "measured." So Lippmann, in 1980, rates higher on objective scale than Frankfurter and Broun. The 1927 writings on Sacco and Vanzetti by Frankfurter and

Broun rate lower than Lippmann's because they are not free of "passionate intensities." Lynn prefers Lippmann to Frankfurter. [69] [Lynn, Emeritus Professor of English, Harvard University, is on the editorial board of The American Spectator.]

Bruce Allen Murphy. The Brandeis/Frankfurter Connection. 1982

... [T]he Massachusetts State Police had wiretapped the headquarters of the Citizens' National Committee, located in the Hotel Bellevue in Boston, Massachusetts, as well as Frankfurter's cottage at Duxbury, Massachusetts. [80]

The recently discovered wiretap transcripts reveal that Felix Frankfurter performed one last service for the justice [Brandeis] in this case. In a telephone conversation with Judge Julian Mack, the professor mentioned that Brandeis was "being hammered widely and getting some very abusive letters" because of his announced decision to withdraw from the consideration of the case.

To counteract this criticism, Frankfurter asked that Mack have an editor for The New Republic "put a paragraph in this week's N.R. that L.D.B.'s refusal to act for [the] defense is a striking rebuke to ... [Judge] Thayer, and point out that it would be a grave wrong for him to have acted." Frankfurter then suggested that this comparison of Brandeis's "purity" with the alleged prejudicial behavior of the trial judge in the case would "please L.D.B. and probably educate a little those that need educating." [81]

[Ed. Murphy's Note #25 on p. 384 refers to transcript of wiretap, Sept. 6, 1927.]

It is now apparent that Mack wasted no time in carrying out the instructions to the letter. In the following issue of The New Republic, this item defending Brandeis appeared in the editorial section. [81]

Murphy quotes from editorial in TNR, September 14, 1927, p. 83.

Bitter criticism of Justice Brandeis for refusing to act in the Sacco-Vanzetti case has been heard from many of the friends of the condemned. It is said that he should have laid aside the scruples arising from the fact that he had intimate personal relations with some of those interested in the defense, that, in a case of this significance, legal niceties were of less importance than anything which might have helped to avert the tragedy of the execution. Nobody can deny that possibly Sacco and Vanzetti had to suffer because Justice Brandeis possessed the same kind of scruple which Judge Thayer should have had, and did not, when he insisted on passing on the question of his own prejudice [Motion 8 built from affidavits by Lois Rantoul and others].... . Would it not be more to the point for those who are shocked and outraged by the conduct of the case in Massachusetts to insist that no judge, whatever he may consider the importance of a cause, should sit in a case where his own prejudice may be involved, and to cite Justice Brandeis' action as a strengthening of this principle? [81][Ellipsis by editor.]

[Murphy, Fred Morgan Kirby Professor of Civil Rights, Department of Government and Law, Lafayette College.]

William Young and David E. Kaiser. Postmortem: New Evidence in the Case of Sacco and Vanzetti. 1985

[Young died in 1980]. By this time [October 1926] interest in the case was reaching unprecedented heights. Communists and other left-wing groups made it a cause celebre in Europe and all over the world, and American liberals, whose favorite journals, the Nation and the New Republic, had always followed the case with interest, began to regard the two men's innocence as an article of faith. [5]

Thus Walter Lippmann, then a New York World editorial writer, had initially enraged many liberal friends, including Frankfurter, by refusing to blast the Lowell Committee's report. One reason, his letters now show, was that he suspected Sacco's involvement. [6]

Most of these witnesses saw the car around the South Braintree railroad crossing. They included Roy Gould, a salesman, who took a bullet through his overcoat from the man next to the driver and gave his story to the police but was never called. Later he swore an affidavit that the man who fired at him at a distance of ten feet was definitely not Sacco. A glassblower, Frank Burke, testified that a bandit moved from the back seat to the front seat as the car approached the crossing, leaned out, pointed a revolver at Burke from a distance of a few feet, and yelled, "Get out of my way, you son of a B," in English. He also gave a good description of another bandit in the back of the car. He had seen Sacco, Vanzetti, and Orciani at Brockton, where he had once been associated with the police, immediately after their arrest. He said the defendants were not the men he had seen. [62]

Both Sacco and Vanzetti presented substantial alibis for 15 April...although a notable proportion of Sacco's alibi witnesses were fellow anarchists whose motives are inevitably suspect. [79]

[T]he carpenter Ricci and the grocer Affe were both subscribers to the Cronaca Sovversiva and therefore presumably anarchists. Ricci had lived in Somerville, Massachusetts, at the same address as Carlo Vandinocci [sic], thought by some to have blown himself up in the 2 June 1919 bombing of A. Mitchell Palmer's house. Authorities also identified John Williams as a "prominent I.W.W. and socialist speaker." [80] [Kaiser's Note #7 on p. 173 is to FBI file.]

Hayes was recalled [to the witness stand] and told Katzmann that he had sat on the left-hand side of the car. The story seems too good to be true, and apparently it was. According to Upton Sinclair, Moore subsequently told him that Hayes's story was a fabrication. An undated note in Moore's pretrial papers refers to Hayes as "a Communist who doesn't believe Sacco is guilty," and a desperate Fred Moore apparently yielded to temptation in an effort to strengthen his case. [83] [See Notes #20 and #21 on p. 173.]

That Moore and the defense committee felt it necessary to bolster Sacco's alibi with Hayes, and conceivably with other perjured witnesses as well, does not mean that the essence of his story was not true. [83]

Despite some holes and contradictions in the prosecution's argument, the juryman John Dever [Dever manuscript, BPL] was persuaded that Vanzetti's gun had been taken from Berardelli, which suggests that the rest of the jury was similarly convinced. But documents newly released from the state police files show that Vanzetti's revolver was very definitely not Berardelli's... . [T]hey show that the prosecution sent Vanzetti to the electric chair on evidence they knew to be false. [85]

... [T]he conclusion [is] that all these [6 murder]bullets were fired from the same weapon—and that bullet III, ... could not have been fired from a different gun. [96]

... [A]ll the shots that struck the two men were fired by one bandit, ... [104]

New documentation provides substantial confirmation for the theory that bullet III and shell W were not genuine exhibits but were substituted by the prosecution. Available evidence indicates that the four bullets originally taken from Berardelli's body—as well as the two taken from Parmenter's—were actually fired from **the same weapon** and that only three rather than four shells were originally found on the ground near Berardelli's body. The minutes of the trial show how District Attorney Williams took careful precautions to make sure that the substitution of a new bullet III was not discovered. There is no exact proof, and there almost certainly never can be, of exactly how, when, and by whom a switch was made, ... [106] [See Note #5 on p. 178.]

Kaiser cites Dr. Magrath's testimony to the grand jury—9/10/1920.

Q. In your opinion were those bullets all fired by the same gun? A. I have an opinion that they all may have been fired by the same gun, but I have no proof. [107]

Magrath's testimony, while inconclusive, tends to indicate that the original Berardelli bullets did not include one with a left twist and that a switch subsequently took place. [108]

When did **the switch** take place? It must have taken place between September 1920 and February of 1921.... . The switch could have been perpetrated either by Captain Proctor or by Charles Van Amburgh, a second expert whom the prosecution apparently brought into the case because it was dissatisfied with Proctor's opinion about the bullets, or by Chief Stewart and State Police Officer Albert Brouillard, the officers who actually investigated the case. [112]

In the authors' opinion, the switch was probably perpetrated by Stewart and Brouillard sometime before Van Amburgh's examination in December 1920. The two men presumably test-fired Sacco's gun, substituted the resulting bullet for the original bullet III [in custody of the Commonwealth], and added the resulting shell to the three original shells at that time. [113]

More than sixty years after the crime, it seems clear that the substitution of bullet III cannot physically be proven... . The examination [of the 4 Berardelli bullets] was conducted by Professor Regis Pelloux of the M.I.T. Metallurgy Department in his laboratory on 2 August 1982 in the presence of Lieutenant John McGuinness of the ballistics laboratory of the Department of Public Safety. Unfortunately, microscopic enlargements of the bullets were not conclusive [on the question whether "the three scratches on bullet 3 had indeed been made by a different instrument."] [119]

From a strange source ... comes evidence that such tampering with firearms evidence would hardly have been unique in contemporary Massachusetts. In 1946 the Boston University Law Review published "Common Sources of Error in the Examination and Interpretation of Ballistics Evidence" by none other than Charles Van Amburgh himself, who had died shortly before the publication of the article. [119]

The Sacco-Vanzetti case had made Van [119] Amburgh's career... . Commenting on his long experience in 1946, Van Amburgh discussed problems in the proper handling and marking of exhibits [pp. 240-241 in B.U.L.R].

Kaiser quotes from Van Amburgh's B.U.L.R article on "Handling Exhibits."

One old Medical Examiner refused to surrender a bullet for laboratory examination because thirty years before in the Eastman-Grogan case at Cambridge, Massachusetts, a bullet was stolen during a court proceeding in which he was a witness... . It appears that the theft, substitution, or defacement of exhibits was and is a sharp trick resorted to at times [emphasis added]. [122]
[Ed. End of Kaiser's quote from B.U.L.R. Kaiser italicized the 20 words underlined here.]

Two other neighbors ... did say that they had seen Boda driving a Buick. One was the fourteen-year-old Napoleon Enscher [sic], whose testimony at the Bridgewater trial was most unconvincing. The other neighbor was Paul MacDonald, a seventeen-year-old boy who delivered milk to Boda and the Coaccis. Interviewed by Defense Attorney Callahan on 28 December 1920, MacDonald remembered his Italian customers warmly. He confirmed that he had never seen any car but the Overland at Puffer's Place but maintained very definitely that on two occasions, which he could not date precisely, he had also seen Boda driving a Buick. [135]

In 1928, while imprisoned on the island of Lipari, Boda spoke at length to Edward Houlton [sic] James, a case aficionado who had carefully read the defense papers relating to him. Boda bluntly denied Enscher's and MacDonald's statements, saying that he had never driven any car but his own Overland. [135]

The authors of this book have attempted to avoid psychological speculation and base their conclusions on concrete evidence to the maximum extent possible, ... It is impossible to know what went on inside the minds of Stewart, Brouillard, Katzmann, and Williams, but evidence leaves room for some hypotheses regarding their motives. [158]

Williams does not seem to have taken long to realize that something was rotten in the prosecution's case. One of his loose-leaf notebooks, prepared in the first months of 1921, contains a brief outline of the Bridgewater and Braintree cases. The outline, which may have been prepared to help argue appeals of Vanzetti's Plymouth conviction, begins with a quick chronology of the key dates of the two crimes and a summary of the state's evidence against Vanzetti... .

> 5 Elements of Frame-up
>   a—Proctor description given to newspapers [160]
>   b—Witnesses all bear marks of coaching
>   Bowles
>   Cox
>   c—Hat matter
>   d—Cap matter
>   e—Salsedo-Elia
>   f—Johnson-rew———
>   Stewart—
>   g—Defendants State———
>   to May 5———
>   h—Police story that trap ready to spring
>   i—Bullets

Of this list, 5a presumably refers to the original descriptions of the bandits released to the newspapers, which did not fit Sacco and Vanzetti... . The notation of 5e indicates considerable prosecution knowledge of the defendants' radical connections—probably furnished by the Bureau of Investigation—and seems to indicate that the prosecution understood the real reasons for the defendants' behavior at the time of their arrest... . 5h seems to suggest that the whole story of Stewart's having asked Simon Johnson to call him if Boda ever came for his car was not true; ... [161]

Kaiser's conclusion: The case is destined to remain controversial, but the truth should not be in doubt. The overwhelming probability is that a substitution of bullets did take place and that Sacco and Vanzetti were completely innocent of the South Braintree murders. [164]

Kaiser's Note #51: Moore was particularly interested in tentative confessions by Jimmy Mede and Frank Silva, two East Boston men, that they had planned the Bridgewater holdup attempt and that Silva had committed it with "Doggy" Bruno, "Guinea" Oates, and Joe Sammarco. In 1922 Moore went to the Atlanta Federal Penitentiary to try to secure an admittedly false confession from Silva, then serving time under the name of Paul Martini. He failed, but in 1928 Silva sold an article to <u>Outlook</u> confessing his role. More than thirty years later Joe Sammarco, who had spent more than thirty years in Charlestown State Prison for killing a policeman ... told Francis Russell that there was not a word of truth to this story and, according to John Conrad, passed a lie detector test on this point. [183]

[Kaiser, once in the history department at Carnegie-Mellon University, is now Professor in the Strategy and Policy Department of the Naval War College. In 2000 he published <u>American Tragedy: Kennedy, Johnson, and the Origins of the</u> <u>Vietnam War.</u>]

Hugh Brogan. "New convictions." <u>Times Literary Supplement.</u>
December 27, 1985.

<u>Postmortem</u> carries conviction not only because of the cogency of its reasoning and the thoroughness of its research, but because of its plain and economical style... . Kaiser ... takes ample note of the writings of others, particularly Herbert Ehrmann, who over the year did more than any other writer to establish a presumption of Sacco's and Vanzetti's innocence... . From now on it will be unnecessary for the friends of Sacco and Vanzetti to be defensive. The established likelihoods are now overwhelmingly on their side. The onus of proof is once more on their enemies' shoulders, and a heavy burden they will find it. Perhaps, rather than struggle with it, they will at last give up the bad job, and honourably admit defeat. [1474]

[Brogan, Chair of History Dept., Univ. of Essex, exchanged letters on this <u>TLS</u> review with the editor. See Felix's letter to <u>TLS</u> ("The Sacco-Vanzetti Case") 2/21/1986, p. 191. And see Kebabian's letter, <u>TLS</u>: 5/31/1985, p. 607.] [See research topic #36.]

Francis Russell. <u>Sacco and Vanzetti: The Case Resolved.</u> 1986

Summary.

In a letter to Carlo Tresca, convicted murderer Vanzetti told Tresca that his anarchist paper <u>Il Martello</u> sent a militant cry that pierced his Charlestown prison wall. Convicted murderer Sacco, jailed at Dedham (October 1921), told Tresca he simply devoured <u>Il Martello</u>, whose English title is The Hammer. Later, this Sacco letter was published in <u>Il Martello</u>. [25-26]

Maugre that, Tresca, defender of the murderers, declared Sacco guilty before he was gunned down in 1943. Curious, Russell quizzed James Rorty, who wrote a favorable review of Montgomery's 1960 book in <u>The New Leader</u>. Following Rorty's advice, Russell interviewed Max Eastman at Martha's Vineyard. There Eastman told Russell how, when he begged for the truth, Tresca blurted out to him: "Sacco was guilty but Vanzetti was innocent." [27]

When <u>The Nation</u> and <u>The New Republic</u> would not publish Eastman's revelation about Tresca, it was published on October 21, 1961, in <u>National Review</u>, one conservative publication the former communist, Eastman, had studiously avoided. [27]

Russell calls this interview "a turning point." Now he knew he would have to revise his position on Sacco and Vanzetti. This item on p. 27 and pp. 32-42 constitutes his apologia.

Russell says Isaac Don Levine, Norman Thomas, and John P. Roche also heard Tresca speak of Sacco's guilt. Roche, in his 1972 letter to Russell, confirmed that he heard Tresca—in the home of Norman Thomas—declare Sacco guilty and Vanzetti innocent. Roche said nobody in the social group argued with Tresca. [28-29] (Is this the very John P. Roche who ghosted speeches for Adlai Stevenson, John F. Kennedy, and Lyndon Johnson? Russell does not say.)

Napoleon Ensher testified at Vanzetti's Plymouth trial that Mike Boda drove a Buick near the Coacci house (Puffer's Place) before the Braintree crime "when the roads were muddy." [Appel, VI: 143] According to Russell's reading of Moore's papers in the Boston Public Library, the Buick Ensher saw once Paul MacDonald saw twice. This was reported to defense lawyer William Callahan by MacDonald, but Callahan and Moore **did not tell anybody** what P.M., the 17-year-old milkman, had said to Callahan. [58] [See Kaiser, pp.135, 181.]

If Kropotkin was a philosophical anarchist, he declared one thousand pamphlets inferior in propaganda to one bomb. That, says Russell, is your "anarchist high priest." [68]

Defense witness Frank Burke claims he saw the bandit car approach the Rice & Hutchins factory. The Brockton glassblower Burke had been in Moore's employment before he testified, but this fact was not known by anybody. [119] Roy Gould, the itinerant peddler Burke found after the trial, signed an affidavit that created Motion 2 for a new trial. By Gould's account, the gunman who fired at him missed his body but hit and penetrated his overcoat. [119]

Burke and Gould were IWW cronies. It seems "a curious coincidence" to Russell that both old friends would witness the crime on Pearl Street at 3:05 P. M., each oblivious of the other. Later, a female reader of Russell's book told Russell by telephone that Gould, her uncle, "was a rogue." The overcoat through which Gould said one Pearl-Street bullet had passed she watched Gould burn in the incinerator. [120]

Frankfurter's March 1927 article in the <u>Atlantic Monthly</u> and his subsequent 118-page book "gave the case a vast and receptive national and international audience." To William O. Douglas, liberal associate justice of the U. S. Supreme Court, Frankfurter's book "had been our bible." Prestigious Harvard University could point with pride to Felix Frankfurter, their highly respected professor of law. That's weighty. Uncritically, those purported to be among the intelligentsia, together with hundreds "in the literary and academic worlds," judged Sacco and Vanzetti innocent. [134]

Ehrmann did not accept the result of Jury and Weller's ballistics test of October 1961, which concluded that Sacco's Colt fired Bullet 3 and Shell W. [158] In an attempt to discredit the test, Ehrmann engaged Shelley Braverman, whose reputation in ballistics was disparaged by the three experts who conducted the ballistics test of 1983. Russell says Braverman had no better reputation in ballistics than Albert Hamilton. [159]

Similarly, Musmanno disparaged Jury and Weller's test. He challenged the authenticity of guns, shells, and bullets. Serial numbers on the guns proved them authentic, says Russell, who inspected "original official envelopes" holding shells and bullets, noting rusted metal clips that kept these envelopes closed. These trial exhibits were repeatedly photographed. [160]

A 3-day ballistics test of the Dedham trial exhibits at Boston in March 1983 was conducted by Anthony Paul, Marshall Robinson, and George Wilson. D'Attilio annoyed these esteemed firearms examiners with questions unrelated to ballistics. [160] Russell, given recognition by the examiners, asked if Bullet 3 and Shell W connected to Sacco. [161]

Ballistics studies by Goddard, Roche [see 159], Gunther, Jury, and Weller were validated by the 1983 test. Sacco's Colt fired Bullet 3 and Shell W. Speaking to a TV audience, Robinson noted that these repeated tests always brought the same conclusion.

Wilson said the 1983 test brought a new discovery: "Some of the cartridges found in Sacco's pocket were made on the same machine as two of those shells found at the scene of the crime." [161]

Jim McGuinness, who headed the state ballistics laboratory, told Russell that application of new knowledge and technique could now determine "by the markings" whether "bullets had been made on the same machine." This technique was hardly new but was not known by Jury and Weller in 1961. Then Wilson recited the laboratory dictum: "Each machine puts its signature on the cartridge rim, just like a gun barrel or breechblock." Wilson invited Russell to the lab. [161]

Russell visited McGuinness at his laboratory several days later.

The lab microscope, complex and monumental, impresses Russell. McGuiness unlocks a box containing the two guns of the Dedham trial and takes Dedham shells and bullets from "marked envelopes." He tumbles Sacco's 16 Peters cartridges from one envelope. From another envelope he produces the four spent shells of the crime scene, two being of Peters manufacture. McGuiness says "[t]hese six Peters cartridges [161] and the two Peters shells were made on the same machine." The microscope brings one Peters cartridge and one Peters shell together, intricate threadings of cartridge and shell wedded in perfect union on the eyepiece of the microscope. Then five more Peters cartridges (from group of six) are matched with the second Peters shell. [162]

To double check, McGuinness shows Russell that the other ten Peters cartridges found on Sacco **do not** match a Peters shell from the crime scene. Again, Russell sees the evidence in the eyepiece of the microscope. [162]

Russell calls this revelation "the end of the ballistics road." If ballistics tests from 1927 to 1983 show that Sacco's Colt fired Bullet 3 and Shell W, Sacco is further condemned in this latest revelation: having on his person six Peters cartridges that tie him to the crime scene. The 1927 hypothesis of a substitute bullet is disproved by tests of both the single Winchester shell and two Peters shells. [162]

Russell turns to Berardelli's 38 Harrington & Richardson and reviews the Dedham testimony on this gun. Did Berardelli's gun come from Fraher, as Russell stated two times? The gun, in Russell's narrative, had scorings "on the butt." That is, the original owner of the gun, Fraher, "told his brother of the scorings." Russell says: "Vanzetti's Harrington & Richardson, which I examined in 1961 and again in 1983, had such scorings." [163]

Russell surmises: Orciani stole Berardelli's H. & R. revolver on April 15, 1920, at South Braintree. [163] [See. p. 409.]

Russell does not believe the Madeiros story. He speculates that Ehrmann himself may have lost faith in his theory of the Morellis. Why would the Morellis, who lived their lives by slyness and calculation, clock 180 needless miles in two trips from Providence to Boston? By Erhmann's theory, the Buick was not seen in Braintree on the morning of April 15. And positioning the Morellis in a South Braintree speakeasy and a Boston speakeasy is another incongruity in Ehrmann's theory. Would Mike Morelli, an astute man, have driven the Buick back that evening to dump it in those woods—some two miles from the Coacci house?

The confession of Madeiros, "cunning but ill-informed," does not bear scrutiny. [167]

Russell quotes from a letter A. Lawrence Lowell wrote to a <u>TNR</u> editor in 1936:

After nine years' history [he wrote Bruce Bliven], I am perfectly satisfied with the position our Committee took in the Sacco-Vanzetti case. I have seen no reason to change my mind that the evidence proved these men guilty of the crime of which they were charged.

If I could re-live that part of my life with the knowledge that I have now, that I should suffer persecution for doing my duty as a citizen, I should nevertheless do it as I did before. [202]

[Russell's 1986 volume is dedicated to Ideale Gambera, son of Giovanni Gambera, said to be an anarchist friend of Aldino Felicani and Professor Guadagni. Russell visited Ideale in California. (Russell told editor of Ideale's stay with him in Massachusetts.) In a footnote, Russell wrote:

"Later I was to hear a tape-recording of [Giovanni] Gambera repeating in his old voice: 'Sacco was guilty! Sacco was guilty!'" (13) See pp. 11-18 in S & V: The Case Resolved.]

Charles E. Wyzanski, Jr., Senior District Judge. United States District Court. Boston, Massachusetts. Letter to Francis Russell. March 31, 1986.

This letter has no claim to parallel the exciting and valuable qualities of a communication you once received from Ideale Gambera.

I want to express my appreciation of both your article in the March 13, 1986 issue of The New York Review of Books and your just published "Sacco & Vanzetti The Case Resolved."

I myself am persuaded by your writings that Sacco was guilty. It seems to me that Vanzetti was not proven guilty either of murder, or being an accesory before the fact. If he were merely an accessory after the fact he ought not to have been convicted of a capital crime and electrocuted. Even if he were guilty of some crime, the evidence was not such as to prove guilt beyond a reasonable doubt of any crime whatsoever. But that conviction was not on that ground a violation of the U. S. Constitution, nor ground for review by The Supreme Court of the United States or by any federal court. Probably it was not under the then law of Massachusetts an error upon which the Massachusetts Supreme Judicial Court could properly have reversed Judge Thayer's original judgment... .

Subjectively, Harold Williams did not, I feel sure, intend to act or have Proctor act deceptively, unethically, or to proceed without such notice of Proctor's attitude as the prosecutor under present-day standards would be required to give to the defense and to the Court... .

[Judge Wyzanski presided 45 years at the Federal District Court in Boston, Massachusetts. Of him Frankfurter said: Wyzanski "was one of my most brilliant students" at Harvard. (NY Times obit., 9/5/86.) Wyzanski told Russell he read books on the S-V case by Frankfurter, "Brute" Ehrmann, an old friend, Montgomery, and Joughin-Morgan.

Morgan was one of his Harvard professors. Ehrmann and Montgomery gave him copies of their books. Separately, he heard Ehrmann, Montgomery, and Dos Passos discuss the Sacco-Vanzetti case. He said he "had testified in both the trials of U.S. v. Hiss." Wyzanski was one of Frankfurter's "Hot Dogs."] [See. #49 on p. 630.]

Paul Avrich. "Anatomy Of A Murder." The New Republic. April 7, 1986.

[Ed. Avrich reviews both Postmortem and Sacco and Vanzetti: The Case Resolved.]

The district attorney, Frederick G. Katzmann, conducted a highly unscrupulous prosecution, coaching and badgering witnesses, withholding exculpatory evidence from the defense, and perhaps even tampering with physical evidence... . [H]e played on the emotions of the jurors, arousing their deepest prejudices against the accused. Sacco and Vanzetti were armed; they were foreigners, atheists, anarchists. This overclouded all judgment. [31]

Not surprisingly, then, it is a case that refuses to die. The appearance of two new books on Sacco and Vanzetti attests to its extraordinary vitality... . Actually, they [Kaiser and Russell] tell us little that was not available from other sources, much less offer a fresh interpretation... . In general, the authors press their claims too far, exaggerating both the significance and the novelty of their findings. [32] [Ed. Page 32 must be scrutinized.]

They are also niggardly in acknowledging the research of other scholars, notably Robert D'Attilio, perhaps the leading authority on the case, and Lincoln Robbins, who first called attention to the significance of Harold Williams's notebook. [33] [See Avrich's 1991 book.]

Francis Russell. "Why I Changed My Mind about the Sacco-Vanzetti Case." American Heritage (June/July, 1986).

My first lapse from this dogma [dogma of the innocence of Sacco and Vanzetti] came as I read through the trial transcript. Reluctantly I had to admit that, judging by the printed record, the trial had been proper, the verdict reasonable. Sacco and Vanzetti were armed when arrested—for all their explanations, a telling point against them. [107]

Sacco's story on the night of his arrest did not ring true. On the day of the crime he had been absent from work, and alibi witnesses who testified to having seen him in Boston on that day were Italian radicals. [107]

I became more ambivalent when I discovered that Moore had in the end doubted his clients' innocence... . Finally my doubts crystallized on my learning that Carlo Tresca, the anarchist leader who brought Moore into the case, had later said flatly that Sacco was guilty ... [107]

While writing my book [1962], I let the founder of the Committee to Vindicate Sacco and Vanzetti, Tom O'Connor, read my manuscript chapter by chapter, even the last one in which I stated that Sacco was guilty. He said nothing at the time, though later, when he passed me on the street, he refused to speak to me. After his death, when his papers were given to Brandeis University, I discovered that he and Judge Musmanno had launched what they called Operation Assault to persuade book editors not to review my "meretricious" book. [108]

I have been the only one writing about the Sacco-Vanzetti case who has changed his mind. Though I was at first tied to the dogma, the facts turned against me. [108]

James E. Starrs. "Once More Unto the Breech: The Firearms Evidence in the Sacco and Vanzetti Case Revisited." Part II. Journal of Forensic Sciences. (July 1986).

[Ed. Starrs reviews 1983 ballistics test conducted by Anthony Paul, Marshall Robinson, and George Wilson. See Russell, S & V: The Case Resolved, p.160; and see Starrs' note in Journal of Forensic Sciences (April: 649) on Report published in Association of Firearms and Toolmarks Examiners' Journal. AFTE Journal (vol. 17, Number 3), July 1985. Starrs has 264 reference Notes in July article.]

Abstract: This paper is the second and concluding segment of a report and analysis of a 1983 reevaluation of the vast array of firearms evidence at the trial of Sacco and Vanzetti... . The author finds that the evidence and the arguments militate against the bullet switching hypothesis. [1050]

[B]aseless charges of tampering with evidence are demonstrably easy to make but devilishly difficult to rebut. [1051]

... Albert H. Hamilton, a defense expert ... has been quite reliably proved accountable for a switching of the barrel in the Sacco Colt for another, newer one of Colt manufacture, all quite brazenly perpetrated in open court in the unsuspecting presence of Judge Thayer and Prosecutor Williams. [1053] [Ed. See JFS (April, p. 635).]

Anomalously, Ehrmann sought to reason that the failure of trial counsel to draw Dr. Magrath's "attention ... to any ostensible differences between the marks" {198} on the base of the bullets leaves room for argument that Dr. Magrath might have discerned a dissimilarity if his attention had been directed to that possibility. Yet Dr. Magrath could have been called to appear before the Lowell Committee, at which time he would have had the opportunity to expatiate quite fully on this entire matter.... . Still, no one, not the state nor, more unaccountably, the defense, summoned him to appear. Such a failure seems more premeditated than careless and speaks volumes against the defense's bullet substitution theory. [1063]

Captain Proctor was conceded to be the sole custodian of the firearms evidence until it was produced at the trial... . Proctor, therefore, was presumptively the most likely culprit if the mortal bullet were to have been switched. But if that was in fact what happened, what motive did he have to do so? The case did not become an admixture of fame and infamy until much later. If he expected to profit from his forging the evidence to insure a conviction, what tangible reward did he anticipate? [1068]

Then, again, Proctor was, in today's firearms terms, bumble-footed as an expert. According to his trial testimony, he did not know even the basic operation or parts of a firearm. Was [1068] such an inexpert expert to be the chosen one to fabricate a case against Sacco and Vanzetti, a case which could withstand close and careful inspection by genuine firearms experts at the trial? The fabrication of physical evidence is at best risky business, but to have Proctor mastermind the scheme would be foolhardy in the extreme. [1069]

... [T]he defense's arguments are both contradictory and indefensible. On the one hand, it is suggested that Sacco's Colt was the instrument from which the switched bullet was fired. Yet, that possibility is belied by the testimony of defense experts Burns and Fitzgerald at the trial as well as that of Albert Hamilton during the posttrial proceedings. It is beyond cavil that the defense cannot seek to buttress its bullet-switching submission when, on the one side, it maintains the mortal bullet was fabricated by being discharged through Sacco's Colt and on the other proclaims that Sacco's Colt was not the weapon from which the mortal bullet was discharged. The argument is so feeble that it is its own refutation. [1069]

Matching

... Matching means that a person is connected to a crime by the similarity of objects from the crime scene with objects known to be possessed by that person. The closer the similarities in these objects, the more certain we can be that the person is justly charged. [1071]

Fraher Cartridge Case Matching—In the Sacco and Vanzetti trial, matching occurred when it was noted that of the four types of unfired cartridges found on Sacco at his arrest (Peters, U.S.C., W.R.A., and Rem.-U.M.C.—Exhibit 31), three were also discovered among the Fraher cartridge cases (Peters, Rem.-U.M.C., and W.R.A.—**Exhibit 30**). There is a group aspect in evidence here which can be read to link Sacco to the South Braintree crime... . [1071]

The Obsolete Winchester Bullet Matching—... As the Committee saw it: [1071]
   The fatal bullet found in Berardelli's body was of a type no longer manufactured and so obsolete that the defendants' expert witness, Burns, testified that, with the help of two assistants, he was unable to find such bullets for purposes of experiment; Yet the same obsolete type of cartridge was found in Sacco's pockets on his arrest... . Such a coincidence of the fatal bullet and those found on Sacco would, if accidental, certainly be extraordinary. [1072]
[Ed. Starrs has quoted from Fuller's Committee Report in Appel, V: 5378w-5378x.]

The Peters Cartridge Cases' Matching.
   It will be remembered that Sacco had **32** .32 caliber cartridges on his person at his arrest. Sixteen of those were of Peters manufacture. Two Peters spent shells were also found at the crime scene... . The Committee [Paul, Robinson, Wilson] has now established that the same striations appearing in the extractor groove on **6** of the 16 Peters cartridges taken from Sacco also appear on the **2** Peters shells

discovered at the crime scene. This determination, which is very convincingly illustrated in Photographic Exhibit VVV, more closely connects Sacco to the murders, even without any precise knowledge of the number of rounds manufactured by Peters with the same die-cutting tool and without any gleanings as to the geographical distribution or availability of them in or about 1920. [1073] [Ed. See p. 28 in AFTE Journal (Vol. 17, No. 3) July 1985. Title of article is **EXAMINATION OF FIREARM RELATED EVIDENCE: THE NICOLA SACCO AND BARTOLOMEO VANZETTI CASE.**]

The Other Five Bullets and the Other Three Cartridge Cases—The evidence from the six bullets taken from the two victims and the four Fraher cartridge cases demonstrates that at least **two guns** were used in the melee. One of these was evidently a Colt .32 semi-automatic, on account of the six lands and grooves with a left twist found imprinted on Bullet III. The other five bullets all bore the impress of six lands and grooves with a right twist, signifying a non-Colt manufactured weapon was employed in firing them. [1073]

Concerning the five .32 caliber bullets with a right twist, the Select Committee has adduced convincing proof through striation matching {263} that all were fired from the same weapon. A Harrington and Richardson .32 caliber self-loading pistol has rifling characteristics duplicating those found on these five bullets, all of which points invitingly to the conclusion that a Harrington and Richardson .32 self-loader was employed as a second, and only a **second gun.** [1074] [Ed. #263 is Starrs' penultimate endnote.]

Conclusion

In fine, then, we now have significant and credible evidence from a most prestigious panel of firearms experts that Nicola Sacco was probably guilty as a perpetrator or, at the very least, as a conspirator in the commission of these wanton murders. The Select Committee is deserving of unstinting credit, particularly for taking the initiative and the effort to uncover the toolmark identity between six of the Peters cartridges found on Sacco and the **two Peters shells** recovered at the crime scene. [1074]

[Starrs, Professor of Law and Forensic Sciences, The George Washington University.]

Daniel Boorstin. Hidden History. 1987

"Recent immigrants from Italy, these were gentle men, philosophical anarchists ... . Sacco and Vanzetti were executed in 1927, and entered the folklore of American martyrdom, alongside Nathan Hale, John Brown, and Barbara Fritchie." [216]
[Dr. Boorstin, Librarian of Congress Emeritus, was formerly the Preston and Sterling Morton Distinguished Service Professor of History at the University of Chicago.]

Dorothy Gallagher. All the Right Enemies: The Life and Murder of Carlo Tresca. 1988

For more than a decade after their executions, the innocence of Sacco and Vanzetti remained an article of faith for their defenders, unblemished by the earlier rumors of guilt. But in the late 1930s, and until shortly before his own murder in 1943, Tresca would tell a number of people that Sacco had been guilty. At Norman Thomas's apartment, Tresca told John Roche, who asked his opinion of Maxwell Anderson's play based on the case, Winterset, that Sacco had murdered a good comrade. Vanzetti, Tresca said in great agitation, was innocent; Sacco had refused to plead guilty because he thought they could win.

More than once during this period Tresca repeated his accusation against Sacco: to Norman Thomas he said that he had known of Sacco's guilt from the beginning and had urged him to admit it in the defiant anarchist tradition. Late in 1942, in response to a question from Max Eastman, Tresca said that Sacco was guilty, Vanzetti was not... . [T]o no one did Tresca offer supporting evidence, ... [90]

One historian [Russell], assuming that Tresca, of all people, would know the truth, has used his word to make the case for Sacco's [90] guilt. [91]
[Gallagher wrote in Harper's, New York Times, Village Voice. For another opinion by Gallagher, see "The Next-to-Last Word," The Nation (August 29, 1986, pp. 87-90).]

Encyclopedias: Six Opinions on the Sacco-Vanzetti Case

Dennis F. Strong. "Sacco-Vanzetti Case." <u>Encyclopedia International</u>. Vol. 16. 1981.

In July, 1921, Judge Webster Thayer sentenced them to death, after a trial in which the prejudice of the judge and the jury against immigrants and radicals appeared to have more weight than the evidence. Prominent intellectuals such as Felix Frankfurter, John Dos Passos, and Edna St. Vincent Millay challenged the decision... . In 1977, acting on the recommendation of lawyers and historians who had examined new evidence, Gov. Michael Dukakis of Massachusetts proclaimed that the two men had not been fairly tried, and that doubt existed about their guilt. [72]
[Strong, Professor Emeritus, University of Washington, was instructor in history, Princeton Univ., when he wrote the Sacco-Vanzetti article for <u>Encyclopedia International</u> in 1964.]

Louis Joughin. "Sacco-Vanzetti Case." <u>Collier's Encyclopedia</u>. Vol. 20. 1989.

Paraphrase: Joughin says American reaction to the Sacco-Vanzetti case from 1920 to 1930 revealed ethnic bias. He says Americans disliked foreigners and feared radicals. Radicals Americans detested. Joughin calls the two aliens, Sacco and Vanzetti, "philosophical anarchists." Joughin says the public thought the anarchist either a "bomb-thrower" or a "Communist." (See Joughin's S-V entry on p. 319, column 1, lines 29-35.)
[Joughin, in 1951, became assistant director, American Civil Liberties Union. He launched <u>Collier's</u> Sacco-Vanzetti article in 1962. It has not been revised.]

"Sacco-Vanzetti Case." <u>Compton's Encyclopedia</u>. Vol. 21. 1989.

The judge was openly biased. Sacco and Vanzetti were convicted because they were radicals and because they were Italian. [3] [Author unknown. <u>Compton's</u> Sacco-Vanzetti article began in 1989. Their Fact Index has had an item on Sacco-Vanzetti for six decades.]

"Sacco-Vanzetti case." The New Encyclopaedia Britannica. Vol. 10. 1989.

Final Paragraph: "Sacco-Vanzetti agitation continued, and as late as April 1959 a legislative committee sat in Boston giving a full day for hearing on a proposal by Rep. Alexander J. Cella to the legislature to recommend to the Governor a retroactive pardon. The committee and the legislature declined to take such a step. Evidence, nevertheless, pointed to the guilt of Morelli and his gang." [285]

[In 1991 Encyclopaedia Britannica deleted this paragraph, revised its appended bibliography, and cited Francis Russell. Morris L. Ernst wrote Britannica's initial S-V article in 1929. See #5 on p. 604.]

Osmond K. Fraenkel. "Sacco-Vanzetti Case." Encyclopedia Americana. Vol. 24. 1989.

Sacco's alibi was strong. He testified that he had gone to Boston on the day of the murders to inquire about a passport at the Italian consulate, and this was corroborated.... Some writers have claimed that Vanzetti was innocent but Sacco guilty. This opinion rests mainly on ballistic tests made many years after the trial, which are not conclusive. [73]

[Encyclopedia Americana launched their Sacco-Vanzetti article in 1950. Fraenkel, counsel for ACLU, wrote it, using items in his 1931 book. Fraenkel's revision in 1973 is used today.]

James D. Forman. "Sacco-Vanzetti Case." The World Book Encyclopedia. Vol. 17. 1989.

Their supporters also argued that Sacco and Vanzetti had been convicted mainly because they approved of anarchism.... Today, many historians believe that Sacco may have been guilty, and that Vanzetti was probably innocent. But in either event, it is thought that the evidence was insufficient to support conviction. In 1977, Governor Michael Dukakis of Massachusetts signed a proclamation that recognized the faults of the trial and cleared the names of Sacco and Vanzetti. [5]

[Forman is the author of Anarchism: Political Innocence or Social Violence?.] [See editor's challenge to World Book on Author page. Letters to Paul Kobasa—09/15/2005, 05/11/2006—filed.]

The World in Arms: Time Frame AD 1900-1925. **Time-Life Books.**
1989.

In 1920, in the industrial town of South Braintree, Massachusetts, a messenger carrying the payroll for a local firm was robbed and murdered. Two Italian immigrants, Nicola Sacco and Bartolomeo Vanzetti, were charged with the crime. Sacco, a shoemaker, and Vanzetti, who sold fish from a cart, made no secret of their interest in anarchist ideas; the authorities opined that anyone capable of subscribing to such a dangerous philosophy was equally capable of murder in cold blood. Only the slenderest circumstantial evidence linked the pair to the shooting, but they were found guilty and—despite massive public protests—were executed in 1927. [157]
[Author unknown. Consultant for chapter 5, "America Comes of Age," is Hugh Brogan.]

Melvin I. Urofsky. **Felix Frankfurter: Judicial Restraint and**
Individual Liberties. 1991

Both Sacco and Vanzetti had been armed at the time of their arrest, but both also had witnesses who vouched that they had been far from South Braintree at the time of the robbery. The conflicting testimony should have been enough to raise some doubts among the members of the jury, but as people recognized then and later, Sacco and Vanzetti stood trial not for the payroll robbery but for being aliens and anarchists. The presiding judge, Webster Thayer, and the prosecutor, Frederick Katzmann, both displayed considerable prejudice against the pair, as did at least one of the jurors. Walter Ripley, the jury foreman and a former police chief, indicated his belief in the defendants' guilt even before the trial began. When a friend expressed some doubts, Ripley exploded, "Damn them, they ought to hang anyway." [22]
William G. Thompson, a respected member of the Boston bar, ... urged Frankfurter to write an article exposing the legal irregularities that had occurred. Originally, Frankfurter planned to publish the piece in the New Republic, which had taken a major role in defending Sacco and Vanzetti. But when Ellery Sedgwick, the editor of the very proper and prestigious Atlantic Monthly, expressed interest, Frankfurter quickly agreed to publish it there.

The article appeared in March 1927 and was all that the defenders of Sacco and Vanzetti could have desired. Frankfurter coldly analyzed the trial and painstakingly set out proof after proof that Katzmann, with Thayer's support, had undermined the integrity of the criminal justice system in this case. [23]

Urofsky's conclusion: The controversy over their guilt or innocence has not died, and one can still find well-reasoned articles on both sides of this issue. [191]

[Urofsky, Professor of History, Virginia Commonwealth University.]

Paul Avrich. Sacco and Vanzetti: The Anarchist Background. 1991

Then, in 1917, he [Vanzetti] ... took out his first papers for American citizenship. [41]

Luigi Galleani, ... during the first two decades of the twentieth century, was the leading Italian anarchist in America. [48] A revolutionary zealot, he preached a militant form of anarchism which advocated the overthrow of capitalism and government by violent means, dynamite and assassination not excluded. [51] As followers of Galleani Sacco and Vanzetti considered themselves anarchist-communists, ...[52] Far from being the innocent dreamers so often depicted by their supporters, they be-[56] longed to a branch of the anarchist movement which preached insurrectionary violence and armed retaliation, including the use of dynamite and assassination ... Such was the position of Sacco and Vanzetti, as it was of their mentor Galleani, who showered praise on every rebellious deed and glorified the perpetrators as heroes and martyrs, ... [57]

In an article entitled "Matricolati!" (Registrants), published in Cronaca Sovversiva on May 26, he [Galleani] alerted his followers to the dangers of registration [after military conscription act passed by Congress on May 18, 1917].

Towards the end of May, immediately after the publication of "Matricolati!," Sacco quit his job at the Milford Shoe Company, ... Though devoted to his wife and son, he remained foremost an anarchist: Galleani had given the order and [59] he obeyed. Going to Boston, he attended a meeting of Galleanists who were planning to leave for Mexico. It was here that he met Vanzetti for the first time, . . During the ensuing months the two became intimate friends. [60]

It was during the Hopedale strike of 1913, ... that he [Boda/Buda] first met Sacco; and he met Vanzetti in Plymouth during the Cordage strike of 1916. [63]

Such were the companions of Sacco and Vanzetti in Mexico. Of the sixty or so who had made the journey, perhaps half, including Buda and Valdinoci as well as Sacco and Vanzetti, occupied ... adobe houses on the outskirts of Monterrey, ... [65]

Their code of honor taught that revolutionaries should retaliate against the repressive use of force, that submission to the state was cowardly ... [97]

In 1914, under the title of Faccia a faccia col nemico (Face to Face with the Enemy), the Gruppo Autonomo [autonomous group] of East Boston had published a collection of Galleani's articles defending propoganda by the deed and exalting its practitioners—wielders of dagger, pistol, and bomb... . Mere possession of the book, with its striking red cover and gilded lettering, branded one as a dangerous subversive. [97] [Ed. See Sinclair's Boston, p. 456.]

Galleani ... did more than glorify the memory of terrorists and assassins. In 1905 he published a forty-six-page bomb manual entitled La Salute'e in voi! (Health Is in You!) in the Library of Social Studies. [98] [Ed. See The New Leader, Sept. 26, 1960, pp. 12-13.]

The arrest of Galleani in June 1917 stirred his followers in Mexico into action... . Between June and September 1917 a **conspiracy** took shape among the Mexican exiles for the purpose of armed retaliation. Coda ... was a key participant, along with Buda [Mike Boda] and Valdinoci. Their confederates included ... Sacco and Vanzetti of Boston. [102]

By October 1917 Valdinoci, Buda and most of their comrades had returned to the United States. Arming themselves, often assuming new names, they plunged into an underground existence... . They refused to acknowledge any authority save that of their own code of honor, the code of secrecy and self-reliance, ... [104]

The same Draconian spirit permeated the new immigration law, ... The ob-[132]ject of the law, signed on October 16, 1918, was to "exclude and expel from the United States aliens who are members of the anarchistic and similar classes." [133]

High on the list of undesirables remained the Cronaca Sovversiva anarchists. Armed with the October 1918 law, the government renewed its efforts to expel Galleani... [134] On June 24, 1919, the nine anarchists, having been transferred from Boston to Ellis Island, were deported to Italy.... [135] Galleani, at the time of his expulsion, had been living in the United States for eighteen years. [136]

The package bombs. On the morning of April 28, 1919, a amall package arrived by mail in Mayor Hanson's office. [Hanson, Seattle mayor, spoke out against anarchists.] [140] [Ed. Citizens targeted to get package bomb listed on p. 143.]

Far from being part of a widespread revolutionary conspiracy, the package bombs were the work of a small group of Galleanists, centered in New York and Massachusetts. [146]

The shock created by the package bombs had barely worn off when a new round of bombings took place. On Monday night, June 2, 1919, there were explosions in seven cities: Boston, New York, Paterson, Philadelphia, Pittsburgh, Cleveland, and Washington. Unlike the May 1 bombs, which had been sent in the mail, these were delivered by hand to the doors of the intended victims. Moreover, they were much more powerful than the package bombs.... Once again ... copies of a leaflet were found at every [bombing] site, clearly pointing to an organized conspiracy. [149] [Ed. See "The Death of Salsedo," in Montgomery, pp.145-154.]

The leaflet, printed on pink paper ... bore the title <u>Plain Words</u> and was signed "The Anarchist Fighters." ... You have provoked the fight, <u>Plain Words</u> declared. You have jailed, deported, and murdered us.... [It read] "There will have to be bloodshed; we will not dodge; there will have to be murder: we will kill, because it is necessary; ..." [149]

The most sensational of the June 2 bombings occurred in Washington, D.C., at the home of Attorney General Palmer.... The entire house trembled [after detonation], its front was demolished, ... The bomb had blown to bits the man who had carried it [Carlo Valdinoci]. [153] Rosina Sacco [Sacco's wife] considered him [Valdinoci] "a great anarchist." [156]

Although the complete story of the **bomb plot** remains to be unraveled, the following seems a plausible reconstruction. Originating with Valdinoci and Buda [Boda], it centered in the Gruppo Autonomo of East Boston, which met in the hall of the Italian Independent Naturalization Club on Maverick Square. The members of this group, some forty or fifty strong, came from all over the Boston area—Coacci from Quincy, Sacco from Stoughton, Vanzetti from Plymouth, and so on. [157] ... Anarchists who had been in Mexico played a key role in the [bomb] conspiracy, Buda and Valdinoci among them. [158]

Was Vanzetti himself involved in the conspiracy? Though the evidence is far from satisfactory, the answer almost certainly is yes. The same holds true for Sacco. **Both were ultra-militants**, believers in armed re-[159] taliation. They carried guns; they had gone to Mexico; they were associated with known participants in the plot. Buda reckoned them the "best friends" he had in America, ... [160]

Sacco and Vanzeti lived at once a legal and a clandestine existence—one of earning a living and devotion to family, on the one hand, and of underground insurgency, on the other... . Those who perceived Vanzetti as a mere dreamer, ... saw only one side of his complex personality. He liked to talk, it is true. But he was every bit as militant as Sacco. He was also better acquainted with Galleani, who told Edward Holton James ["The Story of Mario Buda"] that he knew Vanzetti well but had met Sacco only twice. [160]

Sinclair came to Boston [to get background for his novel on Sacco and Vanzetti] convinced that Sacco and Vanzetti had been merely "philosophical anarchists" and that there was "no possibility of either being guilty of any crime," as he wrote to Creighton Hill. In the course of his research, however, he found that he had been mistaken... . [H]e concluded that, far from being pacifists, both men "believed in and taught violence." Of this Sinclair was "absolutely certain." [161] "I became convinced from many different sources," he wrote, "that Vanzetti was not the pacifist he was reported under the necessity of **defense propaganda**. He was, like many fanatics, a dual personality, and when he was roused by the social conflict he was a very dangerous man." [161] [See Avrich's Notes 47-49 on p. 238.]

The same applied equally to Sacco. Both, Sinclair was convinced, had been involved with dynamite... . His [Sinclair's] conclusions, . . . are unassailable. [W]hen <u>Boston</u> came out in 1928, Sinclair was taken to task by [161] sympathizers of the executed men for suggesting that they had been dynamiters.

That Sacco and Vanzetti were involved in the 1919 bombings is, indeed, a virtual certainty, ... [162]

At their trial Sacco and Vanzetti testified that they had gone for Buda's automobile in order to move radical literature to a safe hiding place. This, however, was an evasion. "Radical literature," Upton Sinclair tells us, was a euphemism for explosives. Fred Moore, chief counsel for the defense, told Sinclair that "Sacco and Vanzetti admitted to him that they were hiding dynamite on the night of their arrest, and

589

that that was the real reason why they told lies and stuck to them."
[204] [See Russell, S. & V.: C. R., p. 105.]

On September 11 indictments were returned against both Vanzetti
and Sacco, ... At this Buda went into action... . On reaching New
York, Buda acquired a horse and a wagon, in which he placed a large
dynamite bomb... . On Thursday, September 16, Buda drove the
wagon to the corner of Wall and Broad Streets, the symbolic center of
American capitalism... . Buda parked his horse and wagon at the curb
... directly across the street from the House of Morgan ... and
disappeared. A few moments later a tremendous explosion occurred,
... Ambulance men counted thirty dead, and more than two hundred
were injured seriously enough to be taken to the hospital... . [T]hree
more died of their wounds. [205] [See Joughin, Legacy, pp. 216, 379.]

His mission accomplished, Buda left New York for Providence.
There, shedding his pseudonym "Mike Boda," he secured a passport
from the Italian vice-consul... . By the end of November he was back
in his native Romagna, never again to return to the United States. [207]

Avrich's note #32. That Buda was the Wall Street bomber cannot
be proved; documentary evidence is lacking. But it fits what we know
of him and his movements. I have it, moreover, from a reliable source
and believe it to be true. [See Sinclair's letter, 02/08/1928.]
[Professor Avrich told the editor, 11/4/ 92, that his source was an old
Italian anarchist. Avrich's judgment about the case appears on page 6:
"The issue of guilt or innocence awaits definitive treatment, but, alas, it
may never receive it." Avrich, Distinguished Professor of History,
Queens College, and the Graduate School, the City University of New
York.] [Ed. See Avrich's chapter on revenge in this book, p. 593.]

Reviews of Sacco and Vanzetti: The Anarchist Background
Martin Blatt. "Two Good Men." The Nation. June 3, 1991. #1

"Although I believe that Sacco and Vanzetti were the victims of
judicial murder, their innocence of the charges brought against them
does not mean that the men were romantic innocents. The actions of
the Galleanists call into question ... the appropriatenesss of employing
violence in the cause of humanity... . [T]he Wall Street bombing, ...
harmed many passers-by." [748]
[Martin Blatt wrote Free Love and Anarchism: The Biography of Ezra
Heywood.]

Nick Salvatore. "How Innocent Were They?" <u>New York Times</u>
<u>Book Review</u>**. March 17, 1991. #2**

[T]he idea of Sacco and Vanzetti as innocents caught in a web of
intrigue not of their own making is less certain [than such an argument
made by Sacco-Vanzetti partisans in 1927]. [10]

[Salvatore, Professor of American Studies and Industrial & Labor
Relations at Cornell Univ.]

George Woodcock. "Tracking the Elusive Truth," 74 <u>The New</u>
<u>Leader</u>**, July 15-29, 1991. #3**

... Avrich has patiently put together an intricate and convincing
picture of the world of self-confessed subversives that Sacco and
Vanzetti lived in—a world where truth was expected between comrades
and lies were enough for the enemy... . I used to maintain the
innocence of Sacco and Vanzetti as a matter of radical faith... . Paul
Avrich has convinced me ... their innocence must be accepted. [21]

[Woodcock "founded and edited the anarchists' journal <u>Now</u>, in
London from 1940 until 1947." He published <u>Anarchism: A History of</u>
<u>Libertarian Ideas and Movements</u> in 1962.]

"Sacco-Vanzetti case." <u>Webster's New World Encyclopedia</u>**.**
College Edition. Prentice-Hall 1993

The two accused men were philosophical anarchists... . Modern
ballistics evidence suggests that one of the fatal shots was fired from
Sacco's gun. [917] [Author unknown.]

Janet McDonnell. <u>America in the 20th Century: 1920-1929</u>**.**
Marshall Cavendish Corporation 1995

Sacco and Vanzetti were Italian aliens and professed anarchists.
Their trial included flimsy evidence, questionable eyewitnesses, and an
apparently prejudiced judge... [310] The case is still debated to this
day, but most would agree that the anti-foreign attitude in the United
States played a part in the deaths of Sacco and Vanzetti. [311]

George Brown Tindall/David E. Shi. <u>America: A Narrative History</u>. 4th edition. W. W. Norton & Co. 1996

The question of the two men's guilt remains in doubt, and the [1092] belief persists that they were sentenced for their political ideas and their ethnic origins rather than for any crime they had committed. [1093] 7th ed.: [E]vidence convicting them was compelling.

[Tindall, Professor Emeritus of History, Univ. of North Carolina; Shi, Professor of History and President of Furman University.]

Mark C. Carnes, General Editor. Book XII "The Great Crusade and After, 1914-1928" by Preston W. Slosson. In <u>A History of American Life</u>. Abridged. Consulting Editor, Arthur M. Schlesinger, Jr., Scribner, 1996

Nicola Sacco [1073] and Bartolomeo Vanzetti, Italians with anarchistic views, were accused of murdering a shoe-factory paymaster in April 1920 and were convicted on rather **flimsy evidence** the following year... What gave the Sacco-Vanzetti case its special notoriety was the use of the radicalism of the accused as an argument by both friends and foes. Judge, jury, and community were prejudiced against them from the start; ... [1074]
[Except for changes in punctuation, this 1996 analysis reprints the analysis in pp. 89-90 in <u>The Great Crusade and After 1914-1928</u>, by Preston William Slosson, Professor of History, Univ. of Michigan, and member of ACLU. Slosson's **1930** work is volume 12 of <u>A History of American Life</u> (Macmillan), a series edited by Arthur M. Schlesinger, Sr. and Dixon Ryan Fox. Sam Tanenhaus (<u>Whittaker Chambers</u>, p. 497) calls A. M. Schlesinger, Sr. "a loyal champion of Sacco and Vanzetti." Both the footnote of 1930 (p. 90) and endnote #53 of 1996 (p. 1354) say Frankfurter's <u>The Case of Sacco and Vanzetti</u> "is an acute analysis by a legal scholar." Carnes, Professor of History, Barnard College, Columbia University, is one of two General Editors of <u>American National Biography</u>.] [Professor Carnes and Professor Paul S. Boyer, University of Wisconsin, have received documents by email which show that Oxford University Press publications have factual errors on the Sacco-Vanzetti topic. See **ADDENDA**.]

**Paul Johnson. A History of the American People. HarperCollins.
1997**

Johnson writes: "But the organized left decided to make the case a
cause celebre, pulling out all the literary stops both in America and in
Europe … From 1925 the worldwide agitation was directed by Willi
Muenzenberg's official Communist International propaganda machine
in Paris, and produced spectacular results… . Upton Sinclair, …
privately admitted that his researches while preparing the book
[Boston] left him in no doubt that the men had committed the murders.
The left profited enormously from the case, as they were later to do
over the Rosenbergs and Alger Hiss." [669] [See Neville, p. 656.]
[Paul Bede Johnson, British historian and biographer and freelance
journalist for many years, has published a number of books.]

**Nunzio Pernicone. "SACCO, Nicola … Bartolomeo Vanzetti."
American National Biography. Vol. 19. 1999**

The testimony of more than twenty witnesses who had seen
Vanzetti selling eels on the day of the Bridgewater crime was
discounted because the individuals were all Italians. [174]
[Ed. On p. 176 Pernicone cites books on the S-V case by Frankfurter
(1927), Fraenkel (1931), Joughin/Morgan (1948), Montgomery (1960),
Russell (1962), Russell (1986), Young/Kaiser (1985), Ehrmann (1969),
and Avrich (1991). He does not cite Protest: Sacco-Vanzetti and the
Intellectuals (1965), although he had labelled its author, David Felix,
one of four "revisionists" in his article in The Journal of American
History (Dec. 1979). Pernicone states that Russell "subsequently
asserted Vanzetti's guilt in numerous articles and in Sacco and
[Vanzetti: The Case Resolved (1986)."]

**Paul Avrich. "Sacco and Vanzetti's Revenge." Chapter 6 in
The Lost World of Italian American Radicalism, 2003**

[Ed. Chapter 6 provides more background on Sacco and Vanzetti.
Historically pertinent is the opinion of Judge Webster Thayer by Dr.
Avrich's Italian anarchist friend, Valerio Isca. Avrich died Feb. 16,
2006.]

Richard Newby

PROLEGOMENA TO THE STUDY OF RANNEY
The Sacco-Vanzetti Case Papers: Reel 21

Dudley P. Ranney, Assistant District Attorney for the Commonwealth of Massachusetts since 1925, read affidavits by Albert H. Hamilton, a firearms expert whom defense counsel Fred Moore engaged in 1923 to conduct tests on Sacco's pistol (Fifth Supplementary Motion for new trial). Moore also told Hamilton to scrutinize Vanzetti's revolver. (Frankfurter cited Hamilton on pp. 74-75 in The Case of Sacco and Vanzetti, March 1927). Facing Fuller's three Commissioners on July 25, 1927, Ranney attacked Hamilton's credentials and affidavits, citing the poor analysis of ink marks in Hamilton's affidavit (transcript, 3577) in support of the Ripley motion (transcript, 5345). Ranney's attack followed Hamilton's testimony before Governor Fuller's Commission in Boston on July 12, 1927. On July 13, Ranney cross-examined Hamilton, concluding with this question:

Q. And you testified in the case of the people of New York against Charles Stielor [Stielow]? A. Yes. I would like to add, if the committee are interested in my veracity and integrity, there is two exhibits on file before the Governor that could be offered to the committee. [5018] [Ed. See #25 on p. 617.]

An unsigned letter in Ranney's files (09/28/1923) sent from New York City to the County Prosecutor, Norfolk County, reported that Hamilton's ballistics testimony in the Stielow trial was erroneous, that Charles Stielow, wrongfully convicted of murder in 1915 through Hamilton's error, was later set free by New York Governor Charles S. Whitman.

On July 11, 1927, Ranney received data on Hamilton from Frank Nelson Nay, a Boston lawyer. In his letter of July 14, 1927, Ranney thanked Nay, calling Hamilton "this obvious fraud and quack." Ranney's files include a letter (06/17/1921) to the District Attorney, Dedham, Mass., from C. C. Palmer of Dexter, Maine. Palmer, Automobile Inspector for the Maine State Police, reported his findings on Atwater and Slater. See p. 413. Ranney had letters from Goddard (see p. 478) in June 1927. Ranney's letters to Fuller (June 8) and A. L. Lowell (July 6) cite Goddard's ballistics test on June 3, 1927. In his letter to Lowell, Ranney said Proctor used the word "consistent" when he testified at a 1915 trial in Essex County. This was Ranney's direct response to Thompson's complaint (transcript, 4967). On pp. 5188, 5339 Ranney offered to recall Dr. Magrath.

TOPICS FOR DISCUSSION, DEBATE, AND WRITING

Good writing is organized, clear, precise, specific, correct, complete, cogent, and honest.

SHORT PAPERS

A. Examine one of the trial witnesses for (1) credibility and (2) probative value. Many witnesses also make valid topics for discussion or formal debate. ILLUSTRATION. Resolved: The testimony of Shelley Neal (is, is not) credible. Cite evidence to support your position. Choose 25 or more witnesses (prosecution or defense) for papers or debate.

B. Evaluate the credibility of a corroborative or supporting witness.

EXAMPLE 1. The testimony of Augustus Pecheur corroborates the testimony of Frank Burke, who testified defendants were not in the bandit car in South Braintree on April 15, 1920. Yes or No.
EXAMPLE 2. The testimony of Alphonsine Brini (or LeFavre Brini) corroborates the testimony of Joseph Rosen about the cloth sold to Vanzetti. Yes or No. Debate numbers 1 and 2.

C. Write a short paper on the conflicting testimony of Lola Andrews and Julia Campbell. Do Campbell, Kurlansky, Fay, Labrecque, and Allen negate the testimony of Andrews?
D. Write a short paper on Goodridge. Is the testimony of Goodridge nullified by Arrogni, Manganio, Magazu, and Damato?
E. Write a short paper on Levangie. Is the testimony of Levangie severely weakened by Carter, McCarthy, John L. Sullivan, and Alexander G. Victorson? See Transcript of the Record, 419-425. Debate C, D, and E.
F. Write a paper on Joseph Scavitto. Is he important? See Transcipt of the Record, 1531-1537, 2221, 2229.
G. Write a paper on the five primary sources Newby found at Dexter and Bangor. What inferences can be drawn? See p. xxvii.

TOPICS FOR DEBATE OR DISCUSSION

Bracketed numbers are from Appel's 1969 publication of the <u>Transcript of the Record</u>.

1. The cap which Fred Loring found near Berardelli's body (was, was not) Sacco's cap. [798]
2. The gun found on Vanzetti when he was arrested (was, was not) Berardelli's. [757] See Topp's 2005 book in bibliography.
3. Sacco's testimony on the history of the shotgun shells in his house (is, is not) credible [1863].
4. Vanzetti's testimony that he and Boda would have gone to Plymouth on the night of May 5 had they been able to obtain the Boda car (is, is not) credible. [1811]
5. Vanzetti's testimony that he told lies to Chief Stewart on the night of his arrest to protect his friends who had anarchist literature in their homes (is, is not) credible. [1731]
6. Sacco's testimony on the loaded .32 calibre Colt automatic pistol and the twenty-three live rounds taken from him at the Brockton police station (is, is not) credible. [1903]
7. Guidobone's testimony that he bought fish from Vanzetti (1587) (is, is not) verified by Vanzetti.
8. Testimony by Tracy is discredited in cross-examination. [501-518]
9. Sacco's testimony that he did not follow Ruth Johnson to the Bartlett house (is, is not) credible. [1908]
10. Sacco's testimony that he was afraid of deportation on May 5 (is, is not) credible. [1866]
11. Vanzetti's testimony that he bought a revolver for self-defense (is, is not) credible. [1715]
12. Sacco (is, is not) credible in testifying "I did not know" in response to Moore's question: "What did you think you were being held for, then, by Mr. Katzmann?" [1846]
13. Vanzetti's testimony that he and his friends would pick up radical literature "in Bridgewater, ... in Brockton, ... in Sacco house, ... in Orciani house, ... in Haverhill, ... in Salem, and many other places that I don't know" (is, is not) credible. [1760]
14. The behavior of Sacco and Vanzetti at the Johnson house (shows, does not show) that they carried consciousness of guilt about the murders at South Braintree [677-683, 705-708, 876].

15. Fred H. Moore's statement, "It is manifest from the record that Sacco did his best to tell Mr. Katzmann all the truth as he was best able to recollect it," (is, is not) credible. [2145]

16. Defense witnesses Brenner, McCullum, and Constantino (impeach, do not impeach) the testimony by Pelser. [1122, 1149, 1166]

17. Sacco's answers to Katzmann's questions about a passport (are, are not) credible. [1939]

18. Vanzetti (is, is not) credible in his answer—"That is not my fault, because I don't know where Boda is or [if] Orcciani lives with Boda"—to Katzmann's question: "Couldn't you have met Boda in the morning as well as at the dark of night?" [1746]

19. Sacco (is, is not) credible in his answer—"Never, I never did for certain"—to Moore's question: "Now, did you know at any time the place or town where this man Boda lived?" [1963]

20. Sacco's testimony on letters he received from Sabeno and his father (supports, does not support) his innocence. [1933, 1964-1966, 1969-1970, 1974-1976]

21. Testimony by photographer Maertens (seems, does not seem) to exonerate Sacco. [1979]

22. Vanzetti's answer—I don't hear nobody call out "His wife"—(is, is not) credible. [1776]

23. Gatti's denial of knowing Orciani (is, is not) credible. [1219]

24. The cross-examination of Heron (demonstrates, does not demonstrate) that Heron is a weak witness for the prosecution. [520-540]

25. The credibility of Austin Reed (is, is not) virtually destroyed in cross-examination. [598-617]

26. The credibility of Faulkner (is, is not) severely damaged by McAnarney's introduction of a photograph, [444-445], in cross-examination. [See 738, 1530-1536, 2221, 2229.]

27. In his review of Ehrmann's The Untried Case, 2nd edition, in The Boston Globe (Dec. 7, 1960, p. 52), Gardner Jackson (is, is not) accurate and evenhanded.

28. In his review of Montgomery's book, Sacco-Vanzetti: The Murder and the Myth, in The New Leader (Sept. 26, 1960, pp. 12-13), James Rorty shows insights (inferior, superior) to Jackson's in The Boston Globe.

29. Whose Boston Globe review is sounder, Jackson's or Stein's?

30. Katzmann's speech on Faulkner (is, is not) sound. [2229]

LONG PAPERS
Write a well-reasoned paper which argues:

1. Sacco's nine alibi witnesses—and back-up witnesses—demonstrate that Sacco (was, was not) in Boston on April 15, 1920. Choose one side and support it.
2. Testimony by Vanzetti's alibi witnesses shows indisputably that Vanzetti was in (a. Plymouth, b. South Braintree) at 3:00 P.M. on April 15, 1920. Argue a or b.
3. Testimonies by Atwater, Slater, and Falzini (and testimony by defense witnesses on the Plymouth train) destroy the credibility of Faulkner. Argue pro or con. See Appel, V: 5225.
4. The guilty verdicts against both Sacco and Vanzetti (are, are not) just. Argue pro or con.
5. Sacco and Vanzetti had a fair trial at Dedham. Argue pro or con.
6. Vanzetti (had, did not have) a fair trial at Plymouth. Argue pro or con. Is Topp's book in bibliography (2005) helpful?
7. The trial testimony on ballistics (is too weak to justify, is strong and justifies) a guilty verdict against Sacco. See Starrs, "Once More Unto the Breech: The Firearms Evidence in the Sacco and Vanzetti Case Revisited." Part I. JFS (April 1986), 630-654. See Gunthers' book.
8. The closing arguments by defense counsel Moore and McAnarney raise reasonable doubt about the guilt of Vanzetti (or both defendants). Choose one or both defendants. Argue pro or con.
9. The closing argument by District Attorney Katzmann (shows, does not show) that Sacco and Vanzetti were indisputably guilty of the South Braintree crime. Choose one and defend.
10. The attendance of Luigi Falzini at meetings of the Gruppo Autonomo in East Boston on April 18, 1920, April 25, 1920, and May 2, 1920 (a. discredits, b. does not discredit) his Dedham testimony. See Avrich, pp. 188-191, 215. Argue a or b.
11. Thayer's note on ink marks (transcript, 3712, 3577) surely exemplifies Thayer's bias. Argue pro or con.
12. Sacco and Vanzetti are martyrs sacrificed to our criminal justice system. Pro or con.
13. "Heartbreakingly" on p. 45 in The Sacco and Vanzetti Case (a. is; b. is not) the right word. Prove a or b. See Topp, p. 656.

14. Sacco and Vanzetti are martyrs in the cause of social revolution. Pro or con. [Consider Alexander Meiklejohn, "In Memoriam." The New Republic, (September 5, 1928): 69-71.]

15. Clements, reviewing Felix, (is, is not) serious when he says Frankfurter is "their solon."

16. The ACLU (made, did not make) an error of judgment on the Sacco-Vanzetti case on February 19, 1921. See letter by New England Civil Liberties Committee in Montgomery, pp. 61-63.

17. The gun which Vaughn took from Vanzetti (was, was not) the Mogridge gun. (Consider Appel, IV: 4212. Can you get help from James F. Simon in The Antagonists? See Kaiser, p. 90.)

18. Grant, Lowell, and Stratton (had a right, had no right) to say Rosen lied (transcript, 5378y).

19. The 1999 edition of American National Biography (has, does not have) a reliable overview of the Sacco-Vanzetti case. Argue pro or con.

20. The commentary by Andrew Kopkind (this handbook, p. 551) on Invitation to an Inquest gives strength and credibility to Kopkind's analysis of Felix's Protest. Argue pro or con. (See Herbert Romerstein and Eric Breindel, "Atomic Espionage—The Rosenberg Case" in The Venona Secrets: Exposing Soviet Espionage and America's Traitors, pp. 231-254. And see the Schneirs on p. 234.)

21. Kebabian's letter in TLS—31 May 1985, p. 607—(is, is not) relevant to the Sacco-Vanzetti debate. Pro or con. b. Orciani (did, did not) plead in Dextrer, Maine. See p. 571 in this handbook.

PREVIEW OF NOS. 1-52. a. Vanzetti's letter from Charlestown Prison (June 13, 1926—Dear Comrade Blackwell) creates dramatic irony. Identify the ironic relationship created between Vanzetti's views and those of a knowledgeable 21st-century reader. Pinpoint the irony in Vanzetti's first three sentences. See Letters from Prison at Linder's UMKC Web site: Famous Trials And see The Letters of Sacco and Vanzetti (Penguin Books, 1997). Is Linder more accurate than The History Channel? b. Find six egregious errors in Doreen Rappaport's The Sacco-Vanzetti Trial, excluding the four factual errors on p. 155. Note Rappaport's omissions. c. Find Judy Monroe's egregious error on Sacco in The Sacco and Vanzetti Controversial Murder Trial. How did Monroe blunder on Sacco? List Monroe's factual errors.

LUMINARIES 1989 - 2001

SPECIAL EDITION OF FRAENKEL
1989 INTRODUCTION BY DERSHOWITZ

Evaluate the two-page Introduction which Professor Alan M. Dershowitz wrote for the 1990 copyrighted reprint of Fraenkel. The Introduction—dated December 29, 1989—appears in The Sacco-Vanzetti Case, a special edition of Fraenkel's 1931 book "privately printed for the members of The Notable Trials Library," Division of Gryphon Editions, Inc. Ask a librarian to help you find a copy of this book. You may wish to write this essay assignment after you have given considerable attention to the 52 research topics. See next page. Cite books and articles by Professor Dershowitz that best reveal his credentials on this disputed topic. Show how each cited book and article is useful to your evaluation of this 1989 analysis by Dershowitz. See pp. 757-799 in the Bentley edition of Sinclair's Boston, which is in the editor's bibliography (at 1928). See research Topic 10-k.

VIDEO: VHS DOCUMENTARY
THE HISTORY CHANNEL - IN SEARCH OF HISTORY
TRUE STORY OF SACCO AND VANZETTI
1998 A & E TELEVISION NETWORKS

Does the 1998 video, True Story of Sacco and Vanzetti, vindicate Sacco and Vanzetti? Explain fully. See Felix, The Journal of American History (Dec. 1980, p. 754), on the notion that the 1928 Holt Transcript might inspire "scholarly vindication."

FAMOUS CRIMES REVISITED
Dr. Henry Lee & Dr. Jerry Labriola

Does the Lee/Labriola book vindicate Sacco & Vanzetti? What does edition 2004 tell you? How would Dr. James E. Starrs respond to Dr. Lee's last four lines on page 96? Can you defend Dr. Lee's use of "presumably" on page 17, line 9? Evaluate pp. 77-91 as if you were a history teacher. Will pages ix, 5, 13-76 bear scrutiny? How does the revelation of the fire in Dexter, Maine, affect your judgment of pp. 5-98 in the Lee and Labriola book?

52 RESEARCH TOPICS

Books and articles on the Sacco-Vanzetti case challenge you to separate the true from the false. Keep in mind that all authors on the case, even those with high rank and/or outstanding credentials in the intellectual community, are subject to error. Knowing that, be deferential only to truth. Hold to this ideal: Researchers try to be impartial and accurate, are rigorous in checking facts, respect the rules of evidence, test all conclusions harshly, and omit no critical item. They determine whether reviewers have ties of loyalty to the author they review or ties to a narrow cause, and whether such ties give a bias to their judgment.

These research topics can sharpen your reading, analytical, and debating skills, as well as your writing skills. They help you to see American history, American politics, the American criminal justice system, the writing of history (especially the gatekeeping of the Sacco-Vanzetti case)—and human nature.

Honor rules for documentation and paraphrasing. Use wisely the bibliography and other research materials in this handbook. Use the Holt or Appel volumes for primary support. See "Critically Analyzing Information Sources," Cornell University Library; "Evalutating Sources of Information," Purdue University, Online Writing Lab; "Evaluating Sources of Information." San Diego University; or Evaluating Information, UW-Madison Libraries.

Research, sort, connect items, test credentials of all writers. Get your facts straight. Then judge. Challenge every sentence written about this case. Create your own research topics.

1. Evaluate Vanzetti's Plymouth trial. Read Appel (VI: 1-377); Fraenkel (The Sacco-Vanzetti Case, pp. 183-201); Joughin-Morgan (The Legacy, pp. 4, 10, 45-57,158, 300); Ehrmann (The Case That Will Not Die, pp. 4-18, 50-52, 67-142); Montgomery, pp. 11-55; Frankfurter, p. 7; Kaiser (Postmortem, pp. 27-36, 183); Russell (Tragedy in Dedham, pp. 70, 93-106). a. Does Avrich (Sacco and Vanzetti: The Anarchist Background, pp. 62, 87) help or hinder you in judging testimony by Casey (Appel, VI: 106,111), Ensher (VI: 143), Stewart (VI: 180), Johnson (VI: 203-204)? Does the argument by Katzmann (VI: 159, 213-214) help on the Boda question? Was Boda at the crime site in Bridgewater on December

24, 1919? b. Who is right about the weight of Mrs. Brini's testimony at the trial—Ehrmann (The Case, pp. 341, 518); Fraenkel, p. 69; Feuerlicht, pp. 225, 379; or Montgomery, pp. 19-20? Does p. 305 in the Plymouth transcript help? c. In his opening statement, Graham (VI: 219-221) did not promise that Vanzetti would take the witness stand. Does this matter? d. Does Ehrmann (The Case, pp.137-140) make a convincing argument on the question of Vanzetti's failure to take the stand? Explain precisely. e. What challenges would Vanzetti have faced had he taken the witness stand at his Plymouth trial? f. Read the transcript to test Ehrmann's comments on McDonald (The Case, p. 70, line 15); Boda (73.10 and 97.4)); the expressman (116.19-23); Mrs. Fortini (120.31). g. Feuerlicht (p. 173) says that Katzmann, in cross-examination of Mrs. Fortini, was "amusing himself and the jury." Feuerlicht (p. 174) calls his cross-examination of Mrs. Fortini "sadistic flaying." Do you agree with Feuerlicht? Explain. h. Does the testimony of Vittoria Papa (VI: 221-223) support Vanzetti at his Plymouth trial? Does it bear on the Dedham trial? i. Is Kaiser's analysis (p. 35) of testimony by Casey, Stewart, and Johnson more objective than Montgomery's? Has either scholar omitted critical items, inconvenient facts? j. Does Background of the Plymouth Trial exculpate Vanzetti? Is Vanzetti's explanation here (pp. 34-35) for not testifying at Plymouth credible? See his second explanation in his letter of July 20, 1927. l. Are Vanzetti's alibi witnesses more credible than the eyewitnesses? Can you get help from Sacco-Vanzetti: Developments and Reconsiderations—1979? (S-V: D. & R.) m. Show how C.C. Palmer's letter is relevant. See #8.

2. Should The World Book Encyclopedia have reported in 1956, the year of their initial Sacco-Vanzetti article, that Sacco and Vanzetti were "philosophical anarchists"? a. Did Horace Meyer Kallen write this unsigned article for World Book? [Background: Kallen wrote the article "Anarchist" in volume I of World Book (1956). Martin H. Bush says "educator Horace Kallen...had been deeply involved in the Sacco-Vanzetti case during the trial." For Kallen's speech "at the first memorial meeting," see Joughin (The Legacy, p. 330, and note #64, pp. 548-549; and 575.)] Why did World Book cite David Felix's book Protest in "Additional Resources"

appended to their article in 1985-1987 and not later or earlier? b. Why did <u>World Book</u> call Sacco and Vanzetti "philosophical anarchists" in editions 1956-1987? Why did <u>World Book</u> wait until 1988 to cite a book by Russell and to drop the term "philosophical anarchists"? c. Should <u>World Book</u>, in the mid-sixties, have cited either Russell's 1962 book on the case or Montgomery's book? d. Should the editorial staff of <u>The World Book Encyclopedia</u> have assigned James D. Forman to write the article "Sacco-Vanzetti Case" for their 1988 edition? Does "Sacco and Vanzetti" (pp. 64-65,122) in Forman's 1975 book, <u>Anarchism,</u> earn Forman respected editorial authority? Did Felix have stronger credentials on the Sacco-Vanzetti case than Forman in 1988? See letter by Felix in <u>TLS</u> (2/21/1986, p. 191). e. Should <u>World Book</u> have cited Monroe's book in 2001? Why didn't <u>World Book</u> cite Judy Monroe's book on Sacco and Vanzetti in edition 2007?

3. Editors of <u>Compton's Encyclopedia</u>, in their initial article on the Sacco-Vanzetti case (1989)—more detailed than their longrunning entry on Sacco-Vanzetti in the Fact Index—allude to Vincent Teresa's book <u>My Life in the Mafia</u> (1973), a book written in collaboration with crime writer Thomas C. Renner. Teresa says, pp. 44-46, he heard Butsy Morelli confess that the Morelli gang alone killed Parmenter and Berardelli. a. Read <u>My Life in the Mafia</u> to see whether it confirms the Morelli hypothesis (Motion 6). Evaluate <u>Compton's</u> editorial use of Teresa's allegation in a reference book for elementary school children. b. Why would it be useful to know the author of the unsigned Sacco-Vanzetti article in <u>Compton's Encyclopedia</u>?

    c. Is the Sacco-Vanzetti article in <u>Compton's Encyclopedia</u> (1) derivative, (2) evenhanded? To what other encyclopedia did <u>Compton's</u> unidentified contributor(s) turn for editorial help?

4. <u>Encyclopedia International</u>, a subsidiary of Grolier (publisher of <u>Encyclopedia Americana</u>), advises readers of their Sacco-Vanzetti article to consult Ehrmann's 1969 book and the 1962 edition of Frankfurter's book. Identify the credentials of author Dennis F. Strong. Is Strong's Sacco-Vanzetti article in <u>Encyclopedia International</u> (1981) evenhanded? Why did Strong not join the

ACLU? One clue is The Nation's rebuke of the ACLU on August 20, 1977. See Transcript of the Record, 4904-4905.

5. Review the article "Sacco-Vanzetti case" in Encyclopaedia Britannica from 1929 to 2000. Evaluate the bibliography appended to the S-V article in Encyclopaedia Britannica for 1929. What item in Fraenkel's book weakens Britannica's bibliography in 1929-1960? Explain. a. Did Morris Leopold Ernst have editorial control of Britannica's Sacco-Vanzetti article for 45 years? Do you find footprints of Ernst in edition 2000? Compare the first paragraph of the Sacco-Vanzetti entry—unsigned in the 1929 edition—with that in the 1961 edition (initialed M.L.E.). Is it relevant that Ernst took Joe Morelli to his home overnight (Ehrmann, The Case, p. 429)? See Montgomery, p.65; Russell (Tragedy in Dedham, pp. 303-305, 308-309, 314, 462). b. Of what relevance is Ernst's work with O. G. Villard (New York Times, 8/11/1927/ 3)? Does Ernst's article "Deception According to Law" (The Nation, 6/1/1927) help you to judge Ernst's Sacco-Vanzetti article for fairness? Is Ernst's review (Yale Law Journal) of Frankfurter's book relevant? See Ernst at "f" in #20 and in American National Biography (vol. 7, p. 565). c. Since Encyclopaedia Britannica cited The Untried Case and Weeks's textbook from 1961 to 1973, was Britannica obligated to cite a book on the case either by Montgomery, Russell or Felix? Do you agree with Britannica's conclusion in their entry of 1985-1990: "Evidence ... pointed to the guilt of Morelli and his gang"? [Note: Their entry, 1961-1973, uses "pointing," not "pointed."] d. Why did Britannica append no bibliography to their Sacco-Vanzetti article from 1974 through 1978? On June 14, 1988, the editor told Encyclopaedia Britannica that their bibliography appended to the S-V article was "fiercely tendentious." On June 22, 1988, one signature (documented) in the Editorial Offices replied: "It would appear that the bibliography appended to the article 'Sacco-Vanzetti case' in the Encyclopaedia Britannica is unintentionally biased in favor of the more outspoken side of the controversy. I have turned your letter over to our bibliography staff, and their revision will be put into work as soon as our editorial schedule permits." e. In what printing year did Encyclopaedia Britannica mention 1. Vanzetti's Plymouth trial, 2. the defendants' guns and

ammunition found upon them at their arrest, 3. the lies the defendants told about their guns and live ammunition to Katzmann on May 6, 1920? Write a paper on the topic: The Sacco-Vanzetti case and the Editorial Offices of Encyclopaedia Britannica. Give your paper an original title. See #10-k, #22-b, #20.

6. In 1950 Encyclopedia Americana published their article on the Sacco-Vanzetti case and left it unchanged through 1972. a. Does the author of this unsigned article use phrasing from Fraenkel's 1931 book? If so, what is the implication? Note that some phrases in Americana's S-V article, editions 1950-1972, match phrases in the three columns given to Sacco and Vanzetti in the Dictionary of American Biography (1935). Did Sylvester G. Gates, author of the DAB columns, write the S-V article of 1950 for Encyclopedia Americana? Or do you conclude that the S-V article in Americana (1950-1972) had two or more authors? b. Should Encyclopedia Americana have reported, 1950-1972, that Luigi Galleani, who knew Vanzetti well, professed "philosophical anarchy"? How is Pernicone's 1979 rebuke of liberal historians relevant? Is Pernicone right? (See S-V: D. & R., p. 60) c. In 1973 Encyclopedia Americana attached the name Osmond K. Fraenkel to their S-V article. Identify key items in Walker's biography of Fraenkel (ANB, vol. 8, pp. 353-354) that help you to judge the credentials of Fraenkel. What do you conclude? d. For how many years did Americana fail to mention Vanzetti's Plymouth trial? In what year did Americana first mention the defendants' guns and their lies about their guns and bullets? f. Did Americana strengthen their credentials on the "Sacco-Vanzetti" topic when they made Eric Foner one of their Advisory Editors? See Foner at #10-b. e. Study the Sacco-Vanzetti article, virtually unchanged in editions 1973-2000. Test each of the 14 paragraphs in this article for fair and accurate reporting of the Dedham transcript, for any distortion of fact. g. Of what relevance is S. G. Gates's review of Fraenkel's The Sacco-Vanzetti Case in The New Republic (Dec. 9, 1931, pp. 103-104)? Evaluate Gates's review for balance and accuracy. See Fraenkel at #21. Determine if p. 1822 and p. 1919 in the Transcript of the Record confirm Fraenkel's paragraph 5 in the S-V entry, 1973-2005.

7. Louis Joughin launched the article "Sacco-Vanzetti Case" for Collier's Encyclopedia in 1962. What opposition has Joughin stirred by labeling Sacco and Vanzetti "philosophical anarchists" in 1962? In 2000? Is it relevant that Joughin became assistant director, American Civil Liberties Union, in 1951? How are Joughin's chapters (pp. 201-514) in The Legacy relevant? Should Collier's "Sacco-Vanzetti Case" have been assigned to Joughin? Explain. See #23, #46.

8. Frank Silva's confession. From 1929 to 1960, Encyclopaedia Britannica cited the October 31,1928 editorial in Outlook and Independent: "The Truth About the Bridgewater Hold-up," pp.1053-1055. Read this editorial and "Frank Silva's Story," pp.1055-1060. Read articles in O. and I. by Jack Callahan (pp. 1060-1063, 1070) and Silas Bent (pp. 1071-1075). Then read Brine's article in the Boston Herald (Jan. 13. 1929). Get a range of opinion on Silva's confession from Musmanno, p. 82; Montgomery, pp. 37-50; Feuerlicht, pp. 296-297; Kaiser, p.183; Russell (Tragedy, pp. 270-279); Felix, pp.129-132; Ehrmann (The Untried Case, pp. 51-52); Joughin-Morgan, pp. 51-55; and The New Republic, Nov. 7, 1928, pp. 317-318. See Fraenkel's discovery (The Sacco-Vanzetti Case, p. 199) of a factual error in the Outlook editorial, and see pp. 200-201). Can Lovett's "Vanzetti Was Innocent" editorial in The New Republic be defended? Give evidence that Lovett wrote this unsigned editorial. Explain why you can, or cannot, verify Silva's confession. Is O'Connor helpful: VLR (June 1961), 996-997? Does this alternate hypothesis (Silva hypothesis) exonerate Vanzetti? See #1.

9. Read summaries of the Sacco-Vanzetti case in these reference books: The Oxford Companion to American Literature (5th ed.); The Almanac of American History (Schlesinger); An Encyclopedic Dictionary of American History (Hurwitz); The Oxford Companion to American History; Dictionary of American History (Martin & Gelber); Dictionary of American Biography, VIII: 279-280; Family Encyclopedia of American History (The Reader's Digest); The Encyclopedic Dictionary of American History, 3rd ed., 1986 (J. M. Faragher); The Dictionary of Cultural Literacy (Hirsch/Kett/Trefil); Benet's Reader's Encyclopedia; Encyclopedia

of American History, 7th ed. (R. B. Morris/Morris); The Reader's
Companion to American History (Foner/Garraty); American
National Biography 1999 (Garraty/Carnes); The Great American
History Fact-Finder (Yanak/Cornelism); A Short Chronology of
American History 1492-1950 (Kull/Kull); The Encyclopedia of
American Crime, pp. 633-634 (Carl Sifakis); Crime Dictionary
Revised and Expanded Edition (Ralph de Sola); Dictionary of
Criminal Justice (pp. 307-308, George E. Rush); Encyclopedia of
World Crime, IV: 2649-2652 (Jay R. Nash); The Oxford
Companion to Law; American History Desk Reference (The New
York Times Public Library); The American Heritage Encyclopedia
of American History 1998 (John M. Faragher); Bartlett's Familiar
Quotations. Does Russell, in S & V: The Case Resolved, p. 3,
correctly assess editorial opinion on Sacco and Vanzetti: "Their
innocence has been taken for granted [in reference books.]"? See
#10-r. b. Evaluate Kevin Mattson's article, "The Smoking Gun
That Wasn't," in The Chronicle Review (March 3, 2006). Focus on
the last sentence in the third paragraph from the end: (Neither . . .
American history should nurture).

10. Potpourri. a. Do you agree with Dos Passos on Carlos Affe (see
excerpt)? Did Dos Passos believe Madeiros? b. Read closely Eric
Foner's essay in The Nation (Aug. 20, 1977, pp. 136-141): "Sacco
and Vanzetti: The Men and the Symbols." Then judge The Nation,
making Foner's essay a litmus test of the journal's accuracy and
fairness. c. Do Tindall and Shi (America, 1999) honor core facts
in the Dedham transcript and in post-trial scholarship? Do they
challenge Leuchtenburg's 1958 statement on Sacco and Vanzetti:
"Felix Frankfurter punched holes in the case."? Do these three (T.
S. & L.) challenge the statement by the New England Civil
Liberties Committee (2/19/1921)? What does this tell you? d.
Should Kadane and Schum (A Probabilistic Analysis ...) have said
they are not combatants of the case (p. 22) if they invoke Kaiser's
authority (p. 103), find neither defendant guilty (p. 283), and state
that Starrs is "hedging" (p. 22)? Do their six factual errors (Heron
and Andrews: 91; Ricci, Affe, Hayes: 95; Mrs. Melvin Corl: 96)
weaken their NSF study? Is their scrutiny of Rosen (p. 96) a
reliable test of their "conceptual microscope" (p. 22)? e. Should
the ACLU have supported Sacco and Vanzetti after hearing the

report of Mary Heaton Vorse? See pp. 330-340 in Vorse's <u>A Footnote to Folly;</u> and see <u>ANB</u> (vol. 22, p. 413). f. What does the statement by Ralph L. Deforrest tell you (Appel, VI: 452-455)? Why did Katzmann not call Deforrest as a prosecution witness? See Kaiser, pp. 60-61, 146. And see Appel, V: 5082. g. Albert H. Hamilton is identified as a "microscopist" in <u>The New International Year Book 1927</u> (p. 710). According to <u>TNIYB</u>, Hamilton demonstrated "that micro-photographs" [made it] "impossible that the bullet that killed Berardelli could have come from the pistol carried by Sacco." What lesson does this 1927 entry in <u>TNIYB</u> teach? See #26. h. All ballistics items of Dedham trial (Sacco's gun, Vanzetti's gun, bullets, and shells) are in a secure vault. They will be put on display when the State Police build their Museum, which is in the planning stage. Be patient. Address: Massachusetts State Police Academy, 340 West Brookfield Road, New Braintree, MA 01531. i. Does Grossman's article, "Lord Jowitt and the Case of Alger Hiss" (<u>Commentary</u>, Dec. 1953, pp. 582-590), help you to evaluate Grossman's credentials in 1962? Explain. What does Grossman's work with <u>Partisan Review</u> tell you? See Diana/Lionel Trilling. j. Is <u>Academic American Encyclopedia</u> authoritative and reliable in their two entries: "Sacco and Vanzetti case" and "Shahn, Ben"? Precisely what did Syracuse University endorse when it put Ben Shahn's 'crucifixion' mosaic, <u>The Passion of Sacco and Vanzetti</u> (60' x 12'), on the east wall of the Huntington Beard Crouse Building in 1967? Discuss. k. Evaluate the 1977 Report to the Governor in the Matter of Sacco and Vanzetti, pp. 757-796 in Bentley's edition of <u>Boston</u>. Keep to the question of innocence or guilt. Which review group wins the debate—Fuller's 1927 Advisory Committee or Dukakis's 1977 Taylor commission (p. 757)? Explain. One of seven assisting Taylor, Rep. Alexander J. Cella, is cited in <u>Britannica</u>, 1961-1973, 1985-1990. See Starrs (<u>JFS</u>, July: 1056.) l. Is harm done by the factual errors of Cleanth Brooks, R. W. B. Lewis, and R. P. Warren in <u>American Literature</u>: <u>The Makers and the Making</u>, II, St. Martin's Press (1973), p. 2443? Explain. m. What is Howard Zinn's debatable point in <u>A People's History of the United States 1492—Present</u>, pp. 366-367 (1995)? n. E. L. Doctorow contends each of "the most important trials in our history ...: Scopes, **Sacco and Vanzetti**, the Rosenbergs ...

shimmers forever with just that perplexing ambiguity characteristic of a true novel." What lesson does Doctorow's contention teach? See American Review 26 (Nov. 1977), p. 227. o. Is Mark C. Carnes' edition of A History of American Life "a milestone in the road toward a better knowledge of the past," as Professor Schlesinger claims on p. 24? Test this claim in pp.1073-1074. p. How reliable is the Internet on Sacco and Vanzetti? q. Is D'Attilio 100 percent reliable? r. Determine whether the entry on Sacco and Vanzetti is accurate and balanced in these 10 reference books: The Cambridge Biographical Encyclopedia, Second ed., ed. David Crystal, Cambridge Univ. Press (1998), p. 820; The Cambridge Encyclopedia, Third ed., ed. David Crystal, Cambridge Univ. Press (1997), p. 931; The New American Desk Encyclopedia, Fourth ed., Signet, (1997), p. 1129; Oxford's Family Encyclopedia (1997), p. 584; An Incomplete Education, Judy Jones and William Wilson, Ballantine Books, (1995), p. 50; What Every American Should Know About American History, Dr. Alan Axelrod and Charles Phillips, Bob Adams, Inc., (1992), p. 273; Oxford Dictionary of Quotations, Revised 4th edition, Angela Partigan (1996), p. 708; West's Encyclopedia of American Law, IX (1998), pp. 99-101; Great American Trials, Edward W. Knappman, ed. (1994), pp. 288-293; Encyclopedia of the American Left, 2nd ed., (1998), pp. 713-716. s. Which book has the best factual account of the case? Prove it. t. Generally speaking, do you find editorial bias in favor of the Commonwealth (prosecution) in reference books? Explain.

11. Read closely Frankfurter's The Case of Sacco and Vanzetti, then test it against both trial transcripts. See Leonard Baker, Brandeis and Frankfurter, New York: Harper & Row, p. 270: "Occasionally the accuracy of Frankfurter's book is challenged, but such challenges consistently are rebutted." [Baker restates Ehrmann's claim (The Case, p.173) of Frankfurter's "complete accuracy."] a. Is Frankfurter's book free of factual errors and other flaws listed in #30?

b. Did both Montgomery and Felix fail "to discredit Frankfurter's great authority," as Ehrmann argues in The Case That Will Not Die (p. 534)? Does it matter, as Paul Johnson states (A History of the American People, p. 767), that Frankfurter "was indeed perhaps the most influential law professor in US history"?

c. Here is the Atlantic's March 1927 editorial assessment of Frankfurter's S-V article in the March 1927 issue of the Atlantic Monthly (p. 406): "This paper by **Felix Frankfurter** is the first effort to give the public a complete and accurate re´sume´ of the facts of the case.... . The paper represents a necessary abridgment, ... but [is] compressed accurately and fairly by a trained and responsible lawyer." The Atlantic's March cover states: "A Comprehensive Analysis of a Trial of Grave Importance." Did Montgomery have a legitimate complaint (S-V: The Murder and the Myth, p. 294, lines 21-27) against the Atlantic Monthly? Explain. d. Did Ernst know Frankfurter? e. Rate the Urofsky-Levy assessment of Frankfurter's book (The Letters, p.270). f. What weight do you give former Judge Samuel R. Stern's evaluation of Frankfurter? (See "From a Lawyer's Standpoint" in The Outlook, Sept. 7, 1927, pp. 17-18.) Did Joughin (p. 325) misquote Stern? How is Frankfurter's opinion of Hamilton (pp. 74-75) answered by Starrs in JFS: (April): p. 635? g. Test Parrish's claim in American National Biography, vol. 8, p. 376: "... [T]he verdict of historians has vindicated Frankfurter's position [on the case]." h. Identify and evaluate Frankfurter's five weakest points. Put all in a paper. See Appel, V: 5295, lines 4-9 & #49.

12. Read Bruce A. Murphy's account of Frankfurter's instructions to Judge Julian Mack on how one Sacco-Vanzetti item——Brandeis's decision not to act for defendants——should be written in The New Republic. Explain what light Murphy's research (The Brandeis/Frankfurter Connection, pp.78-81) sheds on Frankfurter's 1927 book. See Urofsky's 1991 book, p. 25. Does Murphy's book affect your judgment of Frankfurter and Montgomery? Is Felix's charge against The New Republic, June 4, 1966, valid? Why does it seem appropriate that A. M. Bickel should review Felix's book in TNR? What does "Bickel vs. Felix" really mean? Who is more reliable on Sacco and Vanzetti, Felix or Michael Miller Topp?

13. In November 1931, Max Lerner said of Louis D. Brandeis in the Yale Law Journal (p. 25): "And to many in radical circles his refusal, on ethical grounds, to intervene in the Sacco-Vanzetti case seemed equivocal." What lesson does Lerner's 1931 statement

teach? Why did Lerner, elsewhere, write about Frankfurter's "Hot
Dogs"? See Murphy, pp. 9-14.

14. Joseph Rosen, peddler of woolens, testified at the Dedham trial
(1921) that he made a cash sale to Vanzetti in North Plymouth on
April15, 1920. On July 21,1927, Rosen told Fuller's Advisory
Committee: "I registered in some boarding house [at Whitman on
April 15, 1920] ... I put down my name and my address, according
to my best recollection, which I proved to District Attorney
Katzmann." Then Rosen spoke of the action he took when he read
of Vanzetti's arrest: "But a few weeks after this ["this," by the
1921 testimony, means his overnight stay at Whitman] I pick up a
Boston paper and see a picture of this Vanz-[Appel, V: 5254] etti; I
didn't know his name before that, but he was the only fish peddler
in town, so I was wondering how he could be connected with this
crime. So when I came back to Plymouth once again I went in up
to the house, you know, that I sold him the piece of cloth, to a
party I think by the name of Miss Brini, and I ask her what was the
matter with this Vanzetti, I says, 'I have been in Plymouth; I sold
him a piece of cloth at about noontime.'" [V: 5255] When Rosen
completed his testimony, Ranney (Assistant District Attorney)
said: "No questions." [V: 5256] Then Lowell asked Rosen: "Do
you desire to change any of the testimony that you gave at the
trial?" Rosen said: "No." [V: 5256] Write a paper in which you
explain (a) whether Rosen's testimony of July 21,1927, possesses
value for Fuller's Advisory Committee, (b) whether this testimony
seems to exonerate Vanzetti, (c) whether Fraenkel's summary (p.
505) of Rosen's 1927 testimony at Boston is accurate, (d) whether
Kaiser's examination of Rosen (p. 79) will bear scrutiny.

15. Study this statement that William G. Thompson made to Fuller's
committee on July 21, 1927. "Yesterday I saw the brother of
Boda. His real name is (spelling) B-u-d-a. He is in the employ of
the Daloz Cleansing Company in Boston. He said that his brother
has been living for several years with his mother in a town in Italy
which he mentioned, and he says he will gladly cable to his brother
to come back to America, and he thinks he will come if his
travelling expenses are paid, and that he will do his best to get him
back. He said his brother has nothing to fear except the Federal

officials, and if that were arranged he would be glad to get here and get back again. I will dictate into the record the present address as I have ascertained it from his brother. It is Mario Buda, Savignano di Romagna, Province Favi, Italy." [V: 5256] a. What does Thompson's statement to Grant, Lowell, and Stratton teach you? b. Does Thompson's reference to Joseph Scavitto (Appel, V: 5369) help you answer "a"? c. Are Montgomery's pp. 252-254 relevant? Are pp. 5307-5308 in vol. 5 of Appel useful? See #21.

16. Thompson told the Advisory Committee that Bullet 3 of the Dedham trial was not Bullet 3 of Dr. Magrath's autopsy (Appel, V: 5038). See accusatory letter on substitute bullet and shell in Appel, VI: 357-358. And see Appel: 5186-5188, 5292, 5314, 5317, 5339. a. Does Fraenkel, pp. 334-335, resolve the dispute between Ehrmann and Lowell (V: 5319-5320)? (Note: Fraenkel, p. 335, refers to p. 77 in the transcript.) b. Does Dr. Jones's reference to a "slightly flattened" bullet (VI: 415) at the April 17 inquest and his other remarks on pp. 414-415 help you to assess Kaiser's argument (p. 113, line 5) about "the switch" of bullets? c. Is the April 17 observation by Dr. Frazier on p. 395 helpful? Evaluate Kaiser, pp. 106-123, 158; Felix, pp. 119-127; Russell (S. & V: C. R., pp. 152-153); Ranney's comments (Appel, V: 5188, 5339); Grossman's article in Commentary (Jan., 1962) and Grossman's reply to Musmanno's challenge in Commentary (Sept. 1962, pp. 254-256). d. Read Starrs, "Once More Unto the Breech: The Firearms Evidence in the Sacco and Vanzetti Case Revisited" Part II, Journal of Forensic Sciences (July 1986):1050-1078. Tell why Starrs **is** or **is not** fair to Kaiser in JFS (April): 650? To Jackson (April): 646? Is Starrs fair to Ehrmann in JFS (July): 1053, 1063? To Thompson (July): 1056? e. Excluding Bullet 3, what three pieces of evidence, one of which is in Part I (April issue), prompt Starrs to reject the bullet switching hypothesis? Is Starrs sound? f. Is Kaiser's debate with Russell in "Sacco and Vanzetti: An Exchange" in the NYRB (May 29, 1986, pp. 52-55) a useful summary? Explain. In his letter to Newby (June 29, 1988), Russell responded to Kaiser's challenge in the NYRB, p. 52, column 4: "That 6 Peters cartridges found in Sacco's pocket and two spent cartridges found at the scene of the crime were manufactured on the same machine is indisputable. Kaiser argues

that for that to mean anything we should have to know the number of machines involved. But I have learned since from a Remington superintendent that the dies of a machine have to be changed once or twice a day. Once they are changed, the markings are different. So the six cartridges and the two shells were made on the same machine on the same day, too obvious to be a coincidence." g. Evaluate the Thompson-Ehrmann allegation, the allegation Kaiser renewed in 1985. See Montgomery, pp. 88-93, if you like. See #35. See Appel, IV: 3673-3677. And see #25.

17. Write a "Dear Walter" letter in response to Walter Lippmann's editorial in The World, August 19, 1927. The editorial appears in Corbett, Classical Rhetoric for the Modern Student, 235-241. Was Corbett's Modern Student in1965 able to evaluate fully (see Readings on pp. 176-177) Lippmann's "Doubt That Will Not Down" without access a. to the 1928 Holt transcript, b. to Steel's research on Lippmann's reversal of editorial opinion, c. to the August 9 Goddard report, d. to Lippmann's remarks on the guns (p. 237), e. to studies by Pernicone's four "revisionists"? Show how Corbett's citation to Weeks's textbook (p. 235) is, or is not, helpful to students. Is Corbett a disinterested student of this topic? Show evidence. See Weeks at #29 and Pernicone at #44. Enrich your letter with your adventures in S-V research.

18. a. Identify facts from the trial transcripts that support the argument in Babette Deutsch's sonnet in The New Republic (April 7, 1986, p. 32). Is the sonnet factually correct? Explain why TNR reprinted this 1927 sonnet in 1986. b. Create an imaginary conversation (after the method of W. S. Landor) between Walter Lippmann and Judge Wyzanski; between P. W. Slosson and D. Felix; between Prof. Starrs and Prof. Douglas Linder; between E.M. Morgan and Russell Aiuto. Aiuto on Internet: The Legacy. Charles C. Palmer and Herbert B. Ehrmann.

19. Evaluate Sinclair's Boston [Bentley ed.] for objective reporting on the Sacco-Vanzetti case. Evaluate Zinn's Introduction to Boston, including note #5 on p. xxviii. Evaluate Zinn's Reading List on p. xxxi. a. Do you accept the judgment of Peter Hansen (Brandeis University)—in Fox and Kloppenberg's A Companion to

American Thought, p. 629—that Sinclair's Boston "contributed to
the apotheosis of anarchists Nicola Sacco and Bartolomeo
Vanzetti, folk heroes of the mythic left"? Why? Why not? b.
How important, for understanding Boston, is Sinclair's debate with
the anarchist editor of The Road to Freedom, June 1929, pp. 6-7?
c. Does the scene of Henry Cabot Winters and his mother-in-law
(Boston, pp. 453-460) support D'Attilio's thesis: "the neglected
anarchist dimension of the case" (S-V: D. & R., p. 77)? Does
Boston come under scrutiny in S-V: D. & R.? d. Is Russell (S. &
V: C. R., p. 105) helpful? e. See Sinclair's letter to Robert Minor,
Feb. 8, 1928, p. 480. See Louis Joughin in The Legacy, p. 448.

20. Ehrmann. Read The Untried Case: The Sacco-Vanzetti Case and
the Morelli Gang. See Morelli/M motion (Appel, V: 4361-4721);
Thayer's decision on Morelli/M motion (V: 4722-4777); briefs on
Morelli/M motion (V: 4782-4877); Morgan's review of Ehrmann's
book in the Harvard Law Review, (January 1934), 538-547;
Morgan's 1960 Introduction to Ehrmann's second edition, pp. xvii-
xxii; Montgomery, pp. 205-250; Russell (Tragedy, pp. 278-314,
461-62; S & V: The Case Resolved, pp.127-131,164-172); Felix,
pp.133-140; Kaiser, pp. 150-152; chapter 6 and Appendix A in
Frankfurter; Grossman's article in Commentary (Jan. 1962). a. Is
Grossman (p. 36) fair to Ehrmann's characterization of Madeiros
in the concluding "Da Vinci" passage, pp. 203-204? How does
Ehrmann's "perfect Calvary" (p. 141) apply? b. The Untried Case
never states that the Buick and the Bridgewater and Braintree
plates were all stolen at Needham. Is Russell's theory of towns (S.
& V: C. R., pp. 171-172), more credible than Ehrmann's theory of
the Morellis? c. How far does Morgan's Introduction to
Ehrmann's second edition depart from his 1934 review? d. Does
Morgan's excerpt, p. xxii, mislead uninformed readers? Explain.
Why does Hughes attack Morgan in vol. 49 of The Georgetown
Law Journal (Summer 1961)? e. Does Ehrmann's "After Forty
Years," pp. 261-268, rebut Montgomery? f. Does Joseph Morelli's
1939 letter to M. L. Ernst, p. 238, exonerate Sacco and Vanzetti?
See Ernst in #5. g. Evaluate "A Letter From the Secretary of
JUSTICE OLIVER WENDELL HOLMES" (October 29, 1934) on
the back jacket of the 1960 edition of The Untried Case. Is it
somber? h. Does Ehrmann, in The Case That Will Not Die, give

expert attention to 1. Grossman's review of Montgomery's book (Commentary, Jan. 1962); 2. Morgan's review of The Untried Case (Harvard Law Review, Jan. 1934); 3. James Burns's correction of his Dedham testimony (Boston Evening Transcript, Aug. 10, 1927 and Bridgeport Post, Aug. 4, 1927), 4. Pecheur? Explain. See #27. i. Do Kaiser (p. 83) and Russell (S. & V.: C. R., p. 120) have documentation which suggests that Ehrmann (The Case, pp. 367-370) withheld embarrassing truth about James Hayes? Do you agree with Ehrmann's judgment of Affe (p. 366) and Hayes (p. 367)? j. What does Ehrmann's shift of opinion on Katzmann (S & V: The Case Resolved, p.153) show? k. Does Palmer's letter, p. 413, help you judge pp. 245-246 in The Case That Will Not Die? Is Ehrmann's title for chapter 15 ironic?

21. In The Sacco-Vanzetti Case, Osmond K. Fraenkel wrote (p. 5): "Both men [Sacco and Vanzetti] belonged at the time to the Galleani group of philosophical anarchists." See Avrich on Galleani: pp. 41,48, 56-57, 97-98,135, 160-162. See Pernicone, p. 60, and D'Attilio, p. 81, in Sacco-Vanzetti: Developments and Reconsiderations—1979; Grossman (p. 40); and Thompson in Appel, V: 5307-5308. a. Test Fraenkel's 1931 statement on "philosophical anarchists." b. How does Fraenkel's 1931 portrait of Boda (The Sacco-Vanzetti Case, p. 10) differ from Avrich's 1991 portrait of Boda/Buda on pp. 137,157, 159, 188, 204-207 (S & V: TAB)? See Pernicone's portrait in ANB (vol. 19, 174)? How does Vecoli's biography of Galleani in ANB (vol. 8: 646-647) help? c. Have Sacco-Vanzetti scholars given proper attention to Fraenkel's "absence due to sickness" (p. 11, line 7)? Is this a minor point? Is p. 14, line 8 relevant? d. Why are Fraenkel's witnesses on p. 191, lines 24-26, a big item? e. Have Fraenkel's 1931 statements on defense witnesses Williams, Affe, and Hayes (pp. 507-508) withstood the test of time? Explain. (See Kaiser, pp. 80, 83) f. Does Samuel Johnson (Appel, V: 5161-5165) shed light on Boda? g. Why is Walker's biography of Fraenkel in ANB (vol. 8, 353-354) useful? Is Walker an A.C.L.U. stalwart? Will Fraenkel's diary, accessible in 2033, exonerate Sacco and Vanzetti? Explain. h. Test Fraenkel's evaluation of Scavitto. See Fraenkel, pp. 67-68, 218. And see "Summary" on p. 307. Show conclusion. See Fraenkel at #6, Thompson at #15, Felix at #32.

22. In <u>After Twelve Years,</u> chapter 35, Musmanno recalled his argument before Attorney General Arthur K. Reading of Massachusetts. He said (p. 371): "[T]hese equivocating eleven" [witnesses for the Commonwealth: Andrews, Tracy, Heron, Pelser, Splaine, Devlin, Goodridge, Faulkner, Levangie, Reed, Dolbeare] "could never have overcome the testimony of the forthright hundred and five [defense witnesses] if the trial had been conducted with all the safeguards provided for by the Constitution and the law." a. Write an official reply Reading could have sent to Musmanno. b. What does Musmanno's speech in the State House in April 1959 tell you? See "Massachusetts: The Restless Ghosts," <u>Newsweek</u> (4/13/1959): 38. See p. 644.

23. When Henry A. Yeomans published <u>Abbot Lawrence Lowell, 1856-1943</u>, he was challenged by Louis Joughin (<u>The Legacy</u>, p. 309): "[W]hy does Professor Yeomans pass over in silence the Bosco-Guadagni episode (the failure to insert in the record of the proceedings a rehabilitation of this part of Sacco's alibi),—which constituted the most formidable specific charge against Lowell?" Evaluate the Bosco-Guadagni episode. Did Lowell blunder? If so, did his blunder weaken the Advisory Committee report sent to Fuller? Did Lowell unwittingly help to rehabilitate "this part of Sacco's alibi"? How does Katzmann join to this episode? See Appel, V: 5085-5106; Feuerlicht (pp. 363-365); Ehrmann's "President Lowell Destroys a 'Serious Alibi'" in <u>The Case</u>, pp. 374-387. Write a paper in which you assess the validity of Joughin's challenge in 1948. See #7.

24. Does the U. S. Department of Justice have evidence in its files that exonerates Sacco and Vanzetti? See Thompson in Appel, V: 4500-4507; 4377-4392; Judge Wait in V: 4893; Hill, Field, and Evarts in V: 5443; Thayer in V: 4748-4750, 4753-4777; Grant, Lowell, and Stratton in V: 5378l, 5378m, 5378t, 5378u. And see Frankfurter, p. 68; Montgomery, pp. 278-280; Felix, p. 253; Feuerlicht, pp. 326-327; Kaiser, pp. 124-125, 129-130, 133; Russell (<u>S & V: The Case Resolved</u>, pp. 110, 173-182). Were Sacco and Vanzetti innocent victims of the Red Scare? When did the Red Scare begin to fade? See <u>The FBI Files</u> (Linder: #52). See <u>The Red Scare</u> at

Douglas Linder's Website: <u>Famous Trials—Trial of Sacco and Vanzetti</u>.

25. Research Albert H. Hamilton. What opinions do you get of him from Frankfurter (pp. 74-75); J. and C. Gunther (pp. 228, 241, 244); Montgomery (p. 88); Felix (pp. 120-121, 143); Ehrmann (<u>The Case</u>, p. 277); Kaiser (p. 93); Joughin-Morgan (pp. 173-175,190, 537); Starrs (April): 635; (July): 1053; Russell (<u>Tragedy</u>, pp. 234, 249, 376-377), (<u>S & V: The Case Resolved</u>, pp. 150-151); Musmanno (p. 176)? Is the 1957 Hatcher-Jury-Weller book useful? When Hamilton was challenged at Boston on July 13, 1927, he told Ranney he had been a trial expert witness in chemistry, handwriting, firearms and bullets, gunshot wounds (external and internal), and inks; but he was not "a graduate of a medical college." Compare Hamilton's affidavit on ink marks with affidavit by William E. Hingston in Appel, IV: 3577-3578. Switch of Gun Barrels is in Appel, IV: 3732bb-3732tt. See Joughin-Morgan (p. 537) on Hamilton's testimony in the trial <u>People v. Strewl</u>, and Appel (V: 5018, 5345) for Ranney's challenges to Hamilton. How is "Sacco and Vanzetti" in Forman's book <u>Anarchism</u> (p. 65) relevant? Be specific. Do you get help from "Stielow and Green" (pp. 245-256) in Edwin M. Borchard's <u>Convicting the Innocent</u>, New Haven: Yale University Press, 1932? See transcript, 5018, & Russell, p. 402. See p. 224.

26. Gill and Burns. Montgomery, p. 87; Grossman, p. 37—(repeated in <u>Commentary</u>, September 1962, p. 255)—Russell (<u>Tragedy</u>, p. 376) and Felix, p.126, state that Gill, who conducted ballistics tests in 1923, accepted Goddard's report on his ballistics study made with the comparison microscope (June 3, 1927). Russell (pp. 376-377) and Felix (p. 126) state that James Burns, defense ballistics expert at the trial, conceded in 1927 that Bullet 3 had been fired from the Sacco gun. a. Does Kaiser mention these concessions of Gill and Burns? Do Joughin and Morgan mention these concessions in <u>The Legacy</u>? b. Does Ehrmann make a valid point on Gill in <u>The Case</u>, p. 283? Does Ehrmann mention Burns' concession? c. Should Joughin (<u>The Legacy</u>, p. 352) have been more specific about "error" and "new information" in <u>True Detective Mysteries</u>? d. Do you accept Joughin's statement on

Gill in his 1963 review of Russell's book in <u>American Historical Review</u> (Jan. 1963), p. 488? Explain. e. Do you find useful information on Burns in the <u>Boston Evening Transcript</u>, Aug. 10, 1927, pp. 1,16, and the <u>Bridgeport Post</u>, Aug. 4? f. Is Van Amburgh accurate on Burns in the September 1938 issue (p. 119) of <u>True Detective Mysteries</u>? Fraenkel does not say Burns conceded. Fraenkel does say, p. 160: "Gill was reported as having expressed doubt about the correctness of his earlier views after seeing Goddard make his test." g. Is Grossman responding to Fraenkel? e. How important are Gill and Burns in the post-trial debate? State a precise conclusion and defend it.

27. Two principals in the Sacco-Vanzetti controversy are Roy E. Gould, who did not testify at the Dedham trial, and Frank J. Burke. Write a well-reasoned paper in which you compare Kaiser's evaluation of Gould and Burke (p. 62) with evaluations of them by Montgomery (pp.167-171); Felix (p. 112); Ehrmann (<u>The Case</u>, pp. 395-398); Russell (<u>S & V: The Case</u> Resolved, pp. 119-120); Frankfurter (p.75); Fraenkel (pp. 297-301; 316-317). Thompson called Gould "a perfectly reputable man" (Appel, V: 5275). Your paper should explain a. what these divergent views tell you, b. whether Thayer was justified in denying the Gould motion, c. whether Ehrmann, in <u>The Case</u>, included or omitted Pecheur, Burke's working companion, in his evaluation of Burke; whether Ehrmann's description of the IWW as "the far left labor organization" (<u>The Case</u>, p. 152) is useful; d. whether Joughin-Morgan give a sound analysis of Burke and Pecheur; e. whether testimony by the trio—Burke, Gould, and Pecheur—seems credible; f. whether Montgomery read the affidavits for Motion 2 more closely than Thayer (Appel, IV: 3496-3527). How does the map ("Witnesses West ...") help?

28. Is there a definitive, standard reference work on the Sacco-Vanzetti case? Discuss.

29. Compare <u>Commonwealth vs. Sacco and Vanzetti</u>, edited in 1958 by Robert P. Weeks, with this book. a. In what areas is Weeks's book superior to this book? b. How much attention does Weeks give to Sacco's alibi witnesses? To Vanzetti's? To Atwater,

Slater, and Falzini? To Pecheur? To Lola Andrews and George Kelley? To Carlo Tresca? To Goddard's test on June 3, 1927? To Sinclair's post-execution talk with Fred Moore? c. Evaluate the claim on the cover that Weeks's college text is "A Book of Primary Source Materials." d. Is it significant that Weeks's quotations from the Joughin-Morgan book are limited to Joughin's paragraphs on pages 203-204 and two lines from p. 205? e. Evaluate Weeks's bibliography, pp. 274-275, after you have read page 68 in Vincent Ruggiero's The Art of Thinking. f. Evaluate Davidson and Lytle's claim (After the Fact, p. 287, 5th ed.): "The trial records, though available in some libraries in six volumes, may be found in adequate length in Robert Weeks, ed., The Sacco-Vanzetti Case."

30. Read three reviews of Francis Russell's book Tragedy in Dedham. (1) American Historical Review, LXVIII (January, 1963), 487-89, by G. Louis Joughin; (2) "The Sacco-Vanzetti Case: With Critical Analysis of the Book Tragedy in Dedham by Francis Russell" in Kansas Law Review, 11 (May, 1963), **481-525**, by Michael A. Musmanno; (3) Saturday Review, XLV, (September 8, 1962), 56, by Roger Baldwin. See Baldwin at #32. Evaluate these reviews after you have read chapters 9-13 in Russell's 1962 volume. a. How well does Russell's book stand up to criticism? Do you find—either in Russell or in his reviewers—misleading statements, misstatements, misrepresentation, misinformation, distortion, misperception, errors of fact, errors of omission, or unsound inferences drawn from the transcripts of the trials or from other sources? b. Is Grossman's comment on Tragedy in Dedham in Commentary (Sept. 1962, pp. 254-255), that of a partisan or a disinterested scholar? How can you tell? c. What do Russell's shifts of opinion on the S-V case from 1955 to 1986 reveal about Russell? d. Does Russell's 1962 book honor Avrich's 1979 belief in the high importance of "the anarchist dimension," set forth in Sacco - Vanzetti: D. and R., p. 61? Explain. In a letter to the editor (1993), Felix wrote of Russell: "The attacks of the case partisans later drove him to a more realistic view of the anarchists and their martyrs. But, like many others, he let Vanzetti seduce him. His last thoughts on Vanzetti seemed to be that Vanzetti was involved in the holdup [at South Braintree] but did not shoot

anyone. This is innocence only by a dispensation the courts do not grant." e. What weight does Felix's letter to the editor carry? In a letter of August 1, 1988, Russell told the editor he challenged one S-V partisan to bring him "facts proving the two men were innocent." f. How do these two letters shed light on Sacco and Vanzetti: The Case Resolved? See Pernicone's statement on Russell's 1986 book in ANB (vol. 19, p. 176). Evaluate Gallagher's use of the terms "dreamer" and "scholar" in "The Next-to-Last Word," The Nation, August 2/9, 1986, pp. 87-90. What do you learn from Gallagher?

31. A. J. Ayer, reviewing Russell's book in the New Statesman (5 July 1963, 15-16), said Vanzetti's letters from prison reveal "a man of great sweetness and nobility of character," that "the crime was entirely foreign to his character." Lippmann wrote in Lantern (August 1929): "By every test that I know of for judging character, these are the letters [The Letters of Sacco and Vanzetti] of innocent men." How do Felix and other scholars—Pernicone, D'Attilio, Grossman, Vecoli (ANB, v. 8: 646-647), and Avrich— speak to these evaluations by Ayer and Lippmann? Why is a second look at Appendix I in the published letters of 1928 helpful (see bibliography)? Did Ayer worship Bertrand Russell? Or is Noel Annan wrong? Draw a conclusion and support it.

32. In Roger Baldwin: Founder of the American Civil Liberties Union, Peggy Lamson (p. v) says Morris Ernst and Osmond K. Fraenkel "worked closely ... with Roger..." Does Lamson's documentation of the Baldwin/Ernst/Fraenkel connection (pp.173-174, 225-226) affect your decision-making about the Sacco-Vanzetti case? Are tributes to Baldwin by Max Lerner and William O. Douglas (p. 268) useful? Is Russell's correspondence with Baldwin useful (S. & V.: The Case Resolved, p. 124)? Are Baldwin's visits to Sacco and Vanzetti in prison (p. 169) relevant? How is Felix's response to Baldwin (Columbia University Forum, Winter 1964, p. 46) relevant? See Ernst at #5 and Fraenkel at #6.

33. On a teeter-totter sit ten experts who reviewed Felix's Protest: Sacco-Vanzetti and the Intellectuals. One side seats five who are critical of Felix's book: Bickel, #2; Fraenkel, #7; Lorenson, #9;

Musmanno, #13; Joughin, #4. The other side seats five who praise Felix's book: Cort, #1; Clements, #3; Toomin, #5; Hughes, #14; Chamberlin, #16. Which side has the weightier argument? Check credentials of each critic. Which side gets the higher rating as disinterested critics (people with no axe to grind)? Answer in a well-reasoned paper.

34. Give a close detailed study to Phil Stong's "The Last Days of Sacco and Vanzetti" in The Aspirin Age, pp. 169-189, ed. by Isabel Leighton. Decide whether Felix (pp. 178-182, 252-253) makes a valid criticism of Vanzetti's much-cited speech (p.188 in Stong): "If it had not been for this thing, ..." Like Stong, Corbett (p. 387) attributes the speech to Vanzetti and notes its "moving eloquence" and "rhetorical effectiveness." Why do M. Frankfurter-Jackson make Vanzetti's speech to Stong the epigraph for their book and assign it, mistakenly, to April 9, 1927? See Feuerlicht, pp. 339-345; Russell (Tragedy, p. 388), and (S. & V.: The Case Resolved, pp. 126, 222); "The Testament of Vanzetti," National Review, (Jan. 14, 1961), pp.15-17; and Polenberg's Introduction to The Letters of Sacco and Vanzetti (Penguin Books, 1997), pp. xxiii-xliii. Does Polenberg mislead on p. xxxix? See Starrs, JFS (April): 650. Does Tanenhaus's footnote on Ben Huebsch (Whittaker Chambers, p. 342) affect your judgment of Polenberg's Introduction to the Penguin edition of the letters? See Corbett at #17. Is Feuerlicht's analysis better than Corbett's?

35. Kaiser found in a loose-leaf notebook left by Harold Williams, Katzmann's assistant, "a quick chronology of the key dates of the two crimes and a summary of the state's evidence against Vanzetti." Item "5h" in Williams' chronology reads: "Police story that trap ready to spring." Kaiser concludes: "5h seems to suggest that the whole story of Stewart's having asked Simon Johnson to call him if Boda ever came for his car was not true." a. Evaluate both Kaiser's suggestion on "5h" and Kaiser's opening comment on Williams' notebooks: "Williams does not seem to have taken long to realize that something was rotten in the prosecution's case" (pp.160-161). b. Where is Kaiser's blunder on p. 79? What is his factual error on p.105? c. Does p. 25 accurately represent testimony in Appel, V: 5085? d. Does Kaiser's judgment of

Hamilton (p. 93) hold up against judgments of him by Russell (Tragedy, pp. 233-234, 249; S. & V: C. R., p. 152); Felix, pp. 125-126); Starrs, JFS (July): 1053); Joughin-Morgan, pp. 173-75, 190, 537; and Grossman, pp. 36-37? e. Did Goddard have "to admit error" (Kaiser, p. 95)? f. How does Kaiser's account of Edward H. James (p.135) compare with Russell's account (S. & V.: C. R., p. 57)? g. Is Kaiser's excerpt (p.122) from Van Amburgh's essay a strong point for him? h. Can Kaiser (p.177) justify his accusation against Russell (see S & V: The Case Resolved, 148) on the subject: "breechblock markings on shells"? Are you helped by the paragraph on "breechface markings" by Starrs in Journal of Forensic Sciences (April 1986, p. 648)? Why did Van Amburgh give so little emphasis to the breechblock when he testified on June 21,1921? See True Detective Mysteries (Sept., 1938, 119). i. Is Kaiser's debate on Gambera in "Sacco and Vanzetti: An Exchange" in the NYRB (May 29, 1986, p. 53) critical? On p. 52 of NYRB Kaiser challenges Russell on the 16 live Peters cartridges found on Sacco (S. & V.: C. R., p. 162). How does Starrs respond in July of 1986? j. Is Kaiser's "one bandit" shooter (p. 104) validated by Starrs? (See "same weapon" on p. 96, line 21.) k. Does Kaiser recognize Grossman's article in Commentary (Jan. 1962)? l. Does one Kaiser item on p. 62 touch on Pecheur? m. Kaiser claims (p. 175) that Michael Stewart's "word cannot be trusted." Test his claim by reading Stewart's memorandums, which you can obtain from The Commonwealth of Massachusetts, Archives Division, 220 Morrissey Boulevard, Boston, MA 02125. Refer to Sacco and Vanzetti Case File, 1920-1947 (Series PS11/2084X). Note this paragraph in the Memo by M. E. Stewart, May 31, 1921 ["Courtesy of Massachusetts Archives"]: "On the 30th of April word came from Johnson that he [Boda] had stated that he was coming for the car the following day, May first. I notified State Officer Scott and he in company with Arthur Wells, also a state officer at that time, spend [sic] the entire day in the Selectman's office at Bridgewater waiting for word from Johnson that they had come for the car. [Officer] Warren Laughton was laying close by in West Bridgewater. Boda didn't come [on May 1, 1920]." Does Avrich honor any Stewart memorandum? Does Frankfurter? n. Why did Judge Wyzanski (#49) fail to mention the Young-Kaiser book? o. Does Kaiser omit two inculpatory items from Stewart's memorandum titled "Nicola Sacco"? Explain. p. Evaluate Kaiser's speculation (p. 24) that Sacco and Vanzetti "might ... have wanted to conceal ... an incriminating person such as Carlo Valdinocci" on May 5, 1920. Does the Young-Kaiser book, cited by <u>Britannica</u> in 1991, hold up to scrutiny? Explain. See #1, #16, #25, #33.

36. Evaluate Brogan's review of Kaiser's book <u>Postmortem</u> in the <u>Times Literary Supplement</u> (Dec. 27, 1985, p. 1474.) In <u>The Longman History of the United States of America</u> (1985), Brogan says Sacco and Vanzetti were "found guilty of murdering and robbing a paymaster in South Braintree" (p. 513). Does Brogan's statement in his U. S. history book add authority to his <u>TLS</u> review? Did Brogan [his letter to Illinois State Univ. (22 Sept. 1988) and email (24 Jan. 2001)] twice weaken (withdraw?) his 1985 support of Kaiser's book? See letter by Felix in <u>TLS</u> (2/21/1986, p. 191). Judge Brogan.

37. Is Vanzetti accurate and persuasive in the first three numbered items of his letter to Fuller, July 28, 1927. (See <u>The Letters of Sacco and Vanzetti</u>, pp. 381-397.) When the three Irish Carbarn Bandits were executed on January 6, 1927, for the murder of a watchman on October 5, 1925 (<u>Boston Herald</u>, Jan. 6), Vanzetti said Fuller refused to commute the death sentences of these Irish Americans in order to make invalid—on the grounds of consistency—an anticipated plea of clemency for Sacco and himself (Letter, Jan. 10, 1927, p. 234). Was Vanzetti correct in his imputation? Had 26 men died in the electric chair at Charlestown State Prison since 1901? Is Fraenkel's reference to "the Catholic element" (<u>The Sacco-Vanzeti Case</u>, p. 19, line 34) useful for tracking authorship? See <u>Tragedy in Dedham</u>, pp. 349-350. And see Joughin (<u>Legacy</u>), pp. 332-334. See #6.

38. Page 84 of <u>The Court Years 1937-1975: The Autobiography of William O. Douglas</u> (1980) has Douglas's statement: I know of no more serious danger to our legal system than occurs when <u>ideological</u> trials take place behind a facade of <u>legal</u> trials. Perhaps the most eloquent statement on this subject comes from Bartolomeo Vanzetti when he was asked [April 9, 1927] if he had

"anything to say." [Clerk Worthington asked the regular court question: "Bartolomeo Vanzetti, have you **anything to say** why sentence of death should not be passed upon you?" See Appel, V: 4896]

Vanzetti's last words in court to Thayer—quoted by Douglas.

This is what I say: I would not wish to a dog or to a snake, to the most low and misfortunate creature of the earth—I would not wish to any of them what I have had to suffer for things that I am not guilty of. But my conviction is that I have suffered for things that I am guilty of. I am suffering because I am a radical and indeed I am a radical; I have suffered because I was an Italian, and indeed I am an Italian; ... but I am so convinced to be right that if you could execute me two times, and if I could be reborn two other times, I would live again to do what I have done already. [Source is Appel, V: 4904.] Report, in a paper, what this statement by Douglas tells you; and be aware that H.S. Commager-Cantor put this speech in <u>Documents of American History</u>, II: 218-219.

39. a. Feuerlicht wrote (p. 431): "Not only did the Puritan legacy kill Sacco and Vanzetti, but their ultimate executioners [Lowell and Holmes] were its two most prominent legatees." Write an intelligent response, noting Feuerlicht's other villains on p. 430. See pp. ix,160,170, 177, 223, 225. Does the interview of John Dever in 1950 (New Bedford <u>Standard-Times</u>) support Feuerlicht's thesis on the 1630 Puritan migration (p. ix)? b. Show why Porter's "Afterword" in <u>The Never-Ending Wrong</u>, pp. 58-63, is (is not) in harmony with Feuerlicht's <u>Justice Crucified</u>. Is Porter's "locomotive of history" (pp. 19-20) identical to Lash's "locomotive" (<u>ANB</u>, v. 8, col. 2, line 17)? What does this <u>ANB</u> item tell you about Lash? About Parrish? Should <u>Encyclopaedia Britannica</u> have cited Feuerlicht's book (or Porter's) in its 1979 edition? Explain.

40. a. Are Dominick Ricci (Transcript 1679) and Domenico Ricci (Avrich, pp. 64,172,215, 244) one and the same person? Or are they two distinct individuals? (Dominick is the English spelling, Domenico the Italian.) b. Are Luigi Falzini (Transcript: 1629) and

Luigi Falsini (Avrich, pp. 158, 188-189, 215) one and the same person? c. Explain why p. xxxi in Mennel and Compston's Holmes and Frankfurter helps you evaluate Sylvester Gates' review of Fraenkel's book in TNR. See p. 506.

41. Does Avrich's book overpower the argument of Montgomery's book? Evaluate Avrich's 1991 charge (p. 3) that Katzmann "conducted a highly unscrupulous prosecution ... perhaps even tampering with physical evidence." See Appel, V: 5187-89, (Ehrmann in V: 5314, 5320); (Stratton in V: 5228); (Ranney in V: 5188, 5339); Russell, S & V: The Case Resolved, (pp.153, 155). a. Is Wyzanski (#49) useful? b. Should Avrich (p. 162) have mentioned Vanzetti's reference to Hippolyte Havel (Letters, p.163), who agreed with Sinclair in 1929 that Sacco was a "Militant Anarchist"? c. Why does Avrich (p. 210) keep Orciani, the quondam motorcyclist E. H. James visited in 1928 and 1932, out of his Epilogue? d. What does Avrich's use of the word tilting on page 159, line 5, tell you? e. Does Avrich (p. 162), by inference, validate and broaden Grossman's 1962 observation on idealism (p. 44)? Explain. f. Does Avrich have two dubious points on pp. 202-203? g. Is chapter 14, "The Arrest," accurate, evenhanded, and complete? h. Did Avrich find new evidence in The Sacco-Vanzetti Case Papers, Microfilm, 23 reels, an item in his bibliography, p. 252? i. What lesson do you learn from reviews of Avrich by Blatt, Woodcock, and Candace Falk? Evaluate Falk's use of "courage" in the penultimate sentence of her review (JAH: Dec. 1991, p. 1123). Why do you agree or disagree with Falk? j. What does Avrich attempt to do in his book? Answer in about 10 words. Does Avrich succeed in this attempt?

42. Review the literature on recantations by Commonwealth witnesses Pelser and Andrews. What do these two episodes tell you about the Sacco-Vanzetti case? See Montgomery, pp. 172-175, 181-187, 302; Russell (Tragedy, pp. 225-228, 231-233); Kaiser, pp. 54-55, 155; Joughin-Morgan, pp. 132-134, 174. Is the statement by Mrs. Hewins relevant (Appel, V: 4540)? See Appel, V: 5564-5597; IV: 3892-3960. Do affidavits by Kennedy [Appel, V: 4508-4509] and Kelly [V: 4513] and judgment by Lowell [V: 5034] impeach the testimony of Lola Andrews? See Judge Grant at V: 5037. Does

Thompson win at V: 4804, 4852? Is President Lowell's statement about Lola Andrews (Appel, V: 5114) relevant? Explain fully.

43. Evaluate Edmund Wilson's public statement in Felicani's journal Lantern (August 1929) against his private comment on the Sacco-Vanzetti case in a letter to John Peale Bishop, October 22, 1928. Did Wilson decline to write a book on the case because he had not read the transcripts of the two trials or because he did not like research? Or both? Why did Wilson not join the protesters at Boston? See [S-V: D & R., p. 21]. What was Wilson's "moral top of the world"? Which Nobel winner noted this?

44. Evaluate the Russell-Pernicone dispute over Carlo Tresca. Read articles by Eastman (National Review, Oct. 1961); Pernicone (The Journal of American History: Dec. 1979); chapter 3 in Russell's 1986 volume; and page 90 in Gallagher. a. After you master #10-b, write an analysis of Pernicone's footnotes 6 and 7 on p. 536 in JAH. Show how Pernicone's footnotes 6 and 7 connect to the editorial staff of the ANB. Do footnotes 6, 7, and 10 present a consistent or fair argument? Explain—after you have read Russell (S & V: The Case Resolved, pp. 26-29). b. Why did Pernicone's JAH article have an 18-year gestation? c. How should Pernicone's reference to the longevity of the "pro-Sacco-and-Vanzetti interpretation" (p. 535) be read? d. Do you approve of Pernicone's terms "revisionists" and "traditionalists" on pp. 535-536? Explain. e. Does the clash between Felix and Pernicone in JAH (Dec. 1980, pp. 753-755) shed light on the Russell-Pernicone debate? Explain. Is Felix right about the publication of the Holt edition (p. 754)? f. What does Pernicone's 5-column biography of Sacco and Vanzetti in American National Biography (v. 19) reveal in respect to his 1979 insistence that history be examined coldly? g. List the four most vulnerable statements by Pernicone in the ANB entry. Show the flaw of each statement. Should he have called Sacco and Vanzetti atheists? h. Precisely what does Pernicone's analysis of the Plymouth trial in ANB teach you? i. How is Pernicone's ANB article indebted to Frankfurter? Does the ANB (vol. 24, p. 803) call Sacco and Vanzetti murderers? j. Is the ANB biography of Galleani useful? How do Vecoli and Avrich differ with Pernicone on the 1919 bombings? k. Does Pernicone's 1993 book (Italian

Sacco and Vanzetti "were revolutionary anarchists"; 2. "there has been much **falsification of the history of Sacco and Vanzetti**, for a variety of political and ideological reasons." a. Do these 1979 statements validate Dr. Boorstin's judgment (Hidden History, p. 216) that Sacco and Vanzetti were "gentle men, philosophical anarchists"? b. Did papers from this two-day conference show important developments? Identify them. Did Pernicone and Wieck provide information in 1979 significantly different from information in Sinclair's letters, typified by this item Avrich adduces in Sacco and Vanzetti: The Anarchist Background (p. 161): "I became convinced from many different sources that Vanzetti was not the pacifist he was reported under the necessity of defense propaganda." If Avrich, Pernicone, and Wieck all drew from the same sources—Sinclair's letters at the Houghton Library and the Lilly Library—for how many years had this information been available to scholars? c. Did the first generation Sacco-Vanzetti scholars seek out Sinclair, whose "chief obligation," says Avrich, "was to the truth" (S. & V: A. B., p.161)? Recall that an anonymous critic for the anarchist journal, The Road to Freedom (April 1929), declared Sinclair an unfit historian "not in possession of all the facts" when he published Boston. Sinclair replied angrily in the June issue: "It is a fact that Sacco was a '**Militant Anarchist**', and gloried in the fact, ... That is one of the facts I had to deal with in 'Boston'" (p. 6). Editor Hippolyte Havel replied (p. 7): "Of course, Sacco was a militant... ." Did Fraenkel or Gates talk to Sinclair before publishing in 1931 and 1935 (DAB)? Is Fraenkel's 1925 trip to the Soviet Union relevant (ANB, vol. 8: 353)? d. Did conference speakers at Boston adduce evidence that seems to exculpate Sacco or Vanzetti? Specify. e. Why did Francis Russell decline to speak at this Boston conference? f. Has the historian met D'Attilio's ideal (S - V: D. & R., p. 89)? g. Write your consideration on this Boston conference. h. Will the next movie on Sacco and Vanzetti match the historical accuracy of Guiliano Montaldo's Sacco and Vanzetti (1971)? Explain. Have developments **since 1979** provided the next filmmaker and scriptwriter with new evidence that will exonerate Sacco and Vanzetti? Explain. See #19.

49. Evaluate the 5-page letter Judge Charles E. Wyzanski, Jr. sent to Francis Russell on March 31,1986. The letter is filed with the Francis Russell Papers, Library of the Boston Athenæum, 10.5 Beacon Street, Boston, MA 02108. a. Is there a useful fact in the report Jeremiah Smith, Jr. made to Gus Hand (Judge Augustus N. Hand and two other judges of the Second Circuit affirmed the Hiss conviction.)? b. Why did Wyzanski tell Russell he testified at both Hiss trials, adding that, initially, he thought Hiss innocent? c. Why did Joseph Lash call Judge Wyzanski a Frankfurter "hot dog"? (See From The Diaries of Felix Frankfurter, p. 236.) d. Do references to Wyzanski—in Bruce A. Murphy's book, pp. 114, 118-119, 149,167, 168, 200, 315-318, 335-336—affect your judgment? Do tributes to Wyzanski in Harvard Law Review (February 1987, pp. 705-727) seem relevant? Do references to Wyzanski in Allen Weinstein's Perjury, pp. 163, 376, 383-4, 448, 563, put Wyzanski in perspective vis-`a-vis the Sacco-Vanzetti case? e. To what scholars does Wyzanski, by inference, direct his vindication of Harold P. Williams? Does Wyzanski show deference to Dukakis? f. How is his letter ironic? g. Do you dispute any item in Wyzanski's letter? Explain. Does Wyzanski's "not proven" verdict on Vanzetti carry a stigma? h. Why did Frankfurter campaign to get Wyzanski appointed to the federal bench (Murphy, pp. 315-316)? i. Do the American National Biography entries—"Frankfurter, Felix" and "Wyzanski, Charles Edward, Jr."—by University of California historian Michael E. Parrish teach a lesson? Choose "yes" or "no" and defend. j. John Henry Schlegel says Roscoe Pound, dean of the Harvard Law School, took "the wrong side" in that touchstone of "liberal sensibility [known] as the Sacco and Vanzetti case." How should Schlegel be tested and judged? (See The Journal of American History (March 1999: 1623). And see Newby's letter in JAH 87 (June 2000: 321). k. What lesson do you gain from five Columbia University historians—Alan Brinkley, Mark C. Carnes, Eric Foner, John A. Garraty, Richard B. Morris—in re this Wyzanski letter? See #9, #11, #41. l. Wyzanski's letter links the Alger Hiss case to the Sacco-Vanzetti case. Show how William A. Reuben's 9-item bibliography ("Further Reading") appended to the entry "Hiss Case" in Encyclopedia of the American Left links to the debate on the Sacco-Vanzetti case. (See 2nd edition—edited by Buhle,

Buhle, and Georgakas, Oxford Univ. Press, 1998, p. 318.) Tell precisely but fully how certain researchers/authors—Reuben, his editors, others—make up this linkage. m. Could he speak, what would R. H. Montgomery say about Wyzanski's letter? Is Montgomery, on the S-V topic, outclassed intellectually by history professors? n. May one call 1986 the <u>annus</u> <u>mirabilis</u> of the Sacco-Vanzetti debate? From whose perspective? Is Topp's book, superior to Montgomery's book? How did M. Buhle aid Topp?

50. Have authors of American history textbooks given evenhanded summaries of the Sacco-Vanzetti case? (1) <u>The National Experience: A History of the United States</u>—John M. Blum, McFeely, Morgan, Schlesinger, Stampp, Van Woodward—p. 620; (2) <u>The United States Becoming a World Power</u>, II—Leon F. Litwack, Jordan, Hofstadter, Miller, Aaron—pp. 609-610; (3) <u>A History of the American People</u>—Norman A. Graebner, Fite, White—p. 662; (4) <u>A People & A Nation</u>—Mary Beth Norton, Katzman, Escott, Chudacoff, Paterson, Tuttle—p. 686; (5) <u>The Growth of the American Republic</u>—Samuel Eliot Morison, Commager, Leuchtenburg—pp. 411-412, 458; (6) <u>Land of the Free: A History of the United States</u>—John W. Caughey, J. H. Franklin, May—p. 539; (7) <u>America: A Narrative History</u>—George Brown Tindall, Shi—pp. 1092-1093. (8) <u>The Making of American Society</u>, II—Edwin C. Rozwenc—p. 295; (9) <u>Nation of Nations: A Concise Narrative of the American Republic</u>—James W. Davidson, Gienapp, Heyrman, Lytle, Stoff—pp. 671-672); (10) <u>A History of the American People</u>—Paul Johnson—p. 669; (11) <u>The American Pageant</u>, 10th ed.—Thomas A. Bailey, D. Kennedy—p. 746; (12) Add the nontextbook—<u>200 Years: A Bicentennial History of the United States</u>, II—Books by U. S. News & World Report, p. 296. a. Which book in this group is the most evenhanded on Sacco and Vanzetti? Show evidence. b. Is Stephen Jay Gould's statement—"Once ensconced in textbooks, ..." [This View of Life, "*Abscheulich!* (Atrocious!)," <u>Natural History</u>, March 2000, p. 45, and modified in red ink on p. 46] relevant? Explain. c. John C. Burnham, Professor of History, Ohio State University, "is the contributor of Unit 35: The 1920s," pp. 350-373 in <u>The Study of American History</u>, vol. 2, The Dushkin Publishing Group (1974). Does Unit 35 win Burnham

respected editorial authority for his entry on the Sacco-Vanzetti case in <u>The Encyclopedic Dictionary of American History</u>? Does the imprimatur of Yale University's John M. Faragher boost Burnham's authority? Who is closer to the objectivity of the chemist, Burnham or Tindall-Shi? Explain precisely. How would you interview Burnham, Faragher, and Tindall-Shi on this topic? Evaluate summaries of the Sacco-Vanzetti case in 21st-century textbooks created for survey courses in U.S. history. Write conclusions.

51. a. If we exclude die-hards, can the innocence or guilt of Sacco and Vanzetti be determined with certainty in the twenty first century? If "[t]here is no absolute knowledge" (Jacob Bronowski, <u>A Dictionary</u> of Common Fallacies, p. 102), who has won this debate, vindicators of the Commonwealth or champions of Sacco and Vanzetti? Can common readers, unassisted by university professors and encyclopedias, give—in the words of Avrich (p. 6)—"the issue of guilt or innocence ... definitive treatment"? Is it useful to consider Tanenhaus's "must be innocent" (<u>Whittaker Chambers</u>, p. 434) and Russell's "<u>had</u> to be innocent" (<u>Tragedy</u>, 1971 ed., p. xii)? End this debate! Vote "guilty" or "not guilty." Tell why you are right. b. One professor of note argues that "some" S-V studies in the last 25 years raise a trivial distinction (quibble) "over guilt and innocence." Such quibbling, says the professor, is proper work for antiquarians, not historians, who now invest the case with symbolic meaning. Explain why you agree or disagree with this professor, whose reference-book entry on the case sowed seeds of doubt about the Dedham verdict. Is the "quibble" argument valid or phony?

52. After you have reviewed Ben Shahn's "23 satirical gouache paintings based on the trial," express your insights in your own creative works on the topic: a series of paintings that depict scholars at the very moment they "became uncoupled from the locomotive of history" in the Sacco-Vanzetti debate; a Sacco-Vanzetti mural; sculpted pieces for a campus quad; a tapestry BY YOU that shows Sacco-Vanzetti paladins and villains; prints joined to penny broadsides; a ballad; a play; brief lives of S-V principals (after Aubrey); a new chapter for Richard Shenkman's

Legends, Lies & Cherished Myths of American History; a
journalist's longitudinal report; a revamping of Boston; a new
Swiftian battle of the books. Design a set before which you
entertain as a storyteller of the Sacco-Vanzetti legend (a PBS
Special?). Do a "Who's Who in Sacco and Vanzetti." Do a
handbook: "100 Fictions of the Sacco-Vanzetti Case." Write a
monologue that resonates with ironic scenes from the evolving
debate. Write a short story with a Sacco-Vanzetti theme, and let it
be told by an obtuse narrator. Compose a Marvellian poem: The
Last Instructions to a Historian. Do a comparative analysis to
determine which publication gets closer to the truth about Sacco
and Vanzetti—Kill Now, Talk Forever: Debating Sacco and
Vanzetti or The Trial of Sacco and Vanzetti (1921). The latter has
been assembled by Professor Douglas Linder, UMKC School of
Law, and put on the well-used Web site: Famous Trials. Click on
these items: Excerpts from Trial Transcript, Summary of Evidence,
Chronology, The Red Scare, Bibliography and Links, and The
Sacco-Vanzetti Case: An Account by Doug Linder. Explore
Linder's Web site fully. Has Newby or Linder published factual
errors of consequence? If so, identify them. Next, imitating the
style of William Hogarth, paint a scene which depicts "state of the
art" scholarship ensconced in the entry **SACCO AND
VANZETTI CASE** (p. 681) in The Oxford Companion to United
States History (2001).

UPTON SINCLAIR
STATION A
PASADENA. CALIFORNIA

August 29, 1929.

John Beardsley
610 Rowan Bldg.,
Los Angeles, Calif.

Dear John:

I will write you a few notes about the matter concerning which we were talking last night.

When I went to Boston the last time in October 1928 I was completely naive about the Sacco-Vanzetti case, having accepted the defense propaganda entirely. But I very quickly began to sense something wrong in the situation. There was an air of mystery about the Boston anarchists, and I saw they had something to conceal. Then in Sacco's cross-examination in the record I detected what seemed to be a slip in his alibi. I began asking catch questions, and ultimately I got the admission from one of the leading defense witnesses that his testimony had been framed. I got a virtual admission of the same thing from another witness. . . .

. . . Alone in a [Denver] hotel room with Fred [Moore] I begged him to tell me the full truth. His reply was, "First tell me what you have got." I decided to take a chance at the worst, and I told him that I knew that the men were not merely terrorists, but that they were guilty of the holdup. His reply was, "Since you have got the whole story there is no use my holding anything back," and he then told me that the men were guilty, and he told me in every detail how he had framed a set of alibis for them. . . .

I faced the most difficult ethical problem of my life at this point. I had come to Boston with the announcement that I was going to write the truth about the case. If I had dropped the project it would have been universally said and believed that it was because I had decided the men were guilty. I had, of course, no first hand knowledge of their guilt, but I did have first hand knowledge of the framing of testimony. I decided that I would write the story on the basis of telling exactly what I knew. I would portray all sides, and show all the different groups and individuals telling what they knew and what they believed. . . .

. . . [W]ord spread among the committee in Boston what I was doing, and they flew into a panic, and I had a long string of horrified and indignant letters and telegrams. They strenuously denied that there had ever been any perjury in the case--which, of course, I knew to be perfectly absurd. They also denied that Sacco had ever been a terrorist--though on this point I was finally able to back Gardner Jackson down. I saw him in New York before the book went to press, and we went all over various points line by line, and argued for hours. Gardner admitted that I was all right about Sacco, but he claimed that I was doing Vanzetti an injustice. Charles Boni had listened to our discussion. I asked him his opinion, and he said that Gardner had admitted everything that I was claiming, and a little more. Vanzetti as a pacifist was a perfect absurdity, because I talked with a Socialist whom he had chased with a revolver, and young Brini told me of having witnessed a similar scene as a child in his home.

The rumors of Sacco's guilt were very general in the Italian colony in Boston, and there is no possible question that these rumors, brought to Thayer and Fuller and Lowell in a thousand forms by the police, were the real reason for the execution. . . . I asked Roger Baldwin, who is, himself, an anarchist, and knows the whole crowd. He told me there was no possible doubt of the guilt of Sacco and Vanzetti, . . .

Bob [Minor] said that he had heard these rumors from the beginning, and had investigated them carefully, and was convinced that they were not true about Sacco and Vanzetti.

This letter is for yourself alone. Stick it away in your safe, and some time in the far distant future the world may know the real truth about the matter.

Sincerely, (Signature of Upton Sinclair)

[Ed. Beardsley was Sinclair's attorney. Albert & Charles Boni published Sinclair's "Boston" in 1928. Paul Hegness sent the editor a copy of this letter, noting it was public domain.]

ADDENDA

1. Fault Watson's "Crackdown!" in <u>Smithsonian,</u> 2/02, pp. 51-53. b. Test McGirr's Harvard Freshman Seminar 46k (2004).

2. See <u>America: A Concise History,</u> vol. 2: Since 1865, 2nd ed., for Dumenil's analysis of S-V case. Other editors: Henretta/Brody. See "SACCO AND VANZETTI CASE" in <u>The Oxford Companion to United States History.</u> And see Dumenil's <u>The Modern Temper,</u> pp. 23-24, 225. Draw a conclusion.

3. Compare Ch. 6, "The Sacco-Vanzetti Case," in Page Smith's <u>Redeeming the Time</u> to studies of the case by other historians. Where is Smith strong? Where is he weak? Find two serious factual errors. See #7 below.

4. Does Dershowitz trip himself in Note #11 on p. 519 of <u>Shouting Fire</u>? See "Stielow and Green," Topic #25.

5. Aaron (<u>The New Republic,</u> 5/24/99, p. 49) calls Evans's <u>The American Century</u> "The work of a very knowledgeable journalist." Do pp. 178-179 in Evans's book support Aaron's claim? Explain.

6. Show how the 3-page letter Ehrmann sent to E. M. Morgan, 1/20/34, dramatizes Ehrmann's combativeness in the Sacco-Vanzetti case. See documents by Ehrmann, Morgan, Holmes, and others. Write: Ehrmann Collection: #3609, Box 1, "Miscellaneous" Folder, American Heritage Center, Univ. of Wyoming, P. O. Box 3924, Laramie, WY 82071.

7. On p. xxiii in Brief 4th Edition of <u>America Past and Present,</u> vol. 2: From 1865, Divine, Breen, Fredrickson, Williams, and Roberts ask: "And how does a student of history approach documents, sources, and textbooks with a critical and discerning eye?" Read their handbook: <u>Learning to Think Critically: Film, Myth, and American History.</u> (See "Author" page.) Next, see Divine's statement on Sacco and Vanzetti, p. 455. Then answer their question. Last, do pp.729-730 in the 12th edition of <u>The American Pageant</u> (Kennedy/Cohen/Bailey) illustrate Gould's red-ink thesis on p. 46 in <u>Natural History</u> (3/00)? See Bailey's 1st edition (1956). See p. 168.

8. See Marion Frankfurter's undated letter to Vanzetti on pp. 126-127 in Lisa Baker's book <u>Felix Frankfurter</u>: " . . . I did not go to Dedham that day [April 9, 1927]. I did not think I could bear to be there. But when my husband [Felix Frankfurter] came home and told me what had happened, I knew I had missed a rare experience. He had been uplifted by what he saw and heard there, through you and through Mr. Sacco; and I was lifted up and sustained when he told me about it. . . . That is what you give us--a sense of beauty of spirit that abides above the bitterness and ignorance and confusion that give us so much pain. . . ." In closing, Mrs. Frankfurter expressed her "gratitude" to Sacco and Vanzetti. Why is this letter important?

9. a. Why does Ehrmann cite "Phaedo" in The Untried Case (1960), p. 241? b. What does INTERLUDE, p. 168, reveal?

10. What does p. vii in Pernicone's book, <u>Carlo Tresca</u>, reveal?

11. Write a new entry **SACCO AND VANZETTI CASE** for The Oxford Companion to United States History that reflects 2006 scholarship. Honor the advice Eric Foner gave Roger Shattuck on Nov. 19, 1998: Foner urged "scholars to get their facts straight." Get your facts straight! Submit your entry to Paul S. Boyer, Editor in Chief.

12. Do Atwater and Palmer help you get to the truth about Vanzetti's revolver? b. Evaluate Schlesinger's use of "objective sketch" in his address, April 2, 1959. See p. 452.

13. **SUMMATION.** Show how letters (04/26/1927; 05/02/1927) from Edwin M. Borchard to Frankfurter, Law Library, Univ. of Iowa, sharpen your understanding of <u>The Case of Sacco and Vanzetti</u> (1961). See Borchard's letters (12/26/1930; 10/24/1931; 12/17/1931) in The Papers of Felix Frankfurter, Reel 15. See Borchard's letter in the <u>Yale Daily News</u> (04/26/1927). See Frankfurter's letter to Borchard (11/09/1933). Show in detail how these letters shed new light on Frankfurter's Note on Republication, June 5, 1961, p. xxxvii.

ANNOTATED BIBLIOGRAPHY

THE DEBATE IN CHRONOLOGY

"Suicide Bares Bomb Arrests." Special Dispatch to the Herald. Boston Herald. May 3, 1920. Federal agents make Galleani group the prime suspects of 1919 bombings.

Beffel, John Nicholas. "Eels and the Electric Chair." The New Republic, December 29, 1920. Beffel says Vanzetti, "a philosophical anarchist," was prevented by his attorneys from testifying in his own defense at his Plymouth trial.

Vorse, Mary Heaton. "Sacco and Vanzetti." The World Tomorrow. (January 1921):14-15. Vorse finds Sacco "clean-cut as a Roman coin" in Dedham jail, exuding "confident innocence." She counts 18 witnesses who testified to Vanzetti's sale of eels on Dec. 24, 1919.

Davis, Anna N. "To American Friends of Justice." New England Civil Liberties Committee. February 19, 1921. Parent of the NECLC is the ACLU. NECLC and ACLU conclude Sacco and Vanzetti are being put on trial because they are "influential radicals."

Vanzetti, Bartolomeo. The Story of a Proletarian Life. Tr. Eugene Lyons. Boston: Sacco-Vanzetti Defense Committee, 1923. Vanzetti: "I am and will be until the last instant … an anarchist-communist." Vanzetti says he's innocent.

_____. Background of the Plymouth Trial. Boston: Road to Freedom Group, 1926. Vanzetti contends his lawyers kept him from testifying at his Plymouth trial.

Frankfurter, Felix. "The Case of Sacco and Vanzetti." Atlantic Monthly. 139 (March 1927): 409-432. "Sounded a clarion call to all liberal minds, all academics."—Francis Russell. Note p. 406.

Frankfurter, Felix. The Case of Sacco and Vanzetti: A Critical Analysis for Lawyers and Laymen. Boston: Little, Brown, March 1927. Argues both innocent. Frankfurter is confident that the Joe Morelli gang committed the South Braintree crime. See Wyzanski (1986). See p. xxxviii and p. 457.

Grabill, Ethelbert V. Sacco and Vanzetti in the Scales of Justice. Boston: The Fort Hill Press, April 22, 1927. Argues both guilty. Advises Fuller not to appoint a review committee.

Ernst, Morris L. "Deception According to Law." The Nation, June 1, 1927. Ernst argues prosecution withheld exculpatory evidence.

Ernst, Morris L. Rev. of The Case of Sacco and Vanzetti, by Felix Frankfurter. Yale Law Journal (June 1927): 1192-1194. Ernst repeats argument he made in The Nation. He finds Gould credible.

Bliven, Bruce. "In Dedham Jail: A Visit to Sacco and Vanzetti." The New Republic. June 22, 1927. Bliven says the odds make these men with faith of philosophical anarchism innocent of South Braintree crime.

Dos Passos, John. Facing the Chair: Story of the Americanization of Two Foreignborn Workmen. Boston: Sacco-Vanzetti Defense Committee, 1927. Finds testimony by itinerant grocer Affe credible. Facing the Chair has Dos Passos' New Masses articles on the case.

"Bridgeport Man Thinks Shell Photos Beat Sacco-Vanzetti: James E. Burns, Ballistic Expert At Remington Arms Co. Says Pictures Speak For Themselves. Tells How Marks Were Same On Both Shells. Testified As Defence Witness At Trial. Questioned by Governor Fuller When He Started to Review the Case Recently." Bridgeport Post (Aug. 4, 1927): 1. Photos of shells on separate page. Burns defends Thayer. Calls defendants disruptive.

Broun, Heywood. "Sacco and Vanzetti." New York World (Aug. 5, 1927). Broun: "It is not every prisoner who has a president of Harvard University throw on the switch for him."

Howie, Wendell D. "How the Sacco Bullet Was Fingerprinted." Boston Evening Transcript, August 9, 1927. Report of Goddard's ballistics test on June 3, 1927. Howie cites Aug. 4 article in Bridgeport Post.

Lippmann, Walter. "Doubt That Will Not Down." New York World, Aug. 19,1927. In Edward P. J. Corbett. Classical Rhetoric for the Modern Student. New York: Oxford University Press, 1965, pp. 235-241. Corbett asks students to analyze rhetoric of Lippmann, Edmund Burke, Vanzetti, et al. He praises rhetorical skill of Vanzetti. See Steel at year 1980 on p. 647.

Stern, Samuel R. "From a Lawyer's Standpoint." Outlook 7 Sept. 1927: 17-18. Stern, formerly Judge of the Superior Court of the State of Washington, writes: "Professor Frankfurter is so steeped in what he thinks are the wrongs of the laboring people that he has lost his perspective of what is right and fair, ..."

Sinclair, Upton. Boston: A Documentary Novel of the Sacco-Vanzetti Case. 2 vols. New York: Albert and Charles Boni, 1928. Reprint. Cambridge, Massachusetts. Robert Bentley, 1978. Finds defendants innocent. This fictional treatment of the case angers anarchists. Excellent photographs in Bentley edition.

The Sacco-Vanzetti Case: Transcript of the Record of the Trial of Nicola Sacco and Bartolomeo Vanzetti in the Courts of Massachusetts and Subsequent Proceedings 1920-27. 5 vols. With a supplemental volume on the Bridgewater Case. Prefatory essay by William O. Douglas. Mamaroneck, N. Y.: Paul P. Appel, 1969. Published by Henry Holt & Co., New York. 6 vols., 1928-29. Holt publication omits episode on switch of gun barrels.

Sacco, Nicola, and Bartolomeo Vanzetti. The Letters of Sacco and Vanzetti. Ed. Marion Denman Frankfurter and Gardner Jackson. New York: Viking, 1928. Appendix I, "The Story of the Case," excerpts large segments of Frankfurter's book The Case of Sacco and Vanzetti. Jackson says these letters vindicate S and V.

Bellamy, Francis Rufus. "The Truth About the Bridgewater Holdup: The First of the Crimes for Which Vanzetti Was Convicted." Outlook and Independent (October 31, 1928): 1053-1055. In 1931, Fraenkel cites a factual error in this editorial that exonerates Vanzetti. Agreement is made to pay Silva for his I-was-at-Bridgewater affidavit. This "Truth About" article is cited in Encyclopaedia Britannica, 1929-1960.

"Frank Silva's Story." Outlook and Independent (October 31, 1928): 1055-1060. Silva exonerates Vanzetti. E. M. Morgan says, (The Legacy, p. 54): "Silva was acting... for a money reward."

Callahan, Jack. "How I Found Frank Silva." Outlook and Independent (October 31, 1928): 1060-1063, 1070. Callahan, an ex-con, says "Silva's story is the truth." Silva's wish to be paid for confessing to Bridgewater crime is not mentioned. Callahan meets Dr. Horace M. Kallen. See Kallen at 1929.

Bent, Silas. "Checking Up the Confession." Outlook and Independent (October 31, 1928): 1071-1075. Bent: "Frank Silva, alias Paul Martini, has told the truth." Joughin says (The Legacy of Sacco and Vanzetti, p. 318) Bent had "an excellent reputation for accuracy and veracity" as a newspaperman.

[Lovett, Robert Morss.] "Vanzetti Was Innocent." The New Republic (November 7, 1928): 317-318. Lovett vouches for accuracy of

Outlook editorial of October 31, 1928. See Lovett in American
National Biography (vol. 14, pp. 20-21).

Brine, Fred R. "Contradicts Story Clearing Vanzetti in Bridgewater
Crime: Silva's Affidavit to Hurwitz Opposite to Version in
Outlook." Boston Herald (Jan. 13, 1929): 1, 6.

Book Review. "Boston by Upton Sinclair." The Road to Freedom
(April 1929): 6. Anonymous reviewer in this anarchist journal
says Sinclair is a false historian.

Sinclair, Upton. "Sinclair Protests." The Road to Freedom. (June
1929): 6-7. Sinclair responds in anger to April issue of TRTF that
challenged his credentials. Calls Sacco a "Militant Anarchist."

Kallen, Horace M. "Fear, Freedom, and Massachusetts." American
Mercury 18 (November 1929): 281-92. Questions Fuller's
integrity. See entry on Kallen in Joughin-Morgan bibliography
(1948), p. 575. See obit. in NY Times and ANB (vol. 12, pp. 351-
352).

1930

Fraenkel, Osmond K. The Sacco-Vanzetti Case. New York: Alfred A.
Knopf, 1931. Says Boda is "[p]erhaps not a radical." Claims
Sacco and Vanzetti were philosophical anarchists.

Gates, Sylvester G. "A Formidable Shadow." Rev. of The Sacco-
Vanzetti Case, by Osmond K. Fraenkel. The New Republic 69
(December 9, 1931): 103-104. Gates, Frankfurter's pupil, says
Fraenkel's book is "as fair, accurate and well-balanced ... as it is
possible to make."

Allen, Frederick Lewis. Only Yesterday. New York: Harper, 1931.
Argues it is almost impossible to think a philosophical anarchist
like Vanzetti could commit murder.

Borchard, Edwin M. "Stielow and Green." Convicting the Innocent:
Errors of Criminal Justice. New Haven: Yale Univ. Press, 1932.
245-256. On p. 252 Borchard writes: "The experts, Mr. Bond, and
the Governor concluded that the trial testimony of Mr. Hamilton
that the death bullets had come from the Stielow pistol was clearly
erroneous.... It appeared, moreover, that the Stielow revolver had
not been fired for some years." See reviews of Borchard by M. L.
Ernst (Nation, June 8, 1932, p. 657); O. K. Fraenkel (TNR, May

25, 1932, p. 52); W. G. Thompson (Columbia Law Review, Dec. 1932, pp. 1460-1462). See Stielor in Transcript, 5018, line 31.

James, Edward Holton. "New Light Coming on the Sacco-Vanzetti Case." Unity (Aug. 15, 1932): 327-329. Reports that Orciani, living in Italy after the executions, is "really afraid" of Katzmann.

Ehrmann, Herbert B. The Untried Case: The Sacco-Vanzetti Case and the Morelli Gang. New York: The Vanguard Press, 1933. Argues the South Braintree crime was committed by members of the Morelli gang. The 1960 edition has Morgan's Introduction and Secretary Howe's letter, 10/29/34, on the back of the jacket.

Morgan, Edmund. M. Rev. of The Untried Case, by Herbert B. Ehrmann. Harvard Law Review 47 (January 1934): 538-547. Morgan says Ehrmann fails in his aim to convict the Morelli gang of the South Braintree crime.

Grant, Robert. Fourscore: An Autobiography. Boston: Houghton Mifflin Co., 1934. "All of us [Fuller's committee] regarded the story [Motion 6 on Madeiros/Morelli] as flimsy and falling far short of the probative value which would justify a new trial."

Gunther, Jack D. and Charles O. The Identification of Firearms from Ammunition Fired Therein. New York: Wiley, 1935. Gunthers challenge Burns, Gill, and Hamilton—three ballistics experts for defense. Photos of comparison microscope on pp. 21-22.

Gates, Sylvester G. "Sacco, Nicola ... and Bartolomeo Vanzetti." In Dictionary of American Biography, VIII: 279-280. Ed. Dumas Malone. New York: Charles Scribner's Sons, 1935. See entry on H. B. Phillips (1960). DAB succeeded in 1999 by ANB.

Van Amburgh, Charles J., and Thompson, Fred H. "The Hidden Drama of Sacco and Vanzetti." True Detective Mysteries, XXIV (April, 1935), 7-13, 79-82; (May, 1935): 50-53, 106-08, 111-112; (June, 1935): 32-37, 108-110, 112, 114; (July, 1935): 50-53, 83-86; (August, 1935): 50-53, 100-103; (September, 1935): 58-61, 115-116,118-20. Argues defense ballistics expert Burns had to admit Sacco's guilt when he met Fuller's committee in July 1927. Good photo of Rice & Hutchins in April issue.

Cowley, Malcom. "Echoes of a Crime." TNR, Augh. 28, 1935.

Lyons, Eugene. [Morris Gebelow] Assignment in Utopia. New York: Harcourt, Brace and Company, 1937. In Italy, Lyons finds Coacci, "a terroist of the Galleani school," his shelves full of bomb manuals. Lyons reveals his disillusionment with Soviet Union.

Lovett, Robert Morss. "Sacco-Vanzetti—After Ten Years." Unity (August 16, 1937): 220-221. Lovett says publication of the 1928 Holt transcript "has convinced educated opinion of the innocence of these victims [Sacco and Vanzetti]."

White, William Allen. Forty Years on Main Street. New York: Farrar & Rinehart, 1937. White finds both defendants guilty in 1927. Later he is "satisfied" they were innocent.

Seldes, George. You Can't Do That. New York: Da Capo Press, 1938. Seldes, dubbed "a Media watchdog" by the AP, proclaims Sacco and Vanzetti innocent.

Musmanno, Michael A. [Judge of the Court of Common Pleas State of Pennsylvania] After Twelve Years. New York: Alfred A. Knopf, 1939. Argues: "They called themselves philosophical anarchists …and did not believe in violence." See p. 178.

1940

Pesotta, Rose. Bread Upon the Waters. Edited by John Nicholas Beffel. New York: Dodd, Mead & Company, 1945. Pesotta, a lifelong anarchist, pickets the State House at Boston in 1927. She vouches for Beffel's "painstaking accuracy with regard to … historical facts."

Van Amburgh, Charles J. "Common Sources of Error in the Examination and Interpretation of Ballistics Evidence." Boston University Law Review 26 (April 1946): 207-248. Says doctors should not try to analyze ballistics evidence. Dismisses Ehrmann in a footnote.

Yeomans, Henry A. Abbott Lawrence Lowell, 1856-1943. Cambridge: Harvard Univ. Press,1948. Argues: "Socialists, communists, and anarchists here and abroad jumped to the conclusion that the convicted defendants were martyrs."

Joughin, G. Louis, and Edmund M. Morgan. The Legacy of Sacco and Vanzetti. New York: Harcourt, Brace, 1948. Reprint with an Introduction by Arthur M. Schlesinger. Princeton Univ. Press, 1978. Morgan says Vanzetti's Plymouth trial was fair, the verdict just, that "a group of Italians [may have] framed an alibi for Vanzetti." Joughin honors Gates's three columns on the convicted murderers in Dictionary of American Biography. He holds out hope "that time will bring vindication."

1950

Howe, Mark de Wolfe, ed. Holmes-Laski Letters, vol. 2. Cambridge, Mass.: Harvard University Press, 1953. Holmes is cold to Laski's defense of Sacco and Vanzetti.

Sinclair, Upton. "The Fishpeddler and the Shoemaker." Institute of Social Studies Bulletin 2 (Summer 1953): 13, 23-24. Sinclair reports that Fred Moore told him "Sacco was guilty ... possibly Vanzetti also was guilty." He describes Moore's defense trial tactics.

Murray, Robert K. Red Scare: A Study in National Hysteria, 1919-1920. Minneapolis:Univ. of Minnesota Press, 1955. Says: "By the fall of 1920 the Great Red Scare was dying."

Russell, Francis. "The Tragedy in Dedham: A Retrospect of the Sacco-Vanzetti Trial." Antioch Review 15 (Winter 1955-56): 387-98. Russell argues Sacco and Vanzetti were innocent.

Dever, John F. Papers relating to his memoirs as a member of the jury which convicted Sacco and Vanzetti. Mss. & typescripts. 3 boxes. Boston Public Library. Boston, 1955-1960. Dever says jury had no doubt that both defendants were guilty. Defends Thayer.

Hatcher, Julian S., Frank J. Jury and Jac Weller. Firearms Investigation Identification and Evidence. Harrisburg: The Stackpole Co., 1957. Authors claim Goddard's photographs of shells, pp. 464-465, confirm Sacco's guilt.

Schlesinger, Arthur M., Jr. The Age of Roosevelt. Vol. I: The Crisis of the Old Order 1919-1933. Boston: Houghton Mifflin Co., 1957. Scholars have noted Schlesinger's factual errors on the arrest of Sacco and Vanzetti.

Weeks, Robert P., ed. Commonwealth vs. Sacco and Vanzetti. Englewood Cliffs: Prentice-Hall,1958. Textbook cover makes the claim: "A book of primary source materials."

Leuchtenburg, William E. "Red Scare." In The Perils of Prosperity, 1914-1932, pp. 66-83. Chicago: University of Chicago Press, 1958. Argues: "Felix Frankfurter punched holes in the case."

Zelt, Johannes. Proletarischer Internationalismus im Kampf um Sacco und Vanzetti. (East) Berlin: Dietz Verlag, Institut fuer Gesellschaftswissenschaften beim Zentralkomitee der S.E.D [German Democratic Republic] 1958. World-wide demonstrations for Sacco and Vanzetti were organized and directed by communists. See Johnson (1997).

Record of Public Hearing Before JOINT COMMITTEE on the JUDICIARY of the MASSACHUSETTS LEGISLATURE on the RESOLUTION of REPRESENTATIVE ALEXANDER J. CELLA RECOMMENDING A POSTHUMOUS PARDON for NICOLA SACCO and BARTOLOMEO VANZETTI. Gardner Auditorium. Massachusetts State House, Boston. April 2, 1959. COMMITTEE for the VINDICATION of SACCO and VANZETTI. See addresses by Cella, pp. 6-12; Musmanno, pp. 31-76; Ernst, pp. 94-110; Roche, pp. 112-113; O'Connor, pp. 131-157. In 1961-1973 and 1979-1990 Encyclopaedia Britannica cited this 1959 hearing. See Britannica on p. 584 in this handbook.

"Massachusetts: The Restless Ghosts." Newsweek 53 13 Apr. 1959: 38. Alexander J. Cella failed in his effort to get a posthumous pardon for Sacco and Vanzetti.

1960

Montgomery, Robert H. Sacco-Vanzetti: The Murder and the Myth. New York: Devin-Adair, 1960. Argues both defendants guilty and publicizes his 1958 dispute with Justice Frankfurter on the failure of Vanzetti to take the witness stand at his Plymouth trial.

Ehrmann, Herbert B. The Untried Case: The Sacco-Vanzetti Case and the Morelli Gang. 2nd ed. Foreword by Joseph N. Welch. Introduction by Professor Edmund M. Morgan. New York: Vanguard, 1960. Ehrmann offers an 8-page rebuttal of Montgomery's book. See The Boston Globe, 12-7-1960, p. 52.

Phillips, Harlan, ed. Felix Frankfurter Reminisces: Recorded in Talks with Dr. Harlan B. Phillips. New York: Reynal & Company, 1960. On tape, Frankfurter says (p. 258) biography of Sacco and Vanzetti in DAB shows the "quality" of his pupil Sylvester G. Gates.

Aaron, Daniel. Writers on the Left: Episodes in American Literary Communism. New York: Harcourt, Brace & World, Inc., 1961. Useful on Malcolm Cowley, Max Eastman, Michael Gold, Upton Sinclair, Lincoln Steffens, and Edmund Wilson.

Eastman, Max. "Is This the Truth About Sacco and Vanzetti?" The National Review, October 21, 1961. Eastman says editors of The

645

New Republic and The Nation refused to publish his article. Eastman claims he heard Tresca say Sacco was guilty, Vanzetti innocent.

Grossman, James. "The Sacco-Vanzetti Case Reconsidered." Commentary 33 (January 1962): 31-44. Correspondence: Ibid. (May 1962): 443-444; 34 (July 1962): 72-73; (September 1962): 253-256. Sacco guilty, Vanzetti innocent. In the September issue, Grossman rejects Musmanno's criticism (253-254) and praises Russell's 1962 book.

Russell, Francis. Tragedy in Dedham: The Story of the Sacco-Vanzetti Case. New York: McGraw-Hill, 1962. Sacco guilty, Vanzetti innocent. Says Valdinoci bombed Palmer's home. See photos of guns, shells, bullets. See also photos in Kaiser's 1985 book.

Felix, David. "Apotheosis in Boston: Sacco and Vanzetti, from case to legend." Columbia University Forum, 6 (Fall 1963): 33-38. Correspondence: Ibid., 7 (Winter 1964): 3, 46-48. Argues investigations by Fuller and Fuller's committee "could not shake the cast-iron structure of guilt with a single substantial doubt."

Felix, David. Protest: Sacco-Vanzetti and the Intellectuals. Bloomington, Ind.: Indiana University Press, 1965. He implies Sacco and Vanzetti are guilty. Says Dedham trial fair. See composite photograph of Shell W and test shell, opposite p. 39.

Bush, Martin H. Ben Shahn: The Passion of Sacco and Vanzetti. With An Essay and Commentary by Ben Shahn. Syracuse, N.Y.: Syracuse University Press, 1968. Shahn: "This was a crucifixion itself—right in front of my eyes."

Ehrmann, Herbert B. The Case That Will Not Die: Commonwealth vs. Sacco and Vanzetti. Boston: Little, Brown, 1969. Concludes that his book "may help clear the names of the dead men." Pernicone gives this book high praise in American National Biography.

Baker, Liva. Felix Frankfurter. New York: Coward-McCann, 1969. Baker says the TNR editorial of June 9, 1926, was written by Sylvester G. Gates, Frankfurter's pupil.

1970

Russell, Francis. Tragedy in Dedham: The Story of the Sacco-Vanzetti Case. Fiftieth Anniversary Edition. New York: McGraw-Hill, 1971. Sacco guilty, Vanzetti innocent.

Gambino, Richard. Blood of My Blood: The Dilemma of the Italian-Americans. Garden City: Doubleday & Company, Inc., 1974. Concludes: "But, guilty or innocent, they received a good deal less than a fair trial."

Forman, James D. "Sacco and Vanzetti." In Anarchism: Political Innocence or Social Violence?, pp. 64-65. New York: Franklin Watts, 1975. In 1988 Forman revises the S-V article for World Book. See Forman on switch of gun barrels, p. 65. And see entry on Starrs at (1986).

Lash, Joseph, ed. From the Diaries of Felix Frankfurter. New York: W. W. Norton, 1975. Lash dedicates his book to Frankfurter and his "Hot Dogs," not knowing that both Jeremiah Smith (footnote, p. 125) and Judge Wyzanski (footnote, p. 236) are fated to challenge Frankfurter's article and book on the case. See Lash in ANB (vol. 13, pp. 217-220).

Lamson, Peggy. Roger Baldwin: Founder of the American Civil Liberties Union. Boston: Houghton Mifflin Company, 1976. Lamson calls M. L. Ernst an ACLU stalwart.

Feuerlicht, Roberta Strauss. Justice Crucified: The Story of Sacco and Vanzetti. New York: McGraw-Hill, 1977. Feuerlicht is rebuked by Pernicone at 1979 Boston conference for rigid partisanship. Feuerlicht says Sacco-Vanzetti case began with Puritans in 1630.

Porter, Katherine Anne. The Never-Ending Wrong. Boston: Atlantic-Little Brown, 1977. Commemorates 50th anniversary of the executions. Recalls how she saw communists at Boston in 1927 exploit Sacco and Vanzetti. Grudgingly concedes Sacco's guilt.

Foner, Eric. "Sacco and Vanzetti: The Men and the Symbols." The Nation, August 20, 1977. 50-year review. Dr. Foner, destined to be De Witt Clinton Professor of History, Columbia University, says: "... [D]efense produced thirteen witnesses, all Italian, to testify that Vanzetti had been selling fish on the day of the [South Braintree] crime."

Rabinovitz, Barbara. "Sacco and Fuller: The Debate Goes On." The Boston Herald American (Aug. 22, 1977): 1. "Sacco's grandson, Gov. Fuller's son differ on fairness of the trial." **The occasion is Dukakis's Proclamation of August 23, 1977.**

Pernicone, Nunzio. "Carlo Tresca and the Sacco-Vanzetti Case." The Journal of American History 66 (December 1979): 535-547. Answers Eastman's article of 1961. Challenges Tresca's credentials on Sacco and Vanzetti. See Felix's response in <u>JAH</u> 67 (Dec. 1980): 753-755. See Pernicone in <u>ANB</u> entry below (1999).

D'Attilio, Robert. "La Salute'e in Voi: The Anarchist Dimension." In <u>Sacco-Vanzetti: Developments and Reconsiderations—1979</u>, pp. 75-89. Boston: Boston Public Library, 1982. He claims a 25-cent bomb manual is significant. He concedes that Valdinoci bombed Palmer's home.

Russell, Francis. "Sacco and Vanzetti: Was the Trial Fair?" Modern Age. Winter 1975.

1980

Steel, Ronald. <u>Walter Lippmann and the American Century</u>. Boston: Little, Brown, 1980. Reports Lippmann told Judge Learned Hand he "was never convinced that they [Sacco and Vanzetti] were innocent." Steel recalls Frankfurter as a persuasive force.

Lynn, Kenneth S. "Versions of Walter Lippmann." <u>Commentary</u> 70 (October 1980): 69. Argues both defendants were "probably guilty." Lynn contrasts Lippmann's "measured opinions" on the case against Frankfurter's "passionate intensities."

Jackson, Brian. <u>The Black Flag</u>. London: Routledge & Kegan Paul, 1981. David Kaiser judges Jackson's book to be "the most inadequate treatment" of the case. Though riddled with factual errors, <u>The Black Flag</u> is useful on Kropotkin.

Murphy, Bruce A. <u>The Brandeis-Frankfurter Connection: The Secret Political Activities of Two Supreme Court Justices</u>. New York: Oxford University Press, 1982. Discloses a new reason why Brandeis had to recuse himself. See letters edited by Urofsky-Levy (1991).

Parrish, Michael E. <u>Felix Frankfurter and His Times</u>. New York: The Free Press, 1982. Argues: "The evidence of guilt, although vigorously disputed by the defense, was not trivial." See Parrish's entries—"Frankfurter" and "Wyzanski"—in <u>ANB</u> (1999).

Davidson, James West, and Mark Hamilton Lytle. "Sacco and Vanzetti," In <u>After the Fact: The Art of Historical Detection</u>. New York: Alfred A. Knopf, 1982. These Bard College professors say textbook by Weeks is a reliable source on Dedham trial if Holt's or Appel's volumes cannot be accessed. The fifth edition (2005) omits Felix and cites <u>Kill Now, Talk Forever</u>.

Perrett, Geoffrey. "The Red and the Black." In America in the Twenties: A History. New York: Simon and Schuster, 1982. Says Galleani "virtually worshipped by men who normally despise idolatry." Covers ground Avrich takes up in 1991. Honors Beffel's article.

Baker, Leonard. Brandeis and Frankfurter. New York: Harper & Row, 1984. Responds to Murphy. Baker credits Sacco with the historic speech that some attribute to Vanzetti.

Brogan, Hugh. "Murder after murder." TLS. May 10, 1985, p. 513. In his review of Ludovic Kennedy's The Airman and the Carpenter: The Lindbergh Case and the framing of Richard Hauptmann, Brogan writes: "Hauptmann's ghost can only be laid by some official, legal determination that he was innocent: such atonement as Massachusetts made to Vanzetti and Sacco."

Felix, David. Letter. TLS. May 31, 1985, p. 607. Felix responds to Brogan's review: "Hugh Brogan writes incorrectly that Massachusetts vouchsafed 'atonement ... to Sacco and Vanzetti' in the form of an 'official, legal determination' of innocence. ... In the event [Proclamation] Mr. Dukakis had no more authority to make a legal determination, ... than an office charwoman."

"Examination of Firearm Related Evidence: The Nicola Sacco and Bartolomeo Case." Report of Firearm Examination Panel: Henry C. Lee, Anthony L. Paul, Marshall K. Robinson, George R. Wilson. Select Committee on Sacco and Vanzetti, October 11, 1983. AFTE Journal. (Volume 17, Number 3) July 1985, pp. 13-42. Professor Starrs (1986) draws from this Report. Dr. Henry C. Lee gives administrative support. The Panel of four experts concludes on p. 28: "Of the caliber .32 Auto cartridges in possession of Nicola Sacco at the time of his apprehension (Exhibit #31), sixteen (16) were manufactured by The Peters Cartridge Company; and, of the sixteen cartridges, six (6) were made on the same machine that made the two Peters fired cartridge cases (Fraher shells) that were recovered from the crime scene." Photo of Exhibit M, the leather holster, is on p. 32. See Lee at 2000.

Young, William, and David E. Kaiser. Postmortem: New Evidence in the Case of Sacco and Vanzetti. Amherst: University of Massachusetts Press, 1985. Kaiser argues Bullet 3 and Shell W were false trial exhibits. Says both defendants innocent. Kaiser claims (111-112) Harold Williams used deception at Dedham trial.

Brogan, Hugh. "New Convictions." TLS. December 27, 1985, p. 1474. Brogan says the Young and Kaiser book contains the historical truth about Sacco and Vanzetti. In his letter of 22 September 1988 Brogan is less confident in pronouncing on forensic matters. In his e-mail to Newby on 24 January 2001, Brogan is less willing to praise the Young and Kaiser book.

Felix, David. "The Sacco-Vanzetti Case." Letter. Times Literary Supplement. February 21, 1986, p. 191. Felix: Conspiracy theory in Young/Kaiser book is hollow, and Brogan's review of the Y/K book in TLS, 12/27/1985, has factual errors. Felix concedes that Vanzetti "had been only a little bit pregnant with guilt."

Russell, Francis. Sacco and Vanzetti: The Case Resolved. New York: Harper & Row, March 1986. Sacco, guilty; Vanzetti, an accessory after the fact. Pages 140-142 detail World-Wide Protests in 1927.

Russell, Francis. "Clinching the Case." The New York Review of Books 33, Number 4 (March 13, 1986): 33-36. Russell's argument on Sacco's sixteen Peters cartridges is answered by Kaiser on 5/29/86.

Wyzanski, Charles E. Jr. Senior District Judge. United States District Court at Boston. Letter to Francis Russell. March 31, 1986. Filed with the Francis Russell Papers at the Boston Athenæum. Praises Russell. Argues Sacco "guilty," Vanzetti "not proven guilty." Vouches for the integrity of Assistant District Attorney Williams. The Judge recalls his friend from boyhood, Herbert "Brute" Ehrmann, who had argued cases before him in his District Court. He says he testified at both Hiss trials. Wyzanski tells Russell that "... which might startle you is what Jeremiah Smith, Jr. told Gus Hand. When Jerry had finished his service as High Commissioner in Hungary, he, before A. L. Lowell, [underlined two times] was asked by Governor Fuller to serve on the Commission to Advise the Governor. Jerry consulted his doctor who told him that he must not serve because at any moment he might die (though in fact he lived another year or two). Jerry told Gus that he felt so badly at declining to perform the civic obligation that he privately undertook to read the entire record, and concluded that both Sacco and Vanzetti were guilty and had not been denied a constitutionally adequate trial, ..." See entry on Hull at (1997).

Starrs, James E. "Once More Unto the Breech: The Firearms Evidence in the Sacco and Vanzetti Case Revisited," Journal of Forensic

Sciences 31 (April 1986): 630-654; (July 1986):1050-1078. Starrs
says: (1) "Hamilton had been discredited in the earlier murder trial
of Charles Stielow" (635); (2) Hamilton, a charlatan, switched gun
barrel of the Sacco Colt (635, 1053). Starrs says the Young and
Kaiser book is "crippled" because it ignores "the findings of the
1983 Select Committee" (650). Starrs claims Sacco is linked to the
crime and crime scene by "the cartridges found in his possession
on his arrest" (1050).

Avrich, Paul. "Anatomy Of A Murder." The New Republic, (April 7,
1986): 30-34. Argues both Kaiser (Postmortem) and Russell (S &
V: The Case Resolved) make claims they cannot support. Declares
D'Attilio "perhaps the leading authority on the case."

David E. Kaiser and Francis Russell, "Sacco and Vanzetti: An
Exchange." The New York Review of Books 33, Number 9 (May
29, 1986): 52-56. Kaiser asks how many machines manufactured
Peters bullets. Russell answers in letter to Richard Newby,
6/29/88.

Russell, Francis. "Why I Changed My Mind about the Sacco-Vanzetti
Case." American Heritage (June/July, 1986): 106-108. "Though I
was at first tied to the dogma [of innocence], the facts turned
against me."

Gallagher, Dorothy. "The Next-to-Last Word." Rev. of Sacco and
Vanzetti: The Case Resolved, by Francis Russell, and Postmortem,
by Young/Kaiser. The Nation 243 (Aug. 2/9, 1986): 87-90. Says
book by Russell, a "dreamer" and revisionist, "is a shabby job of
work." Gallagher finds a more convincing presentation of
evidence in Kaiser's book.

Boorstin, Daniel. Hidden History. New York: Harper & Row, 1987.
Boorstin labels Sacco and Vanzetti "philosophical anarchists."

Russell, Francis. Letter to Richard Newby. June 29, 1988. Fronting
Kaiser, Russell gives added information on bullet manufacturing.
Hopes to republish his S-V books in soft cover. Letter filed with
the Francis Russell Papers, Library of the Boston Athenaeum.

Gallagher, Dorothy. All the Right Enemies: The Life and Murder of
Carlo Tresca. New Brunswick: Rutgers University Press, 1988.
Takes up Tresca's allegation: Sacco, guilty, Vanzetti innocent.
Gallagher says Russell overrated Tresca's authority.

Simon, James F. The Antagonists. New York: Simon and Schuster,
1989. Simon says Braintree crime occurred (p. 54) "outside the

factory of the Slater Morrill Shoe Company." Simon, Martin
Professor of Law at New York Law School, says (p.55) "... Sacco
and Vanzetti carried weapons that the prosecution later linked with
the bullets found in the bodies of the murdered men." In 1989
Simon was Dean at NYLS.
C.C. Palmer to District Attorney of Norfolk County, June 17, 1921.
The Sacco-Vanzetti Case Papers. Microfilm, Reel 21. Frederick,
Md.: University Publications of America, 1986.

1990

Dershowitz, Alan M. "Introduction." The Sacco-Vanzetti Case. Ed.
Osmond Kessler Fraenkel. The Notable Trials Library. New
York: A.A. Knopf, 1931. Birmingham, AL: Leslie B. Adams Jr.,
1990. iii-iv. Dershowitz says that when Sacco and Vanzetti were
arrested, " ... they were carrying pistols and anarchist literature."
Dershowitz also says: "Indeed, there may have been a legal
miscarriage of justice even if it were to turn out that Sacco and
Vanzetti were factually guilty."
Naveh, Eyal J. Crown of Thorns: Political Martyrdom in America from
Abraham Lincoln to Martin Luther King, Jr. New York: New
York University Press, 1990. Sacco's and Vanzetti's "martyrdom
was meaningful only to a few alienated intellectuals and radicals."
Urofsky, Melvin I., and David W. Levy, eds. "Half Brother, Half Son":
The Letters of Louis D. Brandeis to Felix Frankfurter. Norman:
Univ. of Oklahoma Press, 1991. Reader learns that Brandeis got
his copy of Frankfurter's book on March 7, 1927, and wrote: "It
will prove an event of importance ... perhaps a turning point."
Urofsky, Melvin I. Felix Frankfurter: Judicial Restraint and Individual
Liberties. Boston: Twayne Publishers, 1991. Argues: "[O]ne can
still find well-reasoned articles on both sides of this issue" [of their
guilt or innocence]. Urofsky is cited in ANB under Editors and
Advisers.
Avrich, Paul. Sacco and Vanzetti: The Anarchist Background.
Princeton: Princeton Univ. Press, 1991. Concludes Sacco and
Vanzetti have not been proved guilty, nor have they been proved
innocent. Avrich concurs with Russell: Valdinoci bombed Palmer's
home. He hopes (p. 6) "new evidence will be discovered."

Meredith, Isabel. A Girl Among the Anarchists. London: Duckworth & Co., 1903. Reprint. Bison Book Edition. Introduction by Jennifer Shaddock. Lincoln: University of Nebraska Press, 1992. This novel by Helen and Olivia Rossetti relates "their actual experience as adolescent editors of ... The Torch," an anarchist newspaper. They call "Propaganda by Deed" (pp. 188, 212) the "deeds of violence"—a phrase that is metamorphosed to "retaliatory violence" by D'Attilio. These nieces of D. G. Rossetti met Kropotkin.

Lucie-Smith, Edward. American Realism. New York: Harry N. Abrams, Inc., 1994. Argues: "Sacco and Vanzetti were convicted of murder on the flimsiest of evidence in 1920."

Kadane, Joseph B., and David A. Schum. A Probabilistic Analysis of the Sacco and Vanzetti Evidence. Wiley: New York, 1996. Told his book has factual errors, Dr. Schum on 2 Sept. 1998 gave Newby a lecture about "facts."

Tindall, George Brown, and David E. Shi. America: A Narrative History. 4th edition. New York: W. W. Norton & Co., 1996. These professors wonder: Were Sacco and Vanzetti convicted because they were anarchists? No change in 1999 edition.

Johnson, Paul. A History of the American People. New York: HarperCollins, 1997. Johnson sees Sinclair's loss of faith in innocence of defendants. Says: "[W]orldwide agitation [for Sacco and Vanzetti] was directed by Willi Muenzenberg's official Communist International propaganda machine in Paris." He notes that America's Left links Sacco and Vanzetti, Hiss, and the Rosenbergs as victims. See Zelt (1958).

Hull, N. E. H. Roscoe Pound and Karl Llewellyn: Searching for an American Jurisprudence. Chicago: The Univ. of Chicago Press, 1997. Hull says (p. 165): "President Lowell of Harvard had been chosen to chair the governor's 'independent' panel to review the Sacco and Vanzetti case. Lowell, however, came to the panel predisposed to condemn the two men.... Lowell had actually confided to Pound, before the former had been appointed to chair the commission, 'that he did not care whether they were guilty or not, public confidence in the institutions of Massachusetts required that the sentence be carried out.'" In footnote #134 Hull concedes that documentation is not firm on this point. In his e-mail of 15 November 2004 David Felix "pointed out the lack of proof in

Hull's claim" on p. 165. Felix maintained Lowell was "not fool enough to say something of the sort and heartless enough to believe it." Hull's claim, Felix said, is "characteristic of the bad-mouthing exercised on such honorable persons as Lowell, who were trying to do their duty upholding justice in the Sacco-Vanzetti case." See Wyzanski entry at (1986) for reference to the eminent Justice Augustus N. Hand, for whom Wyzanski clerked.

Sacco, Nicola and Bartolomeo Vanzetti. The Letters of Sacco and Vanzetti. Ed. Marion Denman Frankfurter and Gardner Jackson. New York: Viking, 1928. Reprint. New York: Penguin Books, 1997. Introduction by Richard Polenberg. Polenberg endorses Kaiser's hypothesis of the substitute bullet and shell. Vanzetti, 05/15/26, writes of "the criminals who testify against us,..."

Brinkley, Alan. The Unfinished Nation: A Concise History of the American People. 2nd ed. New York: Alfred A. Knopf, 1997. Brinkley, Allan Nevins Professor of History, Columbia University, argues: "The case against them was questionable."

Tanenhaus, Sam. Whittaker Chambers: A Biography. Modern Library Edition. New York: Random House, 1998. "[T]heir martyrdom helped radicalize a generation of intellectuals." Tanenhaus's 1997 edition is reviewed in December 1996. For update, see Tanenhaus's attack on The Nation in The New Republic (July 5, 1999): 35-36.

Evans, Harold. "Martyrs or Enemies of The American Way?" The American Century. New York: Alfred A. Knopf, 1998. Citing Avrich, Evans calls Sacco "ultramilitant." He concludes: "[I]t was probably guilt of violent anarchism, not of robbery and murder for which they were executed." He finds the Sacco plea of innocence credible. Photos.

Parrish, Michael E. "Frankfurter, Felix." American National Biography. Eds. John A. Garraty and Mark C. Carnes. New York: Oxford Univ. Press, 1999. Parrish: "[T]he verdict of historians has vindicated Frankfurter's position." Garraty is Gouverneur Morris Professor Emeritus of History, Columbia University.

Pernicone, Nunzio. "Sacco, Nicola ... and Bartolomeo Vanzetti." American National Biography. Eds. John A. Garraty and Mark C. Carnes. New York: Oxford Univ. Press, 1999. Pernicone says The Case That Will Not Die is "[t]he most thorough and well-balanced study of the case." Pernicone says Russell's 1986 book declares Vanzetti guilty as well as Sacco. Honoring Avrich's research (interview of "an old Italian anarchist"), Pernicone concedes Boda/Buda is guilty of Wall Street explosion. Pernicone's egregious factual error is in vol. 19, p. 174.

Parrish, Michael E. "Wyzanski, Charles Edward, Jr." <u>American National Biography</u>. Eds. John A. Garraty and Mark C. Carnes. New York: Oxford Univ. Press, 1999. Parrish: "... [Wyzanski] shared with one of his mentors, Learned Hand, the distinction of being among the ablest of American jurists who never sat on the U. S. Supreme Court." Parrish is cited in <u>ANB</u> under Editors and Advisors.

D'Attilio, Robert. "The Sacco-Vanzetti Case" (overview). www.english.upenn.edu/~afilreis/88/sacvan.html. 10 August 1999.

Newby, Richard. "Judge Wyzanski Makes History: Sacco and Vanzetti Reconvicted." www.english.upenn.edu/~afilreis/50s/newby-sacvan.html. 29 August 1999. Newby cites Judge Wyzanski's1986 letter to Russell, a document not mentioned in the <u>ANB</u>.

2000

_____. "To the Editor." <u>The Journal of American History</u> 87 (June 2000): 321. This letter responds to John Henry Schlegel's book review in <u>JAH</u> (March 1999): 1623. Schlegel's failure to acknowledge Wyzanski's March 1986 letter is noted by Newby.

Lee, Dr. Henry and Dr. Jerry Labriola. "Sacco-Vanzetti." <u>Famous Crimes Revisited: From Sacco-Vanzetti to O. J. Simpson</u>. Southington, CT: Strong Books, 2001. 1-98. The "Sacco-Vanzetti" section has factual errors and raises serious questions about documentation. It fails to cite two articles by James E. Starrs (<u>JFSCA</u>, 1986). It omits a key article in the <u>AFTE Journal</u> (Vol. 17, No. 3, July 1985), on p. 30 of which is the signature: HENRY C. LEE, 31 Oct. 1983. Authors omit Atwater and Slater.

Topp, Michael Miller. <u>Those without a Country: The Political Culture of Italian American Syndicalists</u>. Minneapolis: Univ. of Minnesota Press, 2001. Topp has useful information on Carlo Tresca. His bibliography on Sacco and Vanzetti, p. 307, is biased.

Linder, Douglas. "The Trial of Sacco and Vanzetti" by Doug Linder (2001). See <u>Famous Trials</u> (UMKC Web site): <u>The Sacco-Vanzetti Trial 1921</u>. Linder finds Sacco guilty, then concludes his analysis

(Account): "Vanzetti undoubtedly knew who the Braintree bandits were; he may have had some limited role in planning the crime, or perhaps had advance knowledge of the crime—but it seems likely that Bartolomeo Vanzetti was, as he told the jury, selling fish in Plymouth on April 15, 1920."

Avrich, Paul. "Sacco and Vanzetti's Revenge." The Lost World of Italian-American Radicalism. Eds. Philip Cannistraro and Gerald Meyer. Westport: Praeger, 2003. 163-169. Avrich concludes Chapter 6 with "information" he received about Judge Thayer from his "old friend Valerio Isca ... the last of the Italian anarchists in New York, ..." Avrich learns how Sacco and Vanzetti "received a posthumous measure of revenge." Avrich places his discovery in his last sentence (p. 168): "For Thayer, he [Isca] said, died on the toilet seat, 'and his soul went down the drain.'"

Newby, Richard. "Sacco & Vanzetti: Were They Really Innocent?" History News Network at George Mason University, April 19, 2004. The new evidence is the fire that gutted Frank Morgridge's grocery story in Dexter, Maine, on February 1, 1914.

Neville, John F. Twentieth-Century Cause Celebre: Sacco, Vanzetti, and the Press, 1920-1927. Westport: Praeger Publishers, 2004. Praeger: "Neville argues that, while casting about for a case to champion in 1926, the Cominterm of the USSR discovered in Sacco-Vanzetti the perfect vehicle to discredit and shame the United States." Neville says (p. 83) Frankfurter's article in the Atlantic Monthly is "lacking in serious supporting documentary evidence." Neville says (p. 82): "Munzenberg had Frankfurter's essay reprinted and distributed en masse throughout major European cities." Neville misses irony when he describes Vanzetti's excitement over a certain TNR "splendid editorial" (p. 68). Neville claims Vanzetti "was innocent" (p. 150). His note on Mucci, p. 51, enriches p. 337 in Kill Now, Talk Forever. Although Neville cites Musmanno (p. 176) and fails to cite James Grossman's 1962 review of Montgomery's book on Sacco and Vanzetti in Commentary, he does note Beffel's inaccuracy (pp. 21, 23). Neville's book invites comparison with Topp's 2005 book to see which has the more disinterested analysis.

Topp, Michael M. The Sacco and Vanzetti Case: A Brief History with Documents. The Bedford Series in History and Culture. Boston: Bedford/St. Martin's, 2005. On the back of this Bedford/St.

Martin's book Paul Avrich writes: "Topp's book is well written and scholarly yet accessible to the general reader. Clear, comprehensive, and fair-minded, it provides as full and as objective a history of Sacco and Vanzetti as we are likely to see for some years." Publisher's Foreword (Davis, May, Hunt, Blight) states that this book would " ... be a reasonable one-week assignment in a college course." That is debatable. Topp is niggardly in providing testimony from the transcript of Vanzetti's Plymouth trial and the transcript of the trial of Sacco and Vanzetti at Dedham. Topp believes (p. 24 and p. 193) Kaiser has the facts on Vanzetti's revolver. The bibliography is thin. Neither Dr. Topp nor his "very careful" manuscript reader, "compatriot Nunzio Pernicone," (p. ix) will acknowledge that Columbia Encyclopedia, Sixth Edition, says the 1961 ballistics text "... seemed to prove conclusively that the pistol found on Sacco had been used to murder the guard" (p. 2476).

Pasco, Jean O. "Sinclair Letter Turns Out to Be Another Expose'." LA Times. 24 Dec 2005, California section, Part B, p. 3. Pasco reports how a California attorney, Paul Hegness, found a letter Upton Sinclair sent to John Beardsley on August 29, 1929.

Newby, Richard. Letter to the Editor. The New York Sun. June 21, 2006, p. 10. Letter cites new evidence on Vanzetti's revolver that Newby discovered on microfilm in 2005.

Tindall, George Brown, and David Emory Shi. America: A Narrative History. 7th ed., vol. 2. New York: W. W. Norton & Company, 2007. Tindall/Shi say (p. 969) " . . . the evidence convicting them was compelling; . . ." Further Reading section, p. 990, has this update: "The controversial Sacco and Vanzetti case is thoroughly explored in *Kill Now, Talk Forever: Debating Sacco and Vanzetti*, edited by Richard Newby (2002) [revised 2007]."

INDEX

About the Author

Richard Newby was born on 15 June 1924 in Bridgeton, Indiana. He grew up in Ridge Farm, Illinois.

He earned his B. A. in English in 1950 and his M. A. in English in 1953 from Southern Illinois University and his Ph. D. in English in 1970 from the University of Colorado, Boulder.

He joined the Illinois State University faculty in 1958 and took on the role of detective during his13-year stint, 1976-1989, as teacher of creative writing, Thomas Mallon (Stolen Words) and Alistair Cooke being his silent mentors. His work in judging short stories by ISU students proved to be excellent training for the warring Sacco and Vanzetti arena.

He gained insight into Sacco and Vanzetti studies in May 1986 when a member of the Illinois State University history department assured him that the prosecution presented two false exhibits at the Dedham trial of Sacco and Vanzetti. He took her opinion seriously and resolved to scrutinize all documents.

On June 14, 1988, he told the Managing Editor of Encyclopaedia Britannica that Britannica must revise its entry on the Sacco-Vanzetti case because the appended bibliography was biased. On November 2, 1990, Britannica's General Editor, Robert McHenry, told him that the entry on Sacco and Vanzetti and the appended bibliography were revised in April, that both revisions would be in the 1991 printing.

In 2003 he found new evidence in Dexter and Bangor.

Then he found the undated pamphlet by Randy Roberts and Robert E. May of Purdue University: LEARNING TO THINK CRITICALLY: Film, Myth, and American History. In #2 under "Thinking Critically About American History," Dr. Roberts teaches: "Read and view historical documents on your own. Don't be satisfied with what books, movies, and historical exhibits tell you about the past. Discover your own answers by tracking down diaries, letters, newspapers, deeds, wills, court records, government documents, artifacts, and icons."

Inspired by Paul Avrich's zeal for "the truth" about Sacco and Vanzetti, he added letters by Palmer, Ranney, Frankfurter, and Borchard to the canon. Then he stumbled upon factual errors and plagiarism in a book cited by The World Book Encyclopedia. Recalling 1988, he sent documentation to the Editor in Chief of World Book, Inc.

Printed in the United States
86445LV00007B/1/A